HOOSIER CARAVAN

GEORGE ADE
HOAGY CARMICHAEL
ELMER DAVIS
THEODORE DREISER
EDWARD EGGLESTON
LOGAN ESAREY
A. B. GUTHRIE, JR.
KIN HUBBARD
EMILY KIMBROUGH
ROSS LOCKRIDGE, JR.
MEREDITH NICHOLSON
JEANETTE COVERT NOLAN
GENE STRATTON PORTER
ERNIE PYLE
JAMES WHITCOMB RILEY
CORNELIA OTIS SKINNER
BOOTH TARKINGTON
EDWIN WAY TEALE
DAVID WAGONER
LEW WALLACE
JESSAMYN WEST
WILLIAM EDWARD WILSON
JOHN WOODS
KURT VONNEGUT, JR.
SAMUEL YELLEN
MARGUERITE YOUNG
AND MANY OTHERS

HOOSIER CARAVAN

A Treasury of Indiana Life and Lore

Selected, with comment,
by R. E. BANTA

INDIANA UNIVERSITY PRESS Bloomington & London
NEW AND ENLARGED EDITION

Published in Canada by Fitzhenry & Whiteside Limited, Don Mills, Ontario

MANUFACTURED IN THE UNITED STATES OF AMERICA

Library of Congress Cataloging in Publication Data
  Banta, Richard Elwell, ed.
    Hoosier caravan.
    1. American literature—Indiana.   2. Indiana—Literary collections.   I. Title.
  PS571.I6B3   1975   810'.8'09772   73-16521
  ISBN 0-253-13862-0 deluxe edition, slipcase
  ISBN 0-253-13861-2 regular cloth   75 76 77 78 79 1 2 3 4 5

To my good friend
LEE McCANLISS
Parke County Hoosier by birth and nature
New Yorker by Fortune's whim

Contents

Foreword

Kurt Vonnegut, Jr.'s *Cat's Cradle*, which won the 1964 Indiana Authors' Day award for fiction, contains this passage:

> Crosby asked me what my name was. . . . I told him, and his wife Hazel recognized my name as an Indiana name. She was from Indiana, too.
>
> "My God," she said, "are you a *Hoosier?*"
>
> I admitted I was.
>
> "I'm a Hoosier, too," she crowed. "Nobody has to be ashamed of being a Hoosier."
>
> "I'm not," I said. "I never knew anybody who was."

True enough—but an understatement. With the possible exception of Texans, no state's citizens are more chauvinistic than Indiana's; and they might well go so far as to claim (allowing no exceptions) that none have better reasons for their chauvinism. Hoosiers are proud of their basketball teams, of Brown County, of Indiana limestone, of many other things, but most of all they are proud of their writers.

Writing springs from Indiana so naturally and abundantly that it is difficult to resist the conclusion that there may actually be something in the Hoosier air that induces authorship. Kin Hubbard is one who reached this conclusion: his Abe Martin's discourse on "Indiana's Fame and Industries" ends with this sentence:

> I'm told by transcontinental tourists who cross Indianny west on the ole historic National road that they no sooner hit Richmond on

the Eastern border till plots fer novels an' rhymes fer verses come
o'er 'em so fast an' thick that they kin hardly see the road, an' often
go in the ditch.

It was the inspiration of R. E. Banta, Indiana author, rare book
dealer, publisher and humorist, to put this collection together. It's a
wonder the idea, such a natural one, hadn't already occurred to some
earlier Hoosier, but it's no wonder, considering the extent and scope
of Hoosier literary accomplishment, that Banta's plan worked out so
successfully. *Hoosier Caravan* was originally published in 1951; it was
one of the books on the first fall list of Indiana University Press. The
anthology was widely acclaimed by critics (non-Hoosier as well as
Hoosier) and has been zealously treasured by the readers who bought
out the 1951 printing. It was high time the Press brought out a new
edition. The book might have been re-issued this year just as it stood,
simply to satisfy the demand that it be made available again. That
wouldn't do, however, for the flow of Hoosier writing has never
stopped, and it would have been unthinkable for the 1975 edition not
to be considerably expanded (some 150 pages have been added) to include samples of new Indiana literature, samples that prove that the
Hoosier propensity for putting words effectively on paper has not
diminished.

Mr. Banta has supplied a new preface, but his entertaining, informative and often irreverent comments between the selections have been
retained—and his remarks introducing the added pieces are in the same
vein. And what Corbin Patrick said of the 1951 edition remains true:
"Banta did not produce this anthology to instruct or impress. Its main
purpose in this naughty world is to give delight, and that it will do in
overflowing measure."

Inevitably, every single reader of this volume will protest that some
favorite Indiana author of his is not represented; such complaints go
with the anthologist's territory. But just consider what Banta was up
against with such a plethora of material to choose from, what painful
decisions he must have forced himself to make! One of these limiting
decisions, not to include any prose for children, is certainly understandable, for after all, this is an adult book. Yet Indiana's writers have always been pre-eminent in juvenile literature, too, and some of them

should at least be mentioned in this foreword—some of the early ones, that is, for it wouldn't be feasible (or safe) to attempt to list the hundreds of outstanding contemporary Hoosier authors in this field. There was Martha Finley of South Bend, whose first Elsie Dinsmore book came out in 1867; in 1896 the Little Colonel series, by Annie Fellows Johnston of Evansville, began to appear; in 1911, Lucy Fitch Perkins of Maples launched her popular series with *The Dutch Twins*. And more and more Hoosier books for young people have been coming out ever since—and better and better ones from, say, 1914, the year which saw the publication of both Tarkington's *Penrod* and *Bambi* by Marjorie Benton Cooke of Richmond.

Hoosier Caravan is indeed a treasury, a generous and varied collection of published work, both serious and humorous, both gloriously good and uproariously bad, by Indiana's sons and daughters from 1816 to 1975. Glance at the Table of Contents. How will you be able to decide what to read first?

ROBERT W. MITCHNER

Preface to the Second Edition

Updating *Hoosier Caravan*

UPDATING A REPORT on Hoosier writing is simple enough. Updating Hoosiers and Hoosierland is something else again. We Hoosiers seem to remain much the same, as does our land, still served by the Ohio, White, and Wabash Rivers and, under new ownership, the Monon Railroad. There seems to be a balance and lack of hysteria in the Hoosier which keeps us on an even keel, except for some minor effects of world cataclysms such as war, peace, and pieces of wars, which have a temporary economic influence on the prices we get for our corn, soybeans, and hogs and affect the market for the steel ingots and other bibelots and nicknacks we manufacture.

Perhaps the above statement is oversimplified and, thus, is not completely accurate. There have been *some* changes since 1951. Take this writer, for instance. He's now been a native son for over seventy years, not for forty-seven, and supposes his cantankerous Hoosier traits have expanded, or hardened, or whatever traits do with the passing of years. But even that change is comparatively modest.

So let's just say we can't expect to update Hoosiers themselves significantly. They continue much as usual: in the winter, they devote their attention to basketball, a sport exceeded in interest only by playing politics, which continues to be the favorite year-round pastime.

The early spring months are devoted to watching for the burgeoning green shoots of the pieplant (called "rhubarb" by the uninformed); to searching out, rolling in cornmeal, and frying in bacon grease the succulent morel (true scientific name for what we know to be mush-*er-oons*); and to trimming sassafras roots into useable chunks. Thanks to James Buchanan Elmore, the latter comestible has gained more literary fame than the morel; Jim Buck, who worshipped the muse of poesy about equally with the god of digestive processes (see Chapter Fourteen, "When Katie Gathers Greens"), either wrote or did not write a lyric tribute to the root which ran:

> In the Spring of the year, when the blood is thick
> There's nothing so good as a sassafras stick.
> It quickens the liver and strengthens the heart
> And to the whole system doth new life impart.
> Oh sassafras, oh sassafras
> Thou art the stuff for me.

That statement to the effect that Jim "either wrote or did not write" the lines may be confusing, but here are the facts. When the deathless opus first saw print in the *Crawfordsville Journal* over Elmore's name, he hotly denied authorship and attributed it to some daring blatherskite member of the press; later, when the little masterpiece had been picked up and reprinted in some dozens of newspapers all over the country, Jim Buck decided that he must have written it after all, and included it in subsequent collections of his works.

That these gustatorial preferences remain in vogue is evidenced by no less authoritative source than the columns of the *Crawfordsville Journal and Review*, which recently carried the following advertisement:

JEST LIKE GOIN
TO GRANDMA'S SASSAFRAS KITCHEN
Bridgeton, Indiana
Friday & Saturday nights 5–9 P.M.
Salad smorgasbord $1.50
Ham steaks   German sausage
Deep fried perch

Served with old fashioned fried biscuits; also,

FRIED MUSHROOMS

Homemade butterscotch and chocolate pie

HOT SASSAFRAS TEA

Across from the Bridgeton covered bridge

Old time Sunday dinner 11:30 to 3

GEORGE & KITTY HILAND & FAMILY

In between the seasons for winter sports and growing things—with a bit of time off for bass fishing and coon hunting—the Hoosier apparently devotes himself almost entirely to writing books. Three thousand or so of us have had books published in the past twenty-three years, and many of us had more than one book each, so that we may estimate that there have been at least fifteen thousand titles. Since all know that not every book begun is ever finished, and since not every finished manuscript finds a publisher, we may surmise that one whale of a lot of writing is done each year within the confines of Indiana.

And it covers every imaginable field. Fiction still holds its own, as do history, biography, and poetry; all sciences are covered, including some that were unheard of and others known only in the imaginations of Jules Verne and H. G. Wells up to fifty years ago. Only sermons and tracts seem to be in short supply, and perhaps their place has been partially filled by Richard Lingeman's book *Campfollowers Guide* and Kurt Vonnegut, Jr.'s, *Canary in a Cat-House*. Judging by titles only, these may be laying the foundation for a new class of contribution to our learning.

The original Chapter One contained some failures to report coming events—for some of which failures your petitioner accepts responsibility: he knew that R. C. Buley had just received a Pulitzer Prize for *The Old Northwest*, but he could not know that A. B. Guthrie, Jr., was about to be voted another for *The Way West*. He could not anticipate the fact that Jessamyn West, whom he gave a typical, smart-aleck Hoosier brush-off by calling a "poet and essayist," was about to add half a dozen of her novels to the best-seller lists during the next two decades.

No one need apologize for failing in 1949 to expect the rise of Kurt

Vonnegut. The young man was laboring to brighten the public image of the General Electric Corporation in that day. He may have dreamed of highly successful novels, but he had published none and the name Vonnegut meant only hardware in Indiana. Nor could we have been expected to anticipate the rise of Marilyn Durham, now known as author of *The Man Who Loved Cat Dancing* and *Dutch Uncle*, but who in 1951 was still an innocent young daughter of Evansville.

So let us forget previous errors of omission and commission and state, immodestly enough, that literature still flourishes on the banks of the Wabash.

R.E.B.

ACKNOWLEDGMENTS

For arrangements made with authors, publishers, and authors' agents, the following acknowledgments are gratefully made:

"Indiana and Her People" and "The Rural Type and the Dialect" reprinted with permission of Macmillan Publishing Co. Inc. from *The Hoosiers* by Meredith Nicholson, copyright 1915 by MacMillan Publishing Co. Inc., renewed 1943 by Meredith Nicholson.

"Indiana Names" used by permission of the author, Virginia Scott Miner.

"A Game of Piquet," "Under the White Flag," "A Suspension of Hostilities," and "The End of Ah-Mah-Nac-O" from Caroline Brown's *On The We-a Trail*, copyright 1902 by MacMillan Publishing Co., Inc. and used with their permission.

"Why Tecumtha Fought" and "The Fall of the Prophet" from *True Indian Stories* by Jacob Piatt Dunn used by permission of Caroline Dunn and Eleanor Dunn Moore.

Selection from *The Big Sky* by A. B. Guthrie, Jr., copyright 1947, is reprinted by permission of the publisher, Houghton Mifflin Company.

Selection from *Angel In The Forest*, by Marguerite Young, copyright 1945 by Marguerite Young. Reprinted by permission of McIntosh and Otis, Inc.

The selections from *Raintree County* by Ross Lockridge, Jr., and *Abraham Lincoln* by Albert J. Beveridge are reprinted by permission of and arrangement with Houghton Mifflin Company, the authorized publishers.

"The Battle of Finney's Ford" from *The Friendly Persuasion*, by Jessamyn West, copyright 1940, 1943, 1944, 1945 by Jessamyn West, used by permission of Harcourt Brace Jovanovich, Inc.

A part of Chapter XXIII from *An Autobiography* by Lew Wallace, copyright 1906 by Harper & Row, Publishers, Inc., reprinted by permission of the publisher.

"Family Albums" and "Swiss Bell Ringers" from *Abe Martin's Broadcast*, by Kin Hubbard, copyright 1927, used by special permission of the publishers, The Bobbs-Merrill Company, Inc.

The selection from *Pony Wagon Town*, by Ben Riker, copyright 1948, used by special permission of the publishers, The Bobbs-Merrill Company, Inc.

The selection from *The Magnificent Ambersons*, by Booth Tarkington, published by Doubleday & Company, Inc., copyright 1918, 1946 by Booth Tarkington, used by permission of Brandt & Brandt.

Hour of Victory by Margaret Weymouth Jackson, © 1946, The Curtis Publishing Company, reprinted by permission from *The Saturday Evening Post*.

"We Lived In Indiana Too" by Elmer Davis, copyright © 1950 by American Heritage Publishing Company, Inc., reprinted by permission from *American Heritage*, Autumn, 1950.

The selections from *The Ideas Of A Plain Country Woman* by Juliet V. Strauss, copyright 1908 by Doubleday & Company, Inc., are reprinted by permission of the publisher.

The selections from *Abe Martin's Town Pump*, by Kin Hubbard, copyright 1930, used by special permission of the publishers, The Bobbs-Merrill Company, Inc.

The selections from *The Red Gods Call*, by C. E. Scoggins, published by The Bobbs-Merrill Company, copyright 1936 by C. E. Scoggins, used by permission of Brandt & Brandt.

The selection from *The Stardust Road* by Hoagy Carmichael, copyright 1946 by Hoagland Carmichael and reprinted by permission of Mr. Carmichael.

The selection from *How Dear To My Heart* by Emily Kimbrough, reprinted by permission of Dodd, Mead & Company. Copyright 1944 by Dodd, Mead & Company, Inc. Copyright renewed 1972 by Emily Kimbrough.

The selection from *The Song Of The Cardinal* by Gene Stratton Porter, published by Doubleday & Company, used by permission of Jeannette Porter Meehan.

The selection from *Dune Boy* by Edwin Way Teale, reprinted by permission of Dodd, Mead & Company. Copyright 1943 by Edwin Way Teale.

"Staying Alive" from *New and Selected Poems* by David Wagoner, copyright © 1969 by Indiana University Press, is reprinted by permission of David Wagoner. This poem originally appeared in *The New Yorker*.

The selections from *A Home In The Woods: Oliver Johnson's Reminiscences of Early Marion County* as related by Howard Johnson (Indianapolis: Indiana Historical Society, © 1951, reprinted 1972) were used with the permission of the Indiana Historical Society.

The selections from *Cress Delahanty*, copyright 1953 by Jessamyn West, are reprinted by permission of Harcourt Brace Jovanovich, Inc.

"Times Change" by Kurt Vonnegut, Jr., first published in *Esquire* Magazine, is reprinted by permission of Donald C. Farber for the author.

The selection from *The Desperate Hours* by Joseph Arnold Hayes, copyright 1954 by Marrijane and Joseph Hayes, is reprinted by permission of Random House, Inc.

The excerpts from *Crescent City* by William E. Wilson, copyright © 1947, copyright renewed 1975 by William E. Wilson, are reprinted by permission of the author and his agent, James Brown Associates, Inc.

"The Deaths at Paragon, Indiana" is from *Turning to Look Back* by John Woods, copyright © 1972 by Indiana University Press, and reprinted with the author's permission.

"The Shooting of John Dillinger Outside the Biograph Theater," from *New and Selected Poems* by David Wagoner, copyright © 1969 by Indiana University Press, is used by permission of the author.

"First Grade, Room 1, South Case School" from *The Convex Mirror: Collected Poems* by Samuel Yellen, © 1948 by The New Yorker Magazine, Inc., copyright © 1971 by Indiana University Press, is reprinted by permission of the author.

"The Mystic Presences" from *The Passionate Shepherd* by Samuel Yellen, copyright © 1957, is reprinted with the permission of the author and the Ann Elmo Agency, Inc.

Chapter 8 of *Our Hearts Were Young and Gay* by Emily Kimbrough and Cornelia Otis Skinner, copyright 1942 by Dodd, Mead and Company, Inc., copyright renewed 1970 by Cornelia Otis Skinner and Emily Kimbrough, is reprinted by permission of Dodd, Mead and Company.

"Referee Again Saves Israel From Victory" (October 23, 1973) and "Oh, Henry Really Has Tales to Tell" (November 12, 1973) by Bob Collins, reprinted by permission of the author and *The Indianapolis Star*.

HOOSIER CARAVAN

CHAPTER ONE

What Makes
Hoosier Authors Tick?

What makes Hoosier authors tick? Well, don't ask me, I've only been here forty-seven years and, besides, my Hoosier lines of ancestry have begun to sort of play out: we don't put vinegar on our greens any more, and we haven't had a dried apple pie since 1908.

The only answer I could give would be to the effect that they *do* tick and have been ticking in print since 1816, when the Federal Government peeled the State of Indiana out of the Territory Northwest of the River Ohio and put us Hoosiers on our own. I don't know what Hoosier authors did before 1816—probably sat on Indians and made them listen while they recited odes, told stories to the tulip trees or wrote essays on slippery-elum bark—but it's a safe bet that they managed to express themselves and that they had an audience, restrained by force if necessary.

Observers agree that Hoosiers have two marked characteristics: an overweening desire to see themselves in print and an uncontrollable appetite for politics. Observers have, of course, also pointed out other Hoosier peculiarities but they were often hasty in their conclusions; it is foolish to claim that we Hoosiers are second only to Texans in demanding recognition for what we claim to be the virtues of our state, or that our writers are driven to create fiction by the desolation of the local landscape. Who ever heard of a Hoosier who was anything but modest and self-effacing? Or of a desolate landscape in Indiana?

During the first hundred years of statehood more than nine hundred Indiana authors produced something like seven or eight thousand books—exclusive of text books, sermons and purely technical works on medicine, law, science or religion.* Production has fallen off little, if any, since 1916 and, Hoosiers having increased in numbers through natural processes, the total of both authors and books has probably doubled since that date. And these books, in the first as well as the latter period, have been singularly successful, for outlanders read Hoosier books even more avidly than do Hoosiers. The total of best sellers, of prize winners, and recently of book club selections has been truly astounding!

Why this should be true is the question, and as far as I am concerned there is no satisfactory answer. Masters' theses, doctoral dissertations, monographs by the wastebasketful which purported to analyze and establish a *raison d'être* for the phenomenon have been written by outlanders from Massachusetts to California. Mainly they proved nothing except that it is possible for the persistent student to earn a degree or for the serious scholar to immortalize himself in a learned journal without contributing perceptibly to the sum of human knowledge. But the fact remains: Indianians have written a lot of books—perhaps it is something in the good, productive soil, perhaps it is the pollen from the horseweed on the Wabash (horseweed was always more plentiful than sycamores on that stream), perhaps it is an Inner Urge (Indianians, except Theodore Dreiser, have never tended much to analyze their Inner Urges)—anyway they have done it and, as far as most of them are concerned, that is that.

Indiana authors have written about many subjects. One very early specimen liked to translate romantic verse from the Persian; another invented a central European principality—Graustark, remember?—and wrote several best sellers about it; their romances laid in Timbuctoo, Alaska, Batavia and Tibet, not to mention various units of the British Commonwealth of Nations, have been myriad indeed. Hoosiers have written about politics, government, history, the sciences, spiritualism, sociology, temperance and road-building; they have composed novels, short stories, sketches; they have rhymed

* See *Indiana Authors and Their Books*. Wabash College, Crawfordsville, Indiana, 1949, for details of the 1816–1916 period.

odes, acrostics, sonnets and commemorative poems of all classes, from those distinguished for their artistry to those immortal because of their heroic inadequacy. But always many Hoosiers have written of Indiana, and it is this production that we will examine here.

The greatest popularity of the largest number of Indiana writers came in the first decade of the Twentieth Century but success has continued. Occasionally a writer arises to sing the praises of some specific great day of Indiana letters and to add that, sorry as he is to say it, the day has gone. Such a dictum is, thus far invariably, the signal for an immediate and brilliant renaissance of Indiana writing.

In 1876 an anonymous contributor to the Cincinnati Gazette listed and praised the Indiana writers who had gone before, and he implied, in so doing, that the big crop was probably harvested. In 1900 Meredith Nicholson devoted a good part of a book to the mention of Hoosier writers who had flourished before that day, probably feeling as he wrote that it was all pretty well a matter of history. In 1945 another wrote in praise of the remarkable literary production since 1900 —and he knew that the Hoosier soil was farmed out! In the Saturday Review of Literature for January 6, 1945, said Hoosier

HEATH BOWMAN

Those, Those Hoosiers

CULTIVATION IN INDIANA ISN'T CONFINED TO CORN

JUST AT THE TURN of the century, it blossomed. There was hardly a literate soul in the country who was not reading one or more of the sudden outpourings by Indiana authors. Their sales ran into thousands, their titles headed the lists: Charles Major's "When Knighthood Was in Flower"; Meredith Nicholson's "The House of a Thousand Candles"; Gene Stratton Porter's "Song of the Cardinal"; George Barr McCutcheon's "Graustark"; George Ade's "Fables in Slang"; Booth Tarkington's "The Gentleman from Indiana"; even Riley's "An Old Sweetheart of Mine" sold more than any other single poem ever had. And, although very few people found copies to read, at the same time came Theodore Dreiser's "Sister Carrie." All of them published practically at once, within a year or so. Dreiser had ushered the old century out with an epitaph for a type that would vanish, and Tarkington brought the new one in with a manner appropriately gay for this best of all possible centuries, as they were sure it would be.

Immediately, when one talks of the Hoosier tradition, one begins to ask questions rather than to answer them dogmatically. And if you are not a Hoosier, you are bound to ask: Why should it have happened *there*, to those—those Hoosiers? In the very manner of your asking lies one clue, even though you may never have heard of the opprobrious origin of the name that has come to be recognized as widely as the New England "Yankee."

Only two or at the most three generations before this outburst of Hoosier prose, the early Indianians were guiding their flatboats along the Ohio and down the great Mississippi to New Orleans. And there it was that they received the name "hoosier": an epithet that had come originally from Lancashire, that meant a tall and green and gawky lad. A yokel, a hick. A backwoodsman who obviously didn't know much about book larnin'.

Was Indiana writing therefore a kind of compensation for that laughter? A kind of determination to show the world? Unquestionably that motive went into the molding of the Hoosier character, and is important to remember. But, even as the flatboats glided south, a man by the name of Samuel Merrill came out from Vermont with his books, and established in Indianapolis, the new capital, the only publishing firm west of the Alleghanies which still ranks with the great houses. Many another early citizen was widely read, and articulate, despite the aspersions cast by Baynard Rush Hall when he wrote "The New Purchase." Still, there *were* aspersions. . . .

Historically speaking, the Hoosier tradition began in 1871 with the appearance of "The Hoosier Schoolmaster," by Edward Eggleston, a preacher's son who grew up in one of the most charming of Ohio river towns, Vevay, where the Swiss had come to plant their vineyards. For the period, it was an unvarnished account of a strident regionalism.

Just about that time a happy-go-lucky kid was peddling Dr. McCrillus's Popular Standard Remedies, which he had helped make household words from the St. Mary's to the White River. As he rollicked along behind that buckboard, the waters of the Mississinewa, of all the myriad creeks, the golden acres of the land sang out—and he sang, too. At home in Greenfield on the National Road, his trunk began collecting verses. For many years to come those verses would be doled out, for this was his greatest period of production; the first published one would shortly appear in *Hearth and Home*. He sang of the simple things he knew, unashamedly, without the need of the philosophical explanation he heard Robert G. Ingersoll deliver: "Nothing is more marvellous than the everyday facts of life. . . ." For James Whitcomb Riley had discovered that truism by intuition.

Most of those future Hoosier authors knew Jim Riley as his fame spread, all of them knew his verses by heart; they rocked with laughter or grief at his recitations up and down the land with Bill Nye. For they heard those slightly gnarled words as they should be spoken, as the less privileged later generations could never experience them. And the goal was painted for these aspirants, they saw it brightening the way. It was possible, they began to understand, that writing also could make you not only respectable but respected. Respected, because you could make money at it.

For another of theirs had proven that fact beyond doubt in the early eighties: General Lew Wallace, of Covington and Crawfordsville and the Civil War, had written "Ben Hur." He had recopied it in purple ink by night after his labors as a solemn Governor of far-off New Mexico Territory.

But these three—Eggleston, Riley, and Wallace—rather afforded an inspiration, perhaps, than pointed a tradition. For here lay three precedents, not one: would they follow realism, lyricism, or romanticism? It was the mere encouragement these younger writers wanted:

for them, the zest to write—to write anything—was more potent than an inner necessity to describe and explain their peculiar milieu. And most of those best sellers of the early nineteen-hundreds dwelt on castles and kings and exotic lands, or the strangeness Hoosiers felt when they went forth to the Big Cities.

Dreiser, of course, was the great anomaly. Brought up on the wrong side of the tracks, among coal miners and madames of sporting houses, it was a long time—not until 1916—before he could bring himself to don a linen duster and go all the way west again, mentally and physically, to make his "A Hoosier Holiday." It was even much later before he could set down those early agonizing years in "Dawn," one of the most remarkable autobiographies America has yet seen. Booth Tarkington, on the other hand, felt few of these strictures, and came home almost immediately from Princeton to drive his red-wheeled runabout behind his handsome pair of trotters and to view his countryside with mingled love and amusement. Although "Monsieur Beaucaire" already had been written and accepted by *McClure's*, it was "The Gentleman" which the Hoosiers first read. And a lot of folks didn't much like his opening chapters about that dusty, sleepy little Hoosier town of "Plattville," and the talk of political corruption and the terrorism of the "white caps." Tark had something there, though, and the nation acknowledged it. Best of any of his contemporaries, he would combine the various expressions of his earlier mentors.

All of them must have had a yearning not as clear to us today as it was in that more tentative age—a yearning not only for expression but to prove to themselves and the world that "cultivation" in Indiana didn't always mean tending corn or tomatoes. They and their readers together yearned for a more exciting world, and they were proud and confident from the battles they had won: against that early opprobrium attached to the flatboatmen, against the poverty of the log cabin, against the Eastern political bosses—even against the literary Brahmins of Boston. The Indiana tradition did not profess to include much soul searching. It was spacious and pleasant as their wide lawns, and as consciously limited as if curtained by those elegant cast iron fences. There were a few iron deer, too—good enough imitations of non-indigenous elements—in their stories. But, like those spreading lawns and hospitable ginger-bread houses, their works began to dwindle, were encroached upon by forces outside their favorite state. The smoke of the factories and the First World War seemed to wither them; and there were no new contenders for the old honors. . . .

Fie! and for shame, Mr. Bowman! We Hoosiers are good but we must not infringe upon the prerogatives of Divine Providence—especially in the matter of killing off Indiana's "purely literary expression" so precipitately!

Even as Mr. Bowman wrote, other Hoosiers were writing too—several of them—and four years later (only a reasonable period to allow for final revisions, signing contracts, printing, binding and a few bookstore autographing parties) several of them combined to prove Mr. Bowman's prophecy utterly and completely in error, as witness a piece by Corbin Patrick, literary editor of the Indianapolis Star, in which he views the Indiana triumphs of 1949 and 1950.

CORBIN PATRICK

The Indiana Literary Tradition at Midcentury

Of ALL THE SNIDE REMARKS that irk us, the worst is the moss-back lament that nothing worthwhile is being written anymore. This complaint originates, we suspect, with people who gave up reading when they bought their first radios. They pretend to believe that Indiana's literary tradition flowered and withered shortly after the turn of the century.

If they will listen, we should like to suggest that said tradition is flourishing today as seldom before and that a group of writers as fine as ever represented Hoosierdom are just catching their breath following an almost unprecedented outburst of fruitful creative effort less than two years ago. Time has not hallowed them or assayed the gold they panned, but Indiana has every right and reason to be proud of its 49ers.

The magnitude of their achievement should have been obvious even to the most hardened cases last year when two of them shared the major literary awards for books published in 1949. Critics of the nation, voting in the *Saturday Review of Literature* poll, gave first place in the field of fiction to Bedford-born A. B. Guthrie's pioneer novel, "The Way West," and declared "Lincoln Finds a General," by K. P. Williams of Indiana University, the outstanding historical work. Guthrie's splendid contribution also won the Pulitzer Prize and Williams' rich two-volume Civil War Study went on to receive what many dyed-in-the-wool but discerning Hoosiers will consider the highest tribute of all—selection for the state's "Book of the Year" award at the Indiana Author's Day program last summer.

But the best test of a book is readability, not the list of its honors, and other good ones stemmed from the same period. One introduced a relative newcomer, Richard E. Banta of Crawfordsville, with a vigorous and dramatic history of "The Ohio." Another was William E. Wilson's "Abe Lincoln of Pigeon Creek," a delightful account of the future president's boyhood years on a Hoosier homestead. Heath Bowman, a chief mourner of what he considers the faded glory of Indiana's literary tradition, once stated that wide aspects of the Hoosier scene, both historical and contemporary, have never been done justice. Wilson, and others, have accepted that challenge. "The smoke of the factories and the First World War seemed to wither them," said Bowman, in reference to Indiana's past masters, "and there were no new contenders for the old honors." The 49ers have changed that. . . .

The vitality of this revival was further demonstrated by the appearance late in 1950 of R. Carlyle Buley's magnificent two-volume history, "The Old Northwest," which subsequently won the Pulitzer Prize. As completely unexpected as it seems to have been, generally speaking, the award did not exactly flabbergast the few people around the country who had read the book—the first edition published by the Indiana Historical Society was limited to 3,000 copies. What surprised them was the Pulitzer Committee's unusual discernment. Prof. Buley's contribution was the one lasting monument produced by the Indiana Territory Sesquicentennial observance of 1950.

Those we have named in this brief review, along with Jessamyn West, Jeannette Nolan, Marguerite Young, Emily Kimbrough, Ross Lockridge Jr. (whose "Raintree County" we think is a novel of major and lasting importance), and the group of active writers they represent, have made Indiana's literary tradition a thing of today and tomorrow as well as yesterday. We no longer need look back; we can look forward with confidence.

Except for that Cincinnati Gazette article of 1876 and a few similarly fugitive pieces all this discussion stems from the charming little 1900 book, already mentioned, which came from the pen of the distinguished Meredith Nicholson.

Called The Hoosiers, it was filled with essays about Indiana and Indianians which described this fortunate state and these chosen people as pleasantly as could be desired.

Nicholson was as sure at analyzing the peculiar virtues of Hoosierdom as a Hoosier could ever be (a large contract, as any citizen of the state will admit), and for a sound reason: he himself had most of them. Indiana reveres its authors; Nicholson was a brilliant essayist, a highly successful novelist and a writer of more than passable verse. Playing politics is the favorite Indiana sport; Nicholson, prominent in Democratic Party affairs, spent his last active years as minister to Paraguay, Venezuela and Nicaragua. Hoosiers admire a man with business sense; Nicholson took excellent care of his affairs in this field.

And in his career as a writer he followed, though not by choice, a suitable program of migration; he was born and spent his childhood at Crawfordsville in the waxing literary light of Lew Wallace, Maurice Thompson, and the sisters Krout, and he moved with his family to Indianapolis in time to join the great days of Riley, Tarkington, and the capital city group.

In addition to these felicitous circumstances of talent and fortune he was something many writers of fiction are not, a careful and thorough scholar. What he has to say is, Indianawise, gospel.

MEREDITH NICHOLSON

The Hoosiers
[1900]

CHAPTER I INDIANA AND HER PEOPLE

THE RISE OF INDIANA as an enlightened commonwealth has been accompanied by phenomena of unusual interest and variety, and whatever contributions the State may make to the total of national achievement in any department of endeavor are to be appraised in the light of her history and development. The origin of the beginners of the State, the influences that wrought upon them, the embarrassments that have attended the later generations in their labors, become matters of moment in any inquiry that is directed to their intellectual history. It is not of so great importance that a few individuals within a State shall, from time to time, show talent or genius, as that the general level of cultivation in the community shall be continually raised. Where, as in Indiana, the appearance of artistic talent follows naturally an intellectual development that uplifts the whole, the condition presented is at once interesting and admirable. Owing to a misapprehension of the State's social history an exaggerated importance has been given to the manifestations of creative talent perceptible in Indiana, the assumption being in many quarters that the Hoosier Commonwealth is in some way set apart from her neighbors by reason of the uncouthness and ignorance of the inhabitants; and the word "Hoosier" has perhaps been unfortunate as applied to Indianians in that it has sometimes been taken as a synonym for boorishness and illiteracy. The Indiana husbandmen, even in the pioneer period, differed little or not at all from the settlers in other territorial divisions of the West and Southwest; and the early Indiana town folk were the peers of any of their fellows of the urban class in the Ohio Valley.

The Indianians came primarily of American stock, and they have been influenced much less than the majority of their neighbors in other states by the currents of alien migration that have flowed around and beyond them. The frontiersmen, who carried the rifle and the axe to make way for the plough, were brave, hardy, and intelligent; and those who accompanied them and became builders of cities and framers and interpreters of law, were their kinsmen, and possessed the natural qualities and the cultivation that would have made them conspicuous anywhere. The Indianians remained in a striking degree the fixed population of the territory that fell to them. They were sustained and lifted by religion through all their formative years, and when aroused to the importance of education were quick to insure intelligence in their posterity. The artistic impulse appeared naturally in later generations. The value of the literature produced in the State may be debatable, but there is no just occasion for surprise that attention to literary expression has been so general.

Indiana has always lain near the currents of national life, and her beginnings were joined to the larger fortunes of the national destiny. Three flags have been emblems of government in her territory, and wars whose principal incidents occurred far from the western wilderness played an important part in her history. Early in the eighteenth century the French settled on the Wabash, which was an essential link in the chain of communication between the settlements of the St. Lawrence and Great Lakes and those of the Lower Mississippi; and the *coureurs des bois*, as they guided their frail navies up and down the stream, or sang their *chansons de voyage* as they lay in lonely camps, gave the first color of romance to the Hoosier country. The treaty signed at Paris, February 10, 1763, ended French dominion and brought British rule. The American Revolution made itself felt on the Wabash when, in 1779, George Rogers Clark effected the capture of Fort Vincennes from a British commander. The first territorial governor of Indiana became the ninth president of the United States after the rollicking hard cider campaign of "Tippecanoe and Tyler too"; and when, years afterward, Benjamin Harrison, his grandson, was elected twenty-third president, the bonds between State and Nation were close and strong. . . .

The victories of George Rogers Clark were not only of great

importance in determining the future political relations of the Northwest Territory, but they defined the character of the population that should dominate in the region he conquered. The Ohio was the highway that led into the new world, and the first comers to Indiana in the years immediately following the Revolution were mainly drawn either directly from Pennsylvania, the Carolinas, or Virginia, or were of that fascinating band of hunters and frontiersmen of similar origin, who had only a few years earlier begun the redemption of Tennessee and Kentucky from savagery. Kentucky was a temporary resting-place for many who later drifted West and Northwest; and their descendants, markedly of Scotch-Irish origin, are still clearly defined in Indiana. Philadelphia and Charleston were the two ports to which these Presbyterian Irish came in greatest numbers in the early years of the eighteenth century. They at once left the seaboard settlements and spread along the Alleghanies, the Pennsylvanians moving southward until they met their Carolina brethren, when the united stream swept with fresh strength boldly into the Ohio Valley. . . . The Germans, also derived from Pennsylvania and the Carolinas, joined the westward stream; the English, the Dutch and the Swiss added to it in varying degree, but the North-Irish element, dating from the earliest settlement, was long potent in politics, society, and religion, and became a most important factor in Indiana history.

Northern Indiana was settled much more slowly than the southern half of the State, owing primarily to the fierce resistance of the Miami Confederacy, which barred ingress by way of the lakes, rivers, and portages, and defeated successive armies that were sent against it. When the way was opened, the Middle States and New England slowly contributed to the population. Many of these immigrants paused first in the Western Reserve of Ohio, and a smaller proportion in Michigan. It is a question for the scientists whether the differences still observable between the people of the northern prairie region in Indiana and those of the woodland areas—differences of thrift, energy, and initiative—are not due as much to natural conditions as to racial influences; and they may also have an explanation of the fact that Indiana's literary activity has been observed principally in the southern half of the State, below a line drawn through

Crawfordsville. The seniority of the southern settlements is not a
wholly satisfactory solution, and the difference in antecedents in-
vites speculation. . . .

The rural and urban classes produced a first generation that realized a type drawing strength from both farm and town and destined
to steady improvement throughout the century. New people poured
in from the Eastern States and from Europe; but in no old community of the seaboard has loftier dignity been conferred by longer
residence or pioneer ancestry than in Indiana. This pride was brought
in more particularly from the Southeast, and there are still communities in which the stranger will be sensible of it. . . . In the
larger cities, as Indianapolis, Evansville, and Fort Wayne, the Germans had an important part from the beginning, and the Irish were
well distributed; but before the Scandinavians and Slavs had begun
to seek homes in America, the land values in Indiana had so appreciated that this class of immigrants could find no footing. The centre
of population in the United States, which lay just east of Baltimore
in the first decade of the century, moved gradually westward, until,
in the last decade, it lay in Indiana at a point sixty-five miles south
of Indianapolis.

The older Indiana towns enjoyed in their beginnings all the benefits that may be bestowed upon new communities by a people of
good social antecedents. Many of these towns have lost their prestige, owing to changed political or commercial conditions; the departed glory of some of them is only a tradition among the elders;
but the charm of many remains. Indiana, as Territory and State,
has had three political capitals, Vincennes and Corydon having enjoyed the distinction before Indianapolis finally attained it. Vincennes, however, refused to fall with her political dethronement, but
built upon her memories, and became "no mean city." In 1847 the
railway connecting Madison with Indianapolis was completed. Madison was thus made the gateway of the State, and one of the most
important shipping points on the Ohio, with daily steam packet
to Cincinnati and Louisville; but this prosperity was only temporary,
for east and west lines of railway soon drew the traffic away from the
river. Madison retains its dignity in spite of reverses, and is marked
by an air of quaint gravity. It may be called picturesque without

offence to the inhabitants, who rejoice in its repose and natural beauty, and do not complain because their wharves are not so busy as they used to be. The social life there had a distinction of its own, which has not vanished, though the names identified with the town's fame—Lanier, Hendricks, Bright, King, and Marshall—have slowly disappeared, and few of the old regime remain. The juxtaposition of Kentucky was not without an influence in the years of the town's ascendancy, and there was no little sympathy with Southern political ideas in the antebellum days.

Brookville is another town which, like Madison, sent forth many men to bring fame to other communities. It lies in the White Water Valley, amid one of the loveliest landscapes in all Hoosierdom. The Wallaces, the Nobles, and the Rays were identified with the place, and each of these families gave a governor to the State. Abram A. Hammond, still another governor, lived there for a short time, as did James B. Eads, the distinguished engineer, who was a native of Lawrenceburg; and William M. Chase, the artist, also a native Hoosier, is one of Brookville's list of notables. . . . Centerville lives principally in its memories, having been the home of the Mortons, and of others who attained distinction. . . . The family of Robert Underwood Johnson was prominent in Wayne County; and though the poet and editor was not born there, he lived in the community from early infancy until his graduation in 1871 from Earlham College, whose seat is Richmond. His cousin, Mrs. Alice Williams Brotherton, the author of two volumes of verse, and a contributor to the periodicals, lived as a young woman at Cambridge, in the same county. . . .

Salem, in Washington County, is another of the older towns that contained in its earliest years families of marked cultivation. John Hay, the author, diplomat, and cabinet officer, and Newtown Booth, governor of California and senator in Congress from that State, were born there. . . .

The successes of several Indiana authors were a great stimulus to literary ambition in Indiana; and the literary clubs were an additional encouragement. Poetry seems to the amateur much more easily achieved than prose, and poets rose in every quarter of the State in the years following the general recognition of James Whitcomb

Riley and Maurice Thompson. There was a time in Indiana when it was difficult to forecast who would next turn poet, suggesting the Tractarian period in England, of which Birrell writes that so prolific were the pamphleteers at the high tide of the movement that a tract might at any time be served upon one suddenly, like a sheriff's process. At Indianapolis the end seemed to have been reached when a retired banker, who had never been suspected, began to inveigle friends into his office on the pretence of business, but really to read to them his own verses. Charles Dennis, a local journalist, declared that there had appeared in the community a peculiar crooking of the right elbow and a furtive sliding of the hand into the left inside pocket, which was an unfailing preliminary to the reading of a poem. Rhyming is, however, the least harmful of amusements, and so fastidious a poet as Gray expressed his belief that even a bad verse is better than the best observation ever made upon it.

"But Time, who soonest drops the heaviest things
    That weight his pack, will carry diamonds long;"

and as the office of the discourager of genius is an ungrateful one, it is doubtless well that many should implore the gods, in the faith that an occasional prayer will be answered.

CHAPTER II THE RURAL TYPE AND THE
DIALECT

THE ORIGIN OF THE TERM "Hoosier" is not known with certainty. It has been applied to the inhabitants of Indiana for many years, and, after "Yankee," it is probably the sobriquet most famous as applied to the people of a particular division of the country. So early as 1830, "Hoosier" must have had an accepted meaning, within the State at least, for John Finley printed in that year, as a New Year's address for the Indianapolis *Journal*, a poem called "The Hoosier's Nest," * in which the word occurs several times. It is a fair assumption that its meaning was not obscure, or it would not

* Finley's poem is given in full in Chapter Four.

have been used in a poem intended for popular reading. "Hoosier" seems to have found its first literary employment in Finley's poem. Sulgrove, who was an authority on matters of local history, was disposed to concede this point. The poem is interesting for its glimpse of Indiana rural life of the early period. Finley was a Virginian who removed to Indiana in 1823 and had been living in the State seven years when he published his poem. He was an accomplished and versatile gentleman, and his verses, as collected in 1866, show superior talents. . . .

. . . Both Governor Wright and O. H. Smith were of the opinion that "Hoosier" was a corruption of "Who's here" (*yere* or *hyer*); and Smith has sought to dramatize its history:—

> "The night was dark, the rain falling in torrents, when the inmates of a small log cabin in the woods of early Indiana were aroused from their slumbers by a low knocking at the only door of the cabin. The man of the house, as he had been accustomed to do on like occasions, rose from his bed and hallooed, 'Who's here?' The outsiders answered, 'Friends, out bird-catching. Can we stay till morning?' The door was opened, and the strangers entered. A good log fire soon gave light and warmth to the room. Stranger to the host: 'What did you say when I knocked?' 'I said, Who's here?' 'I thought you said Hoosier.' The bird-catchers left after breakfast, but next night returned and hallooed at the door, 'Hoosier;' and from that time the Indianians have been called Hoosiers."

This is the explanation usually given to inquirers within the State. The objection has sometimes been raised to this story, that the natural reply to a salutation in the wilderness would be "Who's there?" out of which "Hoosier" could hardly be formed; but careful observers of Western and Southern dialects declare that "Who's hyer?" was, and in obscure localities remains, the common answer to a midnight hail.

Sulgrove related the incident of an Irishman, employed in excavating the canal around the falls at Louisville, who declared after a fight in which he had vanquished several fellow-laborers that he was "a husher," and this was offered as a possible origin of the word. The same writer suggested another explanation, that a certain

Colonel Lehmanowski, a Polish officer who lectured through the West on Napoleon's wars, pronounced Hussar in a way that captivated some roystering fellow, who applied the word to himself in self-glorification, pronouncing it "Hoosier." Lehmanowski's identity has been established as a sojourner in Indiana, and his son was a member of an Indiana regiment in the Civil War. The Rev. Aaron Woods is another contributor to the literature of the subject, giving the Lehmanowski story with a few variations. When the young men of the Indiana side of the Ohio crossed over to Louisville, the Kentuckians made sport of them, calling them "New Purchase greenies," and declaring that they of the southern side of the river were a superior race, composed of "half-alligator, half-horse, and tipped off with snapping turtle!" Fighting grew out of these boasts in the market place and streets of Louisville. An Indiana visitor who had heard Lehmanowski lecture on "The Wars of Europe" and been captivated by the prowess of the Hussars, whipped one of the Kentuckians, and bending over him cried, "I'm a Hoosier," meaning, "I'm a Hussar." Mr. Woods adds that he was living in the State at the time and that this was the true origin of the term. This is, however, hardly conclusive. The whole Lehmanowski story seems to be based on communication between Indiana and Kentucky workmen during the building of the Ohio Falls Canal. The original canal was completed in 1830; and . . . the Polish soldier was not in this region earlier than 1840, ten years after the appearance of Finley's poem. . . .

It is clear that the cultivated people of Indiana recognized the nickname in the early half of the century. Wright and Smith, as mentioned above, had sought to determine its genesis; and Tilghman A. Howard, when a congressman from Indiana, writing home to a friend in 1840, spoke casually of the "Hoosier State." The word occurs familiarly in Hall's "New Purchase" (1855), and it is found also in Beste's rare volume, "The Wabash; or, Adventures of an English Gentleman's Family in the Interior of America," published at London in the same year, and in Mrs. Beecher's "From Dawn to Daylight" (1859). . . .

No reader of Hoosier chronicles can fail to be impressed by the relation of the great forests to the people who came to possess and tame them. Before they reached the Indiana wilderness in their advance before civilization, the stalwart pioneers had swung their axes in Pennsylvania or Kentucky, and had felt the influence of the great, gloomy woodlands in their lives; but in Indiana this influence was greatly intensified. They experienced an isolation that is not possible today in any part of the country, and the loss of nearly every civilizing agency that men value. These frontiersmen could hardly have believed themselves the founders of a permanent society, for the exact topography of much of their inheritance was unknown to them; large areas were submerged for long periods, and the density of the woods increased the difficulty of building roads and knitting the scattered clearings and villages into a compact and sensitive commonwealth. . . .

The pioneers could not see then, as their children see now, that the wilderness was a factor in their destiny; that it drove them in upon themselves, strengthening their independence in material things by shutting them off from older communities, and that it even fastened upon their tongues the peculiarities of speech which they had brought with them into the wilderness. But their isolation compelled meditation, and when reading matter penetrated the woodlands, it was usually worth the trouble of transportation in a day of few roads and little travel. . . .

It has been insisted by loyal Indianians that the speech of the later generations of natives is almost normal English; that the rough vernacular of their ancestors has been ground down in the schools, and that the dictionaries are rapidly sanctioning new words, once without authority, that inevitably crept into common speech through the necessities of pioneer expression. It may fairly be questioned whether, properly speaking, there ever existed a Hoosier dialect. The really indigenous Indiana words and novel pronunciations are so few as to make but a poor showing when collected; and while the word "dialect" is employed as a term of convenience in this connection, it can only be applied to a careless manner of speaking, in which novel words are merely incidental. A book of colloquial terms, like Green's "Virginia Word Book," could hardly be compiled for Indiana without infringing upon the prior claims of other and older States to the greater part of it. The so-called Hoosier dialect, where it survives at all, is the speech of the first American settlers in Indiana, greatly modified by time and schooling, but retaining, both in the employment of colloquial terms and in pronunciation, the peculiarities that were carried westward from tide water early in the nineteenth century. The distinctive Indiana countryman, the real Hoosier, who has been little in contact with the people of cities, speaks a good deal as his Pennsylvania or North Carolina or Kentucky grandfather or great-grandfather did before him, and has created nothing new. His speech contains comparatively few words that are peculiar to the State or to communities within it; but in the main it shares such deviations from normal or literary English with the whole Southwest.

In his book "The Wabash" Beste describes his interview with an Indiana carpenter, who questioned whether the traveller was really an Englishman, because his speech was unlike that of the usual English immigrants whose trouble with the aspirate had evoked derisive comment among the Americans. This occurs in his chapter on Indianapolis, in which the carpenter is quoted thus:

" 'You do not say 'ouse' and 'and' for 'house' and 'hand'; all the children, and all of you, pronounce all these words like Americans, and not as real English pronounce them. Their way of speaking makes us always say that we talk better English than the English themselves.' I had, indeed, often heard the Americans laughed at for saying so; but now the matter was explained. My carpenter repeated with great accuracy various instances of provincialisms and vulgarisms which he and all of them had noticed more or less, in all the English emigrants who had come amongst them. Seeing none of any other class, they naturally supposed that all English people pronounced the language in the same manner, and so prided themselves upon the superiority of American English. For notwithstanding the disagreeable nasal tone and drawling whine in which most of them speak, and notwithstanding a few national phrases and the peculiar use and pronunciation of certain words, it must be admitted that the American people, in general, speak English without provincial dialect or vulgarisms. Whence, in fact, could they acquire such, since all the emigrants they see came from different parts of England, and the provincialisms of the one neutralize those of the other." . . .

Lapses in pronunciation have never been punishable with death on the Wabash, as at the fords of the Jordan, where the shibboleth test of the Gileadites cost the Ephriamites forty and two thousand. The native Indianian is not sensitive about his speech and refuses to be humble before critics from the far East who say "idea-r" and "Philadelphia-r." . . .

It is likely that during the next quarter of a century the continued fusion of the various elements of Western population will create a dead level of speech, approximating accuracy, so that in a typical American State like Indiana local usages will disappear, and the only oddities discernible will be those of the well-nigh universal slang, which even now reach Colorado and California almost as soon as they are known at the Atlantic seaboard. At the South and in New England, where there is less mingling of elements, the old usages will probably endure much longer; and it is a fair assumption that in the Mississippi Valley and in the Trans-Missouri country, a normal American speech free of local idiosyncrasies will appear first. Our keen sense of humor and our love of the conveniences of speech are likely to continue to be national traits, leading to the creation and adoption of slang from time to time; but where a people imply quotation marks in all their lapses from propriety, they anticipate and destroy criticism.

Not being gifted with the power of prophecy, Meredith Nicholson could no more anticipate that the very year he published, 1900, was the beginning of a Golden Age of Indiana letters than Heath Bowman could know, in 1945, that it was not yet over. It is scarcely necessary to note that, within ten years after he wrote The Hoosiers, *Nicholson himself, Booth Tarkington, George Barr McCutcheon, David Graham Phillips, George Ade, Gene Stratton Porter, Maurice Thompson and Charles Major would not only be among America's most celebrated, most successful writers of fiction, they would, by any reasonable standard, be the most celebrated!*

Apparently, by the evidence of Nicholson, Bowman, and Patrick, it is only necessary to let the Hoosier fields lie fallow for a spell, every decade or so, to guarantee a continuing production of one of Indiana's most valuable crops.

There are contributing factors of course; something besides the soil must be right for book production. Perhaps the poetry and romance which has marked so much of Indiana writing has been prompted by the names of Indiana places. Whether or not there is a connection,

VIRGINIA SCOTT MINER

had some pleasant things to say about those names:

Indiana Names

Sing your songs of the eastern sea,
    And make your redwood boast,
But the fairest names in the land to me
    Are not of the country's coast.

Neither the Yankee white-spire towns
    Nor the shores of blue Carmel
Can savor the glory that still abounds—
    With an almost magic spell—

In the great old Indian names that star
    These towns and lakes and springs,
As rich and strange as the feathers are
    In a mallard's breast and wings.

And these are the names where arrowheads
    Are lying close by the rushes,
Where the bluegills rise from off their beds,
    And there's singing of the thrushes!

Manitou and Wawasee,
    And Ken-a-po-co-mo-co,
And Papakeechie, mad with glee
    When the fire-water sent him loco.

Menominee, who preached of God,
    The white man's God, to his race—
And vanished into the nameless sod
    Of some Tipton halting place.

And Winamac—a deadly one
    Grown bitter for his kind;
The other, friend of Harrison,
    And bold to speak his mind.

Pokágon chieftains, brave and wise,
    Tecumseh and his brother—
And one they called the Great Snake lies
    Now still as any other . . .

Except about these, legends grew,
    A wealth of debated story,
From the Wabash banks to the Tippecanoe—
    From Vincennes to Buzzards' Glory!

CHAPTER TWO

The Fight for Indiana

War for the possession of good Indiana lands did not begin—as did so many other ills—with the arrival of civilized men of European origin. Abundant evidence exists to prove that conquest had been carried on intermittently since the first skin-clad beings slunk fearfully in along the courses of the Wabash and Ohio Rivers to seek food and shelter for themselves, their women and their children.

When whites came to Indiana they found Indians of appearance and culture similar to those whom the first American settlers had met and conquered upon the Atlantic seaboard and Gulf Coast: simple folk, satisfied with little, not harassed by ambition, easily imposed upon and ready victims of the white man's greed and vices.

But there were traces of earlier people, some of quite primitive culture and others obviously of a greater day from which the Indians of historic times seemed to have degenerated. Most obvious monuments to the passing of the greatest of the modern Indians' predecessors were the mounds, which appeared remarkable even to the most ignorant whites who visited the wilderness. These mounds were, and are, of all shapes—conical, pyramidal, circular and square. Some were small, some were of tremendous size, but all were obviously beyond either the capacity for planning or the imaginable concerted effort of the Indians known to white men. Buried in these mounds were the skeletons of their builders, with their beautifully carved pipes and images, handsome pottery, ornaments, weapons and utensils expertly worked in copper, and the remnants of fine cloth—goods of workmanship and quality far superior to the best of those imagined by the historic Indians of Indiana. Furthermore the historic Indians had only vague traditions as to how or when the mounds had come to

be. Of what had happened either to their makers or to the spirit
which had prompted their making they had no idea whatever.

As the state began to be peopled by educated men who were aware
of the antiquities of Europe, Africa and Asia, the mounds attracted
great interest. They were measured, excavated, and described in newspapers and periodicals by amateur archeologists who were, otherwise,
doctors, lawyers, farmers and businessmen—private individuals all,
working for the love of it.

Following this tradition Eli Lilly, Indianapolis manufacturer, in
1937 gathered together his own studies and those of his predecessors
in a book which presents the accumulated knowledge of these Indiana
mounds and the people from beyond "sombre clouds obscuring the
past" who constructed them and who left mementos of their arts
within. The following passages sketch the high points of Indiana's
prehistory:

ELI LILLY

Prehistoric Antiquities of Indiana

Due to the many and varied attacks made upon the problems
of prehistory, it may be said that certain vague, shadowy forms seem
to be taking shape through the somber clouds obscuring the past,
especially near the border of the misty curtain and in the ghostly
middle distances. Relatively inadequate tribal traditions, mythology,
unrelated pieces of archaeological work, language structure, burial
customs, and skeletal characteristics are sandy foundations upon
which to build theories as to the migrations of the tribes, and the
resulting story may be of "such stuff as dreams are made on." It is
extremely interesting, nevertheless, to attempt to anticipate what
the findings will be and to explain the methods that are being followed with the hope of final success in working out the mystery.

The persistence, perception, and the spades of the archaeologists
have classified the known mounds and village sites of the Ohio
Valley into two and possibly three main "patterns." They are the

"Mississippi," the "Woodland," and a third which has not been satisfactorily named, but which embraces the "Hopewellian phase" and the "Adena aspect." Some authorities think this third pattern should be included in the "Woodland" pattern, for to them it would appear that Hopewell in the North is basically Woodland, modified by Mississippi and other as yet unidentified influences from the South. These patterns each reveal certain sets of characteristics of the cultures of the different peoples formerly inhabiting this great valley. . . .

Mr. Lilly's scholarly listing of all the identifying points of the three cultures is probably a bit beyond the interest of the layman. Perhaps it will suffice to say that:

The people whose lives followed the "Woodland Pattern" occupied temporary round houses and constructed mounds only for burial purposes. They buried their dead sometimes in ordinary graves, sometimes in the mounds, with the bodies usually in a flexed posture but sometimes extended, dismembered or even cremated. Not much in the way of goods were placed in the graves but items found about their large village sites include stone arrow and spear points, pestles of the roller, bell or muller types, pipes made of stone or clay in several styles, and simple tempered pottery.

The production of those who followed the "Mississippi Pattern" was much more elaborate; their cultural development was much higher and their government and village organization must have been quite efficient. They lived in rectangular, semipermanent houses constructed of clay, mats and thatching on a log frame; their villages were surrounded by earthen walls, reinforced with logs and sometimes including bays spaced two bow-shots apart so that defenders could cover every part of the wall with their volleys of arrows. The structures which most distinguish this culture are the flat-topped pyramid mounds, many of enormous size, which they built as substructures for their houses and public buildings. They used stone, horn, bone, shell, clay, copper and wood to make tools, utensils, weapons and ornaments, and their workmanship and design was careful and artistic. Their pottery was especially interesting since it was of a great variety of finish and decoration and was frequently made in the shape of animals, men and women. They made copper beads, ear

*spools and gorgets and sometimes overlaid wood and metal objects
with thin sheets of copper.*

Not much is yet known of the houses built by the people of the
"Hopewellian Phase," but they used their mounds for burial purposes and often built elaborate earthworks in geometrical designs.
They also buried their dead in a variety of positions and sometimes
encased the bodies in stone or log tombs. The Hopewell people used
materials from all over the continent and were particularly fond of
beautifully designed ornaments, jewelry and headdresses made of
copper and mica and decorated with freshwater pearls. They made
good cloth and a considerable variety of pottery, but it was as workers in copper and in pearls and other decorative material that they
were most distinguished.

Resuming Mr. Lilly's account:

With the slowly accumulating knowledge regarding these patterns
and their traits, and many sidelights flashed by related sciences
through the murky darkness surrounding the subject, some progress
has been made in attacking the problem from both the archaeological
and the traditional-historical angles. . . .

Judging from the archaeological evidence in this and surrounding
states, it is believed that Indiana must have been first inhabited by
a few primitive, longheaded, hunter-fisher folk of one or several
origins, some of them possibly related to the Ozark bluff dwellers
and to the inhabitants of the Kentucky rock shelters and caves.
Possibly one of these early groups built the stone mounds border-
ing the Ohio and its tributaries. Those along the Whitewater River
are of special interest to the people of Indiana. . . . These primitive
groups had no corn nor tobacco, little pottery, and they buried their
dead in many ways. Possibly some of these early groups may have
made the very characteristic projectile blades known as Folsom
points. . . . This particular type of point has been found at . . .
locations in the Southwest, so closely associated with the bones of
prehistoric animals as to leave no doubt as to their having been
contemporaneous.

Let us say, then, to begin our speculations, that between approx-
imately 10,000 and 1000 B.C., Indiana was inhabited by a slowly
growing number of roving, primitive men who gained their living by

hunting and fishing, and whose known traits have been briefly mentioned above. This period saw great changes in the climate, flora, and other factors in the environment of Indiana. In 10,000 B.C., a cold and humid climate supported thick forests of spruce, pine, and fir, a background befitting wandering hunters. From 8000 to 5000 B.C., the weather conditions were cool and dry, the evergreen forests giving place to dense, mixed woodlands. From 5000 to 1000 B.C., less humid conditions resulted in oak-hickory savannas. The optimum conditions favoring the culture of maize prevailed in 1000 B.C.

Then let us say that these primitive groups were followed by, driven out by, or amalgamated with, tribes showing Hopewellian cultural characteristics. It may even be that they themselves developed Hopewellian culture. First came the Adena or early Hopewellian period, which was brought to full flower in the later Hopewellian (commonly called Hopewell) culture. Influences from the South, either through tribal migration or diffusion of traits from one tribe to another, helped to produce the different intensities of Hopewell in the North. . . .

The path of the Hopewellian influence into Indiana was along the river valleys, the Ohio, Wabash, White River, the Whitewater, and into northern Indiana and Michigan along the Illinois, Kankakee, and St. Joseph rivers. Traces are found toward the north in Iowa, Illinois, Indiana and especially in Ohio. The shapes of their skulls varied. In some sites the prevailing types were longheaded, and in others they were round, while in still others they were mesocephalic. This may indicate a mixture of races which may in turn account for the ensuing cultural climax. The shadowy mists surrounding these groups are still so dense as to be almost impenetrable. It may be that the dawn of this culture was as early as that of Pueblo I, or about two thousand years ago. More orthodox opinion would probably assign a later date, say in the middle of the first Christian millennium, and place its culmination in the fourteenth or fifteenth century. Be that as it may, to the Hopewellian people we attribute certain forms of beautiful ceremonial stonework and most of our Indiana mounds, such as those at Winchester, New Castle, Anderson, Vincennes, groups in Greene and Porter counties and along the Whitewater, and many of those situated upon the banks of the Ohio River. These people also secured by trade or raid the ruddy metal from the Michigan copper mines, obsidian from the Yellowstone, mica from the Carolinas, and shells from the Gulf of Mexico.

This stimulating period began when Indiana's warm, dry climate had fostered oak-hickory savannas, and summer-green deciduous forest lands furnished the most favorable conditions for the cultivation of Indian corn. These important factors were very possibly the underlying causes that led the Hopewellian people to invade such "Islands of the Blest," or to increase and multiply amidst such prosperity. By the beginning of the historic period, the increasing humidity had thickened the mixed woodland to an almost impenetrable forest, making the growing of maize much more difficult.

With "controlled imagination" still at work, and stimulated by the knowledge conveyed by several stratified sites in Illinois, Wisconsin, and Iowa, and certain indications within our own borders, let us proceed to account for the period lying between 1000 A.D. and historic times. Early in this era, it may be assumed, tribes of the so-called Middle Phase of the Mississippi Pattern were well established, along our southern border in particular. They inhabited southern Illinois and had an outpost as far north as Wisconsin.

The present state of our knowledge would lead us to believe that the linguistic stocks of this period in southern Indiana, having Middle Mississippi culture traits, numbered two—the Muskhogean and Siouan. . . . A hazarded guess would be that the southeastern Muskhogean people were responsible for the great Angel group of mounds six miles east of Evansville, including a large, terraced, flat-topped mound, and that there they probably built well-thatched temples and caciques' dwellings of wattlework so characteristic of that group. The mound and village were presumably surrounded by a tall, forbidding, mud-plastered palisade made of tree trunks, with protruding bastions at regular intervals. They built a great flat-topped mound at Murphy Landing in Posey County, measuring at the top one hundred by two hundred feet, and were responsible for many villages. These works resemble those at Etowah and in many other places to the south and east long held by the Muskhogean tribes.

On the other hand, the village and burial site near the mouth of the Wabash yielded so many artifacts similar to the Oneota culture, such as limestone disk pipes, copper ear coils, tubular beads, and characteristic triangular arrow points, that Siouan relationship seems almost certain. Probably the village at Bone Bank and the "citadel" at Merom, both on the lower Wabash, were also Siouan sites. . . . Their pottery was extremely well developed into many shapes . . . hooded bottles, some in the form of squatting, hunchbacked women; effigies of fish and other real and imaginary creatures, with the heads on one side of the opening and the tails on the other. . . .

At this particular point, it is probably fair to let history and tradition have their innings on the subject of the early inhabitants of the Ohio Valley. A thorough search for, and co-ordination of, information on tribal migration in archaeological and ethnological literature points to the Siouan-speaking peoples as the earliest known highly developed group in the upper Ohio Valley. That they were driven out by an inthrust, probably by the Iroquoian-speaking peoples, is indicated by their peripheral position when first encountered by the whites—the eastern coast in Virginia and North and South Carolina on the one hand, and the western branches of the Missouri and middle and upper Mississippi rivers on the other. The traditions of some of these western Siouan tribes tell of a migration down the Ohio to their present habitats. Early French reports say that the Ohio was called the "river of the Akansea [Quapaw]" after one of the Siouan tribes whose village on the Mississippi was visited by De Soto in 1540.

To continue this picture: It would seem that the Iroquois had a part in driving out the Sioux. A suggestion of this is made by Adair, who says: "The six united northern nations [the Iroquois] have been from time immemorial engaged in a bitter war" with the Catawba, a Siouan tribe. Of course real proof as to which linguistic stock first occupied the upper Ohio Valley, the Siouan or the Iroquoian, is nonexistent. . . .

From the traditional-historical angle it would seem that the Iroquois-speaking nations (including the Cherokee) were followed by the inpouring of the Algonquian hordes from the north and north-

west, who, in turn, pushed eastward through the Iroquoian linguistic stock in the Ohio Valley, leaving them on the sidelines, as
it were, along the St. Lawrence on the one hand and, in the case of
the Cherokee, in the mountains of Virginia and North and South
Carolina on the other. . . .

The beginning of the main invasion of the Algonquian peoples
brings us fairly close to historical times. . . . According to the tradition repeated by the great Miami chief Little Turtle, members of
that tribe were masters of the whole of Indiana, and of Ohio east to
the Scioto River, and had possession of our fertile valleys where they
built their villages and planted their waving, fragrant corn. Portions
of the tribe subsequently pushed to the northwest into Wisconsin.
It is quite probable that the Miami have lived longer continuously
in Indiana than any other modern tribe. William De Lisle's map,
published in Paris in 1718, shows Miami villages on the Wabash at
Ouiatenon near Lafayette, and at Vincennes. The former town was
said to have had a sizeable population. Except during the latter half
of the seventeenth century, when Indiana is said to have been practically denuded of population, their residence was uninterrupted
until they were sent beyond the Mississippi in 1832.

About the time that La Salle first visited northern Indiana, savage depredations by the fierce Iroquois had practically stripped Indiana of inhabitants, from about 1650 until about 1700. This federa-
tion enjoyed the blessings of gunpowder, receiving it from the Dutch
in 1630, while the other tribes, still equipped with aboriginal weapons, could not stand against them and retired to Illinois and Kentucky. La Salle found very few Indians in the northwestern part of
our state in December, 1679, but the French took steps to arm their
allies and they swarmed back into the empty forests after successfully repulsing the Iroquois about the year 1700.

In the eighteenth century the roving Shawnee hunted through
and harassed the settlers in the southern part of the state. The
Lenápe or Delawares came back from their eastern migration to the
central eastern section, and the Potawatomi swung down the west
shore and around the southern end of Lake Michigan in the last
quarter of the 1700's to build their wigwams and light their fires in

our northern lake region. The Miami, Illinois, and Kickapoo gradually worked back into the western and southwestern sections from Illinois just before 1700.

Such were the positions of the tribes when the white settlers came and began to crowd the forest people toward the West. . . .

The first white men to enter the undefined borders of Indiana were, possibly, a wandering conquistador or two, strays from De Soto's bloody band after it had begun to reap some of the horror it sowed among the southern Indians.

Once the seaboard colonies had been planted, English bond-servants were brought to America. Naturally, with freedom so readily available, they soon began to disappear into the great woods beyond the coastal plain. Those who were most apt to run away were of two opposite types: the intelligent and ambitious or the ignorant and desperate. Before 1700, when the French made the northern detour through the Great Lakes and established settlements in the Mississippi Valley, such runaways could find only one sanctuary—with the Indian tribes. Some of them married Indian women and either sank to the level of their in-laws or set new standards, introduced new ways, among the people of their adoption. Some of these certainly reached Hoosier territory.

At least one Dutchman from Albany, Arnout Viele, traded along the Indiana bank of the Ohio in 1693 and 1694; shortly after that the French moved in from the north to establish, in time, the posts at Vincennes, Ouiatenon and present Fort Wayne.

The French and Indian War had little effect upon the Indiana scene; those three French posts were abandoned (by their military but not by their civilian population) but the British were in no hurry to occupy them and life went on as before. In fact wars of a national scope touched Indiana only three times in the early days; there were raids, expeditions, massacres and counter measures, but only during the American Revolution, the Indian wars of the seventeen-nineties, and at the opening of the War of 1812 did the state see full-scale military action.

CAROLINE VIRGINIA KROUT

(a member of the Crawfordsville houseful of Krout sisters who in the eyes of Hoosiers held a rank similar, intellectually, to that of the sisters Brontë in England) laid the scene of a novel in Vincennes during the stirring times of the Revolution.

As the story opens George Rogers Clark, the dashing Virginia red-head, had brought a tiny rag-tail army into present Indiana and Illinois, had captured the British governors of Kaskaskia, Cahokia and Vincennes and had won over the congenitally anti-British French of those towns. Eventually he hoped to go on north to capture that British stronghold, Detroit, in the present state of Michigan, from which Indian raids against the Ohio were directed and where the raiders returned to be paid for American prisoners and/or scalps taken.

But Clark had spread his little force too thin. When Governor Henry Hamilton of Detroit (called the "Hair-buyer General," although he was not a general at all) came down to Vincennes with a large force of Canadians, British regulars and Indians, the fort at Vincennes was manned only by Captain Leonard Helm and two or three Americans. Middle-aged Helm was no fool; he surrendered, although he demanded full military pomp and pageantry for the occasion, sent a message to Clark at Kaskaskia, and sat, a prisoner in the fort, to await Clark's coming.

He was not to be disappointed, as Miss Krout points out:

On the We-a Trail

CHAPTER XXXV A GAME OF PIQUET

It was a muggy night after a period of drizzling, wet days when the grass had been soaked from dull green (for it had been an "open" winter) to the duller brown of ultimate decay, to which nature brings everything, animal and vegetable, high and low, at last.

The mud in the fort grounds would have been knee deep but for Hamilton's timely application of gravel. The sky was lowering and thick with mist that needed but a waft of colder wind to distil it into drops, as a peevish child melts to tears at the one trifle too much.

It was eminently a night for pleasure indoors, and Hamilton vaguely pitied the unlucky wight who had business out; as he heard the dull tread of the sentries, and thought of Lamothe, whom he had sent off that morning on a scouting expedition. When he reached Helm's quarters he found pleasant company, and he threw off his cloak and hat without waiting for his host (who called out a cheery greeting) to rise from an occupation that promised much. Helm was crouched over the hearth, in the full heat of the fire, though not in need of warming, as his flaming face testified.

He was watching a row of red-cheeked apples fade in the glow, like rosy girls in the perfervid fire of life, into an ugly brown, all their lusty color scorched from them as he turned them slowly before the hot bank of coals. When the odor of pleasant juices reached him, Hamilton sniffed unctuously as a cat sniffs catnip. He drew near the hearth, and placing himself to one side where he could watch the agreeable task of his host, rubbing his chill hands, smacking his lips, he remarked:—

"If I mistake not all the signs, Helm, we are in for one of your incomparable brews. Eh?"

"I design nothing else, general, though most soldiers in my case would prefer a 'brew' of another sort!" he replied, with a scarcely perceptible straying of the eye toward Major La Grasse and Captain Bosseron, paroled residents of O Poste, who at that moment entered together, coming in from the town.

Bellefluille, the interpreter, answered to Helm's remark.

"Small chance of any other kind this night, captain, unless it be of rain,—which le bon Dieu avert! We have had more than a stomach full of that."

All the guests, but the newcomers, were gathered about the table dicing. Hamilton retired from the fireside and seated himself apart from the others at the extreme end of the table, a long slab of puncheon, and fell to sorting over a pack of cards, preparatory to getting satisfaction out of Helm for his last defeat at piquet, by that worthy. He counted aloud absently, "ace," "deuce," "tray," as he threw them into two piles.

Hay sat on a corner of the table, idly swinging his foot in the pauses of the game he was engaged in, watching intently each step of the toddy making.

Bosseron approached the hearth, his back to the rest, and stretched out his hands to the blaze to warm them. As he did so Helm glanced up casually at him and met a look so meaning, so triumphant, he read it, with the intuition of a woman, as a message of import. Tact silenced his lips, but his eyes flashed the question, "Good news?"

Bosseron's lips silently formed the word "Yes."

The next moment his interest centred on his row of apples, now done to a turn, their thin skins bursting, showing the foamy white inside. With a hand that trembled slightly he nicely blended the brandy, water, sugar, and spice (a modicum of dried sassafras and spice-wood bark doing duty), turned it into the great iron brewing cup, and thrust the long nozzle into a bed of living coals well inside the fireplace. He hung over it as solicitously as a young mother over a sick babe, but managed meantime to keep up a volley of chaffing with his guests. Noticing Hamilton's occupation, he cried:—

"Don't hope to beat me at piquet, general. By the Eternal! I've come to think my victory over you foreordained."

This "double entente" was not lost on La Grasse and Bosseron, who smiled broadly.

Hamilton glanced up from the cards and said somewhat testily,—

"Destiny in battle is not foretold by a pack of dirty cards, begad!"

"Spoken like a soldier. No! by Heaven, 'tis by courage, endurance in the face of every difficulty and danger. God prosper the right!"

Hamilton looked surprised at this outburst, and remarked dryly:—

"This post is rather a hard billet, but I've no reason to complain except for this cursed dullness. Much I owe you, Helm, for becoming my prisoner."

There was a very slight emphasis on the last word.

"And I you for being my guest," Helm replied, with irresistible bravado, which puzzled the Frenchmen and made the Englishmen laugh.

"Besides, it will be livelier soon," said Hamilton, with unmistakable meaning.

"I doubt it not," acquiesced Helm, nonchalantly, turning to his brew. He lifted it to a hotter bed, and was just settling it to his satisfaction when there was a crack from a gun, a rattle, and a great lump of dried mud fell down the chimney and splashed into the mixture. Helm started back to get out of the cloud of hot aromatic steam. The vessel had turned sideways and had spilt most of the posset on the fire; but he carefully righted it, skimmed off the mud, and roared out:—

"By the God of heaven, gentlemen, that's Clark's soldiers. And they'll take your fort. But," he added whimsically, "they ought not to have spoiled this apple-toddy!"

Dice turned up double sixes in vain. Cards were flung to the wind. Hamilton rushed to the parade ground, followed by all but Helm. Balls whistled about his ears. A sergeant fell, shot dead. An instant more and the drums sounded a wild alarm,—the fort was roused. For a brief space there followed a state of seeming confusion, then the well-disciplined men were in position,—gunners and swabbers at the cannon; musketeers at the port-holes; lights out.

At the first alarm a detail had rushed forward to barricade the gate toward the church, when, to their consternation, it burst open. It was only McBeth, the post surgeon, who entered in furious haste. . . .

Helm and the handful of prisoners were forgotten in the suddenness of the attack, and the wild excitement following upon it. His quarters were deserted of all who had been his guests but a short ten minutes before. Mild domestic peace had given place to fierce, cruel war. Helm stood by his hearth, tranquilly sipping a glass of the scalding toddy, now and then blowing upon it to cool it, and listening to the din noising outside.

"I'm neither a prophet, nor the son of a prophet! But, by the Eternal! I was right that time!"

He swallowed a draught in silent toast, and smacked his lips loudly in appreciation of the merits of both the prophecy and the brew. . . .

A quiet now ensued, so perfect that the angry rush of the river, full to the brim, not fifty feet back of Helm's cabin, could be distinctly heard. Then followed a mighty blare of cannon, shrill cries, and loud huzzahs,—the tremendous harmony of battle!

The loud cheers roused Helm. They were the blended voices of his old comrades, as he well knew. He ran to the nearest block-house in the thick of it, the one overlooking the church. He mounted the ladder and stood by the grimy gunner as he rammed home the charge and touched off the vent. The flame leaped outward. The ball sped with a sharp hiss; the gunner peered on the instant through the embrasure. His shadow fell across it. Ping! a bullet sang. He fell dead! Before his shot had reached its aim a musket-ball had pierced his breast.

"It's the Virginians, no doubt after that!" said Helm, proudly. "They are the only soldiers that can shoot at a shadow and kill a man!"

Without hesitation, the man swabbing out the bore of the gun took the dead man's place, pushing to one side with his foot the out-flung arm of the gunner that he might not tread upon it. He bent forward. Before he could ram home the charge, a bullet bored through his skull near the corner of the eye.

"By all the fiends of hell! these fellows shoot at your shadow and leave you a shade," muttered Helm, looking down at the slain men. "I must have a care that I'm not plugged myself! But this fellow mustn't be silent. He can only tell tales, as Pat would say, by keeping still!" He dragged the dead out of the way. . . .

The air was swart with smoke! The rayless darkness was lit mo-mently into horrid brilliancy by flamings of cannon, and from every port-hole to the east rifles flashed a narrow jet of fire.

Each impotent volley from within was received with jeers and taunts by the Americans without. Clark's men were firing inter-mittently; now and again their long squirrel-rifles carried swift death within through every crack and crevice. Outside the fort, intermingled with the noise of battle, were sounds of chopping, followed by a crash; dull blows were succeeded by the ripping apart of timbers. But to those within the fort worse than all these were the periods of perfect quiet, lasting but a few moments, but to their strained and anxious ears seeming to be hours long.

They set the nerves a-quiver; the teeth a-chatter with dread of what might come next. The besiegers were so close under the stockade their movements could not be seen. They slipped like shadows following the sun, from one point to another, and after an interval of racking suspense the attack would come from a new quarter. Then swivels must be turned, cannon shifted, to meet the new attack. After volley-firing would come, at long intervals, the deadly single shots of the sharp-shooters, when the shadow of some incautious, curious gunner darkened the port for an instant, peering out to behold—death! Scarcely a missent shot was fired by Clark's men.

Hamilton pervaded the fort, cool and brave. But he was secretly chagrined to have been caught napping by an army of backwoodsmen, such as he conceived Clark's to be. He was a good officer and knew what his men were about. When the cannon in the southwest blockhouse rang out sharply and regularly, he gave no further attention to it, for he was needed elsewhere.

At last the blackness of the long night began to yield to the graying of dawn. Trembling shafts of light began to part the curtain of smoke and let the morning in. The Americans seemed to have withdrawn; their rifles were quiet after a terrible night of action. The cannon in the fort paused as if to catch breath. The dominant sound was the rush of the river, muddy and swollen, which spread wide on the farther shore to the very lodges of the Piankeshaws. . . .

The wan light proved truly the beginning of another day. The sun appeared a glittering blotch on a dull gray sky and gradually penetrated the sulphurous smoke that hovered over the fort. With the day's return was revealed to Hamilton the true significance of the dull blows and crashings heard in the night. Three hundred yards before the gate, toward the village, the Americans had thrown up a barricade of trees and earth, and were strongly intrenched behind it. They had pulled down the adjacent barns and cabins, leaving a broad space between the fort and village. How they could have accomplished all this and have kept up so galling a fire amazed Hamilton. His wonder would have increased had he known that these 154 men stood up to the work after a march of fifteen days of incredible hardship, the last week up to the armpits through water over the Drowned Lands, covered for six miles by the overflow of the Ouibache; and that, after eating the first full meal they had had for six days, wet, ragged, wayworn, without a thought of rest, they had commenced the attack and kept it up so hotly all night that he was put on his mettle with his fresh troops to meet it. The invincible, unconquerable spirit of the Americans might have warned him and his compatriots of the inevitable outcome of the struggle, not only here but in the colonies.

Hamilton strongly suspected that the villagers had given aid. Clark forbade them to take part in the assault; but they had indeed been of great assistance, melting pewter utensils into bullets, felling trees, tearing down buildings, throwing up earthworks, and above all, by unearthing a goodly store of buried powder.

The Americans seemed indeed insensible to fatigue. With the return of day they renewed the assault with unabated energy. Now it was at the price of life a figure passed before a port-hole. Ping! spoke the bullet. Death answered.

Helm, stripped to the waist, grimy and sweating, sorely puzzled, had watched each move of Clark's with amazement. But he knew the wonderful sagacity of the man, and had perfect faith in him, while he had not the clew to his actions. He dully wondered what would be his next move. But even he, man of strong faith, was unprepared for it.

Another appalling silence fell, significant of fresh disaster; and Hamilton, well convinced his weakened garrison could not stand to the guns much longer, ascended to the top of the southwest blockhouse,—for the enemy had shifted to that quarter,—and anxiously used his glass. He almost dropped it in bewilderment; for he saw a man approaching the gate bearing a white flag.

CHAPTER XXXVII UNDER THE WHITE FLAG

As THE TRUCE BEARER approached nearer the gate, a calm fell upon the fort more impressive than the clangor of arms or the roar of cannon. The heavy sulphurous smoke was weighed earthward by the mist from the sullen river.

Hamilton, with his aide, Hay, had retired to his own quarters to receive Clark's messenger with due impressiveness. His face was flushed with gratification, and he turned to Hay and said with boastful elation:—

"The insolent varlets! It takes but a taste of true soldiership to subdue them."

"Yes, general. No doubt they see the noose before them and would make terms,—the dastards!—to keep their heels from dangling."

They looked arrogant with victory.

The heavy puncheon gate was thrown wide with a triumphant flourish, and Clark's orderly entered. He was ushered into the presence of Hamilton and Hay and saluted respectfully. There was an affronting pause. Could contempt kill, the orderly had been a dead man, so disdainful were the looks the two British officers bent upon him.

Wholly unmoved, he asked with a courteous inclination,—

"I have the honor to speak to General Hamilton?"

Hamilton, who disdained to speak, nodded a curt affirmative.

"I am Captain Nicholas Cardinal, at your service; and I have the honor to deliver to you Colonel Clark's message, and am commissioned to bear to him your reply, if it please you."

Hamilton cavalierly accepted the note he tendered, carelessly opened it, and began to read. After the perusal of the first few lines his manner turned from haughty contempt to furious anger. His eyes flashed. His lips worked. He muttered fiercely beneath his breath. The cool audacity of the message made him raging mad, so widely at variance was it from what he had expected,—*humble surrender*. What he read was this:—

"Sir:—In order to save yourself from the impending storm that now threatens you, I order you immediately to surrender yourself, with all your garrison, stores, &c., &c. For if I am obliged to storm you, you may depend on such treatment as is justly due a murderer. Beware of destroying stores of any kind, or any papers or letters that are in your possession, or hurting one house in town, for, by heaven! if you do, there shall be no mercy shown you.

G. R. CLARK."

The unparalleled arrogance, the matchless effrontery, the impudent confidence—the antithesis of his anticipation—struck Hamilton dumb. But he recovered his wits and dashed off these words,—

"Lieutenant-governor Hamilton begs leave to acquaint Colonel Clark that he and his garrison are not disposed to be awed into any action unworthy of British subjects."

Cardinal, surmising its tenor, accepted the note composedly, and retired with strict military courtesy.

Hamilton looked for an immediate reply, but got none, nor did Clark make any demonstration whatever. The suspense was unbearable, and after enduring it for two or three hours Hamilton himself sent the white flag to the Virginia colonel. His aide bore a letter asking for a truce of three days and for a private conference between himself and Clark within the fort, each to have one witness. He ended the document by saying, "If Colonel Clark makes a difficulty of coming into the fort, Lieutenant-governor Hamilton will speak to him by the gate."

Clark was surprised at the character of this missive; and while he suspected there was some secret motive for it, he was not slow to reply, and his note was decisive:—

"If Mr. Hamilton is desirous of a conference with Colonel Clark, he will meet him at the church with Captain Helm."

Clark and his officers were discussing this strange turn of affairs, not without a tinge of suspicion, as the messenger walked off to the fort, when a wild war-cry sounded from the hills back of the village, and a band of savages in warpaint and feathers appeared upon the lower terrace, returning from a successful foray, driving before them their wretched captives. From their belts dangled the blood-sodden scalps of men, women, and children. A crack of musketry followed the war-cry, a salute to the British flag, hanging limp above the fort like a thing sentient of disaster. They descended to the broad level on which the town stood, and not until then were they aware of the presence of the Americans. They turned in panic and fled to the forest behind them. Clark immediately ordered a squad to pursue them.

CHAPTER XXXVIII A SUSPENSION OF HOSTILITIES

S HORTLY AFTER NOON Clark, accompanied by Bowman, entered the little slab church. He much mistrusted whether his arrogant demand would be complied with; but he had scarcely had time to become impatient when Hamilton appeared, accompanied not only by Helm, but Major Hay as well. Perhaps no more momentous conference ever took place, one more fruitful of results, than this which was held in the little slab church that gloomy February day. On it followed the cession of the great Illinois country to Virginia, all owing to the tremendous courage and fidelity of Clark and his little army of 130 men. The success of the colonies was not yet assured, but Clark proceeded as if it were an accomplished fact.

When the English general faced Clark, he could not but forebode the end of British rule. This man and his puny army had forced their way through insuperable obstacles; fifteen days had they marched on a journey which ordinarily required three, through bottomless mud and unremitting rain; six days wading to their necks or floating on improvised rafts over the Drowned Lands, where the Ouibache spread six miles in an angry flood. Without food six days; with but four hours' rest after this tremendous exertion, to commence an assault,—could such men be conquered? Hamilton could not but feel humiliated in the presence of this wet, mud-splashed giant, who, when other men would have been foot-sore and weary and discouraged, defied the king as sturdily as if he had had at his back a great army instead of a puny company of 130 backwoodsmen.

The conference began at once by Hamilton's producing written terms of capitulation.

Clark gave these articles deliberate perusal while Hamilton watched his countenance for sign of assent.

"I reject it as a whole!" said Clark, equably.

"Sir, may I beg you to make some proposition?" asked Hamilton, no little disturbed by his calm, unqualified refusal.

"I have no other to make, than that already submitted—your surrender as prisoners at discretion."

Hamilton flushed hotly and began a protest which Clark silenced by a wave of the hand, and resumed his interrupted speech.

"Your troops have behaved with spirit, and you cannot suppose they will be worse treated in consequence of it, viewing us as savages, as they have been taught to do—"

Hamilton would have interposed a word, but was again denied speech, while Clark dispassionately proceeded:—

"It is vain to make any proposition to me. By this time you must be sensible the garrison will fall. Both of us must view all blood spilled in the future as murder. My troops are already impatient and call aloud for permission to tear down and storm the fort. If such a step be taken, many of course will be cut down, and the result of an enraged body of backwoodsmen breaking in would be obvious to you."

Clark paused, that his hearers might fully grasp his meaning, and realize his implacable determination, and all that hung on Hamilton's own decision. Then he resumed with slow impressiveness, "It would be out of the power of an American officer to save a single man!"

For an instant they gazed at Clark dumbly. A purple color suffused Hamilton's face, he thrice attempted to speak before he burst out furiously.

"For this cursed defiance of the king you may yet pay dearly, sir! For the present I am hard beset. But a time of reckoning will come, when this rebel war is put down. Then, sir, you will meet the fate of all traitors!"

Clark bowed with the utmost civility, and said coolly:—

"It is my decision. If you choose to comply, perhaps the sooner the better."

Helm, always easily moved, was pricked by the soldier's shame on Hamilton's face, and interposed with swift kindness,—

"Cannot you moderate your demands, colonel?"

"Captain Helm," answered Clark, with the severity of a superior toward an offending inferior, "I would remind you, sir, that you are a

British prisoner! As such, it is doubtful if you may with propriety speak on the subject!"

This rebuff Helm received with a crestfallen air, while mentally admiring the inflexible attitude of his chief.

Hamilton, perceiving a chance for help, quickly said, turning to his prisoner,—

"Captain Helm is from this moment liberated, and may use his pleasure!"

Clark sternly regarded Helm: "I will not receive you on such terms. You must return to the garrison, a prisoner, as you came, and await your fate." Amazed at his stern obduracy, Helm had no boldness left to make reply.

Turning fully to Hamilton, Clark directed his speech to him, ignoring the others. Unseen, Helm, the irrepressible, made a grimace at Bowman, who had been respectfully silent during the entire interview, and who with difficulty commanded his countenance at the sly impertinence of his brother-at-arms that could not be overawed for long by any one.

Clark addressed Hamilton with the calm decision of finality, and the Englishman was troubled and mortified beyond measure. "Sir," the American said, "hostilities shall not commence until fifteen minutes after the drums sound the alarm."

Saluting conventionally, the two parties moved off a few paces,— one to return to the fort, the other to the rude breastworks. Hamilton turned about and asked Clark irritatedly, but with rather more deference than he had hitherto shown,—

"Will you be so kind, sir, as to give me reasons for refusing the garrison on any other terms than those I have offered?"

Clark mused a moment, then answered unflinchingly:—

"I have no objections to giving my real reasons, which are simply these: I know that the greater part of the Indian partisans are with you. *I want an excuse to put them to death,* or otherwise treat them as I think proper. The cries of the widows and the fatherless on the frontiers, which they have occasioned, now require *their* blood from *my* hands." He paused to note the effect.

The dispassionate decision, the inflexible purpose, conveyed by his scarcely lifted voice, fell like a clammy coldness on them, that chill which tells of death.

His own officers, Helm and Bowman, stared at him incredulous, and Hamilton and Hay were moved from their military comport.

Fully alive to the impression he had made, Clark continued:—

"I do not choose to be so timorous as to obey the absolute command of their authority. I would rather lose fifty men than not empower myself to execute this piece of business with propriety. If you choose to risk the massacre of your garrison for their sakes—it is at your pleasure. I might, perhaps, take it into my head to send for some of those widows to see it executed."

He bent on them a look of such scathing rebuke, such terrible vengefulness, that for an instant they quailed.

Major Hay, who had listened closely, with a countenance of dismay, burst out insolently,—

"Pray, sir, who is it you call 'Indian partisans'?"

"Sir, I take Major Hay to be one of the principals!" replied Clark, urbanely, as if passing an idle compliment.

A greenish paleness passed over Hay's countenance; his limbs trembled so they could hardly bear him up. Hamilton, seeing him in such sad plight, blushed for very shame. Bowman looked first at Hay with disdain, then on Hamilton with respectful sympathy, while Clark remained utterly unmoved.

As they stood thus, like men under doom, a shout from the returning American squad was heard, and without another word Clark walked hastily off to his intrenchments.

Hamilton and Hay, with Helm still in attendance, retraced the few rods to the fort, to await the beat of the drum.

CHAPTER XXXIX THE END OF AH-MAH-NAC-O

THE RETURN OF THE SQUAD with their captives threw the fort and town into violent excitement. The French villagers had retired behind barred doors and windows, as ordered by Clark, before hostilities had begun, and up to this time—two hours past noon—had remained close in their houses. But now wooden shutters were parted a crack, barred doors opened a tiny space, and eager faces were pressed against them.

The villagers supposed the shouting mob to be one of Hamilton's war-parties, sent out against the pioneers, returning victorious, and with deep anxiety they awaited events.

Within the fort the spirits of the English were at the lowest ebb, which the gloom of the day did not tend to mitigate. They augured ill from the disturbed countenances of Hamilton and Hay. From the blockhouses they watched the Americans drive before them the defiant savages into the very presence of Clark. He was intrenched but thirty yards from the front gate, and the wind bore his sonorous voice to their ears. Now and then a chance word reached them, from which, and his significant actions, they could gather his intention.

When the captives were brought face to face with Clark, he gave them one brief glance. His determination was already taken, and his orders were short and stern.

To the officer in command of the squad he said,—

"These five Indians are to be executed, even as they have killed their victims,—by the tomahawk, before the big gate at the fort, at once."

Bowman looked as if he would have remonstrated. Clark, reading his intention, said sagely and coolly,—

"It may convince the Indians generally that Governor Hamilton cannot give them that protection which he has made them believe he can."

The savages gathered their fate from the stern countenance of the "Big Knife," and accepted it stoically.

They were led to the place designated. Profound silence prevailed as the names of the men detailed for the execution were called. They stepped forward with firmly set lips and stern eyes; there was not one among them who could not tell a fearful tale of cruelty toward his kinsmen.

The prisoners squatted on the ground, and all but one threw their blankets over their heads, ready to finish life bravely. That one, frightfully smeared and stained, turned imploring eyes to the guard nearest him and broke into agonized appeal, as the man raised his hatchet to brain him.

"Oh, save me! save me!" he screamed.

The executioner turned pale, his weapon fell. He rushed to the spot where Clark stood and cried piteously:—

"Oh, sir, spare him. He is a spy, but he is my unhappy son. The hope of my old age. Be merciful!"

Clark was not unmoved by this woeful appeal; but it alone would not have saved the wretch. He had a whole village of wavering Frenchmen to deal with. The condemned man was one of them, though an English partisan. The suppliant, his father, had labored all night in the intrenchments. Mercy in this case would bind the easily moved Frenchmen to his cause; and Clark ordered the prisoner released.

"For your sake, and because of the service his brave countrymen have rendered us this day, he is free. But send him from the village."

The Indians had uncovered and watched this scene with faces as impassive as red stone images. It only strengthened their purpose to die bravely. Clark signed for the business to proceed, and then withdrew.

The savages again swathed themselves in their blankets, and the first one chanted a weird death song:—

"O Great Spirit, I go toward the sun-setting, beyond which lie the Happy Hunting Grounds. O Manitou of my Fathers, when I come to the Happy Hunting Grounds make me fleeter than the doe, braver than the panther, wiser than the fox. There I shall feel no more the keen frosts of winter. There hunger will gnaw me no more. There the sword-leaved maize grows green and fresh forever. On those wide plains the buffalo are numberless, and the deer cannot be counted. There the sun shines warm, nor ever hides behind a cloud. There the Pale Face comes not. There I shall be forever strong and forever young. I go joyfully! I go bravely! I am ready!" He dropped into silence. Crash! The hatchet fell—the scalping-knife flashed! The body sank backward easily.

Unmoved, the second warrior began his death song. It ended. Crash! The second skull was split.

Without faltering the third warrior broke into his dirge, and met the grisly terror calmly as the last note died upon his lips.

But one remained alive, a stripling with the proud bearing of the best of his race, and with the cruelty of the most brutal. He threw off the end of the blanket and faced his executioner uncovered. No death song was on his lips, mocking malice parted them in a hideous, smiling grimace. Wolfish hate gleamed from his steady eye. Had his executioner approached near enough, his gleaming teeth would have shredded his flesh. Whether his contemptuous defiance, or whether the silent appeal of youth for continued life unnerved the arm that directed it, the blow was not strong enough; it did not kill. Ah-mah-nac-o himself tore the hatchet from the gaping cleft in his skull and handed it back to the man. Twice, thrice it fell before its work was accomplished. Hardened men turned away from the ghastly sight, sickened. . . .

Behind the peepholes of Fort Sackville many a heart contracted with fear and dread. Never before had they beheld such atrocities; *they had only sanctioned them! instigated them! rewarded them!* Their ears were terror-struck by the crash of the tomahawk. Their eyes widened with horror at the glistening circle described by the scalping-knife. They were appalled by the hideous spectacle enacted before them, *not upon them.* Yet *they* beheld, *not torture,* but swift death.

They might well tremble behind the frail barriers of the fort at this tame repetition of the atrocities of their own mercenaries. The example was as efficacious as Clark had surmised it would be. By set of sun, which went down dully in dark skies, Hamilton sent a messenger bearing a note of surrender.

As a postscript to Miss Krout's sketch it may be well to add that Governor Hamilton and his staff were presently incarcerated in the jail at Williamsburg, Virginia (which did not offer accommodations to meet the Governor's exacting demands), and the United States has held Vincennes ever since. But George Rogers Clark never reached Detroit—thanks to the red-tape, jealousy within the armed services, and personal prejudices which marked American government in the Revolutionary period—even as it has occasionally since!

Several military forays were made against the Indians between the days of George Rogers Clark's campaign in the Revolution and the War of 1812, but the most important engagement resulted from the brave stand of Tecumseh, the Shawnee. He should be called "Tecumtha," according to the writer of the following piece, but whatever the spelling of the name he was one of the greatest of Indian statesmen. His leadership and wit, with the sound morality preached by his brother, The Prophet, deserved better reward than the defeat at the Battle of Tippecanoe which broke the last stand of the Indians on Indiana soil. That battle—in which our government was unquestionably the aggressor—is considered by many historians to be the opening engagement of the War of 1812. The cause of the United States against the British in that war was just: sad it is that so little justice attached to the initial campaign against the Indians.

JACOB PIATT DUNN

was a newspaper man, for many years Indiana State Librarian, and always a scholar engrossed with the Midwestern historical scene. This selection is from his book

True Indian Stories

CHAPTER IV WHY TECUMTHA FOUGHT

No INDIAN'S NAME is more inseparably linked to the history of Indiana than that of "Tecumseh," and none is more familiar to American readers, but it is remarkable how little is definitely known about this celebrated man. . . .

Drake probably is right in his statement that Tecumtha was born at the old Shawnee town of Piqua, on Mad River, Ohio; that his father was Puck-e-shin-wau (something that drops), a Shawnee of the Kiscopoke clan, and that his mother was Me-tho-a-tas-ke, Shawnee of the Turtle totem. Her name signified a turtle laying eggs in the sand.

But Drake says the name is properly "Tecumtha," and that it means "a shooting star." Other authorities say it means "a comet," "a panther leaping on its prey," and "an obstacle in the path." . . .

There is little truth in the common ideas of the cause of Tecumtha's hostility. He was a warrior, but he . . . was also a statesman, and his chief end in life was to prevent a wrong to his people. The cause of this originated in the treaty of Greenville. At that time General Wayne forced the assembled tribes to accept a boundary line which gave most of Ohio to the whites and threw the Ohio tribes back into Indiana. The Ohio Indians—Wyandots, Ottawas, Six Nations of Sandusky, Delawares and Shawnees—unanimously asked General Wayne to divide the land between the several tribes. . . .

But General Wayne declined to do this, and with remarkable disregard of the point of the request said: "You Indians best know your respective boundaries," and urged them: "Let no nation or nations invade, molest or disturb any other nation or nations in the hunting grounds they have heretofore been accustomed to live and hunt upon, within the boundary which shall now be agreed on."

This decision they were forced to accept, and therefore the Ohio Indians were thrown back among the more Western tribes without having any lands set off for them. They mixed largely with the Indian tribes, many of the Delawares and Shawnees making their homes in the hitherto unoccupied parts of southern Indiana, but they advanced the theory that under the new arrangement the land belonged to all the tribes in common, and this was generally accepted.

In 1802 Governor Harrison wrote: "There appears to be an agreement amongst them that no proposition which relates to their lands can be acceded to without the consent of all the tribes."

But the only treaty in which he undertook to get this general consent was the one of June 7, 1803, and its cessions of land were very slight . . . although by 1806 he had negotiated five other treaties. . . .

These treaties were made with the "chiefs and head warriors" of various tribes, and four of them had only five Indian signers each. It was these treaties that raised the wrath of Tecumtha and his sympathizers, for not only did none of the Ohio Indians consent to them, but none received any part of the compensation, although the Indiana and Illinois Indians had shared equally in the compensation at the treaty of Greenville. It was clear that the Shawnees and other Ohio Indians were being shut out entirely; and when the treaties of 1809 were made, by which 3,000,000 acres were added to the cessions, Tecumtha became defiant and said that these treaties should not be carried into effect.

It was then that Tecumtha came to Vincennes and had his dramatic interview with General Harrison. He came to Vincennes on August 12, 1810, with a retinue of 75 warriors, and for several days there were interviews and councils between him and Governor Harrison. On the 20th . . . he charged Harrison with having incited the trouble. He said:

"It is you that are pushing them on to do mischief. You endeavor to make distinctions. You wish to prevent the Indians to do as we wish them, to unite and let them consider their lands as the common property of the whole. You take tribes aside and advise them not to come into this measure; and until our design is accomplished we do not wish to accept your invitation to go and see the President. The reason I tell you this is, you want, by your distinctions of Indian tribes, in allotting to each a particular tract of land, to make them to war with each other. You never see an Indian come and endeavor to make the white people do so. You are continually driving the red people; when, at last, you will drive them into the great lake, where they can't either stand or work." He declared that the warriors represented the will of the Indians, and that unless the treaties were rescinded he would call a great council of the tribes to deal with the treaty chiefs.

At the close of his speech Governor Harrison began to reply. He was dwelling on the uniform justice which the United States had shown in its dealings with the Indians, when Tecumtha sprang to his feet and denounced the statement as untrue, and charged that Harrison and the United States had cheated and imposed on the Indians. With defiant gesticulation he said to the interpreter, Barron, "Tell him he lies." Barron hesitated and sought to soften the expression, but Tecumtha reiterated, "No, no. Tell him he lies."

But the stir interrupted the proceedings. Several of the warriors arose and stood in a threatening attitude. General Gibson, Secretary of the Territory, who understood the Shawnee language, directed Lieutenant Jennings to advance with the guard of twelve men, who had stood at a little distance. As soon as order was restored Tecumtha's words were translated, and Governor Harrison indignantly reproached him for his conduct, and ordered him to return to his camp, saying that the council fire was extinguished. . . .

With cooling time, Tecumtha realized that he had made a diplomatic blunder. In the morning Barron visited him in his camp, and found him very desirous of a further interview and an amicable settlement. Governor Harrison consented to the interview on condition that Tecumtha would apologize for his insult, and in the afternoon the council was resumed. With perfect dignity, but in a respectful manner, Tecumtha disclaimed any intention to offer insult, and explained that he had perhaps been misinformed as to the sentiments of the white people, who, he had been told, were divided in their opinion as to the treaties; but he said he knew they already had more land than they could use. . . .

On the next day, Governor Harrison, accompanied only by Barron, visited Tecumtha's camp, where he was politely received, and another long interview was held, but without different result. Tecumtha restated his position, and when Governor Harrison assured him that his claims would never be admitted by the President, he replied:

"Well, as the great chief is to determine the matter, I hope the Great Spirit will put sense enough into his head to induce him to direct you to give up the land. It is true, he is so far off he will not be injured by the war. He may sit still in his town, and drink his wine, while you and I will have to fight it out."

This closed the conferences of 1810, but, in June, 1811, Governor Harrison sent a message to Tecumtha and The Prophet, warning them of the consequences of hostilities. To this Tecumtha replied, protesting that no hostilities were intended, and saying that he would come to Vincennes in hope of a peaceable adjustment of all differences. . . .

CHAPTER V　THE FALL OF THE PROPHET

NOTWITHSTANDING THE ELOQUENCE, magnetism and high repute of Tecumtha among the Indians, there is little room for question that the chief element of strength in his confederacy was the influence of his brother, The Prophet . . . Tems-kwah-ta-wah, or He Who Keeps the Door Open. American writers have commonly denounced him as an impostor, and a conscious humbug, but there is in fact no more reason for questioning his sincerity, though he may at times have resorted to trickery to enhance his reputation, than there is for questioning the sincerity of Mahomet or Joan of Arc or our own Mrs. Eddy. . . .

Among the white contemporaries of The Prophet, almost the only ones who credited his sincerity were the Shakers, who are among the few sects who accept literally the prophecy that "your old men shall dream dreams." They sent three missionaries to the Shawnees in 1807, and one of these, Richard McNemar, records The Prophet's own story of his divine calling as follows:

"He [The Prophet] had formerly lived on White River; had been a doctor and a very wicked man. About two years ago, while attending on sick people at Attawa, in a time of general sickness, he was struck with a deep and awful sense of his sins; cried mightily to the Good Spirit to show him some way of escape, and in his great distress fell into a vision, in which he appeared to be traveling along a road, and came to where it forked. The right-hand way, he was informed, led to happiness, and the left to misery.

"This fork in the road, he was told, represented that stage of life in which people were convicted of sin; and those who took the right-hand way quit everything that was wicked and became good. But the left-hand road was for such as would go on and be bad, after they were shown the right way. They all move slow till they come here, but when they pass the fork to the left then they go swift. On the left-hand way he saw three houses—from the first and second were pathways that led into the right-hand road, but no way

leading from the third. This, said he, is eternity. He saw vast crowds
going swift along the left-hand road, and great multitudes in each
of the houses, under different degrees of judgment and misery. He
mentioned particularly the punishment of the drunkard. One presented him a cup of liquor resembling melted lead; if he refused
to drink it he would urge him, saying: 'Come, drink—you used to
love whisky.' And upon drinking it his bowels were seized with an
exquisite burning. This draught he had often to repeat. At the last
house their torment appeared inexpressible; under which he heard
them scream, cry pitiful and roar like the falls of a river.

"He was afterward taken along the right-hand way, which was
all interspersed with flowers of delicious smell, and showed a house
at the end of it, where was everything beautiful, sweet and pleasant; and still went on learning more and more; but in his first
vision he saw nothing but the state of the wicked, from which the
Great Spirit told him to go and warn his people of their danger, and
call upon them to put away their sins and be good. . . . Whereupon
the Great Spirit told him to separate from these wicked chiefs and
their people, and showed him particularly where to . . . make provision to receive and instruct all from the different tribes that were
willing to be good. Accordingly all that believed had come and
settled there, and a great many Indians had come to hear, and
many more were expected. That some white people were afraid, but
they were foolish, for they would not hurt any one."

The moral teachings of The Prophet were not objectionable, as
the sins he specially condemned were witchcraft, lying, stealing,
poisoning people, fighting, murdering, drinking whisky, beating
their wives and lewdness, but he taught also that acceptance of the
customs of the whites was a sin for Indians, for which they were
being punished. And these have always been the general lines of
the teachings of Indian prophets. . . . It is the natural hope of a
people who feel themselves being crushed by a superior power that
the Almighty will in some way intervene in their behalf, if they
repent and abandon their sins. But this also naturally encourages
hostility to the superior race among the younger and more warlike
individuals, and it certainly had that effect in this case.

In the spring of 1808 The Prophet and his followers moved from

Greenville to the Wabash, just below the mouth of the Tippecanoe. Their town there is commonly called Kethtippecanunk. . . .

At the new home on the Wabash, The Prophet's religion prospered greatly, and its fame spread far. . . . Hundreds gathered to the village, where the life was of religious solemnity. There were public services morning and evening, with speakers who discoursed on the duties of man, the pauses of their sermons being noted by a loud "seguoy," or sort of "amen," from the hearers. . . .

With the growth of the new religion the alarm of the whites increased. Temskwhatawah protested to General Harrison that his designs were peaceable, but depredations on the frontier continued, and from friendly Indians on all sides came assurances that he meant open war as soon as he was strong enough. Tecumtha himself openly declared that the boundary lines of the treaty of 1809 should not be run. Finally, in 1811, Governor Harrison and the national authorities decided that the safety of the frontiers demanded the breaking up of The Prophet's town.

In September, the chief part of the forces for the expedition having been assembled, they moved up the Wabash to a point two miles above Terre Haute, where Fort Harrison was built. After completing it, and being reinforced by the rest of the troops called for, the expedition proceeded on October 28 . . . the entire force aggregating a little over one thousand, of whom one-fourth were mounted. On October 31, having passed Big Raccoon Creek . . . the army crossed the Wabash near the present town of Montezuma. From this point it kept to the prairie country on the west side of the river, to avoid possibility of ambush. On November 2, the army camped two miles below the mouth of the Big Vermillion, and erected a blockhouse twenty-five feet square, at which a small guard was left to protect the boats that had been used in bringing the supplies thus far. The army then proceeded through the prairies, usually at some distance from the river, and on November 6 came in sight of The Prophet's town. The scouts were sent forward to ask a conference with The Prophet, but as some Indians appeared and seemed to attempt to cut them off, they were recalled, and the army moved forward. It had come to about one hundred and fifty yards from the town when some Indians came out and asked a halt and a conference. It was agreed that the troops should go into camp over night at what is now known as "the battle ground," and that hostilities should be suspended until a conference could be held on the following day. . . . Although no attack was anticipated, all preparations were made for it, except fortifying the camp, and Harrison said this was omitted for lack of axes. The men slept on their arms, and explicit orders were given for forming the lines in case of attack.

There has been some contention as to the intent of the Indians, and the events of that night, but the truth was probably told later by White Loon, one of the leading chiefs present. He said that there was no intention to attack until the Potawatomi chief Winamac (Cat Fish—literally mud fish), arrived and insisted on it. A council was convened and most of the chiefs opposed attack, but Winamac denounced them as cowards, said it was now or never, and threatened unless the attack was made to withdraw and take with him the Potawatomis, who formed about one-third of the town. Then the attack was agreed to. White Loon, Winamac and Stone Eater were put in command, the Indian force being about equal to that of the whites. The Prophet made a speech, in which he assured them of success, saying that his charms would protect them from the bullets of the whites, and the warriors went into the battle as confident of supernatural protection as any religious fanatics that ever lived.

They had intended to attack on three sides simultaneously, but a sentinel, Stephen Mars, caught sight of them as they crept in close to the lines, up the bank from Burnetts' Creek, at the northwest angle, and fired the alarm shot. The Indians who were close enough attacked at once, breaking the lines at some points and in two or three instances penetrating to the tents. Mars was killed as he fled. The recklessness of the assault showed their faith in The Prophet's protection, and it took two hours of stubborn fighting to convince them of its futility.

Governor Harrison was quickly at the point of attack after the first firing, and, finding the lines at that point somewhat broken, ordered up two companies for support. By that time a heavy firing began at the northeast angle, and Harrison, turning there, found

Maj. Jo Daveiss (this is the correct spelling—not Daviess, as it has been handed down) anxious to charge the enemy. After two refusals he was given permission to charge, and dashed forward with only twenty men. The Indians fell back from the front and gathered on their flanks, pouring in a heavy fire that drove back the charging party, with Major Daveiss mortally wounded. The firing now extended all around the camp, and was especially heavy on the left flank, where, as on the right flank, the Indians could approach on high ground under cover of the trees. The morning was dark and cloudy, and it had rained intermittently during the night. The campfires gave the Indians the advantage in aiming, and they were extinguished as soon as possible. The lines were reinforced wherever needed, and held intact. So the fight went on in the dark, from a little after four o'clock till daybreak, when gallant charges were made on the right and left flanks, and the Indians were chased into the marshes where the horsemen could not follow. They did not return.

The pursuit was not extended far, for the army had its hands full. Thirty-seven men had been killed, and 151 wounded, of whom twenty-five afterwards died. The cattle had escaped, and had been driven away; and the troops had recourse to horseflesh for meat. A report was started that Tecumtha was on his way to the place with 1,000 warriors. November 7th was occupied with burying the dead, caring for the wounded, and throwing up breastworks of logs. On the 8th the mounted men advanced to the town, and found that the Indians had deserted it in haste, leaving almost all their possessions. After gathering up the copper kettles, with what corn and beans they could carry, the troops applied the torch and destroyed all that was left. There remained no doubt that the Indians knew they were whipped. Their force in the fight was probably about equal to that of the whites, and although reports as to their loss varied widely, it is certain that it was no less than that of the troops. Tecumtha was not in the vicinity, having gone south to try to secure the alliance of the southern tribes, and it is very well established that The Prophet had given battle in defiance of Tecumtha's express orders.

He had met defeat, and it was more than a mere defeat. A religion was shot and bayoneted to death on that field . . . he lost all; for even his most devoted followers realized that, if there was any divine interference at that time, the stars in their courses fought against Temskwahtawah. . . .

CHAPTER THREE

Take t' th' Timber, Boys, Them's Injuns!

Far more fearsome than organized warfare on the frontier were the Indian raids on solitary cabins and outlying fields; the scalping, captivity and sometimes torture of individuals or small groups and—it must be admitted—the murders, burnings and mayhem perpetrated by whites in reprisal.

Periods most marked by activity of this kind were, first, that which extended from the beginning of the American Revolution until the defeat of the Midwestern Indians by Mad Anthony Wayne in 1794; second, those years following the Battle of Tippecanoe during which many able-bodied men of Indiana, Kentucky and Ohio were occupied fighting the British and Indians around Detroit and in Canada.

Very early it became the fashion of returned captives of the Indians to write or to dictate accounts of their adventures. These narratives form a considerable literature. The three Kentuckians celebrated in the following sketch (two of whom survived and presently became Indianians) did not need to write their story, they only had to tell it, time and time again, until its details were fixed in the mind of a lad who was the grandson of one and a more distant kinsman of the other.

This lad, a cripple from childhood, was born in Wayne County, Indiana, about 1812 and was brought to the western part of the state in 1824. As a young man he became a teacher of country schools and a contributor to newspapers; eventually he gathered together a selec-

*tion of his articles on pioneer life—not forgetting the story of his
relatives' captivity—and published them in 1860:*

SANDFORD C. COX

Recollections of the Early Settlement
of the Wabash Valley

NARRATIVE OF THE CAPTIVITY BY THE
INDIANS OF RICHARD RUE, GEORGE
HOLMAN, AND IRVIN HINTON

ON THE 11TH DAY OF FEBRUARY, 1781, a wagoner by the name of
Irvin Hinton was sent from a blockhouse at the village of Louisville,
at the Falls of the Ohio river, to Harrodsburg for a load of provisions
for the fort. Two young men, named Richard Rue and George Holman, the former aged nineteen years, and the latter sixteen, were
sent as guards to protect the wagon from the depredations of any
hostile Indians that might be lurking in the canebrakes or ravines
through which they had to pass in going to and returning from
Harrodsburg. There had been no late reasons for apprehending danger from the Indians so early in the season, although there was a
general expectation that about the time the leaves were as large as
a squirrel's ear, there would be a general attack on the frontier inhabitants of Virginia, Pennsylvania, and Kentucky.

Soon after the party set out on their journey, a severe snow storm
set in, which continued with unabated fury until after noon, filling
the wagon ruts, and wreathing the copse and canebrakes in a rich
white robe, until mother earth appeared to lie prone in a winding-
sheet of spotless purity. Lest the melting snow might dampen the
powder in their rifles, the guards fired them off, intending to reload
them as soon as the storm ceased. Hinton urged on his horses, while
Rue walked briskly a few rods ahead of the wagon, and Holman

about the same distance behind. As they ascended a hill about eight miles from Louisville, Hinton heard some one say "ho" to the horses. Supposing that something was wrong about the wagon, he stopped, looked around and asked Holman why he called to him to halt. Holman said that he had not spoken. . . .

At this time a voice cried out, "I will solve the mystery for you. It was Simon Girty that cried 'ho!' and he meant what he said!" at the same time emerging from a sink-hole a few rods from the roadside, followed by thirteen Indians, who immediately surrounded the three Kentuckians, and demanded them to surrender or die instantly. Rue instinctively raised his gun to his face to shoot down Girty, but on remembering that it was empty, he took it down, and the little party, making a virtue of necessity, at once surrendered to this renegade white man and his Indian allies. Being so near two forts, Girty made all possible speed in making fast his prisoners. He stripped the harness from the horses, selecting the lines and such ropes and leathern straps as might be needed on the journey, and prepared for an immediate flight across the Ohio river. After securely binding the prisoners, by passing ropes under one arm and over the opposite shoulder, they cut off the legs of their pantaloons about four inches above the knee, and started them off through the deep snow, as fast as the horses could trot. . . . The party arrived at the Ohio river before dark that evening, where three large bark canoes were secreted in a cove on the south bank of the river some twelve miles above the Falls. The prisoners, weary and benumbed with cold, were placed in one of the canoes under the care of Girty, their respective captors and two other Indians who paddled the canoe. The rest of the Indians brought over the other crafts, swimming the horses over by the lower side and stern of the canoes.

After crossing the Ohio river, the prisoners were hurried with great speed into the wilderness of the North-Western Territory, towards Wa-puc-ca-nat-ta. The party made no halt until late the first night, when they encamped without striking a fire, about half a mile from the trace, some twenty miles north of the Ohio river. Here a brief parley was held. . . . Finally it was decided to make a feint by traveling awhile in the direction of Vincennes, then change their course and steer through the White river country to the Auglaize. . . .

Girty was morose and taciturn. The few words he spoke were generally in the Delaware language. Rue had been in several campaigns against the Indians, and had obtained a smattering of several of the Indian dialects. Girty at length thought he could perceive by the shades that passed over Rue's countenance at times, that he was not entirely ignorant of the Indian language, and took occasion during his temporary absence (which he artfully contrived for the purpose) to enquire of his fellow captives if he had not been in some of the campaigns and battles against the Indians. They were admonished to tell the truth—that if the Indians ever caught them in a lie death would be the inevitable consequence. They hesitated giving an answer. The question was pressed with a menacing flourish of the tomahawk. They replied that he had been in several campaigns against the Indians. How many? Three or four, was the response. Rue chanced to overhear this colloquy. He thought his hour had come. But knowing that bravery was esteemed one of the highest virtues by the savages, he approached the camp fire as if he knew nothing of what had transpired, sat down his brass kettle of water he had been ordered to bring, and took a seat on a log by the side of Girty in a quiet, confident manner. The old bogus savage appeared moody. At length he muttered out, "Rue, was you ever out in a campaign against the Indians?" "Yes, I was." "How many?" "Four," replied the captive. "Was you with General Clark at the taking of Vincennes?" "Yes." "Was you with him when he made his dash against Chillicothe, and destroyed the Piqua towns and Loramie's store?" "I was," was the ready reply. At this Girty sprung from the log, rage convulsed his whole frame, while with a ghastly frown he muttered: "You played h—l there! didn't you! I have a mind to split your skull with this hatchet!" but he changed the weapon in his hand, and struck the prisoner a blow on the head with the handle.

Simon Girty was a white man, a Pennsylvanian by birth. He was brave, ambitious, and unscrupulous. He espoused the cause of the Indians (whose prisoner he had been for many years in his early boyhood), and led them to many bloody massacres of his white brethren. From the time of his treacherous apostacy, he vied with the most cruel and relentless savages to circumvent his old friends, and put them to death by the most cruel and ingenious tortures. . . .

The third day after crossing the Ohio, the party, finding that they were not pursued, relaxed their speed, and turned aside for the purpose of browsing their horses, and resting themselves and their prisoners, who were all much fatigued by the forced marches and lack of rest the two preceding days and nights. . . .

. . . hunters were sent out, who, after a few hours' absence, returned with a small deer and two turkeys. These were dressed and hastily broiled on the coals, without salt, and were divided out among the company . . . the famished, travel-worn prisoners now felt they were beyond the reach of aid from their friends, and were doomed to a fearful captivity among exasperated savages, who considered themselves and the whole Indian race trampled upon and abused by the steady and systematic encroachments of the white man. . . . The prisoners remembered the cruel circumvention and cold blooded murder, a few years before, of the noble Cornstalk, a leading Chief of the Shawnees, his brave son Ellinipsico, and the young Chief Red Hawk, near the mouth of the Great Kanhawa, and did not know but they might be the three victims that would be sacrificed to appease the manes of these lamented chieftains.

From this point the party changed their course for Wa-puc-ca-nat-ta, on the Auglaize, passing through the White river and Blue river countries, crossing the head waters of the Wabash east of where Fort Wayne was afterwards built. On arriving within a day's journey of Wa-puc-ca-nat-ta, on the Auglaize, a runner was dispatched to inform the Indians of the return of Girty and his party, and to make preparations to have the prisoners run the gauntlet on entering the town. When the party had arrived within a few miles of the town, they were met by several Chiefs and warriors, who came out to do themselves the honor of meeting the returning band, and assist in arranging the preliminaries of the gauntlet, a time-honored custom of the savages. A brief parley ensued. Girty called the prisoners before him. He told them that within a few hours they would arrive at the village where they would find the Indians drawn up in two lines, one line on each side of the path, for two or three hundred yards from the council-house. They must pass between these two lines of warriors, who would strike at them with clubs and knives as they passed. If they were knocked down, it was against the rule to hit them. . . . They must get upon their feet again, and run for the council-room with all speed. When they gained the goal, they were free from further assaults. There they would be tried for their lives. . . .

On arriving within sight of the village, they saw the lines drawn up on either side of the path, and the grim, painted savages awaiting the approach of the prisoners.

It was decided that Hinton should first run the gauntlet. He received severe whacks and blows over the head and shoulders, from the clubs and sides of the tomahawks of the Indians, before he reached the council-house, which afforded much sport to the Indians, who evinced their hilarity in the most vociferous yells, and roars of laughter. . . . Rue was next started down between the lines, and an Indian after him with an uplifted tomahawk. He far outstripped his pursuer, dodged most of the blows aimed at him as he passed, and gained the council-house amidst the noisy shouts of the savages.

Holman was reluctant to enter the race. He told Girty that he would not be able to pass through so severe an ordeal—that he thought it unfair to put a stripling like himself, wasted with famine, and worn down with hardships, to so severe a test. A pow-wow was held. The programme was changed. The men retired from the lines, and their places were filled by squaws and boys, with knives, clubs and switches in their hands. . . . The chase was spirited. Switches and clubs rattled over his head, shoulders and body, as he darted between the lines to the council-house, amidst the loud and prolonged whoops and *ha ha's* of old and young, who looked upon the last race as the lighter after-piece or farce, that succeeded the weightier tragedy. . . .

The savage sanhedrim was soon in session. An old dark-visaged Chief presided. Speech after speech was made, during which many violent gestures were made, and angry glances cast toward the corner of the room where the prisoners sat which boded no good for the unfortunate trio, who understood but little of their harangues. The council broke up. The prisoners were told that their cases were not

finally disposed of, but were continued for the presence of other
Chiefs and warriors, who lived on the Scioto and Big Miami, who
were expected to arrive in a few days.

Hinton's mind was filled with gloomy forebodings of a cruel fate
impending over him. He thought he saw in the trial (which had
been continued for the presence of other chieftains, equally and perhaps more cruel than those who had sat in the former council) unmistakable signs of a hard fate. Visions of his wife and children at
home were in his slumbers by night, and filled his thoughts by day.
Could he escape from the ruthless savages, and again press these
loved ones to his bosom? . . . His fellow prisoners remonstrated
against his attempting to escape, as hazardous in the extreme. They
advised him to remain with them and abide the trial—that some
circumstance might transpire to their advantage. But Hinton was
determined in his plans, which were kept entirely secret, and a few
nights afterward it was announced that "Red Head," as the Indians
called him, had escaped, taking with him an Indian's gun and ac-
coutrements. . . . Pursuit was immediately instituted. Scores of
infuriated savages thronged the woods in every direction to find
some trace of the fleeing fugitive, who it was supposed would aim
for the Falls of the Ohio, but as a matter of precaution might in
the outset start in some other direction to elude pursuit.

A stricter guard was placed over the remaining prisoners, who were
plainly told that should they attempt to escape and fail to do so
they would immediately be put to death, and they could not promise
how mild or severe a manner; that Hinton's escape had exasperated
the tribes, and that the two remaining prisoners would most likely
receive less clemency at their pending trial.

Next morning most of the pursuers returned. Some eight or ten
only had pressed on to a point where they expected to intercept
Hinton on his way to the Ohio river. They were right in their calculations, for late in the afternoon of the second day after his escape,
a man was seen gliding through the woods about half a mile from
the trace that led from Sandusky to the old Chillicothe town. At
times he would stop, and from some log or high piece of ground
overlook the surrounding country, as if he were a spy. Thus he
walked into the midst of an ambuscade of his wily pursuers, who,

after watching his motions for a while, crawled from one hiding place to another until they had completely invested him, before he was aware of danger. They uttered a simultaneous and prolonged yell, and rushed upon the lone, fatigued traveler, whom they recognized to be Hinton, firing two or three shots as they pressed around him, without any other effect than increasing his consternation at his truly appalling condition. He was seized and disarmed, and told to prepare for a cruel death; that they had often admonished him of the danger of attempting to escape, and that "Indians would not lie"—they would be found as good as their word; that night he would be burned at the stake, that the severity of his punishment might deter others from attempting an escape. He told them that he did not care so much for his own life; that it was his love for his wife and children in Kentucky that caused him to break away from his captivity; that as for himself, he could soon have become reconciled to their mode of life, and made himself happy by hunting and fishing. His touching appeal to the heart of the husband and father in behalf of the dear ones far away, whose welfare now caused a deeper solicitude than his own desperate condition, failed to excite the sympathy of his inexorable captors, who immediately set about making preparations to burn their devoted victim. He earnestly implored them to shoot or tomahawk him, and not protract his sufferings unnecessarily; but they turned a deaf ear to his entreaties, and consummated their arrangements for his death. After partaking of their evening repast, which they shared with their fatigued and hungry victim, they drove a stake into the ground in the center of a circle of dry sticks and brush which they had gathered for the purpose. They then proceeded to strip and black the prisoner—a preliminary usually attended to in such sacrifices. After tying the prisoner to the stake, burning faggots were applied to the brush in several places; the war-whoop thrilled through the dark surrounding forest like the chorus of a band of infernal spirits escaped from Pandemonium, and the scalp-dance was struck up by those demons in human shape, who for hours encircled the roasting victim, brandishing their tomahawks and war-clubs, and venting their indignant execrations on the helpless sufferer who meekly submitted to his immolation and died about midnight from the effects of the slow intense heat, which literally roasted him to death. As soon as he fell upon the ground, the Indian who first discovered him that evening in the woods sprang in, sunk his tomahawk into his skull above the ear, and with his knife stripped off the scalp, which he bore back with him to the town as a trophy, and which was tauntingly thrust into the faces of Rue and Holman, with the interrogation, "Can you smell the fire on the scalp of your old red-headed friend?—We cooked him and left him for the wolves to make a breakfast upon: that is the way we serve runaway prisoners."

Shortly after the cruel murder of Hinton, a deputation arrived from Detroit, stating that the contemplated movement against the whites on the Kentucky borders had been postponed; that calls had been made for a general rendezvous of the Indians at Detroit; and for those at Wa-puc-ca-nat-ta, Chillicothe, and intervening points to come on, bringing with them any captives they might have in their possession. Girty and his party, with the principal portion of the warriors then at Wa-puc-ca-nat-ta, took up their march for the point designated. At the end of the third day's march, the party approached an Indian village situated on the Maumee river, a few miles above the spot where the city of Toledo now stands. It was determined that the prisoners should be made to run the gauntlet again at this place; and as the Chillicothe Chiefs and those residing at the Mad river towns were present, it was determined that the postponed trial of Rue and Holman should be brought to a final conclusion. A general halt was made. Their approach was heralded to the town. The usual lines of painted savages were drawn up on either side of the path. The order of the chase was the same as at Wa-puc-ca-nat-ta, except that Holman's portion was not diluted with women and switches. A tall, active Indian was placed behind Rue with an old sword in his hand. At the given signal Rue darted down the line, receiving many blows from the clubs and hatchets of the Indians in the line, which stunned him so that his pursuer overtook him and hit him a couple of severe strokes over the head, which well nigh felled him to the ground. At this point he had reached a brush fence that enclosed several angles of the village and, making a bound, cleared the fence and alighted on the other side; but finding his pursuer had crossed the fence at almost the same instant of time, Rue affected to stumble and fall to the ground. The Indian waved the sword over his head and motioned for him to get up and run. The prisoner laid still. The Indian stepped off eight or ten paces, and again told him to get up and run. The prostrate prisoner motioned with his hand for him to get back over the brush fence which the Indian did, Rue feigning inability to proceed. The Indian with the sword then walked back some ten or twelve paces from the fence, and urged the prisoner to run. As nimble as a cat Rue sprang from the ground, and darted into the council-house before his pursuer could get within ten paces of him, amidst the deafening yells of the savages, who seemed to admire the stratagem used to avoid the ponderous blows of his pursuer. Holman was then passed down the lines, and made the goal with about as much flagellation as his savage tormentors thought he would be able to bear.

The usual feast was then spread. After the feast was over, the Chiefs and warriors indulged in the scalp dance, which the prisoners regarded as an ill omen to precede the council that was to decide their fate for weal or for woe. . . .

The vote was finally taken, and it was evident to the prisoners that a hard verdict had been rendered against them. The glances, gestures, and general demeanor of the council spoke the language of doom. In about a quarter of an hour after the council broke up, Girty informed the prisoners of their impending fate. The council had decided that they should be burned at the stake that night. . . .

An unusual excitement appeared to run through the fragments of the assembly, that lingered around the council-house. High words and angry looks evinced a want of unanimity among the different tribes that composed the assembly. What was the cause of the dissatisfaction the prisoners could not learn, nor could they ascertain that it had any connection with the sentence in their case. At a pause in the contention, a noble looking Indian approached where the prisoners were sitting and spoke a few words in the Mingo language to the guards. He then took Holman by the hand, lifted him to his feet, cut the cords that bound him to his fellow prisoner, caused the black to be taken off his face and hands, put his hand kindly upon his head, and said:—"I adopt you as my son, to fill the place of the one I have lately buried—you are now a kinsman of

Logan, 'the white man's friend,' as he has been called, but who has lately proven himself to be a terrible avenger of the wrongs inflicted upon him by the bloody Cresap and his men." Girty, with evident reluctance, interpreted what he said. . . . But the sad fate that awaited his companion, neutralized his excess of joy and he felt that life itself would be dear if he had to witness the excruciating torture and death of his friend, whom he loved as a brother.

The commutation of Holman's sentence, and the adoption of him into a family nearly related to Logan, sent a momentary thrill of pleasure through the breast of Rue, who, although doomed to die in a few hours, still entertained a faint hope that something might transpire to avert, or at least postpone his doom; and should he even that night suffer at the stake, his friend might be spared to tell at some future time of the sad fate of Hinton and himself.

After a brief interval, two Indians approached Rue with leathern thongs in their hands, cut loose the cords that bound his feet, raised him from the ground, stripped him, passed a cord under one arm and over the opposite shoulder, which they tied securely; around this they passed the long, coiled leathern strap, and made it fast. . . .

Rue was then led to one of the stakes in the center of the circle of dried brushwood to which he was tied fast. At this time a general contention pervaded the encampment—not a few tomahawks were brandished in the air, and scores of knives were seen glittering in the hands of exasperated Indians, who seemed to be in a general ferment.

Just as the lighted faggots were about to be applied to the dry brush that encircled the devoted prisoner, a tall, active young Shawnee, a son of the victim's captor, sprang into the ring, and, with his tomahawk, chopped off the cord that bound him to the stake, led him out of the ring amidst the deafening plaudits of a part of the crowd, and the execrations and threats of others who appeared determined that the death penalty should be executed on the prisoner forthwith. The cool, defiant manner of the young Indian who released the captive from the stake, held at bay the more cruel and bloody-minded who, at a respectful distance, gnashed their teeth and inveighed against the lawless rescue, which the young brave had the temerity to make in the face of the very council that had condemned the prisoner.

Regardless of threats and remonstrances, he caused water to be brought, and the black to be washed from the face and hands of the prisoner, whose clothes were again placed upon him, when the young brave said: "I take this young man to be my brother, in the place of one I lately lost. I loved that brother well, I will love this one too. My old mother will be glad when I tell her that I have brought her a son, in place of the dear departed one. We want no more victims. The burning of 'red-head' ought to satisfy us. These innocent young men do not merit such a cruel fate. I would rather die myself than see this adopted brother burnt at the stake." . . .

This sudden and unexpected change of affairs, although it resulted in the rescue of the prisoners from a cruel death, nevertheless produced some discord among the different tribes composing the party, some of whom abandoned the trip to Detroit, others returned to Wa-puc-ca-nat-ta, a few turned their course towards the Mississinnewa and the Wabash towns, while a portion continued on to Detroit. Holman was taken back to Wa-puc-ca-nat-ta, where he remained the most of the time during his captivity. Rue was taken first to the Mississinnewa, then to the Wabash towns. Two years of his eventful captivity were spent in that region of country watered by the Wabash and Illinois rivers and their tributaries. He gave accurate descriptions of many localities along these rivers after a lapse of over fifty years. The mouth of Tippecanoe River; the Wea Town, and Prairie; Black Rock; the mouth of Big Pine Creek . . . and the Kankakee swamps were also frequently spoken of in his descriptions of the West. . . .

The last few months of Rue's captivity were spent at Detroit. I shall not attempt to give a full description of the various incidents of his long and painful captivity, which lasted three years and a half, and was terminated in the following manner: Rue and two of his fellow captives, whose names are not recollected with sufficient certainty to give them a place in these pages, came to the conclusion to make their escape, if possible. In anticipation of such an attempt, they had for some time been secretly preparing for their departure. At the time there were three or four different tribes of Indians assembled at the Trading House on the Lake shore near Detroit. A circumstance occurred during the drunken revels of the Indians which produced great excitement. One of the Indians lost a purse containing some ninety dollars in silver. Search was instituted in vain for the lost treasure.—Who was the thief? Various were the conjectures and insinuations of the exasperated tribes, who were about to make it assume a national character, when it was announced that there was a Soothsayer, or Prophet present, who belonged to another tribe from either of those who were disputing about the lost treasure, who, by conjuration, could detect the thief and tell where the lost money was secreted. . . . The professor of the black art, looking as solemn as an owl, unrolled a deer-skin upon the ground with the flesh side up. He then drew from his belt a little bag of fine sand, which he emptied upon the deer-skin. With a magic wand about the size and length of an ordinary rifle ram-rod, he spread the sand smoothly over the whole surface of the skin. The eager and deeply interested crowd with a solemn awe depicted in their countenances, encircled the magician and awaited with breath-less silence the result of his divination.—Meanwhile the Prophet, as he was termed, silently gazed at the glittering surface of the sand for many minutes, without any definite result. Then after mutter-ing over some half articulated spell-words and looking awfully wise, he took another long, steady gaze into the sand. Ureka! Ureka were not the words uttered by the venerable seer, but he said, "I see the thief, and the stolen treasure." "Who is he? Who?" shouted a dozen voices—"tell his name, point him out, be it whomsoever it may." But the Prophet . . . gravely declared the impropriety of divulging a fact that might terminate so disastrously. He exonerated all those who had been charged with the theft and said that the lost money had been taken and carried away by a member of a different tribe from any of those embroiled in the quarrel. . . .

Rue and his comrades being witnesses of this display of the Prophet's professional skill, concluded at the first convenient op-portunity to interrogate him in regard to the number, age, sex, and condition of their respective families at home; and whether they were all still alive, and resided where they did when they were captured.

A private chance occurred within a few days afterwards, the fee was agreed upon and paid, and the three prisoners and the seer seated themselves around the outspread deer-skin, covered with the enchanted sand. After a long silence, during which the Prophet looked steadily into the sand, he remarked that he saw Rue's folks passing about through the door-yard, giving the number of males and females, and their age and appearance with such accuracy that Rue at once considered him a genuine wizzard. The conjurer then lifted his eyes from the sand and remarked: "You all intend to make your escape—and you will effect it soon." Then gazing into the sand he continued: "You will meet with many trials and hardships in passing over so wild a district of country, inhabited by so many hostile nations of Indians. You will almost starve to death; but about the time you have given up all hope of finding game to sustain you in your famished condition, succor will come when you least expect it. I see dimly the carcass of some wild animal taken as game, what it is I can't clearly see. It will be a masculine of some kind—after that you will find plenty of game, and you will all arrive safely at your homes." They stoutly denied any intention or desire of escaping; but at the same time told the wizzard that as they had paid him for his professional revelations, that they had implicit confidence that he would not divulge, except to themselves, any shadowings of the future that flitted over his sand-covered deer-skin. . . .

At length the set time for their departure arrived and they commenced their dubious journey thro' the wide wilderness, infested with wild beasts, and wild and bloody-minded savages whose tender mercies (with a few noble exceptions) they had long since learned were cruel. They knew that as soon as they were missed they would be pursued, and they pushed ahead as fast as possible the whole of the first night and encamped about daybreak, without fire, in a thicket almost surrounded by a swamp. Here they lay concealed the whole day. Having eaten the scanty amount of victuals they had been able to stealthily abstract from the camp the morning they left, they began to feel pressed with hunger, but dare not venture from their concealment. . . . The morning of the third day found them so weak and exhausted by travel and hunger that it was determined that Rue, who was a good hunter, should venture out in quest of game. He spent the most of the day in hunting but found no game, not even a bird nor a squirrel to appease their gnawing hunger. By this time they had reached the streams that led into the Wabash river, which Rue knew abounded with fine fish, but having no fish hooks with them, nor wire to construct any out of, they deemed it too hazardous to attempt to spear any by torch-light. . . . Their hunger now began to become insupportable and, although the woods and streams showed strong and fresh signs of Indians, it was determined that Rue, their Nimrod, must go in quest of game at all hazards. He scoured the woods for miles around, up hill and down dale, but strange to say, he could find no game of any description. . . . At length another one of the fugitives arose from his prostrate position on the ground, and said, "Suppose I try my luck, or lack of luck, once more." Then, shouldering the best gun in the company, he walked slowly off and was soon hid in the darksome forest that surrounded them. But this persistent effort on the part of their comrade brought no hope to the minds of Rue and the other man, who well knew the want of skill on the part of the departed hunter. But the race is not always to the swift nor the battle to the strong . . . less than three hours after he started from the camp, the amateur hunter returned tottering under a small three-pronged buck, which he had killed and partly dressed. As he threw it upon the ground the words of the conjuerer—"It is a masculine—after killing it you will find plenty of game, and your hardships will mostly be over" flashed across the mind of Rue, who now felt fully confirmed in the oracular wisdom of the old Indian, whose prophetic ken had so far penetrated the future as to see the carcass of that deer, which was so opportunely killed to save them from death by famine. If it was a mere coincidence, or shrewd guess of the seer, they considered it strange beyond parallel. A fire was soon kindled, and a small portion of the deer was broiled. The experience and sound judgment of the prisoners prevented their eating too much of the delicious repast. They now had enough to last them several days, until they could kill more, and the last words of the conjurer threw the rainbow hues of hope over the remainder of their toilsome journey. . . . Had they been discovered by the Indians who inhabited the different portions of the country through which they passed, they would most likely not have been recognized as white men, for their dress, gait, manners and general appearance were completely Indian, from the painted feathers and porcupine quills that crowned the turban that encircled their foreheads, to the beads and ribbons that adorned their moccasins, and variegated the fanciful belts that surrounded their waists, bristling with scalping-knife and tomahawk. . . .

On the twentieth day after they made their escape from near Detroit, they struck the Ohio river, about fifty miles above the Falls. The sight of this beautiful river, which they had not seen for over three years, sent a thrill of joy through their bosoms, and they set to work to construct a rude raft out of logs to bear them down its sparkling current to the village of Louisville, where their toilsome and dangerous journey would be brought to a close. But before they had floated half the way to Louisville their frail raft was dashed to pieces by the white-caps raised by a stiff gale that swept up the river, and the three passengers with their guns, blankets, and provisions were spilt out into the river. With difficulty they reached the Kentucky shore, and crawled up the bank looking, as they afterwards said, like drowned rats. . . .

Rue married a relative of George Holman, his companion in captivity; and was in several campaigns against the Indians after his escape from captivity.

On the return of Holman's party of Indians to Wa-puc-ca-nat-ta, much dissatisfaction existed in regard to the manner of his release from the sentence of condemnation pronounced against him by the council. Many were in favor of recalling the council, and trying him again; which was finally agreed to, and the young man was again put on trial for his life, with a strong probability of his being again condemned to the stake. Both parties used strenuous efforts, one to condemn, and the other to acquit him. The votes were counted. The party in favor of the prisoner's acquittal prevailed by a majority of one, and the young captive was again rescued from the stake.

About three years and a half after Holman was taken prisoner, there was a cessation of hostilities for about one year. The protracted war had brought great distress upon the Indians, who wished to recruit themselves and get more trading houses established to furnish

them with the necessary supplies. Holman understanding their
wishes, proposed if they would send a young Indian with him who
knew the way to the Falls of the Ohio, he would make application
to a rich uncle of his in Kentucky, from whom they could obtain
as much goods as they wanted. Their necessities induced them to
comply with Holman's proposal. He, in company with another prisoner and a young warrior, started from Wa-puc-ca-nat-ta for the
vicinity of Harrodsburg, Kentucky. They struck the Ohio river a
few miles above Louisville, Ky., where General Clark was then stationed with troops and military stores. On arriving at the river,
Holman and his two companions lashed their guns and blankets
upon their backs, and taking advantage of the current, swam over
to the Kentucky side of the river. They stayed all night with Gen.
Clark, at Louisville, who, after learning the object of their mission,
told them to call for whatever they wanted to procure the ransom
of the two captives. Thus Holman and his fellow captive, for a small
sum, paid in powder, lead, salt, handkerchiefs, &c., were ransomed
by Gen. Clark and in a few days Holman met his friend and fellow
captive, Rue, at Edward Holman's residence, in the vicinity of Harrodsburg, Ky. Rue had arrived only three days before, and the
reader can imagine, better than I can describe, the transports of joy
that thrilled the bosoms of those two noble young Kentuckians,
on being released from the perils, toils, and sufferings of their protracted captivity. . . .

Both Rue and Holman lived many years in Woodford and Henry
counties in Kentucky; and in the year 1805, they, with their families,
removed to Wayne county, Indiana Territory, and settled and lived
close neighbors, on the same section of land, the remainder of their
lives, about two miles south of where the city of Richmond now
stands. . . .

Many years after peace had been established, their old Indian
relatives, as they called them, were in the habit of paying Rue and
Holman annual visits, staying from one to two weeks at a time. I
recollect that grandfather [Rue] and Mr. Holman made a great
parade over the old wrinkled Indian men and squaws that visited
them; and ordered their ponies to be well cared for. For hours to-

gether these old companions of the forest would sit and converse in broken English, and in the Indian dialect, by signs, motions, looks, and all manner of ways, which used to both astonish and amuse the younger members of the family, who were often called in to light their pipes, and report the condition of the ponies. First at Rue's, then at Holman's, and back again, once or twice during their stay, was the usual order of these periodical visits, which were continued during the lifetime of their Indian relatives. Nothing that Rue or Holman possessed was deemed too good for these guests from the forest, who were always dismissed with the utmost affection, and their ponies were loaded with presents in the shape of tobacco, salt, flour, and other nicknacks. . . . When we reflect that their lives had been spared, and their necessities supplied by these, their adopted relatives, to the full extent of their abilities—we are constrained not only to approve, but to admire such demonstrations of gratitude for favors conferred in the hour of extreme need. . . .

That second period of frequent Indian raids, which took place during the War of 1812, is described by Indiana's first historian,

JOHN BROWN DILLON

whose lonely life is worthy of a full-scale biography of its own. He was born in Wellsburg, Virginia (now West Virginia), in 1807 or 1808. Little is known of his youth or, for that matter, of his later life. He was respected by his contemporaries, and something tragic in his bearing and manner apparently elicited their sympathy, but no one seems to have been in his confidence: no one on terms better than acquaintanceship with him.

He always lived alone, in bachelor quarters reported to be more notable for the quantity of books, papers and notes with which they were strewn than for order or comfort. Lonely in life, he left no relative or close friend to fill in the outline of his biography.

He became an orphan at nine and existed precariously, there is reason to believe, until he was apprenticed and learned the printer's trade. As a journeyman he worked in Cincinnati and it was there that a personal tragedy occurred which prompted his poem "The Burial of the Beautiful." The loss of his sweetheart is probably the key to the mystery of his lonely life, but the poem, published in a Cincinnati newspaper, earned Dillon his first regard as a writer.

Before 1834 he went to Logansport, Indiana. There he read law and was admitted to the bar. He became an authority on American colonial legislation, but he did not practice law; instead, he and Stanislaus Lasselle (supposed to have furnished capital to match Dillon's technical knowledge) founded the newspaper, Canal Telegraph, of which Dillon acted as editor.

It was during this period that he completed and published the most important historical work relating to the Old Northwest Territory produced to that time or for a century following. His Historical Notes on the Discovery and Settlement of the Territory . . . Northwest of the River Ohio was published in Indianapolis in 1843 and was immediately recognized for what it was—a sound, scholarly, readable compilation of the facts of settlement gathered from original sources and carefully checked, in many cases by some of the men who had taken leading parts in the events described.

The authorship of this work had much to do with John B. Dillon's appointment to the post of Indiana State Librarian in 1845. Although the possibilities of profit in a newspaper published in a town as thriving as Logansport were certainly greater than those offered by the library post, Dillon accepted. Income necessary to maintain anything beyond the most Spartan existence was of no interest to him; the "Beautiful," whoever she was, had by then been buried many years.

During the rest of his life Dillon held various minor appointments in Indianapolis and Washington—assuring an existence and time to write—and he carried out his duties with meticulous care for detail. Before he died (in 1879) he produced another important book and in 1859 published a second and enlarged edition of his first work under the title:

A History of Indiana

CHAPTER XL PIGEON ROOST MASSACRE . . .
GENERAL HOPKINS' ILLINOIS
EXPEDITION . . . GEN. HOPKINS'
WABASH EXPEDITION

Within the present limits of the county of Scott, there was, in 1812, a place that was called "the Pigeon Roost settlement." This settlement, which was founded by a few families, in 1809, was confined to about a square mile of land, and it was separated from all other settlements by a distance of five or six miles. In the afternoon of the 3d of September, 1812, Jeremiah Payne, and a man whose name was Coffman, who were hunting for "bee-trees" in the woods . . . were surprised and killed by a party of Indians . . . ten or twelve warriors, nearly all of whom were Shawnees, then attacked the Pigeon Roost settlement, about sunset, on the evening of the 3d of September; and, in the space of about one hour, killed one man, five women, and sixteen children. The bodies of some of these victims of savage warfare were burned in the fires which consumed the cabins in which the murders were perpetrated. The persons who were massacred, at this settlement, were Henry Collings and his wife, Mrs. Payne, wife of Jeremiah Payne, and eight of her children, Mrs. Richard Collings, and seven of her children, Mrs. John Morris, and her only child, and Mrs. Morris, the mother of John Morris. Mrs. Jane Biggs, with her three small children, escaped from the settlement, eluded the vigilance of the Indians, and, about an hour before daylight, on the next morning, arrived at the house of her brother, Zebulun Collings, who lived about six miles from the scene of carnage. William Collings, who had passed the age of sixty years, defended his house for the space of three-quarters of an hour against the attacks of the Indians. In this defense, he was assisted by Captain John Norris. There were two children in the house. As soon as it began to grow dark, Mr. Collings and Captain Norris escaped with the two children (John Collings and Lydia Collings) from the house, eluded the pursuit of the Indians and, on the morning of the next day, reached the house of Zebulun Collings.

A number of the militia of Clark county immediately proceeded to the scene of the Pigeon Roost massacre, where they found several of the mangled bodies of the dead, surrounded by the smoking ruins of the houses. These remains of the murdered persons were brought together and buried in one grave.

On the afternoon of the 4th of September about one hundred and fifty mounted riflemen, under the command of Major John McCoy, followed the trail of the Indians about twenty miles, when "the darkness of the night" compelled them to give up the pursuit. A small scouting party under the command of Captain Devault discovered and made an attack on the retreating Indians, who, after killing one of Captain Devault's men, continued their flight through the woods and eluded the pursuit of the scouting party.

On the 6th of September, the militia of Clark county were reinforced by sixty mounted volunteers from Jefferson county, under the command of Col. William McFarland, and on the evening of the 7th about three hundred and fifty volunteers from Kentucky were ready to unite with the Indiana militia of Clark and Jefferson counties for the purpose of making an attack on the Delaware Indians— some of whom were suspected of having been engaged in the destruction of the Pigeon Roost settlement. It seems, however, that a spirit of rivalry which prevailed among some of the officers defeated the intentions of those who, at that time, proposed to destroy the towns of the friendly Delawares who lived on the western branch of White river. After the time of the Pigeon Roost massacre, many of the settlers on the northern and western frontiers of Clark, Jefferson, Harrison, and Knox counties lived in a state of alarm until the close of the war, in 1815. Mr. Zebulun Collings . . . says: "The manner in which I used to work, in those perilous times, was as follows: On all occasions I carried my rifle, tomahawk, and butcherknife, with a loaded pistol in my belt. When I went to plow, I laid my gun on the plowed ground, and stuck up a stick by it, for a mark, so that I could get it quick in case it was wanted. I had two good dogs. I took one into the house, leaving the other out. The one outside was expected to give the alarm, which would cause the one inside to bark, by which I would be awakened, having my arms always loaded. I kept my horses in a stable close to the house, having a porthole so that I could shoot to the stable door. During two years I never went from home with any certainty of returning—not knowing the minute I might receive a ball from an unknown hand; but in the midst of all these dangers that God who never sleeps nor slumbers has kept me."

The hostile Indians who began to assemble in considerable numbers around Fort Wayne about the 1st of September, 1812, continued to invest that fort until it was relieved, by the approach of Kentucky and Ohio troops, from the danger of a general attack.

In the month of August, 1812, General Harrison received from the Governor of Kentucky the appointment of major-general, by brevet, of the Kentucky militia; and, as such officer, he was requested to take the chief command of all the troops which had been raised in that State for the defense of the northwestern frontiers. About two thousand Kentuckians, and seven hundred citizens of Ohio, marched under the command of General Harrison from the place of rendezvous at Piqua, in Ohio, and arrived at Fort Wayne on the evening of the 12th of September. On the approach of the army, the hostile Indians retired, after having burned a few houses in the vicinity of the fort. . . .

On the 19th of September, General Harrison gave up the command of the troops at Fort Wayne to Brigadier-general James Winchester, who was a citizen of Tennessee, and who had been an officer in the revolutionary war. On the 24th of the same month, however, General Harrison . . . received dispatches by which he learned that the President of the United States had assigned to him the command of the northwest army . . . [under] the following orders: "Having provided for the protexion of the western frontier, you will retake Detroit; and, with a view to the conquest of Upper Canada, you will penetrate that country as far as the force under your command will in your judgment justify."

Before Governor Harrison was invested with the command of the northwestern army he had requested the governor of Kentucky to send from that State a military force sufficient not only to aid in the protection of the frontiers of Indiana and Illinois but strong enough, when reinforced by the militia of those territories, to carry on offensive operations against the hostile Indian tribes of the northwest. . . .

In the latter part of September, 1812, there were at Vincennes about two thousand mounted volunteers from Kentucky under the command of General Samuel Hopkins, a gentleman who had acquired an honorable distinction as an officer of the revolutionary war. Gen. Hopkins was invested with the command of the troops which were intended to operate against the enemy . . . on the borders of the river Wabash and in the vicinity of the river Illinois; and he was requested and instructed to make strenuous efforts to break up and destroy the settlements and villages of the hostile Indians who resided on the borders of those rivers.

Early in the month of October, General Hopkins moved from Vincennes, and made an attempt to carry an expedition against the Kickapoo villages in the Illinois territory. . . . The following particulars concerning the failure of this expedition are copied from a letter which was written by Gen. Hopkins, at Fort Harrison, on the 26th of October, 1812, and addressed to Governor Shelby, of Kentucky:

"The expedition, with the mounted riflemen, has terminated. The Wabash was re-crossed yesterday, and the whole corps are on their way to Bosseron, where the adjutant-general will attend, in order to have them properly mustered and discharged; and where their horses may get forage during the delay necessary for this object. Yes, sir, this army has returned, without hardly getting the sight of an enemy. A simple narrative of facts, as they occurred, will best explain the reasons that led to this state of things. The army, having finished crossing the Wabash, on the 14th instant, marched about three miles, and encamped. I here requested [the presence] of the general field officers and captains, to whom I imparted the objects of the expedition, and the advantages that might arise from a fulfillment of them. The nearest Kickapoo villages were from eighty to one hundred miles distant; and Peoria not more than one hundred and sixty miles. . . . Breaking them [up,] or as many as our resources would permit, would be rendering a service to all the territories; that, from their number, this tribe was more formidable than any other near us; and, from their situation and hostility, had it more in their power to do us mischief. Of course, to chastise and destroy these, would be rendering real benefit to our country. It was observed by some officers, they would meet the next morning, consult together, and report to me their opinions—desiring, at the same time, to be furnished with [an interview with] the persons on whom I had relied for intelligence of the country. This council was held, and all the intelligence furnished that had been requested; and I had a report highly favorable to the enterprise. This, to me, was more gratifying, as I had found, as early as our encampment at Vincennes, discontents and murmurings that portended no wish to proceed further. At Bosseron I found an evident increase of discontent, although no army was ever better or more amply supplied with forage and rations than at this place. At Fort Harrison we encamped on the 10th, where we were well supplied with forage, etc. I found, on the 12th and 13th, many breaking off, and returning without applying to me for a discharge; and, as far as I know, without any notification to their officers. . . .

"Thinking myself secure in the confidence of my brother officers and the army, we proceeded on our march early on the 15th, and continued it four days—our course near north, in the prairie—until we came to an Indian house, where some corn, etc., had been cultivated. The last day of the march to this place I had been made acquainted with a return of that spirit of [discontent] that had, as I hoped, subsided; and when I ordered a halt near sunset, (for the first time that day,) in a fine piece of grass in the prairie, to aid our horses, I was addressed in the most rude and dictatorial manner, requiring me immediately to resume my march, or his battalion would break from the army and return. This was a Major. . . . I mention him, in justice to the other officers of that grade; but, from every information, I began to fear that the army waited but for a pretext to return. This was afforded the next day, by our guides, who had thought that they had discovered an Indian village at the site of a grove, about ten miles from where we encamped on the fourth night of our march, and turned us about six or eight miles out of our way. An almost universal discontent seemed to prevail, and we took our course in such a direction as we supposed would atone for the error in the morning. About or after sunset, we came to a thin grove, affording water. Here we took our camp; and about this time arose one of the most violent gusts of wind I ever remember to have seen, not proceeding from clouds. The Indians had set fire to the prairie, which drove on us so furiously, that we were compelled to fire [the prairie] around our camp to protect ourselves. This seems to have decided the army to return. I was informed of it in so many ways, that, early the next morning, October 20th, I requested the attendance of the general and field officers, and stated to them my apprehensions—the expectations of our country—the disgrace attending the measure—the approbation of our own consciences. Against this, I stated the weary situation of our horses, and the want of provisions—which, to me, seemed only partial—six days only having passed since every part of the army was furnished with ten days' ration in bacon, beef, or breadstuff. The reasons given for returning, I requested the commandants of each regiment, with the whole of the officers belonging to it, to take fully the sense of the army on this measure . . . and to report to me in writing—adding, that if five hundred volunteers would turn out, I would put myself at their head, and proceed in quest of the towns; and the balance of the army might retreat, under the conduct of their officers, in safety, to Fort Harrison. In less than an hour the report was made, almost unanimously, to return. I then requested that I might dictate the course to be pursued that day only, which, I pledged myself, should not put them more than six miles out of their way—my object being to cover the reconnoitering parties I wished to send out for the discovery of the Indian towns. About this time—the troops being paraded—I put myself in front, took my course, and directed them to follow me. The columns moving off quite a contrary way, I sent Captain Taylor and Major Lee to apply to the officers to turn them. They were told that it was not in their power—the army had taken their own course, and would pursue it. Discovering great confusion and disorder in the march, I threw myself in the rear, fearing an attack on those who were there from necessity, and continued in that position the whole day. . . .

"I am certain we were not twenty miles from the Indian village, when we were *forced* to retire; and I have many reasons to prove we were in the right way. I have, too, myself, (superadded to the mortification I feel at thus returning,) been in a bad state of health from first to last; and am now so weak, as not to be able to help myself on my horse." . . .

Immediately after the discharge of the mounted volunteers, whose mutinous conduct was deeply deplored by General Hopkins, that officer began to organize a military force composed mainly of infantry, for the purpose of penetrating the Indian country as far as the Prophet's Town, and destroying the Indian villages which had been rebuilt in that quarter. . . . The main body of this army moved from the place of rendezvous at Vincennes and arrived at Fort Harrison on the 5th of November. In a letter, dated "November 27, 1812," and addressed to Governor Shelby, of Kentucky, General Hopkins says:

"On the 11 of November the army marched from Fort Harrison, on the road formerly made by Governor Harrison's army; and the boats set out at the same time. The length of time the enemy had expected us made it necessary to guard ourselves in an especial manner. The rise of the waters, from the heavy fall of rain preceding our march, and some large creeks, left us no doubt of considerable difficulty and embarrassment; insomuch that not until the 14th did we pass Sugar creek, three miles above the road. From every information, I had no hesitation in moving on the east side of the Wabash. The Vermillions, Pine creek, and other impediments on the west side, superadded to the presumption that we were expected, and might more easily be annoyed and ambuscaded on that route, determined me in this measure. The boats, too, with provisions of rations, forage, and military stores . . . encamped with us on the bank of the river, almost every night. This so protracted our march, that we did not reach the Prophet's Town until the 19th.

"On the morning of this day, I detached three hundred men to surprise the Winnebago town lying on Ponce Passu [Ponceau pichou] creek, one mile from the Wabash, and four below the Prophet's. This party, commanded by General Butler, surrounded the place about break of day, but found it evacuated. There were, in the main town, about forty houses, many of them from thirty to fifty feet in length, besides many temporary huts in the surrounding prairie, in which they had cultivated a good deal of corn.

"On the 20th, 21st, and 22d, we were embarked in the complete destruction of the Prophet's Town, which had about forty cabins and huts, and the large Kickapoo village adjoining below it, on the west side of the river, consisting of about one hundred and sixty cabins and huts—finding and destroying their corn, reconnoitering the circumjacent country, and constructing works for the defense of our boats and army. Seven miles east of us, on the Ponce Passu creek, a party of Indians were discovered. They had fired on a party of ours, on the 21st, and killed a man by the name of Dunn, a gallant soldier in Captain Duval's company. On the 22d, upward of sixty horsemen, under the command of Lieutenant-colonels Miller and Wilcox, anxious to bury their comrade, as well as gain a more complete knowledge of their ground, went on to a point near the Indian encampment, fell into an ambuscade, and eighteen of our party killed, wounded and missing. . . . On the return of this party, and the information of a large assemblage of the enemy, who, encouraged by the strength of their camp, appeared to be waiting for us, every preparation was made to march early and engage the enemy at every risk; when, from the most violent storm and fall of snow, attended with the coldest weather I ever saw or felt at this season of the year, and which did not subside until the evening of the 23d, we were delayed until the 24th. Upon arriving on the ground, we found the enemy had deserted their camp before the fall of the snow, and passed the Ponce Passu. . . .

"After reconnoitering sufficiently, we returned to camp, and found the ice so accumulated as to alarm us for the return of the boats. I had fully intended to have spent one more week in endeavoring to find the Indian camps; but the *shoeless, shirtless state of the troops*, now clad in the remnants of their summer dress— a river full of ice—the hills covered with snow—a rigid climate, and no certain point to which we could further direct our operation— under the influence and advice of every staff and field officer, orders were given and measures pursued for our return on the 25th.

"We are now progressing to Fort Harrison, through ice and snow, where we expect to arrive on the last day of this month. . . . Before

I close this, I can not forbear expressing the merits of the officers and soldiers of this command. After leaving [at] Fort Harrison, all unfit for duty, we had, in privates of every corps, about one thousand—in the total, twelve hundred and fifty, or thereabouts. At the Prophet's Town, upward of one hundred of these were on the sick report. Yet, sir, have we progressed in such order as to menace our enemy, free from annoyance; seven large keel boats have been covered and protected to a point heretofore unknown in Indian expeditions; three large Indian establishments have been burnt and destroyed, with near three miles of fence, (and all the corn, etc., we could find) besides many smaller ones. The enemy have been sought in their strongholds, and every opportunity afforded them to attack or alarm us; a march on the east side of the Wabash, without road or cognizance of the country, fully one hundred miles perfected; and this has been done with a naked army of infantry, aided by only about fifty rangers and spies. All this was done in twenty days. No sigh, no murmur, no complaint. . . ."

On the 18th of December, 1812, General Hopkins announced, in general orders issued at Vincennes, his determination to retire from military life. He said—"The commander-in-chief now closes his command, and, in all probability, his military services for ever. With tender and sincere affection he bids his brother officers and soldiers farewell—their virtue, courage and patriotism, he has justly represented to their country."

———

From John Dillon's account of the period, based upon the evidence of the military gentlemen most directly involved, the fact is all too obvious that warfare against the Indians in Indiana during the War of 1812 resulted only in great success for Indian arms.

Other Hoosiers and Kentuckians—and at that only a few thousand more of them than poor, doddering, old General Hopkins commanded—were invading Canada and winning a victory over British regulars, Indian allies under no less a commander than Tecumseh, and Canadian militia; but at home all was confusion as Hopkins and his harum-scarum army were losing themselves in what is now the Indiana-Illinois corn country, running into ambushes on Wildcat

Creek, suffering terrific thirsts as whiskey rations were cut and encountering other miscellaneous horrors of war! Since most Shawnees had joined the British in Canada long since, the actually hostile Indians against whom all these expeditions were directed probably never exceeded a very few hundred warriors.

But these facts did not make life any easier for the families in the widely scattered cabins along the outer fringe of settlement in the state: they, poor devils, were as open to attack as they would have been had General Hopkins never come out of retirement at all!

———

The trouble with most published reminiscence, pioneer or otherwise, is that it is usually composed at a time when the author has grown old and full of rectitude—or at least when he is anxious to appear full of rectitude to his neighbors, his grandchildren and his Maker.

No such mincing considerations deterred Sam Ginger of Ridgeville and the Mississinewa. He wrote his pieces for the Ridgeville News at about the turn of the century and, when he had accumulated enough of them and the public displayed a rewarding interest in the discreet and indiscreet doings of their own and their friends' ancestors, he put them in a little paper-covered volume.

Those sketches display the pioneer on the Mississinewa in what is probably a spitten image; neither so harassed by his sexual motivation as he would later appear to Dreiser and Lockridge nor so engrossed in thoughts of his future salvation as the early "home missionaries" hoped he was. Sam Ginger was an honest man; a glance at the portrait, circa 1905, which serves as frontispiece in his book, proves that beyond shadow of doubt. Slender, still jaunty at eighty or so, silken white mustaches of the kind made famous by William F. Cody, the broad-brimmed black hat and regimental badge of the Civil War veteran, what appears to be a tulip at his lapel and the devil in his eye—if he hadn't been an innately honest man, if he had pretended to possession of a life-long odor of sanctity, he would never have permitted publication of that photograph!

There follows an episode of later Indian trouble from

SAMUEL GINGER

Reminiscences of Ridgeville
and the
Mississinewa Country

Wizards know their times; deep night, dark night, the
silent of the night, the time of night when Troy was set
on fire; the time when screech owls cry, and ban dog howl,
and ghosts break up their graves.—KING HENRY VI.

Puccachee, in the Indian language means, Forward march! Git
up and git! Skedaddle! Vamose the ranch! So the six warriors, six
squaws, and six papooses started west to find a more congenial
hunting ground. Before the next autumn's hunting season came
around, all the camps on that creek were burned to the ground. No
one knew who did it, but the strong presumption was that Jesse
Gray knew something about it; and to this day that creek is known
as burnt camp creek and it was while camped on the banks of that
creek, in company with Jesse Gray, my father, elder brother, uncle
Joe and several others, that I heard many of the thrilling adventures
which are related in the "Reminiscences," from Jesse Gray himself,
the great hunter and Indian slayer and noblest Roman of them all.

It was while encamped here with Gray, my father and many
others, that occurred one of those peculiar, and to this day, laughable
incidents that so vividly illustrated the superstition of the hunter
of that day, and in fact may still be found with many hunters, actors
and gamblers of the present time. My father was an old Virginia
dutchman, and as full of dreams, signs and tokens as an egg is of
meat, and the rest of the party were much like him in that respect.
Father was always recognized as the Grand Sachem or boss of the

party; and it being necessary for Gray to go home for a few days to attend to some urgent business, after which he would join us and finish up the hunt, as he shouldered his gun just at peep o'day, he turned to my father and said:

"Now, Lew, if an old devil and wizard, named Harshish, should come here in my absence, which he is almost sure to do, don't under any circumstances, give him anything, for if you do he will spell your guns, and you will not hit another deer this hunt." With this parting injunction the old man took his leave. After Gray left some of the party laughed rather lightly at the old man's warning, but the most of them considered it more seriously. My brother Jim, who was considered the best hunter in the party concluded that he knew more about "spelling" guns than father, Gray, or anyone else, and said that the idea that a gun could be "spelled" was too absurd to be talked of for a moment; and if he was at the camp when Harshish called, he would give him the whole camp just to show them that they were all superstitious lunatics. But Jim changed his mind before thirty-six hours had passed.

It was about four o'clock in the evening of the day that Gray left for his home. I, a boy of twelve or thereabout, and the camp keeper of the party, was stirring the fire preparatory to setting on the coffee pot, and hanging over the blazing logs, the dinner pot, well filled with young venison. I was startled by an apparition of, well I will not say a man, yet it was a living, moving, breathing animal of the genuine homo. I would like, if possible to describe that singular looking being for the reader, but alas the pen is unequal to the task, and I pause dumfounded, not knowing where to begin or what to say. Nay, not even the hasty little kodak of today could catch him so uncertain were his movements, so restless his motions, so glittering and piercing his little deep sunken eyes; indeed he was one that might well appall the devil, and what of a twelve year old boy; I presume that had it not been that Gray's description had prepared me for such a sight, these "Reminiscences" would never have been written, and yet I had as much grit as the average boy of that day and age.

I assure you that his greeting was not calculated to nerve me, as his first words were in a tone of voice something between the screech of a locomotive and the plaintive wail of a Scotch bag-pipe. "What the devil is the matter, boy, did you never see a man before?" "N—, n—, no" I managed to say, I never had. I suppose I meant such a man as that. He was about five feet in height, slimly built and could not have weighed over ninety pounds, with a shock of grizzly gray hair, a snow-white beard that covered every inch of his repulsive features, and neither hair nor beard had ever known the use of a comb. His little deep-set piercing eyes reminded one of two holes cut in a venison ham, or two holes burnt in a blanket. But now to attempt to describe his dress; a hunting shirt which at the beginning, was buck skin, but now from the numerous patches sewed on, tied on with strings, tied on with hickory bark, patch upon patch, until all the colors of the rainbow were blended into one inconceivable butternut hue; moccasins of a pre-historic type, were tied upon his feet with leatherwood bark, while his pants out-generaled his coat for color and patches. His hands, which scorned the use of soap, reminded one of the talons of a chicken hawk; on his head he wore what had once been a cap, made of deer skin with the hair side out, but now it looked somewhat like a last year's inverted bird's nest after the breaking up of a hard winter; but comparisons are vain, and I'll give it up in despair.

An old U. S. flint-lock musket was slung over his shoulder, a dilapidated, greasy shot-pouch and powder horn hung by his side, while a much-worn shoemaker's knife, in a leather scabbard, was tied to his belt. His next words were:

"Give me something to eat, boy; I'm hungry as a bar."

But by this time I had partially regained my senses, and told the ghoul or goblin, that there was not a morsel of cooked food in the camp, but if he would tarry awhile, the hunters would be in and by that time I would have supper ready, and would be very much pleased to have him sup with us. This invitation he readily accepted, and standing his gun against a tree with a satisfied grunt, sat down on a log to await the return of the hunters and supper.

In a short time, all returned and as they greeted the visitor it was plain to be seen, they knew who he was from Gray's description; and indeed he introduced himself as Harshish, the oldest and greatest hunter of the classic Loblolly; had killed more deer and bear than any man in the world. While he would be talking to one, the rest would be out behind the camp discussing the situation. It was finally decided that allowing the wizard to take supper with us would not be giving him anything anyway, and moreover was any man ever known to come to the home of father, hungry, and go away empty? So Harshish took supper with us. He did not tarry long after supper, but picked up his gun to start; for the sake of good manners, father asked him to stay all night; no, he would go to his own cabin, which was not more than a mile away, and he had traveled those woods darker nights than that.

Just before leaving he turned to father rather carelessly and said he had always made it a point when he was having good luck hunting, to divide with his less fortunate neighbors, and he had been hunting several days and killed nothing, and his family being entirely out of meat and nothing else in the house to eat but a little unground corn, he would be very thankful for a small piece of venison. Now of course father could not refuse that appeal especially when the wizard referred to his family, and had his mind fully made up to offer him meat without asking, regardless of the wishes of the others, but he wisely concluded to have their consent, so if any disaster followed the gift, he would not bear all the blame. And moreover we could not plead scarcity, as there right in front of the gent, hung three fine deer, the fruits of the day's hunt. So father said, "Well 'tis true we have the venison, and to spare, but I am only one and as for me you can have the meat, and welcome." Then Jim, the man who did not believe in "spells," spoke up, "Certainly, give him all the meat he wants, and we can kill more when this is gone." Uncle Joe was of the same opinion, and gave his assent. Old Coon Thompson, the next oldest, to father, and the most superstitious of the party was the hardest nut to crack. But as all the rest were against him, gave a reluctant consent, saying he thought any man who was not too d—n lazy might get all the game he wanted without begging it. If Harshish heard this remark he did not heed it, and father stepped out to one of the deer hanging on the pole, cut off a fore-quarter and handed it to the apparently thankful Harshish, who speedily took his departure. For hours after he was gone the men lay there discussing the pro's and con's, and wondering what the morrow would bring forth, which interesting question will be answered in the next chapter.

CHAPTER X

They ripped and tore, cussed and swore, and swore they wouldn't stay there any more.—OLD NEGRO MELODY.

A BETTER TIME for stalking deer never dawned, than the morning after the wizard of Loblolly left the camp with his quarter of fat venison. A crisp white frost covered the ground and hung like sparkling diamonds from the trees and underbrush; just such a morning as gladdens the heart of a hunter, and sends him forth with the assurance that before the frost has melted from the leaves he will get a shot; for on such a morning any old deer-hunter will tell you that every deer in the woods is on the move, especially in the height of rutting time.

It was not more than a half hour, until bang, went a gun. "That's father," said I, "and I'll bet my boots there's one deer less in the woods." I wish to explain here that after being in the woods a few days, hunters can tell the crack of each other's guns as well by the sound, as if they saw them fired. In five or ten minutes more, bang, bang, I heard Jim's gun fire two shots in quick succession, and in less time than it takes to record it, the shots became so fast and furious that it reminded one of a skirmish line, and I began to wonder what we would do with all the deer killed that morning. But before dinner time my mind was set at rest on that subject. The first to get into camp was father; he came tearing through the woods like a mad steer; as he threw off his shot-pouch and slammed his gun down in the tent, he muttered, "D—n old Harshish; what in the dickens did them fellows mean by giving him meat anyway; two broadside shots and not a hair touched."

Next came Uncle Joe puffing and blowing with the same refrain, "D—n that old scoundrel! Three as fair shots as I ever had in my life and not a hair or drop of blood. Lew, what in the thunder ever possessed you to give that old d—l that quarter of venison?"

"I didn't give it any more than the rest of you" replied father hotly.

Next came Jim the wise man, that did not believe in the hoodoo art. Oh, but he was hot! "What do you think" said he; "I stood right in my tracks and shot five times at the biggest five point buck that runs the woods and never made him bat his eye. I knew I took as good sight, and had as steady a nerve as I ever had, and I did not shoot an inch over sixty yards. That villian has spelled my gun, I am ready to swear, for I never miss a deer that distance, you all know."

This was a fact for Jim was known as the greatest deer hunter of that day, and had the proud distinction of standing in his tracks, and piling up five full grown deer, and that with the old fashioned muzzle loading, single barreled rifle, which would be a considerable feat to-day, even with the improved Winchester. In fact it was not uncommon for Jim to kill more deer than all the rest of the party, and as a matter of course when he reported having missed five fair shots, something had to be wrong with his gun, that was dead sure. After each one related his terrible luck, and blamed old Harshish with it, father says, "Well we will wait for old Coon Thompson, and if he missed we may as well hang up the fiddle and break for home."

They had not long to wait, for last came not Satan, but something worse. It was old Coon. You might have heard him swear for a mile or more; he fairly turned the woods blue with profanity. "Didn't I warn you, Lew, not to give that old devil anything? Didn't Jesse Gray tell you that if we gave him anything, our luck was done and our goose was cooked? Why I would have seen the old son of a gun starve before I would have given him a crumb of bread to save his cussed old life. We may just as well pull up stakes and start for New Paris, (where we lived at that time). If I only had that old devil here for one minute he would never spell another gun" said old Coon.

"Why, have you forgotten, John, that nothing but a silver bullet will kill a witch or wizard?" said father, half jeeringly, half earnest.

"I'd risk it" replied old Cooney; "I'd take the ax, chop him into mince meat and throw him into the fire."

"Well" said father "you have not told us yet what your luck has been; we heard you cannonading, and thought you had a wagon load of deer hung up."

"Deer" said Cooney, "devil a deer have I touched this day, though I have shot away every bullet in my pouch. The first chance I had was a doe and two fawns; they ran up within twenty steps of me; I could see their very eye winkers, and knew if I could knock the doe down in her tracks, I was about sure of all three of them. I held for the doe's heart, when fiz went the cap. They never stirred. I put on a new cap, and click, it went again. There them three deer stood until I busted seven caps, and then galloped away without even seeing me. I then concluded the powder in the tube had got damp, and sighted at a spot on a tree, and the gun cracked as clear as a bell. I loaded again, and had not gone two hundred yards, until six deer came running and stopped within sixty yards of me. There I stood and banged away, shot after shot, while them deer circled around me until I hadn't a bullet left in my pouch. I'll take my oath I did not shoot over twenty-five yards at some of the deer, and never touched a hair. It's all your fault, Lew; I told you not to give that old cuss anything, but you would have your own way, and now you see what's come of it. Our guns are spelled and we will not kill another deer."

I should have stated that the other two hunters, one of them, Hust Porterfield, of New Paris, and the D. G. of the same place had come in just before old Cooney, and had about the same experience to report; plenty of shots, or snaps, but no game. Especially was D. G. badly demoralized; he had got a half mile from camp, when a large black bear came running and jumped up on a log not over fifteen steps away and on seeing the hunter, raised up on his haunches and took a hasty survey of him. The hunter aimed for his heart, when click went the cap; he snapped again and again, and the gun failed to fire. He went to put on a new cap, and in his great haste and excitement allowed the cap box to slip from his hand and roll away in the leaves, and as he stooped to recover it the bear took the alarm and jumped the log and in a very brief time was lost in the underbrush.

Thus it was each man had a story more dismal than the one preceding him. So they jawed and quarreled. Crimination and recrimination was the order of the day; each one positively denying that he had been responsible for the bad luck in giving the wizard the venison. So after they had quarreled until they became tired of that sport, father said the witch did not live that could put on a charm that he could not break, that he was not born right in the shadow of the natural bridge in old Virginia to be out-generaled by such a little shriveled up wizard as old Harshish, and if they would all be governed by him he would break the spell. To this they readily assented you may be sure.

Each man took his gun barrel out of the stock; this being done, the vents or tubes were closely plugged up; a pole was placed over the big log fire, high enough for the lower end of the barrels to hang a foot or more above the fire. A piece of hickory bark was tied around the muzzle and was filled with a fluid readily obtainable, then each barrel was suspended from the pole, until they should boil dry, while an incantation or witch jargon, something like the following was repeated thrice:

Boil away, boil away, till the pot boils dry;
Away to the clouds the charm will fly;
If the witch comes back, the witch will die;
Howly poke, up in smoke, and all's well.

The guns having all boiled until they were perfectly dry, were taken down, thoroughly washed out with hot water and ashes, and wiped dry with tow. They were then fitted to their stocks and were ready for the next morning's hunt. About sundown Jesse Gray returned, and laughed heartily, when told of the morning adventures, he himself having killed a large five point buck on his way to camp. We staid there three more days, and had more game than we could haul home. Besides the deer killed, we had six or eight wild turkeys, and nearly a barrel of honey.

I am aware that some of my readers will think Old Timer is exaggerating, but I can assure them that while the language is my own, the facts as here set down are substantially true as Holy Writ. . . . In fact things every whit as absurd and unreasonable are believed by many people of today, and not the most ignorant people either.

CHAPTER FOUR

Those Big, Dark Indiana Woods

Thus far we have seen only scattered outposts of the original Indiana settlement, mainly on the southern border along the Ohio River. Shortly after the War of 1812 those people who would eventually make up the bulk of the population began to arrive. Most of them could not come by river this time, for there were no navigable streams other than the Wabash. These folks, bringing household goods and tools for farming, often driving a few hogs, and more rarely leading a cow or two, had to move through the thick, mainly hardwood, forests following what they called "traces." That was a good term, the word "road" did not apply, for these were wild animal routes of emigration, adapted by Indians in their travels and now widened laboriously to wagon-width with axe and hoe.

In 1816 Indiana was admitted to statehood, but this had no effect, yet, on transportation; hopeful residents were expected to find their own way in if they wished to become Hoosiers. Arrivals previously had been mainly from Kentucky, Virginia, and, to a lesser degree, North Carolina; now they came from all over—from the Eastern Seaboard, New England, even, some of them, of first or second generation descent from overseas. There were, already present, a scattering of Canadian French along the Wabash and in the northern half of the state and until the 1830s a considerable number of Indians, members of the various subtribes of the Miami Confederacy, Potawatami and, recently arrived after having been driven out of their homes in the eastern states, some Shawnees, Delawares, and a few members of less important tribes.

The new whites who were arriving were a typical mixture'in character: some were good, some so-so, some undesirable, and a few very bad
indeed. As usual they were in the main an indifferent lot, too good to
hang but not too well worth praying for. They varied widely in individual attainments: some could read, some could not; some had mastered a trade, others were good only for common labor. One in a great
number was college-bred, or what equalled that state of questionable
salubrity.

One of the first mile-by-mile accounts of travel through the big woods
of Indiana is preserved in the journal of

THOMAS DEAN

by a New York state gentleman who came to Indiana in the hope of
helping the Brothertown Indians buy a tract of land which would
replace their reserve in central New York on which, as usual, whites
were encroaching. Dean built a boat which could be propelled by sails
or oars, as conditions made necessary. He set out, accompanied by five
leading men of the Brothertowns and the wives of two of them. Dean
was a young man of thirty-four years.

The party set sail on Oneida Creek on June 10, 1817 and by taking
advantage of Lakes Ontario, Erie, Chatauqua, and tributary streams
and no small number of portages, they reached the Allegheny River,
which took them into the Ohio and, eventually, the Wabash. It was a
long, arduous, sometime hungry and (oddly enough) thirsty voyage, but
not of particular interest to us until on July 23rd they reached Ft. Harrison, a few miles north of Terre Haute, which had just been laid out.

At this point the boat was docked and Dean and his Indian friends
started out afoot on a trace that began on the north bank of Raccoon
Creek. Now they would travel as did most others in this part of the
country at the time, except that they did not have the worries occasioned by possessions, wagons, and livestock. They had only their personal gear to transport.

The Journal of Thomas Dean

JOURNEY FROM FORT HARRISON...

July 31. We prepared by washing our clothes, baking bread for our journey, and storing our goods. The women finished washing the clothes that were not washed yesterday, and we began to unload our goods and stored them at John A. Lafond's, where we put up. Major Chunn [commandant of the fort] offered to put our boat under the care of the guard at the fort, that it should not be injured or taken away.

We had our goods all stored, made a chain, fastened our boat near the fort to a stump, put the oars, poles, etc., into the blockhouse, and prepared to start, but we could not get ready until it was too late in the afternoon. The Indian who was going to wade Eel River and pilot us agreed to wait until morning, so we made preparations to start early in the morning. In the evening John A. Lafond and another man informed me that we had best not start too early, as an Indian had told them that twenty or thirty of the Pottawottomis had come from Chicago, were hostile, and if they came across us they might injure us. We thought it was a false report and concluded to start as soon as we could.

August 1st. We put up what clothes we wanted to take with us and some bread. They told us we could go through in three days if we had horses, it being one hundred miles, so we concluded to take three days' provisions and get horses if we could, but it happened that there was not more than one pound of meat put up. We took three guns and an ax, started about 10 A.M., and our guide went on with us. The weather was very warm, and we had to go through the prairie, about seventy-two miles, which was very hot and uncomfortable. We could get no water to drink until we went about thirteen miles, where there was good water and a family lived. Here they gave us some milk to drink. After we had refreshed ourselves we left two guns and proceeded on. We traveled very fast until we came to Raccoon Creek, a large stream that runs into the Wabash twelve or fifteen miles above the fort. It was deep. Our guide went across and got a bark in the form of a canoe, took packs across, and Jacob Dick rode his horse across; the others waded. It was near up to their arms. I got some wet, as well as the rest, and it was very warm. We went on in our little path through the woods up the creek three or four miles, made a fire, and lay on the ground. Being very sweaty, and having no shelter, I took cold. We ate a piece of meat and laid down.

August 2d. We took a piece of bread and a small piece of meat for breakfast. It thundered, and as we went on in the little path it soon began to rain. I was very sore and stiff, so that I could hardly travel. It rained very hard, which made it worse going, and being wet with sweat all night, and now wet with rain, I was very uncomfortable. We went on some miles and stopped under the trees to rest, then went on again until fatigued, then stopped and made a shelter of bark and built a fire. Our guide would not wait for us, so we let him go on. It was so bad going through weeds and brush that we stayed about one hour until it stopped raining, went on through mud and water some miles, and then came another shower. We reached a shelter of bark, made a fire, and stayed until the rain was over. As we went on we met an Indian man, woman, and boy, with two horses, going to the fort with skins, etc. We traveled until near night, made a shelter and fire, and camped for the night. We had a good fire, took a small piece of meat and a piece of bread, and obtained what rest we could to meet the fatigues of another day.

August 3d. In the morning we refreshed ourselves with some bread and water and started on our journey, it being the first day of the week. We followed our little path, crossed Raccoon Creek and its branches two or three times, and expected soon to come to the Wea village. About 12 o'clock we came to three or four bark cabins of the Weas [possibly this was Cornstalk Town], where our guide lived with his relations. None of them could speak English. They brought us about a quart of boiled corn, which we soon made way with. We tried to get a horse, but they made signs that we must stay there that night, for we could not get through the village. I did not feel like traveling much farther on foot that day, and towards night one of the family who could speak some English arrived. He said we could have a horse to go through to the village next day for $2, and some one would go with us. They gave us some blackberries to eat and at night they sweetened some for us, and showed us some barks we could lay on in a cabin by ourselves. We lay on a kind of stage, with barks on, with our own blankets to cover. As near as we could tell we were about sixty miles from the fort.

August 4th. This morning it thundered and there was a hard shower of rain and some hail. It soon cleared off, and they gave us about three pints of boiled corn, which we ate. We had but two spoons to use among five of us at this place. The women boiled some dried venison for us. We could only get one horse. My companions went forward and left me to follow. When we started, which was about 8 o'clock, the old man went on foot to ride my horse back, and his son, the one that came from the fort with us, rode with me and took part of our baggage. We traveled hard through the woods, brush, weeds, etc., in a small path, it being very muddy and in some places swampy for many miles. We overtook the old man, and then my company. They went very fast, sometimes on the run. We startled many turkeys in our way, one of which Fowler killed with his staff, having left the other gun and the ax where we stayed, but we took a hatchet. Jacob Dick took a turn on horseback. I went on foot awhile to rest him. We continued traveling rapidly until we came to the village, about 5 P.M. The village is on a prairie containing thirty or forty houses in different places [must have been Thorntown]. I had a letter of introduction from Lt. Lafond to the French trader at the village. He invited us to his cabin to lodge. The man who rode with me shot a young deer as we rode along. We had some of it cooked for our supper. There were many Indians who came to see us where we put up, and we engaged two horses to go to White River, one for me and one for Jacob. We came about thirty-five or forty miles this day.

August 5th. We took breakfast early this morning. Thomas, Paul, and R. Fowler started on foot and left Jacob and me to come with the horses and bring the packs. We had to give $1.50 for each horse. We started about 9 A.M., in company with four or five Indians, men and women, and passed the woods as fast as we could. The path was bad, over a swamp or muddy ground. We traveled all day as hard as we could, but did not overtake the rest of our company. We startled many turkeys. We camped on the ground at night, made a fire near the other and lay by it, and there came up a man and woman, who camped a little way off. They brought us about a pint of sweetened hoecake, which was very good, have nothing to eat since morning. We ate that, drank water and laid down for sleep. At dark a young Indian came up to our camp, who was going to take my horse back. He had killed a young raccoon as big as a cat. They burned the hair off of it, then boiled it without salt and gave us some, which we were glad to eat. We then tried to get some sleep under the trees, so that we had not much dew on us, but many fleas.

August 6th. They brought us a little piece of raccoon and some other food which we thought was made of roots, which answered as bread, but I was not fond of it. We went on rapidly until we got through. Traveling along, the Indian who killed the raccoon walked before me and shot a turkey that would weigh fifteen or twenty pounds. We left the settlement about 10 A.M., gave up our horses, and understood that my other three companions had crossed White River. We therefore took the packs, rode through the river and went to the house of William Conner, a French trader, whom I found had gone to Phila-delphia. His partner, William Marshall, had gone to Muncie, a town twenty-five miles up the river. The women could not speak English, but we found they had gone down the river. We went down across the prairie about a mile, crossed the river and went about four miles to a settlement of the Delaware Indians, carried our packs, and then met them at the lower village. They gave us some bread and milk to eat. We invited them to go to Fort Harrison to the council, but they did not agree to go. We returned, crossed the river, and went to Conner's to get a horse to the upper town, but got none. Joe, Paul, and Rudolphus started on foot about half past 5 P.M.; the rest concluded to stay, and soon after William Marshall came home. He said we could not get any of the Delawares to go to Fort Harrison, they were all going to Fort Meigs to a treaty there the 15th of September, so we concluded to go up in the morning. Marshall would furnish me with a horse to ride.

It is about forty or forty-five miles from the Weas to the White River, making about 40 miles from Fort Harrison to White River, and five down and five up makes ten miles.

August 7th. We took breakfast, hired a horse, and proceeded on up to the other town. We reached the settlement about 10 o'clock P.M., obtained some bread and buttermilk, then went on toward the principal Indian village and met Paul Dick with horse going for us. He said the council must be held at the village where Anderson lived. We went up and met several at his house, was appointed a council on the morrow. We were furnished with supper, which consisted of bread and herb tea made sweet, with which we refreshed ourselves. There was a heavy shower of rain, with hail and thunder, and a violent tempest, so that it was near blowing some of the cabins down. We put up at the house of the principal chief. It was as good as any in the village, and he a plain, majestic looking man, sixty or sixty-five years old. Paul and F. Fowler were directed to another house to lodge, and the rest of us lodged at the chief's. I had the most comfortable place. It was some boards or staves put on benches, and bullrushes laid on them, and a small pillow, through it was wet in the shower.

August 8th. We got together in the morning and were served with some boiled corn and venison for breakfast. After breakfast the people began to come in, and we were soon served with another dish of squashes, made sweet with sugar, and some bread, which we partook of. After the chiefs and councilmen and principal men of the nation came in they informed us that they were ready to hear what we had to say. . . .

There were twenty or thirty Indians who attended the council, which lasted about four hours. We went to look for the horse that I rode, but did not see it. We mentioned that we wanted some provisions to take on our journey, and we were informed that they would be brought in the morning, so we put up for the night, myself, T. Isaac, and T. Dick at the chief's, P. Dick and R. Fowler at another house.

August 9th. Our provisions soon came in. They were hoecake and Indian bread. We received two or three pairs of moccasons. Thomas Isaac found the horse and after breakfast we took our leave. . . .

We have already met

SANDFORD C. COX

in the piece beginning on page 61. He was a youth, crippled from birth, who in his maturity became a teacher and wrote charming extracts from his memories for local newspapers. In October 1824, he set out by wagon with his parents and two brothers from Wayne County to the new town of Crawfordsville. They saw sights on the way which were still vivid to his memory thirty-six years later.

Recollections of the Early Settlement of the Wabash Valley

In furnishing some extracts from the Journal of the Black Creek School Master, in relation to the early settlement of the Wabash Valley, I will first give a few entries made by the young journalist while on the road moving to this country. The first memorandum of any particular interest reads thus:

Falls of Fall Creek,
Madison Co., Ind., October 24, 1824.

Mr. Corey, the sheriff, took us in to see the Indian murderers— Bridge, Sawyer, Hudson, and John Bridge. Hudson is now under sentence of death. He sits apart from the rest, reading a small Bible. Old man Bridge, his son John, and Sawyer, are reclining on the jail floor, dressed in brown pantaloons and blue linsey hunting shirts. Hudson has on a black woolen wamus, fastened with a leathern belt. He is quite penitent, talks but little, and appears to be about forty years old—heavy set, and inclines to be corpulent. Old man Bridge and Sawyer talked freely with father and others on the subject of their confinement. They each appear to be over fifty years of age, and are thin and cadaverous.

John Bridge is an over-grown boy of about twenty, who says his father and uncle Sawyer were the cause of his guilt. Last night they attempted to choke him to death in prison for disclosing their guilt—so say the guards, who relieved him from their murderous hands.

These prisoners, with one Harper (who escaped arrest), in cold blood, murdered nine friendly Indians, most of whom were women and children, while their husbands and fathers were absent on a hunting excursion—cruelly shooting and stabbing the women, and knocking out the brains of the children against trees; concealed their dead and mangled bodies in a sink-hole hard by, then plundered their camp of furs, deer skins, and other valuables, which were afterwards found concealed under the floor of Sawyer's cabin. One of the Indian women, after remaining in the water in the clay-hole amongst the dead bodies of her slaughtered relatives for two days and nights, was taken out alive. She said Bridge and his son, Sawyer, Harper, and Hudson were the murderers—lived a few hours, and died.

It is thought here that Harper incited the others to participate in the bloody tragedy. Moses Cox, clerk of the court, shot at Harper with a rifle as he escaped precipitately down a hill.

The jail is enclosed with pickets—logs placed on end in the ground, about sixteen feet high, forming an area around the prison of about eight rods square, in which is a guard house, wherein four sentinels are stationed, who keep watch day and night over the prisoners. The sad condition of these wretched prisoners is another melancholy proof of the truth of the scripture declaration—"the way of the transgressor is hard."

A little brother of mine, who arrived too late to gain admittance with the rest of us, mounted one of the pickets, climbed over the top, and descended to the ground on the inside. A sentinel who witnessed the dexterous feat, raised his gun and yelled, "out with you,"—the little chap, alarmed at either the whiskers or firearms of the "soger," instantly "obeyed orders," and as nimbly as a squirrel, mounted to the top of the picket, grinned defiance at the sentinel, and descended outside.

To-morrow we start for Crawfordsville, on Sugar river, some sixty miles distant. We expect to cross White river near Strawtown, then take the wilderness road by Thorntown, Wisehart's, and thence down Sugar river to the Crawfordsville settlement.

All the above named prisoners, except John Bridge, were executed on the scaffold at the Falls; he was reprieved by Governor Ray, under the gallows, after witnessing the execution of his father, and uncle Sawyer. He survived his double tragedy but a short time, and died in about a year afterward of a broken heart.

We may excuse Mr. Cox if he took poetic license with the "broken heart."

According to other accounts, this was not quite all of the features of this event. The governor carried out some histrionics of which even an elected official should have been ashamed. Riding his horse up before the lad who awaited the noose, he is reported to have said something like this:

> Only two persons can save you now, young man. One is God Almighty and the other is the Governor of Indiana! The latter person stands before you. I am Governor Ray of this state. You are pardoned. Go forth and sin no more!

Young Sandford failed to report this; perhaps in his youth and innocence he believed that governors were supposed habitually to talk like this, and did not realize that he had witnessed an 1824 miracle.

The Cox family journey continued and their mishaps and adventures were probably not uncommon for the day and place. Traveling by wagon on the Thorntown Trace in 1824 seems to have been little less strenuous than travel on the Raccoon Creek Trace and had been seven years before. Two boys and a herd of sheep lost in sixteen or eighteen hours probably established no record for the course.

On the morning of the 25th of October, 1824, we made an early start from the Falls, and in the evening arrived at Abbott's Ford, on White river, where we encamped for the night. Next morning, the 26th, we crossed the river and took the old Strawtown road, or rather Indian trace, which emigrants had widened into a rough wagon road.

Soon after crossing the river we passed Beckworth's place. Mr. Ogle, who drove the team, told us to take a good look at the cabin, as it was the last house we would see for forty miles on our journey. This was an unwelcome announcement to the younger members of our family; but father and mother, who were inured to frontier life—having been the first white family that ever settled in Wayne county, now the most populous and wealthy county in Indiana—seemed to care but little for the hardships and privations of the wilderness.

Our ox team moved slowly along the narrow road, which wended through a vast, primeval forest, clothed in the rich drapery of Autumn. A more gorgeous and beautiful landscape I never beheld, sleeping in the golden haze of Indian Summer. But alas! how true the couplet of the song, which reads:

> We should suspect some danger nigh,
> When we possess delight,

for while I was wrapt in admiration of the beautiful scenery that surrounded me, I neglected to watch for a minute or two our flock of sheep, which brother John had placed under my especial charge, while he attempted to kill a buck. The result was, the sheep, sixteen in number, were lost. Without letting the rest know of the matter, John and myself scoured the woods on both sides of the road in search of them. In my eagerness to succeed, I wandered too far from the road and became lost! Oh, horrible! The idea of being lost in that deep wilderness, full of Indians and wild beasts, was appalling beyond description. I could hear my heart beat distinctly, and felt a dimness come over my eyes, shutting out every glimpse of the autumnal glories of the woods, which not two hours before had so enchanted me. I ran, and hallooed at the top of my voice till I was hoarse, without any response. None but those who have been lost themselves can form a correct idea of the deep, dreadful import of the word "Lost"—even in this world.

In a few hours I was found and brought back to the road, which looked more lovely to me than a bar of gold of the same width and length, though it might extend from Strawtown to the mouth of the Columbia river.

We made no further search for the sheep, but left them to the mercy of the wolves, and pursued our journey.

In the evening it grew cloudy and threatened rain. We struck camp about twilight near the road side. About eight o'clock the rain descended in torrents, accompanied by a heavy wind which roared dismally among the tree-tops, rousing us from our slumbers by its wild, deep moanings.

The weather became clear during the night, and on the morning of the 27th a white frost lay on the logs and newly fallen leaves. This morning we aimed to make an early start, but another unfortunate and unlooked for event threw our whole company into the deepest consternation. Jesse (my little brother who climbed the pickets at the Falls) followed Mr. Ogle and brother John into the woods, when they went to bring in the oxen and other cattle. Upon their discovering him following them, they told him to go back to camp, for which he immediately started, but took a wrong direction. He was not missed until we were ready to start. Imagine the panic produced when it was known he was lost! Another energetic search was immediately instituted for the lost child. The woods for miles around echoed with "Jesse! Jesse!" from more than half a dozen voices. He heard us, but supposed we were Indians, and hid in the underbrush until we got close to him, when he emerged, mounted on a log, and said: "It is quite a frosty morning"—declared he had not been lost; that he saw the smoke of the camp all the time, and heard us calling, but took us to be Indians, and was determined to make no noise nor let himself be seen until he was certain we were not Pottawatomies. . . .

After bringing the lost boy into camp, we soon started on our journey. About noon we reached Cicero creek, and encamped for dinner at an unextinguished camp fire where some persons had stayed the previous night. They had killed a deer, dressed and cooked what they needed of it, and with a commendable regard for the comfort of their fellow-travelers through the wilderness, they had salted and baked one side of the ribs of the deer previous to leaving, and turned the other side to the fire to be properly cooked for the next emigrants who might chance to pass that way. We were the lucky travelers who found it, done brown; and manna and quails to the children of Israel during their pilgrimage through the wilderness, were not more unexpected nor acceptable, than were these cooked venison ribs to us.

After crossing the creek, we passed a fine looking horse lying dead near the roadside. Doubtless some poor traveler had to pack his saddle on his back for miles, or hand it over to be "toted" by some more lucky comrade; or, it may be, some family of movers here lost one of their best team horses, and were compelled to pursue their journey with a weakened and less efficient team.

We drove hard to reach a stream called "Brown's Wonder" that night, which was the only place we could obtain water before we reached Clayroot spring, near Thorntown. The weather was clear and warm, and the magnificent forest, clad in its variegated robe of Autumn, was beautiful and picturesque beyond description. By the middle of the afternoon several of us began to suffer with thirst, occasioned either by partaking freely of the baked venison, or the warm weather. Search was instituted for water on both sides of the road, but none could be found except the black puddles in the horse tracks and wagon ruts. My thirst became so intense that I could not refrain from stooping down and drinking out of a horse track in the road, shutting my eyes lest I might see wigglers in the water.

Failing to reach "Brown's Wonder," we camped a few miles east of it—suffering much through the night for want of water. Early on the morning of the 28th we reached that stream, and refreshed ourselves and team with its sparkling waters. Here we met four old acquaintances from White Water, on their return from exploring the Wabash country, with which they were higly pleased. They spoke in most enthusiastic terms of the Wea, Wild Cat, and Shawnee prairies, and declared that "the Wea plain was the prettiest place this side of Heaven,"—a fact which has never been disputed by any one who ever saw it.

Among these men was Wright I.——, who once basely maltreated me at school. A sight of my ancient enemy fanned afresh the smouldering embers of my wrath, and I felt like drawing him from his saddle and administering such a castigation as his former abuse of me merited; but the fact that Wright had reformed, joined church and preached sometimes, and perhaps might be a better man than he was a boy, so allayed my anger that I let him pass without any hostile demonstration on my part—although I confess I felt that I weighed something less than a ton, when I recollected that he once spit tobacco juice in my eye.

In the evening we arrived at Clayroot spring, and encamped, as well pleased as were the Israelites when Moses smote that rock at Horeb, and they had water in abundance.

The rising sun on the morning of the 29th, found us pursuing our journey. About eight o'clock A.M. we arrived at Thorntown, once a large Indian and French village, which sent its hundreds of warriors to the battle-field. It is now deserted; or, rather, its inhabitants are all absent on a hunting expedition. Wigwams composed of poles and bark cover many acres of this beautiful and salubrious plain, on which Thorntown is situated.

We soon struck Sugar river, and followed the road on its southern bank to a Mr. Wisehart's—the first house we had seen since we left Beckworth's on White river, full forty miles back. About four o'clock P.M. it turned cold and cloudy, and by the time we arrived at Kinworthy and Lee's neighborhood, it began to snow briskly.

About dark we concluded our journey by arriving in the midst of a snow storm at John Dewey's, about a mile and a half east of Crawfordsville....

For more detailed information on the life of the settler, once he had found a satisfactory tract to buy, if he had money—or to squat on if he had not—there is no more reliable nor spritely source than

LOGAN ESAREY

—for many years a beloved professor of American history at Indiana University. Dr. Esarey was reared on an Indiana farm where living conditions closely approximated those of the pioneer days. His yarns of the simple life, which delighted generations of his students, were published after his death in a book entitled

The Indiana Home

THE SETTLER BECOMES A CITIZEN

THE FIRST PUBLIC AFFAIR that interested the settler was the militia. Although the poor Indians had learned at last that it was bad business to harm a settler they still roamed over this country, hunting.

They were sullen and the settlers feared them. Every man had to join the militia and about the first stranger who appeared at the new settler's door was the captain who had come to enroll him in the militia. This was the first law he became acquainted with. It required him to have a gun, a shot-pouch with a half-pound or so of powder, thirty to fifty bullets, a good ramrod and cleaning stick with a bunch of tow, bullet moulds and a hunting knife or hatchet. This last was usually called a "tommy hawk." The captain took the settlers name and age and told him when and where to meet the other "boys" for training. This meeting was always called the "muster" or "training day."

The militia usually met twice a year, spring and fall. In the spring there was the company meeting—from forty to one hundred men under a captain. In the fall all the men in the county met as a regiment under a colonel. In the early days there were always a few men in the neighborhood who had done some service in the Indian wars, maybe in the Revolution or War of 1812. The men elected their own officers and generally chose such a man. The adjutant had a list of all the men and as he called their names they took their places in line. The captain then "inspected" the men to see that each had what the law required. In the afternoon they might practice marching through the woods, either in so-called Indian file, or the whole company abreast and dodging from tree to tree. There was some target firing to see that each man's rifle was in good condition and that he knew how to use it. The men couldn't afford much of this practice, for powder and lead were scarce. The most valuable feature of these meetings was the renewing of acquaintance.

These men were not strangers to the frontier or frontier ways. As one told about the Tippecanoe campaign, another told of the Pigeon Roost massacre; some had been with Harrison in Ohio, some with Jackson in Alabama, and those who had never seen an Indian had "hear'n tell." As they ate their lunches and passed the bottle, the stories grew more marvelous, the Indians larger and more ferocious, and as Indians grew in size and number the more of them they killed. The poor Indian hadn't a chance and was slaughtered shamelessly. The new settlers, "strangers," were properly sized up as the "soldiers" gathered in little groups for the neighborhood gossip. If the womenfolks came, and they usually did, they traded out all their information along with their garden seeds and remedies for all kinds of ailments. . . .

The fall meeting was called the county muster or training day. It was no new thing. These folks had had it in England and had kept it up in the colonies and the states. It was held at the county seat and often lasted two days. If the October weather was nice the settler came in his wagon, maybe bringing something to trade at the store. . . . This might be the only time during the year when friends from distant parts of the county would see each other and renew old acquaintances or make new ones. The work depended entirely upon the officer. If the officers were good ones, the men "fell in" at ten in the morning and actually trained until noon. Then they had two hours for dinner.

There was generally one company of mounted men in each county. All young men with good horses were eager to get into this outfit, for it was considered the best. They were called dragoons. If there should be a call to fight Indians these men would go first. They were supposed to be able to fire and reload their rifles from horseback.

Each captain tried to have his company make as good an appearance as possible for it was quite an honor to be elected a colonel. There were no uniforms, though occasionally the members of a company would have caps, belts or jackets alike. . . .

The first settlers had never used roads for hauling. What little produce they had for sale was carried to market on pack horses, driven on foot, or taken by boat. So when they settled in Indiana they usually built their houses off the trails. They soon learned they could not market corn or hogs on pack horses and that they had to open roads. Perhaps one settler in five came in a wagon. The United States Government gave the state three dollars out of every one hundred taken in at the land office but this was not enough to build many roads. If a number of settlers wanted a road they prepared a petition and gave it to the commissioners. These officers then sent three "viewers" to see whether a road was needed and, if so, they marked it off among the trees. The commissioners then ordered the supervisor of that road district to call out the "hands" and open the road. Not a dollar of money was spent on these "county" roads. The commissioners divided the county into road districts and over each district appointed a supervisor. Each man had to work on the roads at least six days each year.

So, sometime in summer or fall after the corn was "laid by," the supervisor would call at the cabin in the clearing and "warn" the man where and when to come to help make or mend a road. On the day named the settler took his axe, or his mattock, and started to perform his public duty. He received no pay, only a mark on the supervisor's little book to show that he had worked one day. Twelve hours, or "from sun to sun" was a day's work. Here, perhaps for the second time, he met all of his neighbors. After a week's work with them he began to feel as if he were acquainted.

First they cut all of the underbrush from the roadway. If a large tree, rock or other bad place was in the way, they just cut the road around it. The road did not have to be straight and it probably ran largely on government land. Along most of the way after the road was finished, the limbs of the larger trees overarched it completely. Sometimes, at the crossing of creeks, a bank would be dug down, just a little. If there was a wet place, a swamp or "drene"—a branch or small stream—the workers would cut poles, five or six inches in diameter and ten or twelve feet long, and lay them side by side to keep the wagon wheels or horses' feet from going down into the mud. . . . If the stream was too deep to ford, a quiet deep pool and a ferry was best. When the "cricks" were up wise people just didn't cross. Those who knew the stream swam their horses across and occasionally someone was drowned. . . . Roads built thusly were poor roads but the settler had enjoyed a week's visit with his neighbors and another tie had been woven around the little neighborhood community.

One afternoon a strange, barefoot, tow-headed boy of twelve walked slowly up the path to a cabin. After making friends with Towser he said his "mother reckoned as how you all might want to hear the preacher. He left a printment at Brother Blank's house over on the Paoli road just across Big Pizen (Creek) for a meetin' at early candlelight comin' next Wednesday. Mother hopes you all 'll come."

It was only three miles by the path through the woods, and on the appointed evening our pioneer folks left home about three o'clock and by dusk were at the meeting place. If it was nice warm weather the children all came—even the babies. . . . By six o'clock there would be twenty grown persons present and meeting would begin. First, they would warm up with a psalm or hymn. The preacher would line it, that is, read the first line—"On Jordan's stormy banks I stand"—then they would sing that line. Then the preacher would read: "And cast a wistful eye"—and the folks would sing that line and so on—never omitting a stanza, if it took all night. . . .

Next came the prayer. Like all things pioneer, no one could tell what it would be like. If it were some old Peter Cartwright he might roar like Goliath as he called down the wrath of a just God on guilty sinners or it might be as sweet and sad as the Sermon on the Mount as he pleaded for mercy for his children in the lonesome wilderness. Then, after another hymn, came the sermon, one or two hours long. The preacher usually stood in front of the fireplace with his Bible on a chair, if one could be found. The audience sat or stood in the little room, in the doorway, stuck their heads in the windows, or sat on the ground outside. All could hear, 'for as the preacher "warmed up," his voice rose until he could be heard a quarter of a mile. After the sermon they sang a doxology and if five or six church members were present, they organized a class and arranged for regular preaching. After a session of visiting the mother hunted up her baby and the father picked out one or two of the smaller children, took them under his arms or set them on his shoulders, and set out on the dark path for home. Many a youngster of ten who had been eager to come was not so eager on the return trip.

As the neighborhood grew, the men got together and built a log meeting-house—a chapel—down at the crossroads, by the creek, so they could have water handy for baptizing. Here the little group met for preaching, when they could find a preacher; here those that belonged to the same church (denomination) met as a "class" and talked over church affairs, perhaps sang, if someone could "lead"; here later was the Sunday school and here later were the blacksmith shop and country store.

After the work was over, the little group of church members might decide to hold a camp meeting. It would bring folks from miles away and two, three or maybe four "big" preachers. Some Saturday in September the men gathered at the appointed place with axes and cleared off two or three acres for the campground; logs, ten feet long and one foot in diameter, were cut and laid on cross logs the same size for seats. Someone with a foot-adz dressed the bark and knots off the tops of the logs to make the seats as comfortable as possible. In front of the log auditorium they built a stand six or eight feet high, and perhaps ten feet square, for a speaker's platform. On the sides and at the back large heaps of dry logs and brush were piled to furnish light for the night meetings. A large space had to be cleared off for wagons and for cooking. There might be fifty or one hundred wagons. There was plenty of work, but the pioneers were not afraid of work. Everybody was supposed to bring his own food but not all of them did. Some came only to spend a day and stayed a week. . . .

Preaching usually began at ten in the morning. By that time those who lived near, four or five miles, could be there, and those who camped could cook their breakfasts, water and feed their horses and "brush up." If there were three preachers, one spoke forenoon, one afternoon, and one at night. The sermons were long and powerful. After each sermon, exhorters or local preachers went up and down the walks urging the people to "jine" the church, while everybody sang or shouted. It usually took a day or two to get the meeting under full headway, but when it did, it excelled any circus in interest. Sometimes a great preacher—and some of the very best were heard in Southern Indiana—held the large crowd spellbound and silent for two hours—until scores dropped to the ground from exhaustion. Sometimes a half-dozen "exhorters" would be shouting at the same time, like "barkers" at a street fair. Sometimes a dozen would be praying at the same time, some of them merely mumbling through sobs and tears, others yelling like hussars leading a cavalry charge. . . .

Others would try to "shin it" up the trees to get as near to heaven as possible. Sometimes, completely worn out, many would fall to the ground either sound asleep or in a trance and have to be carried away to keep them from being trampled on. Sometimes the preacher would have to stop in his sermon, get down from his scaffold pulpit, join with other men and chase some drunken rowdies away. The rowdies didn't always run, and fists and clubs were used. The bootleggers, then as now, always hung around with their jugs and cups and many a scoffer who came for fun and was made bold by too many drinks, found himself tied hand and foot to a tree to listen to the sermon. Long into the night the singing, exhorting, praying and shouting continued until all were tired out. Then the fires burned low, the folks went home or to sleep in their wagons or under the big trees, the katydids and whippoorwills took up the singing, and the stars twinkled as usual. Ten or twelve men, selected for that purpose, kept guard over the camp. It was a great place for horse thieves to ply their trade. Nor must we forget that the young folks had a good time, the younger ones playing and the older ones caring for them and sparking as best they could. Men in small groups sat at a distance and talked politics or farming; candidates then as now were always on hand, especially attentive to the new settlers. Altogether it was the greatest social event of the year. . . .

At the camp meeting one of the pioneer mothers had met an elderly neighbor who lived two or three miles away and who had spoken of a newspaper. One morning some days later, after her husband had gone to work, she called her ten-year-old son. "Do you mind the house way down the road at the foot of the big hill? Well, Miss Brown lives there. She was tellin' me they all git a newspaper from Vincennes. Comes down to the county seat and they go down every week or two and git 'em. You heered pa say how a man at the land office wanted him to take it but he didn't have any money left. Ken you run down and ask Miss Brown fer the loan of it fer a day or two. I'll do your work this mornin'."

"I know where it is; Pa and I was past there t'other day squirrel huntin'."

"Now tell her yore name when you git down there, and where you live."

Some time later the boy arrived at the Brown cabin.

"Miss Brown, my ma wondered if you mightn't let her read your paper. She ain't had nothin' to read since we moved out here."

"Law, does yore ma read! I spec she gits right lonesome way up thar in the woods."

"Yep, course she works all day, but I hear her and pa talkin' after us children has gone to bed and they wonder about things I don't know about."

"Well, well, come to think about it, I mind now I lent them papers to Squire Smith, last Sunday two weeks past. Law, I thought he'd already brung 'em back. You know where he lives? Out on the Polk Patch road 'bout a mile; second house to the right. You kin just run by there and tell him I sed to let you have 'em. That's a little man."

"Ma said for me to say thank 'e."

"You tell yer ma to h'ist herself down this way sometime. I declare, here it is six month and she ain't never been to see me. You say yer ma reads? Hain't you been to school yit?"

The question was too much for the boy. He had heard of schools but couldn't make out just what one was.

"They tell me Mis' Simpson is thinkin' of takin' in some scholars this fall. I hear'n she reads right peart. Some say she used to read out loud at a literary or something like that back where they come from. Her man, you know, preaches."

But the boy was hopelessly at sea and could only stammer a few "uh-huh's."

From the squire the boy got not one but four copies of the *Western Sun* and hurried home, proud of his adventures, for the squire was not too busy to ask all manner of questions about the new family.

That evening after supper, and after a small blaze had been kindled in the fireplace, the father stretched out lazily, half on the floor and half up against the log wall. The mother sat on a low stool, sidewise to the blaze, and the children nestled around, getting closer and closer as the mother read slowly, almost painfully picking out the words. It made no difference that the papers were two or three months old, and the advertisements were as interesting as the news about Bonaparte. . . . The men did not show as much interest in a school as they had in a church but finally ten or twelve children were subscribed and the wife of a local preacher agreed to teach them. There was no money to be had but the teacher was paid in corn, meat and other produce. They added a mud and stick chimney to the log "chapel" and used it for a schoolhouse. School began about the first of September and lasted until the middle of October. After that the weather was too bad for the children to go so far through the woods. . . . By the end of the six weeks a ten-year-old boy was slowly but very delightfully spelling out and reading with many strange pronunciations the simple stories of the Bible—his only reader. In the meantime, boys and girls had perfected their counting, had learned the addition and subtraction tables, but were hopelessly stalled by "carryin'" in addition and "borrerin'" in subtraction. Next year they would have a book—maybe a speller or maybe a reader—and learn to write. In three six-weeks terms they would read, write and cipher and be ready to meet the big world on even terms.

Our typical pioneer had probably had but little practice in local government and politics until he moved to Indiana. A squire and a constable were all the officers he knew outside of the militia. So when in the late summer he rode down to the county seat he heard much strange talk and saw some strange sights. The county seat town had a log courthouse with two rooms. Around it was a yard about three hundred feet square cleared of underbrush. Over on the corner of the large lot was a heavy log pen some twelve by twenty feet with only a heavy puncheon door. This, he was told, was a jail. . . .

Across the road from the courthouse was the store, a little one-room log house. A bag of green coffee, a bushel or so of salt, some plug tobacco, a can of gunpowder, some bars of lead, a can of tea, two or three hoes without handles and about the same number of axe-handles with axes composed his stock. In a box were five or six letters and three or four newspapers—the United States post office. . . .

While the newcomer was chatting with the postmaster an elderly man came in and introduced himself as the treasurer of the new county. He asked our settler if he had been listed.

"I dunno what you mean," replied the latter, "but I reckon not, leastwise not as I know on."

After asking where he lived and where he came from, how long he had been there and how he was comin' on, the treasurer said he would send the "lister" around to see him.

"You'll be clearin' a passel of new ground come fall and winter most likely?" inquired the treasurer.

"I calkilate on't," returned the settler.

"Be needin' any help?"

"Not as I knows on."

"You know this man Glack, squatted over toward Big Injuns, had the shakes all spring and summer and wuz turned 'vagrant' on us. We're havin' an auction over at my place on t'other side the square this evenin'. Thought as how you might want to bid on 'im."

"Could shore use him and got plenty of grub, but I reckon I couldn't find anywhere he could sleep."

The treasurer was also serving as overseer of the poor and that afternoon our settler saw the unfortunate man sold to a man who agreed to give him food, shelter and clothes and pay him a small amount if he got able to work. The contract was to last for a year. At the same time two little children who had been left homeless were "sold out" to the lowest bidder to take care of for the "time bein'" until homes could be found or until someone would "take 'em to raise."

When the sun was about an hour high the loud talking at the courthouse ceased, the folks separated into little groups, everybody talking to everybody else. Finally our settler, as folks began to leave, got on his horse and rode slowly away to his cabin home.

He had not long to wait. One afternoon the following week the lister, a rather active middle-aged man, rode up and "halloed" the house. The settler invited him to "light and hitch your nag."

"Nope, no use, just want to talk a spell," said the stranger as he dismounted and passed his arm through the bridle reins. "I hearn you be a newcomer and I kim by to list ye. Yer name? How old might ye be? Uh huh. How much land did ye enter? Uh huh. Paid fer? No tax on yer land till four years after it's paid fer. Any hoss beast? Uh huh; one critter. No other beasts? No. Come next spring yer tax'll be, poll fifty cents, critter tax ten cents. Pay ter the treasurer next May."

So our settler was enrolled as a taxpayer.

For an hour or so the men talked of neighborhood affairs, of old times, those who had been there the previous year or longer, of newcomers, those who had moved in that season, of sickness, of the weather, of growing crops and finally of politics.

"I reckon as how you all ha' hearn about the big 'lection this fall?"

"Naw, not much. I been so busy cuttin' sprouts and workin' the corn I just ain't give no heed. I mind now as I did hearn some talk down at the meetin'."

"Ye been hearin' about Andy Jackson?"

"No."

"Mr. Potts ut lives down on Musky was over at Salem to the big convention. He said Jackson was the man fer president. When the Indians was cuttin' all kinds o' capers down in the South Old Andy gethered up a posse of men from Tennessee and marched down into Alabam'e and jist naturally cleaned them varmints out. Guess he must o' killed thousands of 'em. They say the woods air full of 'em up state. We got to get rid of 'em and Old Andy'll do it."

"I dunno," returned our settler, "they ain't never harmed me. Course I don't like 'em any better'n you do. They was a passel of 'em by here yisterday; ragged, dirty, hungry looking. I give 'em a hand full o' salt and the woman cooked 'em a pone o' bread. Seemed to do 'em a power o' good."

"That's the way o' them varmints, I tell you," broke in the lister. "Can't put no 'pendence on 'em. They come draggin' their lips around yer in daytime ter see what ye got and then come back at night un git it. . . . Jo Potts said he hearn, too, down to the convention at Salem, if Jackson was elected he'd turn all the rich men out of office and give 'em to the pore men like you and me and most likely we'd have free land fer the settlers; specially fer the squatters. That ud help the western country powerfully. Jackson's shore a friend to the pore man. Ken I put ye down fer Jackson?"

"I dunno," drawled the settler. "I've dun contracted fer my land and I shore ain't hankerin' fer any office. It does seem bad to drive these pore Injuns out uv the only home they got. There's right plenty o' huntin' yit in these woods. But I cain't say as the women folks wants 'em strollin' around, though. I guess I'll go fer Jackson."

Late in October when the trees had put on a riot of red and yellow our settler and his family started at daybreak and went over to the county seat to a rally of Jackson men. . . .

This was just a beginning in politics. That fall the county commissioners divided the county into townships and in the spring trustees, secretaries, treasurers, fence-viewers, stray-keepers, poor overseers, road supervisors and school trustees were to be elected. In the summer or early fall county and state officers had to be elected. It seemed everybody and everybody's friends were candidates. But here we must leave our settler. With the opening of spring he became an oldtimer. He was now really a citizen of Indiana.

Messrs. Dean, Cox, and Esarey have described the arrival and settlement of people who became, once in the big woods, "Hoosiers," although they did not know how or why. (And no more, pardon the thought, do all the learned gentlemen who have since written upon the origin of that term!)

Hoosiers they were called, and Hoosiers they soon admitted themselves to be. The name sounded harsh at first but, after a reasonable number of Hoosier boys had knocked out a sufficient quantity of Buckeye and Kaintuck and Old Dominion and York State teeth which had let the term slip by them with an uncomplimentary cast to the tone of it, "Hoosier" gained some favor even among the refined citizens of the state. After 1830, when John Finley, the editor-poet over at Richmond, wrote his appreciation of a good solid, hospitable, Hoosier family, and it was reprinted in newspapers all over the country, the die was cast: people who lived in Indiana were Hoosiers and proud of it!

JOHN FINLEY

The Hoosier's Nest

I'm told, in riding somewhere West,
A stranger found a Hoosier's nest—
In other words, a Buckeye cabin,
Just big enough to hold Queen Mab in;
Its situation, low, but airy,
Was on the borders of a prairie;
And fearing he might be benighted,
He hailed the house, and then alighted.

The Hoosier met him at the door—
Their salutations soon were o'er.
He took the stranger's horse aside,
And to a sturdy sapling tied;
Then, having stripped the saddle off,
He fed him in a sugar-trough.

The stranger stooped to enter in—
The entrance closing with a pin—
And manifested strong desire
To seat him by the log-heap fire,
Where half a dozen Hoosieroons,
With mush-and-milk, tin cups, and spoons,
White heads, bare feet, and dirty faces,
Seemed much inclined to keep their places.
But Madam, anxious to display
Her rough but undisputed sway,
Her offspring to the ladder led,
And cuffed the youngsters up to bed.

Invited shortly to partake
Of venison, milk, and johnny-cake,
The stranger made a hearty meal,
And glances round the room would steal.

One side was lined with divers garments,
The other spread with skins of "varmints";
Dried pumpkins overhead were strung,
Where venison hams in plenty hung;
Two rifles placed above the door;
Three dogs lay stretched upon the floor—
In short, the domicile was rife
With specimens of Hoosier life.

The host, who center'd his affections
On game, and range, and quarter sections,
Discoursed his weary guest for hours,
Till Somnus' all-composing powers
Of sublunary cares bereft 'em;
And then—

No matter how the story ended;
The application I intended
Is from the famous Scottish poet,
Who seemed to feel as well as know it,
That "buirdly chiels and clever hizzies
Are bred in sic' a way as this is."

As early as the eighteen-forties the eyes of Indianians turned to the Far West; some turned their steps as well as their eyes, and of these a few—being Indianians—were impelled to return and write books about the marvels of the new country.

Some of the best known early accounts of lands beyond the Rocky Mountains came from the pens of Hoosiers William H. Winter and Overton Johnson, of Joel Palmer and Joseph Williams: Cincinnatus Hiner Miller (who called himself "Joaquin") was also Indiana born. In the 'seventies Ezra Meeker and John Hanson Beadle wrote voluminously of the West; recently Oscar Winther has contributed fine historical writing about the Northwest.

These gentlemen wrote only of the West, however, and their famous works are thus not eligible for inclusion as we survey writing on Indiana. Not until 1947 did an Indiana writer come along who managed, also, to include a glimpse of Hoosierdom as he viewed the trans-Mississippi scene. Any Hoosier or Westerner would readily con-

cede that such a combination of locale was likely to result in a phenomenal success. It did.

A. B. GUTHRIE, JR.

Indiana born, Western reared and Kentucky resident, produced first
and second novels which gathered in almost all the honors for which
twentieth century books are eligible—book club selections, critics'
choice; for the second a Pulitzer Prize in literature, and for both
fabulous sales of moving picture rights of the kind that came into
being, incidentally, with the price paid for Hoosier Lew Wallace's
old Ben Hur.

It is Guthrie's first book from which we quote, as his hero under-
goes a rather harrowing experience with the backwoods justice which
our forefathers probably did administer upon occasion under the
early judicial system. We look at The Big Sky.

As this selection opens in 1830, young Boone Caudill, seventeen
and by no means yet his own man in the eyes of nineteenth century
Kentucky law, is passing across Indiana on the old trail from Louisville to St. Louis.

He has already knocked out his bullying father (killed the old man,
he thinks), stolen a boat to paddle across the Ohio at the Falls, over-
set it in the flooded river and reached the Indiana shore half dead
but still clutching his father's fine Kentucky rifle, with which he had
endowed himself before he ran away from home. He has spent several
nights on the road, has extended the hospitality of his campfire to a
New Orleans sharper named Bedwell, has awakened next morning to
find both Bedwell and his rifle gone, has set out in pursuit and is about
to catch up with that smooth city-slicker.

The Big Sky

He LISTENED as he went on, and watched the back trail, ready to
slip into the woods and hide, and before he had gone a mile he
caught a glimpse of movement behind him. A horseshoe rang against

rock. The woods were thin here, but off to the left a thick stump squatted. He ran to it and threw himself down behind it, watching through a fringe of grass, hearing a long outward snuffle of the horse before he could see it. From behind a cluster of trees rode a dove great-coat and a white beaver hat, and under it a sharp, lined face. Boone saw Old Sure Shot, tied to the saddle. He lay there until the horse and man had passed him and lost themselves in the woods ahead, reminding himself as they went by that a man couldn't outrun a horse or go up against a rifle unarmed, either. Then he got up and set out after them, trotting to keep close.

He came on Bedwell suddenly an hour later. Making a turn at the edge of a grove that had hidden the way, he saw the horse drinking at a creek that crossed the road, and Bedwell on the ground with his back toward him, flicking his snug leg with the switch he carried in his hand. They were no more than a stone's throw away. While Boone watched, Bedwell opened his breeches and made water, buttoning up slowly afterwards.

Now was the time, Boone told himself, but careful, careful! His hand dropped the poke. He felt his legs running under him and a breeze fanning his face. His feet kicked up a noise in the road. Bed-well straightened his trousers and turned and saw him and set him-self, waiting, not trying to get the rifle from the saddle. He stood there and met the charge, and they went down, rolling into the little stream and out of it. Boone heard the horse snort and saw the hoofs dance away. He felt the man's hand slip under his cap and clamp on his hair. The other hand came up and the thumb of it found Boone's eye, and now the two hands worked together, the one holding his head while the thumb of the second pushed into the socket. Pain was like a knife turning in his skull. The eye started from its hole. He let go of Bedwell's throat and tore himself free and scrambled to his feet. Bedwell stood blurred before him, stood dripping, his lips a little open, not saying anything, the lines mak-ing small half circles at the corners of his mouth. His eyes studied Boone. Boone lunged in, swinging at the face. Bedwell's knee jerked up, and his hands pushed Boone away as if the last lick had been struck. Boone doubled and stumbled back. A straining noise came out of his throat. He tried to straighten against the fierce pain in his groin.

"Well?" asked Bedwell. His hand brushed at the mud on his coat.

"You taken my rifle!"

"So?"

"I aim to git it back."

"Aim ahead."

"I ain't through yit."

Bedwell's eyes slid off Boone, looking over his shoulder, and a sudden glint came into them that Boone did not understand. He was smiling now, smiling on one side of his face. "Afraid, aren't you, pup?"

Boone's shoulder caught him in the chest. The man went over, easy this time, with Boone on top of him. The strength seemed to have drained out of Bedwell. He tried to squirm from under and fell back, grunting. His hands fluttered, fending Boone's thumbs from his eyes. He was yelling, making a roar in Boone's ears. "Help! Help!" Boone got his hand beneath the flutter. His thumb poked for an eye. It had just found it when a voice like a horn sounded. "Stop it, damn you! Stop it!"

A hand grabbed Boone's shoulder and jerked him loose. The man in the black coat stood over him, and now Boone saw there was a star on the coat. "I'm the sheriff."

"Thank God, sheriff!" It was Bedwell speaking. He got to his feet and picked up his white hat from the water and brushed at it. "He would have killed me." He pointed at Boone. "Must be crazy."

The sheriff's gaze went to Boone. "I seen him afore, sneakin' through the woods."

"He slipped up on me. I was letting my horse drink, and he charged me from behind."

"What's the idee, boy?" the sheriff asked, and answered his own question. "Robbery, that's what." His eyes went to Bedwell's horse, standing hip-shot across the creek. "Wanted to get the gentleman's horse and rifle and outfit, didn't you?"

"No."

Bedwell was nodding his head. "I hadn't thought of that, sheriff."

The sheriff went on, "I bet you'd've jumped me, only you seen my pistol."

"He stoled my gun. I aimed to git it back," Boone said.

The sheriff's voice was a pounding in Boone's ears. "That why you got to go sneakin' through the woods like a varmint?"

"He stoled it."

"What you doin'"—the sheriff's eyes went over Boone's dirty homespun—"with a handsome piece like that?"

"He stoled it, I said."

Bedwell gave the sheriff a small smile. "Poor excuse."

"Worser than none. Come along, both of you."

The sheriff's thumb signaled the direction. "March!" he said. "No funny business, now." He had his pistol in his hand. To Bedwell he said, "You climb on your horse and go ahead. We'll keep him 'twixt us." He strode back, keeping his eyes fixed over his shoulder on Boone, and caught up his own horse. Bedwell grinned at Boone. He said softly, "Looks like you won't get to St. Louis for a spell." They set off, Bedwell and the sheriff, mounted, at head and tail of the line and Boone, afoot, between them.

They came into a town a mile further on. Boone took it for Paoli. Alongside Louisville it was a little place, but it was still big enough, and it was all eyes and moving lips. The eyes looked at Boone from windows and doorways and the lips said things, and people closed the doors and walked over to fall in with the sheriff, and he could feel their eyes boring at his back and hear their lips talking.

"What is it, sheriff?"

"That young'n there."

"Looks rough, sure enough."

"Is there gonna be a trial?"

The sheriff's big voice said, "Could be."

"The jury ain't been excused, from yesterday."

"The president judge went off to Corydon, but the side judges are around."

"All side and no judges."

The voices cackled. They were making fun behind him, like going to a quilting or a bee. Bedwell seemed to like it. He squirmed around on his horse, smiled at the men following, and said to the sheriff, "I hope we can get this over with quick. I got to get on."

The courthouse was a long, low building, made of logs. "Tie up here," the sheriff said to Bedwell, and hitched his own horse at the rack. "I'll take the rifle, and your horn and pouch." He motioned them inside. "Git the coroner for me, will you?" he asked one of the men before he went in.

Boone found himself in that part of the room meant for judges and lawyers and the jury and people who were lawing. At the front of it were a platform and a high bench, and behind the high bench was another bench, with a back to it, to sit on. Out from the platform were three tables and some chairs, and at the side of it were places for the jury to sit. The section was separated from the rest of the room by a pole which ran from side to side and was tied to the walls. Beyond the pole were hewn benches for those who wanted to watch and listen. A few people already sat there, and more were coming, entering through a door at the other side of the pole. The sheriff motioned, "Set down." A dark little man with eyes like wet acorns touched the sheriff on the arm. The sheriff said, "Hello, Charlie. We got to get set. Seen Eggleston and the judges?"

"They're across, havin' one."

The sheriff took Bedwell by the arm. "Watch this here boy, will you, Charlie?" he said to the dark little man. The man sat down. The sheriff and Bedwell went out.

The section beyond the pole was filling. The voices made a single, steady noise in the room, a noise without words, rising and falling but still steady, coming at a man like waves and washing up on him. The people stopped and looked up front as they came in and then went and sat down and looked up again and began to talk, their voices going into the wave.

After while the door beside Boone opened to let in the sheriff and Bedwell and half a dozen other men. Two of them stepped up on the judges' platform and sat down and waited there, quiet and open-eyed, like owls in the light. One of them had a body like an egg, and a red face and eyes with little rivers of blood running in them. The other was pale and had eyes like a sick hound. He slumped back when he sat down and didn't make a motion, letting his eyes go over everything as if nothing mattered. A third man went to a little table and put a big book on it and sat down behind it and got out a pen. The sheriff nudged Boone to his feet and pushed him over in front of the judges. The red-veined eyes fastened on him. "What's your name, boy?"

"Boone Caudill."

"You are charged with assault and battery. Guilty or not guilty?"

"I ain't done nothin'."

"Not guilty, then. Ready to stand trial?"

When Boone didn't answer the red eyes flicked impatiently. "Here, this boy needs counsel." The eyes picked out a man. "Squire Beecher."

One of the half-dozen men who had just come in stepped forward. "Yes, your honor." He wore a brown coat with a rolling collar and underneath it a lighter-colored vest. His hair was thick and straw-colored, and at the nape of his neck it flowed into a queue, tied with some kind of skin, which reached to his tail. He looked to be twenty-five or twenty-six years old.

"Can you take the defense? The court doubts if there's a fee in it." The man nodded slowly, and the judge went on, "Eggleston says the state's ready. We got a jury, from yesterday."

"Give me a minute," asked Squire Beecher.

"Sure thing. Take the defendant into the grand jury room. Then we'll git on."

"Suppose you tell me all about it," said Squire Beecher after they had sat down in the other room. There was a table in it, and twelve chairs, and five or six spittoons that reared up, wide-mouthed, as if begging for a squirt. "Well?" prompted Beecher.

"That gun, he stoled it from me."

"How?"

"He just taken it, and I was aimin' to git it back."

"That's why you tackled him?"

"To git it back."

The squire hitched himself in his chair. "Look, boy! I'm on your side, but unless you tell me the facts of the case I can't help you. Start at the first now, and tell the whole story."

"Ain't nothin' to tell, savin' he came up on me two nights ago and gave me his name and took supper with me."

"Where?"

"Two days away, yonder."

"Then what?"

"He sneaked off in the night, takin' my gun and my horn and bullet pouch."

"When he came up on you, do you mean it was at your house?"

"Outside."

"How did you happen to be outside?"

Squire Beecher waited for an answer. "You mean you were traveling?"

"To St. Louis."

"From where?"

Again the squire waited. "Is this all you're going to tell me, just that this man Bedwell came up on you while you were camping out, and shared your supper and later stole off with your gun while you slept?"

Boone said, "That's all there is."

Squire Beecher bent his head and brought his queue around in front and fingered it while he thought. It was eelskin, likely, it was tied by. Beecher said, "You don't give yourself much chance. How do you happen to be tramping through Indiana with no money? You haven't any money, have you? No food? No horse?"

The sheriff's horn of a voice came into the room. "Court's ready, Beecher." While Beecher looked at him Boone said, "It don't matter. He stole my rifle, I told you." The young lawyer got up, a frown wrinkled his smooth face. "Come on, then."

"Ready?" asked the red-faced judge. Squire Beecher nodded. "Ready as can be, Judge Test." To the sheriff the judge said, "Summon the jury." The sheriff strode to the door and bellowed "Jury!" like a man calling hogs. Afterward he came back and pounded on a table. "Oyez! Oyez!" There was a scuffling of feet as everybody stood. The voice boomed around the room. Beecher motioned Boone toward one of the tables. They sat down by it. Bedwell was seated at the other, and with him was a lean-faced man who kept fiddling with his chin. The man's eyes were so gray they were almost white, like glass, and, like glass, they looked hard and cool.

The fat man called Judge Test sat forward on his seat, his arms crossed on the bench in front of him. The other judge stayed slumped back, looking tired. Judge Test had his hand up and was saying something to the jurymen, seated over to the right against the side wall. Boone wondered if the pale judge was as sick as he looked. Beecher and the cold-eyed man were putting questions to the jury. A man might get as white as that if he never let the weather touch him. The red-veined eyes swung around. "Let the witnesses be sworn. Stand up! Hold up your hand there, boy!"

". . . sweart'ell the truth, the whole truth and nothing but the truth, s'helpyouGod?"

As the judge said "God" a queer look flashed over his face. His eyes flicked wide, as if he had been poked in the behind, and his jaw fell down and his mouth made a round hole in his face. His hands fluttered. There was the sound of wood splintering. Boone just caught a glimpse of the wide eyes and open mouth and the hands grabbing, and then the judge's face dropped out of sight behind the bench as if he were playing fort and had ducked a rock. Boone heard his rump thump on the platform. The pale judge seized the bench in front of him and held himself up while the other end of the seat beneath him went down. Judge Test got up, blowing and redder than ever. He said, "Dammit!" and looked at the sheriff. "It's the sheriff's job to see that this here courtroom is kept in repair."

The sheriff said something that Boone couldn't hear because people had begun to laugh. Judge Test pounded for silence. The cold-eyed man at the other table nodded wisely. He muttered, "It appears that this is a mighty weak bench."

They hollered then, the people at the other side of the pole did, and slapped each other and whooped while Judge Test pounded. The judge's eyes flashed redly, but the cold-eyed man just grinned at him and by and by the judge swallowed and made himself grin, too. A man brought in a block of wood, and they set the end of the bench on it, and Judge Test lowered himself slowly, trying it out. "All right, Eggleston," he said, "if you're through with your funnin'," and the cold-eyed man said, "Come around, sheriff."

The sheriff handed Old Sure Shot to another man and came over and sat down in a chair beside the judges' bench, facing the crowd.

Eggleston asked, "You are Mark York, sheriff of Orange county?"

"Sure."

A thumb motioned toward Boone. "Ever see this defendant before?"

"Sure."

"When and where?"

"First time, he went sneakin' around me, on the Greenville road. That was about noon."

"What were you doing there?"

"Matt Elliott got a cow stole. I was coming from there."

"What do you mean when you say he sneaked around you?"

"He left the road and circled behind me. I just got a flash of him makin' off."

"Do you know any reason why he would want to sneak by you?"

Squire Beecher jumped up. "Objection!"

Eggleston said, "Oh, all right," and went on. "When did you see him for the second time?"

"Up the road a piece. He had this here gentleman down and was gougin' him."

"They were fighting?"

"Sure."

"Who would you say was the aggressor?"

"This young feller here was on top."

Squire Beecher cried "Objection!" again. Judge Test looked at him, then said, "This court isn't going to tie itself up with a lot of fiddle-faddle. It's the truth we want. Go ahead, Eggleston."

"And you brought them in?"

"Sure." He pointed at Boone. "He was fixin' to get the gentleman's horse and outfit."

"Objection!"

Eggleston turned his white eyes on Squire Beecher. "Pass the witness."

The squire said, "Sheriff, so far as you know, the man Bedwell might have started the fight, might he not?"

"Could be."

"Actually you couldn't tell who the aggressor was?"

"This one was on top."

"But that doesn't prove anything?"

"Proves he was gettin' the best of it."

The answer set people to nudging one another and giggling and talking at the corners of their lips. The sheriff grinned back at them and made a slow wink. Judge Test rapped.

"That's all."

The sheriff got up and walked over to the side and took Old Sure Shot from the man he had handed it to.

"Bedwell."

The dove greatcoat switched, the tight breeches scissored, the white hat swung from one hand.

The prosecutor looked at his papers. "You are Jonathan Bedwell, of New Orleans?"

"The same."

"You know the defendant here?"

"I saw him, just the once."

"Tell the court about it."

"He attacked me."

"Go on."

"It was about noon today. I had stopped and got off my horse while I let him drink."

"Where?"

"On the Greenville road, a mile or so out."

"Yes?"

"I heard someone running, and turned around, and it was this man, charging me."

"Ever see him before?"

"No."

"Why would he attack you?"

"I object," called Beecher. Except for one flicker of the veined eyes, Judge Test gave him no notice.

"I don't know. The sheriff said it was robbery, but I don't know."

The lean face of the prosecutor turned on Boone. "He looks like he needed something of everything, all right." People smiled at that, and some of them cackled while Beecher objected and Judge Test pounded on the bench. There was just one man who didn't smile. He was an Indian in the first row beyond the pole, sitting straight and unmoving, his hands holding a pair of quilled moccasins which he had brought to town to sell, likely. The pale judge came out of his slump and fixed his sad eyes on the prosecutor. "That ain't law, Eggleston, and you know it."

Eggleston went on. "At any rate, he charged you and knocked you down and was trying to do you bodily injury when the sheriff happened on the scene."

"He would have killed me, I think."

"You have a horse?"

"A good one."

"And a rifle?"

"A good one, but a little light."

It wasn't light, either, Boone said to himself, but heavy enough for even b'ar or buffler.

"I guess any robber—" the cold eyes were on Boone—"would be glad to get them."

"I suppose so."

"I object." It was Beecher again, standing and shaking his head so that the queue swung behind his back. Judge Test moved one finger. "No fiddle-faddle."

"You can have him," said Eggleston to Squire Beecher.

Beecher asked, "Did you say you had never seen this boy before?"

"Never."

Beecher aimed a finger at Bedwell. "But, as a matter of fact, you shared his supper with him night before last, didn't you?"

"No."

"You shared his supper with him and spent the night at his campfire, and you got up early, while the boy still slept, and made off with his rifle and horn and pouch, didn't you?"

"No. I did not."

Eggleston interrupted. "The state objects to this line of questioning."

"Go on," said Judge Test to Beecher.

"And the boy attacked you just in the hope of getting his rifle back?"

"It wasn't his rifle."

The questions went on. Through a window Boone could see a tavern across the street, and, at the side of it and farther on, the wooded knobs lifting to the horizon. He thought of the cave where he had spent the night, and the rain whispering on the rocks while he stayed dry inside.

"That's all," said Beecher. Bedwell started to get up, but Eggleston motioned him back. Eggleston's thick mouth worked carefully. "Just a minute. Can you identify the rifle?"

"Of course. It was made by old Ben Mills at Harrodsburg, Kentucky. I bought it from him."

"Sheriff," Eggleston asked, "bring the rifle around, will you?" He looked at the piece, held it for Beecher's inspection and then handed it to the jurymen. It made the rounds among them while they nodded their heads. The prosecutor let himself smile.

Squire Beecher was on his feet. "Wait! Wait!" His finger leveled at Bedwell. "You could have memorized the name of the maker after you had stolen the rifle, couldn't you?"

"Yes," said Bedwell. "If I had stolen it."

"As a matter of fact, that would probably be the first thing you would do, wouldn't it?" asked Beecher, his eyes going from one juror to another. They looked at him and looked away, as if they couldn't be jarred loose from an idea.

Bedwell said, "Probably. If I had stolen it."

Eggleston pointed his lean face at the bench. "That's the case."

Squire Beecher turned to Boone. "All right," he said. His finger showed the way to the witness stand.

Boone got up and went over and sat down. At one side of him were the jurors, at the other the judges' bench. In front of him were the attorneys and Bedwell and the clerk with his big book and pen, and beyond them were the townspeople, staring at him, turning to talk behind shielding hands out of eager, curling mouths. The eyes came together on him, as if everything was just one big eye and he was all there was to see. Only the Indian sat quiet, looking at him out of eyes that caught a gleam from the window, his hands idle in his lap, holding the moccasins. He wouldn't be a real western Indian, but a Miami, or maybe a Pottawatomi. Far back in the room a man was smiling at Boone, like a body would smile at a friend. In the whole passel of faces his was the only friendly one, unless it would be the Indian's.

"What is your name?" asked Beecher.

"Boone Caudill."

"In your own words," said Beecher quietly, "will you tell the court about your fight this morning and the circumstances surrounding it?"

"It's my gun. He stole it." ·

"Wait a minute, now. Start at the first."

"I was fixin' my supper—"

"When and where?"

"Night before yistiddy. Down the road a piece."

"The other side of Greenville?"

"I reckon so."

"Go on."

Boone made a little gesture at Bedwell. "He came ridin' up."

"Yes?"

"He gave me his name and asked if he could put up, too."

"Yes?"

"Come mornin', he was gone, and the rifle to boot."

"And so," said Squire Beecher, "when you came upon him to-day you tried to get your rifle back?"

"Yes."

Eggleston barked, "Objection!"

"Quit coachin' him," ordered Judge Test.

"That's the way it was," Boone said.

"Can you identify the rifle?"

"Ben Mills made it, at Harrodsburg."

Squire Beecher got up. "Your honors," he said, while a frown wrinkled his face, "we believe a motion for dismissal is in order. As to the identification of the gun, the court simply has a contradiction, without supporting evidence on either side. Neither does the charge of assault and battery stand up. There again the court has a contradiction, and the testimony of the sheriff on the one side does nothing to enforce the accusation. The sheriff simply saw the men fighting. Any conclusion he has drawn or implied is pure assumption, without weight before the law. The only thing of actual proof is that a fight took place."

Eggleston had arisen, protesting. "We want to cross-examine the witness."

Judge Test waved them both back. "Go on, then," he said to the prosecutor, but Squire Beecher said, "Wait, your honor. We're not through." His eyes came back to Boone. "Have you any other way of identifying the rifle? Are there any other marks on it, or scratches that would identify it?"

"It's got nary a scratch on it."

Squire Beecher rested his chin on his fist. His eyes studied the table in front of him. "Maybe," he said after a pause, "you can establish your claim to the rifle through the horn or pouch." His head came up. "How many bullets in the pouch?"

"There was eleven, and I shot a rabbit. Ten, there would be."

Beecher motioned, and the sheriff brought over the pouch. Eggleston came and stood over Beecher as Beecher emptied the pouch on the table. "One, two, three . . ."

Eggleston broke in, "There's eight. Just eight."

Beecher's hand fumbled in the pouch and came out empty. "Of course," he said to Boone, "anyone who stole it could have fired it a couple of times, couldn't he?"

Eggleston looked down at Beecher, grinning, and said, "I ought to object. You're coaching him again." He went back over to his seat, still grinning.

Beecher said, "That's all."

Judge Test's red face turned on Eggleston. "Go on."

Eggleston leaned forward toward Boone, like a snake with a stand on a bird. "How long have you owned this rifle?"

"A spell."

"How long?"

Boone heard the pen scratching as the man at the little table wrote in the big book. It scratched and stopped, and he saw the pen raised, waiting. From the back of the room, the man still smiled at him, like someone who was on his side.

"I asked how long. Good Lord, boy, if the rifle is yours you must know how long you've owned it."

"I couldn't rightly say as to that."

"Oh, you couldn't rightly say. Where did you get the rifle, anyway? Is it really yours?"

The pen was scratching again, and stopping again. Boone felt his hands knotted between his knees. His tongue came out and wet his lips.

Eggleston yelled, "Is it?" and pounded on the table with his fist.

"Your honors," Squire Beecher complained, "we object that the questioning amounts to abuse."

"He won't answer."

The judge's red eyes rested on Boone. "Boy, a defendant can't be made to incriminate himself—but I'll have to warn ye, if you don't answer, the jury's likely to hold it against you."

Boone said, "My pap gave it to me."

The prosecutor's hand fiddled with his chin. After a silence he said, "How old are you, boy?"

"Comin' eighteen."

"You're seventeen, then." Eggleston's light eyes studied him. "You're a runaway, aren't you?"

Boone heard Beecher cry "Objection!" and Judge Test answered, "He's cross-examinin'."

"Where you from?"

Boone brought his hands from between his knees and took hold of the bottom of his chair. "St. Louis."

"What are you doing here?"

"Goin' back."

"From where?"

"Around."

"Just around, eh?"

"Reckon so."

The prosecutor looked at the judges, his eyebrows up, making wrinkles in his forehead. "He ought to be held for investigation. Probably a bound boy."

Squire Beecher came forward, and again the yellow queue swung. "The charge is assault and battery. No other accusation is before the court."

"Let's git on with it, first," Judge Test said to Eggleston. "Ready for pleadin'?" There was a little buzz of whispers in the crowd and a shifting of butts on the benches. They sat forward, as if this was what they had been waiting for. While Boone looked, the man in the back nodded his head, as if to say everything would be all right.

"You can come here," Squire Beecher said, not unkindly, and Boone left the witness chair and sat at the table by him.

Beecher got up and stepped over in front of the jury and began to talk. His voice, lighter than Eggleston's, seemed to turn on and off like a spigot as he faced one way and then another. It was a sight, the way his pigtail joggled. Beyond him, through the window, was the tavern and, farther on, the woods against the sky and the sky itself clear and blue as water. Boone made out a bird against it, probably just a buzzard, but sailing free and easy like keeping up was no trick at all. The spigot turned on and off. "Only one man's word. . . . No case has been proved . . . all that has been shown, all you can be sure of, is that a fight took place. . . . In the circumstances you must resolve the doubt in favor of the defendant. . . ." Out beyond the pole everybody was looking at Beecher, except when he pointed, and then the eyes all moved over, as if they were on a string, and bored at Boone. And everybody was listening, too, and sometimes smiling and sometimes frowning, and whispering once in a while. Maybe a man would find it easy enough to listen, to keep his mind to what was being said, if he was out there. Maybe it was right pleasant, watching and listening and not having fingers aimed at you and eyes putting holes through you, knowing you could get up and go any time you wanted to, to St. Louis or wherever. ". . . this innocent and friendless boy. . . ." He didn't want anyone to be friends, unless it was Jim Deakins. And he wasn't a boy, but a man, growed and out on his own. ". . . ask the jury in its wisdom and mercy to return a verdict of acquittal."

Beecher was sweating when he sat down.

Eggleston lifted himself from his chair and went over toward the jury with his hands in his pockets and head down. When he got there, though, the hands came out and the head lifted. His voice was loud, so that Boone could hear it plain, if he set himself to listening, no matter how Eggleston faced. Eggleston marched back and forth in front of the jurymen, his arms swinging. Once in a while he turned and pointed and fixed Boone with his whitish eyes, and, when he did, his voice boomed in Boone's ears, saying "ragged rascal" and "plain piece of banditry" and "murderous tramp." When he turned back his words hit the wall first and seemed to run like echoes in the room. Beyond him, way beyond him, the buzzard was still circling, light as a feather, not moving its wings but just tilting, round and round, with the wind. Words came at Boone again, like rocks being pitched. He felt the eyes on him and his skin trying to be small inside his clothes. "I submit, gentlemen, that you can come to only one verdict, and that is the verdict of guilt." The arm swung over, like a loose limb in the wind. "Look at him! Look him over well! Ask yourselves what a man like this—" a finger pecked at his clothes—"would be doing with a piece like that." Then it was the echo again, bouncing from the wall. "The penalty, gentlemen, I leave to your good judgment."

Eggleston turned around and went to his seat, giving Squire Beecher a smile on the way. Boone reckoned they were pretty good friends outside of court.

Judge Test rapped once. "The jury can retire." They got up, stretching, and filed out. Through the window Boone could see them cross the street and go into the tavern. The crowd began to shuffle out, most of them making for the tavern, too. The Indian arose, his dark face still as set as a picture, and got his blanket closer around his neck and went through the door, letting the moccasins dangle from his hand. The smiling man in the back was among the last to go out. Watching him, Boone saw that he was crippled. One shoulder was withered, and one leg dragged on the floor. He was still smiling as he drew closer, but smiling a fool's smile, Boone could see now, smiling without meaning out of an idiot's face. Before he passed through the door he turned and stuck his tongue out at Boone. Bedwell tidied his beaver and after a final look around left the courtroom. Judge Test came down from the bench and cut himself a chew of tobacco. He and the sheriff began to chaff.

After while the sheriff said, "This was just a one-drink case." He motioned out the window, to the jury coming from the tavern. Beecher shook his head but didn't say anything.

The jurymen lagged in. Judge Test lifted himself back on the platform and sat at the bench pulling at his dewlaps. The pale judge sat with his jaw in his hand. His eyes opened slowly as the jury tramped by him. The clerk came and sat down before his book.

"Gentlemen, have you come to a decision?"

One of the jurors got up and stood framed in the window, shutting out the woods and the sky and the bird soaring. "We have."

"Let the court hear it."

"Judge, your honor, we say the boy's guilty, but not too orful guilty."

The judge pursed his lips while his red eyes waited on the speaker.

"We figger," said the juror, "that he'll have to work it out, if'n you fine him, so we say about five dollars, or seven days."

Judge Test whispered to the pale judge and they both nodded, and Judge Test said, "Let it be seven days." The clerk's pen scratched in his book. To Eggleston Judge Test added, "That'll give you time enough to run him down."

Boone felt that hand of the sheriff on his arm. "Come along!" Eggleston looked up as they were about to pass him. "Maybe you can get something out of him, sheriff." One cold eye winked. The sheriff said, "Sure." As he passed out the door he said to the little man named Charlie, "Git Little Betsy, will you?"

The jail was a log cabin with a heavy oak door. The sheriff sprang the lock with a rusty key. It was a big lock, as big as a terrapin. For a minute Boone couldn't make things out after he had got inside. Then he saw a plank bunk with a ragged cover on it, and a broken table, on which a half-burned candle was stuck.

A voice outside said, "Here's Betsy." The sheriff said, "Thanks. Watch the door." The door whined as it closed.

The sheriff was a big man, tall and bony, with a look of power about him. Boone hadn't noticed before how stiff his face could be. It was like a rock face, like Pap's when the devil got in him.

"Time we get well acquainted," said the sheriff, "maybe you'll feel more like talkin'." The right hand came away from his side, holding something that for a minute dragged on the floor. "Turn around!"

Boone cried, "You ain't going to whale me, mister!"

Before he had finished, the whip whistled.

CHAPTER FIVE

Spare the Rod

Schools were generally taught by males in the early days and most teachers fell into one of three classes: 1) the very young—whose tenure usually was brief; 2) the middle-aged Irish fiddle-players and worshippers of the jug; 3) the honest, sincere (and often ill-prepared) who taught as a means of livelihood because they could not support themselves in another profession.

It was of a very young schoolmaster that

EDWARD EGGLESTON

wrote, and his example of the species was able (in Eggleston's fiction, at least) to overcome the crudities of the Indiana frontier and to triumph in the end. Examining the facts of Eggleston's life and reading his fiction, one reaches the conclusion that his hero, the young "Hoosier School-master," was Eggleston as he saw himself—except that he had assumed the role of Bible Agent rather than teacher in southern Indiana, and followed that with preaching and other pursuits there and in Minnesota before he went to Chicago and later to Eastern cities as an editor, sometime minister and author.

While Edward Eggleston was born in Vevay, Indiana, in 1839, attended Indiana schools and made the state his headquarters during frequent bouts with ill health and despondency in his young manhood, he never became a true Hoosier. Either the state was too crude or Eggleston was too sensitive—anyway he never quite achieved a sympathetic or even a reasonably tolerant attitude toward Indiana or Indianians. He saw nothing beneath the surface faults; he never succeeded in coming even near to transcribing the speech, or understanding the motives of Midwesterners; he was pretentious and he was a bit spiteful.

All this would have been of little significance except that, as one of the first Hoosiers to return to the East and establish himself as an editor, his analysis of the peculiarities of the former fellow citizens he described in The Hoosier School-Master was accepted on the seaboard as gospel!

Some Midwesterners either failed to note Eggleston's biases and misrepresentations, forced themselves to accept his critical opinion, or showed an unnecessary deference. In 1900 a man of no less stature than Meredith Nicholson remarked, that, probably "The Hoosier School-Master represented Indiana in her darkest years!"

I wonder: were those Indiana years really so dark, or was it Mr. Eggleston, new-rich in elegance as a result of his recent contacts with the Eastern literati, who viewed darkly the Indiana scene of his frustrated youth?

The Hoosier School-Master is unquestionably short on realism in matters of speech, mental processes and improbable behavior of its heroic characters: does this augur accurate portrayal of the less elegant members of the cast? Eggleston based his studies of the uneducated southern Indianians on his assumption that they were a "semi-nomadic people, descendants of the colonial bond-servants." It was a beautiful theory, but it was nothing more: the parts of his first nineteen years which he spent in Indiana could have allowed for no very profound research into the antecedents of his neighbors but, had such a project occurred to him, he would have been surprised to learn that among the class of whom he speaks a great many individuals bore names prominent in the Colonial history of Virginia and the Carolinas and that their bearers then (as now) could give a reasonably plausible account of the unfortunate but not at all "base-born" generations through which the names had been inherited. Negro slaves often took the family names of their masters: white bond-servants did not, for they had names of their own.

But in spite of the errors of detail found in The Hoosier School-Master, it at least demonstrates some of the problems which faced a frail young intellectual who elected to face a career as an educator.

EDWARD EGGLESTON

The Hoosier School-Master
[1871]

CHAPTER IV SPELLING DOWN THE MASTER

"I 'LOW," said Mrs. Means, as she stuffed the tobacco into her cob pipe after supper on that eventful Wednesday evening: "I 'low they'll app'int the Squire to gin out the words to-night. They mos' always do, you see, kase he's the peartest *ole* man in this deestrick: and I 'low some of the young fellers would have to git up and dust ef they would keep up to him. And he uses sech remarkable smart words. He speaks so polite, too. But laws! don't I remember when he was poarer nor Job's turkey? Twenty year ago, when he come to these 'ere diggin's, that air Squire Hawkins was a poar Yankee school-master, that said 'pail' instid of bucket, and that called a cow a 'caow,' and that couldn't tell to save his gizzard what we meant by *'low* and by *right smart*. But he's larnt our ways now, an' he's jest as civilized as the rest of us. You would-n know he'd ever been a Yankee. He didn't stay poar long. Not he. He jest married a right rich girl! He! he!" And the old woman grinned at Ralph, and then at Mirandy, and then at the rest, until Ralph shuddered. Nothing was so frightful to him as to be fawned on by this grinning ogre, whose few lonesome, blackish teeth seemed ready to devour him. "He didn't stay poar, you bet a hoss!" and with this the coal was deposited on the pipe, and the lips began to crack like parchment as each puff of smoke escaped. "He married rich, you see," and here another significant look at the young master, and another fond look at Mirandy, as she puffed away reflectively. "His wife hadn't no book-larnin'. She'd been through the spellin'-book wunst, and had got as fur as 'asperity' on it a second time. But she couldn't read a word when she was married, and never could. She warn't overly smart. She hadn't hardly got the sense the law allows . . . when Squire Hawkins married Virginny Gray he got a heap o' money, or, what's the same thing mostly, a heap o' good land. And that's bet-ter'n book-larnin', says I. Ef a gal had gone clean through all eddi-cation, and got to the rule of three itself, that would-n buy a featherbed. Squire Hawkins jest put eddication agin the gal's farm, and traded even, an' ef ary one of 'em got swindled, I never heerd no complaints."

And here she looked at Ralph in triumph, her hard face splinter-ing into the hideous semblance of a smile. And Mirandy cast a blush-ing, gushing, all-imploring, and all-confiding look on the young master.

"I say, ole woman," broke in old Jack, "I say, wot is all this 'ere spoutin' about the Square fer?" and old Jack, having bit off an ounce of "pigtail," returned the plug to his pocket.

As for Ralph, he fell into a sort of terror. He had a guilty feeling that this speech of the old lady's had somehow committed him be-yond recall to Mirandy. He did not see visions of breach-of-promise suits. But he trembled at the thought of an avenging big brother.

"Hanner, you kin come along, too, ef you're a mind, when you git the dishes washed," said Mrs. Means to the bound girl, as she shut and latched the back door. The Means family had built a new house in front of the old one, as a sort of advertisement of bettered circumstances, an eruption of shoddy feeling; but when the new building was completed, they found themselves unable to occupy it for anything else than a lumber room, and so, except a parlor which Mirandy had made an effort to furnish a little (in hope of the bliss-ful time when somebody should "set up" with her of evenings), the new building was almost unoccupied, and the family went in and out through the back door, which, indeed, was the front door also, for, according to a curious custom, the "front" of the house was placed toward the south, though the "big road" (Hoosier for *high-way*) ran along the north-west side, or, rather, past the north-west corner of it.

When the old woman had spoken thus to Hannah and had latched the door, she muttered, "That gal don't never show no gratitude fer favors"; to which Bud rejoined that he didn't think she had no great sight to be pertickler thankful fer. . . .

Every family furnished a candle. There were yellow dips and white dips, burning, smoking, and flaring. There was laughing, and talking, and giggling, and simpering, and ogling, and flirting, and courting. What a full-dress party is to Fifth Avenue, a spelling-school is to Hoopole County. It is an occasion which is metaphorically inscribed with this legend: "Choose your partners." Spelling is only a blind in Hoopole County, as is dancing on Fifth Avenue. But as there are some in society who love dancing for its own sake, so in Flat Creek district there were those who loved spelling for its own sake, and who, smelling the battle from afar, had come to try their skill in this tournament, hoping to freshen the laurels they had won in their school-days.

"I 'low," said Mr. Means, speaking as the principal school trustee, "I 'low our friend the Square is jest the man to boss this 'ere consarn to-night. Ef nobody objects, I'll app'int him. Come, Square, don't be bashful. Walk up to the trough, fodder or no fodder, as the man said to his donkey."

There was a general giggle at this, and many of the young swains took occasion to nudge the girls alongside them, ostensibly for the purpose of making them see the joke, but really for pure pleasure of nudging. The Greeks figured Cupid as naked, probably because he wears so many disguises that they could not select a costume for him.

The Squire came to the front. Ralph made an inventory of the agglomeration which bore the name of Squire Hawkins, as follows:

1. A swallow-tail coat of indefinite age, worn only on state occasions, when its owner was called to figure in his public capacity. Either the Squire had grown too large or the coat too small.

2. A pair of black gloves, the most phenomenal, abnormal, and unexpected apparition conceivable in Flat Creek district, where the preachers wore no coats in the summer, and where a black glove was never seen except on the hands of the Squire.

3. A wig of that dirty, waxen color so common to wigs. This one showed a continual inclination to slip off the owner's smooth, bald pate, and the Squire had frequently to adjust it. As his hair

had been red, the wig did not accord with his face, and the hair ungrayed was doubly discordant with a countenance shrivelled by age.

4. A semicircular row of whiskers hedging the edge of the jaw and chin. These were dyed a frightful dead-black, such a color as belonged to no natural hair or beard that ever existed. At the roots there was a quarter of an inch of white, giving the whiskers the appearance of having been stuck on.

5. A pair of spectacles "with tortoise-shell rim." Wont to slip off.

6. A glass eye, purchased of a peddler, and differing in color from its natural mate, perpetually getting out of focus by turning in or out.

7. A set of false teeth, badly fitted, and given to bobbing up and down.

8. The Squire proper, to whom these patches were loosely attached.

It is an old story that a boy wrote home to his father begging him to come West, because "mighty mean men get into office out here." But Ralph concluded that some Yankees had taught school in Hoopole County who would not have held a high place in the educational institutions of Massachusetts. Hawkins had some New England idioms, but they were well overlaid by a Western pronunciation.

"Ladies and gentlemen," he began, shoving up his spectacles, and sucking his lips over his white teeth to keep them in place, "ladies and gentlemen, young men and maidens, raley I'm obleeged to Mr. Means fer this honor," and the Squire took both hands and turned the top of his head round half an inch. Then he adjusted his spectacles. Whether he was obliged to Mr. Means for the honor of being compared to a donkey was not clear. "I feel in the inmost compartments of my animal spirits a most happifying sense of the success and futility of all my endeavors to sarve the people of Flat Creek deestrick, and the people of Tomkins township, in my weak way and manner." This burst of eloquence was delivered with a constrained air and an apparent sense of a danger that he, Squire Hawkins, might fall to pieces in his weak way and manner, and of the success and futility of all attempts at reconstruction. For by this time the ghastly pupil of the left eye, which was black, was looking away round to the left, while the little blue one on the right twinkled cheerfully toward the front. The front teeth would drop down so that the Squire's mouth was kept nearly closed, and his words whistled through.

"I feel as if I could be grandiloquent on this interesting occasion," twisting his scalp round, "but raley I must forego any such exertions. It is spelling you want. Spelling is the corner-stone, the grand, underlying subterfuge, of a good eddication. I put the spellin'-book prepared by the great Daniel Webster alongside the Bible. I do, raley. I think I may put it ahead of the Bible. For if it wurn't fer spellin'-books and sich occasions as these, where would the Bible be? I should like to know. The man who got up, who compounded this work of inextricable valoo was a benufactor to the whole human race or any other. . . .

"I app'int Larkin Lanham and Jeems Buchanan fer captings," said the Squire. And the two young men thus named took a stick and tossed it from hand to hand to decide which should have the "first choice." One tossed the stick to the other, who held it fast just where he happened to catch it. Then the first placed his hand above the second, and so the hands were alternately changed to the top. The one who held the stick last without room for the other to take hold had gained the lot. This was tried three times. As Larkin held the stick twice out of three times, he had the choice. He hesitated a moment. Everybody looked toward tall Jim Phillips. But Larkin was fond of a venture on unknown seas, and so he said, "I take the master," while a buzz of surprise ran round the room, and the captain of the other side, as if afraid his opponent would withdraw the choice, retorted quickly, and with a little smack of exultation and defiance in his voice, "And I take Jeems Phillips."

And soon all present, except a few of the old folks, found themselves ranged in opposing hosts, the poor spellers lagging in, with what grace they could, at the foot of the two divisions. The Squire opened his spelling-book and began to give out the words to the two captains, who stood up and spelled against each other. It was not long until Larkin spelled "really" with one *l*, and had to sit down in confusion, while a murmur of satisfaction ran through the ranks of the opposing forces. His own side bit their lips. The slender figure of the young teacher took the place of the fallen leader, and the excitement made the house very quiet. Ralph dreaded the loss of prestige he would suffer if he should be easily spelled down. And at the moment of rising he saw in the darkest corner the figure of a well-dressed young man sitting in the shadow. Why should his evil genius haunt him? But by a strong effort he turned his attention away from Dr. Small, and listened carefully to the words which the Squire did not pronounce very distinctly, spelling them with extreme deliberation. This gave him an air of hesitation which disappointed those on his own side. They wanted him to spell with a dashing assurance. But he did not begin a word until he had mentally felt his way through it. After ten minutes of spelling hard words Jeems Buchanan, the captain on the other side, spelled "atrocious" with an *s* instead of a *c*, and subsided, his first choice, Jeems Phillips, coming up against the teacher. This brought the excitement to fever-heat. For though Ralph was chosen first, it was entirely on trust, and most of the company were disappointed. The champion who now stood up against the school-master was a famous speller.

Jim Phillips was a tall, lank, stoop-shouldered fellow who had never distinguished himself in any other pursuit than spelling. Except in this one art of spelling he was of no account. He could not catch well or bat well in ball. He could not throw well enough to make his mark in that famous Western game of bull-pen. He did not succeed well in any study but that of Webster's Elementary. But in that he was—to use the usual Flat Creek locution—in that he was "a hoss." . . . Bud Means, foreseeing that Ralph would be pitted against Jim Phillips, had warned his friend that Jim could "spell like thunder and lightning," and that it "took a powerful smart speller" to beat him, for he knew "a heap of spelling-book." To have "spelled down the master" is next thing to having whipped the biggest bully in Hoopole County, and Jim had "spelled down" the last three masters. He divided the hero-worship of the district with Bud Means.

For half an hour the Squire gave out hard words. What a blessed thing our crooked orthography is! Without it there could be no spelling-schools. As Ralph discovered his opponent's mettle he became more and more cautious. He was now satisfied that Jim would eventually beat him. The fellow evidently knew more about the spelling-book than old Noah Webster himself. As he stood there, with his dull face and long sharp nose, his hands behind his back, and his voice spelling infallibly, it seemed to Hartsook that his superiority must lie in his nose. Ralph's cautiousness answered a double purpose; it enabled him to tread surely, and it was mistaken by Jim for weakness. Phillips was now confident that he should carry off the scalp of the fourth school-master before the evening was over. He spelled eagerly, confidently, brilliantly. Stoop-shouldered as he was, he began to straighten up. In the minds of all the company the odds were in his favor. He saw this, and became ambitious to distinguish himself by spelling without giving the matter any thought.

Ralph always believed that he would have been speedily defeated by Phillips had it not been for two thoughts which braced him. The sinister shadow of young Dr. Small sitting in the dark corner by the water-bucket nerved him. A victory over Phillips was a defeat to one who wished only ill to the young school-master. The other thought that kept his pluck alive was the recollection of Bull. He approached a word as Bull approached the raccoon. He did not take hold until he was sure of his game. When he took hold, it was with a quiet assurance of success. As Ralph spelled in this dogged way for half an hour the hardest words the Squire could find, the excitement steadily rose in all parts of the house, and Ralph's friends even ventured to whisper that "maybe Jim had cotched his match, after all!"

But Phillips never doubted of his success.

"Theodolite," said the Squire.

"T-h-e, the, o-d, od, theod, o, theodo, l-y-t-e, theodolite," spelled the champion.

"Next," said the Squire, nearly losing his teeth in his excitement. Ralph spelled the word slowly and correctly, and the conquered champion sat down in confusion. The excitement was so great for some minutes that the spelling was suspended. Everybody in the house had shown sympathy with one or the other of the combatants, except the silent shadow in the corner. It had not moved during the contest, and did not show any interest now in the result.

"Gewhilliky crickets! Thunder and lightning! Licked him all to smash!" said Bud, rubbing his hands on his knees. "That beats my time all holler!"

And Betsy Short giggled until her tuck-comb fell out, though she was on the defeated side.

Shocky got up and danced with pleasure.

But one suffocating look from the aqueous eyes of Mirandy destroyed the last spark of Ralph's pleasure in his triumph, and sent that awful below-zero feeling all through him.

"He's powerful smart, is the master," said old Jack to Mr. Pete Jones. "He'll beat the whole kit and tuck of 'em afore he's through. I know'd he was smart. That's the reason I tuck him," proceeded Mr. Means.

"Yaas, but he don't lick enough. Not night," answered Pete Jones. "No lickin', no larnin', says I."

It was now not so hard. The other spellers on the opposite side went down quickly under the hard words which the Squire gave out. The master had mowed down all but a few, his opponents had given up the battle, and all had lost their keen interest in a contest to which there could be but one conclusion, for there were only the poor spellers left. But Ralph Hartsook ran against a stump where he was least expecting it. It was the Squire's custom, when one of the smaller scholars or poorer spellers rose to spell against the master, to give out eight or ten easy words, that they might have some breathing-spell before being slaughtered, and then to give a poser or two which soon settled them. He let them run a little, as a cat does a doomed mouse. There was now but one person left on the opposite side, and, as she rose in her blue calico dress, Ralph recognized Hannah, the bound girl at old Jack Mean's. She had not attended school in the district, and had never spelled in spelling-school before, and was chosen last as an uncertain quantity. The Squire began with easy words of two syllables, from that page of Webster, so well known to all who ever thumbed it, as "baker," from the word that stands at the top of the page. She spelled these words in an absent and uninterested manner. As everybody knew that she would have to go down as soon as this preliminary skirmishing was over, everybody began to get ready to go home, and already there was the buzz of preparation. Young men were timidly asking girls if "they could see them safe home," which was the approved formula, and were trembling in mortal fear of "the mitten." Presently the Squire, thinking it time to close the contest, pulled his scalp forward, adjusted his glass eye, which had been examining his nose long enough, and turned over the leaves of the book to the great words at the place known to spellers as "incomprehensibility," and began to give out those "words of eight syllables with the accent on the sixth." Listless scholars now turned round, and ceased to whisper, in order to be in at the master's final triumph. But to their surprise "ole Miss Meanses' white nigger," as some of them called her in allusion to her slavish life, spelled these great words with as perfect ease as the master. Still not doubting the result, the Squire turned from place to place and selected all the hard words he could find. The school became utterly quiet, the excitement was too great for the ordinary buzz. Would "Meanses' Hänner" beat the master? beat the master that had laid out Jim Phillips? Everybody's sympathy was now turned to Hannah. Ralph noticed that even Shocky had deserted him, and that his face grew brilliant every time Hannah spelled a word. In fact, Ralph deserted himself. As he saw the fine, timid face of the girl so long oppressed flush and shine with interest; as he looked at the rather low but broad and intelligent brow and the fresh, white complexion and saw the rich, womanly nature coming to the surface under the influence of applause and sympathy —he did not want to beat. If he had not felt that a victory given would insult her, he would have missed intentionally. The bull-dog, the stern, relentless setting of the will, had gone, he knew not whither. And there had come in its place, as he looked in that face, a something which he did not understand. You did not, gentle reader, the first time it came to you.

The Squire was puzzled. He had given out all the hard words in the book. He again pulled the top of his head forward. Then he wiped his spectacles and put them on. Then out of the depths of his pocket he fished up a list of words just coming into use in those days—words not in the spelling-book. He regarded the paper attentively with his blue right eye. His black left eye meanwhile fixed itself in such a stare on Mirandy Means that she shuddered and hid her eyes in her red silk handkerchief.

"Daguerreotype," sniffed the Squire. It was Ralph's turn.

"D-a-u, dau——"

"Next."

And Hannah spelled it right.

Such a buzz followed that Betsey Short's giggle could not be heard, but Shocky shouted: "Hanner beat! my Hanner spelled down the master!" And Ralph went over and congratulated her.

And Dr. Small sat perfectly still in the corner.

And then the Squire called them to order, and said: "As our friend Hanner Thomson is the only one left on her side, she will have to spell against nearly all on t'other side. I shall therefore take the liberty of procrastinating the completion of this interesting and exacting contest until to-morrow evening. I hope our friend Hanner may again carry off the cypress crown of glory. There is nothing better for us than healthful and kindly simulation."

Dr. Small, who knew the road to practice, escorted Mirandy, and Bud went home with somebody else. The others of the Means family hurried on, while Hannah, the champion, stayed behind a minute to speak to Shocky. Perhaps it was because Ralph saw that Hannah must go alone that he suddenly remembered having left something which was of no consequence, and resolved to go round by Mr. Means's and get it.

———————

Higher education was available in Indiana even before Eggleston's young School-master underwent his ordeal. The Indiana Seminary (scheduled to become Indiana University as soon as enough students could be prepared) had opened its doors in Bloomington in 1824. By 1828, when the little seminary had crammed the heads of a few young Hoosiers with the Latin, Greek and mathematics required for college admission, it received its college charter.

Baynard Rush Hall, graduate of Union College and Princeton Theological Seminary, came to Bloomington and was elected principal of the Indiana Seminary. The election was in the hands of the trustees of the institution, and—as is intimated in Mr. Hall's report of the interviews of other candidates—he was chosen as the only qualified man available. Had the generality of Bloomington's citizens been permitted to vote the result might have been otherwise; most considered Mr. Hall a smart aleck, and thus ineligible for the post.

Hall served four years as principal of the Seminary and three years
as professor of ancient languages at Indiana College before his resignation and return to the east in 1831. Some residents of Bloomington
still considered him a smart aleck.

In 1843, writing under the name of Robert Carlton, Esq., he published a book in which he gave his unflattering opinion of the town
(called Woodville), the Seminary, and of those who had been his
friends and enemies there. At last, opinion regarding Mr. Hall became unanimous in Bloomington. There was no longer a dissenting
voice: Mr. Hall was a smart aleck.

As we take note of his supercilious criticism of those who had supported him, of his snobbery, of his refusal to make allowance for
good intentions—and, worst of all, of his elephantine playfulness,
the strained quality of his humor and his cute apostrophes to his
"Dear Reader!"—we can but join the good folk of Bloomington in
their unanimity of view after 1843:

BAYNARD RUSH HALL

was smart-alecky; painfully so, as witness this passage from

The New Purchase

or

Early Years in the Far West
[1855]

CHAPTER XI [BLOOMINGTON—OR WOODVILLE—IN THE
EIGHTEEN-TWENTIES]

ON THE MORNING of the fourth day, about ten o'clock, A.M., we
emerged from the forest upon a clearing one mile in length, and a
half a mile in breadth: and nearly in its centre stood Woodville, the

capital of the NEW PURCHASE—a village just hewed and hacked out of the woods, fresh, rough, and green. . . .

Woodville was now almost three years old; large, however, for its age, and dirty as a neglected urchin of the same years, and rough as a motherless cub. It was the destined seat of a University: hence when Mind whose remarkable tramp was now *being*—(hem!) —heard, halted here in its march some years after, in the shape of sundry learned and great men, we were all righted up, licked into shape, and clarified. But to day, never were strange animals so stared at, walked around and remarked upon near at hand by the brave, and peeped at by the modest and timid from chinks and openings, as were we, tame and civilized bipeds, Mr. and Mrs. C., by our fellow creatures of Woodville. Why, we could not then conjecture—unless because Mr. C. wore a coat and was shaved—or because Mrs. C. had on no cap, and a cap there was worn by all wives old and young—a sign in fact of the conjugal relation—and so it was "suspicioned" if Mrs. C. was not my wife, she ought to be. . . .

But here comes Dr. Sylvan, and we must introduce him. First, however, be it understood that Woodville, even then, had two classes, the superior and the inferior; the former *shaved* once a week, the latter once in *two* weeks, or thereabouts. At our first meeting, which was accidental, I was at a loss where to class my friend; and had we not already acquired some art in decyphering character by studying the countenance and the mien, and not by looking at the dress, or rather the want of it, we should have fallen into a great mistake about this true Christian and gentleman.

Shoes he wore, it is true—but one a coarse cow-hide laced boot, the other a calf-skin Jefferson, or some other presidential name. And this latter was well blacked, though not shiney; but the cow-hide had been too stiff, stubborn, and greasy, to receive its portion. Above the Jefferson was a stockingless ancle—presumptive, and even *a fortiori* evidence that the ancle in the boot was in a natural condition. Coat he wore none; but he had on a Kentucky-jean vest, open to its lowest button, and allowing the display of a reddish-yellow flannel shirt bosom, his arms being encased in sleeves of thick cotton something, and all unembroidered. As a rare extravagance, and which placed him in the aristocratic class of democrats, the Doctor *wore*, not *carried*, a pocket-handkerchief; and he wore it circumambient—the cotton bandana going over one shoulder, and under the opposite arm, and then both ends met and were tied just above the *os femoris*. This luxury, however, was used only as "a sweat rag," and not as "a nose-cloth,"—delicate names applied appropriately to a handkerchief, as it was employed to wipe off perspiration or to blow the nose. As to the Doctor's nose, it was, in its necessities, most cruelly pinched and twisted between his finger and thumb; and these were then wiped on the rag just mentioned—on the plan of the man that topped the candle with his fingers, and deposited the burnt wick in the snuffers. The operation was certainly performed with great skill, yet it seemed unnatural at the time; and it was not till we had seen the governor himself in a stump speech, and the judge on the bench, perform the same instinctively and involuntarily, that we came to regard the affair as natural, and to conclude that, after all, handkerchiefs were nothing more than civil conveniences.

Such was the leaden casket—the outer man; but reader, within was a rare jewel. With a little fixing, this gentleman would easily have adorned and delighted the best company in the best places. He was a brave soldier, an able statesman, and a skillful physician; and if not learned, he was extensively and even profoundly read in his favourite studies, medicine and politics. His person, disfigured even by his dress, was uncommonly fine, his countenance prepossessing, and his conversation easy, pleasant, and instructive. . . . As a husband and a father, no man ever was more affectionate; and as a physician, none more kind, tender, and anxious—indeed he not only prescribed for a patient, but as far as possible, nursed him. It was strange, however, that so brave a man in the field, should have been occasionally cowed in the presence of political foes—but so it was; and this was the only blemish in a man otherwise so good, noble, and generous.

Other citizens may be introduced hereafter; at present we shall speak of Woodville itself. This was, as has been stated, the capital of the New Purchase—the name of a tract of land very lately bought from the Indians or the Abor'rejines, as the Ohio statesman had just then named them, in his celebrated speech in the legislature:—

"Yes, Mr. Speaker, yes, sir," said he, "I'd a powerful sight sooner go into retiracy among the red, wild, Abor'rejines of our wooden country, nor consent to that bill." The territory lay between the north and south Shining rivers—called sometimes the Shinings, sometimes the Shineys, from the purity of the waters and the brightness of the sands—and it contained fine land, well timbered and rolling. The white population was very sparse, and mainly very poor persons, very illiterate, and very prejudiced, with all the virtues and vices belonging to woodsmen. . . .

South of Woodville—distance according to the weather—and in the very edge of the forest, were at this time, two unfinished brick buildings, destined for the use of the future University. As we passed to-day in our vehicle, the smaller house was crammed with somebody's hay and flax; while the larger was pouring forth a flock of sheep—a very curious form for a college to issue its parchments— which innoxious graduates paused a moment to stare, possibly at a future trustee, and then away they bounded, a torrent of wild wool, to the shelter of the woods.

The larger edifice was called Big College— But—

But—hark!—the rattle of our carriage! We must then hastily wind up with saying, that east of Woodville was a wilderness, and uninhabited for forty miles; south, cabins were sprinkled, on an average, one to the league; south-west, the same; but north and north-west, settlements and clearings were more abundant.

CHAPTER XXXIV [INDIANA UNIVERSITY COMES
TO BE—IN THE PREPARATORY
STAGE]

OUR BOARD OF TRUSTEES, it will be remembered, had been directed by the Legislature to procure, as the ordinance called it, "Teachers for the commencement of the State College at Woodville." That business, by the Board, was committed to Dr. Sylvan and Robert Carlton—the most learned gentlemen of the body, and of—the New Purchase! Our honourable Board will be more specially introduced hereafter; at present we shall bring forward certain rejected candidates, that, like rejected prize essays, they may be published, and *thus* have their revenge.

None can tell us how plenty good things are till he looks for them; and hence, to the great surprise of the Committee, there seemed to be a sudden growth and a large crop of persons even in and around Woodville, either already qualified for the "Professorships," as we named them in our publications, or who *could* "qualify" by the time of election. As to the "chair" named also in our publications, one very worthy and disinterested schoolmaster offered, as a great collateral inducement for his being elected, "*to find his own chair!*"—a vast saving to the State, if the same chair I saw in Mr. Whackum's school-room. . . .

The Committee had, at an early day, given an invitation to the Rev. Charles Clarence, A.M., of New Jersey, and his answer had been affirmative; yet for political reasons we had been obliged to invite competitors, or *make* them, and we found and created "a right smart sprinkle."

Hopes of success were built on many things—for instance, on poverty; a plea being entered that some thing ought to be done for the poor fellow—on one's having taught a common school all his born days, who now deserved to rise a peg—on political, or religious, or fanatical partizan qualifications—and on pure patriotic principles, such as a person's having been "born in a canebrake and rocked in a sugar trough." On the other hand, a fat, dull-headed, and modest Englishman asked for a place, because he had been born in Liverpool! and had seen the world beyond the woods and waters too! And another fussy, talkative, pragmatical little gentleman, rested his pretensions on his ability to draw and paint maps . . . !

But of all our unsuccessful candidates, we shall introduce by name only two—Mr. James Jimmey, A. S. S., and Mr. Solomon Rapid, A. to Z.

Mr. Jimmey, who aspired to the mathematical chair, was master of a small school of all sexes, near Woodville. At the first, he was kindly, yet honestly told, his knowledge was too limited and inaccurate; yet, notwithstanding this, and some almost rude repulses afterwards, he persisted in his application and his hopes. To give evidence of competency, he once told me he was arranging a new spelling-book, the publication of which would make him known as a literary man, and be an unspeakable advantage to "the rising generation." And this naturally brought on the following colloquy about the work:—

"Ah! indeed! Mr. Jimmey?"

"Yes, indeed, Mr. Carlton."

"On what new principle do you go, sir?"

"Why, sir, on the principles of nature and common sense. I allow school-books for schools are all too powerful obstruse and hard-like to be understood without exemplifying illustrations."

"Yes, but Mr. Jimmey, how is a child's spelling-book to be made any plainer?"

"Why, sir, by clear explifications of the words in one column, by exemplifying illustrations in the other."

"I do not understand you, Mr. Jimmey, give me a specimen—"

"Sir?"

"An example—"

"To be sure—here's a spes-a-example; you see, for instance, I put in the spelling-column, C-r-e-a-m, *cream*, and here in the explification column, I put the exemplifying illustration—*Unctious part of milk!*"

We had asked, at our first interview, if our candidate was an algebraist, and his reply was *negative*; but, "he allowed he could *'qualify'* by the time of election, as he was powerful good at figures, and had cyphered clean through every arithmetic he had ever seen, the rule of promiscuous questions and all!" Hence, some weeks after, as I was passing his door, on my way to a squirrel hunt, with a party of friends, Mr. Jimmey, hurrying out with a slate in his hand, begged me to stop a moment, and thus addressed me:—

"Well, Mr. Carlton, this algebra is a most powerful thing—aint it?"

"Indeed it is, Mr. Jimmey—have you been looking into it?"

"Looking into it! I have been all through this here fust part; and by election time, I allow I'll be ready for examination."

"Indeed!"

"Yes, sir! but it is such a pretty thing! Only to think of cyphering by letters! Why, sir, the sums come out, and bring the answers exactly like figures. Jist stop a minute—look here; a stands for 6, and b stands for 2 and c stands for 4, and d stands for figure 10; now if I say $a + b - c = d$, it is all the same as if I said, 6 is 6 and 8 makes 14, and 4 subtracted, leaves 10! Why, sir, I done a whole slate full of letters and signs; and afterwards, when I tried by figures, they every one of them came out right and brung the answer! I mean to cypher by letters altogether." . . .

The most extraordinary candidate, however, was Mr. Solomon Rapid. He was now somewhat advanced into the shaving age, and was ready to assume offices the most opposite in character; although justice compels us to say Mr. Rapid was as fit for one thing as another. Deeming it waste of time to prepare for any station till he was certain of obtaining it, he wisely demanded the place first, and then set to work to become qualified for its duties, being, I suspect, the very man, or some relation of his, who is recorded as not knowing whether he could read Greek, as he had never tried. And, beside, Mr. Solomon Rapid contended that all offices, from president down to fence-viewer, were open to every white American. . . .

Naturally, therefore, Mr. Rapid, thought he would like to sit in our chair of languages, or have some employment in the State college; and hence he called for that purpose on Dr. Sylvan, who, knowing the candidate's character, maliciously sent him to me. Accordingly, the young gentleman presented himself, and without ceremony, instantly made known his business thus:—

"I heerd, sir, you wanted somebody to teach the State school, and I'm come to let you know I'm willing to take the place."

"Yes, sir, we are going to elect a professor of languages who is to be the principal, and a professor—"

"Well, I don't care which I take, but I'm willing to be the principal. I can teach sifring, reading, writing, joggerfree, surveying, grammur, spelling, definitions, parsin—"

"Are you a linguist?"

"Sir?"

"You of course understand the dead languages?"

"Well, can't say I ever seed much of them, though I have heerd tell of them; but I can soon larn them—they aint more than a few of them I allow?"

"Oh! my dear sir, it is not possible—we—can't—"

"Well, I never seed what I couldn't larn about as smart as any body—"

"Mr. Rapid, I do not mean to question your abilities; but if you are now wholly unacquainted with the dead languages, it is impossible for you or any other talented man to learn them under four or five years."

"Pshoo! foo! I'll bet I larn one in three weeks! Try me, sir,—let's have the furst one furst—how many are there?"

"Mr. Rapid, it is utterly impossible; but if you insist, I will loan you a Latin book—"

"That's your sorts, let's have it, that's all I want, fair play."

Accordingly, I handed him a copy of Historiae Sacrae, with which he soon went away, saying, he "didn't allow it would take long to git through Latin, if 'twas only sich a thin patch of a book as that."

In a few weeks to my no small surprise, Mr. Solomon Rapid again presented himself; and drawing forth the book began with a triumphant expression of countenance:—

"Well, sir, I have done the Latin."

"Done the Latin!"

"Yes, I can read it as fast as English."

"Read it as fast as English!!"

"Yes, as fast as English—and I didn't find it hard at all."

"May I try you on a page?"

"Try away, try away; that's what I've come for."

"Please read here then, Mr. Rapid," and in order to give him a fair chance, I pointed to the first lines of the first chapter, viz: "In principio Deus creavit coelum et terram intra sex dies; primo die fecit lucem," etc.

"That, sir?" and then he read thus, "in prinspo duse creevit kalelum et terrum intra sex dyes—primmo dye fe-fe-sit looseum," etc.

"That will do, Mr. Rapid—"

"Ah! Ha! I told you so."

"Yes, yes—but translate."

"Translate!" (eyebrows elevating.)

"Yes, translate, render it."

"Render it!! how's that?" (forehead more wrinkled.)

"Why, yes, render it into English—give me the meaning of it."

"*MEANING!!*" (staring full in my face, his eyes like saucers, and forehead wrinkled with the furrows of eighty)—"*MEANING!!* I didn't know it *had* any meaning. I thought it was a *DEAD* language!!"

Our honourable board of trustees at last met; and after a real attempt by some, and a pretended one by others, to elect one and another out of the three dozen candidates, the Reverend Charles Clarence, A.M., was chosen our principal and professor of languages; and that to the chagrin of Mr. Rapid and other disappointed persons, who all from that moment united in determined and active hostility towards the college, Mr. Clarence, Dr. Sylvan, Mr. Carlton, and, in short, towards "every puss proud aristocrat big-bug, and blasted Yankee in the New Purchase."

CHAPTER XLII　FOURTH YEAR

[THE COLLEGE LEVEL AT LAST!]

OUR FOURTH YEAR introduces an epoch, the Augustan age of the New Purchase—the opening of the State College!

And now comes on the stage, as one principal actor, my friend, the Reverend Charles Clarence, A.M., Principal and Professor of Ancient Languages. This gentleman had accepted our appointment, not for the paltry stipend paid as his salary, but wholly because he longed to be in the romantic West, and among its earliest literary pioneers; and hence, early this spring, he was with us, and not merely ready, but even enthusiastically impatient to commence his labours. . . .

. . . if ever man was influenced by disinterested motives, and fired with enthusiasm for advancing solid learning—if ever one desirous of seeing western institutions rival, if not excel, others—if ever a person came willing to live and die with us, and to sacrifice eastern tastes and prejudices, and become, in every proper way, a Western Man, my friend Clarence was he. . . .

Be it remembered, that Uncle Sam is an undoubted friend of *public* education, and that, although so sadly deficient in his own; and hence, in the liberal distribution of other folks' land, he bestowed on us several entire townships for a college or university. It was, therefore, democratically believed, and loudly insisted on, that as the State had freely received, it should freely give; and that "larnin, even the most powerfullest highest larnin," should at once be bestowed on every body! and without a farthing's expense! Indeed, some gravely said and argued that teachers and professors in the "people's college ought to sarve for the honour!" or at least be content with "a dollar a day, which was more nor double what a feller got for mauling rails!" The popular wrath, therefore, was at once excited almost to fury when necessity compelled us to fix our tuition fee at ten dollars a year; and the greatest indignation was felt and expressed towards Clarence "as the feller what tuk hire for teaching and preaching, and was gettin to be a big-bug on the poor people's edicashin money". . . .

Proceed we, however, to open the college. And my narration may be depended on, as Clarence has reviewed the whole and says it is substantially correct,—indeed, in some respect I was a *quorum-pars*.

The institution was opened the first day of May, at 9½ o'clock, A.M., anno Domini 1800, and so forth. And, some floors being unlaid, and the sashes all being without glass, the *opening* was as complete as possible—nearly like that of an Irish hedge school! When the Principal—so named in our minutes and papers, but by the vulgar called *master*, and by the middle sort, *teacher*—appeared, a clever sprinkle of *boy* was in waiting; most of which firmly believed that, by some magic art, our hero *could*, and being paid by government, *should*, and without putting any body to the expense of books and implements, touch and transmute all, and in less than no time, into great scholars.

"Boys and *young gentlemen*," said Mr. C. compounding the styles of a pedagogue and professor, "I am happy to see you; and we are now about to commence our State College, or, as some call it, the Seminary. I hope all feel what an honour attends being the first students in an institution so well endowed; and which, therefore, by proper exertions on our parts, may eventually rise to the level of eastern colleges, and become a blessing to our State and country. You have all, I suppose, procured the necessary books, of which notice was given at *meeting*, and in several other ways, for the last four weeks."

"I've got 'em—"

"Me too—"

"I've brung most on 'em—"

"Master—Uncle Billy's to fetch mine out in his wagin about Monday next—"

"Father says he couldn't mind the names and wants them on a paper—"

"Books!—I never heern tell of any books—wont these here ones do, Master?—this here's the Western Spellin one—and this one's the Western Kalkelatur?"

"Mr. Clarinse—I fotch'd my copy-book and a bottle of red ink to sit down siferin in—and daddy wants me to larn book-keepin and surveying."

"Order boys—order!"—hem!—"let all take seats in front. There is a misunderstanding with some, both as to the books and the whole design and plan of the school, I perceive. This is a Classical and Mathematical School; and that fact is stated and fully explained in the trustees' public advertisements; and no person can be admitted unless one intending to enter upon and pursue the prescribed course; and that includes even at the start Latin, Greek, and Algebra. Now, first, let us see who are to study the dead languages—"

"I do—I do—me too—me too," etc., etc.

"Do you, then sit there. Well—now let me have your names for the roll—A. Berry—S. Smith—C. D., etc., etc.—ten names—I will attend to you ten directly, so soon as I have dismissed the others. I regret, my young friends, that you are disappointed—but I am only doing my duty; indeed, if I wished, I have no power to admit you, unless to the course of studies—nay, even the trustees have power to do only what they have done. I hope, therefore, you will now go home, and explain the matter to your friends—"

By several—

"Daddy says he doesn't see no sort a use in the high larn'd things —and he wants me to larn Inglish only, and book-keepin, and surveying, so as to tend store and run a line."

"I allow, Mister, we've near on about as good a right to be larn'd what we wants, as them tother fellers on that bench;—it's a free school for all."

"I am sorry, boys, for this misunderstanding; but we cannot argue the subject here. And yet every one must see one matter plainly; for instance, any man has a right to be governor, or judge or congressman; yet none of you can be elected before the legal age, and before having some other qualifications. It is so here, you all have a right to what we have to bestow; but you must be '*qualified*' to enter; and must be content to receive the gift of the State in the way the law provides and orders. You will please go home now."

The disappointed youngsters accordingly withdrew; and with no greater rudeness than was to be expected from undisciplined chaps, full of false notions of rights, and possessed by a wild spirit of independence. Hence, Mr. C. heard some very flattering sentiments growled at him by the retiring young democrats; but which, when they had fairly reached the entry, were bawled and shouted out frankly and fearlessly. And naturally after this he was honoured with some high sounding epithets by certain hypocritical demagogues in rabblerousing speeches—sneaking gentlemen, who aimed to get office and power by endless slanders on the college, and most pitiful and malicious slang about "liberty and equality, and rights and tyranny, and big-bugs, and poor people, and popular education," and the like. . . .

Clarence, therefore, was now hated and vilified as the supposed instrument of pride and aristocracy, in drawing a line between rich and poor; and for a while his person, his family, his very house was abominated. On one occasion he was in Woodville when a half-drunken brute thus halloed against him—"thare goes that high larn'd bug what gits nine hundred and ninety-nine dollars and ninety-nine cents of the people's eddekashin money for larnin ristekrats' sons high-flown words—gimmie that 'are stone and I'll do for him." Whether this was fun or earnest, Clarence did not care to ascertain;

for hearing the sneers and derision of the bystanders, and fearing it might become earnest, he took shelter in my store. . . .

But the reader may wish to know how Mr. Clarence got along with "the Few." Well, as the warm weather approached, the "boys and young gentlemen" came to recitation without coats; and, as the thermometer arose, they came without *shoes*—

"What! in the State college? Could your Mr. Clarence not have things ordered with more decency?"

Softly, Mr. Dignity—in a world where our presiding judge, a man of worth and great abilities, sat in court without his coat and cravat, and with his feet modestly reposed on the upper rostrum, thus showing his boot-soles to by-standers and lawyers; where lawyers were stripped and in shirt-sleeves; and where even Governor Sunbeam, in a stump speech gave blast to his nose pinched between a thumb and finger, and wiped said pinchers afterward on the hinder regions of his inexpressibles; do you, sir, think our Mr. C., or all eastern dignitaries combined, could have compelled young bushwhackers to wear coats and shoes in recitation rooms? He indeed ventured once as follows:—

"Young *gentlemen*"—(hem!)—"why do you attend recitations without coats and shoes?"

" 'Tis cooler, sir!"—with surprise.

"Ay! so it is—perhaps it would be still cooler if you came without your *pantaloons*."

Haw! haw!—by the whole ten.

"And *did* they, Mr. Carlton, come *without* their indispensables?"

Oh! dear me! no; on the contrary, the young gentlemen were so tickled at our professor's pleasant hint direct, that next day they not only came in their breeches but also with shoes and coats on!

CHAPTER SIX

Utopia, Posey County, Indiana

In order to look into the strange doings at Harmonie, later New Harmony, in Posey County on the Wabash, we must make the acquaintance of George Browning Lockwood, who was first to make a scholarly, unbiased, study of the communistic societies sponsored there by religio-mystic George Rapp and, later, by atheistic Robert Owen.

Mr. Lockwood, born in Illinois, came to Indiana with his parents in his boyhood. He attended the Peru public schools, graduated from DePauw University and spent most of his life as a newspaper editor and publisher in Terre Haute, Marion and Muncie. He became interested in the history of New Harmony before 1894, followed *very lead then available for information about the place and, in 1902, he published his findings.

GEORGE BROWNING LOCKWOOD

The New Harmony Communities

THE RAPPITES IN INDIANA

"When Rapp, the Harmonist, embargoed marriage
    In his harmonious settlement which flourishes,
Strangely enough as yet without miscarriage,

Why called he Harmony a state sans wedlock?
Now here I have the preachers at a dead-lock.

"Because he either meant to sneer at harmony
    Or marriage, by divorcing them thus oddly.
But whether Rapp learned this in Germany
    Or not, 'tis said his sect is rich and godly:
Pious and pure beyond what I can term any
Of ours. * * *"
                —Byron, *Don Juan*, Canto XV, Verse 25.

ALL THAT WE KNOW of the history of the Rappite community on the Wabash is gleaned from the accounts of travelers who visited the settlement, which immediately attracted wide attention in the West, and became the largest town in the territory of Indiana. The last of the thousand persons who were members of the original community died some years ago, and the Harmonists have kept no record of their proceedings.

The Rappites found themselves pleasantly situated on the Wabash. . . . Favorably to Rapp's ideas, they were further removed from enervating contact with the outside world, and the simple peasants were here less liable to become dissatisfied with their mode of life by the contemplation of that of others. There was little in the hard life of the pioneers who inhabited the surrounding country to tempt the Rappites from their comfortable homes, and though the squatters regarded with contempt the servile allegiance of the Harmonists to Father Rapp, they must have envied them the oasis which they soon created in the wilds of Indiana. . . .

The Rappites soon discovered, however, that their new home was not a serpentless Eden. The first breaking up of the bottom ground released the germs of malaria, and the death rate was enormous during the first five years of the settlement. While the ratio decreased in later years, it is claimed by some authorities that the Rappites held to a resolution made during the first year of their residence in Indiana to remain only long enough to improve the land sufficiently to make it salable. In the last year of their residence on the Wabash, it was officially stated that but two members of the community died, —a surprisingly low death rate, showing the establishment of healthful conditions.

It was not long until Harmonie began to show evidences of German thrift. Numerous log, frame and brick buildings were erected, orchards and vineyards were planted. Among the first buildings constructed was a large frame church, having a belfry with a clock striking the hours and quarters. This was replaced as a place of worship in 1822 by a huge brick structure. One entire block was given to manufacturing purposes, and among the buildings were a cocoonery and silk factory, a saw-mill, brick-yard, brewery, distillery, woolen mill and an oil mill. The power in several of the smaller manufacturing establishments was derived from a tread mill propelled by dogs. The brick dwelling houses erected by the Rappites still stand as monuments to the faithful work of their sturdy builders. The frames were made of very heavy timbers, and the spaces between the weather-boarding and the plastering were filled with cement and brick. Four large buildings were erected to serve as community houses. What was known as "Number 1" has been torn down; "Number 2" is now a general store; on its south wall is an old-fashioned sun-dial which has been faithfully telling the time since community days. "Number 3," partially rebuilt, is used as a hotel, "The Tavern." "Number 4" has been converted into an opera house. A large brick house was built as a residence for Father Rapp. Near it was a brick and stone structure used as a granary, and intended also for a fort, or refuge for the population in case of invasion by the squatters, of whom the Rappites stood in much dread. This structure was provided with loopholes, and was so substantially built that its defense would have been easy. . . .

George Flower, one of the founders of an English settlement in Edwards county, Illinois, describes the village as he saw it in 1819. A large portion of the land included in the estate, he says, was of the best quality, between two and three thousand acres being under cultivation and fenced. The town consisted of several brick and frame two-story houses for the use of small families, all built after one model, with ample gardens, well fenced and neatly cultivated, and a vast number of log cabins, neatly kept. There were also five or six very large buildings, three-stories high, which contained the community families, of sixty to eighty individuals each. Rapp had a brick mansion, a large building, with a granary of the most solid masonry, and a large brick church, itself a curiosity, the plan, it is said, being given to Mr. Rapp in a dream. There were four entrances to the church, closed by folding doors; the doors were about one hundred and twenty feet from each other. The upper story was supported by twenty-eight pillars of walnut, cherry and sassafras, the walnut pillars being six feet in circumference, and twenty-five feet high; the others were twenty-one feet high and of proportionate circumference; a surprisingly large building, Mr. Flower declared, for this country. William Herbert, a London traveler, writes of this church: "I can scarcely imagine myself to be in the wilds of Indiana, on the borders of the Wabash, while passing through the long and resounding aisles and surveying the stately colonnades of this church." There were shops for every occupation, Mr. Flower tells us, represented in the community, magnificent orchards of grafted fruit in full bearing, and extensive vineyards.

"This singular community of Germans," Mr. Flower writes, "had little or no communication with the outside world, except through the miller, the store-keeper, the tavern-keeper, and Mr. Rapp. All who went to Harmony, with surprise observed with what facility the necessaries of life were acquired and enjoyed by every member of Rapp's community. When compared with the privations and discomforts to which individual settlers were exposed in their backwoods experience, the contrast is very striking. The poor hunter that brought a bushel of corn to be ground, perhaps from a distance of ten miles, saw with wonder people as poor as himself, inhabiting good houses, surrounded by pleasant gardens, completely clothed with garments of the best quality, supplied regularly with meal, meat and fuel, without any apparent individual exertion, and he could not fail to contrast the comforts and conveniences surrounding the dwellings of the Harmonists, with the dirt and discomfort of his own log hut, and it opened to his mind a new train of thought. One of them said to me in his own simple language: 'I studies and I studies it,' an expression that depicts the feeling of every person that obtained a sight of Rapp's colony at Harmony."

At the time of the founding of the community in Pennsylvania, a record was made of the amount of property contributed by each member, and it was agreed that at the withdrawal of any member, this amount, or its equivalent, should be returned to him. In 1808, as before stated, this agreement was abrogated, and in 1818, after the removal of the Harmonists to Indiana, the record was destroyed, on motion of George Rapp, unanimously adopted by the society. With its consignment to the flames, the last tie which bound the Rappites to the system of individual property was dissolved.

We are not at a loss to explain the wonderful authority acquired by George Rapp as leader of the Harmonists. Nearly six feet in height, with patriarchal beard and stately walk, he commanded the reverence of the members of his sect as a prophet among them, while his cheerful and kindly manner, his sympathetic and plain-spoken way of talking over with the Harmonists their smallest trials, made him beloved as well. Father Rapp shrewdly maintained a nominal cabinet, or board of advisers, chosen from among the more intelligent members of the community, such as might be able to set up a rival leadership. He gained great prestige by playing on the superstitions of the peasantry. He professed to be guided on many occasions by communications received in visions, as noted by Flower, for instance, in building a great structure in the form of a Greek cross on plans supposed to have been handed down from heaven. . . .

There still remains in New Harmony what is known as "Gabriel's Rock"—two lime-stone slabs, originally one stone, ten feet by five, and five inches thick. Upon one a square figure is traced, occupying the center, and upon the other appears, seemingly, the imprint of two feet,—the print of the right foot being perfect, while the forepart of the left foot has disappeared. The tradition is that Father Rapp informed his followers that these were imprints of the feet of the angel Gabriel, who had alighted upon earth to convey to the society a message from heaven. David Dale Owen concluded that the figures were chipped in the stone by Indians. Another theory is that the slab was hewn from the pictured rocks along the Mississippi. . . . The Duke of Saxe-Weimar, who visited New Harmony only two years after the departure of the Harmonists, says: "This piece of stone was hewed out of the rock near St. Louis and sold to Mr. Rapp." This theory, therefore, seems to have the weight of authority.

Father Rapp taught humility, simplicity, self-sacrifice, neighborly love, regular and persevering industry, prayer and self-examination. He also demanded that each evening anyone who had sinned during the day should come to him and confess his transgression. No quarrels were allowed to pass through the night uncompromised, the rule which declares, "Let not the sun go down upon thy wrath," being literally enforced. Persons seeking admission to the community were compelled to make full confession of their sins, this being considered requisite to the forgiveness of God. . . .

The day's work was conducted after a fixed routine. Between five and six the people rose, breakfasted between six and seven, lunched at nine, dined at twelve, ate an afternoon lunch (vesperbrod) at three, and supped between six and seven. At nine o'clock the curfew bell was rung. Women as well as men labored in the fields, as many as fifty sometimes being employed in a body, harvesting wheat, or breaking flax in the streets. Often they marched to the fields to the music of a band which was one of the regular institutions of the community. On summer evenings this band, stationed in the public garden, discoursed the old German hymns while the women busied themselves with their house-work, the stolid peasants dozed upon the door-steps, and the children shouted at play in the streets. It is said that this band often played upon the hillsides while the peasants labored in the valley. A hundred acres of wheat were harvested by the sickle in a day,—a remarkable result for that time.

John Woods, a member of the settlement at English Prairie, twenty miles from "Harmonie" on the Illinois side of the Wabash, visited the Rappites in 1820. He says that the value of their property was then estimated at a million dollars. "Each lives in his own house," writes Woods, "but all dine at one hour and take their meals in the same manner." Woods says that the homes were distributed among the Harmonists by lot, but "though there was of necessity much difference in the size and equipment of the various buildings, there was no dissatisfaction or disturbance over the apportionment." He declared them to be a most industrious people, but said the greater part of them were not very enlightened. "As I approached the place in July, I met their plow teams, sixteen in number, just entering a field of wheat stubble. I was much pleased with their appearance." Woods counted eighty-seven milch cows going to pasture, driven by a herdsman who, according to another authority, lived in a house on wheels, called "Noah's Ark." "The dress of the Harmonists," writes Woods, "is uncommonly plain, mostly of their own manufacturing. The men wear jackets and pantaloons, with a coarse hat; the women a kind of jacket and petticoat, with a skull cap and straw hat made in the factory here. As this society do not marry, I presume they depend upon immigration from Germany to keep up their numbers, as the Americans are not likely to join them; most of them regard the Harmonists with jealousy on account of their engrossing most of the business of this part of the country." Woods' surmise as to the method employed in keeping up the numbers was correct. In 1817 one hundred and fifty recruits from Würtemburg swelled the membership. . . .

Connected with George Rapp in the leadership of the Harmonists was Frederick Rapp, who for many years served as manager of the business interests of the Rappites. Frederick Rapp was the adopted son of George Rapp, and a man of intelligence and education. He met a violent death in 1834, some allege at the instigation of George Rapp, incensed at his son's refusal to put away his wife. A more probable story is that he was fatally injured by a falling tree at Economy, Pa. Frederick Rapp contributed to the community most of its attractive features. By nature an artist, he was the originator of plans which made Harmony one of the most attractive villages in America. Had it not been for his influence upon George Rapp, amusements would have been few in the place and the unrelieved monotony of the community might have impelled even the stolid Rappites to renounce their allegiance and seek happier homes.

While Father Rapp was king of the community Frederick Rapp was his secretary of state. Father Rapp controlled internal, Frederick Rapp external affairs. Through Frederick Rapp the community held business and political connection with the outside world. Frederick Rapp was a member of the convention which met under the famous oak at Corydon and framed the first constitution of Indiana, preliminary to the admission of the territory to the Union. He was afterwards a member of the state legislature. Among the important committees upon which he served was that which located the state capital at Indianapolis in 1820.

Under the younger Rapp's administration, Harmony became a garden of neatness and beauty in the wilderness. The gabled roofs of the buildings were lifted above the forest of black locust trees which the Rappites seemed to love so well. The broad river, the vine-covered hills, the fertile valley with its peaceful town, the stately church and the fruitful orchards, furnished a scene of Acadian beauty which seemed a vision of promise to the Owenite communists who succeeded to the ownership of the estate. . . .

A short distance from the village was a famous horticultural design which visitors came miles to see. . . . A labyrinth of vines and shrubs was constructed about a summer house. . . . Robert Dale Owen says: "It contained many circuitous walks, enclosed by high hedges and bordered with flowering shrubbery. It was arranged with such intricacy that without some Daedalus to furnish a clue, one might walk for hours and fail to reach a building erected in the center. This was a temple of rough material, but covered with vines of grape and convolvulus, and its interior neatly fitted up and prettily furnished. Thus George Rapp had sought to shadow forth to his followers their final state of peace and harmony; and the rough exterior of the shrine, and the elegance displayed within, were to serve as types of toil and suffering, succeeded by happy repose."

The Rappites carried out strictly in every-day life, the moral laws and religious observances prescribed by Father Rapp. Any transgression of these regulations was punished, not by Father Rapp, but by a refusal of the remaining members of the society to associate with the wrongdoer until full forgiveness had been obtained. There is no account of a single infraction of the law of celibacy. In later years, elopements were not unknown, but the care with which the sexes were separated prevented a frequent repetition of the offense, and such transgressors were not again admitted to the society, except after the performance of prolonged penance. The character of Father Rapp has never been questioned, and his example went far towards insuring good conduct on the part of his followers. The reputation for honesty borne by the Rappites was one of the secrets of their commercial prosperity. Flour, woolen goods or distillery products bearing the Harmony brand, were known to be of the best quality, and this fact secured them trade from all parts of the country. . . .

It is related that when on one occasion Frederick Rapp made his regular trip to Pittsburg for supplies, he found himself denied credit by merchants of that city. In deep discouragement and humiliation, he went to the river side to weep and pray. He was found there by a merchant, who was so touched by Rapp's dependence on prayer to release him from his troubles, that he offered him all the supplies he could transport in two four-horse wagons. The offer was accepted with thanksgiving, and in a short time the merchant was paid in full. Several years later this man was on the verge of financial embarrassment during a period of business depression. When the news reached the Harmonists, Frederick Rapp filled his saddle bags with coin, and hastening to Pittsburg, saved their benefactor from bankruptcy. . . .

Robert Dale Owen, in "Threading My Way," gives us the last information we have of the Rappites in their Indiana home, describing them just as his father found them before their departure from the Wabash valley:

"Harmony was a marvelous experiment from a pecuniary point of view, for at the time of their emigration from Germany, their property did not exceed twenty-five dollars a head, while in twenty-one years (i.e., in 1825), a fair estimate gave them two thousand dollars for each man, woman and child, probably ten times the average wealth throughout the United States; for at that time each person in Indiana averaged but one hundred and fifty dollars' worth of property, and even in Massachusetts the average fell far short of three hundred dollars for each adult and child. Socially, however, it was doubtless a failure; as an ecclesiastical aristocracy, especially when it contravenes an important law of nature, must always be. Rapp was an absolute ruler, assuming to be such by virtue of a divine call, and it was said, probably with truth, that he desired to sell Harmony because life there was getting to be easy and quiet, with leisure for thought, and because he found it difficult to keep his people in order excepting during the bustle and hard work which attended a new settlement. At all events, he commissioned Mr. Flower to offer the whole property for sale.

"When my father reached the place, he found among the Germans, its sole occupants, indications of plenty and material comfort, but with scarcely a touch of fancy or ornament, save the flowers in the gardens and what was called the labyrinth.

"The toil and suffering had left their mark, however, on the grave, stolid, often sad German faces. They looked well fed, well clothed (so my father told me), and seemed free from anxiety. The animal had been sufficiently cared for, and that is a great deal in a world where millions can hardly keep the wolf from the door, drudge as they will; where hundreds of millions, manage as they may, live in daily uncertainty whether in the next week or month (chance of work or means of living failing), absolute penury may not fall to their lot. A shelter from life-wearing cares is something; but a temple typifies higher things,—more than what we shall eat, and what we shall drink, and where withal we shall be clothed. Rapp's disciples had bought this dearly,—at the expense of heart and soul. They purchased them by unquestioned submission to an autocrat who had been commissioned,—perhaps as he really believed, certainly as he alleged,—by God himself. He bade them do this and that, and they did it,—commanded them to forego wedded life and all its incidents, and to this also they assented."

Rappites were odd enough, Heaven knows, but they were stuffy adherents to the norm by contrast with those who replaced them in the village on the Wabash after Robert Owen bought the place and issued an invitation to all who wished a Better Life to join him—for free! Under Owen's proposed New System of Society his followers were to reduce labor to the minimum necessary for existence; property was to be held in common; the development of the intellect was to be the major aim; art, music, literature, the drama and the free interchange of ideas were to be encouraged; stultifying religion was to be frowned upon; reforms in dress, diet, manners and morals were to be instituted. Most attractive feature of all was Robert Owen's promise to feed, clothe and shelter the population until it could become self-supporting. That, figured the hundreds who flocked to New

Harmony, was exactly what their exceptional qualifications merited—someone to support them until their worth should be recognized.

Things went at New Harmony as could easily have been anticipated. There were endless meetings, discussions, elections, impeachments, more discussions, jealous charges of favoritism, reorganizations, new elections, further discussions—and no work whatever. When Owen's money ran low (there were limits to his purse if not to his misguided zeal) most of his followers returned to their old homes and their previous sources of livelihood: those sources, in most cases, were long-suffering relatives and friends. Much of this is discussed by Marguerite Young, who wrote Angel in the Forest, A Fairy Tale of Two Utopias—a book which delighted critics, irritated historians and embarrassed a good many ladies' literary clubs—all with good and sufficient reason.

Her "Two Utopias" are the Harmonie of the Rappites and the New Harmony of Robert Owen and his motley crew of followers, both located on the same site beside the Wabash in Indiana's Posey County. Her knowledge of the whys, wherefores and personalities of the characters in both movements was sketchy or mistaken; her sense of accurate reporting did not exist. That irritated the historians. The ladies' literary clubs were alienated by Miss Young's treatment of her subject, which was consistently fey and earthy in spots, to boot. Possibly those two factors, though, account for the applause from the more rarefied strata of critics.

However, Miss Young should not be taken to task for either her confusion of fact, the faerie lilt of her prose or her earthiness when she is writing of the Owenite period in the little town in Indiana's Pocket Country—that point of the state which is the peninsula between the Wabash and Ohio Rivers. Heaven knows there was confusion enough and the inhabitants were, universally, both fey and earthy. Nothing more suitable than her style could be conceived for the purpose of describing the season in which William Maclure's "Boatload of Knowledge," freighted with Robert Owen's dreamy son, Robert Dale Owen, and a crew of subsidized intellectuals, advanced on the town to participate in the final days of the New Moral World on the Wabash. What matter if William Maclure was actually a geologist, instead of a geographer as Miss Young occasionally states? if she has confused French Madame Marie Duclos Fretageot, who was Maclure's very dear friend, with the Russian lady in black who was making her pass at no one less than Robert Owen

himself? if there is, and always has been, a pronounced shortage of
birch trees on the lower Wabash? if she spells the name of Constan-
tine Samuel Rafinesque with a double f?—such aberrations are not
at all inappropriate to the scene she describes on the Philanthropist
("Boatload of Knowledge," her "Noah's Ark") as it struggled through
the Ohio ice down from Pittsburgh and, later, the strange things its
passengers encountered in New Harmony.

MARGUERITE YOUNG

Angel in the Forest

CHAPTER XXIII

Land of the West, we come to thee,
Far o'er the desert of the sea;
Under thy white-winged canopy,
Land of the West, we fly to thee!
Sick of the Old World's sophistry,
Haste then across the dark, blue sea.
Land of the West, we rush to thee!
Home of the brave: soil of the free—
Hurrah! She rises o'er the sea.
—Sung by the Owenite party on the Boatload of Knowledge

LIFE ITSELF was to be the masterpiece of art, a rich fountain of
unsullied happiness, untainted by personal desires—in a universe
of which man may be only an insignificant atom, but an atom loving the whole of which he forms the part. While the Pears family
were lamenting in New Harmony, and had all but lost faith, Robert
Owen and a party of scientists waited in Pittsburgh for the waters
to rise.

The boat, when it was embarked upon the Ohio flood, was
dubbed, by bystanders, Noah's Ark, the Maid of Mist, the Boatload

of Knowledge. Rarely had the Ohio borne such passengers as these—opposers to slaveholding oligarchies, hostile laws, white supremacy, suspension of natural rights. Oriental dream, whisky trade, non-existent township, nonexistent centaur, the Four Horsemen of the Apocalypse, irrationalism, capitalism, marriage, monasteries, money, deception in every form. No wonder the people who watched Noah's Ark set sail were as amazed as if all God's messengers were gathered aboard. Some said this group might establish a great new American commerce, with the virtue that the goods it dealt in would be intangible.

Nothing can be conceived which can be called good without qualification, except a good will. About eight miles from the new Rappite location in Pennsylvania, the ice closed in, arresting Noah's Ark for a month which seemed eternity. . . .

Thomas Say, naturalist, lay on a makeshift bed, imagining conch shells and other harmonies. His grandfather, a Quaker physician, had been transported from Philadelphia upward to heaven by choirs of angels, and, having passed beyond the seventh crystal wall, had beheld the face of an old black cook, bearded with lichen. Even in heaven, he had been outside neither time nor space. Thomas Say looked not for such supernatural revelations, one's self-objectified—but only for the Spirit of Nature, a woman who binds together Heaven, Earth, and Hell, and who is the invisible sum total of delicate nuances and shades, the rock goose, the sleep of flowers, a wilderness unprofaned by the pruner's ax. Charles Lesueur, fellow naturalist, looked for white animals in a blinding snowstorm, but nothing human, as human nature was not his province. The action of brutes expressed merely the character of the species, not of the individual—unlike that of man, Lesueur believed. The problematical Mr. Whitwell discoursed on the papery edifices of Byzantium, with many citations from Gibbon to prove the decline of the Roman Empire—while he erected, to take the place of Rome, a community palace on paper—our characters to be regarded as the temporal unfolding of the extra-temporal. William Maclure, mountain climber, who was aware of no veil drawn over the face of nature, and could therefore not wish to penetrate beyond the veil, and who had invested a large sum in Thomas Say and Lesueur, utilized this opportunity to balance his financial records—liabilities in one column, assets in another. Liability, six pairs of paper-soled shoes, one empty convent—asset, Thomas Say, a hundred preserved butterflies. Robert Owen embellishing Mr. Whitwell's papery palaces with the science of society, considered that perhaps underneath space and time, all beings were identical, multiplicity and individuality being the quality of illusion only. To be man was a certain way of being an animal—to be happy, the satisfaction of natural wants. Excessive joy and excessive sorrow were both unnecessary.

Robert Dale recalled the enforced delay of the Boatload of Knowledge as the happiest period of his life—when, if ever, the chaff was swept out, and harmony realized. . . .

William Maclure was, in fact, a man of such great common sense as to seem almost senseless. Having decided that the mind is the source of most of the evils the flesh is heir to, he wanted to stamp out most of the mind. He attributed the world's downfall to the flowers of rhetoric. On the altar of his society, therefore, he was willing to sacrifice the peacock with its crown feathers of the trinity, the word of God, and other ornaments. William Maclure condemned, most wildly, imagination, which, he said, "has been so beaten up, mixed, and compounded with the wisdom of our senses that it is difficult to draw the line of separation between them." He drew the line between ornamental and useful studies, rejecting all assumptions as to the universe's being a project of the human mind, whether rational or irrational, good or bad, white or black. Man was but a raindrop. The study of natural sciences, he believed, might be pursued, in all countries and all climates, at the least expense to money or morals. As to his idea of the science of society, it was largely important for what it excluded—fishing, shooting, horse racing, bull baiting, corporal punishment, capital punishment, Jehovah, Rousseau, the histories of ancient nations, luxurious living, the universe, and such excesses. William Maclure urged, quite simply, the revival of Spartan character—every child to learn shoemaking—for though every child should not turn out to be a shoemaker, still he might be, in time's necessity, grateful for a knowledge of this art.

The old geographer knew what he knew. He had studied rocks and had picked up, in the course of his travels, quite a fortune, was richer than any Spanish grandee in the realm of the imagination, or Mohammedan prince lugging the tomb of a scrofulous saint over the high Himalayas. By sheer republican simplicity, he had acquired enough territory to make a diamond-studded, emblazoned Austrian potentate in a glass-paneled carriage look rather sick. He, the true American spirit, could have bought and sold the Duke of Ciudad Rodrigo, laurel-crowned monasteries of the Jesuits in Ireland, the Persian mob, the Australian bush, and half of Texas. He owned, in fact and not in fancy, Spanish castles among dusty olive groves, the Valley of Murada, the estate of Carman de Croix, an Irish convent occupied by nuns and doves, a Mexican monastery occupied by priests and buzzards, Virginia Big Lick plantations shaggy with grapevines, Texas ranchos limitless as the horizon's blue, Indian villages occupied by flea-bitten dogs, many gold, silver, and copper mines, an island off the coast of Florida, various speckled birds' eggs in various nests. To say nothing of a million reals in Spanish securities, forty-one thousand francs French securities, and other intangibles. . . .

What was he doing on his way to Utopia in the pocket country? Among his many travels and adventures, this was, for the great student of material rocks, nothing final, but only another attempt in the right direction. At Alicante, Spain, he had financed a communal farm but, a revolution uprising in that country, had been fortunate to escape with the amount of his investment. This same sum he was willing to sink over and over again in Utopia or perhaps his own division of it, the shoemaking department, which he considered had most important implications as to the whole of man's welfare. . . .

CHAPTER XXIV

Now Vice and Crime no more shall stalk
Unseen in open day,
To cross our silent, peaceful walk
Through life's enchanting way.
Old Ignorance with hoary head
Must seek his everlasting bed.

Each warrior now may sheath his blade
And toil in vain no more
To seek fair Virtue's genial shade,
For now all wars are o'er.
The battle's done, the day is won,
The victory's gained by Truth alone.

—Owenite song in New Harmony

PRESUMABLY, THE ICE BROKE, and the struggle of love with hate began again. Noah's Ark pursued its course on the Ohio, carrying many philosophers, many notebooks, and the supplies which William Owen had asked for—all but what he had most wanted, a black cook.

There was great rejoicing at New Harmony, as the communicants awaited a solution, now imminent, of their many difficulties. A voice had once shaken the earth, but now it was to shake heaven, that those things which could not be shaken might remain. All old drunks were to put on new garments at last, it seems. Their faith was to make them whole. A Russian wheelwright declared that he saw, stemming out from New Harmony, a tree which would shadow the world.

Even Robert Dale was deceived, at first, by the idyllic vision. It was a pleasant life at New Harmony, with little suspicion that the beginning must be so near the end. There was a great charm in the good-fellowship and freedom from class distinctions. He was delighted by the solidarity of the human race, particularly as it expressed itself at evening balls and concerts. The young people, if not especially cultivated, were at least genial, as passionately fond of dancing as he was. He had not expected sophistication on the American frontier, so could not be disappointed with the simplest fare, the rudest accommodations. He "cared no more for the absence of luxury than young folks usually care who desert pleasant homes to spend a summer month or two under canvas—their tents on the beach, perhaps, with boats and fishing tackle at command, or pitched in some sylvan retreat, where youth and maiden roam the forest all day, returning at nightfall to merry talk, improvised music, or an impromptu dance on the greensward." New Harmony was a place for the sporting of virtues in the shade, a moral holiday, a release from narrow horizons. . . .

What a wonderful scene of spontaneous existence was this, so far from the supernatural! Every season was a mating season. Boys and girls would stroll in the moonlight in groups, sometimes in pairs. Naturally, there were a few ill-timed marriges—a few who mistook the transient love for permanence, which is the most difficult thing in the world. His own heart, Robert Dale said, was occupied by Jessie, placed far above price, a pearl. Otherwise, he might have fallen victim to the proximity of a charming partner at ball or picnic—one, in particular, a lusty creature, who afterwards married the Chief of Cincinnati's fire department, but no rival to the ghostly beauty at his side. By comparison with some of these buxom creatures of the frontier, Jessie seemed very refined, almost a creature of snow and light. . . .

Yet it was a Pentecost of politics, this New Harmony—a grand hallelujah, every man being a sword of angelic flame and every man a chariot, whose winged horses were courage and desire. The extreme of skepticism was the extreme of mysticism.

In the Rappite cruciform church, for which the plans had been handed down, it may be remembered, from heaven, the problematical Mr. Whitwell, airy builder of nothingness perhaps, proposed his papery palaces to replace present cities, his rational nomenclature to replace the present names of present cities. He had noted, we are told, the incongruities of American names, such as a Banquo and a Bean Blossom to describe twin cities in this wilderness, though there was neither a ghost in the first nor a bean in the second, but vice versa. According to this plan, which seems to have been most seriously presented and accepted, each city was to have a distinctive name, a compound word expressing latitude and longitude, so that its location in space would be self-evident—cities which have no location in space not to carry such names, and thus would be shown the impossibility of ever going there. Letters were to be employed as substitutes for the numerals used in expressing latitude and longitude. The first part of the town name was to express the latitude, the second, the longitude. The letter "S" inserted in the latitude would indicate that it was south latitude, its absence, that it was north—the letter "V," west longitude, its absence, east. This system, though it might present difficulties at first, especially to the uninitiated, had the great virtue that it would make obsolete such monstrosities and confusions as the name of a neighboring Indian chief, a poor fellow without a tribe, one Occoneocoglecococacheco-dungo, familiarly known, at least among squatters, as Dungo or Dusty.

A committee was appointed to consider the entire problem. New Harmony, 38.11 N., 87.55 W., received, accordingly, its rational name—Ipba Veinul. New York emerged as Otke Notive, Pittsburgh as Otfu Veitoup, Washington as Feili Neivul, London as Lafa Vovutu. . . .

Rational nomenclature was not the only diversion away from the job at hand. An intoxicated engineer—but not, it may be hoped, Captain Macdonald, who dreamed of a return to pastoral sanctuaries —suggested that by the improvement of the steam engine, it would be possible to reduce the distance between one place and another, London to be not much farther from Berlin than a stone's throw, figuratively speaking, and all cities to be joined in everlasting harmony.

During such lectures, tatterdemalions sat up close to the platform or draped themselves at Robert Owen's feet, as if they loved him— the better-educated members keeping to themselves, as if they had their private pews. Meetings were generally closed by the recitation of an Ode to Co-operation, a goddess with long green hair, who would shed her radiance over the earth when the workers were united and all cities rectangular. Meetings were closed only to be assembled again—smaller units taking up the discussion where it had been left off. . . . A Scotch coffinmaker, who had no following, decided to remain in New Harmony—he could keep busier here, outside of latitude and longitude, he said, than any place he knew of on earth. There seemed to be numerous Biblical patriarchs lurking about. There seemed to be numerous drunks. There were many sciences of society, in fact, and even a few plans to scrap the rectangle entirely, in favor of a semicircle or a hollow tree or a fox's hole—each science in the guise of a ragged, though perhaps rugged, individualist, alight with heaven's flame, who might stagger a little, but who had his own sweet version of reality, and his own quirks and fancies, often at odds with harmony, considered rationally.

Our focus, however, can be only on a few revealing characters—complicated, adventuresome, temporary, at large.

Constantine Raffinesque, Athenian nomad, a gentleman of Greek, Turkish, Hebrew, and French extraction, a walking league of nations, came to New Harmony late and left early. The period of his visit was a little before Utopia or a little after. According to Audubon's report, Raffinesque was "extremely remarkable" in appearance. He wore a long, loose coat of yellow nankeen, a waistcoat of the same, with enormous pockets and buttoned up to the chin, a pair of tight pantaloons, the lower part buttoned over his ankles, and his beard long, where birds might nest, and his long hair hanging loosely, like an ancient prophet's, over his shoulders. Ordinarily, he was stooped like a burro under a bundle of herbs. . . . He was a picaresque scientist, a walking museum. He had gathered shells, plants, and fishes on every shore from the Hellespont to the Wabash and, carried away by his imagination, had made up for the deficiencies of nature by describing nonexistent species as if they were existent. Nature abhorred, however, as much as he did, a vacuum—years later, what everybody had scoffed at turned up as big as life. Raffinesque was publisher, editor, and sole subscriber to a number of magazines devoted to nature's wonders. None was so wonderful as he. He carried upon his person, not only nature in futurity, but also his own version of the science of society, a kind of exaggerated old-age insurance plan. As he believed the social order to be merely a human fabrication or invention, he had had his plan patented in Washington. There was a fine for imitating it. . . . While in New Harmony, he advised that drinking water, as it was full of invisible bodies, should be sterilized—and soon, under his burden of grass, had slipped into the wilderness from whence he came. . . .

Frances Wright, a link between the Rappites and the Owenites, a friend of both Frederick Rapp and Robert Dale, wished to combine the virtues of these two orders at Nashoba, for the freeing of Negro slaves. Bentham's ward, the friend of Shelley, the friend of Lafayette, Frances had been educated a rebel, who fit into no domestic map or moral sphere—her only goal, an infinite progress. Fortunately, she was rich, and able to arise above even that circumstance, and the circumstance of being a lady by birth. "She had," Robert Dale recalled, years after their estrangement over financial matters, "various personal advantages—a tall, commanding figure, somewhat slender and graceful, though the shoulders were a little bit too high; a face the outline of which in profile, though delicately chiseled, was masculine rather than feminine, like that of an Antinous, or perhaps more nearly typifying a Mercury; the forehead broad, but not high; the short chestnut hair curling naturally all over a classic head; the large blue eyes not soft, but clear and earnest." At the time of her coming to New Harmony, he could not have guessed her later development, those peculiarities of character which caused her downfall—"the courage untempered by prudence, the philanthrophy untempered by common sense, the enthusiasm untempered by sound judgment, the inordinate estimate of her own mental powers, the obstinate adherence to opinions once adopted." She was known largely as the author of a small book entitled *A Few Days in Athens* and of a diary recording her travels in the American wilderness—though she was already what she would always be, a fighter. Mercury was restless . . . Mercury, like a slave pursued, carried everywhere the glad tidings of freedom and racial, sexual, political, economic equality. Frances or Mercury was lonely. At New Harmony, she hoped to find, if possible, a "few kindred spirits," who should join her at Nashoba, where each was to occupy a small brick house with a piazza, and each was to write poems and essays for the advancement of the human race. The Negroes, meanwhile, would render such services to themselves and to the few kindred spirits as would pay Frances a return on her investment, with which she would then buy other slaves at the auction block, these to be run in turn through the sieve at Nashoba, until such time when all members of the black race should have attained their freedom. Slaves, once freed, and the amount of their passage having been included in the price of their freedom, would be transported to another country. It was a long-time program. Frances hoped, however, that Southern planters, inspired by her example, would set up other Nashobas far and wide, so that the Negro might remain in America as the equal of his white brother. . . . At New Harmony, Frances blazed the trail, not only for Negro freedom, but also for that of woman. The Minerva Society, made up of many wingless creatures, met in a Rappite celibate dormitory, where Frances, determined to break up the time-hardened soil of conservatism in this field, urged, as woman's life was then so short in comparison with man's, the practice of birth control, that an ounce of prevention is worth a pound of regret. . . .

Other ambiguous characters on the streets of New Harmony: A long-bearded Irishman who believed himself a thing not seen and eternal, a philosophic nonresistant who slept with a revolver under his pillow, a woman in a black silk dress with a Greek cross around her neck and a pair of inglorious diamond earrings, a skeptic wrapped in the cocoon of mysticism, a whisky merchant or two, a terrestrial Elysianist, a necessarian circumstantialist. . . .

Joseph Neef, ex-priest, ex-lieutenant under Napoleon, ex-school-master, grappled with problems as great as the science of society. Neef, to put it broadly and boldly, without shame, without disguise, was New Harmony's nursemaid. Question—how to throw the bath out without throwing out the baby. Question—how to fold a diaper in such a way as to insure the greatest happiness to the greatest number. Question—how to spare the rod and not spoil the child. Wherever he went, Neef was surrounded by children—as if he were priest of another congregation, lieutenant of another army. There was neither the threat of hell nor a firing squad—but plenty of ex-citement otherwise, a little community within the community, a little republic within the republic. What protection had Neef against nature? He admitted to the children that his government was that of the worst despot, reflecting his will, though disguised as a democ-racy—but only because the members had not yet discovered the eternal laws of reason within their frames corporeal. Rather, how many noses had to be wiped, and how many knees had to be bandaged! Life was a never-ending struggle of good with evil. . . . He urged that the children should not imitate him and especially that they should not imitate his language. He had a most distressing habit which, try as he would, he could never cure himself of—to burst into a wild volley of oaths, as if he were still Napoleon's lieutenant, to call on the lord, as if he were still a priest at the altar. When the little army retired from a weed patch, scarred, torn, and defeated, unwilling to progress the battle farther, he swore vociferously. When the little congregation seemed about ready to stray from the beaten path, he prayed to God, whose high arm could reach where Neef's could not. As Neef was rarely seen without a squalling brat under each arm, and half a dozen others in his wake, perhaps his excesses were understandable, even the children agreed. Could the teacher of babes be a babe himself?

The Duke of Saxe-Weimar, who, after the failure of the Greek struggle for freedom, had rejected the crown of Greece, was one of the great travelers in the American forest. . . . From the Duke's diary may be gathered several valuable tips on old New Harmony, if one uses his imagination to fill up the empty spaces.

First of all, the Owenite city was a something intangible, a merely proposed rectangular shape, and not in evidence like the Rappite city. The cruciform-shaped church, far from being God's plan, had been Father Rapp's make-work plan, as idle hands might get into mischief, naturally. Rumor persisted—Father Rapp had castrated a son. Yet how not admire, however unwillingly, a man who had had the ability to impose his will on a large population, even to the extent of contravening an important law of man's nature? Two lightning rods were on the house of the man of God—Father Rapp had taken good care of himself. It grieved the Duke that such a good man as Robert Owen should expect to change the course of all governments, all nations, and all peoples—a larger project than Father Rapp's had ever been, and doomed to failure. . . .

Mr. Say, his hands covered with blisters by his work in the potato field south of the back garden, was ridiculous-looking but at least contributed his share of labor, according to the Duke. A correct thinker was bound to be incorrect, the Duke observed.

All in all, New Harmony, due to its circumstance in a melancholy land already denuded of many trees, and scarred by the effects of Rappite industries, was not a place for paradise—unless considered as a place for those human beings who, losing their senses one by one, become marble statues. . . .

. . . New Harmony seemed about to scatter to the four winds, in fact.

"I can hardly believe that this society will have a long duration. Enthusiasm, which soon abandons its subjects, as well as the itch for novelty, contributed much to its formation, as to its dissolution." Some of the most turbulent, with an Irishman who wore a long beard, sat under the Rappite sundial, planning a community for alcoholics to be located in the cold mountains of Mexico—where, however, they would be unable to procure even the ghost of a living, the Duke believed. Mr. Jennings, of Philadelphia, a disfrocked clergyman, yearned for nothing so much as to wear his collar backward once again and represent the Lord, in whom all things move. The elegant Madame Fratageot, of Moscow, had been married for three days when her husband perished, most mysteriously, and for this reason had come to attach herself, like a bride, to Robert Owen's science of society, but still mourned the loss of her first love, and confessed that she had been "egregiously deceived" in her expectations, as the community was too low, and the table so bad as to be beyond criticism. "The good lady appeared to be about to run from one extreme to another, for she added that in the summer she would go to a Shaker establishment in Vincennes." A charming young girl, Miss Virginia, had been interrupted in the midst of her piano playing by a brute laborer, who had demanded that she go take her turn at milking the community cows—music being no work, according to present standards of values, but a mere diversion. Miss Virginia, weeping, had retired from the room—poor darling, who deserved protection! Madame F., perhaps because of just such occurrences, had gathered the young girls of the better class around her, and there they were sheltered, like chicks under the wings of an old hen. Indeed, more seemed to have been lowered than raised by this community. . . .

Was Robert Owen so infatuated with the idea of mankind, the Duke wondered, that he had forgotten sleeping workmen, deceived aristocrats, and other disgruntled specimens who comprised it? Evidently not. "Know thyself" was ever the first rule of this community.

The plates of human character, the Duke saw, were intended to facilitate the business of self-knowledge, as by these each person could be shown, from day to day, his capacities and their development, with the least possible waste of time. The plates bore the superscription, "Scale of Human Faculties and Qualities of Birth." They were marked with ten scales, labeled Self-attachment, Affections, Judgment, Imagination, Memory, Reflection, Perception, Excitability, Courage, and Strength. Each scale was divided into a hundred parts, marked from five to five, with a slide that could be moved up and down to show the measure of the qualities, therein specified, which the measurer possessed or believed himself to possess.

What a clever machine, of which all the parts could be known and studied! Alas, but the sleeping workman might find that he was not deficient in Courage and Strength—though woefully lacking in Imagination and Memory. One such fellow, with his hat drawn over his eyes, and an empty bottle at his side, seemed, so far as the Duke could judge, never to have moved from his position in the grass in front of an unfinished building during the entire length of his stay in New Harmony. Or Madame F., the egregiously deceived, might find that she was free from Self-attachment and Excitability. Or Miss Virginia might need Strength, which fact should have been evident to anyone in his senses. . . .

There was, last but not least among New Harmony's citizens, old Greenwood, a seeker after happiness, who might have been, however, more at home among the Rappite candidates for heaven than among the Owenites. New Harmony experienced, during its second summer, almost a deluge, such as would inspire the imagination to believe that the world might be destroyed by flood again. The Wabash champed like a lion in its cage. During one of frequent thunderstorms, when the whole sky was illuminated by a green light, Robert Dale looked out of the window, expecting nothing but a scene of desolation and the usual Fool of Nature. What did he behold but a vision, most strange, most mysterious? Old Greenwood, thoroughly drenched, was parading up and down, up and down, like a sentinel upon the rain-veiled streets, and obviously going nowhere in particular. He carried upright, as a soldier carries a musket, a slender iron rod, ten or twelve feet long—but where was the war? Over his head, the lightning scrawled zigzags on the sky, and all around him, trees fell—yet he was perfectly calm, perfectly self-possessed, at ease with nature. Robert Dale was puzzled by this display of exaggerated eccentricities. Perhaps old Greenwood had lost his power of reason, and that was why he did not have enough sense to come in out of the rain? Yet there was something even more compelling than the lack of sense—as if old Greenwood had determined on this strange course of action for some perfectly good reason.

Later, Robert Dale questioned old Greenwood—why had he not stayed indoors, why had he walked in the awful floods? Old Greenwood was by this time as dry as dust in a chimney corner, and as melancholy as a bat under the eaves. "Ah, well, young friend," he said, "I am very old. I am not well. I suffer much, and I thought it might be a chance to slip off, and be laid quietly in the corner of the orchard." He had simply not wished to take the responsibility of destroying himself, so had prayed that God would strike him dead. . . . "If God had only seen fit to do it," he concluded, "I'd have been at rest this very minute, all my pains gone, no more trouble to anyone, and no more burden to myself." Only death could now translate him to a better state than New Harmony, a city whose gates are of pearls as big as goose eggs, and where the old do not grow older, and where the lion lies down to sleep with the lamb.

The New Moral World had its day of Armageddon before there was time to harvest two crops—had crops been planted—but there was eventually a happy ending to the New Harmony story. After the exodus of the most inept or vicious of the Owenites; after Owen himself had returned to England—leaving his sons Robert Dale, William, David Dale and Richard to salvage what they could of their father's Indiana investment—New Harmony had its great day.

William Maclure, that mysterious Philadelphia millionaire patron of education and the sciences, had been persuaded by Robert Owen to finance the educational experiments in the community. He had brought out his old friend and companion Marie D. Fretageot and such other teachers of the sciences and the arts as Thomas Say, Charles Alexander Lesueur, Phiquepal d'Arusmont, Gerard Troost and Thomas Neef. He continued to pay their expenses after the disintegration of Owen's New Moral World and some of them, with the Owen sons, carried on some experiments in education, publishing, and the encouragement of the arts which were of great and lasting importance.

Then it was, from about 1828 to the middle 'fifties, that New Harmony had its day as a center of learning and culture—a day more productive than any other town of its size in America has ever experienced.

CHAPTER SEVEN

The Gaudy 'Fifties

Those were fancy years, the 'forties and 'fifties—a kind of intoxication with newly-discovered power in the first decade, and in the second a hell-for-breakfast fling while riding high before the inevitable bust.

Even the most God-fearing Americans went on a sort of reckless spiritual toot but, not having such facilities for sporting life in Indiana as were available, for instance, in New Orleans, they had to play extra hard at such pastimes as politics, waltzing, military drill and taking baths in patent tubs.

Few relish the flavor of that period more keenly than

THEODORE G. GRONERT

of the Wabash College faculty, who wrote the following sketch of

Hoosier Pioneer Society

By 1850 much of the rowdiness of an early period had disappeared. Rowdy elections, drinking, crimes of violence were still too common, but the older communities were feeling the civilizing influence of the missionary teacher and the sober business and professional men who were bent upon settling in permanent locations. Tavern gatherings were less boisterous and fist fights were replaced by shooting matches, the telling of tall stories, and impromptu singing. They sang sad ballads brought from the East or something like the more rollicking frontier-inspired, "Over the Hills in Legions, Boys." Sometimes there was a grimly humorous note in their song, when they sang:

> "Great western waste of bottom-land,
> Flat as a pancake, rich as grease;
> Where mosquitos are as big as toads,
> And toads are full as big as geese!
> Beautiful prairie, rich with grass
> Where buffaloes and snakes prevail;
> The first with hellish-looking face,
> The last with hellish-sounding tail."

But the prevailing note was one of optimism, of young men on the march, putting the faith that was in their hearts in their songs:

> "When we've wood and prairie land
> Won by our toil,
> We'll reign like kings in fairee land
> Lords of the soil."

These songs were still popular in Indiana at Civil War time, but a more settled way of life brought some of the refinements of the East. On the piano rack in the homes of the well-to-do, there were music folios including the words and music of "Old Folks at Home," "Annie Laurie," "O What Do the Birds Say," and "He Never Smiled Again."

Instrumental music included the waltz, the polka and the schottische. Young ladies of the Methodist, Baptist or Presbyterian persuasion were allowed to play the music but were denied the right to dance to these or any other tunes. The schottische was denounced as unusually wicked, because it was taught to Hungarian officers by gypsies and everyone old enough to have the right to express an opinion knew what they knew about gypsies and Hungarian officers. But despite the origins of the schottische and the opinions of elders some young ladies did go to dances. These affairs took the form of military balls, soirées or cotillions. At Crawfordsville, Wabash College students, even including some ministerial candidates, were known to surrender surreptitiously to the "embraces of Terpsichore." May we express the hope that they were never so completely hypnotized by the aforementioned Terpsichore as to engage in the Gavotte Cotillion as described by the Lafayette *Courier:*

"The ladies swing corners. Having done this, the gentlemen place their arms around their [the ladies] necks and kiss them on the left cheek. Young ladies shriek and fall into young gentlemen's arms. Gentlemen seize young ladies in their arms and waltz to their seats."

A decade earlier the description of a rather boisterous quadrille was more idiomatic and equally impressive as the caller sang:

> "Gents bow out and ladies bow under,
> Hug 'em tight and swing like thunder."

Those who avoided the temptations of dance music might find other means of satisfying their musical appetites. Serenaders sometimes disturbed the night air and thrilled some young lady by singing in an approximation of harmony and an excess of zeal "What Do the Birds Say," or "Come Where My Love Lies Dreaming."

There were plenty of other diversions for the Hoosier of the 'fifties. Traveling players gave thespian entertainment by presenting Shakespearean or contemporary dramas. A circus caravan, including the inevitable clown, two or three mangy animals and a few acrobats, made occasional visits to the frontier community. There were Panoramas, Lectures and Museums. One museum boasted a mermaid, and another announced a macabre exhibit in the form of "an illegitimate child, richly dressed"—but deceased. Barnum brought out Tom Thumb and other exhibits, which one editor denounced as a filthy display but others found elevating.

The "Feminine 'Fifties," as some commentator has called it, was still an age of repression for women. Indiana editors joined their brethren everywhere in excoriating Sarah Bloomer, Dr. Mary Walker and other articulate feminists. Woman's place was in the home where, endowed with a knowledge of the three R's and a proper sense of wifely duty, she could polish if not adorn the family hearth.

And the average women of the 'fifties had little time to give to the question of adornment. Western cities were but two decades removed from the frontier and their period, modern enough from their point in time, possessed few of our modern conveniences.

Obviously running water and the modern bathrooms were unknown to mid-Nineteenth-century Indiana—their absence creating very little hardship since all were equally deprived. Even the absence of the bathtub represented no serious deprivation, for as a matter of fact our frontier ancestors had little interest in bathing. For them it was a luxury, not a necessity. The Saturday night bath, if the family observed that function, was taken in the kitchen usually in a wash tub, sometimes in a special zinc contraption with an offset at the low water mark. The bather sat on the offset partially immersed in water and let his feet hunt for the soap in the off-shore depths. This bathtub, the lazy man's luxury, was threatened by the competition of such bathing machines as that advertised by Mick's General Store in the Crawfordsville *Review* of 1853.

The prospective purchaser was assured that bathing was expedient if not necessary, and this particular machine was a paragon of efficiency because "it only takes one bucket of water to supply it for any length of time. The water is poured into the lower part of the bath; the person bathing stands on a platform above the water, and by a slight movement of the body, throwing the weight alternately from one foot to the other, the water is forced up into the sprinkler from which it comes down on the bather with much force.—One bucket of water will answer every purpose—the same water being thrown over the bather in a constant current."

If this appeals to moderns as a rather qualified cleansing process, take heart from the fact that the user got his daily dozen in the same process and besides even one pail of water in constant circulation was better than no water at all. Apparently Mick's store sold a number of these machines; at least Mr. Mick reported satisfied customers.

Internal bathing so eloquently advertised in some of our popular weeklies was unknown—and any bathing of an internal nature was restricted to drinking water, occasional coffee or tea and more than occasional hard liquor. It was the day of free whiskey in the general store and eye openers and night-caps at home. Ladies drank much less than they do now—but the men saw to it that there was no troublesome surplus. Even the temperance addicts worshipped unwittingly at the shrine of Bacchus: witness the twilight zone between sweet and hard cider and the numberless chronic ailments that could be ameliorated, though fortunately never finally conquered, by double doses of Ayres Sarsaparilla or Hostetter's Bitters; alcoholic content 80 to 85 per cent.

It would be unfair to imply that the male of the 'fifties spent all his time in the vicinity of the grocer's whiskey barrel or the drug store counter. Young men attended military balls, cotillions or literary societies and their elders foregathered at lodges, stump speakings or what were elegantly termed "collations." When the gentlemen attended formal social functions they wore the dignified apparel of the period: tail coat and tight-fitting trousers of colored broadcloth, buff waist-coat, high black satin stock, a coat or cape draped about the shoulders, high hat of beaver—set off, when possible, by a gold headed cane. Women wore hoop skirts with ruffles and flounces. (If modern women wore as many clothes and discarded them as quickly as they do now, there would be no textile surplus.) They carried muffs and wore bonnets elaborately ornamented with flowers and other trimming. Laces and brocades were displayed by the fashionable. The merchants offered a variety of goods to intrigue and beguile the female from the paths of pioneer thrift. These goods included: "*Portsmouth Lawns, Berene de Laines, Ginghams, Black Silk, Swiss,* figured and plain, *Victoria Lawns,* figured and plain, *alpaca luster* of all kinds, *Cambric, Jaconett, mull, Muslins, bobinetts, edgings, insertions, bonnet ribbons, cape ribbons, silk fringes* and *laces.*"

The list of goods is elaborate enough to cause the reader to feel that even that age was not without its extravagances. But the list is more imposing to the eye than its component parts were, in practice, to the contemporary citizen. Ladies dressed in style only on rare occasions, and silks and brocades did duty for years instead of months. Dresses for ordinary wear were home-made, as were many home furnishings—such as carpets, hangings and quilts. Elaborate dress as well as eleborate manners were reserved for special occasions;

there was a homely simplicity about the everyday life of the ladies that had its own appeal.

And the men of the 'fifties could not have criticized the most elaborate female costume with a clear conscience, for this was the decade of the voluntary military company, who on occasion could out-dress Field Marshal Goering in all his glory. Indiana did not lag when it came to the "fuss and feathers" of military haberdashery. We instance the City Grays of Indianapolis who appointed a special committee on "trimmings": when their dress uniform was assembled it consisted of gray coat and pantaloons with black cloth trimmings corded with gold, and a bear-skin shako. The company in full dress resembled a convention of drum majors and at their appearance on parade "a general feeling of admiration fell from the lips of men, women and children."

The Lafayette Guards and Indianapolis Guards wore the regulation coat with white trousers as a dress uniform. Their most striking adornments were plumed hats, and the commander of the Lafayette company was especially fond of calling for a parade with "white pants and plumes." Probably the Lafayette Guards were pricked by the spur of rivalry for in addition to a gun squad, a Teutonic company and the Turners, that ambitious young city boasted of two volunteer fire companies. One had a name symbolic of incendiarism and rebellion, in *Kossuth*, but the other in becoming contrast modestly called itself, "The Good Intent Fire Company." Crawfordsville's first fire company and its Wabash Cadets furnished no real rivalry for Lew Wallace's Montgomery Guards, for by 1859 this latter company had adopted a Zouave uniform with red cap, blue jacket and "red breeches like meal bags gathered at the knees."

This attempt to out-dress Solomon in all his glory might have been in behalf of military efficiency and morale, but the weight of evidence inclines to a different conclusion. Dress parades were made over well-travelled streets in the hope that the brave might be viewed by the fair. When the men of the 'fifties dubbed General Scott "Old Fuss and Feathers," they were characterizing an epoch as well as an individual. Men may cherish a suppressed desire to imitate the lilies of the field, but only occasionally find sufficient excuse to gratify that desire. The volunteer military companies of the 'fifties afforded opportunities and the newspaper descriptions indicate that the members made the most of them.

The movement had its social as well as its athletic and patriotic features. After drill there was often a dance in honor "of the God of war and the Goddess of friskers." When a company from Lafayette visited the Crawfordsville Montgomery Guards, the members were entertained by a dinner and dance. They "had plenty to eat and drink, and all arrived home in good time this morning, and of course duly sober." Military encampments were never completely successful unless terminated by a great military ball which visiting companies patronized by sending "a large representation of their beauty and elite."

A Crawfordsville editor stood to bet his pile that Lew Wallace's Zouaves were the best drilled company in the state of Indiana. In this he had support from an Indianapolis observer at the 1860 encampment who praised the "Arab performance" of the Zouaves and proclaimed them "a little ahead of anything similar seen in *these parts*." A Lafayette editor was more impartial when he included all the companies participating in the Tippecanoe encampment of 1859, declaring that, "The military science displayed in the drills, parades and evolutions, is worthy of all praise."

The encampment at which these evolutions occurred was one of the outstanding events of the history of volunteer companies. In 1859, Lafayette, combining the appeal of the Tippecanoe Battleground with the interest in an Independence celebration, announced an inter-state military encampment. The youth of the city began preparations in the spring of 1859. A gun squad, (armament, one cannon) and a company of hussars were formed. Volunteers drilled six days a week, while the gun squad made as much noise as possible with the lone cannon, and the Teutonic Rifles secured a little taste of active service through a raid on a camp of thieving gypsies. Citizens raised money to aid the local companies and the newspapers promised that the fete would be "the most brilliant and pleasing ever held in the middle west."

Twelve military companies from Indiana, Ohio, Illinois and Kentucky attended the encampment. The railroads, in addition to giving reduced fares, had the train crews arrange decorations of flowers, flags and evergreens on the locomotive. All of which was done, according to the reporter, with "exquisite taste." The program alone occupied a column in the local paper. The afternoon and evening of July first was taken up with the reception of visiting companies by the Lafayette military and July second was given over to a trip to the Tippecanoe Battle-ground. July third was the Sabbath and the day was widely observed in Lafayette, representatives from various colleges of the state presiding at the meetings. The climax of the encampment came on July Fourth when the companies under general command of H. W. Ellsworth, famous Zouave commander from Chicago, with Lew Wallace second in command, performed before the crowds. The military evolutions were only incidental, however, for the poet laureate of the occasion recited an original poem lasting over one hour. Following this recital, the Honorable Thomas Corwin of Ohio, speaker of the day, announced that he was too ill to speak, after which he proceeded to edify his hearers for more than two hours. Then, to remind the audience that this was a military encampment, a Louisville company presented the intricacies of Zouave drill.

The climax of the celebration came with the great soirée and festival of Monday night where music was furnished by military bands and "a thousand burners reflected their radiance on the beauty and chivalry." Socially and oratorically the encampment was a complete success, but its military achievements were somewhat less evident. The story of this encampment as well as that of inter-city visits and dress parades indicate that the companies were much more interested in self expression than in efficiency. Drill was incidental to display, and no mimic war was complete unless there were crinolined ladies in the offing.

The record of the encampment might well serve as a summary of social conditions in 1859. Here we find a typical recreation of the post pioneer period with supplementary dancing, speech making, collations and full dress displays. Such military conventions were common throughout the country. Was it a vagary of the American of the period, subconsciously preparing for the cataclysm of Civil War, at the same time striving through a maze of words and social gaieties to forget the inevitable?

As must be evident by now, the overwhelming body of the writing about Indiana by Indianians is of the past in the state.

True, Hoosiers have enjoyed stories of the ancient doings of their ancestors since, in the very earliest of Indiana nights, they sat around the mud-daubed fireplaces in their first crude cabins and swapped yarns about gran'pap's hunting exploits in old Kaintuck' for others about how Uncle Eph whupped the regiment of Redcoats dam' near single-handed, time of the big war back in Car'liny. Early also, Indiana colleges began to stray from the classics occasionally to offer a course in American history and Indiana University was so fortunate as to have a faculty which did not feel that the offering of courses in American history for graduate study was beneath its dignity. (And you'd be surprised at the short period during which such courses have been available in most American universities!)

Whatever the reason for the popularity of Indiana history as a theme for Indiana writers, that popularity is an incontrovertible fact. Even the youngest crop of Indiana authors has been phenomenally successful in writing of the past, as witness the record of

ROSS LOCKRIDGE, JR.

who used a scene which looks remarkably like Henry County, peopled it with characters who are unquestionably Hoosier and saw them through a sizable stretch of the nineteenth century in his best-selling

Raintree County

July 4— —1854

BIG CROWD OF PEOPLE
HAD POURED INTO THE COURT HOUSE SQUARE

of Freehaven for the Fourth of July Celebration. Among them was Johnny Shawnessy, fifteen years old, bony and angular and beginning to bust out of his kneepants. His head looked too big for his body, his hair was a tangled mat of brightness, his cheeks and chin showed the beginnings of a beard and were sprinkled with little pimples. From a platform erected on the court house yard, a military band blasted out number after number, while the people came streaming from every corner of the County, into the foursided, sunflooded morning of the Square. There they walked with shining eyes, looking over their shoulders, craning their necks, bobbing out from behind buildings as if they were hunting for something.

Johnny Shawnessy was hunting for something too. Whenever he came to the Court House Square on festive days, he vaguely hoped for two things: that he would stand before the crowd a hero and be rocked with a thunder of hands; and that he would find in the crowd a lovely girl he had never seen before, who, perceiving at once his great soul through the callow veil of his fifteen years, would go with him to a place remote from the crowd, where she would take off her dress and all her petticoats for him, and he would be her impetuous lover, kneepants and all.

—Hello, Johnny.

The name was said in a manner softly personal. He turned around. A strange girl, half a head taller than he, was standing on the sidewalk with a boy he had never seen before.

—Nell!

Johnny hadn't seen Nell Gaither for years. When he was much smaller, he had gone to school with her and had seen her often at the Danwebster Church with her father and mother. Mrs. Gaither had been a fragile, lovely woman from a Connecticut family of means and culture. She had come with her husband in the great migration West, and they had settled in Raintree County in the late thirties to the hard existence of making a living from the earth. Nell had been the first child, and for a long time the only one. Johnny remembered how Nell had always seemed so much more ladylike than the other girls he knew, probably because of her mother's influence. Then when Nell was seven, Mrs. Gaither had died after the birth of a still-born child, and Mr. Gaither had sent the girl back to her mother's family in the East. And that was the last Johnny had heard of her until now.

—Where did you come from, Nell? he asked.

—I'm back with Daddy, Nell said. He's married again, you know,

and I'm going to live here for a while. O, by the way, Johnny, I
want you to meet a friend of mine, Garwood Jones.

Garwood Jones was a large, sleek, florid boy, perhaps a year older
than Johnny. He had a broad, smooth face, dark, wavy hair fragrant
with oil, and blue eyes filled with faint amusement. He thrust out
his hand and said in an incredibly big voice,

—Happy to make your acquaintance, John.

The greeting was both personal and patronizing.

—Pleased to meet you, Johnny said.

—What part of the County are you from, John?

Johnny told him, and the boy said that he used to live at Way-
cross in the southeast corner but that his family had long ago moved
to Freehaven.

—Garwood is speaking on the program today, Johnny, Nell said.

—Just a few patriotic recitations, the boy said with arrogant humility.

Johnny didn't dislike Garwood Jones, but he envied the smooth,
newly razored face, the deep voice, the long trousers, and the place
on the Program of the Day.

—How did you and Nell get to know each other? Johnny said.

—O, I get to know all the pretty girls, John, Garwood said.

He laughed a throaty laugh. The flat of his hand fell affectionately
between Johnny's shoulderblades.

In the old days, Johnny had never thought of Nell as especially
pretty. Now he looked at her a little more closely. The thin, serious
child was gone. Nell had her hair bound up like a woman's showing
her long white neck. A sort of small crazy hat teetered on her sun-
colored curls. Her face, which was rather small, was studiedly
serene, the chin held high, the unusual, fleshy mouth primly closed.
The very wide-apart green eyes, her most attractive feature, looked
calmly down at him a little sideways past her nose, which was pert
and covered with freckles. She had on a white shortsleeved dress. She
had the steep breasts of a budding girl and was getting somewhat
wide in the hips, although her waist was very slender and her arms
were long, angular, and childlike.

She stood, right hand on hip and left hand over right hand, dangling a parasol, while her left foot was toed out to show her new shoe.

Johnny thought she looked a little dowdy and ridiculous, but when she spoke, her voice was very husky, grave, and sweet. He noticed especially the soft, personal way in which she said his name, as if she had practiced it.

—I'll see you at church, Sunday, Johnny, she said.

The small lofty face smiled. Nell suddenly shot her parasol open. The interview was at an end.

—Well, John, Garwood Jones said, I trust I will have the pleasure of seeing you again.

He removed his straw hat and made a stately bow, and he and Nell walked away toward a lemonade stand. Johnny stood watching Nell walk, her hips softly moving as if revolving around a center, while her long, slender back and primly held shoulders were motionless.

—Hey, Johnny!

His brother Zeke was waving from in front of the Saloon. In the middle of a crowd there, a young man stood, white teeth flashing from a brown bearded face. In one hand he held a beermug, and with the other he kept pushing back the brown shag of his hair. His skintight pants showed off the hard length of his legs and the great breadth of his whiteshirted chest and shoulders. The young man laughed and said in a harsh, high voice, as Johnny approached.

—I can beat any man or boy in the County, and here's five dollars says I can.

He buried his white teeth in the mug and came up, mouth and beard shining. A gold coin glinted in his free hand. A hush fell on the crowd. Two men removed their hats, perhaps to see better. Johnny joined Zeke on the edges of the crowd.

—I said I can lick any man or boy in this County.

—And he can do it too, a solemn, sharpfaced man confided to Johnny. Just like he says, can't none of 'em touch 'im. Flash Perkins kin outrun 'em all.

From this remark, Johnny gathered that the talk was about the annual Fourth of July Footrace by which the fastest runner in Raintree County was determined.

—Our boy from Prairie Township'll make yuh eat them words this afternoon, a voice in the crowd said.

—Who said that? Flash Perkins said.

His forehead shot up into ridges, his mouth went on smiling, his eyes never changed from the childlike, excited look. He shoved his way into the crowd.

—Hot darn! Zeke said. A fight!

The crowd withdrew leaving one man alone in a ring of red faces. The man, a tall gawky fellow, looked embarrassed and put upon. He extended his arm, his finger almost touching Flash Perkins' nose.

—Take it easy now, brother, he said. Better not start nothin' you cain't finish.

His voice was high and nervous.

—You the man that said that? Flash Perkins asked.

—Yes, I am. I said it, and I stick by it.

—Reckon you wouldn't want to cover that there statement with a little coin?

The man looked relieved.

—I cain't cover it by myself, but they's a bunch of us from Prairie will make up a pot for Pud Foster.

—Git a hat, said a voice.

—Here's a hat, said a voice.

—Who's here'll back Pud Foster from Prairie?

—I'll put in, a man said. He can beat any beersot from town any day.

Several men shoved their way in and began to talk bets. There was a frightful blast of sound. It was the band starting up again. They were playing 'Yankee Doodle.'

—Shucks, Zeke said. No fight.

—But that sure ought to be some race, Johnny said.

—What's going on, boys?

It was T. D. He was taller than anyone else in the crowd. His blond pointed beard was bobbing up and down. He was rubbing his hands together and smacking his lips.

—They're betting on a race, Johnny said.

—That's what I thought, T. D. said.

He pushed his way into the crowd.

—Gambling is a sin before the Lord, gentlemen. Put up your money.

—Put up your lip, you old she-goat, a man said.

The crowd roared.

—Pa's gittin' hisself into something, Zeke said. Looks like they might be a fight after all, and us in it.

—No harm done, Pop, Flash Perkins said. Here, give the old guy a drink.

—Who is that crazy old bastard, anyway? the solemn, sharpfaced citizen said to Zeke.

—That's my pa, Zeke said.

Zeke was seventeen and looked a man. His red hair bristled all directions.

—What's that? the man said.

—I said that's my father.

—O, the man said. Is that a fact?

He looked thoughtful and began to move away through the crowd.

—Young man, T. D. said to Flash Perkins, who was holding his beermug in one hand and a hatful of money in the other, don't you know that your body is a temple of the spirit and you defile it and pollute it with that devil's brew you have there?

Flash's forehead made ridges.

—If you say so, Pappy.

—Hello, Johnny.

It was Ellen Shawnessy, her face excited and curious, her small body straining on tiptoes to see over the shoulders of the crowd.

—What's T. D. doing? she asked.

—Pa's preaching a little at them.

T. D. went on talking awhile about the lusts of the flesh and the wages of sin. He clasped his hands behind his back in the usual way and teetered back and forth from heels to toes, smiling amiably at the crowd, his long blue eyes a little absent and noticing things that went on some distance away. His closing remarks were delivered in some haste, like a child's recitation.

—What are they betting about? Ellen whispered to Johnny.

—The Footrace, Johnny said.

—When is it?

—I don't know.

—Be sure not to let me miss it, she said.

—O.K., O.K. Reverend, I get it, Flash Perkins said. We were just foolin'.

T. D. bowed pleasantly, straightened his tie, and walked serenely down the street with Ellen. The crowd went right on arguing and making bets, only now they all moved into the Saloon and got drinks. Johnny could see through the batwing doors how they laughed and swatted each other's backs and how they kept wiping beer out of their mustaches.

—I hope he loses that race, Zeke said.

But Johnny somehow felt that Flash Perkins would win the race. He looked like the winner type.

—Ladies and Gentlemen, spare me a little of your precious time, boomed a rich voice from the court house lawn.

Behind a table loaded with brightcolored bottles, stood a man with noble black mane and heavy beard, unshorn, lustrous, magnificent.

—I trust you all perceive the object which I hold in my hand, the man said, as the boys joined the crowd.

—Yes, we see it, Perfessor.

—What is it?

—Well, what of it?

—It is nothing, the man said, but a bottle, a simple, unadorned, ordinary bottle. And yet, friends, this simple, plain, unadorned, and ordinary bottle contains in it a secret preparation, the miracle-worker of our age. Ladies and Gentlemen, may I have just a little of your precious time to describe to you the extree-ordinary virtues of the elixir contained in this bottle?

—Sure. Go on.

—Get to the point, Perfessor.

—I am getting to the point, the man said serenely, and judging, my good sir, from the condition of *your* scalp and hair, you would be wise to pay special heed to what I have to say.

The man who had said, Get to the point, was standing right beside Johnny. He was a short man, genteelly dressed. Singled out, he put his hand up and smoothed a wreath of hair fitted down on his bare dome.

—Now then, the speaker continued, I trust you will all permit me to indulge in a little personal reminiscence. I am sure that few of you will believe me when I tell you that not many years ago my head was fast approaching the condition of hairlessness that you behold in the gentleman on the front row and in several other domes which I see about me here and which are, in the words of the poet,

> Open unto the fields and to the sky,
> All bright and glittering in the smokeless air.

Now I think we will agree that the good Lord never does anything without a purpose, and if he meant mankind to go about with his skull naked of hair, why did he bestow upon us this lush and luxuriant foliage that in our natural state starts and stands triumphantly, according to the words of the poet,

> With all its fronds in air?

Fellow Americans, the good Lord intended each and every one of us to have his hair and all of it too, for as the fellow said about his wife, She ain't much, but I mean to hang on to her if I can.

The crowd whahwhahed.

—Yes, Ladies and Gentlemen, I was once in the condition of several of you here. For about twenty years, my hair had been turning gray and had become very stiff and unpliant. Bald patches were appearing on my scalp, and the skin scaled off. Each time I brushed my hair, I found the brush matted with dry tufts of hair. I tried all the famous hair restoratives on the market, but they seemed to only aggravate my condition. Then a friend told me about Mrs. Allen's World Hair Restorer and reported to me the marvellous recoveries effected thereby. I will confess to you that I was very skeptical at first, but on the repeated importunities of my friend, I finally gave in and purchased a bottle of Mrs. Allen's World Hair Restorer. Ladies and Gentlemen, need I say more? Within a week or two, a noticeable change was apparent. My hair began to recover the black lustre it had in my younger days when a boy in the hills of western Virginia. My head became entirely clear of dandruff, and new hair grew where the old had been. You see before you today, Ladies and Gentlemen, a man whose pride and hair have been restored together and general health improved. Butler, my acquaintances often remark to me, where did you get the fine wig? But I assure you, friends, it is no wig.

—It looks like a wig to me, friend, the baldheaded man said.

—Pull it, friend, the vender said.

The baldheaded man walked right out of the crowd and carefully examined the speaker's head. He pulled hard.

—No sir, he said, that's no wig.

—You bet it isn't, the speaker said. It's hair, friend, live and lusty, and you can have a head like that too, friend.

—How can I, friend? said the baldheaded man, now standing beside the speaker.

—Very simple, friend. Purchase one bottle of Mrs. Allen's World Hair Restorer for one dollar and fifty cents, and I will personally guarantee that you will have the beginnings of a fine head of hair in a week or two.

—I'll take a bottle of that, the baldheaded man said.

He pulled out a dollar and a half and gave it to the speaker.

—And just to be sure that you get your money's worth, the speaker said, I am going to give away to you free, gratis, and for no extra charge this large bottle of Doctor Hostetter's Celebrated Stomach Waters, guaranteed to cure any and all diseases of the alimentary tract, nervous, respiratory, muscular, and circulatory systems—to wit, stomach ache, heartburn, dyspepsia, diarrhea, dysentery, dizziness, fainting spells, biliousness, piles, pimples, arthritis, lumbago, rheumatism, jaundice, kidney trouble, female complaints, and organic weaknesses caused by youthful indiscretion or the approach of old age. For the next ten minutes, to everyone who can get up here with a dollar and fifty cents, I will make this extra-special-gigantic-double-for-your-money offer of two bottles. Mrs. Allen's World Hair Restorer is also an excellent hair-dressing for the ladies.

—I'll take *two* orders, Perfessor, said the baldheaded man, who was still holding his money and had not yet got his hands on the bottle.

—Here you are, my friend, the man said.

He gave the baldheaded man four bottles and put the money in his pocket.

The baldheaded man opened a bottle of the hair-restorer, shot a little of the brown liquid into the cup of his hand, and rubbed it on his head. There was a silence. A hundred eager faces watched the little man with the shiny bald head.

—It tingles, said the baldheaded man.

—You bet it does, friend, the vender said. It tingles, and that means it's taking already. Use that bottle religiously, friend, and I predict the barbers of this community will get a lot of your money before the year is out.

—But he ain't from this community, a man next to Johnny said.

—Where's he from? another man said.

—I dunno, the first man said, but I never seen him before.

—And, said the vender, let me be the first to. congratulate you on the great discovery which you have just made. You wife will be a happy woman, friend.

—I'm not married, friend, said the baldheaded man.

—You will be, friend, you will be! said the vender magnificently. No woman in town will be able to resist you when you grow the shiny, black, and vigorous head of hair that will spring up in response to the stimulating power of this wonderful hair restorative.

Johnny Shawnessy felt happy because the baldheaded man had discovered the secret for getting back his hair; he was very happy, too, to see how people flocked up and bought bottle after bottle from the vender. He could not remember ever having seen so much money in so short a time.

—How can he make any money, giving that other bottle away? Johnny asked.

—I reckon he does it for fun, Zeke said. Look how he's enjoyed hisself.

—I wish I had a dollar and fifty cents, Johnny said. I'd like to get a couple of bottles.

—But you got all your hair, and you ain't sick, Zeke said.

—Just the same— Johnny said.

Just then the band struck up again, and the two boys moved reluctantly away. They watched the baldheaded man withdraw from the crowd. Moving along close to this person whose scalp now seemed to shine with the promise of reviving hair, they were a little surprised when he stopped at a small tent on the other side of the Square and went in. They waited, and in a moment, he came out again, carrying a large board frame, which he hung over a nail on a maple tree beside the tent. The frame bore a huge picture of a head, seen in profile and with all the upper part, beginning on a level with the eye, divided into sections, in each of which a word was written. Some of the words were Acquisitiveness, Alimentativeness, Amativeness, Cautiousness, Sublimity, Spirituality, Self-Esteem, Approbativeness. Above the picture were the words

PROFESSOR GLADSTONE, WORLD-RENOWNED PHRENOLOGIST

At the bottom were the words

KNOW THYSELF

The little man re-entered the tent and reappeared with a pointer, an armload of small clothbound books, and a cowbell, which he began to ring. A large crowd gathered.

—Allow me, said the baldheaded man, to introduce myself, Ladies and Gentlemen. I am Professor Horace Gladstone. Those of you who may have heard me lecture in the great city of Cincinnati will pardon me if I repeat some of the things I said there to the distinguished company which assembled in the great lecture hall of that metropolis of the West.

Now I have a question to ask each and every intelligent person gathered here. Friend, are you everything today that you would like to be? Are you as rich as you wish? Do you excel in the social graces? Do you radiate that personal magnetism which makes the great to respect you and the humble to acknowledge your superiority? Why, friends, *why* are there so many blighted and unhappy lives, so many stunted souls, so many men and women today in this great and glorious country of ours who are something less than they had hoped to be in the blithe optimism of their youth?

Ladies and Gentlemen, I can answer that question. It is through a simple ignorance of the scientific principles that regulate human life. O, you say, Perfessor, don't go giving me any high-falutin' language about science because I can't understand it. Friends, it is my happy good fortune to have it within my power to open up to each and every one of you all the marvellous secrets of a great new science, by which you can achieve, like thousands before you, complete self-knowledge and self-control. That science, Ladies and Gentlemen, is the great new science of Phrenology.

Now we all agree, do we not, that no man can or does exist in rational society without a brain. May I say that in Kentucky, whence I have lately come, I felt some disposition to modify that statement, but—

The Professor waited for the applause and laughter of the crowd to subside.

—But I see no need to do so for the intelligent and enlightened concourse that I see before my eyes. Now, we all know that the brain is the instrument of every mental act, just as every movement of the body has to be performed by a muscle. Certain areas of the brain control certain human faculties and are large or small in proportion to the development of the faculties they control. Thanks to the great experiments and studies of Professors Gall, Spurheiz, and Fowler, it is now possible to say with the strictest accuracy which part of the brain controls which faculty. These facts are now available to all. Nothing is simpler, once these principles are known, than to apply them.

I have myself become a specialist in the science of Phrenology. I have examined the heads of three Presidents and many other great and distinguished heads here and abroad, not excepting the crowned heads of Europe. By helping people to become better acquainted with their strong and weak points, I have been able to direct them to a fuller exercise or restraint of certain faculties. Many hundreds and thousands of people have already benefited from this instruction. Penniless paupers have become the possessors of uncounted pelf. Timid and backward souls have sought and won the hands of the richest and most ravishing maidens. Old men have recovered the lost joys of their juvenescence. Gentleman and Ladies, I am here in your fair little city of Middletown—

—This ain't Middletown, said a voice in the crowd. It's Freehaven.

—Freehaven, said the Professor. Thank you, friend, for the correction. I am here in this fair little city of Freehaven for a limited time. I have a small stock of books left over from my travels in the great cities of the West, and I should like to get rid of them as rapidly as I can. Now I wish I could give each and every one of you a private and personal analysis of your phrenological faculties. Alas, my friends, due to the small time I have at my disposal, I must forego this signal pleasure. But I have here between my two hands a little book that contains all the advice needful. It is perfectly within the comprehension of every one and each of you. On the inside page of this book is a copy of the chart which you see hanging here, and a table of the phrenological faculties. Now the book is entirely self-explanatory, but I am willing to give a little demonstration here of Phrenological Analysis, if someone in the crowd will be so kind as to volunteer.

There was a silence.

—Come, don't be embarrassed, the Professor said. It's absolutely free of charge, and furthermore I will give to anyone who so volunteers for the instruction of this amiable and enlightened company one of these books at half-price instead of the usual price of one dollar and fifty cents.

Johnny Shawnessy felt himself propelled from behind out of the crowd. He heard Zeke laughing, and he was about to duck back, but the Professor was tapping him smartly on the shoulder with his pointer.

—Yes, my boy. Step right up here. I am about to do you a great favor, my boy. O, that I had had the inestimable blessing of a Phrenological Analysis when I was your age! How old are you, my boy?

—Fifteen, Johnny said. I didn't mean to—

—Perfectly all right, my boy. Just come up on this platform and sit down here on the edge of this table.

A firecracker exploded, and the band struck up a number. The Professor waved his hands to indicate that nothing could be accomplished until the band was through. For the first time in his life, Johnny had the sensation of being extracted from the crowd and placed above it in naked isolation. The Court House Square was converging upon him; he was being absorbed by its manifold bright eyes. The band stopped playing.

—Ladies and Gentlemen, said the little man, we have an interesting head here, a very interesting head. To you, this may be only another head, more or less, but to the practiced eye of the phrenologist, this boy's character and potentialities—nay, his whole past, present, and future—are legible in the geography of his skull. Now, then, just cast your eyes on this chart a moment, friends, and notice this section of the head below the eye.

The pointer touched the glazed, segmented head and underlined the word LANGUAGE.

—According to phrenological principles, friends, we are to measure the degree of prominence which these various areas of the skull possess and we can determine thereby the capabilities of the person we are dealing with. Now then—

A fat hand touched moistly the region below Johnny's eyes.

—Open your eyes, boy. Don't sit there blinking like an owl.

As usual the sun hurt his eyes; there was much light in the Square.

—Extraordinary, the man said. Very.

The crowd drew closer. People gathered from far back.

—Very, very interesting. Please observe, folks. Very long eyes and set somewhat forward in the head. Cheekbones prominent. In a boy of fifteen, the development is quite unusual. Now, then, let us turn to the book.

The man expertly thumbed the book.

—Here we are. 'Such people are (I quote) exceedingly expressive in all they say and do, have a most expressive countenance, eye, and manner in everything, and thoroughly impress the various operations of their own minds on the minds of others; use the very word required by the occasion; are intuitively grammatical, even without study, and say oratorically whatever they attempt to say at all; commit to memory by reading or hearing once or twice; learn languages with remarkable facility; are both fluent and copious, even redundant and verbose,' and so forth, and so forth.

There was a stir in the crowd.

—Here, the man said, are pictures illustrating these developments.

An engraving of the great English author Charles Dickens, whose linguistic characteristics are excessively developed.

—Say, Perfessor, Zeke said from the crowd, you ain't fer wrong about that boy. He's got a head for memorizing like nothin' you ever seen.

—There you are, the little bald man said, Phrenology never lies. And I was about to say that even if the boy hadn't shown any faculty in that direction, it was high time he cultivated his natural aptitude for it. But to pass on.

The Professor went all over Johnny's head, pointing out interesting hills and hollows and putting numbers in a chart that was in the front of one of the books. Finally, the Professor had worked clear over the top of Johnny's head and down to the base of his skull behind.

—Mirthfulness, the Professor said. Very large. This boy ought to be the fiddle of the company.

—Ain't that T. D. Shawnessy's son? a man said.

—Smart little cuss, someone said.

—What a cute boy! a woman said.

The band blew up; it was another march. Everyone began talking very loud and strong. People were laughing violently. Somebody set off a firecracker under a fat man in the crowd and blew his hat off. A horse got scared and began dragging a buggy down the street. The band finished its number, and by that time the Professor had made another discovery.

—Very remarkable! the Professor said in a loud voice. For a boy of his age too. Most extree-ordinary! Unusual, to say the least.

—What is it, Perfessor?

The crowd was now participating freely in the examination.

—Let us in on it, too, Perfessor.

—Has he got lice?

—Ladies and Gentlemen, the Professor said, please observe the remarkable development of this boy's head at the base of the skull. The lump of AMATIVENESS is remarkably distended.

—What does that mean, Perfessor?

—What does that mean, friend? To put it bluntly, this young gentleman is going to be an extra-special catch for the ladies.

The Professor winked and rubbed his hands jovially together. People in the crowd sniggered. Various men felt the back of their skulls.

—Hey, girls, Zeke said, I got a lump back there big as a duck's egg.

—Say, Perfessor, said a little man thrusting forward, and presenting his head for inspection. Feel that there. What do you think of that?

With obliging hand the Professor palped the back of the little man's skull and whistled.

—Hey, Perfessor, how about me? another man said. Feel that.

—Now, wait a minute, folks, the Professor said, suddenly walking back to the platform and grabbing an armload of books. Much as I would like to, I can't subject each and all of you to a personal scrutiny, but this book here will answer all your questions. For those whose various organs and faculties are underdeveloped, rules for enlargement are given. Know thyself, said the great philosopher Socrates to the Athenians in the Golden Age of Greece. And I say to you, Know thyself, fellow Americans, in this great age of Progress and Perfection, in this greatest and fairest republic the world has ever known. God bless her on the day of her birth and glorious founding! One dollar, folks, just one round dollar—reduced from a dollar and a half!

As if by prearrangement, the band exploded with 'Hail, Columbia! Happy Land!' and with moisture in his eyes, the Professor began to distribute books as fast as he could, at the same time dropping dollars into a box on the table. Johnny sat for a while watching from the platform how the people all rushed up and pulled dollars out of their pockets, rudely grabbing for books in their haste.

—While they last! While they last! the Professor said. One dollar, friends, while they last! One hundred and fifty-four illustrations. *Phrenological Self-Instructor.*

People who hadn't even heard what the Professor said fought their way through and bought a book. The pile was almost gone, and Johnny Shawnessy began to feel alarmed.

—Know thyself! Know thyself! One dollar. While they last.

The pile was gone.

—One moment, folks, the Professor said. I have a small reserve supply that I had hoped to save for sale in the great city of St. Louis.

He disappeared in the tent and reappeared immediately with another armload of books. When the last sale had been made, there were still some books left. Johnny went up to the man and put down seventy-five cents.

—It's a dollar, my friend, the Professor said.

—But you said I could have it half-price. Half of a dollar and a half is—

—Unusual development of the bumps of Calculation and Eventuality, the Professor said.

He laughed at his own good joke.

—Here's your book, boy, all marked. You've a good head on your shoulders there, son. What is your name, my boy?

Johnny told him, and the Professor took a pencil from his coat pocket and on the title page where it said THE CHART AND CHARACTER OF he wrote on blank lines provided for the purpose:

John Wickliff Shawnessy

As Marked By

Professor Horace Gladstone,
July 4, 1854

—I predict a great future for you, my boy, the Professor said, tossing the three quarters deftly into the air.

He bit the tip off a cigar.

—Smoke?

—No, thanks, sir.

—Never start it, said the Professor. Filthy habit. Yes, a great future, my boy. Tell me, son, is there a place around here where one can obtain a little liquid refreshment for the stimulation of a jaded physique?

—The Saloon is right over there.

—Good day, boy, the Professor said and walked off briskly, landing smartly on his heels, his toes turned slightly up and out.

—Ladies and Gentlemen, said at that moment a rich, oily voice from the other side of the Square, spare me a little of your precious—

Johnny walked away holding the little book in his hand. For a few bright coins, dropped in a wooden cigar box, a future of wonderful self-mastery had been opened up. In the presence of the people he had become a child of prophecy; his consecration had been sanctified by the majestic adjective 'scientific' and the formidable epithet 'phrenological.' Here, suddenly and by accident on the Court House Square, there had been a confirmation of something Johnny Shawnessy had always secretly believed—that he was destined to be a great man and to find one day the key to all knowledge. For a while, he felt jealous of all the other people who had purchased the same cheap ticket to intellectual beatitude, but when he saw the innocent, shy joy on their faces, as they wandered somewhat confusedly like himself in the Court House Square, clutching their *Self-Instructors*, he was thrilled to think that he was to be one of a whole community of Americans working together toward the creation of a perfect republic.

He didn't have time to look over the book at all, because the Program for the Day was beginning. He and Zeke went over and found seats in a big space in the assembly ground south of the Court House, and all the people sat and listened to a man read the Declaration of Independence. Then the chairman of the program introduced the outstanding boy orator Garwood Jones. Talking in a thundering, artificial way and waving his arms, Garwood brought the crowd down with gems of American oratory, including the peroration of Webster's Reply to Hayne.

Wearing his Mexican War uniform and all his medals, Captain Jake Jackson, Raintree County's war hero, got up and gave a very dramatic speech about the security of the Nation. He was a virile young man, of open, fearless countenance. He stood very straight with one leg slightly forward and spoke with chest expanded. He said that the Union was threatened from within and without, but he reminded his hearers that the last bunch who tangled with the sovereign authority of the United States of America had got one devil of a drubbing, in which he, Jake Jackson, had taken, as they knew, a humble part. And he was there to say that although he was a man who loved peace, he, Jacob J. Jackson, would personally Gird on the Sword and once more Bare his Patriot Breast to the Sleet of Battle ere he would permit one corner of the Dear Old Flag to be Dragged in the Dirt. Johnny applauded violently and was angry when an older man close by said he was getting goddam tired of young Jackson's heroics and fuh Christ's sake, did he think he fought the Mexican War singlehanded?

The Honorable Somebody or Other was introduced for the Address of the Day. He spoke for two hours, beginning in the usual vein but getting louder, hoarser, and more eloquent all the time as he talked about slavery and the South.

In those days everyone was excited about the Kansas-Nebraska Bill. The word had come through only a day or so before that Congress had made the bill a law. Johnny wasn't exactly certain what the bill said, but it appeared that land once saved for freedom was going to be opened up for slavery. The Orator of the Day made it out so that you thought of a poisonous black flood boiling up out of the South, and here were people trying to build walls against it, and then one of the people—and a Northerner to boot—Stephen A. Douglas, had gone yellow on them, and let the flood come through, and now there was nothing to stop it anywhere.

Those days, there was a strange spirit abroad in the land. It was not uncommon for families to stop talking to each other over political questions. T. D., who was always fighting some kind of evil or other, talked with a singular fierceness about certain people who were perfectly willing that part of the human race should be in chains, if it meant a few more dollars in *their* pockets or if they didn't have to see it happen under *their* noses. The problem was spatial, geographical—like Phrenology. In a section of the country below a certain line people kept slaves. You could draw a line across the Nation, and half of it was white and half was black. And now that they had passed the Kansas-Nebraska Bill, it was all right for the black part to go over into the white part if it could.

The man on the platform said that that was exactly what would happen.

—Fellow Americans, he said, I am addressing you in one of the darkest hours that has confronted our great republic since those glorious days when Washington was nursing the tiny flickering flame of our freedom in a tattered tent in the windy wilderness of Valley Forge. It is a time when, if necessary, a man should put aside wife and child, leave the hearth of his home, and go resolutely forth to do battle for the preservation of those great principles upon which this republic was founded and which we have just heard read to us from that immortal document, the Declaration of Independence.

—Let them alone, and they'll leave us alone, shouted a voice from the crowd.

—Throw that guy out! yelled other voices.

—It is a time, said the speaker, to gird on armor and the sword. Our most pious blessing and our most fervent hopes must go with those courageous spirits who are at this moment giving up all they have to rush into the newly opened territories of Kansas and Nebraska to insure that when those territories are petitioning for membership in the Union of the States, no shadow of that cursed blight whose ancient crime has stained the otherwise perfect beauty of our institutions shall sully the virginal banners of their statehood.

The orator went on and on, and the afternoon waned, and when he finished, the formal program was over. But men kept on making speeches. One of them said that he was just passing through on his way to Jackson, Michigan, where a gathering of publichearted citizens was going to talk very seriously about the growing threat to our free institutions and consider the feasibility of creating a new political party. Another man got up and said that the existing Whig party was adequate to meet the threat to the security of the Nation, but he was booed and heckled by Democrats all the way through. A Democrat who succeeded him could not get halfway through his speech and became so angry that he leaped off the platform and got into a fight with one of his persecutors.

Johnny and Zeke rushed over to the neighborhood of the disturbance, and the crowd stormed and shouted. Johnny got lost from Zeke and never did get close enough to see the fight, but he saw some people leading off a man with a bloody mouth, who was weeping and shaking his fist and yelling.

—I'll beat his goddam head off, goddamn him!

Johnny finally found Zeke, who showed where his knuckles were skinned and said earnestly,

—I just got that there from beating up on a damn Democrat.

Later they saw T. D. standing in the middle of a group of men, including the man who was on his way to Jackson, Michigan.

—Friends, the man was saying, I am not just using a figure of speech when I say to you that here in the North we are going to all hang together or hang separately. The South has opened this question up, and they mean to keep it open. It has become a sectional issue. Men, there will be bloodshed before this thing is over.

—God forbid! T. D. said. Personally, I take a hopeful view of the situation. I don't think it will ever come to that. Americans will never fight one another.

—Pardon me, my friend, said the man, a sober white-faced person in a tailcoat and a high black hat. But I'm afraid you take too bright a view of the whole thing. They're fighting now in Kansas, and the whole nation will be at war unless something is done to keep the hotheads of the South in check. It's getting to be all or nothing with them.

—Personally, said another man, whose face was working with anger, I think we'll just have to go down there and beat the hell out of 'em.

—That's just what they're saying about us, the man said. How long do you think we can exist as a nation, pulling two separate ways and fighting over the new territory? Something has got into the life-blood of the Nation. It's a poison, and a black one, and it has diseased the whole body politic. What it will come to I don't know, but I see dark days ahead.

—Say what you will, T. D. said, speaking calmly and brightly, but Americans will never fight each other. We will resolve our difficulties peacefully.

—I hope so, friend, said the man in the top hat. But what will you do if the South prefers to secede from the Union rather than submit to laws that don't protect her peculiar institution?

—They may talk of it, T. D. said, but they will never do it.

Johnny agreed with his father. It really didn't seem possible that a part of the country could separate and not be a part of the country.

How could that be? Could an amputated leg grow a new body? T. D. was right. Yes, it was all only words spoken in the Court House Square. None of those words seemed so important as the word 'Phrenology,' which provided a clearcut, scientific route to individual and social perfection. He was hoping to get an opportunity to read his *Self-Instructor* and see what all the words meant that were parts of his head, but the next thing he knew, Zeke ran up, yelling,

—The race is starting!

Naked to the waist and barefooted, Flash Perkins stood in the middle of a crowd at a street intersection one block from the Square.

—What do you think this is, Flash — a prize fight? someone yelled as the two boys came up.

For answer, Flash struck a pose, balled fists up. The muscles of his cocked arms bulged circularly. The afternoon bathed his body with a young radiance. He seemed stronger and more real than anything else in the exploding vortex of the Fourth of July.

—God, don't he think he's some punkins! said a man next to Johnny.

—Struttin' aroun' like a damn bull on show, said another man. I hope to hell he gets beat and beat proper.

—Pud Foster'll beat 'im, damn 'im, said the first man. They say this here Perkins has been drinkin' his guts full all day and can't hardly walk.

—Seems to me he walks all right, the first man said.

—Yeh, but can he run?

—If he's drunk, maybe it'd be smart to take some of his money, said the first man.

—Damn right it would be!

It got around the crowd that Perkins was filled to the ears and could hardly stand, and a lot of men began to take some of the Perkins money.

Meanwhile Flash Perkins had gone over to a nearby buggy and then back to the starting line. His hairline jumped up each time he smiled. His eyes, full of drunkenness and goodnatured insolence, had never lost the childlike, excited look.

—They's a young lady over here, he said, wants to bet somebody five dollars a certain galoot name of Orville Perkins, better known as

Flash, will win this here race. Person'ly, I respect the sex too much
to doubt this young lady's opinion, and I'll add another five dollars
to her bet and bet anybody here that I can beat any man in Raintree County—or anywhere else, by God!—and let's see the color
of his coin.

—Christ amighty! he's drunk! the first man said.

A rather dowdy girl in the buggy fanned herself vigorously.

—It must be her, that one over there, Zeke said. She's some
looker.

—I'll bet he gets her regular, a man in the crowd said.

Those days, there was always someone in the crowd who took a
cynical view of things.

All of a sudden a man walked into the street with a pistol in his
hand.

—Ladies and Gentlemen, he yelled, the Annual Fourth of July
Footrace is ready to start. The contestants are . . .

The runners lined up, the crowd began pushing out of the street,
the starter's pistol went off, and everyone yelled and pushed and
shoved down toward the Square where the race was to end. Johnny
got a passing glimpse of Flash Perkins, white teeth bared, fists
churning, far ahead of his competitors as he ran toward a distant
string.

There was a vast yelling in the Court House Square, and several
cannon crackers blew up simultaneously. The band played 'Hail to
the Chief.'

When Johnny and Zeke got to the Square, they saw Flash Perkins on the shoulders of a throng. He was borne toward a platform
where a girl sat holding a ring of oakleaves. Bare to the waist, sweating, magnificent, he accepted the circlet of victory and fitted it down
over his tangled hair. His teeth were clenched on an unlit cigar.

—Speech! yelled the crowd.

—It was easy, folks, Flash said. They give me a good race, but
like I said, I can beat any man in Raintree County. . . .

That night there was a fireworks display on the court house yard.
Rockets rose over the dark town, burst into sparks, and went down,
feebly flaming, in distant fields. Some exhibition pieces were hung
on trees, and the climax of the whole day came with a contraption

called 'The Glorious Union.' It was supposed to burn like a lot of stars and stripes in the shape of a shield, but it fizzled at first.

—It ain't goin' to go, everyone said.

Then it did go after all; in fact it caught on fire and blew up all at once with a terrific bang.

As they drove home that night, Johnny told T. D. about the book on Phrenology.

—What do you think about it, Pa? Is it any good?

—Sounds scientific, T. D. said. I seen the man giving you a going-over. Of course, it might of been a fraud. You shouldn't of spent all that money for it, John. You could of looked at someone else's book.

Bob, the oldest boy, said he heard a fellow say that the phrenology man and the vender of hair tonic had both been at Middletown just a day or two before and that they had put on the same act they did in Freehaven. The baldheaded man had pretended to buy hair tonic from the vender just the same way, and they made the same remarks, and the baldheaded man was just as bald now as he was then, no more and no less. Johnny was a little disturbed at this, but T. D. took a serene view of the matter.

—Probably just a story, he said. Why would anybody want to do that? Besides, he was practically giving those bottles away at that price. I have spent my life studying the beneficent effects of botanical medicines, and the ingredients in those bottles sounded good.

T. D. talked a good deal about the condition of the country.

—This here new party they plan to form up there in Michigan may be just what we need, he said. I've voted the Whig ticket faithful for twenty-five years, but it seems to me we need stronger stuff now. If they can just get some big man to head the new party up, some-one, say, like John C. Frémont, who is, in my opinion, the Greatest Living American, why, we might bring the country right out of the fix it's in.

—Things will work out all right, Ellen said.

Johnny Shawnessy looked up at the purple night thicksown with stars that brooded warm and yellow over Raintree County. Yes, things would work out all right. He closed his eyes and seemed to see, ascending in a starless night, the thin, bright streaks of rockets. So would the years go speeding through the purple night of time and bring him all good things before they dropped, feebly flaming, in the distant meadows of the future. So would he too some day know fame and fortune and a great love, and the people in the Court House Square would cheer him. Time and the secret earth of Raintree County would bring all good fruits to him who knew the secret. One day, he would be the fastest runner in Raintree County, because he willed it to be so. One day he would stand with breast expanded, bright with medals, and the crowds would cheer the savior of the Nation. One day he would have the lucid self-understanding that would enable him to say and do everything that he desired, and he would become greater than Charles Dickens or Thomas Carlyle or even William Shakespeare, and he would speak and write words that would resound along the corridors of time forever. And the Court House Square would give place to a more spacious arena, there would be domed tremendous buildings, steps ascending, a platform bigger than was ever seen in Freehaven. And a tall monument would pierce the sky, erected in his memory. All things could be accomplished by him who had the key, who knew the secret, who could pronounce the talismanic word. And in that shining future, he would stand among the greathearted citizens of a perfect America, their heads would be bright with lush and streaming locks, they would all be superbly phrenological in the greatest republic the world had ever seen. And somewhere too in that golden day a vaguely beautiful girl was waiting, her bright hair streamed on delicate shoulders and steep breasts, and on her fruity lips was the highly personal and softly uttered word 'Johnny.'

When they went to get out of the wagon at the Home Place, Johnny knocked something over.

—Careful there, John, T. D. said. Here, let me have that stuff. It was a couple of bottles of

MRS. ALLEN'S WORLD HAIR RESTORER AND
DR. HOSTETTER'S CELEBRATED
STOMACH WATERS

Through the 'fifties the slavery question grew steadily more serious. The value of slaves who fled north over the Ohio to freedom

mounted to hundreds of thousands of dollars a year. Mrs. Harriet Beecher Stowe, living at Cincinnati just across the Indiana-Ohio line, gathered notes on what she saw—or thought she saw—among the slaveholders of Kentucky and what she heard from escaped slaves who were aided by her father, her husband and their friends. Cincinnati was by no means as yet unanimous in its anti-slavery sentiments and Mrs. Stowe's group was sometimes pelted with manure and other convenient missiles as it passed along the public streets, but Mrs. Stowe wrote a book from her notes and when it came out the Abolition movement won a good many recruits from among its readers.

The activities of Abolitionists in aiding slaves to escape from the South by way of the "Underground Railroad" had been established for some time. The "Railroad" operators, though they were often leaders in their communities, were not always highly regarded by their neighbors, even by some of those who had the strongest feelings about the injustice of slave-holding as an institution. This attitude was justified: if it was wrong in the eyes of the Lord to hold human beings in bondage it was equally wrong, in His eyes, to steal valuable property (and Kentucky slaves brought a high price in the 'fifties), to lie, to commit mayhem and murder—all of which the operators of the Railroad sometimes found expedient.

These workers and their methods were, then, not generally viewed with high regard—until after 1850; in that year came one of those great and futile compromises with which United States history is so frequently marked. It was the Fugitive Slave Law which encouraged no-account seekers after the easy dollar to take up the business of recovering runaway slaves, and any Negro they could catch, runaway or freedman, was easy prey. A book by

WILLIAM MONROE COCKRUM

reports an episode of the kind which caused the Underground Railroad to gain respectability in the eyes of the public:

History of the Underground Railroad

THE FUGITIVE SLAVE LAW OF 1850 was so sweeping in its many provisions that every negro found in a free state was likely to be kidnapped, taken out of his neighborhood, and before a commissioner friendly to slavery, put on trial as a fugitive slave, some man in a slave state being named as his owner. The testimony of the kidnapper was all the evidence given, as the negro was not allowed to give testimony any more than a cow would be. The kidnappers became so arrogant and boastful that it was very trying to the people who believed in justice. I well remember them with their whips, handcuffs, and ropes tied to their saddles, and their pistols belted around them. . . .

DR. JOHN W. POSEY AND REV. ELDRIDGE HOPKINS RELEASING KIDNAPPED NEGROES

Along in the early part of the fifties two free negro men who lived in northern Kentucky, not far from Rockport, Indiana, had been working on the Wabash and Erie canal between Washington and Terre Haute for some time, had determined to go to their homes and had got as far as Washington on their way there when they fell in with a man who seemed very friendly . . . asking them where they were going. . . . He told them that he and a friend of his were going in the same direction nearly to the Ohio river in a wagon and that if they wanted to they could go with them . . . but that they would not be ready to start before three or four in the afternoon. . . .

They took the Petersburg road and it was late in the evening when they crossed the White river at the ferry. Mr. John Stucky, who crossed at the same time, knew one of the white men and at once suspected what he was up to but could not draw him into a conversation and could not get a chance to talk to the colored men as he had hold of his horse. He heard them tell the ferryman that they would stay all night in a wagon yard in Petersburg. After they were over, the wagon traveled pretty fast. Mr. Stucky did not keep up with it and reached Petersburg some time after it had put up at the wagon yard. Stucky hunted up Dr. John W. Posey . . . and told him about the white men and negroes that were stopping at the wagon yard. The doctor at once understood the situation and sent a spy to the wagon yard to see what he could find out. The spy soon reported that he found them eating supper and that a noted hotel keeper was some distance away engaged in a conversation with one of the men.

He talked with the negroes, who said that their homes were in Kentucky and that these men were letting them ride in the wagon most of the way. They had no evidence but the doctor resolved to have a watch kept and have the wagon followed up to see what developments might come. About two hours before day the guard who had been on watch came hurriedly to the doctor's home and told him they were ready to start and had their team hitched to a three seated express wagon and that the hotel man was with them and two other fellows whom he did not know. The doctor had three horses saddled and sent for a neighbor to ride one of them . . . one of his hired hands rode another and the doctor the third one. All three were armed. They sent the guard back to watch and report but the express and men had gone. Dr. Posey and the other men hurried on after them on the Winslow road but did not overtake them as they had passed through Winslow a little after sunrise and thirty minutes ahead of the pursuing party. They followed on after them meeting a man about two miles south of Winslow who said he had met the express about one mile south of where they were and that they had two runaway negroes tied together. As there were only three of them and four of the kidnappers and it was supposed that men on such a business would go well armed, they did not feel as if they had an equal chance, but they knew that justice was on their side so they resolved to follow on and when they stopped they would find some one legally qualified to try the case and liberate the poor negroes.

About this time they met Rev. Eldridge Hopkins who told them that he passed the express but a short mile south of where they were and they inquired of him if he could tell them where there was a spring as they wanted to eat an early dinner and feed their horses as they were getting fatigued. Hopkins thought nothing of it as men with runaway negroes were a common occurrence in those days. Dr. Posey told Rev. Hopkins, with whom he was well acquainted, the situation and Hopkins, who was in favor of justice and was good grit all the way through, offered to pilot them around the men if they stopped to feed so that they would be in front of them and could go to a Justice of the Peace on the road a few miles ahead and have papers prepared to stop them and release the negroes.

Coming to the road at the point Hopkins intended, they found that the express had not passed, but they learned that the squire they wanted was away from home and before they could find a legal light who could give them the right to stop the kidnappers they got into Warrick county, where a writ was secured. When the express came up a constable halted them and marched them into a Justice's court. At first the kidnappers were disposed to threaten but by this time a number of men had gathered around in front of them. These fellows were completely nonplussed by the action of Dr. Posey. The two negroes were brought into court and told their story. Dr. Posey retold what the colored men told his man the night before while one of the white men was eating supper with them. The crowd was very much in sympathy with the two unfortunates.

The man who claimed to own them showed a hand bill giving a perfect description of the two men and offering a reward of two hundred dollars for their recapture dated at a point in Tennessee some weeks before. This hand bill was no doubt printed at Washington the day before, while these negroes were waiting for their new found friends. Things now began to look pretty bad for the poor negroes. Hopkins was a ready talker and he volunteered to defend them and made a telling speech in which he had the sympathy of all not interested. The old Justice was against the negroes and he decided that they were nearly all slaves and those who claimed their homes in a slave state were all slaves and whereas their owner had produced a notice of them that had a perfect description and dated several weeks before he would let him (the supposed owner) go with his property.

This infuriated Hopkins and he told Dr. Posey that he would see that the men did not get over the Ohio river with the negroes. While Mr. Hopkins and Dr. Posey were having a consultation, Mr. Hopkins discovered that he had his foot on the hub of a wheel of the express the kidnappers had come in and saw that the wheels were held on with linchpins and that he could easily get one of them out, which he did and put it in his pocket. It was decided that it was best for the doctor and his two men to return home. Hopkins said that in that crowd he could find all the men he wanted to go with him on the raid so having chosen them they secured arms and were soon on the go.

Starting off in an easterly direction . . . to the Boonville road they found that the express had not passed. They took powder and made themselves as black as Nubians; no one would have recognized them. Mr. Hopkins thought that the express might get some distance before the wheel would come off.

They waited for a time but finally started up the road and saw the express with one wheel off about one mile south of where the old squire lived. When they got close to the express they rushed up hurriedly and demanded to know what they had the negroes tied for. The negroes told them that they were kidnapped. The rescuing party leveled their guns at the three white men and made them hold up their hands. One of them had gone back to look for the linchpin. The negroes were untied and the white men searched for guns. They found three old pepper box revolvers of a pattern of that date and several knives. They also found a fine rifle in the bottom of the express. The negroes were made to tie the three men and they all sat down out of sight until the fourth man came back when he was also tied. They then organized a stump court martial to try the kidnappers.

The negroes first told their story as has been above related. The four men were told that they, one at a time could tell their side of the case. The would-be owner produced the hand bills that Dr. Posey told Mr. Hopkins were made in Washington. Mr. Hopkins who was the leading spokesman told them that this was the case and said that that was the worst feature in it.

The court after hearing all the evidence decided that all four of them should die, for such villainy was a menace to good order and the peace of society but told them that any one of them who would tell the whole truth should live. At this one of the men commenced to weaken when the leader told him to remember the oath he took when he was hired and the penalty if he violated that obligation. At this Hopkins took the fellow who seemed ready to tell something away from the rest and where they could not hear and told him that if he would tell the whole truth that his life would be spared. On this assurance he told all he knew. He said that the pretended owner lived at Washington, Indiana, and that it was intended to carry the negroes to Mississippi country and sell them. He also said that they had agreed to pay him and another man whom they hired at Petersburg, one hundred dollars each to go with them and watch the two negroes until they were sold; and that the team belonged to the leader who pretended to own the negroes.

Mr. Hopkins took the man back to the party and put the negroes guard over them. He then re-assembled the court martial and they held another consultation after which he told the white prisoners that they deserved to die for such villainy but they . . . had decided not to kill them, but intended to give them an object lesson they would remember all the rest of their lives.

Hopkins took the leader and the two negroes out in the woods some distance west of the road, cut two good-sized hickory gads and told the negroes to give him twenty-five hard lashes each which they did with a will. They untied the fellow, who was evidently well whipped and told him to go in a north-west direction and not to stop or look back. Then he took the other man from Washington and two negroes to the east side of the road, cut two gads, gave him fifty lashes, untied him and told him to go to the north-east and not to stop or look back under penalty of being shot. The two men who had been hired they gave ten lashes each and then turned them loose toward Evansville. Mr. Hopkins and his party held a final conference and then had the negroes put the wheel on having given them the linchpin. They decided to turn the team over to the two negroes with the pepper box revolvers and the rifle to defend themselves, deciding that they had undergone enough torture to have all the spoils. By this time it was an hour after dark. The two darkies drove away and these rude but just judges went to their homes. . . .

CHAPTER EIGHT

Those Were
the
Troublous Times!

The eighteen fifties ended and Abraham Lincoln was elected President. John Brown, hot-eyed archetype of radical Abolitionists, made his movement against slavery, against the Federal government and against reason. Floods of pamphlets flowed out of New England and the dusky northbound traffic across the Ohio continued to increase.

Presently secession, long threatened by the states of the Deep South, became a reality. The country was dazed; no one had believed that this thing could actually happen. Then South Carolina made it a shooting war and North and South gathered themselves together, rallied from the first shock and set about the grim business of settling the disaffection in blood. To the Union it seemed only a sort of police action (another fond hope, beside that of compromise, of which this country has been guilty more than once) and President Lincoln called for volunteers for a three months' enlistment.

As always the first to go were boys from the towns and villages of the Midwest. Indiana contributed its full share and scenes like that later presented by James Whitcomb Riley in one of his greatest poems were enacted in every small town in the state.

JAMES WHITCOMB RILEY

The Old Man and Jim

Old man never had much to say—
  'Ceptin' to Jim,—
And Jim was the wildest boy he had—
  And the old man jes' wrapped up in him!
Never heerd him speak but once
Er twice in my life,—and first time was
When the army broke out, and Jim he went,
The old man backin' him, fer three months;
And all 'at I heerd the old man say
Was, jes' as we turned to start away,—
    "Well, good-by, Jim:
    Take keer of yourse'f!"

'Peared-like, he was more satisfied
  Jes' *lookin'* at Jim
And likin' him all to hisse'f-like, see?—
  'Cause he was jes' wrapped up in him!
And over and over I mind the day
The old man come and stood round in the way
While we was drillin', a-watchin' Jim—
And down at the deepot a-heerin' him say
    "Well,. good-by, Jim:
    Take keer of yourse'f!"

Never was nothin' about the *farm*
  Disting'ished Jim;
Neighbors all ust to wonder why
  The old man 'peared wrapped up in him:
But when Cap. Biggler he writ back
'At Jim was the bravest boy we had
In the whole dern rigiment, white er black,
And his fightin' good as his farmin' bad—

'At he had led, with a bullet clean
Bored through his thigh, and carried the flag
Through the bloodiest battle you ever seen,—
The old man wound up a letter to him
'At Cap. read to us, 'at said: "Tell Jim
    Good-by,
      And take keer of hisse'f!"

Jim come home jes' long enough
    To take the whim
'At he 'd like to go back in the calvery—
    And the old man jes' wrapped up in him!
Jim 'lowed 'at he 'd had sich luck afore,
Guessed he 'd tackle her three years more.
And the old man give him a colt he 'd raised,
And follered him over to Camp Ben Wade,
And laid around fer a week er so,
Watchin' Jim on dress-parade—
Tel finally he rid away,
And last he heerd was the old man say,—
    "Well, good-by, Jim:
      Take keer of yourse'f!"

Tuk the papers, the old man did,
    A-watchin' fer Jim—
Fully believin' he 'd make his mark
    Some way—jes' wrapped up in him!—
And many a time the word 'u'd come
'At stirred him up like the tap of a drum—
At Petersburg, fer instunce, where
Jim rid right into their cannons there,
And *tuk* 'em, and p'inted 'em t' other way,
And socked it home to the boys in gray,
As they scooted fer timber, and on and on—
Jim a lieutenant and one arm gone,
And the old man's words in his mind all day,—
    "Well, good-by, Jim:
      Take keer of yourse'f!"

Think of a private, now, perhaps,
   We'll say like Jim,
'At 's clumb clean up to the shoulder-straps—
   And the old man jes' wrapped up in him!
Think of him—with the war plum' through,
And the glorious old Red-White-and-Blue,
A-laughin' the news down over Jim,
And the old man, bendin' over him—
The surgeon turnin' away with tears
'At had n't leaked fer years and years,
As the hand of the dyin' boy clung to
His father's, the old voice in his ears,—
   "Well, good-by, Jim:
   Take keer of yourse'f!"

Few of man's foolish activities are more harrowing than his civil wars—especially so when such wars are fought over a point of ideology upon which brother can, and frequently does, differ with brother, father with son; upon which the opponents are not even divided by such distinctions as race or culture.

Free travel was possible throughout the nation for some time after the first of the Southern states had seceded. Northern men were in the South on business, Southerners were in the North. A Hoosier who was in New Orleans as clerk on a steamboat when the Civil War began tells how he got back to Union Territory, how the war began on the Ohio and the part played in it by his battered boat, "The Fanny Bullitt."

JULIUS AUGUSTUS LEMCKE

was a typical representative of the class of educated Germans who emigrated to the United States in the eighteen-forties and 'fifties and settled in river cities from Cincinnati to St. Louis. The Midwest should have been happy to receive them, for most were endowed with great energy, sound education, and an abiding love for good music, good literature, and good food. Some of the marks of these virtues are still observable in the countryside.

In his later years, after a successful career in business and politics, Mr. Lemcke published a little volume of reminiscences for distribution among his friends. The following sketch is a selection from this book which the author, with his characteristic good humor, could not refrain from entitling

Reminiscences of an Indianian. From the Sassafras Log Behind the Barn in Posey County to Broader Fields

WAR TIMES ON A MISSISSIPPI RIVER STEAMBOAT

THE STEAMER "Fanny Bullitt," a side-wheeler of good dimensions and fair speed, of which I was part owner and head clerk at the time the war broke out, cleared port under Confederate sailing papers and made her last departure from New Orleans for Louisville on April 29, 1861. At Memphis, where the rebel authorities looked on us as Yankees, and I was known to be a republican, we barely escaped arrest and . . . confiscation. We arrived at Louisville with an empty cabin; and after discharging a scanty cargo of rosin, turpentine and a little sugar, the boat went to the "boneyard" below the falls at Portland, where, until November of that year, she "choked a ring-bolt." . . .

Our captain, a Kentuckian and southern sympathizer, from constant worry over the deplorable condition of the country, fell sick, and in the early summer, died of a broken heart. At his death, the care of the boat and her considerable indebtedness fell to me; and when the patriotic boys in the north, at the call of the president, shouldered their guns, and with colors flying followed the fife and drum to glory, I found my hands tied and was thus prevented from enlisting. The summer wore on in anxious and irritating inactivity, and when, in the autumn, I proposed to offer the "Fanny's" services to the Union forces then gathering on the lower Ohio, I met with determined opposition from our Kentucky owners, who would not let the boat go into service against their southern friends and kinfolks.

Restive under the situation, and determined to break the deadlock, I bestirred myself. I was fortunate enough, with the aid of a friend, to raise the money in bank wherewith to buy out the disaffected and rebellious partners and thereby increased my already heavy indebtedness. Money in those days was very hard to get, and it took a Caesarian operation to deliver the bank of sufficient cash to satisfy my demand. I thus became the owner of five-sixths of the "Fanny Bullitt," and I also became her commander. The other one-sixth interest remained the property of my friend Captain Ronald Fisher, a stanch Union man, who continued second in command of the boat.

Organized bands of southern sympathizers, in the fall of that year, were operating on the shores of the lower Ohio in southwestern Kentucky. They were engaged in smuggling contraband munitions of war into the Confederacy, and in disturbing the people in the towns and villages on the Illinois side of the river. As yet, along this part of Mason and Dixon's line, no military posts had been established by the federal government.

At Shawneetown, ten miles below the mouth of the Wabash, an Illinois regiment of cavalry had gone into camp for recruiting and organizing purposes. Here I directed my steps, and to the officers of the regiment proposed to bring my man-of-war and help them put down the rebellion "in ninety days," and whip those blustering Johnnies who constantly boasted that each of them could easily whip five of us "northern mudsills." This offer of mine to volunteer was promptly accepted by the colonel and his officers. I knew full well that authority for such service vested in the war department only, and that no pay could be expected. I therefore stipulated that I should be enrolled on the roster of this horse regiment as captain of "horse marines," without shoulder straps, and should have authority to draw rations for my men from the commissary of the regiment, and that oil for the machinery, cordage and oakum should be furnished by the quartermaster; while the necessary fuel I engaged to requisition boldly from neighboring coal mines. These proceedings were altogether irregular, not ordered by the war department, nor authorized in army regulations, but by us hotheads were held to be highly patriotic, laudable and necessary to bring the war to an end and "hang Jeff Davis on a sour apple tree."

The colonel of the regiment, a pet of Governor Dick Yates, was troubled with ingrowing nerve; but he shall be nameless. I may call him "Old Liver-Pad," for in civil life he was a quack doctor. . . .

On taking the boat from her berth at Portland, where she had lain all summer and autumn, I "spared no wisdom" to induce the wharfmaster to take my I. O. U. in liquidation of accumulated port charges instead of cash, which I had not. . . . At our arrival amidst alarums of drums and the huzzas from warriors and citizens on shore, we hoisted the stars and strips at the jackstaff, and never lowered them again from that time on. As I had no money wherewith to pay wages, the crew patriotically went into writings with me, stipulating that unless the state of Illinois or the federal government at some future day paid the boat for her services, no claim for wages should lie against me nor the boat.

We were all of us, the captain as well as his crew, in those days so impecunious that our tobacco was begged from the boys in blue, who were well supplied; of all other delicacies only the Sunday pie remained, which, for want of fruit, was made of beans until bugs and worms were found in the beans. At the little old post of Shawneetown that winter I was looked upon as representing the navy and feted accordingly by the patriotic dames of the town. This secured for me, now and then, a much needed "square meal," in return for which I never failed, in the most engaging manner, to make myself agreeable to maid and matron alike at any of their dances and evening parties.

In support of the proverb that "a sitting hen gathers no moss," we bestirred ourselves strenuously in raids and expeditions along the Kentucky shores, where, under orders from the officers of the regiment and with the aid of its men, we pursued marauders, captured needed forage for the horses of our regiment, and confiscated and destroyed ferry-boats and other watercraft used for purposes of smuggling and disturbing that portion of the people in "Egypt" on the opposite shore of the river who were loyal, and who were not out in the smart-weed and dog-fennel at midnight plotting treason and drilling with their Sons of Liberty and Knights of the Golden Circle.

By the time the federal forces had established military posts at Paducah and Smithland, early in 1862, there came an order from General Grant to report with the "Fanny Bullitt" at headquarters in Cairo. On our arrival there my boat, together with other steamers, was ordered to anchor out in the middle of the Ohio and await orders. Meanwhile I kept up communication with the shore, and during my daily reports to General Grant had, when the tobacco smoke was not too dense, favorable opportunities to observe the silent commander. At Grant's boarding-house, where Charles A. Dana and George Boutwell, the latter an ex-governor of Massachusetts, then in Cairo on a war mission, and myself were the only other boarders, we found the general fairly communicative and genial. . . . I was sent with artillery and ammunition to Fort Henry on the Tennessee river. Here Grant, with the aid of Commodore Foote's gunboats, made his first draw in the game which opened to him the western vitals of the Confederacy. We remained during the fight and then returned to Cairo.

Fort Donaldson on the Cumberland river surrendered on February 15, 1862. I was there with the "Fanny Bullitt" on the day of the surrender, and was ordered the next day to load up and take away from the battlefield to unknown hospital accommodations the first of our seriously wounded men, two hundred of whom completed the cargo. The season was an excessively wet one and the camp and battlefield were knee-deep in yellow clay, which, kneaded into slush, made life very sloppy and disagreeable for everybody.

The Cumberland river, out of banks, with its turbid drift-laden flood, rushed along at millrace speed. Surgeons could not be spared from the battlefield, so that I had to depart without a single doctor or nurse. As there were but few hospitals thus early in the war the "Fanny's" destination was, after reporting to General Sherman at Paducah, mouth of the Tennessee, left entirely to my judgment.

On leaving Donaldson we had not much more than straightened out, laying the boat in her course down stream, when night lowered

her somber mantle upon us, and a stormy, dark and ugly night it
proved to be. Barney Seals, the only pilot on board, was drunk; and
as through Egyptian darkness with lightning speed we rushed down
a bend or rounded a point of that crooked river, the strings of my
heart would tighten until the blood receding, would all but leave it
at a standstill. The intoxicated Barney's catlike eyes, illumined as
they were by the fumes arising from the liquor within, enabled him,
however, to bring us safely past all submerged banks and invisible
death-dealing obstructions. He skillfully managed to keep the boat
out of the woods and away from cornfields, and held her steadily in
the marks.

As in the course of the night, for a short space, I left my post on
the hurricane deck to look in upon the cabin with its hospital of
wounded sufferers, I stumbled over dead bodies brought, as they had
died, from the cabin to the guards of the boiler deck. In the dimly
lighted interior, where two hundred men lay on blood-stained straw,
and feverish moans filled the air, a horrible vision came to my distressed brain. It pictured possible shipwreck. I could see the wounded
men, with broken legs and maimed arms, frantically struggle and
helplessly sink to their death in the merciless waves of the turbid
flood.

Horrified and disheartened at my helplessness and turning to
escape this nightmare, I suddenly came upon a woman, who had
entered through one of the cabin doors. She was of middle age,
broad and stanch of posture, and had a kindly but resolute face. Her
sleeves were rolled up to the elbow, and the skirt of her calico gown
was tucked back. She carried in one hand a pail of hot water, and in
the other an armful of the boat's bed-sheets and pillow-slips, torn
into strips for bandages. Following her were two deckhands, carrying
additional pails of hot water from the boilers below.

Spellbound at the sight of a woman (the only one of her sex on
board) who had come as a volunteer and unauthorized, I followed
her every movement as she dressed wounds, washed the blood and
grime from them, spoke encouraging words to the fever-racked
sufferers, and took last parting messages for widowed wives and sor-
rowing mothers from dying men, until I could see a halo of golden
light encircle and illumine the head of this veritable Mater Dolorosa.

Mrs. Bickerdyke, a woman of great administrative ability and determination, came to Cairo as a volunteer nurse at the time General Grant assumed command. She was at Donaldson when it fell, and on the evening of the "Fanny's" departure for the Ohio river, unaccompanied, she had boarded the boat without orders or asking permission from any one. In the dead of night she appeared amongst us as an angel of mercy, and quietly went to work to relieve suffering. In her efforts she appropriated everything needful, and freely called on the crew of the boat for aid, which was cheerfully given and never refused. From the time she left us at Paducah the next day until the close of the war I never lost trace of this remarkable woman.

In appreciation of her kindly efforts and helpful work among the boys in blue she soon became known as *Mother* Bickerdyke; and when General Grant discovered her eminent executive ability and courage, the lines of his army and doors of the hospitals were opened without restraint; and she was invested with such power as, from that time on, proved a menace to drunken hospital stewards and a warning to dissolute or neglectful army surgeons. . . .

A violet streak in the east, and then a luminous mist, followed by the golden chariot of Apollo, announced that day had come at last, to dispel the horrors of the night and soothe the misery of the afflicted. The blessed light was hailed with satisfaction by all on board; and those who, with closed eyes, lay stiff and stark upon the deck, appeared peaceful and submissive to their lot as their forms emerged from the gloom.

Arrived at Paducah I promptly reported at headquarters to General Sherman, only to learn that he had no place to send me and the poor sufferers in my charge, and over a glass of brandy, in which I joined him, he deplored the utter lack of hospital accommodations. . . .

The scanty and incomplete hospital accommodations at Cairo and Mound City, fifty miles below Paducah, had already been exhausted; and Paducah then had not a single hospital bed prepared. So General Sherman, though powerless "to order," in a kindly and helpful manner, "advised" to try Louisville, where he thought I would find relief. Without doctors or nurses, a further journey of four hundred miles, climbing a six-mile current, in a river filled with heavy drift, meant a tedious trip for the boat, and offered a dolorous outlook for the wounded and suffering men, who, from this time on, had to do without even Mother Bickerdyke. This good woman was needed in Cairo, and she reluctantly left us to our fate.

Anxious to reach sorely needed help I determined to waste no time, and having

> Promptly found my resolution
> I quick put it in execution,

by weighting down the safety valve. With steam raised to the danger point, I now strove to overcome the heavy current of the swollen river.

Arrived at Shawneetown, where everybody knew me, I sent for some of the women and leading business men of the place, and after having told my tale of woe, I was partially relieved. Under the stimulus of their charitable and patriotic impulses all the Illinois men on board were taken ashore.

At Henderson, Kentucky, forty-five miles farther up the river, those citizens of the prosperous little city who were loyal to the Union cause, took what few Kentuckians I had.

At Evansville the authorities took all my Indiana men ashore, where, at the hands of the good women of the place and other patriotic citizens, sorely needed attention was furnished in kindly abundance. . . .

At Louisville I found no difficulty from lack of hospital accommodations. On account of the extraordinary height of the river, however, no landing could be effected until, with much difficulty, I succeeded in sticking the boat's nose into Fourth street, a long ways up among the stores and offices of the city. Here we unloaded the last of our human freight into ambulances and upon spring wagons.

Now that the trip was ended, an inspection showed the condition of the cabin to be that of an abattoir after a hard day's killing. Every stanchion and bulkhead was smeared with human blood, and the boat's decks gave evidence of the abundant loss of the life-giving fluid on the spot where suffering humanity had breathed its last.

On returning to Cairo I was kept on waiting orders, and, like Mahomet's coffin, was hung up until the latter part of March. Then we were ordered up the Tennessee river to Pittsburg Landing with guns and ammunition. After discharging cargo, the "Fanny" was utilized by General Grant, up to the time of the battle of Shiloh, as a ferry between Pittsburg Landing and headquarters at Savannah, where Mr. White, one of my engineers, had two of his fingers shot away by the bursting of a rebel shell. During the days that the battle of Pittsburg Landing was being fought, and it rained bullets, we, under orders and in sight, lay at the landing sheltered from hostile shot by the protecting river bank. . . .

At about the time that Albert Sidney Johnson, the commander-in-chief of the Confederate forces, met his doom in a nearby gully close to our landing, my pilot, Barney Seals, who enjoyed a thirst that was a pippin, was caught, while drunk, stealing chickens from a coop on a neighboring steamer and put in durance vile. I did not intercede in his behalf but left him to sweat in the guardhouse until we were ordered away and the scalawag's services were again needed. Pilots at this time were much in demand, and this insured Barney, in spite of the incorrigible whisky habit, a steady and well-paid job.

Soon after our return to the mouth of the Ohio, together with other transports, and convoyed by United States gunboats, we were dispatched into the heart of the Confederacy, as far south as the mouth of the Yazoo river, just above Vicksburg, where, under a flag of truce, an exchange of prisoners was effected with Confederate States Commissioner Oulds. . . .

By the time our mission had been completed, and the exchanged boys in blue had been brought back, landed and furloughed at Cairo, General Curtis had brought his army through Arkansas to the Mississippi river and gone into camp near Helena. Quartermasters' stores and commissary supplies for his army had accumulated in such quantity at Cairo, that the "Fanny's" share of them made her fairly stagger and drag the guards in the water as I once more turned her head down stream towards the shores of Arkansas.

After arrival at Helena and during a prolonged stay there, I spent much time with the staff and line officers of Generals Curtis and

Osterhaus, some of whom I had known in civil life in St. Louis. The attendance of these warriors at my first "at home" on board the boat, made me think that the Trojan mare "in foal with Greeks" had broken loose, and that the thirsty crowd had brought with it gullets yards in length and open at both ends. . . .

During the operations of the Union forces in the southwest, steamboats were of great importance on the Mississippi, Ohio, Tennessee and Cumberland rivers. While their usefulness was completely paralyzed at the beginning of the war, this large fleet of watercraft afterwards became the main factor in the transportation of troops and the carrying of ammunition, quartermasters' supplies and army stores. The "Fanny," one of this fleet, utilized for all sorts of service, was frequently sent into out-of-the-way localities, where she was exposed to ambuscades from hostile batteries and volleys from the enemy's musketry. From these dangers we strove to protect ourselves by barricading the boilers of the boat with hay and cotton bales and by surrounding the pilot house with boiler iron; and, with the exception of slight wounds received by two of the crew, we succeeded fairly well in protecting life and limb.

My boat had now unremittingly been at work for nigh unto two years, during which time, repairing out of the question, absolutely nothing had been done to offset the heavy abuse and hard knocks she had endured. Much of the nosing around the guards and outriggers was worn off. The gallows frame supporting the starboard wheel, out of plumb, had an ominous leaning outward; and the wheel houses and bulkheads full of bullet holes, with the upper works badly dilapidated, had given her the appearance of a lopsided hobo, staggering under a heavy jag.

Steamboats by this time had again come into demand, but the "Fanny's" scanty earnings up to then were quite insufficient to pay for docking her and cover the large expense of giving the boat and machinery the thorough overhauling they needed. I therefore was glad to find a party who would buy. I consequently sold, and the purchaser immediately went to work on repairs which, when completed, he found had run up to the neat little sum of forty thousand dollars.

President Lincoln's three-months volunteers had been re-enlisted and re-enlisted again; the war had become one of the bloodiest in history, with battles which are still studied by tacticians in spite of almost inconceivable changes in armament and transportation since their day. One of the most famous contests was that at Gettysburg and upon its anniversary President Lincoln gave further fame to the field by making his greatest public address there. Eventually the battle was also celebrated in a poem which, though little known, is an American great.

WILL HENRY THOMPSON

was not a prolific writer. He contributed a few articles to the Century magazine and collaborated with his brother Maurice in two books on the subject of archery. That was all, as far as is known, except that he wrote

The High Tide at Gettysburg

A cloud possessed the hollow field,
The gathering battle's smoky shield.
Athwart the gloom the lightning flashed,
And through the cloud some horsemen dashed,
And from the heights the thunder pealed.

Then, at the brief command of Lee
Moved out that matchless infantry,
With Pickett leading grandly down,
To rush against the roaring crown
Of those dread heights of destiny.

Far heard above the angry guns
A cry across the tumult runs,—
The voice that rang through Shiloh's woods
And Chickamauga's solitudes,
The fierce South cheering on her sons.

Ah, how the withering tempest blew
Against the front of Pettigrew!
A Kamsin wind that scorched and singed
Like that infernal flame that fringed
The British squares at Waterloo!

A thousand fell where Kemper led;
A thousand died where Garnett bled;
In blinding flame and strangling smoke
The remnant through the batteries broke
And crossed the works with Armistead.

"Once more in Glory's van with me!"
Virginia cried to Tennessee:
"We two together, come what may,
Shall stand upon these works to-day!"
(The reddest day in history.)

Brave Tennessee! In reckless way,
Virginia heard her comrade say:
"Close round this rent and riddled rag!"
That time she set her battle-flag
Amid the guns of Doubleday.

But who shall break the guards that wait
Before the awful face of Fate?
The tattered standards of the South
Were shriveled at the cannon's mouth,
And all her hopes were desolate.

In vain the Tennesseean set
His breast against the bayonet!
In vain Virginia charged and raged,
A tigress in her wrath uncaged,
Till all the hill was red and wet!

Above the bayonets, mixed and crossed,
Men saw a gray, gigantic ghost,
Receding through the battle cloud,
And heard across the tempest loud
The death-cry of a nation lost!

The brave went down! Without disgrace
They leaped to Ruin's red embrace.
They only heard Fame's thunders wake,
And saw the dazzling sun-burst break
In smiles on Glory's bloody face!

They fell, who lifted up a hand
And bade the sun in heaven to stand!
They smote and fell, who set the bars
Against the progress of the stars,
And stayed the march of Motherland!

They stood, who saw the future come
On through the fight's delirium!
They smote and stood, who held the hope
Of nations on that slippery slope
Amid the cheers of Christendom!

God lives! He forged the iron will
That clutched and held that trembling hill.
God lives and reigns! He built and lent
The heights for Freedom's battlement
Where floats her flag in triumph still!

Fold up the banners! Smelt the guns!
Love rules. Her gentler purpose runs.
A mighty mother turns in tears
The pages of her battle years,
Lamenting all her fallen sons!

Military action touched the soil of Indiana but once during the Civil War—when John Hunt Morgan led his Confederate raiders across the Ohio River at Mauckport, crossed the state in a wide arc, and entered Ohio north of Cincinnati.

In spite of the glamour that has grown around them, Morgan's men at the time of the raid were a rag-tag outfit, in the main, bent on plunder as much as, or more than, conquest. They were at least the equals, in the matter of collecting cash, silverware, merchandise, and eatables, of the worst of those "bummers" of Sherman's who are

still condemned by the Daughters of the Confederacy. If the opera-
tions of Morgan's men were limited it was only the fault of inef-
ficiency in manpower, command, and tactics.

Morgan's raid has been considered a joke in Indiana—for Hoosiers
can usually laugh at themselves when a laugh is in order—and some
of the inept defensive operations of the Indiana "home guard" were
something less than heroic in practice if not in concept. But the ef-
forts at resistance made here and there by old men and boys, the defi-
ance of housewives and children could, and in sections more romanti-
cally inclined certainly would, have been the subject of an epic
tradition long since.

In the following selection,

JESSAMYN WEST

modern poet, short story writer and essayist of Hoosier background,
tells a story of the affair called

The Battle of Finney's Ford

For JOSH BIRDWELL, no man of war, no man even, if it takes
twenty-one years to make you that, the threat of war had each day
been coming closer. On the morning of the 11th that threat caught
up with and enveloped him. Except for the name of Morgan the
11th had opened up like any other morning in July; clear, with
promise of heat to come. Overhead arched the great cloudless sky
of summer, tranquil above the reports, the rumors, the whisperings,
the fears. And above the true evidence: the evidence brought in by
eye-witnesses; by the boy who had hid himself and horse in the
thicket while Morgan's outriders galloped past; by the girl who had
waded along the branch and was not seen; the stories of the burnings, the shootings, the looting.

Morgan's name had been heard in the southern counties before
July, but it was in July that it began to be heard above everything
else. Women stopped their dashers to listen, children stayed away

from the wood lots, men worked quietly behind their horses fore-going all talk lest their words muffle the approach of Morgan's scouts.

But it was the young men who listened most intently, the skin tightening across their cheekbones. Not with apprehension or fear so much as with wonder. What would they do if the hoofbeats along the woods' trace were made by John Morgan's men? If the press-gang said, "Unhitch your horses, bub, bring out your hams and bacon, show us where the old man keeps his silver"? Would they unhitch, the young men wondered, hand over Prince and Dolly, walk up through the fine dust of the field-path, lay the meat and silver on the outstretched hands? Would they? The young men did not know. They had no way of knowing.

Josh had listened without a word as Ben Whitey talked. "I was there," Ben finished. "I saw it. I saw them burn the Harkness mill. I saw old man Yardley shot. I'll give myself two hours to rest, then I'll head for Vernon. It's my aim to join the Home Guard and fight John Morgan till he's killed or pushed back across the Ohio."

Josh looked, not at his friend, but at his shadow which was long and still upon the dusty lane. Heat waves already rippled across the well-tassled corn; the Whiteys' windmill turned round three or four times with considerable speed, then stopped as if forever.

"I'm going with thee," Josh said.

Ben Whitey lifted himself wearily from against the side of the house. "You're a Quaker. Your folks'll never let you."

Josh didn't argue with him. "I'll meet thee at the Milford cut-off in two hours."

Ben Whitey turned toward the door. "I won't wait for you," he warned. "I'll go straight on if you're not there."

"Thee won't need to wait. I'll be there," Josh said.

He turned homeward, running heavily through the early morning heat.

Breakfast was over when he stepped into the summer kitchen. He was astonished to see the nearly empty gravy bowl, the meat platter with its single egg, the plates crusted with jam and biscuit crumbs. It was a wonder to Josh that on such a morning people had been able to put gravy on biscuits, to spear slices of ham; a morning on which their neighbors were being killed.

He stopped behind the chair in which his brother, Little Jess, sat. He knew, in his self-conscious way, that his family was looking at him and he made a strong effort to control his feelings. He was particularly aware of his brother Labe's calm, cool gaze and he thought of it as being belittling; that Labe, who was muscular, smooth-jointed, supple, considered him a scarecrow with his black hair like a wig, his high-burning cheekbones, his lop-sided mouth which trembled when he was in earnest. It was trembling now.

"What kept thee, son?" his father asked.

"I was over at the Whiteys'."

"Set, set, Josh," his mother bade, bustling up from her place. "I'll fry thee fresh eggs."

"I couldn't swallow an egg," Josh said.

"What do they hear at the Whiteys'?" asked his father.

"Morgan's heading this way, he's following the railroad up from Vienna. He's making for Vernon. He'll be there today or tomorrow."

"Vernon," said his mother. She put the two eggs she had in her hand back in the egg crock. Vernon was home. Josh had as well said the south forty.

"How do they know so much over at the Whiteys'?" his father asked. "Morgan didn't cross the Ohio till evening of fourth day. Morgan's lost out there in the woods . . . got guerrillas trained to stay out of sight. Yet people'll sit at their breakfast tables and say just where John Morgan is. Tell you whether he's shaved yet this morning and where he'll be this time tomorrow."

"People at breakfast tables," Josh began angrily, then stopped. "Ben Whitey was in Harrison County when Morgan crossed over. He's been riding ahead of him for three days."

"Did thee talk to Ben?"

"Yes."

"What'd Ben have to say?"

"Nothing about whether Morgan'd shaved or not this morning."

"Son," said his father, "sit thyself down and tell us."

Josh, without intending to do so, sat suddenly in the chair which was pushed out for him, and also without conscious intent began to chew hurriedly on a cold biscuit. His mother made a gesture toward passing him butter and jam, but Jess shook his head and said, "Well, Josh?"

Josh spoke rapidly, his voice a little muffled by the dry biscuit crumbs. "Ben Whitey passed a dozen of Morgan's outriders last night camped down this side of Blocher. Not more'n twenty miles from Vernon. They're following the railroad. They'll raid Vernon."

"Raid Vernon," said his mother. "What does that mean?" It was a word whose meaning on the page of any book she knew perfectly well. But "Raid Vernon"—the town where she sold her eggs, the church town, the county fair town, with its whitewashed brick houses, its quiet, dusty streets, its snowball bushes dangling their white blossoms over the unpainted picket fences—what did that mean? "Raid Vernon," she said once again as if the words themselves might somehow suddenly focus, as a stereopticon glass did when given just the proper shove, to show a landscape, lifelike in its dimensions, distances—and ruin.

Josh knew what the word meant. Ben Whitey had told him. "Raid means," he told his mother, "burn, kill, take what you want."

"Are Morgan's men killing people?" Eliza asked.

For a second the world his mother saw flickered before Josh's eyes: a world of such loving companionableness that the word war had no other meaning for her than murder; where deliberate killing was as unthinkable as though in her own household son should turn on son; but it flickered for a second only, then disappeared leaving him angry again.

"Doesn't thee know there's a war?" Josh asked with intensity. "Doesn't thee know what a war is?"

"Thy mother knows there's a war, Josh," his father reminded him, "but she don't know what a war is. Let alone what a war in Vernon'd be like. She's more used to think of caring for people than killing them."

"John Morgan thinks of killing them," Josh said. "He shot a boy through the legs who didn't run fast enough. He shot an old man in the back. I don't know how many's dead in Harrison County. Ben Whitey said he could smell the smoke of Morgan's burnings the whole way up. He said he didn't think there was a mill left standing in Harrison County. He said the country's scoured of horses—and anything else in any house a trooper wanted and could carry across his saddle bow."

Eliza leaned across the table. "The earth," she said, "and the fullness thereof, is the Lord's. What's Morgan's men but a ruckus of boys with their pants in their boots? Trying to get something they've never had a taste of before? We've got more'n we need here. High time we're called on to share it with someone. If John Morgan's men came here," Eliza said—and Josh saw his mother's eyes turn toward the door of the summer kitchen as if she saw there a dusty, slouch-hatted trooper, "I'd offer them the best I had on hand. No man's my enemy," she said.

Josh stood up, crumbling in one hand the biscuit he had been swiftly munching. "Some men are my enemies," he said. "Any man's my enemy who kills innocent men and makes slaves. They're my mortal enemies."

Josh felt his sister Mattie's hand, long-fingered—and cold for so warm a morning—touch, then feel its way into his clenched fist, and he gave way to its insistent downward pressure and sat again. "I will share with my friends," he said, "but if thee gives all thee's got to a thief, thy friends will have to go hungry—there's not enough to go round. What's good about that?" he asked. "I'd rather die."

There was a long silence about the breakfast table. Eliza reseated herself. Little Jess looked from face to face with nervousness. He was embarrassed when grownups showed emotion. Mattie, because she oscillated between two ways of seeing, suffered: when she was generous and peaceful as was her mother, she thought herself a coward; when she, like Joshua, was ready to fight (she supposed) she felt herself a renegade, an outcast from faith and the scriptures.

Only Labe sat quietly, his calm face touched neither by sorrow nor eagerness. Only one way open before him, and except that he believed this to be a matter between his mother and brother, and presently his father, he would have spoken and said more convincing words, he thought, for loving all men than his mother had.

In the long silence, while there was no talk, sounds of great clarity filled the room. All, except Little Jess, harkened to them as if they were omens—as if each, properly apprehended, might carry some kind of a revelation: the slow grating start of the windmill easing into rhythmic clicking as the wind freshened; two distant notes as Old Bess, the bell-cow, reached forward toward uncropped grass; the prolonged, sweet morning trill of a small bird which, undesired either by raiders or raided, flew, singing, near the windows, then flipped out of sight.

Jess, from his place at the head of the table, looked down toward his eldest son. He bent upon his a face of so much love and regard—and good humor, too, as if behind this talk of war there were still a few reasons to laugh—that Josh thought he might be unable to bear his father's gaze, would have to lay his arms across the table and bury his face in them, and so hidden, say, "Yes, pa," or "No, pa," to whatever his father had to say. But as his father continued to gaze, quizzically and lovingly, Josh knew that he had left behind him forever the happy time of freedom from decision and sat very straight, back teeth clamped together, lips trembling, quietly waiting his father's word.

"Thee knows, Josh," his father said, "Dying's only half of it. Any of us here, I hope,"—and Jess included Little Jess and Mattie in the nod of his head—"is ready to die for what he believes. If it's asked of us and can be turned to good account. I'm not for dying, willy-nilly, thee understands," Jess said, his big nose wrinkling at the bridge. "It's an awful final thing, and more often than not nobody's much discommoded by it, except thyself, but there are times when it's the only answer a man can give to certain questions. Then I'm for it. But thee's not been asked such a question now, Josh. Thee can go out on the Pike, and if thee can find John Morgan, die there in front of him by his own hand if thee can manage it, and nothing'll be decided. He'll move right on and thee'll be back there on the Pike just as dead and just as forgotten as if thee'd tied a stone around thy neck and jumped off Clifty Falls. No, Josh, dying won't turn the trick. What thee'll be asked to do now—is kill."

The word hung in the air. A fly circled the table, loudly and slowly, and still the sound of the word was there . . . louder than the ugly humming. It hung in the air like an open wound. Kill. In the Quaker household the word was bare and stark. Bare as in Cain and Abel's time with none of the panoply of wars and regiments and

campaigns to clothe it. Kill. Kill a man. Kill thy brother. Josh regarded the word. He explored it, his hand tightening about the case
knife in his hand.

"I know that," he said. "I am ready to fight." But that wouldn't
do. He could not pretend that he was ready for the necessary act so
long as he flinched away—from even the word. "I will kill these
men if I have to."

"No, Josh," Eliza said.

Josh was glad to be relieved of the need of facing his father and
regarding death abstractly. He turned to his mother. "Yes," he said.
"I will. I'm going to meet Ben Whitey at eight. Soon as he's had
two hours of rest. The Governor's made a proclamation. Every man's
to join the Home Guard and help defend his town. We're going
right down to Vernon and join. Morgan'll be there anytime. I'd
ought to've gone a week ago."

"Joshua, Joshua," cried his mother. "Thy great great grandfather
came here with William Penn to establish ways of peace. And he
did," Eliza declared passionately. "With savage Indians. Men of
blood. Now thee proves thyself to be worse than the Indians. They
kept the peace."

Josh felt better. The picture of himself as bloodier than a savage
Indian was so fantastic it hid for the time such savagery and blood-
thirstiness as he did possess—and hid too, what Josh felt to be perhaps even worse, his lack of these qualities, his fear and trembling.
"The Indians," he said, "weren't dealing with John Morgan."

Jess spoke. "Josh," he said, "those who take the sword shall perish
by it."

They were back to dying: only a nicer word. "I am ready to
perish," said Josh.

But Jess wouldn't let them stay there. "Thou shalt not kill," said
Jess.

There it was. "But He said, render unto Caesar the things that are
Caesar's," Josh said desperately. "I live here . . . in Jennings County.
My town is Vernon. The governor said to defend it. My body is my
country's."

"Thy soul, son, is God's."

"God won't want it," Josh said, "if I don't do what I think's my duty." He was standing again, half crying, a horrible way for a man to be starting to war. "Thee can live with God now, maybe, I can't. I don't want to die . . . and I don't even know if I could kill anyone if I tried. But I got to try," he said, "as long as people around me have to. I'm no better'n they are. I can't be separated from them."

He left the table and ran toward the kitchen stairway. "I'm going," he said. "I'm meeting Ben Whitey at eight."

As he went up the stairs he heard his father say, "No, Eliza, no."

Atop his own horse, lumbering, unwarlike Old Snorty, Josh tried to carry himself like a Home Guardsman. He rode down the dusty road toward the Milford cut-off scanning the horizon for signs of Morgan and his raiders, keeping an eye out for single horsemen. If outriders of Morgan's had only been twenty miles away last night they might easily turn up at any crossroads now.

In spite of his conviction that his intention made him a militia-man already, sworn to hunt down and stop—or kill—John Morgan, Josh could not accustom his mind to the idea of shooting a man. He tried to think how it would be: to come upon a man, emerging from the woods, say, or around a sharp turn, and not speak, not pause to pass the time of day, but instantly with raised musket to fire and hope to blow the stranger's head off. The idea made Josh sweat. My God, he thought, or prayed, he didn't know which, I hope it's no boy, no old man. Then remembering that Morgan's raiders were themselves handy with firearms he settled deeper in his saddle and listened more intently.

Ben Whitey was early, waiting at the cut-off, impatient and fuming as Josh rode up.

"I shouldn't've waited," he yelled. "I should've gone on."

"We'll make up for it now," Josh told him, but they were only fairly started when Ben, looking back down the Pike, said, "Looks like your brother Labe on Rome Beauty. He joining too?"

"No," Josh said, "Labe's got convictions the other way."

"Well, you forgot something then," Ben Whitey said with disgust, "and your ma's sending it to you." He rode on while Josh turned back to meet Labe.

Labe came up at a long trot, the only kind Rome Beauty had, dismounted, and said, "Get on. Father said for thee to take Rome.

Old Snorty's no horse to get to war with."

Josh sat atop Old Snorty, unmoving, unbelieving.

"Get down," said Labe. "If thee's going to fight Morgan, fight him. Don't set there like a bump on a log."

"Father's against my going," said Josh.

"He's against it, but that didn't stop thee. Now get on. He says as far as he knows, Rome's no Quaker. From all he can tell, thee and Rome think about alike. Get on."

Josh got off Snorty, transferred his bed roll to Rome's saddle, and stood in the dusty road beside his brother. He was taller than Labe but Labe's shoulders and stance made him feel small.

"Tell father," he began, but Labe interrupted him. "Father said to tell thee most killing's caused by fear. . . . Rome's being under thee ought to help a little. He don't send thee Rome because his mind's changed about anything."

"Labe," Josh asked, "thee don't think about going?"

"No," said Labe, "I don't."

"I got to," said Josh. "Otherwise I'd always think maybe it was because . . ."

"Get on," said Labe, giving him no time to finish.

Astride the big red horse Josh rode after Ben Whitey, but before he overtook him he finished the sentence. "I am afraid," he said.

"You got a fine mount now," Ben Whitey told him when he drew alongside. "If you can just keep his nose headed the right direction you ought to make out."

"Never thee fear," Josh began . . . but he shut his mouth at that point. "Thee don't know," he told himself.

They rode into Vernon together—a roan and a claybank, two raw-boned farm boys. Ben Whitey, a born fighter, and Josh who was trying to do his duty. They entered Vernon and saw it the way a man who thinks he has been dreaming wakes and sees the land-scape of his dream lying all about him; the disaster real, hard, and unmelting as sunlight—and dreaming the only means of escape. Deep in the country, on the farms, they had believed—and not believed. To come here with loaded guns had been an act of faith and now their faith was justified. Morgan was true; he existed; he was killing and looting; he would be here at any hour. There were tens of mouths to tell them.

The town blazed under the July sun; it throbbed with the heat of the season—and the heat of fear and excitement and wonder and resolution. At first Josh thought it was alive as he had seen it for an August fair, or Fourth of July celebration. And there was something of a holiday spirit in the plunging, headlong activity. As if after fifty years of watching the placid alternations of the seasons, Vernon had tired of its placid punkin-butter existence and had turned with relish to something with a sharper flavor.

That was the surface: the movement, the shouts, the numbers of horses in the streets, the vehicles, the laughter even; a holiday roar and the excess movements of a celebration when steps reach higher and higher into the air, bows go lower and lower toward the earth, and smiles strain at the limitations of a single face. But beneath the surface, when Josh came to regard the sights and sounds singly, he saw there was no holiday.

There were spring wagons, gigs, democrats, buckboards, all filled with women, children, and valuables and headed for back country and the hills. There were men digging deep holes, preparing to bury silver, money, keepsakes, whatever they and their wives cherished and thought a raider might fancy. There were boys barricading doors, boarding up windows, reinforcing bolts. There was a man who had turned his house into a store and was now busy trying to make his store look like a house again. There was an old fellow atop the gable of his house, peering off to the south through a long spyglass. The voices, too, when Josh listened to them, were not celebrating anything: they rasped; they started even, then broke; a man began yelling, looked around, ended whispering.

"Let's get out of this," Ben Whitey said. "Let's find the Home Guard."

From across a picket fence an old man beckoned to them. "Want to mix in it?" he asked.

"That's what we're here for. Where's the Home Guard?" Ben Whitey asked.

"Everywhere," said the old man. He picked up the end of his long beard and used it to point with. "Spread thin, but mostly to the south. Morgan could circle us—but reports are he's hitting us solid from the south. Coming up the railroad from Vienna. They got companies posted at every ford, road, and bridge south of town."

"Where you figger we could do the most good?"

"South Fork bridge. I been thinking about this for two days. I figger John Morgan, being the man he is, will come straight in, cross the South Fork bridge, and bust into town from there. If you want to get in some telling licks, that's the place I'd head for."

"That's the place we want," Ben said.

The Muscatatuck where the South Fork bridge crosses it flows between banks of considerable height. Here the Home Guard commander had massed as many men as could be spared from the other approaches to Vernon. Of these the majority, and among them the men Colonel Williams considered most steady and level-headed, were stationed on the west bank of the stream ready to fall upon the raiders should the smaller force which was holding the approaches to the bridge be overpowered. The colonel hoped to stop, if possible by a show of force, if not, by force itself, any thrust the raiders might make before they reached the bridge. Failing this, the guard on the west bank would have a fine chance to pick off the raiders as they debouched from the bridge and headed toward town.

That was the plan. The captain in command of the river could use as many men as he could get, and when Ben and Josh showed up, well mounted, he sent them at once to join the company beyond the bridge. There his men were drawn up in a loose but well planned alignment. He put the two newcomers in the front line. It was his practice to keep untried men, of whom he knew nothing, away from rear lines where in the shock and excitement of a charge they might break and run. Up front, with veterans behind them and an enemy firing into them, they would have very little choice but to steady and fight.

"They're headed this way," the captain told them. "Some of them," he said, pointing, "are sitting right there on top of that hill. Them, we fooled. Our men marched across the cliff road and then out of sight of Morgan—if he's there—a half dozen times over. Musta looked like quite an army to him. But there's likely others and they may be here soon. If we don't stop them, nothing will.

Once they're past us, it will be Maukport and Salem and Lexington all over again. Keep your guns handy. Dismount and rest your horses, but stay by them and keep them quiet. I'm glad you're here. I need you."

Overhead the July sun had weight as well as heat. It lay across Josh's shoulders like a burning timber. Though Ben was on one side of him, and big Gum Anson, a beefy farmer, was on the other, still Josh felt bereft of shelter, unshielded and alone—a naked target.

For a long time he scanned the road before him with rigid and unrelaxing vigilance. There was not much to be seen: the dusty road, the lush growth of summer; dock, volunteer oats, some daisies, a small field of shoulder-high corn, and beyond these a thicket and the road curving out of sight around it. Above earth and river and the river's rank growth were the heat waves, the massive clouds of noon skies, the burning sun. Josh, who felt as if the whole duty of seeing and apprising rested with him, inspected every leaf and shadow. When a sudden movement of air fluttered the leaves of the elders up the road and rasped through the corn he lifted his gun, then put it down shamefacedly. He could feel the sweat trickle down the sides of his chest, then drop to his middle and soak in around his belt.

"Have some cherries," said Gum. "You can't keep that up all afternoon." He held out a big bag. The cherries were cool and firm and Josh took a handful.

"When Nance brought these out this morning," Gum said, "I'd've thrown 'em down except to please her. Goin' off to fight Morgan with a bag of cherries tied to my saddle like a doggone picnicker." He munched away and spat seeds. "Looks like they might be the handiest article I brought."

"Wait'll Morgan gets here, Gum," somebody yelled. "It's gonna take more'n cherry stones to stop that old shite-poke."

"I got more'n cherry stones," Gum called back and the men around him laughed.

Josh looked about, amazed at the sound of laughter, amazed that men waiting to kill or be killed could laugh and joke. He scanned the faces of those who were laughing: old fellows, middle-aged farmers, boys younger than himself. Sweating, chewing tobacco, some dismounted, others lolling in their saddles. Some in uniform, most not. Mounted on farm plugs. Mounted on fast animals he'd seen at county fairs. Every kind of firearms. One man with a bayonet, even. The sight of that lifted Josh up very straight. Did the raiders carry bayonets? His sweating, which he had not noticed for a while, had started up once more.

"Have some more cherries?" asked Gum.

Josh took another handful. "Thanks," he said. "I was awful dry. And hungry, too. I can't remember when I had anything to eat last."

"Go kinda slow on them cherries, then. They don't set too good on'n empty stomach."

"They're setting good on mine," Josh said, chewing and spitting, but keeping his eyes up-road.

"Take it easy," advised Gum again looking at Josh. "You'll be petered out before Johnny gets here. They's scouts up ahead. They'll let us know if anything's twitchin'."

Josh felt a fool not to have thought of that before: rearing up till his backbone was petrified, and staring till his eyes popped, acting as if he were scout, trooper, captain, everything. He noticed that the other men were relaxed, guns dangling, or laid across their bed rolls, some smoking; a man behind him was having a nip of something that didn't smell like switchel.

"Old Morgan'll never come this way," one bearded farmer was saying. "That boy's shiftier than a creased buck. He ain't never goin' to fight his way in the front door when the back door's open."

"Back door ain't so all-fired wide open's you might think."

"Open or shut—what's it to Morgan? With five thousand men you go in where it pleasures you and don't wait for the welcome mat to be put out."

"Five thousand or ten thousand," said a quiet voice, "I'm going to stay right here. I'm going to give Morgan the butt-end of my mind, if nothing else, before he busts over this bridge and into my store."

The afternoon wore on. To the funky smell of the river and the lush river growth was added that of sweating men and horses. Horses and men were growing restless. Josh eased Rome's girth and hoisted his blankets so that a little air could flow under them. Back in the saddle he felt light-headed and detached. Gum had been right about the cherries; they weren't setting right. He felt kind of sick but happy. He'd got here, he was all right, he was where he belonged. By twisting around he could see a curve of the Muscatatuck where it flowed in shallow ripples across a sandbar, then darkened as the channel deepened near the bridge. It was three or four o'clock. The sun went through the water and on to the sandbar, then flashed, pulsing with the movement of the ripples, back into his eyes. He could feel the movement in his temples. He could see the silvery glint of the little minnows, like bullets; a dragon fly ran its darning needle in-and-out—in-and-out—of the flowing water. It was July . . . a summer afternoon . . . the cool water . . . the hot sun . . . the darting silver bullets.

Josh's neck stiffened, his head snapped up, his hand closed round the stock of his gun. A horseman was pounding up the road.

"It's one of our scouts," said Ben Whitey.

The rider, a little fellow in uniform on a lathered black, pulled up beside the captain. Josh couldn't hear what he was saying, but after a minute the captain turned and told them, his voice quiet but with an edge to it, that let them know that this was it, the time had come.

"Boys," he said, "they're closing in. They're up the road a couple of miles. Less of 'em than we figured. I expect them to charge. There's just two things to remember: first, stand steady. Second, don't fire till I give the word." He stood in his stirrups and pounded the words home. "Don't fire till I give the word. If you fire before you can make your shots good, it's all over. They'll ride you down. Hold it. Your guns carry just as far as theirs and you're better shots. Those men've been in the saddle for weeks now, and it's telling on them. Shoot low so's if you miss a man you get a horse. But don't miss."

The scout went on past them at a gallop and Josh could hear the black's hooves ring on the bridge planking, then quiet as he hit the dust of the road on the west bank where the men in hiding were awaiting the news. The captain himself wheeled around to wait the attack with his men.

Josh reached for his gun. Waves of something—he didn't know

what—were hitting his chest. "It's like riding through the woods and being hit by branches that leave thee in the saddle, but so belabored thy chest aches," he thought. Other waves—or perhaps the same ones—pounded against his ears, broke in deafening crashes as if he were deep under water. Then, in the midst of the pain and crashing, Josh thought, "It's thy heart beating. Nothing but thy heart."

Gum said, "Fix those lines, boy." And again, "Get those reins fixed. If your horse jerks his head he'll spoil your aim."

Josh saw that Gum was right. He got his hand out of the reins and rubbed it along Rome's neck. "Good boy," he said. "Good old Rome. Thee'll be all right." He knew he was encouraging himself. Rome didn't need cheering . . . he stood solid as a meeting house, only his big head moving up and down a little.

They were all waiting. Ben Whitey was cussing, a long line of words as if he was dreaming—or singing—in a kind of funny way. But they were mostly quiet—listening. Something came down, or perhaps it came up, out of the earth itself, something very thin and fine, like a spun web, and held them all together. Josh could feel it. Anybody could break away from it if he liked, but while they were headed the same way, and awaited the same thing, it held them. You could lean against it like steel. Josh felt its support . . . the waves beat against him, but he leaned against that fabric and it held him.

It held him until he heard the first sounds: a rebel yell from up the road beyond the elder thicket, then another. Josh never knew a man could make a sound like that. It was a screech such as an animal might make, only it was a man's voice, a voice that could say, "Farewell," or "Rain tomorrow," and that made it worse. It sounded crazy . . . it sounded as if the tongue that gave it could lap blood. It broke the web that held them together, it left Josh alone.

He could hear far away the thud of hooves, and the waves that had beat against his ears before began now to say words: Rome's fast. Rome's mighty fast. Run for it, run for it. The minute they turn the curve, run for it.

He looked around, he picked out the likely path. "Sure wish I had a cherry stone to suck on," said Gum Anson. "Sure am parched."

Gum's words drowned out the others. The hoofbeats came nearer. "What's the worse can happen to thee?" Josh asked himself. "Get a bullet in thy gizzard. Get killed. Nothing else." It was all right. He settled down to wait.

"Hold it, hold it," the captain was calling. "Wait for the word. Hold it, hold it."

From around the bend, very slowly, came a single man carrying a white flag. A few paces behind him were perhaps twenty or thirty other mounted men.

"It's a trick, it's a trick," the Home Guardsmen were yelling. "Watch it, captain. It's funny business."

"Don't shoot," shouted the colonel, who had ridden up. "Don't fire on a white flag. But watch 'em. Keep 'em covered."

He rode forward a couple of paces. "Are you surrendering?" he called.

The man with the white flag called back. "No. No surrender. We want to parley."

"Come on it," said the colonel. "You," he yelled. "You with the white flag. The rest of you stay back."

"Trying to get up inside our range and ride us down," said Gum.

The flag-bearer came up alongside the Home Guard colonel and saluted.

"Keep your guns on those men," the colonel called back, then lowered his own. Josh couldn't hear his words, but could see that the raider was talking fast and earnestly.

"Could be your brother," said Gum.

It was so. The rebel doing the talking was tow-haired and young, a gaunt brown-faced boy, very broad-shouldered and supple in the saddle. Josh's gun, which had been leveled on him, wavered, but he brought it to bear once again.

The Guardsmen grew restless. "Tell him to make up his mind. Surrender and talk—or shut his mouth and fight."

"What's he doin'? Preachin'?"

" 'Lectioneering for Jeff Davis."

"Shut him up, Colonel. Shut him up."

"We'll make him talk outa the other corner of his mouth."

"You the one shot old man Yardell?"

The colonel turned his back on the raiders and rode up to his own men. "Don't take your guns off them," he told them. "He says we're surrounded. He says they've cut around in back of us—that they've got five thousand men circled around Vernon and it's suicide to resist. He says every bridge and ford can be rushed. He says surrender and save bloodshed. He says if we surrender nobody'll be harmed. Provisions and fresh mounts taken only. What do you say?"

The storekeeper who had wanted to give Morgan the butt-end of his mind rose now in his stirrups and delivered a piece of it. "He's lying. Men don't start talking until they're past fighting."

"If he had five thousand men they'd be in Vernon now. Bloodshed, so long's it's your blood, ain't nothin' to a reb."

"Horses and provisions, eh? Who appointed us quartermaster corps to the Confederate Army?"

Ben Whitey gave the final answer. He yelled. His yell wasn't practiced like the rebel screech; it hadn't the long falsetto midnight quaver which could raise the hackles and slide between the bones like cold steel, but it was very strong and it lifted toward the end with a raw, unsheathed resonance of its own. It seemed what they had waited for, it seemed the only answer to give. It drained away the uncertainty, the distrust, the fear that had accumulated during the long wait. Above the quiet river it rose in great volume and flowed in a roiled and mounting current across the summer fields. Josh's musket quivered with the violence of his own shouting.

The colonel regarded his men quizzically, then shrugged his shoulders as if to say to the raiders, "What can I do with such fire-eaters?" and rode back to the rebel leader. There was another conference, shorter than the first one, after which the raiders turned, cantered back down the road up which they had just ridden.

"They give us two hours," the colonel said, "to get our women and children out of town. After which, they attack."

At eight that evening they were still waiting, drawn up, ready. The new moon had set and the night was very dark and warm, filled with soft summer stars which seemed to escape from set star shapes and let light shimmer fluidly—and, it almost seemed, moistly—across the sky. Some time later the captain with the militiaman by his side came up to the group Josh was in.

"Count off here," he said. "I'm sending twenty of you men to Finney's Ford. The rebs could come through there as well as here if they know the crick. There's a company there now—but no use having any if you don't have enough." He turned to the militiaman. "Let some of your men sleep," he said, "but keep a heavy guard posted."

Josh rode with the twenty men slowly and quietly through the night, back across the bridge and to the north side of the river where any party attempting to use the ford could be fired on while in the water. He rode among strangers. Gum and Ben Whitey had been left behind, and he thought, as he had been thinking all day, "Now it begins."

In the darkness the company at the ford seemed very large—the men dismounted, speaking in muffled voices, their horses tethered and resting behind them.

"The crick takes a turn here," the new men were told. "Twenty feet down to the bottom here, so keep your eyes peeled. I'm going to let you men have a couple of hours' sleep then you can relieve some of us. Get out of your saddles and get some rest—but don't rest so hard you can't hear a raider crossin' that branch."

Josh dismounted and felt his way along the bank in the layered darkness. He felt rather than saw the stream below him, smelled it really, he believed, though he could hear the occasional lap of a little eddy against a stone, and see here and there a prick of light reflected from a star. He ate some cold biscuit that he had picked up when he left home, gave Rome a biscuit, then stretched out on his blankets, somewhat withdrawn from the main body of the militia and near the bank of the stream. Rome stood behind him snuffing at the scent of the strange men and horses, mounting the already cropped over grass in search of a neglected tuft.

War, Josh thought, seemed a hard thing to come at. The dying and killing he had declared himself ready for at the breakfast table, and which he had imagined he'd meet face to face as soon as he'd gotten out on to the road, seemed always to lurk round another corner. He had fortified himself for so many encounters—with either or both—that there were now almost no further breastworks he could fling up, or armaments he could assemble. His supply of anticipation was about used up. War appeared to consist not of dramatic and immediate sacrifice, as he had foreseen it at the breakfast table, but of an infinite series of waitings and postponements.

This is it, he had said, and it was only Ben Whitey waiting at the cut-off. This is it, and it was Vernon as much like Fourth of July as war. This surely is it, he had said, and it was the wind in the elder clump. This, this: a man with a white flag. And now in the dark night to defend the ford—and this was not it either—but simply lying at ease on his blankets, his cherry addled stomach settled with biscuit, Rome munching by his side, and the milky way banding the sky familiarly. Except for the gun under his hand it could be any summer night, lying outside for a time to cool off before bedtime. And if John Morgan himself should bend over him, prod him with his toe and say, "*This* is it, bub," he didn't know whether he'd believe him or not. Getting ready for war might be a short horse and soon curried, but war itself was a horse liable to stretch— so far as he could see—from July to eternity . . . head at Maple Grove and hocks in Beulah Land.

Josh closed his eyes to sleep; but beneath his lids there flowed not only the remembered sights of the day, the faces, attitudes, gestures he had seen and noted, but the multitudinous sights that there had been in daylight no time to name, or space within the crowded mind to delineate. Now in darkness, behind shut lids, they lived again. He saw the L-shaped rip in the pants of the raider who had carried the white flag. He saw now, trying to sleep, the controlled drop of a spider—delicately spinning, from the spire of an unblooming head of goldenrod to the yellowed grass beneath it. He heard a voice—the storekeeper's, he thought—say, "I'm a man of peace—but there ain't any peace when your neighbors are being killed. And if it's a question of good blood—or bad—on my hands, by God, I choose bad."

At last he slept—and continued to see and hear . . . a raider was trying to take his mother's starling . . . he had ridden his horse inside the summer kitchen, and overturned the table, trampled the crockery and was snatching at Ebony in his cage and Ebony, above the sounds of confusion, was screaming, "Wake up, wake up."

Josh woke up. He found himself in the center of a great bubbling cauldron of noise: men shouting, screaming advice, cursing; horses neighing; and in the creek below the splash and clatter of men and animals crossing the ford. There was a spattering of shots. Someone was calling over and over, "Mount, mount, mount."

Josh stepped cautiously, felt for Rome in the dark, said his name, doubled his hands hoping to feel them close upon horseflesh, harkened to the billowing roll of sound. Then suddenly the sound fanned out, burst inside his head, roared against the bones of his skull and, breaking through bone and tissue, trickled out by way of mouth and nose; it fluttered a few last times against his ear drums, then left him in quiet.

It was daylight before he was sure what had happened: he had gone over the cliff, through the branches of a willow which grew almost parallel with the stream, and now lay within hand's reach of the creek itself. At first he had tried to call out, but the sound of his own voice had detonated like gunfire inside his head and he was afraid that his skull, which he reckoned was broken, might fall apart with the effort. He was half-conscious, and wholly sick, but between bouts of retching he thought: "This is it. I've come to it at last. This is war. It's falling over a cliff, cracking thy skull, and puking."

It was just after sun-up when Labe found him. He had about given up when he heard sounds from beneath the willow.

"Josh," he cried, "thee's all right."

"No, I'm not," said Josh morosely.

"Oh Josh," Labe said again, and knelt beside him, "thee's all right."

"I wish thee'd stop saying that," Josh told him. "It makes me feel sicker. I'm not all right. My head's split, I think."

Labe looked at it. "It does kind of look that way," he said, "but if thee's not died yet, I reckon thee's not going to."

Josh moaned.

"Why didn't thee call out—get some help?" Labe asked.

"At first," Josh said, "because I didn't know anything. Then when I did, if I even opened my mouth to whisper, my whole head like to fell off. Then I got so's I could talk, but if I did, I puked. I still do," he said, and did. "I wish thee'd go away," he told Labe finally, "and leave me alone. I was beginning to get a little easy."

He lay still for a time. After awhile he asked, "How'd thee come to find me?"

"Rome came home without thee."

"I'd just as lief stay here," Josh whispered bitterly. "Go to war and fall off a cliff."

"Thee needn't let that fash thee," Labe said. "More did than didn't."

Then as if he'd just remembered why he was lying on First Day morning by a crickside with a broken head, Josh asked, "Where's Morgan? Did we get him?"

"He didn't come this way."

Josh lifted himself painfully upon one elbow. "Didn't come this way?" he said. "I heard him. I heard him cross the crick last night."

"That wasn't Morgan," Labe told him. "That was some cotton-headed farmers over'n the south bank who took a freak to drive their stock across to where your company was, to save them from the rebs."

"I was fooled," said Josh. "I thought it was Morgan."

"Thee had plenty of company. They was all fooled."

"Where's Morgan now?" Josh asked.

"Dupont, they say. He gave Vernon the go-by."

Josh lay back. The happiness he felt hurt his head so that for a minute he couldn't speak. They had stood off Johnny Morgan—they had kept him out of Vernon.

When he had first come to, found himself lying at the edge of the crick, he had thought he would hate admitting he'd been hurt, not by gun or saber, but by falling over a bank onto his head. Now it didn't seem to matter. Yesterday morning and his talk of dying and killing seemed almost a lifetime away; the past twenty-four hours, a prolonged campaign from which he had emerged a veteran, with mind much cleared as to what mattered and what did not.

Next time . . . he wouldn't talk so big about fighting and dying. But that didn't matter either, now. What mattered was that he had stood there . . . he had been afraid, but he had stood at the bridge. He had thought of running but he hadn't done it . . . he had stood in the front line not knowing but that Morgan himself might bear down upon them . . . he had stood at the crick's edge in the darkness and confusion and had been hunting gun and horse when he had fallen.

And the things he had learned . . . talk beforehand is no good . . . in the darkness on a twenty-foot cliff it is best not to hurry . . . death when you move toward it, seems to retreat; it is only when you turn and run, that it pursues.

"Labe," he whispered, "we stood them off. We saved Vernon."

There was nothing Labe could say to this. Presently he asked, "If I got some help does thee think thee could move, Josh? They're worried about thee at home. Pa didn't take off his clothes all night. He's on his way here now."

Josh felt his mouth begin to tremble and put his arm across his face as if to keep the sun out.

"If thee'd help me," he said, "I think I could. I'd like to meet pa half way."

CHAPTER NINE

Lincoln Was a Hoosier, Too

Scores, more likely hundreds, of biographies of Abraham Lincoln have been published; of them all, appropriately for our present purpose, the one which gives the most complete, best documented account of the life of the young Lincoln in Indiana is the masterpiece of

ALBERT JEREMIAH BEVERIDGE—of Indiana.

He was born in Ohio and spent his boyhood in Illinois, but after he completed his preparatory schooling he enrolled as a student at De Pauw University. Thereafter until his death he was a Hoosier. His talent for oratory led naturally to the law and to politics. In the course of a distinguished career he eventually reached the United States Senate as a Republican, but he had the misfortune to make a wrong guess in the matter of Theodore Roosevelt's potential as a vote-getter; he joined the Progressive Party and suffered the fate of many another public figure of his day.

Beveridge will be longest remembered not as a statesman but as a biographer: as, in fact, one of the very best biographers of the twentieth century, or perhaps of any other. His first great work was The Life of John Marshall, published in four volumes between 1916 and 1919; his last, only half-completed at the time of his death, was

Abraham Lincoln
[1809-1858]

CHAPTER II INDIANA: BOYHOOD AND YOUTH

Not earlier . . . than the approach of December, 1816, the Lincoln family started for the Indiana solitudes. Two horses bore husband, wife, and children as well as household belongings. Upon one horse rode the father, his little son mounted behind him; on the other horse was Nancy Lincoln, with their nine-year-old daughter. . . . In two days, the ferry was reached, where, leaving the horses, the Lincoln family was taken across the river to Posey's farm on the Indiana side.

There, it is said, Thomas Lincoln borrowed a wagon to take wife, children, and household articles to Pigeon Creek. . . .

Winter was at hand—it may be that the thin snow even then was beginning to fly. Thomas hastily built a shelter for his family. It was a "half-faced camp," such as hunters were wont to throw up as a protection against the weather, not unlike that sometimes found in sugar-camps at a later day. . . . One side of this structure, which was only fourteen feet wide, was not enclosed; and before this open side, a fire, started by steel and tinder, was kept burning, upon which cooking was done. . . . The loose, unhardened earth was the floor, on which leaves were thickly strewn; and over these was spread such bedding as had been brought, skins for the most part and possibly a blanket.

Within and about this camp of poles and brush existed Abraham Lincoln, then in his eighth year, together with his sister and parents throughout the winter of 1816–17. [Dennis] Hanks relates that the second day after the family arrived, the boy killed a turkey "with his farthers Riffle," more by accident than skill, since "Turkies two Numer[ous] to Mention." No other food but game brought in by Thomas Lincoln was possible at first; and water was to be had only by melting the snow, or by carrying in a kettle from the distant spring. Luckily Thomas Lincoln did not have far to go to get sustenance for his family, game filling the thickets that surrounded the small hill on which the half-faced camp was built. "We did not have to go more than 4 or 5 hundred Yards to Kill deer, turkeys and other wild game," Dennis Hanks relates of the following year.

At last came the spring of 1817. Wild rose, swamp lily, wild honeysuckle, blue flag and yellow flag, Sweet William bloomed; crab apple, wild plum, haw trees blossomed; grape clusters began to form; abundant dogwood made spots of white among the brush and trees. The waters of Pigeon Creek rose in their banks and, warmed by the season, invited those begrimed by winter's unwashed months. . . .

In the autumn of 1817, Nancy Lincoln's heart was gladdened by the arrival of her aunt and uncle, Betsy and Thomas Sparrow, who with Dennis Hanks, now eighteen years of age, had come to live permanently with the Lincolns. "Lincoln had Bilt another Cabin By this time," says Hanks, "and got in it a Bout 40 Rods apart" from the half-faced camp. This cabin was of the usual type, round logs with the bark on and roof of poles and slabs. It was larger than any the Lincoln family had lived in, being eighteen feet wide and twenty feet long; and it was high enough for a loft beneath the roof, reached by pegs driven in the log walls.

But no floor was laid, no door contrived, no window; even the roof was not finished when cold weather came. Nor did the approach of another winter quicken the domestic enterprise of Thomas Lincoln; and Hanks chronicles of this and later years, that "we all hunted pretty much all the time, Especially So when we got tired of work—which was very often I will assure you."

In the uncompleted cabin Thomas, Nancy and their children spent the fall of 1817 and the following winter; Thomas and Betsy Sparrow with Dennis Hanks, occupying "that Darne Little half face camp," as Dennis called it, near by. No dogs or cats cheered the Lincoln hut, no chickens, hogs or cows were about. The only light was from hog fat. For most of the day the two men roved with their rifles, they, Nancy, and the children, living well-nigh exclusively on wild animals and birds—"ate them as meat, water and bread," as Hanks told Herndon. Sometimes Lincoln and Hanks varied their hunting by search for wild honey and "found bee trees all over the forest." In the autumn nuts and wild fruit added variety to their fare. Hanks records that "the country was full of chestnuts, Paw paws, . . . wild-turkey peas;" and hickory-nuts, walnuts, hazel-nuts were plentiful. . . .

It was more than a year after he had squatted on the land, that Thomas Lincoln bethought him of the necessity of entering it legally. So he made his way through the forests ninety miles to Vincennes where the land office then was, and, on October 15, 1817, entered the Southwest quarter of Section 32, Township 4 South, Range 5 West, paying the preliminary instalment of sixteen dollars. . . . In December he paid sixty-four dollars more, thus completing his first instalment of eighty dollars, one fourth of the purchase price, the land being sold by the government for two dollars per acre. His right to a patent to the land when he should make the remaining payments thus being established, he rested content and the routine of farming, hunting, and carpentering continued.

Thus dragged along the slow dull weeks. Another winter went by, another spring and summer. Then in the autumn of 1818 a disease, mysterious as forest shadows, came suddenly upon Pigeon Creek. "The milk sick" the settlers called it, because it attacked cattle and particularly milch cows as virulently as men and women. No cure was known and those seized generally died, and died quickly. The nearest doctor lived thirty-five miles from Pigeon Creek and, if accessible, could have done no good, since medical treatment proved wholly inadequate then, or for many years afterward.

Betsy and Thomas Sparrow, who were known in the settlement as "Mrs. Lincoln's father and mother," were stricken in the half-faced camp and there on skins and leaves covering the ground they died, about eighteen months after their coming. A tree was felled, a log of right length cut and whip-sawed into rough, uneven boards. These Thomas Lincoln fashioned into rude boxes, fastening them together with wooden pegs driven into holes made by a small auger, for no nails were at hand. Into these boxes the bodies were placed, and, upon a wooded hill some quarter mile distant, were buried.

To the sick old man and woman Nancy Lincoln had given all the help she could; she had visited, in her last illness, the wife of Peter

Brooner, a hunter chiefly, whose cabin was only half a mile away. Mrs. Brooner died, too; and, at the same time, Nancy Lincoln fell sick. Neighbors attended her and one of them, William Wood, recalls that he "sat up with her all one night." Thus "she struggled on" for a week; and at the last, calling Sarah and Abraham to her side, told them to be good to their father, to each other, and to reverence God. She died in October, 1818, on the seventh day of her illness.

Thomas Lincoln made a coffin for his wife as he had for the others; and on a sled, as the first pioneer woman in that region had been taken to her grave, the body of Nancy Lincoln was hauled to the knoll and buried by the side of her foster parents. No stone or board was placed to mark where she lay, nor during the life-time of her husband or son was a monument of any kind erected over that neglected grave.

Abraham was now nine years old, and there is no evidence that his emotions were unlike those of other children of similar age and in the same situation. Back to their doorless, windowless, floorless cabin, went Thomas Lincoln and his children; and there, with Dennis Hanks, they lived through the remainder of the winter, through the spring, the summer and the autumn of 1819. Sarah, now in her thirteenth year, did the cooking. . . .

Sometime after the death of Nancy Lincoln, an itinerant Baptist preacher, David Elkin, came from Kentucky on a visit to the Pigeon Creek settlement; and while there preached a sermon over the graves of Nancy Lincoln and those who had died from the plague during the fatal days of 1818. Abraham and his sister were present of course, as were Thomas Lincoln and Dennis Hanks, and all who lived in the settlement, about twenty in number. But Abraham had not written to Elkin asking him to come and preach a funeral sermon over his mother's grave, as legend has it; even if the boy had thought of such a ceremony, of which he then could have known little or nothing, he could not write at that time, nor indeed for five years thereafter, "so that he could understand" what he wrote.

Other settlers were taking up claims in the region, cabins of unbarked logs were rising here and there, children multiplying, society forming. In common with most people of the Western country, those on and about Pigeon Creek were very ignorant, rough mannered, vividly superstitious. . . .

The cabins of these wood folk were often ill-kept, dirty in the extreme, infested with vermin. There was no sanitation. Bathing or washing the body in any way was seldom attempted, seldom thought of except, of course, during "swimming time" in warm weather. It is hard to see how, from December to March inclusive, the clothes they wore could have been washed. Food was mostly of flesh, with some corn or wheat broken in stump mortars; and, generally, the cooking was poor and insufficient, frying in grease being a favorite method.

Cabins usually were packed, husband and wife, children, guests, relatives, and hired men living in a single small room—cooking, eating, and sleeping there, a loft sometimes relieving the congestion. The sense of modesty was embryonic, and men took off their clothes before women without a thought by either of any impropriety. Men and boys wore deerskin trousers and coats and coonskin caps; the clothing of women and girls was of linsey-woolsey, home-made from wool and flax. Usually everybody went barefoot during spring and summer; and when they did not, wore moccasins made of hide, until shoes appeared.

Incredible quantities of whisky were consumed, everybody, women and preachers included, drinking the fiery liquid. A bottle was in every cabin—to offer it was the first gesture of welcome, to refuse unpardonable incivility. All used tobacco, chewing, smoking, snuffing; and corn-cob pipes in the mouths of women were a not uncommon sight. Men were quick to fight and combats were brutal. Profanity was general and emphatic.

Yet an innate love of justice, truthfulness, and fair dealing permeated every community, and generous and ready hospitality was the highest ordinance. The desire that their children should get "learning" was well-nigh a passion. . . .

The Lincoln children went to Andrew Crawford's school for a while during the winter of 1818–19. . . . Spelling, reading, writing, and "ciphering to single rule of 3 no further" were taught in the haphazard manner of the period and region. It was a "blab" or "loud school," the children studying vocally. Punishment was ad-

ministered by whipping or making the child wear the "dunce cap."
"When we went to Crawford he tried to learn us manners," relates
Nathaniel Grigsby, showing the pupils how to enter a room, the
formalities of introduction and the like.

But the teacher gave up after one season, it appears, as frontier
school promoters sometimes did. Thereafter Andrew Crawford dis-
appears from the chronicles of Pigeon Creek pedagogy. Lincoln was
then in his tenth year and he did not again go to school until "he
was about 14 or 15." What he learned from Crawford we do not
know; a little simple reading, perhaps, and how to form words with
a quill pen—certainly not much more, since he could not write well
until four or five years later.

Back and forth during the winter months of 1818–19, went the
Lincoln children from the log schoolhouse in the woods to the unfinished cabin on the knoll. Thomas Lincoln and Dennis Hanks
were the providers, protectors, mentors. . . .

Imagination must picture the situation and manner of existence
of these two men living with the girl and boy in that hut in the
brush throughout the year 1819. From trustworthy accounts of
better conditioned families in the same wilderness, it can only be
believed that for the Lincolns 1819 was a year of squalor—mostly
flesh for food, unfit water, wretched cooking, no knives or forks,
bare feet, bodies partly clad, filthy beds of leaves and skins.

A time came when even Thomas Lincoln could stand it no longer.
So back to Kentucky he journeyed for another wife. He knew where
to go, it appears, for he went directly to Elizabethtown where the
woman he had first courted, Sarah Bush, still lived. She was now a
widow, her first husband, Daniel Johnston, having died of the
"cold plague" in 1814, leaving three children for Sarah to care for,
John D., Sarah [Elizabeth], and Matilda. Immediately on coming
to Hardin County, Lincoln must have seen Sarah's brother, Isaac
Bush, and collected from him at least part of the money which he
had paid Isaac for the Sinking Spring farm eleven years before. If
so, it is but natural that the two men should have talked of the
plight of widow and widower and the good sense of their marriage.

Certainly Lincoln made quick work of the business when he saw
Sarah in Elizabethtown, and as certainly he was in funds. As related

by Samuel Haycraft, then deputy clerk of Hardin County Court, Thomas Lincoln, on December 1, 1819, went to the house of Sarah Johnston in Elizabethtown, reminded her of their mutual bereavement and proposed that they get married "right off." The widow said she could not "right off as she owed some little debts which she wanted to pay first." Lincoln asked for a list of the debts "got the list paid them off that evening. Next Morning I issued the license and they were marr[i]ed . . . right off."

Without delay Thomas and Sarah, with her three children, started for Indiana. They took with them the household goods and furniture which had been gathered by the thrifty Sarah during the lifetime of her first husband. In comparison with the store taken by Thomas and Nancy Lincoln in the winter of 1816, Sarah Lincoln's domestic effects must have been opulent; for it took a wagon and team of four horses, borrowed from Ralph Crume, a brother-in-law of Lincoln, to haul the load to the Ohio. Pots, pans, skillets, blankets, covers, a feather bed, a bureau which "cost 45 dollars in K[entuck]y," were among the things piled in the wagon.

So, in mid-winter 1819–20, came Thomas and Sarah Lincoln to the dirty, unkempt cabin near Pigeon Creek, where his neglected children and the vagrant Dennis Hanks were maintaining a bare existence. So, too, began a new and distinct period in the life of Abraham Lincoln. Sarah Lincoln was blessed with energy and sense, was a good housekeeper, prudent, systematic, and with a passion for cleanliness. . . .

No more hunting for Thomas Lincoln and Dennis Hanks until they had split and smoothed puncheons and made a floor, finished the roof, put in a door, cut a place for greased paper to let in the light. The children were washed, combed and "dressed . . . up" so as to look "more human"; the cabin cleansed, decent bedding put on the "bedsteads made . . . of poles and clapboards." The fire-place was overhauled, ample cooking utensils installed; and Thomas was stirred into making a proper table, better stools and, perchance, a hickory chair or two. The change was so pronounced that, nearly thirty-five years afterward, Lincoln remembered and described it.

Eight persons, three adults and five children, now inhabited the Lincoln cabin. Three or four years later, in 1823, John Hanks, the half-brother of Dennis Hanks, joined the Lincoln family and lived with them for four years, thus making nine who dwelt within those crowded walls. But, under Sarah Lincoln's guidance, there were comparative order and harmony. . . .

A year or two after the coming of Sarah Lincoln, another school, about four miles away, was started by one Azel W. Dorsey. It was exactly like that of Andrew Crawford except that Dorsey did not try to "learn manners" to the children. Abraham went to this school for a short time. A schoolmate tells us that he was "long and tall . . . wore low shoes, short socks and his britches made of buckskin" were so short that they left "bare and naked 6 or more inches of Abe Lincoln's shin bone." The school books from which the teacher gave out his lessons were the Bible, Webster's or Dilworth's *Spelling Book*, Pike's *Arithmetic* and a song book.

It was at Dorsey's school that he perfected that clear, distinct chirography, so like that of Washington and Jefferson; and here too he learned to spell with that accuracy which was to become a tradition in the neighborhood. He did all the writing for the family and indeed for everybody in the settlement. Even more important to his avid mind was the fact that he learned to read with ease and fluency.

So ended the education of Abraham Lincoln in schools, except for a short and broken attendance in 1826 at a similar school taught by William Sweeney. . . .

There was, indeed, no reason for him to go longer to these backwoods teachers—they "could do him no further good; he went to school no more."

In the Indiana schools he excelled, it appears, particularly in spelling and could "spell down" the whole class when, at the close of the school every Friday, the older children were placed in line against the log wall for a contest in spelling. . . .

He was notably studious in everything—"head and Shoulders above us all," confesses Dennis Hanks. He would help the other pupils, "would learn us get our cip[h]ers." His stepmother tells us that, when at home, Abraham "cyphered on boards when he had no paper or no slate and when the board would get too black he would Shave it off with a drawing Knife and go on again: When he had paper he put his sums down on it." He made a copy-book by sewing together blank sheets which Dennis Hanks gave him: "I bought the paper [and] gave it to Abe." In this he did his work in arithmetic, scribbling at three places this legend:

> "Abraham Lincoln, his hand and pen
> he will be good but God knows when."

He early showed that kindness of heart which distinguished him throughout life. At Crawford's school the boy reproved other children for cruelty to animals, particularly the placing of glowing coals on backs of turtles; and, even then, wrote "short sentences" against it. While at Dorsey's school he wrote poetry. "Abe took it up of his own accord," relates Grigsby. He kept this up at Sweeney's too, and at both schools also wrote "compositions against Cruelty to animals," which barbarity seems to have been a favorite practice of his schoolmates, and young Lincoln's particular aversion. Indeed, revulsion at brutality, sympathy for the suffering, animals as well as humans, constituted the dominant note of his character, even in boyhood. He always came to school good humored and laughing and "he scarcely ever quarreled." . . .

About the time he learned to read, the boy was big enough to do work upon the ungracious farm, and to labor for others, his earnings going to the father, a legal right which Thomas Lincoln exacted rigidly until Abraham reached the full age of twenty-one. . . .

Between Thomas Lincoln and his son, so different in intellect, character and appearance, there was little sympathy or understanding; and for some reason the father treated Abraham roughly. Sometimes a blow from the old man's fist would hurl the boy "a rod." "I have Seen his father Nock him Down of the fence when a Stranger would call for Information to NeighBour house," testifies Dennis Hanks, who adds that "the Old Man Loved his Childern." Thomas Lincoln also thrashed the lad, who took his punishment in silence, tears the only outward sign of what he felt and thought.

All this led Dennis Hanks to doubt whether "Abe Loved his farther Very well or Not," and to conclude that "I Dont think he Did." . . . A. H. Chapman . . . says, "Thos. Lincoln never showed by his actions that he thought much of his son Abraham when a boy. He treated him rather unkindly than otherwise, always appeared to think much more of his stepson John D. Johnston than he did of his own Abraham."

The father's ill-treatment of the son seems the more extraordinary in view of Abraham's remarkably good nature; for he was conspicuously obliging, eager to please everybody, his parents most of all. "Abe was a good boy . . . the best boy I ever saw," declares his stepmother. "I can say," she continues, "what scarcely one woman, a mother, can say in a thousand . . . Abe never gave me a cross word or look and never refused . . . to do anything I requested [of] him. I never gave him a cross word in all my life. . . . His mind and mine, what little I had, seemed to run together—move in the same channel." Abraham's devotion to Sarah Lincoln, whom he always called "mama," is striking. Many years later he told Chapman of "the encouragement he always had received from his Step Mother" and declared that "she had been his best Friend in this world and that no Son could love a Mother more than he loved her." . . .

The mystery of the father's attitude towards Abraham is deepened by the unanimous and positive testimony to the placid character of Thomas Lincoln. Dennis Hanks, who was devoted to him, describes him as a "good humored, sociable man who took the world easy, loving everybody and everything." Dennis Hanks's son-in-law declares that Thomas Lincoln was "remarkable peaceable . . . good natured;" John Hanks says that "happiness was the end of life with him," and Nathaniel Grigsby recalls that he was "happy, lived Easy and contented."

Yet from his point of view, Thomas Lincoln was, perhaps, not without some excuse for his harshness; for certain it is that Abraham was so absorbed with books that he showed no love for work with his hands, and was not quick to take up any physical task. "Farming, grubbing, hoeing, making fences," as John Hanks describes the boy's work, had no attraction for him. He would carry a book with him when he had to go to work, and over its pages he would pore when rest time came.

Even the alertly partial Dennis Hanks admits that Abraham "was lazy—a very lazy man. He was always reading, Scribbling, writing, ciphering, writing Poetry," etc. This too is the testimony of his step-sister: "Abe was not energetic except in one thing—he was active and persistent in learning—read everything he could—ciphered on boards, on the walls." . . .

The distasteful toil in field and wood was lightened by Abraham's fun and wit; and, although he had no voice for singing, he would join the other hands in shouting the songs of the time and place—in the language of Dennis Hanks, "Hail Collumbia Hap[py] Land if you aint Broke I will Be Damned," or "the turbentuck [turbaned Turk] that Scorns the world and Struts aBout with his whiskers curled for No other Man But himSelf to see and all Such as this." Other and rougher songs there were. Nathaniel Grigsby tells us that: "we sung what is called carnel Songs and love songs. i cannot repeat any of them at this time we sung a song called Barbra allen also we sung the Silk Merchant daughter and others." . . .

So the tall, bony youth, with a coonskin cap on his head and clad in deerskin shirt and homemade trousers which were still always far too short, exposing many inches of "sharp, blue and narrow" shins, went about the countryside doing, in languid fashion, the jobs he was hired to do, or working reluctantly on his father's stumpy farm; but always cracking jokes, telling stories, joining, though poorly, in the songs of the other workers; and, whenever his father or employer was not about, making speeches to his fellows. . . .

Reading, however, was the outstanding phase of Lincoln's life at this time. Much as he loved pranks with other youths, he would forego their jollity and lose himself in some new volume upon which he chanced. "Whilst other boys were idling away their time," says a schoolmate and companion, "Lincoln was studying his books. . . . He read and thoroughly read his books whilst we played." But there was little if any studying by the wavering light from logs in the fireplace or from the dim glow of turnip candle. On the contrary, he studied in the daytime, says his stepmother; "didn't after night much, went to bed early, got up early and then read."

Thus he consumed the scanty store of books brought to the Lincoln cabin by his stepmother, when she came to Pigeon Creek near Christmas time, 1819, wrought in cabin and surroundings the miracle we have witnessed, and rescued the children from the dirt accumulated since their mother died a year before. There had been a few books in her Kentucky household and, although Sarah Lincoln could not read, she knew the value of them, it seems, and brought them with her. There were but four or five volumes—*Robinson Crusoe, Pilgrim's Progress, Sinbad the Sailor, Æsop's Fables.* It appears that this was the first time a Bible found a place in the cabin, for Hanks records that "Thomas Lincoln brought the Bible in 1818 or 19." . . .

In 1823, seven years after Thomas Lincoln came to Indiana and four years after his marriage to Sarah Johnston, he joined, by letter, the Pigeon Creek Baptist Church, a congregation of Primitive Baptists. . . .

To this church, after 1823, the family went when a preacher of that sect came to Pigeon Creek. When Abraham was in his fifteenth year, he would repeat to his companions and others, almost verbatim, the sermons he heard, imitating the delivery of the preacher, for he was an excellent mimic. . . .

Although others of the family became members of the Pigeon Creek congregation, Abraham did not then or afterwards "join church." His stepmother explains that "Abe had no particular religion—didn't think of that question at that time, if he ever did. He never talked about it." "i cannot tel you what his notions of the bible were," wrote Nathaniel Grigsby to Herndon; "he talked about religion as other persons did but i do not now his view on religion he never made any profession while in Ind[iana] that i now of." . . .

There is sharp dispute as to the extent of his reading of the Bible, Dennis Hanks asserting that "Lincoln didnt read the Bible half as much as [is] said," and that although "he did read it, I though[t] he never believed it and think so still." Mrs. Lincoln confirms Hanks's testimony: "Abe read the bible some, though not as much as said." On the other hand Grigsby declares that "he was a great talker on the scriptures and read it a great deal;" and Grigsby is supported by Lincoln's later literary style. . . .

The books at home exhausted, he ranged the countryside in search of more, an intellectual prowler for the sustenance of the printed page. His step-mother asserts that "Abe read all the books he could lay his hands on." In 1823 when Abraham was fourteen years of age, Levi Hall who had married Nancy Hanks, aunt of Nancy Lincoln and mother without marriage of Dennis Hanks, came with his family to the Pigeon Creek settlement. They brought the copy of Bailey's *Etymological Dictionary*, which Mordecai Lincoln had bought in 1793. The fact that this dictionary was at his hand must be borne in mind while considering the books read by Lincoln during the years that he remained in Indiana.

Several books were discovered by the eager youth and made his intellectual property; for, as we shall presently see, Lincoln remembered all he read. Only six of these volumes will here be noted, however, since the influence of these was determinative.

From some source and in some way he got hold of a copy of Grimshaw's *History of the United States*. Of all the American histories in one volume published at that time none had such peculiar qualities as that by William Grimshaw. The first chapter explains the advances made in astronomy, geography, and navigation; and, thus, the reader has before him at the start the existing condition of the world. Then follows the account of the discovery of America and the development of the colonies. . . .

The early New England persecutions are set forth in wrathful terms and an earnest plea made against intolerance. The causes of the Revolution are stated clearly, the patriot writings named, the War for Independence and later events described. The book ends with the cession of Florida to the United States; and, as a climax, the progress of literature, science and art is described. . . .

Abraham had worked for David Turnham, who lived near Grandview on the Ohio. Turnham, six years older than Lincoln, was a prosperous farmer, a Justice of the Peace and a man of uncommon ability. As will presently appear, he had much influence on Lincoln's life. He owned the *Revised Laws of Indiana;* and sometime before he left the State, Lincoln borrowed this formidable volume of nearly five hundred long pages and read it repeatedly and with care. This was the first law book he ever read. . . . Through this volume Lincoln acquired a fair understanding of the elements of law and government.

During this period, too, he read another book which had more and greater qualities making for general culture than any one volume he is positively known to have read. This volume was popularly called "Scott's Lessons." Its formal title was *Lessons in Elocution, or Selections of Pieces in Prose and Verse for the Improvement of Youth in Reading and Speaking,* by William Scott, of Edinburgh. The book opens with short essays upon public speaking, the object of which should be to convey a "precise idea." Scott urges simplicity and intelligence of gesture, distinctness of enunciation, right placing of emphasis, pausing at the end of one sentence before beginning the next, and other items of the technique of delivery.

Then come what the compiler calls "Lessons in Reading," beginning with five pages of maxims. Brief selections from the classics follow. . . . Excerpts from many poems are next; and then a good selection of pieces for recitation. . . . Short and pointed quotations are made illustrative of various forms of speech—antithesis, climax, enunciation, query, and the like.

Lincoln is known to have studied the *Kentucky Preceptor,* a compilation by an unknown hand and not unlike Scott's *Lessons* in general contents. . . . It was a school reader belonging to Josiah Crawford, of whom Lincoln borrowed it, and Mrs. Crawford, in giving the book to Herndon, stated that out of it "Lincoln learned his speeches."

The other two books worthy of note, which are known to have been read by Lincoln while in Indiana, are Weems's *Life of Washington* and the same writer's *Life of Franklin.* It has not been discovered where he got the *Life of Franklin,* but he borrowed Weems's *Washington* from Josiah Crawford, a young farmer of the neighborhood, who had brought the book with him from Kentucky. Abraham worked for Crawford, at times, having "daubed" his fifteen feet square log cabin when the Crawfords arrived in 1824. It seems that the youth left the book where rain injured it, a calamity of which he promptly told Crawford, who gave him the volume and he "pulled fodder a day or two for it." . . .

Such were the volumes, each of which it should be remembered Lincoln read so thoroughly that he could repeat, word for word, parts that best pleased him. "When he came across a passage that struck him he would write it down on boards if he had no paper and keep it there till he did get paper, then he would rewrite it, look at it, repeat it. He had a copy-book, a kind of scrap-book in which he put down all things and thus preserved them."

At Rockport, where Abraham often went, he made the acquaintance of John Pitcher, the first resident attorney of Rockport, who afterwards became prosecuting attorney for Spencer County. Pitcher had a good library which, as he declared sixty years later, included the "standard works of that day," as well as law books; and the use of this library was given to young Lincoln. . . .

Along with the pleasing fiction of midnight study by the log fire, we must dismiss the unhappy legend that Thomas Lincoln interfered with Abraham's incessant reading. The father yielded to the influence of Sarah Lincoln, it appears, and did not disturb his son's devotion to books. "As a usual thing," says his wife, "Mr. Lincoln never made Abe quit reading to do anything if he could avoid it. He would do it himself first . . . he himself felt the uses and necessities of education and wanted his boy Abraham to learn and encouraged him to do it in all ways he could." . . .

Young Lincoln liked to tell what he knew—insisted on telling it. In fact, self-expression was indispensable to the youth, and he became a very geyser of loquacity, talking incessantly to all who would listen—and most were eager to hear him. For he never bored anybody. His talk was informing, to be sure; but it was witty too and full of humor. Nobody could resist his funny stories, and he was as fond of jokes as he was of reading. . . .

He was abnormally gregarious and, when not lost in the pages of some book, made shift to be where other people were, the larger the number the better he was pleased. Yet he did not seek crowds—indeed he shunned them, another of those contradictions of character which so often perplex the student of Lincoln, as they perplexed those who came in contact with him throughout his perplexing life.

Still he went to all the social gatherings—"alway attended house raisings, log rolling, corn shucking and workings of all kinds." There was a small prairie on the South Fork of Pigeon Creek and there members of the local militia gathered for muster. Lincoln was always on hand at these jolly assemblages. And no other person in the now comparatively well populated settlement was so welcome everywhere, for he always was cheerful and tried to make others happy too. . . .

But "Abe did not go much with the girls . . . didnt like girls much, too frivolous," says Mrs. Allen Gentry, then Anna C. Roby, who saw as much of Lincoln at that time as any girl in the settlement except, of course, his sister and step-sisters. . . . The girls liked him, however, because he was "friendly, somewhat sociable, not so much so as we wanted him." Certainly there was nothing attractive in Abraham's appearance, for he was "a long, thin, leggy, gawky boy dried up and shriveled." Even by his sixteenth year he was "6 feet high" and "bony and raw, dark skinned."

Lincoln began to make speeches as early as his fifteenth year. He would mount a tree stump, or stand upon a fence and talk to his fellow workers, who would leave their jobs in fields or woods to listen. "His father would come and make him quit, send him to work," says his step-sister who saw and heard these incidents. Her mother tells us the same thing. "His father had to make him quit sometimes, as he would quit his own work to speak and made the other children as well as the men quit their work."

Of greater moment, however, than the fact that he made them at all, was the arrangement of his speeches and the style of his delivery. Considering the examples of exclamatory and emotional oratory furnished by preachers, lawyers, and candidates to whom he listened, the most reasonable explanation of young Lincoln's method and manner of speaking, is that he had taken Scott's *Lessons* seriously and that the advice of the Scotch schoolmaster was in harmony with his own thoughts on the subject. For all who heard him make these backwoods speeches, lay emphasis on the logical clearness of them and Lincoln's composure in delivery.

"He was calm, logical and clear alw[a]ys," Dennis Hanks told Herndon. Grigsby says the same thing; and adds that he "was figurative in his Speeches, talk and conversation. He argued much from analogy and explained things hard for us to understand by stories, maxims, tales and figures. He would almost always point the lesson or idea by some story that was plain and near us that we might instantly see the force and bearing of what he said."

The clearness and simplicity of these youthful speeches, so striking that all made note of and remembered those qualities, were partly the result of his writing and rewriting what he read and thought. Sometimes he wrote essays on weighty subjects. William Wood, then about forty-five years of age, relates that one such paper, written in 1827 or 1828, was on "national politics," saying that "the American government was the best form of Government in the world for an intelligent people, that it ought to be kept sacred and preserved forever; that general education should [be] fostered and carried all over the country; that the constitution should be held sacred, the union perpetuated, and the laws revered, respected and enforced."

Wood was so impressed by the essay that he gave it to the leading lawyer of Spencer County. "I showed it to John Pitcher who was travelling over the circuit on law business and stopped at my house one night; he read it carefully and asked me where I got it. I told him that one of my neighbor boys wrote it: he couldn't believe it until I told him that Abe did write it. . . . Pitcher said to me 'the world cant beat it.' He begged for it—gave it to him and it was published."

Wood was a member of the United Brethren Church and a foe of hard drinking. He was a subscriber for a temperance paper published in Ohio; and "Abe used to borrow it, take it home and read it and talk it over with me. . . . One day Abe wrote a piece on Temperance and brought it to my house. I read it carefully over and over and the piece excelled for sound sense anything that my paper contained. I gave the article to one Aaron Farmer, a Baptist Preacher: He read it, it struck him; he said he wanted it to send to a Temperance paper in Ohio for publication; it was sent and published. I saw the printed piece, read it . . . over and over again."

One outstanding fact of Lincoln's life at this time is that, although his associates, and indeed everybody, drank a great deal of whisky, Abraham seldom touched liquor. To be sure he "did drink his dram as well as all others did, preachers and Christians included," testifies Grigsby; and his devoted friend and mentor, William Wood, reluctantly admits that "Abe once drank as all people did here at that time." But this slight and casual drinking seems to have been entirely for the sake of comradeship and Lincoln's strong dislike of offending anybody. Equally striking is the fact that, although profanity was general and intense, Lincoln never fell into that habit. "I never knew him to swear," testifies Wood; "he would say to . . . other boys, leave off your boyish ways and be more like men." Wood explains this attitude by concluding that "Abe was always a man though a boy."

Yet, as we have seen, he was no prig; instead he was inordinately sociable, even familiar, and had faults extremely human, such as his love of a certain type of anecdote—a taste which he never overcame and the expression of which, as will appear, was so marked a feature of his manhood and so shocking to the eminent men among whom he did his historic work. . . .

In his seventeenth year his sister Sarah, then aged nineteen, married Aaron Grigsby, son of a farmer and one of the important men in the settlement. Even then social distinctions were sharply drawn and upon the lines of property; and the Grigsbys were of the aristocracy of the backwoods. Abraham composed some doggerel in verse, which, it is said, was sung at the wedding by "the Lincoln family." It was a clumsy rhyme, telling, in eight verses, the story of the creation and marriage of Adam and Eve.

This bridal hymn of Sarah Lincoln argued that since woman was not made of man's feet he must not abuse her; nor should she "rule him," not having been taken from his head; but that he must protect her because "she was taken from under Adam's arm." At the noisy wedding or thereafter, the Grigsby family did or said something which was strongly offensive to Lincoln. Thus was laid materials of a feud, which was to be set blazing by a harsh circumstance two years later.

But in the meantime he adventured far, though briefly, into the world beyond the fifty-mile circuit of the Pigeon Creek settlement. He had seen something of river life, having been hired in 1825 by one James Taylor to help run a ferry boat across the Ohio from near the mouth of Anderson Creek. . . .

Lincoln also built for himself a scow in which he would take travellers to passing steamers hailed in midstream. Another ferryman, John T. Dill, a Kentuckian, angered by this competition, haled Lincoln before a Kentucky Justice of the Peace, Samuel Pate, for running a ferry without a license. Lincoln said that he did not know that it was against the law to take passengers to steamboats in mid-stream, especially when the ferryboat was on the other side and the steamers would not land or wait. The plaintiff pointed out, how-ever, that the jurisdiction of Kentucky ran to low water mark on the Indiana shore. But "Squire" Pate decided that taking persons to passenger craft in midstream, was not "setting them over" the river and, therefore, that Lincoln had not violated the statute. Abraham was deeply impressed and, thereafter, went to this rural court when cases were heard and decided. In such fashion began Lincoln's in-terest in the study and practice of the law.

But running a ferryboat now and then, across the Ohio, taking an infrequent traveller to a steamer, ploughing, splitting rails and killing hogs for Taylor and others, gave Lincoln little more experi-ence of human activities than Pigeon Creek had afforded. Heavy toil was the only lasting impression made upon him. . . .

In his nineteenth year, however, the chance was offered to make a far journey; and the opportunity came as the result of Lincoln's good fellowship and integrity, and the friendship and confidence inspired by these qualities. The richest man in Carter Township was James Gentry, a native of North Carolina who in April, 1818, had come from Kentucky with his young wife to the Pigeon Creek settlement. He entered a thousand acres of land and afterward bought several hundred acres more. . . . Gentry soon began to keep a small stock of goods for sale at his farm house; thus began the town of Gentryville. Soon William David, a blacksmith, came and in time a few cabins were built near by. Gentryville became the so-cial as well as the trading centre of the countryside.

Gentryville was less than a mile and a half from the Lincoln cabin; and to the backwoods hamlet young Lincoln would speed like a homing pigeon when work was done for the day. For there gath-ered other youth and men who craved companionship and the story-telling, talk, and discussion which took place in country stores. About this time, one, William Jones, came from Vincennes and opened a little store. Soon he and Lincoln became fast friends and Jones hired the boy to help him. But it was the village blacksmith who was "Abes pertickler friend." Gentry and Jones formed a partnership, with Abraham sometimes assisting as man of all work. . . .

Lincoln had great physical strength, so great that tales of his performances are well-nigh unbelievable. Long afterward one elderly person recalled that the young Hercules of Pigeon Creek bore away easily heavy posts which "some of the men" were preparing to carry by means of bars. "Abe could sink an axe deeper in wood. . . . He could strike with a mall a heavier blow than any man I ever saw," testifies William Wood. Stature, physical power, good humor, intellect, integrity, are the outstanding features of the picture of Abraham Lincoln during these years.

In April, 1828, James Gentry hired this strong, capable, and trustworthy youth to go with his son, Allen, on a flatboat loaded with produce to New Orleans, then the best market for such things as the upper Mississippi country had to sell. The boat started from Gentry's landing on the Ohio, about three quarters of a mile from Rockport. Lincoln acted as a bow hand, "working the foremost oar and was paid eight dollars per month from the time of starting to his returning home." It was no ignorant lout but a fairly well-informed young person of grasping and absorbing mind, who, with quip and quiddity, droll story and quaint common sense, enlivened the hours, as Gentry's flatboat floated down the Ohio and Mississippi to the great Southern mart.

Nothing happened, it seems, to disturb that placid voyage until one night, when tied to the shore at the plantation of a Madame Duchesne, not far from New Orleans, a company of negroes armed with hickory clubs and bent on plunder, came upon the flatboat when the occupants were asleep. Aroused by the noise, Lincoln seized a club and furiously attacked the marauders. He knocked several into the river and the others fled, Lincoln and Gentry in hot pursuit. They, too, were wounded, it appears, for they were bleeding when they got on board again. Also they feared that the negroes would return; so they "hastily swung into the stream and floated down the river till daylight."

So came Abraham Lincoln to New Orleans, the first city and the first place bigger than the Boonville or Rockport, Indiana, of 1828, he had ever seen. It was then a remarkable city of iron railings, broad avenues lined by handsome houses, a cathedral, and immense warehouses for receiving, pressing, and storing cotton. From the levee, a much used causeway, could be seen nearly two miles of various descriptions of vessels, arks and flatboats from the north, steamboats still giving a sense of novelty, three-masters for foreign trade, with their broadsides to the shore. . . . Lincoln saw and heard the bustle and heaving labor on the river front, sea-going vessels made ready, crews of strange speech. He could note the medley of people and dress—French, Spanish, Mexicans, Creoles, even Indians, and slaves, from the full negro through many degrees of mixed blood. It all gave a new experience to the two youths from the backwoods of Indiana, but there is no evidence of the impression made upon Lincoln by this, his second contact with slavery.

The cargo sold, the young men returned to their Indiana homes in June, making the journey up stream on one of the big and sumptuous steamboats of the time, the elder Gentry paying the fare. On Pigeon Creek Lincoln took up again the old routine . . . doing the familiar work of the backwoods farm, felling trees, splitting rails, ploughing fields, helping Thomas Lincoln now and then in his casual carpentering. But he read and wrote more than ever, and lost no opportunity to hear speeches, especially legal arguments. When court was held in Rockport on the Ohio or at Boonville, county seats of Spencer and Warrick counties respectively, Lincoln would go, making careful notes of all that was said and done. . . .

Thus by reading, listening, absorbing, Abraham's knowledge grew. "How did Lincoln and yourself learn so much in Indiana under such disadvantages?" Herndon diplomatically asked Dennis Hanks. The answer is the best explanation yet given. "We learned by sight, scent and hearing. We heard all that was said and talked over and over the questions heard, wore them slick, greasy and threadbare." This fact must be borne in mind as we follow Lincoln through his remaining years in Indiana.

January 20, 1828, Sarah Grigsby died in child-birth, and Abraham, grieving sorely, blamed Aaron Grigsby and the Grigsby family for his sister's death, which, declares J. W. Lamar, "Abe always thought was due to neglect." Thus was ignited the antagonism which, it seems, had been slowly though silently accumulated since Sarah's marriage two years before.

In the spring of 1829 two sons of Reuben Grigsby, Reuben, Jr., and Charles, were married. Lincoln was not invited to the wedding, nor yet to the infare which was held at the mansion of the elder Grigsby, a house of two stories built of hewed logs. In hot resentment, he contrived through a confederate a confusion of brides and grooms after the festivities, to be corrected the moment the joke was known to the guests.

With this incident for a text, he wrote a scurrilous description of it, entitling the screed "The Chronicles of Reuben." This he dropped at a place on the road "carelessly, lost it as it were" and it was found by one of the Grigsby family. It was anonymous, of course, but everybody knew who wrote it—nobody in the neighborhood but Lincoln could have written it. It was done in imitation of Old Testament narrative, and described the wedding and infare of the Grigsby boys, ending with a bold picture of the mix-up at the close of the merriment.

"The Chronicles" made a tremendous hit throughout the neighborhood. Gossip on swift wings, carried the story of the marital misadventure all over the countryside. Coarse though the satire was, everybody talked about the salacious description; some committed the whole of it to memory and were able to repeat it as long as they lived. . . .

But the success of his trick and Hudibrastic lines did not satisfy Lincoln—he must further castigate the Grigsbys, although they and their friends were already "fighting mad." Lincoln wrote a rhyme about another brother, William Grigsby, who appears to have been bald-headed, very ugly, and, judging from Lincoln's verses, was the butt of rude chaffing. This repellent rhyme was read and repeated as widely as "The Chronicles of Reuben." The meaning could be fully understood only by those who knew the incidents described.

A fist fight was the only possible outcome of these attacks and such a fight took place; but Abraham did no fighting, except, perhaps, in the mêlée that followed. The details of the arrangement of this now famous contest are obscure and confused. All that is certainly known is that John D. Johnston, step-brother of Lincoln, had a savage fight with the outraged William Grigsby, and was soundly thrashed. It is said that Lincoln refused to meet Grigsby because the young giant was so much stronger than his offended opponent; and put Johnston forward in his place, an arrangement to which Grigsby agreed. . . .

As to what happened afterward, however, we have William Grigsby's own account as given directly to his brother Nathaniel Grigsby who, in a letter, repeated it to Herndon: "my old brother W[illia]m Grigsby tells me some things that past betwin himself and Abraham Lincoln which i wil rite . . . after the fite betwen Wm. Grigsby and John D. Johnson Abraham told Wm. Grigsby that he had whiped Johnson but i can whip you but Wm told him that he did not dispute that but if he Lincoln would give him Grigsby a fair c[h]ance he would fite him he Lincoln wish to now how he wish to fite, Grigsby told Lincoln he would fite him a duel Lincoln told Grigsby that he Lincoln was not a going to fool his life away with one shot, so the mater stoped."

In the autumn of 1829 Thomas Lincoln resolved to leave Indiana for Illinois. After staying with the Lincolns in Indiana for four years, John Hanks had gone back to Kentucky and thence in 1828 to Macon County, Illinois. He sent back to Thomas Lincoln and Dennis Hanks the usual reports of a new country. Also the "milk sickness" had come again or was expected. . . .

During the last two years spent in Indiana a change of far-reaching results began to come over Abraham Lincoln. Although most people in Carter township were National Republicans and supporters of Henry Clay, Thomas Lincoln and his family were Democrats and followers of Andrew Jackson as, indeed, were most poor people. Abraham, too, was a Jackson man—a "Jackson Democrat," as Dennis Hanks asserts with emphasis. . . .

Lincoln's friend, William Jones, the store-keeper in Gentryville, who was a staunch Republican, took the *Louisville Journal* and, perhaps, one or two other newspapers. William Wood, too, was a Republican, and, as we have seen, he also took newspapers published at Cincinnati. In these newspapers the speeches of Clay and other public men were printed, and able editorial comment made upon them as well as upon all the questions of the day. Much was reproduced from the Eastern press also, particularly that of New England and Philadelphia. The *Louisville Journal* was violently opposed to Jackson and fervently supported Clay.

Lincoln read these papers to as much purpose as he read books. "Abe read the newspapers . . . at least such as I took," Wood told Herndon; frequently borrowed the *Telescope*, which Wood took from 1825 to 1830. From 1824 to 1830, says Mrs. Lincoln, "newspapers were to be had" and "Abe was a constant reader of them." . . .

In the Presidential campaign of 1828 the National Republican candidate was John Quincy Adams, then President; the Democratic candidate was Andrew Jackson. The outstanding issues were Jackson's wrongs in 1824, when the House of Representatives elected Adams, internal improvements, a protective tariff—"the American system," as Henry Clay called it—and the Bank of the United States as fiscal agent of the government and the supervisor of a stable currency. Discussion of these questions on the stump and in the newspapers was forthright and within the range of popular understanding and credibility. . . .

We "went to political and other speeches and gatherings. . . . We would hear all sides and opinions talk them over, discuss them agreeing and disagreeing," relates Dennis Hanks, and continues in disgust: "Abe turned Whig in 1827-8—think Col. Jones made him a Whig dont know it . . . I opposed Abe in Politics when . . . he became Whig." Worst of all, laments Dennis, he "allways Loved Hen Clay's Speaches I think was the Cause Mostly" of Lincoln's drifting away from Jacksonian Democracy. . . .

Whatever the cause, it appears to be reasonably certain that it was at this point that Lincoln cut loose from the political faith of his fathers. He said little about it, however, at the time, as was the case twenty-four years later when he left the Whig party. With that strange mingling of caution, secretiveness and craft which so confounded his opponents and puzzled his supporters in after years, Lincoln, in 1828–30, kept to himself his changed or changing conviction. . . .

But though he may still have hurrahed for Old Hickory, the forces had been set in motion within his mind which revolutionized his political ideas and shaped his political career. When Abraham Lincoln left Indiana in 1830, he was a Whig at heart and ready to enlist, as he quickly did, under the banner of gallant, dashing "Harry of the West."

Abraham Lincoln returned frequently to the tier of eastern Illinois counties along the Indiana-Illinois state line during the years after his term in Congress. He was one of the more successful members of his profession in Illinois, but his life story was not then well known; perhaps few Indianians who met him were aware that he had grown to manhood in their state.

One young aspirant to fame at the bar who heard and saw Lincoln and was equally impressed by his wit and his odd appearance was a man destined later to give President Lincoln's War Department some moments of satisfaction—and many of anxiety—when, eventually, he bore the military title of General

LEW WALLACE

Of all books written by Indianians there can be little question but that Lew Wallace's Ben Hur has had the greatest sale. Since it continues a remarkably active article of commerce more than seventy years after its first publication, its record is not likely to be challenged. His other two novels, The Fair God and The Prince of India, were reasonably successful but in Ben Hur he struck a note (or rather a chord) which caught the interest of a truly enormous audience.

When Wallace died he was at work on his autobiography. He had assembled sufficient material to fill the two plump volumes which constituted the published work, and his wife, Susan Elston Wallace, and her protégé, Mary Hannah Krout, prepared the manuscript for the press. Lew Wallace's great and abiding love was for things military. More than three quarters of his autobiography is concerned with his heroic, but frequently unorthodox, campaigning as an officer in the Mexican and Civil Wars.

Critics have intimated that Lew Wallace commanded on the field like a romantic novelist and wrote like a rather pompous general. In his later years he did show excessive satisfaction with his personal achievements, but he had grounds for some such feelings: before he died he had enjoyed a distinguished military career, written the best-selling novel of his day, served competently in the diplomatic service, amassed a very considerable fortune, and become a competent painter and violinist. All these things he had accomplished after a childhood marked by tragedy, a terribly neglected boyhood, and a difficult young manhood; if he was able to look back with satisfaction on a successful career made after a beginning under these handicaps, there should be little wonder, no criticism.

It is in the first chapters of Lew Wallace, An Autobiography, when he describes his early years, that he is at his best. By the time he reaches Chapter XXIII, which follows, he has told how he had been moved by his father (one-time governor of the state but otherwise an only middling-good lawyer) from town to town, school to school; how his mother died and a young stepmother replaced her; how he himself developed a wanderlust, a chronic truancy, and an irresponsibility of which his father's example was reasonable root. He had been ordered to give up drawing in favor of reading law, had failed his bar examinations, served in the Mexican War, passed his examinations (by the grace of his status as a veteran and the political friends of his father), married Susan Elston, and was preparing to practice law in Covington, Indiana. His troubles, as he apparently realized, were near their end. He would never be a brilliant lawyer, but with Susan at his side he had now gained something he had lost when his mother died nearly twenty years before: meanwhile, he was certainly meeting some interesting people—among them Mr. Lincoln.

Lew Wallace, An Autobiography

I HAD NOW, it will be observed, three incentives to action—bread, ambition, and the obligations inseparable from the dear soul then mine in solemn covenant.

The first thing in order was to choose a location in which to open a law office. I turned from Indianapolis, for the reason that few things are more trying to a young man than to bring the elders who have known him from childhood to admit the possibility of his knowing more than they even in a specialty. This is certainly true of the elders who may have predestined him to the gallows.

The influences that determine men halting, and which finally give them direction, are sometimes amusing, sometimes trifling, but they are always curious. I did not go to New York or to Cincinnati —Chicago was then only a great city in promise—but Covington, the village on the Wabash already familiar to the reader as my play-ground in childhood. When I remind him of its distance from Craw-fordsville—scant thirty miles—he will at once perceive the influence that drew me there.

It was not merely to be within easy ride of the fair partner of my fortunes; to deny it the chiefest inducement would be a poor return for the devotion she was showing; still there was another motive. Of my eventual success at the bar I had no doubt; so in secret I cherished a wish to make my emergement from obscurity under the eyes, as it were, of the distrustful authority in Elston castle; the naturalness of the prompting must relieve every suspicion of pettiness.

The office I opened in Covington corresponded in furnishment with my means. A table, a stove, the revised statutes of the state, the ordinary text-books, Barbour's *Justice of the Peace*, the Supreme Court *Reports* to date, Blackford's inclusive, constituted my law library. To complete the inventory, I must not forget a violin, to which I was addicted, though not offensively, since my practice in that line was limited to hours when the town was asleep. If Thomas Jefferson and Governor Whitcomb did not disdain the seductions of the bow, why should I?

My "shingle" was in plain black and white—"Lew Wallace, Attor-ney-at-Law." The day I nailed it to the cheek of my office door, I sat down and marshalled my assets in cash. The total was one dollar and seventy-five cents, the dollar being in paper money. That same day came the announcement of the failure of the bank issuing that note. Nothing daunted, I continued boarding at the hotel.

Edward A. Hannegan was the great man of the town, and he ruled it baronially. As United States senator of democratic persuasion, he had distinguished himself in the debate on the boundary-line be-tween our possessions on the Pacific coast and those of the British. The famous utterance, "54—40 or fight," had been his. Could his policy have been resolutely carried out, the tremendous fortification on the northern shore of Vancouver's Island known as the Esqui-malt would not now be dominating the inlet to Puget Sound. More recently he had returned from a residence in Berlin as minister. I have spoken of him as orator. It may be added that he was a man of courtly grace, passionate in his friendships and his hates. To a faculty of attraction, he had the opposite faculty of repulsion, both in larger degree than I have ever seen them in the same person. He and my father had been warm friends in despite of politics. I was much surprised one morning by a visit from him at my office. Besides giving me encouragement, he invited me to make myself free at his house and study. Returning the call, I was astonished at his library, so completely did it cover the world of miscellaneous literature. The privilege of that study was much more than a sounding compliment.

I recall Senator Hannegan as attorney defending a man indicted for murder. In the examination of a witness an objection was offered to one of his questions. The case turned upon the point involved. If the objection were sustained, the conviction of his client was inevitable. He met the opposition with an eloquence so passionate that for years after the speech continued one of the legends of the court. The ruling was in his favor, followed by a verdict of acquittal. His reputation was that of an impromptu speaker. In this instance, however, the argument was so perfect, the sentence so finished, that I smelled the oil of the lamp in it, and to decide a wager he was consulted in his study.

"Mr. Hannegan," my opponent said, "we have come to have you settle a bet. The dispute is whether the speech you made in course of the examination of (giving the name of the witness) was prepared or delivered on the spur of the moment. My friend here says it was carefully prepared; I say it was off-hand. If not offensive, what do you say?"

Hannegan, smiling, went to a drawer and took out a manuscript.

"Here," he said; "if you remember the speech, young gentlemen, this will dispose of the issue between you better than my dixit."

We took the script, and it was the speech word for word without an interlineation or an erasure.

The young gentleman—slightly to modify Senator Hannegan's polite address—thus party of the second part to the wager has since become one of the familiars of the republic. There is little need of more than the mention of his name, so universally known are he

and his career. Daniel W. Voorhees opened a law office in Covington about the time of my appearance for the same purpose. Three
or four years before his death a trifling cloud arose between us,
which, while enough to break our intimacy, failed to weaken the
respect we had for each other. A great political party is a mourner
at his tomb; yet, of the multitude, few outside his children miss him
more than I do, or send sincerer regrets after him. Our bouts, usually in some justice's court, were frequent. They were rough-and-
tumble, or, in wrestling parlance, catch-as-catch-can; sometimes almost to the fighting point. But it was not in his nature to bear
malice. I can yet hear the creak of the door of my office as, without
a knock, he threw it open and walked in—generally the night of the
day of an encounter—a tall man of genuine gladiatorial port. I can
hear the greeting with which he threw himself on a chair: "Well,
Lew, I got you to-day," or "you got me," according to the fact.
"Come, now, put your work up and let's have the fiddle." And with
a word out the fiddle came; whereupon there was truce and presently
a perfected peace. . . .

Mr. Voorhees came to my office one day.

"What are you doing?" he asked.

"Nothing."

"Well, it is the same with me; so I propose we chip in and hire a
horse and buggy and go to Danville."

The reference was Danville, Illinois.

"What's going on there?"

"Court is in session—that's all."

We reached the town about dusk and stopped at the tavern. The
bar-room, when we entered it after supper, was all a-squeeze with
residents, spiced with parties to suits pending, witnesses and jurors.
The ceiling was low, and we had time to admire the depth and rich-
ness of the universal smoke-stain of the wooden walls. To edge in
we had to bide our time. Every little while there would be bursts of
laughter, and now and then a yell of delight. At last, within the zone
of sight, this was what we saw. In front of us a spacious pioneer
fireplace all aglow with a fire scientifically built. On the right of the
fireplace sat three of the best story-tellers of Indiana, Edward A.
Hannegan, Dan Mace, and John Pettit. Opposite them, a broad brick

hearth intervening, were two strangers to me whom inquiry presently identified as famous lawyers and yarn-spinners of Illinois.

One may travel now from the Kennebec to Puget Sound and never
see such a tournament as the five men were holding; only instead
of splintering lances they were swapping anecdotes. As to the kind
and color of the jokes submitted to the audience, while not always
chaste, they never failed to hit home.

The criss-crossing went on till midnight, and for a long time it
might not be said whether Illinois or Indiana was ahead. There was
one of the contestants, however, who arrested my attention early,
partly by his stories, partly by his appearance. Out of the mist of
years he comes to me now exactly as he appeared then. His hair was
thick, coarse, and defiant; it stood out in every direction. His features were massive, nose long, eyebrows protrusive, mouth large,
cheeks hollow, eyes gray and always responsive to the humor. He
smiled all the time, but never once did he laugh outright. His hands
were large, his arms slender and disproportionately long. His legs
were a wonder, particularly when he was in narration; he kept crossing and uncrossing them; sometimes it actually seemed he was trying to tie them into a bow-knot. His dress was more than plain; no
part of it fit him. His shirt collar had come from the home laundry
innocent of starch. The black cravat about his neck persisted in an
ungovernable affinity with his left ear. Altogether I thought him the
gauntest, quaintest, and most positively ugly man who had ever
attracted me enough to call for study. Still, when he was in speech,
my eyes did not quit his face. He held me in unconsciousness.
About midnight his competitors were disposed to give in; either their
stores were exhausted, or they were tacitly conceding him the crown.
From answering them story for story, he gave two or three to their
one. At last he took the floor and held it. And looking back, I am
now convinced that he frequently invented his replications; which
is saying he possessed a marvellous gift of improvisation. Such was
Abraham Lincoln. And to be perfectly candid, had one stood at my
elbow that night in the old tavern and whispered: "Look at him
closely. He will one day be president and the savior of his country,"
I had laughed at the idea but a little less heartily than I laughed at

the man. Afterwards I came to know him better, and then I did not laugh.

———————

One of the best poems about Lincoln was written by a Hoosier, a man of strange qualifications for such an assignment. He was

MAURICE THOMPSON

and since that teller of pleasant tales will appear again, perhaps it is proper to look at his background before quoting his famous poem.

Thompson's experiences in his boyhood were unusual—as, by the same token, were those of his parents! In 1844, when he was born in Fairfield, Indiana, his father held what could only have been an exceedingly poorly-paid pastorate in a local church. Presently the father accepted another pastorate in Missouri (where Maurice's brother Will was born) and later, still another in Kentucky.

Then, before 1854, something happened to the Reverend Mr. Thompson not at all to be anticipated by a man dedicated to the Baptist ministry in the nineteenth century: he found himself suddenly rich. Since none of his pastorates had paid more than the barest of livings we may assume that there was an inheritance, for Mathew Grigg Thompson ceased to minister to poverty-stricken flocks and appeared as a planter in northern Georgia, owner of considerable land, a suitable complement of slaves, and recipient of an income which permitted him to live in luxury and employ what must have been excellent tutors for his sons.

Maurice and Will Thompson took full advantage of this educational opportunity and also of the fine hunting and fishing of the region—which they exploited in company with an old Cherokee Indian. Both the classics they studied indoors and the woodcraft they learned in the hills turned out to be most useful to the Thompsons.

The Civil War began, and they enlisted in the Confederate Army. When the war was over they found that the family plantation would scarcely support their parents. So they—in their turn—made a shift as unusual as had been their father's; they put their belongings into their knapsacks and walked north! The two young rebel veterans had no particular destination in mind, but when they reached Crawfordsville, Indiana, they settled down to stay, in spite of the fact that the town was the home of four recently-returned Union generals. When they had saved some money, married sisters, and brushed up a bit on legal lore, they opened a law office. Both wrote excellent verse (an example of Will's has already appeared), and Maurice had tried his hand at essays on nature study even before the war: by the early seventies the law practice prospered enough to allow him time for further pursuit of his muse.

Eventually Maurice Thompson, through his writings on archery, nature, and the pleasures of camping, had a great deal to do with the forming of American taste for life in the great outdoors. A good case could be made for Thompson as the first to popularize not the philosophical contemplation of nature, in the manner of Thoreau, but its enjoyment by the great majority of us who are neither Brahmin nor blue-stocking. He deserves at least a modest monument somewhere at the expense of the multi-billion dollar American resort industry. He also achieved a respectable reputation as an editor and critic and wrote highly successful novels—including Alive of Old Vincennes.

Thompson's tribute to Lincoln was called

At Lincoln's Grave

May one who fought in honor for the South
Uncovered stand and sing by Lincoln's grave?
Why, if I shrank not at the cannon's mouth,
Nor swerved one inch for any battle-wave,
Should I now tremble in this quiet close,
Hearing the prairie wind go lightly by
From billowy plains of grass and miles of corn,
　　While out of deep repose,
The great sweet spirit lifts itself on high
And broods above our land this summer morn?

I, mindful of a dark and bitter past,
And of its clashing hopes and raging hates,
Still, standing here, invoke a love so vast
It cancels all and all obliterates,
Save love itself, which cannot harbor wrong;

Oh, for a voice of boundless melody,
A voice to fill heaven's hollow to the brim
   With one brave burst of song,
Stronger than tempest, nobler than the sea,
That I might lend it to a song of him!

Meseems I feel his presence. Is he dead?
Death is a word. He lives and grander grows.
At Gettysburg he bows his bleeding head;
He spreads his arms where Chickamauga flows,
As if to clasp old soldiers to his breast,
Of South or North, no matter which they be,
Not thinking of what uniform they wore,—
   His heart the palimpsest
Record on record of humanity,
Where love is first and last forevermore.

His humor, born of virile opulence,
Stung like a pungent sap or wild-fruit zest,
And satisfied a universal sense
Of manliness, the strongest and the best;
A soft Kentucky strain was in his voice,
And the Ohio's deeper boom was there,
With some wild accents of old Wabash days,
   And winds of Illinois;
And when he spoke he took us unaware,
With his high courage and unselfish ways.

He was the North, the South, the East, the West,
The thrall, the master, all of us in one;
There was no section that he held the best;
His love shone as impartial as the sun;
And so revenge appealed to him in vain,
He smiled at it as at a thing forlorn,
And gently put it from him, rose and stood
   A moment's space in pain,
Remembering the prairies and the corn
And the glad voices of the field and wood.

Annealed in white-hot fire, he bore the test
Of every strain temptation could invent,—
Hard points of slander, shivered on his breast,
Fell at his feet, and envy's blades were bent
In his bare hands and lightly cast aside;
He would not wear a shield; no selfish aim
Guided one thought of all those trying hours;
    No breath of pride,
No pompous striving for the pose of fame
Weakened one stroke of all his noble powers.

CHAPTER TEN

Culture: Grant to Harrison

The atmosphere of stifling refinement which swept the nation with recovery from the financial ills attendant upon the Civil War made many changes. It added layers to what once were women's clothes but which now became ladies' toilettes; it raised necklines, brought in high-buttoned shoes, eliminated the female lower limb, multiplied bangs and cork-screw curls, and caused chignons to extend and sag. For the male it expanded whiskers enormously and heightened collars. It caused houses to sprout overhanging eaves, gingerbread borders, colored glass windows, purposeless gables, odd-shaped windows, and multiple chimneys. It brought in plaster dogs and parlor organs.

It was in those days of Grant to Harrison (by way of Hayes, Garfield, Arthur, and Cleveland) that the high arts of the photographic studio and the medicine show came into great favor. Indubitably it was the 'seventies which saw the family photograph album reach the peak of its perfection—if the term "perfection" applies—and only

KIN HUBBARD

speaking from behind the whiskers of Abe Martin of Brown County, could do the subject full justice. Abe and Kin had experienced family albums, as they had experienced most of the other phenomena which affected American life profoundly between 1868 and 1930.

Frank McKinney Hubbard was not Indiana born; he had traveled as a silhouette artist, side-show hand, and minstrel troupe end-man, had served time (one week) in a Detroit art school, and had labored in the postal service before he came to the state. Once settled in Indiana, however, he took over, and before long he was Hoosierdom's favorite cartoonist, humorist, and commentator, through the cast of Brown County characters he invented. By 1906 or 1907 Frank McKinney Hubbard, resident of the state only a matter of a few years, had already become established as Old Man Indiana himself.

Abe Martin's Broadcast

FAMILY ALBUMS

A LOAN EXHIBITION under the auspices o' the ladies o' the Western Star wuz held in the Model Skatin' Rink lately. Ther one could see ole Civil War swords an' guns an' canteens, together with candle snuffers, spinnin' wheels, flint lock eskipets, stuffed owls an' jay birds, sword canes carried by Democrats at the close o' the Civil War, primitive household implements, ole books an' chromos, an' scores o' other relics, some hundreds o' years ole. All are interestin' an' have histories, but the one thing that constantly has a crowd around it is a big, fat, squeaky, faded blue plush family photergraf album belongin' to the ole Bentley family before an' durin' the dark days o' the Civil War, an' now treasured by our own Farmer Jake Bentley. In this ole musty repository o' whiskers, wens, an' retreatin' chins may be seen early likenesses o' Mr. Bentley's forebears an' relatives. One may see a strikin' likeness o' the first Jake Bentley seated on a fringed plush stool with his cornet restin' on one knee. Thrown carelessly across his chest like a fin is his left hand, on which may be seen three rings. The first Mrs. Jake Bentley is shown jest as she appeared at the photographer's studio at Fostoria, Ohio, in 1851. Her hair is combed back to the time of Marie Antoinette, an' the expression on her face makes her look like she was holdin' in till she passed a skunk nest. Ther's a peculiar somethin' in the expressions of all pioneer mothers. Owin' to bears an' Indians an' motherhood an' plowin' they were little given to lookin' pleasant. The ordeal o' havin' a photo struck in the early days wuz a thing to be dreaded. Only when the sun wuz shinin' wuz it possible to git a photo took. The early photographer an' his Windsor tie an' yeller, fluctuatin' windpipe, only attempted full front views. He strived to give one his money's worth by showin' both sides o' the face. He steadied the head with clamps screwed to the skull jest behind the ears. Then he would arrange the arms an' legs, even up to the coat lapels, powder the cheek bones an' nose, bend the ears in place, an' tell you to concentrate on a figure in the wallpaper fer about five minutes. The thing wuz to have photos of all the family connections, cousins, aunts, an' first, second an' third husbands. Sometimes a feller would be took with his favorite gun or croquet mallet. Uncle Milt Bentley's photo shows a snare drum hangin' at his side. He wore long, trailin' side whiskers that looked like live oak moss. Ever'buddy in the album looks sad an' resentful, like they'd been photographed agin their will. But the ole album tells a wonderful story, an' it's remarkable how people dressed the way they did an' lived. Ther's a strikin' family group showin' a band stand, or summer pavilion, in the background. The elder Bentley is in the center with his legs crossed an' his left forward foot is three times bigger than his right foot. His whiskers have evidently been pinned down an' his lapels glued to his coat. The photo proves at least that his wife an' family wuz intact an' available. Early photographers knew nothin' about touchin' out moles, extra chins, hair lips, warts an' scars. On the contrary they emphasized 'em, played 'em up, in other words they made real likenesses. The curious thing is how any young man or woman ever used to git up nerve enough to marry into a home after lookin' through its family album.

———

What she evidently took to be the free bohemian existence of the traveling photographer attracted a lady writer of Indiana as greatly as the processes and products of his art interested Abe Martin, though there was nothing frivolous in her approach. The lady was of considerably more importance to the American literary scene than was appreciated during her life.

MARY HARTWELL CATHERWOOD

came to Indiana as a bride in 1877. She had been writing since her childhood, but she did not achieve significant recognition until the years of her Hoosier residence. Later she found her greatest and most rewarding inspiration in the French who had come to America in the early days and had settled first in Canada, later in the old posts on the Illinois, the Wabash, and the Mississippi. But before she found them she had caught some impressions of the Indiana scene as it was in the 'eighties, particularly of Indiana small town life around the local railroad station. That was realism with a vengeance, for during the early years of her marriage she and her husband lived over a small-town depot, in which he served as ticket agent.

Shortly after her arrival in Indiana she met young—and as yet notably unsuccessful—James Whitcomb Riley and, by her own statement, began a friendship which threatened to become something more than platonic. Mrs. Catherwood's marriage may or may not have been happy but we may speculate, without the slightest implication of scandal, as to what might have resulted had she met Riley—perennial bachelor—while she was still Mary Hartwell. The literary works of both might have achieved even greater brilliance— or, as likely, the conflict of two artistic personalities joined in the permanence of wedlock might have brought ruin to both. But speculating is sometimes fun, isn't it?

Two of Mrs. Catherwood's Indiana stories, written during her closest association with Riley, are marked by a curious similarity of theme. Both are laid in the town of "Fairfield," with the local railroad station prominent in the foreground. No one can believe that Mrs. Catherwood loved an Indiana railroad station (which, incidentally, was, and still is, invariably a "depot") but, having lived in one, she knew its function and its social importance. Both stories have, as principal action, an episode in which a helpless person—a baby in one, a deaf young poet in the other—is struck by a railroad train.

Possibly Mrs. Catherwood saw an accident of the sort while her husband served as station agent in Howard county; certainly she should have been impressed by the danger of such in those days of hand-brakes. But the Freudian interpreter (which, praise be, the present writer is not) would undoubtedly interpret her preoccupation with the theme as evidence that she saw herself, the intellectual, as a

helpless person trapped in the living quarters of the Fairfield depot;
that, having met and knowing she must part from the poet Riley
(who was still himself a rather helpless person), she played with the
romantic idea of release by death under the wheels of a passing train!

Mallston's Youngest
[1880]

THE RAILROAD-VILLAGE of Fairfield woke up one spring morning
and found a clumsy blue car, with a skylight in its roof, standing on
the common near the blacksmith-shop. Horses and tongue were already removed, the former being turned into the tavern pasture and
the latter stowed in the tavern barn. A small sky-colored ladder led
up to the door of this artistic heaven, which remained closed long
after a crowd of loungers had gathered around it.

The Fairfield loungers were famously lazy savages, though to the
last degree good-natured and obliging. They wore butternut overalls
and colored shirts, a few adding the picturesque touch of bright
handkerchiefs and broad straw hats: there were a few coats in various stages of rags and grease, and one or two pairs of boots, but the
wearers of these put on no airs over the long ankles and sprawling
toes which blossomed around them. The whole smoking, stoop-shouldered, ill-scented throng were descendants of that Tennessee and
Carolina element which more enterprising Hoosiers deplore, because in every generation it repeats the ignorance and unthrift
branded so many years ago into the "poor white" of the South.

Those who could read traced the legend "Photographic Car" on
the sides of the vehicle, and with many a rude joke each bantered
the other to have his picter took for such purposes as skeerin' stock
off the railroad-track or knockin' the crows stiff. Their scuffling and
haw-haws waked the occupant of the car, who rose in his bunk and
drew the curtain from a window. The boys saw his face and hushed.
Raising the window, he scattered a bunch of handbills among them,

which set them all to scrambling, and, when they had caught the bills, to struggling with large and small type which announced that an unrivalled photographer would be in that vicinity in a very few days with his beautiful travelling-car, giving everybody an opportunity of securing such tin-types and photographs as only the large cities turned out, and at the lowest possible prices.

Presently the photographer appeared at his own door and looked abroad. The tender spring morning, though it glorified surrounding woods and rich farming-lands, could do little for this dilapidated village, which consisted of one lane of rickety dwellings crossed at right angles by the Peru Railroad, a stern brick building, a wooden elevator and a mill. It was a squalid sight, though the festive season of the year and that glamourous air peculiar to Indiana brooded it. The photographer surveyed his new field with an amused sneer, and descended the steps to go to his breakfast at the tavern, a peak-roofed white frame set among locust trees—the best house on the street. Before it stood that lozenge-shaped sign on a fat post which stands before all country taverns, making a vague, lonesome appeal to the traveller.

The loungers moved in groups on the station-platform, their hands in their pockets and their necks stretched forward, eying the stranger.

Out of the blue distance on the railroad two plumes of steam rose suddenly: then a black object stood up on the track and gave two calls at a crossing. Double-shuffles were danced on the platform, as if the approaching train charged these vagabonds with some of its own strength. It screamed, and bore down upon this dilapidated station to stop for one brief minute, change mail-sacks and gaze pityingly out of its one eye at the howling crew which never failed to greet it there. People in the cars also looked out as if glad they were not stopping, and a few with long checks in their hats, who appeared to be travelling to the earth's ends, were envied by a girl approaching the post-office in the brick block.

She waited near the photographic car until the train passed, her lip curling at this blue van and the pretensions of its owner.

Later she came out of the post-office by a back hall, and, darting a fierce look at Jim Croddy, who ran against her in his performance of the double-shuffle, took her way across the common, crushing her letters in her hand. This time she scarcely looked at the photographic van, but with dilated eyes and set teeth pursued her path into the springing weeds. The photographer, who had returned, looked at her, however, and found her individuality so attractive that he watched her swift step until it took her out of sight within the doorway of a brick residence detached from the village by a meadow and long lawn.

The young man opened his car and prepared for business. His landlady was going to bring her grandchild to be photographed. A locker received his primitive couch, and he further cleared the deck for action by stowing in the back apartment where he prepared his chemicals all remaining litter. Jim Croddy and kindred spirits ventured to look in.

"See here, boys," inquired the photographer, "couldn't one of you get me a bucket of water from somewhere?"

They would all do it. The heartiest and most obliging set of idlers in the world, they almost fought for the pail, and two, taking it between them, cantered to the pump in front of the post-office. The rest were fain to enter, treading each other's bare heels as they tumbled up the steps.

"Don't you want your pictures taken?" inquired the artist, quizzically surveying his shaggy crowd.

"We ain't got no money," replied Bill Stillman, the smallest but readiest-tongued.

"You got money, Bill," retorted Leonard Price, a parchment-colored wisp of nineteen who had recently become a widower.

"I got to git clo'es with it if I hev'. There's Mallston: git him to set for *his* picter."

Mallston was hooted for as he came across the dewy grass on feet of brawn, shaming puny rustics by his huge physique. The photographer mentally limned him: a bushy, low-browed head and dark, reddish, full-lipped face, bearded; muscle massed upon his arms and tatter-clothed legs; a deep, prominent chest; hands large, black, powerful; the whole man advancing with a lightness which in some barbaric conqueror would have been called dignified grace.

Mallston had nothing to answer for himself. He stood folding his arms and looking in. It was said he had African blood in his veins

—barely enough to stain the red of his skin, pinch up his children's hair and give them those mournful, passionate black eyes through which the tragedy of the race always looks. But so vague, so mere a hearsay, was this negro stain, if it existed at all, that he had married a white wife, and moved in society unchallenged by these very fastidious descendants of Carolina and Tennessee.

Mallston's wife had lately added a son to his family. He had two sons before, also two daughters. From any standpoint it seemed an unnecessary addition when the economist considers that he had no means of support except his big-fingered paws, and these, though very willing, depended on chance jobs and days' works given him by other men. In face of these facts the youngest was there as well as the oldest—scarcely seven; the second, scarcely five; and the third and fourth, aged three and a half and two—in his rented house of one room, containing beds in opposite corners, a table and a cooking-stove in front of the fireplace. A generous family and scant provision for it being the mode in Fairfield, however, Mallston may not have seen his desperate position, especially with summer and harvest wages coming. Just now he was out of a job, having finished a ditching contract, and his black, speculative eyes looked anxiously at the photographer.

"Come, clear now!" exclaimed that young man with some authority to his loafers: "I am going to have some sitters."

The landlady and her grandchild were already coming to take advantage of morning sunlight and the domestic lull before dinner. With them came a curious neighbor in ill-made, trailing calico and dejected sun-bonnet, who walked with her hands on her hips and puckered her upper lip, with consciousness of the loss of two front teeth, when she laughed. As they proceeded at a pace regulated by the toddling child, they encountered an old woman with no teeth at all, whose nose and chin leaned very much toward each other: her grizzled hair curled under a still more dejected sun-bonnet, and, setting down a basket of clothes, she stood panting from exertion and wiping her wan face on the bonnet cape.

"I'm a-garn to hick'ry that Bill," she exclaimed weakly. "I tole him to carry me wash-water, and here he is stannin' round thish yer car! George and John's just out, too, and so's Foster. Soon's they git the'r vittles they up and leave me to do the best I kin. Laws! who's garn to pay out money fer fortygraphs? If folks all had to work as hard as I do, they wouldn't have no money fer no such things, so they wouldn't. It 'ud stan' 'em in hand to be savin'."

"Why don't you drive off some yer good-fer-nothin' boys and make 'em do somethin', Mis' Stillman?" bantered the neighbor.

"Well, they've all been a-workin'," relented the mother. "Bill, he's as good a feller to work as ever was if he don't git with a lot of orn'ry boys. Hit hurts Fawt to work stiddy, so it does.—Bill, come here and tote these clo'es home fer me."

Bill came, ruddy and laughing from a scuffle, and walked off with the basket.

"And git the wash-water and make a fire under the kittle," called his mother.

"I'll be apt to," responded Bill.

"Come along into the daguerreyan car, Mis' Stillman," invited the landlady. "You never see the inside o' one, did you?"

"Laws! is that wher' you're garn to? I can't stop but a minute. Hit looks mighty fine. The boys said this feller was drivin' into town last night when meetin' broke. Who's garn to have their picter took?— You, Jane?"

"Me?" replied the neighbor. "Laws! no: I ain't rich."

"Oh, you'll change your minds," drawled the landlady patronizingly, as became a lady of means: "he takes 'em reel cheap."

The photographer met this group at his door and assisted them into the car, from which all his earlier visitors had dispersed except Mallston.

Mallston stood at the steps and watched the landlady's grandchild prepared for a sitting. The rabble had begun their morning business of pitching horseshoes, but his interest was held by that little child—its fresh clothes, rings of black hair and pomegranate coloring. The artist, having placed his camera, was in the farther room preparing his plate. When he came out and was in the act of closing the door he noticed Mallston, and asked, "Do you want a job?"

The barbarian did decidedly.

"Come into the back room, then, and help me."

Mallston went striding through the car, and placed himself in an obedient attitude behind the partition.

"Laws!" exclaimed Mrs. Stillman, standing between the camera, where the artist was burying his head under a black cloth, and the object to be photographed, "when we lived in Bartholomew county —'twas the year after we moved f'm Johnson county—Foster and John they was little fellers then, and I did want the'r picters that bad, so I did. But the'r pap he 'lowed it was a waste o' money. Pore man! he was a mighty hard worker: he'd go a mile'd to make a cent, and then he'd lose it all with bad management, so he would. But I had easy times them days, with everything to my han': I spun and wove all the jeans the men-folks wore, and we milked a dozen cows—"

"Will you please move aside?"

"Git out o' the way, Mis' Stillman: the man can't see through ye."

"Oh!" exclaimed the old woman, jerking herself from the photographer's line of vision, "I didn't go fer to git in the way. But this ain't doin' my washin'," she added, moving toward the entrance. Here, on a little shelf, she found some tiles and brushes, which she took up to examine and hold before the other women, who were seated awaiting the picture-taking. "What's these here things?"

"Artists' materials," replied the photographer, removing his head from under the black cloth, and that from the camera.—"Now, my little man, look straight at the hole in the box, and don't move.— That large brick house—keep perfectly quiet—across the field seems a good point to sketch from. Who lives there?"

"Harbisons," replied the landlady.

"Harbisons, eh? I suppose it was Miss Harbison I saw go past this morning?—Don't move, my little man."

"I do' know," demurred the washer-woman, whose sole recreation in life was the faculty of speech. "I ain't seen Mis' Harbison to town to-day. They's him and her and the boys. Both the boys is away f'm home now. What-fer lookin' woman?"

"It was a young lady in a wide hat."

"Oh, that's Miss Gill: she's some kin to 'em. She's a schoolteacher to Bunker Hill or Peru. Laws! I hate to see anybody so proud."

"That's a good boy!" said the photographer. He removed his plate and carried it to the rear room, where he required the assistance of Mallston, who had watched the process with silent interest. Presently reappearing with the dripping negative, which he held for the women to see, he repeated incidentally, "Proud, is she, this Miss Gill?"

"Yes, she is, kind o'," testified the neighbor who was called Jane. —"It's a reel good one, ain't it?"

"If ye take as good as this all the time," cried the pleased landlady, holding off the negative and giving that excited drawl to the terminal word which may distinguish Kentuckians, for she claimed to be one, "every girl in town 'll be comin' after the'r picter-uh!"

"Except the proud Miss Gill."

The landlady, who had a moustache, bristled it over her square mouth: "I never ast much about her. She's kind o' yaller-complected, but some says she's smart. Bill Harbison was smart too, but he's all broke up now. They don't own nothin' but the house and grounds they're livin' in."

"Laws!" poured in the steady washer-woman, "I used to work fer Mis' Harbison when she was well off—I done knit socks and pieced quilts—and she was always liber'l, so she was. When we fust come here he was gittin' down with his last sickness, and we left a good place in Bartholomew county, fer *his* folks they kep' a-writin', 'Here's the place, Billy: this is wher' you'll find the flitter tree and the honey pond.' And it wasn't never my will, but come we must; and you orto seen Fairfield then. Why, ther' wasn't nothin' but mud, so ther' wasn't.—My soul! if thern don't go Bill, and I know he ain't carried me no wash-water."

The artist helped her down the steps and asked her to come again, which courtesy she distrusted. She 'lowed he was p'tendin'. He throwed his head up like he was big-feelin'. It ruffled her that anybody should be big-feelin' over a pore widder-woman that took in days' washin's, and had a pack o' triflin' boys that et her out o' house and home.

Still, this old woman enjoyed the fruit trees' budding promise as she patted along the railroad, and perhaps some old thrill shot again as a meadow-lark uttered his short, rich madrigal from the weather-darkened fence.

"Ho, Mis' Stillman," called Mallston's wife, standing in her door with the youngest on her arm, "le's go over and see that ther' picter car."

"I done done it," responded the old woman.

By the end of two weeks this photographic car had done good execution on the community. The artist himself appeared friendly, which greatly assisted his trade, openness to familiarity being a prime virtue in all rustic neighborhoods. Every youngster who came to the store after groceries, with a bag slung over the horse's neck in which to carry them, gave pap no peace until means were furnished for a rosy-cheeked tin-type of himself in a pink, green or purple case. The Appledore girls, handsome daughters of a rich farmer, and therefore able to sit for pictures in Kokomo, or even Indianapolis, yet put on all their chains, rings and bracelets and went to the car to test this young photographer's skill. Mrs. Stillman received money from her daughter in Ellwood, together with the written command: "You go and git your fortygraph took fer me, mother: we don't one of us never know what's agarn to happen." So she removed her black alpaca from its peg on the wall for her adornment, and came also, explaining to the neighbors that Kit sent the money, so she did, and was makin' a pore mouth about not havin' no picter of mother. And having got the picture, she used all her past trials and present misfortunes to save half the price, which she succeeded in doing.

Every day the artist had a few sitters. It was surprising how many of the bilious, bare-legged children who collected to gaze at his framed specimens were brought to be photographed, for most of the villagers were squalidly poor and the farmers were entering their busy season. During this time he had opened the Harbison domicile to himself, being son of a friend who had sat in the State legislature with Mr. Harbison. All Fairfield knew that he went there nearly every day, and that it was not to shoot with the long-bow on the lawn. They had no idea how he loved to lounge from one empty room to another of this picturesque, half-furnished house, and how he was gratified by the fitness of the inhabitants to their abode. He liked to see Miss Gill tuck a bunch of peach-blossoms in her coil of hair, and to feel the quickening influences of spring supplemented by her electricity.

Mrs. Harbison took her earth-loving hands from garden-making and went to show the young people the ferns in the woods. She pulled her sun-bonnet over her eyes and trod out with the solid steps of a woman bred to love the soil under her feet. The photographer sketched along the way, but he finally sat down by Little Wildcat where the water boiled over boulders, and Mrs. Harbison went farther to dig ginseng. There was a joyful hurry of birds all around. That leopard of the Indiana woods, the sycamore, repeated itself in vistas.

"Sycamores always look like dazzling marble shafts blackened with patches of moss," said the young man.

"And their leaves," said the girl sitting on the log not far from him, "smell like poetry. I spread them on my face late in summer after a shower and suck up their breath. But I never can put the sensation into words."

"How's that for a sycamore?" he asked, showing a scrap.

She examined it with great satisfaction: "Why do you go about with a photographic car? Why don't you set out to be an artist?"

He laughed: "Because there is so much of the vagabond in me, I suppose. Then I never had any education in art. Folks as poor as Job's turkey."

"But a man can do so much or so little."

"Well, when I'm going about with the car I see a great many odd people, and can pick up little striking things for studies. I get a living, too, such as it is, which I shouldn't do if I set up as an artist. Look here!" He turned over his book and showed an etching of Mallston stepping across the common carrying his youngest, with the four older children at his heels. One had sprawled, and was evidently lifting a howl to the paternal ear. They both laughed at it.

"He's a good fellow," remarked the photographer, "but there's no end to the ignorance and misery such creatures bring upon the world. He couldn't take decent care of himself, and he has a wife and five children hanging on him."

"It is just so with nearly all these people," exclaimed Miss Gill in high scorn. "They have no idea of what life should be—no ambition, and scarcely a soul to divide around among them all. It smothers me!" She threw her arms out impetuously. "I want such different things—the society of the cultivated, the stimulus of great natures. Maybe I could write something that would get before the public then."

"Have you ever sent anything East?" he inquired with a Hoosier's vast respect for older civilization.

"Yes," she answered with a falling inflection of voice and head. "But it's no use: I never shall amount to anything with my surroundings."

The water gurgled over its boulders and the green landscape sent up an exquisite loamy breath. The young people, both representing the afflatus of the State, met in one tragic look which ended in a smile.

Next morning Mallston took his usual post in the car, shifting from one bare foot to the other, while the photographer lounged on his locker waiting for custom. The native frequently parted his shaggy jaws, but considered how he should offer his information. He watched his employer with real attachment, and his dark red face deepened its hue around the eyes as he broke out, "We've got a little feller t' 'r house."

"What! not another one?"

"He's two month ole," explained Mallston.

"Oh, your youngest. Why, yes, I've seen him." Mallston was evidently surprised that so humble a creature as his youngest had attracted the great photographer's notice. "He's a fine youngster," added the latter.

Mallston was then emboldened to blurt out, "We've named him."

"You have? Well, what do you call him?"

"We called him after you."

"Why, here's an honor! How did you come to name him for me?"

"I done it."

"Let me see: what can I do for him? Suppose you bring him over now while we aren't very busy and I'll take his picture."

Mallston grinned with pleasure: "My woman wanted his picter. My woman 'lowed mebby you wouldn't charge for it if you knowed he was a namesake."

"Certainly I won't. So bring him right along and we'll do our best for him."

It was some time before he reappeared, carrying his youngest in his arms, its cheeks polished and its wet hair turning over in rings, decked in its chief finery, a blue quilted cloak. The mother came along to hold her cherub in her lap. She was a long, raw-boned woman, immature in face under all her crust of care and tan, evidently distressed in her free waist by the tightness of her calico dress and in her unfenced feet by shoes.

"What are you going to do with the baby?" inquired Miss Gill kindly as she encountered this group at right angles on her return from the post-office.

"Garn with him to the man to git his picter. Come in and see him took," invited Mrs. Mallston timidly.

The young woman, ready to seize on any distraction, went in, scarcely understanding that her bruised ambition reached for healing to such homely, lowly natures as these.

The artist was glad to see her, and she sat on the locker while preparations went on. She exchanged amused glances with him when the other Mallstons flocked to the steps, bellowing in various keys for their mother, and on their being swung in by one arm and placed in a row on the opposite locker, she gazed at them in turn, wondering what the future held out to such lumps of dirt and sombre black eyes.

Mallston set his youngest on the mother's lap and looked at it with sneaking fondness. The whole tribe seemed equally dear to him, but this youngest appealed to his strength. Mrs. Mallston was not celebrated as a tender mother. She went after pails of water and left her children playing beside the railroad-track; their tattered and ludicrous appearance bespoke her unskilfulness with the needle; she was said to have scalded the eldest boy with a skilletful of hot water in which she had soaked bacon, pouring it out of the window on his head. But she probably did as well as she knew how, and Mallston did much better. The photographer watched him go back a dozen times to straighten the baby's sturdy legs, tap it under the chin with his colossal fore finger, cluck in the laughing red cavern of his mouth and change the folds of its quilted cloak with quite a professional air. What were poverty, the world's neglect, hard labor and circumscribed life to this man? That muscle which gathered and distributed the streams of his body may have been to him a heaven in which these five youngsters ministered as angels.

The young man felt moved with an emotion he resisted: "My God! can it be that this savage is right in his instincts, and I am wrong? Can some peculiar blessing of Heaven rest on the man who dares Fate for family love? Or is the poor wretch's fondness a recompense for his overburdened lot?"

The baby took a fine picture. Mallston stood by a window and gazed at the large tin-type. His full lips dropped apart and his head leaned sidewise. He turned to his wife and said with a foolish expression, "If the little feller 'ud happen to drop off now we got sumpin' to remember him by."

"My children's kind o' sickly," remarked his wife, marshalling forth her quartette, "fer all they look so hearty."

The photographic car remained day after day, although sitters seldom came now, for even the loafers were helping to put in crops. The horses which should have dragged it out almost any dewy morning were not exactly eating their heads off, being turned upon pasture, but the landlord was famous for getting his entertainment's worth. As long as weekly board-bills were paid he said it was none of his business if the man stayed all summer.

On Monday the photographer resolved, "I will start on Wednesday;" on Wednesday he decided, "I will wait till Saturday;" and on Saturday, "It's too late in the week now, but I *must* go next Monday."

Mrs. Harbison, when interviewed about the generous portion of time he spent on her lawn with her summer visitor, answered with downrightness, "Well, what if he does like to come to our place? We know all about his folks. And if them two wants to sit and talk, they're fit company fer each other, and I reckon it won't hurt 'em. So what you going to do about it?"

The village was going to talk about it. The female population gathered at the storekeeper's house, their favorite rallying-place because the storekeeper's wife had no opinions of her own, but made a good echo to whatever was said, and there they judged that Gill girl for taking up with strangers like she done, so stuck up, and hoped it would turn out he was a married man, and wouldn't that bring her down?

Meanwhile, the photographer stretched himself on his oilcloth-cushioned locker and stared at the now fully-unfurled woods, without one mental glance at the vivid moss in its shades, its four varieties of ferns or the ruined cabin with one side thrown down, showing flickers of sunlight through the gaps of its fireplace. He called himself ill names for remaining where he was, and made a crazy picture of a photographic car seesawing along the country roads, with a figure he well knew sitting on the platform beside him as he drove. It was so absurd, but he quoted Mrs. Dalles's song of "Brave Love" while he etched:

> We could not want for long,
>   While my man had his violin
> And I my sweet love-song.

> The world has aye gone well with us,
>   Old man, since we were one:
> Our homeless wanderings down the lanes,
>   They long ago were done.

Then, across some chasm of indefinite time, he saw a studio and himself happy at an easel, with this devoted dark face resting against his side, reciting her work to him and quivering with joy at some sign of success. But the whole panorama dissolved at a breath.

"Now, aren't you a nice fellow," he addressed himself, "a brilliant rascal, a wise genius, to be thinking of such a thing?"

Miss Gill was returning from the woods with a full basket before the morning heat came on. A few women at the storekeeper's fence looked sidewise at each other as she paused to chat under the photographer's window.

The morning was so clear that every object stood in startling relief. A plume of steam far up the leafy railroad vista heralded the Peru express's lightning passage through the town. Scarcely a lounger was left on the platform. Mallston had a job of cleaning the cellar for the storekeeper, and at intervals appeared from its gaping doors with a basket of decayed potatoes on his shoulders. The landscape rung with bird-songs, and the girl, who had skimmed the cream off such a morning, looked up and laughed at her dejected friend. She had purple violets tucked into her coil of hair, her belt and under her collar.

"What are you doing here? Why aren't you out trying to catch the effect of day-twilight in the thick woods?"

"I've been trying," he replied without smiling, "to catch the effect of a rash action—and a woman's face."

"How solemn! Let me see it. Is it Mrs. Stillman's?"

"No, it isn't: it's my wife's."

Her half-lifted hand dropped. While her eyes met his without blenching she turned ghastly white, her face seeming to wither into sudden age.

The express-train whistled. Only a moment before its steam-plume had been her symbol of rushing success in life, and now, for some scarcely apprehended reason, she felt that the train and Fate were running her down. With intuitive resistance and a defiant sweep of her body she turned toward it and screamed aloud.

The photographer could not credit this rapid change to himself when he saw upon the track a small rough cart drawn by Mallston's oldest girl and containing his youngest stretched upon a dirty pillow. The express was coming downgrade at full speed, but at its whistle the oldest child turned off the track and tried to drag her burden across the rail. The cart upset, and the baby sprawled, crying, between the rails, while his sister fled crying toward home.

This whole occurrence was a flash: it seemed to the spectators they had barely started forward with their blood curdling, the engine had but screamed, and Mallston was merely seen dropping a basket of potatoes and leaping with upright hair and starting eyes, before the whole thing was over. The train stopped with such a recoil that many passengers were thrown from their seats: the engineer dropped from his cab, and there was a crowd.

Mallston was jammed into a heap against a tall board fence which surrounded the store-lot. The baby sprawled near him, where he had thrown it when the engine struck him.

"Are you hurt?" asked the photographer, turning him over.

He sat up, looking dazed and ludicrous: "Wher's the little feller?"

"I got him," panted the breathless mother, shaking the child from side to side as she showed it to him.

"*He's* all right," cried the engineer, "but I hit you. Where are you hurt?"

"I ain't hurt no place," said Mallston, crawling up on all fours, " 'cept wher' my back and head hit the fence." He stood up grinning at the excited crowd, and put his sneaking, protecting finger-tips under the baby's chin. The youngest had ceased to yell during the fright, but this touched him off again.

"You skeered the poor little feller," said Mallston severely, but the engineer was already mounting his cab, laughing with relief. The train passed on, people crowding the platforms.

Women felt the baby's limbs: there were no hurts except a bruise on one fat leg and a little more than the usual amount of dirt on its face.

"Are you sure you aren't injured?" urged the photographer, shaking his man.

But Mallston looked into his eyes with a preoccupied mind, and said, as to the only person present who would appreciate the depth of the remark, "I couldn't a-stood that, by jeeminy!" Tears stood in his big bovine eyes.

The group dispersed, many glad to have enjoyed such a genuine sensation, Mrs. Stillman declaring to the neighbor and the landlady she hadn't had such a skeer since the time *he* was took in the dead o' night with bleedin' at the lungs, and not a doctor in ten mile, and every minute like to be his last, so it was.

The artist followed Miss Gill from the spot. She picked up her basket beside the photographic car, her face so sublimated it seemed never to have known any other look.

"I didn't understand human nature," she confessed to the photographer, who had entered his car and again appeared at the window above her. "That fellow has the poetry in him that I can't write out. I'm afraid I'm going to cry."

The artist held down his sketch-book to her. Dabbing back her tears with one hand, she took it with the other and exclaimed at once, "Why, you've sketched *me!*"

"When a man like that dares so much for home happiness in this world, I think I can dare a little, poor, struggling dog as I am. I called that a while ago the picture of my wife; and it shall be—my *woman*," infusing the idiom of his native State with its primitive, tender meaning.

She handed back the book, and he took it, with her hand.

"Do you dare?" trembled the girl with a laugh, mindful that all Fairfield was out.

"I think I do," he replied, smiling also as he followed her eyes toward a group proceeding down the railroad—"even in spite of that."

Mrs. Mallston was walking beside her husband, making a display of ankle-bone under her scant calico wrapper, her sun-bonnet flapping to her nose, the four juveniles able to walk dangling from her fingers or drapery. Mallston, straight as a hickory tree, carried his youngest on his bosom, patting its cheek with his horny, potato-scented palm.

————————

Probably it was in the 'seventies, too, that Indiana began to patronize the stage in what could be called a Big Way.

Already traveling phrenologists had drawn modest crowds, the smaller minstrel and concert troupes had played to not overcrowded houses, and medicine shows had attracted large, though non-paying audiences. But in the 'seventies the influence of the Cultural Movement seeping in from the East through the medium of periodicals, plus an increased affluence on the home front, enabled the state to take up Art for Art's Sake. Who could speak with more authority upon subjects relating to the theatre than Kin Hubbard, through Uncle Ez Pash? Mr. Hubbard himself had enjoyed a wide—and ill-fed—experience in the entertainment world as a blackface minstrel performer before he took up art and philosophy.

KIN HUBBARD

Abe Martin's Broadcast

SWISS BELL RINGERS

"THE FIRST FLOCK o' Swiss bell ringers I ever seen appeared at Melodeon hall in 1867. Then they begun to pour in ever' week or so till 1871," says Uncle Ez Pash, in recountin' all the celebrities an' famous combinations that have appeared in that historic ole playhouse. "Yes, Swiss bell ringers wuz as thick an' common as wild pigeons. Sometimes they'd show up in coveys, an' mebbe sometimes ther'd be as few as four or what wuz called a set. Swiss bell ringers seemed to be susceptible to hot or warm weather, an' were hard to keep in sections where climatic changes were frequent an' violent. Invariably in the spring when the snow began to melt an' the first patches o' green showed up, Swiss bell ringers would migrate to the wild rice fields o' the great northwest. While the bells 'emselves wuz undoubtedly Swiss, I could never be quite sure o' the nationality o' the ringers on account o' ther whiskers, which completely hid ther features, except in rare instances where some effort had been made to curb or train 'em. The women might have been Peruvian so fer as the eye could tell. Swiss bell ringers talked very little an' seemed to take ther ringin' seriously. They huddled together off stage, an' wuz rarely seen in pairs, or walkin' about town alone lookin' at the courthouse an' other points o' interest to the traveler. So fer as I know no explanation—no good reason has ever been given fer the great epidemic o' Swiss bell ringers that swept o'er the United States durin' the period between 1867 an' 1874—how it started, who instigated it, an' how it wuz finally fought back. Our people wuz jest recoverin' from the war between the states, an' ther wuz a great silver agitation becloudin' the minds o' the people, an' ther wuz poverty an' distress on every hand. That the bands o' Swiss bell ringers that swarmed through the country durin' the reconstruction period wuz emissaries o' Providence sent to soften an' reconcile the people o' the north an' south, an' blaze the trail fer a strong an' powerful nation, is the only conclusion I kin come to. Traces o' Swiss bell ringers are still found now an' then along the ole National road as fer west as Saint Louis. In dismantlin' the ole courthouse at Roundhead, Ohio, a program o' the 'Original Spaldin' Brothers' Swiss Bell Ringers' was found along with a copy o' the Philadelphia Ledger, an' in straightenin' a curve o' the National road west o' Terry Hut the skeleton o' a supposed Swiss bell ringer wuz unearthed an' unmistakable evidence showed that his whiskers had attained a length o' forty-two inches. In the late '70's some kindly an' well meaning gentlemen started a movement to conserve a Swiss bell ringer fer the edification o' future generations, but nothin' wuz ever done about it."

Samuel Ginger, described and quoted earlier in these pages, saw the vicinity of Ridgeville uplifted by the disciples of Thespis and Apollo —though the communities along the Mississinewa appear to have attracted a class of talent inferior to that which visited Melodeon Hall and to which Uncle Ez Pash devoted his critical attention. Perhaps the reason for the apparently not-infrequent failure of the theatrical season in Mr. Ginger's locality lay in the violence with which Mr. Ginger himself, and his associates, reacted to any slight lack of capacity on the part of the visiting artists.

SAMUEL GINGER

Reminiscences of Ridgeville and the Mississinewa Country

CHAPTER III, PART TWO

"Can such things be, and not o'ercome us like
A summer cloud without our special wonder."—SHAKESPEARE.

ONE-HORSE SHOWS, magic lanterns, ventriloquism, etc., were always held in the schoolhouse and the gang was generally on hand to investigate the quality of the show. Once upon a time two young fellows stopped with us and advertised that they would give a refined and unequaled entertainment in the school house, consisting of ventriloquism, legerdemain, vocal and instrumental music. The very appearance of the two was enough to convince us that they were frauds; they had no baggage, not even a grip, but the people were hungry for a show and several paid fifteen cents each and went in, but a much larger audience stayed out. . . . They had given a complimentary for a fellow to come with his fiddle, and when the man commenced to sing "Billy Barlow," the fiddler didn't know the tune and got started on the "Devil in the Hay Stack," and the audience joined in the chorus, especially the crowd on the outside, and literally drowned the fellow's voice. He got rattled and gave up the vocal part of the entertainment, and the crowd began to yell for ventriloquism, and many demanded their money back. . . .

The audience clamored louder and louder for the ventriloquist. At last, the poor devil, in sheer desperation, said he would imitate a pig squealing; he raised the window a little way to make the pig appear at a distance; in the meantime the boys had snatched a good sized hog out of a pen nearby and when the showman would try his art the boys would punch the hog with a sharp stick and the ventriloqual pig was no where. By this time pandemonium reigned supreme, both without and within, and the two sharp showmen were glad to give back the money they had taken at the door and . . . get away from that crowd with whole hides and ruined reputations. . . .

But the grandest old round-up in the show business occurred some time later. One warm sultry day in late summer two wagons with a pair of the sorriest looking old plugs of horses and a slim, sickly looking man driving one, and a big fat man driving the other, drove up and stopped on a vacant lot near where the Cash Grocery now stands. They commenced unloading a lot of terrible old dirty show baggage, and without saying a word to anybody proceeded to put up a canvas, a thirty-foot round top—looked like it had just passed through a Kansas cyclone. . . .

After the canvas was up the fat man went to one of the wagons and pulled out two nondescript beings and led, or rather dragged them into the tent. It was conjectured that they were part human at least as they walked upright. They had some old ragged blankets thrown over them and we could only wonder and speculate on what they were but were not long kept in doubt. In a brief time two big flaming pictures, such as we have all seen at the entrance of a side show, adorned the front of the tent and informed the astonished beholder that within the sacred precincts of that tent we might see the possum-headed man from Borneo, and the snake-headed man, who was a man-eating cannibal from the Tonqua Islands. And, also, an immense boa-constrictor from the jungles of South America. Admission, one dime.

Not a word did the fat man nor the slim man utter, but when questioned about the show simply pointed to the awful pictures and softly murmured, "Ten cents." One picture represented a half starved man with the head of a 'possum, curled up in the hollow of a big tree, sound asleep. Another showed a slim, wiry looking man, naked, and half concealed squatting in the tall grass of a big swamp, while the third picture showed an immense serpent coiled up in the branches of a big tree, while the head swung down and had firmly grasped in its strong and wicked-looking jaws, a full grown deer. Notwithstanding the terrific pictures, the thing had such a suspicious look the people were slow to bite. . . .

Well in I went and I hope I may never see the back of my neck, if I did not at the first glance conclude that he had been robbing the cemeteries and putting the corpses on exhibition. On a slightly raised platform on two camp stools, sat two idiots; only this and nothing more. Sumption stepped up to the 'possum-headed man and said, "How de doo, Jack?" The idiot mumbled something that sounded like "yes;" and with that idiotic smile so common to the non compos, said, "Tobacker" . . . he was old Jack Connor, a pauper idiot that was raised up in Ward township and had been in the poorhouse for many years. His head resembled a 'possum about as much as an elephant, only in size.

But the snake-headed man! Shades of Barnum, protect us! He was simply a long, lank, half-starved, ragged, loud-smelling idiot, with an abnormally large tongue, with a deep suture in it, but not in the least forked like the tongue of a serpent, and looked about as much like the head of a snake as it looked like the Goddess of Liberty. He kept his tongue thrust out part of the time, simply because there was more room outside than in for it. On the ground near them lay a dogwood root or rather a stump with many roots. The tree had been grubbed up, cut off near the ground and the bark scraped off the roots. It somewhat resembled a Texas Tarantula. This queer-looking object, Fatty informed us, was the heathen cannibal's god; and on peril of our lives we must not touch it, as it made the heathen very angry, and he was liable to kill all the Christians in sight. I doubted this statement, and determined to test it; so when the slim man called Fatty to the door for some purpose, I quietly and very gently set my foot on the god, all the while keeping my eye on the man-eater, ready to flee at the first sign of hostility. But I did not have to flee; not the least attention paid the snake-headed man to the sacrilegious act; but simply gazed into vacancy with an idiotic stare.

Emboldened by calm indifference on the part of the cannibal, I picked up the god and was proceeding with a lecture on the attributes of the different kinds of heathen gods, when Fatty suddenly made his appearance in our midst. "Drop that god," he shouted;

"drop it quick, it's a wonder you didn't all get killed. You are the first man that has ever handled that god and lived!" . . .

But you should have heard Fatty's lecture on the freaks. "Now gentlemen and ladies," said he, "here is the 'possum-headed man from Borneo. He's a strange critter indeed; he's now tamed down some, but it cost seven men their lives to capture him, he was so savage; he won't touch cooked food but lives on frogs, snails, rats, and mice and little birds he catches in the night. At night he rolls himself up in his blanket to sleep and goes roaming around all night."

On the snake-headed his lecture was brief; after his lecture on the men, he stepped to a little pine box, lifted the lid off and said, "Here, gentlemen, is the great boa-constrictor. He can swallow a whole sheep at one meal; we only feed our snakes twice a year, and as it is nearly six months since he's been fed he's a good deal shrunk in size. Gentlemen you'd hardly believe it, but that snake is thirty-seven feet and nine inches long and as thick as a wooden bucket, when he's at himself."

Gentle reader, as I hope for happiness hereafter, I give facts when I tell you, that the snake was just a common Jay county black snake. . . . It might have been three and a half feet long and was so near dead that it only moved its tail when punched with a sharp stick. . . .

McKew kept everything in his store needed by the inhabitant at that day; among other useful things, old fashioned dinner horns, cow bells, etc. We had at the time a big bass drum with one head stoved in and a dumb bell and horse fiddle left over from a recent charivari . . . armed with the drum, dumb bells, horse fiddle, old tin pans, dinner horns, cow bells and everything possible that would help to make a terrific and discordant noise, we commenced a march . . . in double and single file around the canvas, keeping up a horrible din that would have drowned Hades itself.

We expected to see Fatty get on his ear, but not so; he stood there calmly looking on with a most pleasant smile, as if the music had been gotten up especially to do him honor. Indeed it was prepared for his special benefit. The lean boss canvas man began to get terribly nervous, but Fatty said something which seemed to reassure him. They went to work taking down the canvas and in an incredible short time everything was loaded into the wagons, idiots, snakes and all. They slowly drove west on Main Street to seek new fields to conquer . . . not a word had been spoken by either side during the whole racket. . . .

While on the subject of shows, I might mention the time that G. G. Grady's Circus licked and put to flight the whole town; how the town marshal ran home and hid under the bed; how Jim W. tried to take refuge in the house of Barney Casey; and how Mrs. Casey stood in the door with her skirts expanded the full width of the door and barred his entrance . . . nor how D. M. came running down the alley with a big grubbing hoe in his hand, swearing he was not afraid of all the d—d showmen this side of Hades; and how when he saw two showmen coming meeting him, he wheeled and started north at a rate of speed that would discourage a Nebraska jack rabbit. No, I will say nothing of *this* show as the joke was all on us. . . .

A great patron of drama (he wrote them as well as viewed them) was George Ade, who was born in Kentland on February 9, 1866, and spent a happy and uneventful childhood and youth in that community. In due time he went down to Lafayette and entered Purdue University; his life at Purdue continued happy, but—judging from reports of such observant contemporaries as John T. McCutcheon—it was by no means uneventful.

Ade began newspaper work in Lafayette after his graduation, moved on to Chicago in 1890, was a well-known satirist within two years, the author of best-selling books within two more, and the author of the first of several highly successful musical comedies within another eight.

In spite of the fact that Ade's homeland was in the tallest of the tall-corn section of Indiana, he took naturally to city life, and in Chicago he soon acquired a hard polish and a knowing eye for the foibles of his fellow man which was the genuine Clark Street article. For all evidence to the contrary the polish may have been Mr. Ade's, imparted to Chicago: certainly the people of that windy city had experienced no similar breezy interpretation before his arrival.

He was always amused by the fortunes and misfortunes of the Country Boy who Moved to the Metropolis (if we may borrow his effective style of capitalization). Through his Fables in Slang he loved to poke a deflating finger into the bosom of a stuffed shirt; to dissect an Institution to see what made it tick; to dig down deep in human affairs and to come up with their sometimes sorry motivations. All of this he did in a pleasant way which made the finished product of his cerebrations either an amusing piece of reading or a profound sociological document, depending upon the view his audience chose to take.

Ade was a winner in many fields of writing. He turned out some theatrical box-office successes and in his later years, when he came back to the Indiana soil (as opulent Hoosier émigrés tend to come) he had some authoritative things to say about politics, agriculture and plain good living on the grand scale. Here he appears in some sketches of high society doings in what very well might have been Kentland, Indiana, or some similar prairie metropolis of the Eighties or Nineties.

Those who survive that period or the era in general will no doubt recall a Tobias among their own list of acquaintances. Certainly every small town had a young man who failed to withstand the strains and stresses of prosperity when it came to him by grace of industry even though he fancied he had trained himself to that end by living modestly and committing worthy acts all through his youth.

GEORGE ADE

submits

The Fable of Successful Tobias and Some of His Happy New-Years.

ONCE THERE WAS a Financial Heavyweight, the Mile-Stones of whose busy Life were strung back across the Valley of Tribulation into the Green Fields of Childhood.

Like most of our Aristocrats, he got his Start out among the Corn-Rows.

His Youth was spent very happily, but he did not get on to the Fact until Years later. He used to work Fourteen Hours per for his Board and Clothes, and his only Dissipation was to take in the Swiss Bell-Ringers once every Season.

At the Close of every Year he was permitted to attend a Watch-Meeting at the Mt. Zion Church. The Watch-Meeting is a form of Gayety invented a long time ago by some one who was not feeling well at the Time.

The Outfit were supposed to sit for three or four Hours on the hard Benches, meditating on all the low-down, ornery Things they had done during the Old Year. Some of them had to hurry in order to crowd this Line of Meditation into a brief four Hours.

Now and then a local High-Guy with Throat Whiskers would arise and talk for a short time on the Subject of Death, and wonder how many of those present would be taken in by the Grim Reaper during the New Year.

Just at Midnight the Sexton would toll the Bell so as to cheer every one up. Then each of the Merry-Makers would go home and eat a Piece of Mince Pie and a Belle Flower Apple and retreat to the Feathers, feeling a little Ashamed for having stayed up so Late.

Later On, after Tobias moved into Town and began to wear Store Clothes and Stand-Up Collars and put Oil on his Hair, he encountered another kind of New-Year's Day.

The Era was that of the Open House. All the Women received, and the Men went over the entire Circuit and traded job-printed Cards for something to Eat and Drink.

This made it Fine for those who were not ordinarily invited into the Best Homes.

The Men roamed about in Flocks and usually they had a Hard Finish, for it was customary in those good old Days of Democratic Simplicity for every True Gentleman to take a Drink when it was proffered by the Hand of Lovely Woman.

And Lovely Woman seemed to regard it as her Assignment to put all of the Nice Young Fellows to the Bad.

It was customary to mix Tea, Coffee, Sherbet, Lemonade, Egg-Nog, Artillery Punch, Fizzerine, and Straight Goods until the Happy New-Year looked like a scrambled Rainbow and the last Caller was Sozzled.

Tobe used to go out every New-Year's Day to meet the Good-Lookers and fuss around with them, for those were his Salad Days. He made it a Combination Salad and philandered with about Seven before he took the Big Risk and bought a Home with a Mortgage Attachment and settled down.

Then the Happy New-Year began to have an entirely new Meaning.

He drew a Red Mark around January 1st, for that was the Day when he had to make the Books balance and take up some big Note that was hanging over him like a Storm Cloud.

His usual Plan for celebrating the Happy New-Year was to sit in his Office figuring on how to trim the Pay-Roll and sneak up Selling Prices and keep out of the Sheriff's Hands for another Twelve Months.

But the Time came when Tobias could take out a Pencil on December 31st and compute a Net Profit big enough to fill a Furniture Van.

To all Intents and Purposes he had come to the High Ground where he could afford to sit down for a while and enjoy the Scenery.

He certainly possessed all the Accessories of a Happy New-Year.

He had a Bank Roll and a House on the Boulevard and a Wife who was slowly but surely worming her Way into Society.

He had a Son attending a high-priced University and gradually accumulating an Oxford Accent, while his Daughter was at a School which used the French Novel as a Text-Book.

So, after all these Years of Struggling, Tobias knew what it was to have a genuinely Happy New-Year.

For when the Children came Home for the Holiday Vacation the busy Mrs. Tobias gave a big Dancing Party on New-Year's Eve, to say nothing of a couple of Luncheons and a Formal Dinner.

At these glittering Functions the Family did what it could to keep Tobias in the Background, for while he was a Corker when it came to doing a Fountain-Pen Specialty with a Check-Book, he was a Frosted Turnip when chucked into a Suit costing $100 and put down in a Marie Antoinette Apartment with a lot of Chaunceys who had been educated in the East.

He celebrated the Glad New-Year by standing around in Doorways and looking mournfully at the Light-Weights who were doing the Cotillon, and each of them having the Time of his Life.

He saw his Wife hob-nobbing with a Human Pickerel whose only Excuse for being on Earth was that he looked well in Evening Clothes.

Daughter was dancing with a lovely Specimen of the night-blooming Rounder, and Son was passing Cigarettes. And no one was paying any Attention to the Provider.

So he made a quiet Retreat to his own Room and had a Glass of Milk sent up, and read the Market Report, and managed to put in a Pleasant Evening, after all, seeing the Old One out and the New One in.

MORAL: One New-Year is just about as Happy as another.

Although Ade himself lived out his life in a state of single blessedness he knew that such orgies as he has just reported must eventually end in matrimony for some, even the wary.

He imagines the proceedings leading up to such a climax in

GEORGE ADE

The Fable of What Horace Stood For in Order to Land the Queen

O<small>NCE</small> <small>THERE</small> <small>WAS</small> a Lover who was on the Ragged Edge of the Desert where the Old Bachelors live.

He was good and tired of the Aristocratic Boarding-House, in which one-half of the Women Folks are Private Detectives. This thing of living in a Pigeon-Hole and looking out at a Tin Roof had lost all Rarity and Charm for Horace.

He had gazed into the barren Future and made up his mind to Marry, even if he had to choke some Nice Girl in order to force her to say "Yes." He was all keyed up for Matrimony, and the next thing to do was to choose the Lucky Bride.

Horace had done more or less rehearsing and he was wise to the Fact that it is just as easy to love a Girl who has the Coin as it is to get dippy over the Honest Working-Girl. Some Men imagine that the Foxy Play is to grab off something that never owned any Sunbursts and Sable Wraps, and probably she will be satisfied with Department-Store Belt Buckles and Nearsilk Trimmings.

But Horace observed that those who never had been strong enough to throw on the Lugs while they were living at Home, were the very ones who put Crimps into the Bank Account before the Honeymoon played out.

Horace often suspected that some of them hooked up merely to get a Whack at the Finery. But then, Horace was a regular old Cynic.

So he decided that he would pick one whose Folks had already bought for her about everything she would need.

After travelling the Beat for a Month and putting down Names in his Pocket Memorandum-Book, he drew a Red Mark around the Name of Lucille, and the same day he sent her some Orchids and a New

Book that he knew she would Enjoy, because it had such a Sweet Love-Story running through it.

Soon after that the Girl at Central began to know all about the Progress of the Affair. Lucille was all around the Neighborhood assuring People that, although Horace had been lovely to her and she esteemed him as one of her dearest and kindest Friends, there was really and truly nothing doing. Consequently, every one could see how it was going to turn out.

Horace had fondly supposed that the Recipe for becoming engaged was simply to warm up to the Girl until he could Hold Hands without using Brute Force, and then wait for the Psychological Moment. So one Night when Lucille looked up into his Eyes and said he was different from any other Gentleman she had ever met, he came back with the Speech. Her only Reply was to slip him one of Papa's Business Cards which she had ready for the Occasion.

"Go and square yourself with him," said Lucille.

Next Morning, Horace, wearing his best Bib and Tucker (also 8,000,000 Goose Pimples), was shown into Papa's Office. First he had to tell all about his Assets and his Business Experience, but that didn't take long. Then he told how much he saved every Month. If he swelled it a little, it was because he loved the Girl.

After he had answered all the Questions, he had to sit and listen to that well-known Monologue which is the Prize Specialty of the Self-Made Party who began Life by working for Seven Dollars per Month and saving Five Dollars of it. Lucille's Father said that Young Men nowadays are too extravagant and not half as industrious and Keen as he had been about the Time that he escaped from the farm. He sat there and hurled Bouquets at himself until his Arm gave out, after which he told Horace to go and fix it with Lucille's Mother.

Mother wanted to know, first, if he was willing to be married in the Episcopalian Church. He had to tell all about his Family. She seemed much relieved when she learned that he had Relatives in Virginia. Horace knew that part of it would be all right—unless she should happen to see the Relatives some Day.

She told him why a House was preferable to a Flat and scratched two or three of his Suggestions for Ushers. After letting him know that he would cut but little Ice at the Ceremony, she suggested that he go over and make himself solid with Uncle Samuel, because he had been accustomed to hold Lucille on his Knee when she was a mere Tot.

And, of course, that gave him a right to butt in on all Family Issues.

Uncle Samuel asked Horace what Church he attended regularly. The only thing that saved Horace was that he happened to remember the Name of a Church. Horace tried to side-step the Questions about Drinking and Smoking, but Uncle pinned him down, so he said that he had been tempted but he had not fallen, as yet.

After running the Family Gauntlet, Horace heaved a Sigh of Relief and believed that he had clinched all the Preliminaries. Not so. He had forgotten to fix it up with his own Firm.

An Employé can go on the outside and do almost anything and the Firm will not interfere, but the Minute he talks Marry, then old Mr. Side-Whiskers sends for him to come to the Private Office. The reason for this is that every Antique in the Wholesale District has a lot of cut-and-dried Advice which he loves to unload on any one who is compelled to stand and take it. So Horace learned from his respected Boss that for two or three Years the Couple should live on Cereal Food and make their own Clothes.

The next Bunch of Warning and Advice came from the True Friends at the Club. They put him down at a Table and sat around him and inhaled the Scotch until they were all Pie-Eyed, and then they told him what a Horrible Risk he was taking, and how not more than a half-dozen Married Men in town seemed really happy, and, although she was a Nice Girl, she had been engaged two or three times before, and Mother-in-Law would be a fierce Proposition.

For a Hammer Duet, the Men's Club makes the Boiler-Works seem like the Hush of Death.

The Reader may suspect that Horace was actuated by Mercenary Motives. However, the fact that he went the Rounds and listened to every one and then married the Girl proves that he truly loved her.

Moral: Elope.

At the turn of the century the circus didn't have to come to Indiana; it was already there.

Peru was full of circuses; they wintered there in ever-changing droves. Peru capitalists and horse-traders bought busted circuses and rejuvenated, combined, and renamed them. They made a good thing of it, too.

But the one circus that was an Indiana institution was Gentry Brothers' Dog and Pony Show. It was always the same: same dog acts; same pony acts; same monkeys, and its audiences would have screamed to high heaven if any detail had been changed.

Bookseller

BEN RIKER

Hoosier resident since 1912, describes some of the best-remembered features in his charming

Pony Wagon Town

GOLD LEAF AND RED PAINT

IT WAS FITTING that the Gentrys should come to my father's shop for wagons for their ponies. They [my father's shop and the Gentrys' show] were both getting to be good sized institutions now, and famous far from home; but both had been tiny not many years before, and they had started not far apart in time and place. The show had begun in Bloomington, Indiana, where Henry B. Gentry was a small boy with a knack of teaching tricks to animals.

His first pupil was a smart little ownerless mongrel that he had found on the streets of Bloomington and adopted. The dog learned tricks rapidly and well and the boy and his dog began staging impromptu shows on the downtown corners of the town. Passers-by rewarded them with coins, and before long the young impresario asked and obtained permission to present a more elaborate performance in the local opera house, in which he would offer a whole evening's program of acts starring not only the original dog but several other strays that he had rescued from the streets. He made $9.00 that night, and he had become a showman.

The star of this show was Barney, the dog he had first trained. Among his many accomplishments Barney could turn a back somersault, and his owner had also taught him to walk a tightrope. But before long the prowess of Barney had been surpassed in the esteem of the show's predominantly youthful spectators by a group of white dogs billed as "The Snyder Family." Until the end of its days every Gentry show had a Snyder Family—not the same family, for dogs are mortal, and there were always understudies in training to replace Mr. or Mrs. or Baby Snyder as old age or death removed them from the stage. I remember with pleasure a Snyder Family in every performance of the shows I ever saw.

The three dogs were beautifully trained. They were of proper relative sizes for a family of three, and appropriately costumed to show them as father, mother and child. Mr. and Mrs. Snyder would stroll about the stage on their hind legs wheeling their presumptive infant in a baby carriage and behaving generally as a pair of human parents might; at one point in the act Mrs. Snyder lifted the baby from the carriage and placed him on the floor where he walked, erect but with wobbly infant steps, to a little chair and sat down. The act always drew much hand clapping and many shrill cries of delight.

Four performances soon after the first one in the opera house earned $100 for the young showman and his dogs, and a tour of Indiana and southern Michigan netted him $1800. Ponies added to the show a little later made it possible to describe the outfit as "Prof. Gentry's Equine and Canine Paradox" and it was so labeled on the single railroad car in which it traveled and on the billboards that shouted of its coming in the little towns of its itinerary. After that the proprietor acquired a circus tent and quit showing in theaters, and a little later he added a band, and more railroad cars became necessary for new performers and increasing equipment. . . .

When the World's Fair began Prof. Gentry's Equine and Canine Paradox was about to become the four Gentry Brothers' Dog and Pony Shows, with a brother in charge of each one. "H.B." was the head of the enterprise and it was he who made the deal that added the colorful side line to my father's business. My memory is the only remaining source of information regarding the first years of the relationship, and it is more reliable in respect to the spectacular panorama of gold leaf and red paint than it is where the orderly procession of events is concerned; I remember a good deal about the building of the vehicles, even many of the small details, but I do not always remember which ones came first. I do know that all of the vehicles were ultimately made in lots of four, for the four shows were identical.

When I had my first opportunity to see one of the Gentry shows it had taken on many of the aspects of a full-fledged circus, but with animal performers instead of men and women. There was a street parade in the morning, a gorgeous spectacle made more gorgeous by the bright red and shining gold of the wagons our shop had provided. The performance began with a very grand "grand entry," practically a repetition of the street parade, and it closed with a chariot race, a race usually as fraudulent as its counterpart in the big circus, for the quartet of ponies that kept falling farther and farther behind during the first lap and a half nearly always made a dramatic recovery during the last quarter of the race and finished, to the accompaniment of hysterical screams from the grandstand, winner by four soft little noses. Not always, however. Once in a while, I am told, one of the other teams entered into the spirit of the game, defied its training, made a genuine race and refused to let the laggards catch up and win. Those four ponies ought to have received extra rewards for their honesty, but discipline probably made it necessary to withhold their lumps of sugar on such an occasion.

In between the grand entry and the chariot race came, among other things, a thrilling fire run by a uniformed monkey brigade manning a fire engine, a hose reel, and a hook-and-ladder truck. The fire engine was so constructed that, as the ponies raced to the fire, a rear wheel would come off. The monkey driver would stop his team, climb down, and hold the ponies' bridles, while the crew leaped out and replaced the wheel, whereupon they would resume the interrupted run. At the fire, part of the firemen operated the pumps that threw streams of water from a tank concealed in the body of the truck, while other brave firemen threw up ladders and rescued the monkey family from its flaming home. The house was made ot asbestos; only a paper covering burned.

There was a comic portrayal of the old woman who lived in a shoe, with a gigantic shoe full of monkeys, mounted on a truck drawn by four ponies. Sixteen chariots we made for the Gentrys: the shoe and its truck were our handiwork; the fire equipment all came out of our shop—the only vehicles in history to leave it with defective wheels.

Pudgy ponies went through the movements of the horse-show ring. They tried earnestly, but their short legs and their fat little bodies made of the performance a hopeless, though unintentional, burlesque. And every gaffer who was a child in 1900 remembers with delight the plumpest and broadest-beamed pony of all, who, always under the name of Dottie Dimple, went through her solo routine in every performance of every Gentry show.

There was also, for a time, a trio of elephants until, one day, in a little Illinois town the star of the troupe, appropriately named Satan, killed his trainer and injured a spectator or two. After that the owners decided that elephants had no place in a circus of midgets dedicated to the entertainment of children, and the show knew them no more.

Altogether, it was a happy little show and few children of my generation, in my part of the country, failed to see it at least once. I saw it often when it came to Urbana or Piqua, and even after I had grown up I went out of my way in Indianapolis one day to witness one of the last performances of its career. It was still a good show and I enjoyed it almost as much as I had when I was young. But by that time something was lacking: I was almost the only adult spectator unaccompanied by children, and I felt elderly and out of place. I was twenty-four years old.

CHAPTER ELEVEN

Came the Golden Age

Whatever miracle of Indiana literary production may yet lie ahead, no matter how many poets may beat their fledgling wings against their kindergarten chairs at this very moment, how many future novelists now in Indiana grade schools may be neglecting their arithmetic in favor of day dreams, there can never be another Golden Age.

There was a Golden Age of Letters in Indiana, and while the works of the writers who made it golden may sometime be excelled, there can never again be the concentration in locale which marked it. Indiana has grown too large and travel has become a matter far too simple.

That business of the concentration of authors—swarming, if you like—began in Crawfordsville in a minor way and continued there through 1900. It was a little before the day when the Chamber of Commerce nurtured manufacturing concerns which brought payrolls to town, but writing must have been an industry well worthy of such attention. A good many citizens of the "Athens of Indiana" must have owed their livelihood to the royalty checks which rolled in to Lew Wallace, Maurice Thompson, and the sisters Krout.

But shortly after 1900 came the phenomenal gathering, and it was in Indianapolis. In the year 1901, for example, a casual meeting of only the Indianapolis residents who were major figures in American letters would have blocked a sizeable sidewalk—if those of limited but recognizable stature happened to join them, a call for the riot squad would have been in order. There could have been easily convened—at, say, the intersection of Meridian Street and Monument Circle—James Whitcomb Riley, Booth Tarkington, Meredith Nicholson, and the distinguished statesman-biographer Albert J. Beveridge. And visitors for the day? Well, Charles Major and Mary Hartwell Catherwood might be in town to see their publisher; George Ade, David Graham Phillips, Mary Hannah Krout, and George Barr McCutcheon could very well have been waiting, between trains, on their various ways to see their families in, respectively, Kentland, Madison, Crawfordsville, and Lafayette. General Lew Wallace could have been over from Crawfordsville to look after his Indianapolis real estate investments, and Maurice Thompson might have brought his daughters on a shopping spree. Caroline Krout could scarcely have been present—she seldom left the confines of the Krouts' front yard—and Dreiser, if he was in town, was on some errand other than a visit to his home-folks.

The secondary figures, if any presumed to join the group, would certainly have filled Monument Circle and overflowed into Market Street, East and West. In Indianapolis and within an easy commuting range of forty-five miles there were hundreds of them.

Some of the most successful of the writers of this Golden Age must be excluded from the present survey because we here confine ourselves to writing on Indiana; neither Phillips, McCutcheon, Major (in his best-known works), nor Mary Hannah Krout chose Indiana as a scene. They were writers upon social problems, romance, politics, and reform. The same limitation excluded a contemporary of theirs, Eugene V. Debs, who, significant as he was in the field of labor reform, had little quotable to say about his native Terre Haute.

Of all these Indianians of the Golden Age James Whitcomb Riley was most widely known and admired in his time; probably today as well. Three of his best poems, in the sound opinion of his friend Meredith Nicholson, were "Goodbye Jim" (which we have already included in the literature of the Civil War under its original title, "The Old Man and Jim"), "Little Orphant Annie," and "Nothin' To Say." We now give the latter two:

JAMES WHITCOMB RILEY

Little Orphant Annie

Little Orphant Annie's come to our house to stay,
An' wash the cups an' saucers up, an' bresh the crumbs away,
An' shoo the chickens off the porch, an' dust the hearth, an' sweep,
An' make the fire, an' bake the bread, an' earn her board-an'-keep;
An' all us other childern, when the supper-things is done,
We set around the kitchen fire an' has the mostest fun
A-list'nin' to the witch-tales 'at Annie tells about,
An' the Gobble-uns 'at gits you
    Ef you
        Don't
            Watch
              Out!

Onc't they was a little boy wouldn't say his prayers,—
So when he went to bed at night, away up stairs,
His Mammy heerd him holler, an' his Daddy heerd him bawl,
An' when they turn't the kivvers down, he wasn't there at all!
An' they seeked him in the rafter-room, an' cubby hole, an' press,
An' seeked him up the chimbly-flue, an' ever'wheres, I guess;
But all they ever found was thist his pants an' round-about:—
An' the Gobble-uns'll git you
    Ef you
        Don't
            Watch
              Out!

An' one time a little girl 'ud allus laugh an' grin
An' make fun of ever'one, an' all her blood an' kin;
An' onc't, when they was "company," an' ole folks was there,
She mocked 'em an' shocked 'em, an' said she didn't care!

An' thist as she kicked her heels, an' turn't to run an' hide,
They was two great big Black Things a-standin' by her side,
An' they snatched her through the ceilin' 'fore she knowed what
  she's about!
An' the Gobble-uns'll git you

 Ef you
  Don't
   Watch
    Out!

An' little Orphant Annie says when the blaze is blue,
An' the lamp-wick sputters, an' the wind goes *woo-oo!*
An' you hear the crickets quit, an' the moon is gray,
An' the lightnin' bugs in dew is all squenched away,—
You better mind yer parunts an' yer teachers fond an' dear,
An' churish them 'at loves you, an' dry the orphant's tear,
An' he'p the pore an' needy ones 'at clusters all about,
Er the Gobble-uns'll git you

 Ef you
  Don't
   Watch
    Out!

Nothin' to Say

Nothin' to say, my daughter! Nothin' at all to say!
Gyrls that 's in love, I've noticed, giner'ly has their way!
Yer mother did, afore you, when her folks objected to me—
Yit here I am and here you air! and yer mother—where is she?

You look lots like yer mother: purty much same in size;
And about the same complected; and favor about the eyes:
Like her too, about livin' here, because *she* could n't stay;
It 'll 'most seem like you was dead like her!—but I hain't got nothin'
 to say!

She left you her little Bible—writ yer name acrost the page—
And left her ear-bobs fer you, ef ever you come of age;
I 've alluz kep' 'em and gyuarded 'em, but ef yer goin' away—
Nothin' to say, my daughter! Nothin' at all to say!

You don't rickollect her, I reckon? No; you was n't a year old then.
And now yer—how old *air* you? W'y, child, not *"twenty!"* When?
And yer nex' birthday 's in Aprile? and you want to git married that
     day?
I wisht yer mother was livin'!—but I hain't got nothin' to say!

Twenty year! and as good a gyrl as parent ever found!
There 's a straw ketched onto yer dress there—I'll bresh it off—
     turn around.
(Her mother was jest twenty when us two run away.)
Nothin' to say, my daughter! Nothin' at all to say!

"You never git what you want fer Christmas after you grow up."
                         —Abe Martin's ALMANACK FOR 1909
"Miss Mazie Bud is gittin' t' be so purty she haint got a girl friend."
                         —Abe Martin's ALMANACK

NEWTON BOOTH TARKINGTON

Booth Tarkington was born in Indianapolis in 1869. He attended
Phillips Exeter Academy and entered Purdue University in the happy
days when that young institution was adorned by the undergraduate
presence of George Ade and the McCutcheon boys. Tarkington
transferred to Princeton after two years, where he stood well in his
classes, wrought mightily in literary and dramatic affairs—but left
without benefit of a degree.

Returning to Indianapolis he tried first to establish himself as a
cartoonist and, after making one sale and receiving thirty-one rejec-
tions, switched to writing. He had little luck (though a publisher
bought his novel, Cherry, for $22.50 and stored the manuscript away)
until he undertook to write upon politics, a theme which every Hoosier understands from birth, and to cast Hoosiers in the leading roles.

The result was The Gentleman from Indiana, which became a best seller and long remained in that felicitous state. That was not his last best seller by several dozen, and he would win Pulitzer Prizes in 1919 and 1922 for The Magnificent Ambersons and Alice Adams. Booth Tarkington did not always write great books but he always wrote good ones; all are entertaining and many are important social documents.

He was usually at his best when his scene was a small section of Indianapolis which lies almost in the dead center of Indiana. With its south border on Washington Street (the Old National Road), with Senate Avenue and perhaps a brief deviation on Indiana Avenue (the colored folks' main stem) as the western boundary, and Pennsylvania or Delaware Street as the east, the Tarkington world included only a square mile or so at most. No northern line was permanently established, it varied with the periods in which his plots were laid; Sixteenth Street was suburban in the early days and, for him, Indianapolis never grew much beyond Fall Creek.

Some Indianapolis readers may have cringed a bit at his frequent references to the smoke and dirt which resulted from the city's industrial growth between 1890 and 1920, but Indianapolis was unquestionably smoky, and it was its growth, and the effects of its growth upon its citizens, which really interested Tarkington.

His characters were real—real in that their originals were often recognized by name in Indianapolis, by type everywhere—and especially in the early two-thirds of his production they behaved in a natural manner that caught the interest of the citizens of most American cities which ranged between two thousand and two hundred thousand in population. Residents of such communities throughout the United States added up to a very large audience indeed. There was a Penrod in almost every precinct and most men had once been Willie Baxter for a time. Every down-at-the-heel neighborhood had a bewildered Alice Adams, and most Alice Adamses had ambitious mothers; few were the cities that were not forced to bear with a George Amberson Minafer. Of course, The Gentleman from Indiana was considered a strictly local product, but actually other states than Indiana had sent high-minded young men to Congress, and The Flirt, heaven knows, was a phenomenon universally recognized.

Tarkington was always at his most charming, most telling, as he set a scene and a period in the little section of Indianapolis he had staked out as his own. Witness

The Magnificent Ambersons

CHAPTER I

MAJOR AMBERSON had "made a fortune" in 1873, when other people were losing fortunes, and the magnificence of the Ambersons began then. Magnificence, like the size of a fortune, is always comparative, as even Magnificent Lorenzo may now perceive, if he had happened to haunt New York in 1916; and the Ambersons were magnificent in their day and place. Their splendour lasted throughout all the years that saw their Midland town spread and darken into a city, but reached its topmost during the period when every prosperous family with children kept a Newfoundland dog.

In that town, in those days, all the women who wore silk or velvet knew all the other women who wore silk or velvet, and when there was a new purchase of sealskin, sick people were got to windows to see it go by. Trotters were out, in the winter afternoons, racing light sleighs on National Avenue and Tennessee Street; everybody recognized both the trotters and the drivers; and again knew them as well on summer evenings, when slim buggies whizzed by in renewals of the snow-time rivalry. For that matter, everybody knew everybody else's family horse-and-carriage, could identify such a silhouette half a mile down the street, and thereby was sure who was going to market, or to a reception, or coming home from office or store to noon dinner or evening supper.

During the earlier years of this period, elegance of personal appearance was believed to rest more upon the texture of garments than upon their shaping. A silk dress needed no remodelling when it was a year or so old; it remained distinguished by merely remaining silk. Old men and governors wore broadcloth; "full dress" was broadcloth with "doeskin" trousers; and there were seen men of all ages to whom a hat meant only that rigid, tall silk thing known to impudence as a "stove-pipe." In town and country these men would wear no other hat, and, without self-consciousness, they went rowing in such hats.

Shifting fashions of shape replaced aristocracy of texture: dress-makers, shoemakers, hatmakers, and tailors, increasing in cunning and in power, found means to make new clothes old. The long con-tagion of the "Derby" hat arrived: one season the crown of this hat would be a bucket; the next it would be a spoon. Every house still kept its bootjack, but high-topped boots gave way to shoes and "congress gaiters"; and these were played through fashions that shaped them now with toes like box-ends and now with toes like the prows of racing shells.

Trousers with a crease were considered plebeian; the crease proved that the garment had lain upon a shelf, and hence was "ready-made"; these betraying trousers were called "hand-me-downs," in allusion to the shelf. In the early 'eighties, while bangs and bustles were having their way with women, that variation of dandy known as the "dude" was invented: he wore trousers as tight as stockings, dagger-pointed shoes, a spoon "Derby," a single-breasted coat called a "Chesterfield," with short flaring skirts, a torturing cylindrical collar, laundered to a polish and three inches high, while his other neckgear might be a heavy, puffed cravat or a tiny bow fit for a doll's braids. With evening dress he wore a tan overcoat so short that his black coat-tails hung visible, five inches below the overcoat; but after a season or two he lengthened his overcoat till it touched his heels, and he passed out of his tight trousers into trousers like great bags. Then, presently, he was seen no more, though the word that had been coined for him remained in the vocabularies of the impertinent.

It was a hairier day than this. Beards were to the wearer's fancy, and things as strange as the Kaiserliche boar-tusk moustache were commonplace. "Side-burns" found nourishment upon childlike pro-files; great Dundreary whiskers grew like tippets over young shoul-ders; moustaches were trained as lambrequins over forgotten mouths; and it was possible for a Senator of the United States to wear a mist of white whisker upon his throat only, not a newspaper in the land finding the ornament distinguished enough to warrant a lam-poon. Surely no more is needed to prove that so short a time ago we were living in another age!

. . . At the beginning of the Ambersons' great period most of
the houses of the Midland town were of a pleasant architecture.
They lacked style, but also lacked pretentiousness, and whatever does
not pretend at all has style enough. They stood in commodious
yards, well shaded by left-over forest trees, elm and walnut and
beech, with here and there a line of tall sycamores where the land
had been made by filling bayous from the creek. The house of a
"prominent resident," facing Military Square, or National Avenue,
or Tennessee Street, was built of brick upon a stone foundation, or
of wood upon a brick foundation. Usually it had a "front porch"
and a "back porch"; often a "side porch," too. There was a "front
hall"; there was a "side hall"; and sometimes a "back hall." From
the "front hall" opened three rooms, the "parlour," the "sitting
room," and the "library"; and the library could show warrant to
its title—for some reason these people bought books. Commonly,
the family sat more in the library than in the "sitting room," while
callers, when they came formally, were kept to the "parlour," a place
of formidable polish and discomfort. The upholstery of the library
furniture was a little shabby; but the hostile chairs and sofa of the
"parlour" always looked new. For all the wear and tear they got they
should have lasted a thousand years.

Upstairs were the bedrooms; "mother-and-father's room" the largest; a smaller room for one or two sons, another for one or two
daughters; each of these rooms containing a double bed, a "wash-
stand," a "bureau," a wardrobe, a little table, a rocking chair, and
often a chair or two that had been slightly damaged downstairs, but
not enough to justify either the expense of repair or decisive aban-
donment in the attic. And there was always a "spare-room," for
visitors (where the sewing machine usually was kept), and during
the 'seventies there developed an appreciation of the necessity for a
bathroom. Therefore the architects placed bathrooms in the new
houses, and the older houses tore out a cupboard or two, set up a
boiler beside the kitchen stove, and sought a new godliness, each
with its own bathroom. The great American plumber joke, that
many-branched evergreen, was planted at this time.

At the rear of the house, upstairs, was a bleak little chamber, called
"the girl's room," and in the stable there was another bedroom, ad-

joining the hayloft, and called "the hired man's room." House and
stable cost seven or eight thousand dollars to build, and people
with that much money to invest in such comforts were classified as
the Rich. They paid the inhabitant of "the girl's room" two dollars
a week, and, in the latter part of this period, two dollars and a half,
and finally three dollars a week. She was Irish, ordinarily, or German,
or it might be Scandinavian, but never native to the land unless she
happened to be a person of colour. The man or youth who lived in
the stable had like wages, and sometimes he, too, was lately a
steerage voyager, but much oftener he was coloured.

After sunrise, on pleasant mornings, the alleys behind the stables
were gay; laughter and shouting went up and down their dusty
lengths, with a lively accompaniment of curry-combs knocking
against back fences and stable walls, for the darkies loved to curry
their horses in the alley. Darkies always prefer to gossip in shouts
instead of whispers; and they feel that profanity, unless it be vociferous, is almost worthless. Horrible phrases were caught by early rising children and carried to older people for definition, sometimes
at inopportune moments; while less investigative children would
often merely repeat the phrases in some subsequent flurry of agitation, and yet bring about consequences so emphatic as to be recalled
with ease in middle life.

. . . They have passed, those darky hired-men of the Midland
town; and the introspective horses they curried and brushed and
whacked and amiably cursed—those good old horses switch their
tails at flies no more. For all their seeming permanence they might
as well have been buffaloes—or the buffalo laprobes that grew bald
in patches and used to slide from the careless drivers' knees and hang
unconcerned, half way to the ground. The stables have been trans-
formed into other likenesses, or swept away, like the woodsheds
where were kept the stovewood and kindling that the "girl" and the
"hired-man" always quarrelled over: who should fetch it. Horse and
stable and woodshed, and the whole tribe of the "hired-man," all
are gone. They went quickly, yet so silently that we whom they
served have not yet really noticed that they are vanished.

So with other vanishings. There were the little bunty street-cars
on the long single track that went its troubled way among the cob-

blestones. At the rear door of the car there was no platform, but a step where passengers clung in wet clumps when the weather was bad and the car crowded. The patrons—if not too absent-minded—put their fares into a slot; and no conductor paced the heaving floor, but the driver would rap remindingly with his elbow upon the glass of the door to his little open platform if the nickels and the passengers did not appear to coincide in number. A lone mule drew the car, and sometimes drew it off the track, when the passengers would get out and push it on again. They really owed it courtesies like this, for the car was generally accommodating: a lady could whistle to it from an upstairs window, and the car would halt at once and wait for her while she shut the window, put on her hat and cloak, went downstairs, found an umbrella, told the "girl" what to have for dinner, and came forth from the house.

The previous passengers made little objection to such gallantry on the part of the car: they were wont to expect as much for themselves on like occasion. In good weather the mule pulled the car a mile in a little less than twenty minutes, unless the stops were too long; but when the trolley-car came, doing its mile in five minutes and better, it would wait for nobody. Nor could its passengers have endured such a thing, because the faster they were carried the less time they had to spare! In the days before deathly contrivances hustled them through their lives, and when they had no telephones—another ancient vacancy profoundly responsible for leisure—they had time for everything: time to think, to talk, time to read, time to wait for a lady!

They even had time to dance "square dances," quadrilles, and "lancers"; they also danced the "racquette," and schottisches and polkas, and such whims as the "Portland Fancy." They pushed back the sliding doors between the "parlour" and the "sitting room," tacked down crash over the carpets, hired a few palms in green tubs, stationed three or four Italian musicians under the stairway in the "front hall"—and had great nights!

But these people were gayest on New Year's Day; they made it a true festival—something no longer known. The women gathered to "assist" the hostesses who kept "Open House"; and the carefree men, dandified and perfumed, went about in sleighs, or in carriages and ponderous "hacks," going from Open House to Open House, leaving fantastic cards in fancy baskets as they entered each doorway, and emerging a little later, more carefree than ever, if the punch had been to their liking. It always was, and, as the afternoon wore on, pedestrians saw great gesturing and waving of skintight lemon gloves, while ruinous fragments of song were dropped behind as the carriages rolled up and down the streets.

"Keeping Open House" was a merry custom; it has gone, like the all-day picnic in the woods, and like that prettiest of all vanished customs, the serenade. When a lively girl visited the town she did not long go unserenaded, though a visitor was not indeed needed to excuse a serenade. Of a summer night, young men would bring an orchestra under a pretty girl's window—or, it might be, her father's, or that of an ailing maiden aunt—and flute, harp, fiddle, 'cello, cornet, and bass viol would presently release to the dulcet stars such melodies as sing through "You'll Remember Me," "I Dreamt That I Dwelt in Marble Halls," "Silver Threads Among the Gold," "Kathleen Mavourneen," or "The Soldier's Farewell."

They had other music to offer, too, for these were the happy days of "Olivette" and "The Mascotte" and "The Chimes of Normandy" and "Giroflé-Girofla" and "Fra Diavola." Better than that, these were the days of "Pinafore" and "The Pirates of Penzance" and of "Patience." This last was needed in the Midland town, as elsewhere, for the "aesthetic movement" had reached thus far from London, and terrible things were being done to honest old furniture. Maidens sawed what-nots in two and gilded the remains. They took the rockers from rocking-chairs and gilded the inadequate legs; they gilded the easels that supported the crayon portraits of their deceased uncles. In the new spirit of art they sold old clocks for new, and threw wax flowers and wax fruit, and the protecting glass domes, out upon the trash heap. They filled vases with peacock feathers, or cat-tails, or sumach, or sunflowers, and set the vases upon mantelpieces and marble-topped tables. They embroidered daisies (which they called "marguerites") and sunflowers and sumach and cat-tails and owls and peacock feathers upon plush screens and upon heavy cushions, then strewed these cushions upon floors where fathers fell over them in the dark. In the teeth of sinful oratory, the daughters went on embroidering: they embroidered daisies and sunflowers and sumach and cat-tails and owls and peacock feathers upon "throws" which they had the courage to drape upon horsehair sofas; they painted owls and daisies and sunflowers and sumach and cat-tails and peacock feathers upon tambourines. They hung Chinese umbrellas of paper to the chandeliers; they nailed paper fans to the walls. They "studied" painting on china, these girls; they sang Tosti's new songs; they sometimes still practised the old, genteel habit of lady-fainting, and were the most charming of all when they drove forth, three or four in a basket phaeton, on a spring morning.

Croquet and the mildest archery ever known were the sports of people still young and active enough for so much exertion; middle-age played euchre. There was a theatre, next door to the Anderson Hotel, and when Edwin Booth came for a night, everybody who could afford to buy a ticket was there, and all the "hacks" in town were hired. "The Black Crook" also filled the theatre, but the audience then was almost entirely of men who looked uneasy as they left for home when the final curtain fell upon the shocking girls dressed as fairies. But the theatre did not often do so well; the people of the town were still too thrifty.

They were thrifty because they were the sons or grandsons of the "early settlers," who had opened the wilderness and had reached it from the East and the South with wagons and axes and guns, but with no money at all. The pioneers were thrifty or they would have perished: they had to store away food for the winter, or goods to trade for food, and they often feared they had not stored enough— they left traces of that fear in their sons and grandsons. In the minds of most of these, indeed, their thrift was next to their religion: to save, even for the sake of saving, was their earliest lesson and discipline. No matter how prosperous they were, they could not spend money either upon "art," or upon mere luxury and entertainment, without a sense of sin.

Against so homespun a background the magnificence of the Ambersons was as conspicuous as a brass band at a funeral. Major Amberson bought two hundred acres of land at the end of National

Avenue; and through this tract he built broad streets and cross-streets; paved them with cedar block, and curbed them with stone. He set up fountains, here and there, where the streets intersected, and at symmetrical intervals placed cast-iron statues, painted white, with their titles clear upon the pedestals: Minerva, Mercury, Hercules, Venus, Gladiator, Emperor Augustus, Fisher Boy, Stag-hound, Mastiff, Greyhound, Fawn, Antelope, Wounded Doe, and Wounded Lion. Most of the forest trees had been left to flourish still, and, at some distance, or by moonlight, the place was in truth beautiful; but the ardent citizen, loving to see his city grow, wanted neither distance nor moonlight. He had not seen Versailles, but, standing before the Fountain of Neptune in Amberson Addition, at bright noon, and quoting the favourite comparison of the local newspapers, he declared Versailles outdone. All this Art showed a profit from the start, for the lots sold well and there was something like a rush to build in the new Addition. Its main thoroughfare, an oblique continuation of National Avenue, was called Amberson Boulevard, and here, at the juncture of the new Boulevard and the Avenue, Major Amberson reserved four acres for himself, and built his new house—the Amberson Mansion, of course.

This house was the pride of the town. Faced with stone as far back as the dining-room windows, it was a house of arches and turrets and girdling stone porches: it had the first porte-cochère seen in that town. There was a central "front hall" with a great black walnut stairway, and open to a green glass skylight called the "dome," three stories above the ground floor. A ballroom occupied most of the third story; and at one end of it was a carved walnut gallery for the musicians. Citizens told strangers that the cost of all this black walnut and wood-carving was sixty thousand dollars. "Sixty thousand dollars for the wood-work *alone!* Yes, sir, and hard-wood floors all over the house! Turkish rugs and no carpets at all, except a Brussels carpet in the front parlour—I hear they call it the 'reception-room.' Hot and cold water upstairs and down, and stationary washstands in every last bedroom in the place! Their sideboard's built right into the house and goes all the way across one end of the dining room. It isn't walnut, it's solid mahogany! Not veneering—solid mahogany! Well, sir, I presume the President of the United States would be tickled to swap the White House for the new Amberson Mansion, if the Major'd give him the chance— but by the Almighty Dollar, you bet your sweet life the Major wouldn't!"

The visitor to the town was certain to receive further enlightenment, for there was one form of entertainment never omitted: he was always patriotically taken for "a little drive around our city," even if his host had to hire a hack, and the climax of the display was the Amberson Mansion. "Look at that greenhouse they've put up there in the side yard," the escort would continue. "And look at that brick stable! Most folks would think that stable plenty big enough and good enough to live in; it's got running water and four rooms upstairs for two hired men and one of 'em's family to live in. They keep one hired man loafin' in the house, and they got a married hired man out in the stable, and his wife does the washing. They got box-stalls for four horses, and they keep a coupay, and some new kinds of fancy rigs you never saw the beat of! 'Carts' they call two of 'em—'way up in the air they are—too high for me! I guess they got every new kind of fancy rig in there that's been invented. And harness—well, everybody in town can tell when Ambersons are out driving after dark, by the jingle. This town never did see so much style as Ambersons are putting on, these days; and I guess it's going to be expensive, because a lot of other folks'll try to keep up with 'em. The Major's wife and the daughter's been to Europe, and my wife tells me since they got back they make tea there every afternoon about five o'clock, and drink it. Seems to me it would go against a person's stomach, just before supper like that, and anyway tea isn't fit for much—not unless you're sick or something. My wife says Ambersons don't make lettuce salad the way other people do; they don't chop it up with sugar and vinegar at all. They pour olive oil on it with their vinegar, and they have it separate—not along with the rest of the meal. And they *eat* these olives, too: green things they are, something like a hard plum, but a friend of mine told me they tasted a good deal like a bad hickory-nut. My wife says she's going to buy some; you got to eat nine and then you get to like 'em, she says. Well, I wouldn't eat nine bad hickory-nuts to get to like *them*, and I'm going to let these olives alone. Kind of a woman's dish, anyway, I suspect, but most every-body'll be makin' a stagger to worm through nine of 'em, now Ambersons brought 'em to town. Yes, sir, the rest'll eat 'em, whether they get sick or not! Looks to me like some people in this city'd be willing to go crazy if they thought that would help 'em to be as high-toned as Ambersons. Old Aleck Minafer—he's about the closest old codger we got—he come in my office the other day, and he pretty near had a stroke tellin' me about his daughter Fanny. Seems Miss Isabel Amberson's got some kind of a dog—they call it a Saint Bernard—and Fanny was bound to have one, too. Well, old Aleck told her he didn't like dogs except rat-terriers, because a rat-terrier cleans up the mice, but she kept on at him, and finally he said all right she could have one. Then, by George! she says Ambersons *bought* their dog, and you can't get one without paying for it: they cost from fifty to a hundred dollars up! Old Aleck wanted to know if I ever heard of anybody buyin' a dog before, because, of course, even a Newfoundland or a setter you can usually get somebody to give you one. He says he saw some sense in payin' a nigger a dime, or even a quarter, to *drown* a dog for you, but to pay out fifty dollars and maybe more—well, sir, he like to choked himself to death, right there in my office! Of course everybody realized that Major Am-berson is a fine business man, but what with throwin' money around for dogs, and every which and what, some think all this style's bound to break him up, if his family don't quit!"

One citizen, having thus discoursed to a visitor, came to a thought-ful pause, and then added, "Does seem pretty much like squandering, yet when you see that dog out walking with this Miss Isabel, he seems worth the money."

"What's she look like?"

"Well, sir," said the citizen, "she's not more than just about eighteen or maybe nineteen years old, and I don't know as I know just how to put it—but she's kind of a *delightful* lookin' young lady!"

CHAPTER II

ANOTHER CITIZEN SAID an eloquent thing about Miss Isabel Amberson's looks. This was Mrs. Henry Franklin Foster, the foremost literary authority and intellectual leader of the community—for both the daily newspapers thus described Mrs. Foster when she founded the Women's Tennyson Club; and her word upon art, letters, and the drama was accepted more as law than as opinion. Naturally, when "Hazel Kirke" finally reached the town, after its long triumph in larger places, many people waited to hear what Mrs. Henry Franklin Foster thought of it before they felt warranted in expressing any estimate of the play. In fact, some of them waited in the lobby of the theatre, as they came out, and formed an inquiring group about her.

"I didn't see the play," she informed them.

"What! Why, we saw you, right in the middle of the fourth row!"

"Yes," she said, smiling, "but I was sitting just behind Isabel Amberson. I couldn't look at anything except her wavy brown hair and the wonderful back of her neck."

The ineligible young men of the town (they were all ineligible) were unable to content themselves with the view that had so charmed Mrs. Henry Franklin Foster: they spent their time struggling to keep Miss Amberson's face turned toward them. She turned it most often, observers said, toward two: one excelling in the general struggle by his sparkle, and the other by that winning if not winsome old trait, persistence. The sparkling gentleman "led germans" with her, and sent sonnets to her with his bouquets—sonnets lacking neither music nor wit. He was generous, poor, well-dressed, and his amazing persuasiveness was one reason why he was always in debt. No one doubted that he would be able to persuade Isabel, but he unfortunately joined too merry a party one night, and, during a moonlight serenade upon the lawn before the Amberson Mansion, was easily identified from the windows as the person who stepped through the bass viol and had to be assisted to a waiting carriage. One of Miss Amberson's brothers was among the serenaders, and, when the party had dispersed, remained propped against the front door in a state of helpless liveliness; the Major going down in a dressing-gown and slippers to bring him in, and scolding mildly, while imperfectly concealing strong impulses to laughter. Miss Amberson also laughed at this brother, the next day, but for the suitor it was a different matter: she refused to see him when he called to apologize. "You seem to care a great deal about bass viols!" he wrote her. "I promise never to break another." She made no response to the note, unless it was an answer, two weeks later, when her engagement was announced. She took the persistent one, Wilbur Minafer, no breaker of bass viols, or of hearts, no serenader at all.

A few people, who always foresaw everything, claimed that they were not surprised, because, though Wilbur Minafer "might not be an Apollo, as it were," he was "a steady young business man, and a good church-goer," and Isabel Amberson was "pretty sensible—for such a showy girl." But the engagement astounded the young people, and most of their fathers and mothers, too; and as a topic it supplanted literature at the next meeting of the "Women's Tennyson Club."

"Wilbur *Minafer!*" a member cried, her inflection seeming to imply that Wilbur's crime was explained by his surname. "Wilbur *Minafer!* It's the queerest thing I ever heard! To think of her taking Wilbur Minafer, just because a man *any* woman would like a thousand times better was a little wild one night at a serenade!"

"No," said Mrs. Henry Franklin Foster. "It isn't that. It isn't even because she's afraid he'd be a dissipated husband and she wants to be safe. It isn't because she's religious or hates wildness; it isn't even because she hates wildness in *him.*"

"Well, but look how she's thrown him over for it."

"No, that wasn't her reason," said the wise Mrs. Henry Franklin Foster. "If men only knew it—and its a good thing they don't—a woman doesn't really care much about whether a man's wild or not, if it doesn't affect herself, and Isabel Amberson doesn't care a thing!"

"Mrs. *Foster!*"

"No, she doesn't. What she minds is his making a clown of himself in her front yard! It made her think he didn't care much about *her*. She's probably mistaken, but that's what she thinks, and it's too late for her to think anything else now, because she's going to be married right away—the invitations will be out next week. It'll be a big Amberson-style thing, raw oysters floating in scooped-out blocks of ice and a band from out of town—champagne, showy presents; a colossal present from the Major. Then Wilbur will take Isabel on the carefulest little wedding trip he can manage, and she'll be a good wife to him, but they'll have the worst spoiled lot of children this town will ever see."

"How on earth do you make *that* out, Mrs. Foster?"

"She couldn't love Wilbur, could she?" Mrs. Foster demanded, with no challengers. "Well, it will all go to her children, and she'll ruin 'em!"

The prophetess proved to be mistaken in a single detail merely: except for that, her foresight was accurate. The wedding was of Ambersonian magnificence, even to the floating oysters; and the Major's colossal present was a set of architect's designs for a house almost as elaborate and impressive as the Mansion, the house to be built in Amberson Addition by the Major. The orchestra was certainly not that local one which had suffered the loss of a bass viol; the musicians came, according to the prophecy and the next morning's paper, from afar; and at midnight the bride was still being toasted in champagne, though she had departed upon her wedding journey at ten. Four days later the pair had returned to town, which promptness seemed fairly to demonstrate that Wilbur had indeed taken Isabel upon the carefulest little trip he could manage. According to every report, she was from the start "a good wife to him," but here in a final detail the prophecy proved inaccurate. Wilbur and Isabel did not have children; they had only one.

"Only one," Mrs. Henry Franklin Foster admitted. "But I'd like to know if he isn't spoiled enough for a whole carload!"

Again she found none to challenge her.

At the age of nine, George Amberson Minafer, the Major's one grandchild, was a princely terror, dreaded not only in Amberson Addition but in many other quarters through which he galloped on his white pony. "By golly, I guess you think you own this town!" an embittered labourer complained one day, as Georgie rode the pony straight through a pile of sand the man was sieving. "I will when I grow up," the undisturbed child replied. "I guess my grandpa owns it now, you bet!" And the baffled workman, having no means to controvert what seemed a mere exaggeration of the facts, could only mutter, "Oh, pull down your vest!"

"Don't haf to! Doctor says it ain't healthy!" the boy returned promptly. "But I tell you what I'll do: I'll pull down my vest if you'll wipe off your chin!"

This was stock and stencil: the accustomed argot of street badinage of the period; and in such matters Georgie was an expert. He had no vest to pull down; the incongruous fact was that a fringed sash girdled the juncture of his velvet blouse and breeches, for the Fauntleroy period had set in, and Georgie's mother had so poor an eye for appropriate things, where Georgie was concerned, that she dressed him according to the doctrine of that school in boy decoration. Not only did he wear a silk sash, and silk stockings, and a broad lace collar, with his little black velvet suit: he had long brown curls, and often came home with burrs in them.

Except upon the surface (which was not his own work, but his mother's) Georgie bore no vivid resemblance to the fabulous little Cedric. The storied boy's famous "Lean on *me*, grandfather," would have been difficult to imagine upon the lips of Georgie. A month after his ninth birthday anniversary, when the Major gave him his pony, he had already become acquainted with the toughest boys in various distant parts of the town, and had convinced them that the toughness of a rich little boy with long curls might be considered in many respects superior to their own. He fought them, learning how to go baresark at a certain point in a fight, bursting into tears of anger, reaching for rocks, uttering wailed threats of murder and attempting to fulfil them. Fights often led to intimacies, and he acquired the art of saying things more exciting than "Don't haf to!" and "Doctor says it ain't healthy!" Thus, on a summer afternoon, a strange boy, sitting bored upon the gate-post of the Reverend Malloch Smith, beheld George Amberson Minafer rapidly approaching on his white pony, and was impelled by bitterness to shout: "Shoot the ole jackass! Look at the girly curls! Say, bub, where'd you steal your mother's ole sash!"

"Your sister stole it for me!" Georgie instantly replied, checking the pony. "She stole it off our clo'es-line and gave it to me!"

"You go get your hair cut!" said the stranger hotly. "Yah! I haven't got any sister!"

"I know you haven't at home," Georgie responded. "I mean the one that's in jail."

"I dare you to get down off that pony!"

Georgie jumped to the ground, and the other boy descended from the Reverend Mr. Smith's gate-post—but he descended inside the gate. "I dare you outside that gate," said Georgie.

"Yah! I dare you half way here. I dare you—"

But these were luckless challenges, for Georgie immediately vaulted the fence—and four minutes later Mrs. Malloch Smith, hearing strange noises, looked forth from a window; then screamed, and dashed for the pastor's study. Mr. Malloch Smith, that grim-bearded Methodist, came to the front yard and found his visiting nephew being rapidly prepared by Master Minafer to serve as a principal figure in a pageant of massacre. It was with great physical difficulty that Mr. Smith managed to give his nephew a chance to escape into the house, for Georgie was hard and quick, and, in such matters, remarkably intense; but the minister, after a grotesque tussle, got him separated from his opponent, and shook him.

"You stop that, you!" Georgie cried fiercely; and wrenched himself away. "I guess you don't know who I am!"

"Yes, I do know!" the angered Mr. Smith retorted. "I know who you are, and you're a disgrace to your mother! Your mother ought to be ashamed of herself to allow—"

"Shut up about my mother bein' ashamed of herself!"

Mr. Smith, exasperated, was unable to close the dialogue with dignity. "She ought to be ashamed," he repeated. "A woman that lets a bad boy like you—"

But Georgie had reached his pony and mounted. Before setting off at his accustomed gallop, he paused to interrupt the Reverend Malloch Smith again. "You pull down your vest, you ole Billygoat, you!" he shouted distinctly. "Pull down your vest, wipe off your chin—an' go to hell!"

Such precocity is less unusual, even in children of the Rich, than most grown people imagine. However, it was a new experience for the Reverend Malloch Smith, and left him in a state of excitement. He at once wrote a note to Georgie's mother, describing the crime according to his nephew's testimony; and the note reached Mrs. Minafer before Georgie did. When he got home she read it to him sorrowfully.

"Dear Madam:

"Your son has caused a painful distress in my household. He made an unprovoked attack upon a little nephew of mine who is visiting in my household, insulted him by calling him vicious names and falsehoods, stating that ladies of his family were in jail. He then tried to make his pony kick him, and when the child, who is only eleven years old, while your son is much older and stronger, endeavoured to avoid his indignities and withdraw quietly, he pursued him into the enclosure of my property and brutally assaulted him. When I appeared upon this scene he deliberately called insulting words to me, concluding with profanity, such as 'go to hell,' which was heard not only by myself but by my wife and the lady who lives next door. I trust such a state of undisciplined behaviour may be remedied for the sake of the reputation for propriety, if nothing higher, of the family to which this unruly child belongs."

Georgie had muttered various interruptions, and as she concluded the reading he said:

"He's an ole liar!"

"Georgie, you mustn't say 'liar.' Isn't this letter the truth?"

"Well," said Georgie, "how old am I?"

"Ten."

"Well, look how he says I'm older than a boy eleven years old."

"That's true," said Isabel. "He does. But isn't some of it true, Georgie?"

Georgie felt himself to be in a difficulty here, and he was silent.

"Georgie, did you say what he says you did?"

"Which one?"

"Did you tell him to—to— Did you say, 'Go to hell?' "

Georgie looked worried for a moment longer; then he brightened. "Listen here, mamma; grandpa wouldn't wipe his shoe on that ole story-teller, would he?"

"Georgie, you mustn't—"

"I mean: none of the Ambersons wouldn't have anything to do with him, would they? He doesn't even know *you*, does he, mamma?"

"That hasn't anything to do with it."

"Yes, it has! I mean: none of the Amberson family go to see him, and they never have him come in their house; they wouldn't ask him to, and they prob'ly wouldn't even let him."

"That isn't what we're talking about."

"I bet," said Georgie emphatically, "I bet if he wanted to see any of 'em he'd haf to go around to the side door!"

"No, dear, they—"

"Yes, they would, mamma! So what does it matter if I did say somep'm' to him he didn't like? That kind o' people, I don't see why you can't say anything you want to, to 'em!"

"No, Georgie! And you haven't answered me whether you said that dreadful thing he says you did."

"Well—" said Georgie. "Anyway, he said somep'm' to me that made me mad." And upon this point he offered no further details; he would not explain to his mother that what had made him "mad" was Mr. Smith's hasty condemnation of herself: "Your mother ought to be ashamed," and, "A woman that lets a bad boy like you—" Georgie did not even consider excusing himself by quoting these insolences.

Isabel stroked his head. "They were terrible words for you to use, dear. From his letter he doesn't seem a very tactful person, but—"

"He's just riffraff," said Georgie.

"You mustn't say so," his mother gently agreed. "Where did you learn those bad words he speaks of? Where did you hear any one use them?"

"Well, I've heard 'em serreval places. I guess Uncle George Amberson was the *first* I ever heard say 'em. Uncle George Amberson said 'em to papa once. Papa didn't like it, but Uncle George was just laughin' at papa, an' then he said 'em while he was laughin'."

"That was wrong of him," she said, but almost instinctively he detected the lack of conviction in her tone. It was Isabel's great failing that whatever an Amberson did seemed right to her, especially if the Amberson was either her brother George, or her son George. She knew that she should be more severe with the latter now, but severity with him was beyond her power; and the Reverend Malloch Smith had succeeded only in rousing her resentment against himself. Georgie's symmetrical face—altogether an Amberson face— had looked never more beautiful to her. It always looked unusually beautiful when she tried to be severe with him. "You must promise me," she said feebly, "never to use those bad words again."

"I promise not to," he said promptly—and he whispered an immediate codicil under his breath: "Unless I get mad at somebody!" This satisfied a code according to which, in his own sincere belief, he never told lies.

"That's a good boy," she said, and he ran out to the yard, his punishment over. Some admiring friends were gathered there; they had heard of his adventure, knew of the note, and were waiting to see what was going to "happen" to him. They hoped for an account of things, and also that he would allow them to "take turns" riding his pony to the end of the alley and back.

They were really his henchmen: Georgie was a lord among boys. In fact, he was a personage among certain sorts of grown people, and was often fawned upon; the alley negroes delighted in him, chuckled over him, flattered him slavishly. For that matter, he often heard well-dressed people speaking of him admiringly: a group of ladies once gathered about him on the pavement where he was spinning a top. "I *know* this is Georgie!" one exclaimed, and turned to the others with the impressiveness of a showman. "Major Amberson's only grandchild!" The others said, "It *is?*" and made clicking sounds with their mouths; two of them loudly whispering, "So handsome!"

Georgie, annoyed because they kept standing upon the circle he had chalked for his top, looked at them coldly and offered a suggestion:

"Oh, go hire a hall!"

As an Amberson, he was already a public character, and the story of his adventure in the Reverend Malloch Smith's front yard became a town topic. Many people glanced at him with great distaste, thereafter, when they chanced to encounter him, which meant nothing to Georgie, because he innocently believed most grown people to be necessarily cross-looking as a normal phenomenon resulting from the adult state; and he failed to comprehend that the distasteful glances had any personal bearing upon himself. If he had perceived such a bearing, he would have been affected only so far, probably, as to mutter, "Riffraff!" Possibly he would have shouted it; and, certainly, most people believed a story that went round the town just after Mrs. Amberson's funeral, when Georgie was eleven. Georgie was reported to have differed with the undertaker about the seating of the family; his indignant voice had become audible: "Well, who *is* the most important person at my own grandmother's funeral?" And later he had projected his head from the window of the foremost mourner's carriage, as the undertaker happened to pass.

"Riffraff!"

There were people—grown people they were—who expressed themselves longingly: they *did* hope to live to see the day, they said, when that boy would get his come-uppance! (They used that honest word, so much better than "deserts," and not until many years later to be more clumsily rendered as "what is coming to him.") *Something* was bound to take him down, some day, and they only wanted to *be* there! But Georgie heard nothing of this, and the yearners for his taking down went unsatisfied, while their yearning grew the greater as the happy day of fulfilment was longer and longer postponed. His grandeur was not diminished by the Malloch Smith story; the rather it was increased, and among other children (especially among little girls) there was added to the prestige of his gilded position that diabolical glamour which must inevitably attend a boy who has told a minister to go to hell. . . .

A dozen years later there had been a change in the empire of the Ambersons. Such changes will be recalled by most Americans who were urban residents of the Midwest at the beginning of the present century and will be recognized as a valid historical probability by younger generations. Tarkington describes it in a passage midway through.

CHAPTER XXVIII

NEW FACES APPEARED at the dances of the winter; new faces had been appearing everywhere, for that matter, and familiar ones were disappearing, merged in the increasing crowd, or gone forever and missed a little and not long; for the town was growing and changing as it never had grown and changed before.

It was heaving up in the middle incredibly; it was spreading incredibly; and as it heaved and spread, it befouled itself and darkened its sky. Its boundary was mere shapelessness on the run; a raw, new house would appear on a country road; four or five others would presently be built at intervals between it and the outskirts of the town; the country road would turn into an asphalt street with a brick-faced drugstore and a frame grocery at a corner; then bungalows and six-room cottages would swiftly speckle the open green spaces—and a farm had become a suburb, which would immediately shoot out other suburbs into the country, on one side, and, on the other, join itself solidly to the city. You drove between pleasant fields and woodland groves one spring day; and in the autumn, passing over the same ground, you were warned off the tracks by an interurban trolley-car's gonging, and beheld, beyond cement sidewalks just dry, new house-owners busy "moving in." Gasoline and electricity were performing the miracles Eugene had predicted.

But the great change was in the citizenry itself. What was left of the patriotic old-stock generation that had fought the Civil War, and subsequently controlled politics, had become venerable and was little heeded. The descendants of the pioneers and early settlers were merging into the new crowd, becoming part of it, little to be distinguished from it. What happened to Boston and to Broadway happened in degree to the Midland city; the old stock became less and less typical, and of the grown people who called the place home, less than a third had been born in it. There was a German quarter; there was a Jewish quarter; there was a negro quarter—square miles of it—called "Bucktown"; there were many Irish neighborhoods; and there were large settlements of Italians, and of Hungarians, and of Rumanians, and of Servians and other Balkan peoples. But not the emigrants, themselves, were the almost dominant type on the streets downtown. That type was the emigrant's prosperous offspring; descendant of the emigrations of the Seventies and Eighties and Nineties, those great folk-journeyings in search not so directly of freedom and democracy as of more money for the same labour. A new Midlander—in fact, a new American— was beginning dimly to emerge.

A new spirit of citizenship had already sharply defined itself. It was idealistic, and its ideals were expressed in the new kind of young men in business downtown. They were optimists—optimists to the point of belligerence—their motto being "Boost! Don't Knock!" And they were hustlers, believing in hustling and in honesty because both paid. They loved their city and worked for it with a plutonic energy which was always ardently vocal. They were viciously governed, but they sometimes went so far as to struggle for better government on account of the helpful effect of good government upon the price of real estate and "betterment" generally; the politicians could not go too far with them, and knew it. The idealists planned and strove and shouted that their city should become a better, better, and better city—and what they meant, when they used the word "better," was "more prosperous," and the core of their idealism was this: "The more prosperous my beloved city, the more prosperous beloved I!" They had one supreme theory: that the perfect beauty and happiness of cities and of human life was to be brought about by more factories; they had a mania for factories; there was nothing they would not do to cajole a factory away from another city; and they were never more piteously embittered than when another city cajoled one away from them.

What they meant by Prosperity was credit at the bank; but in exchange for this credit they got nothing that was not dirty, and, therefore, to a sane mind, valueless; since whatever was cleaned was dirty again before the cleaning was half done. For, as the town grew, it grew dirty with an incredible completeness. The idealists put up magnificent business buildings, and boasted of them, but the buildings were begrimed before they were finished. They boasted of their libraries, of their monuments and statues; and poured soot on them. They boasted of their schools, but the schools were dirty, like the children within them. This was not the fault of the children or their mothers. It was the fault of the idealists, who said: "The more dirt, the more prosperity." They drew patriotic, optimistic breaths of the flying powdered filth of the streets, and took the foul and heavy smoke with gusto into the profundities of their lungs. "Boost! Don't knock!" they said. And every year or so they boomed a great Clean-Up Week, when everybody was supposed to get rid of the tin cans in his backyard.

They were happiest when the tearing down and building up were most riotous, and when new factory districts were thundering into life. In truth, the city came to be like the body of a great dirty man, skinned, to show his busy works, yet wearing a few barbaric ornaments; and such a figure carved, coloured, and discoloured, and set up in the market-place, would have done well enough as the god of the new people. Such a god they had indeed made in their own image, as all peoples make the god they truly serve; though of course certain of the idealists went to church on Sunday, and there knelt to Another, considered to be impractical in business. But while the Growing went on, this god of their market-place was their true god, their familiar and spirit-control. They did not know that they were his helplessly obedient slaves, nor could they ever hope to realize their serfdom (as the first step toward becoming free men) until they should make the strange and hard discovery that matter should serve man's spirit.

"Prosperity" meant good credit at the bank, black lungs, and housewives' Purgatory. The women fought the dirt all they could; but if they let the air into their houses they let in the dirt. It shortened their lives, and kept them from the happiness of ever seeing anything white. And thus, as the city grew, the time came when Lucy, after a hard struggle, had to give up her blue-and-white curtains and her white walls. Indoors, she put everything into dull gray and brown, and outside had the little house painted the dark green nearest to black. Then she knew, of course, that everything was as dirty as ever, but was a little less distressed because it no longer looked so dirty as it was.

These were bad times for Amberson Addition. This quarter, already old, lay within a mile of the centre of the town, but business moved in other directions; and the Addition's share of Prosperity was only the smoke and dirt, with the bank credit left out. The owners of the original big houses sold them, or rented them to boarding-house keepers, and the tenants of the multitude of small houses moved "farther out" (where the smoke was thinner) or into apartment houses, which were built by dozens now. Cheaper tenants took their places, and the rents were lower and lower, and the houses shabbier and shabbier—for all these shabby houses, burning soft coal, did their best to help in the destruction of their own value. They helped to make the quarter so dingy and the air so foul to breathe that no one would live there who had money enough to get "farther out" where there were glimpses of ungrayed sky and breaths of cleaner winds. And with the coming of the new speed, "farther out" was now as close to business as the Addition had been in the days of its prosperity. Distances had ceased to matter. . . .

With all its great writing tradition Indiana has boasted comparatively few critics of literature or the drama, in recent years, who have stayed among us. George Jean Nathan, a product of Fort Wayne, does not count for he fled to New York at an early age and has stayed within the confines of that hot-house of the more exotic arts ever since. His career has been brilliant—no question about that—and Indiana honors him as a son, but he had lost whatever Hoosier characteristics he may once have possessed by the time he and H. L. Mencken began to mold American taste in letters through the columns of the old Smart Set at the beginning of World War I.

One of the few critics holding the home front in recent years is

CORBIN PATRICK

who reports theatrical activities, reviews books, and upon occasion writes charming essays for the Indianapolis Star. Mr. Patrick, called upon for a toast in the course of a program honoring Indiana authors in 1949, delivered this appraisal of Indiana's problem child of letters: it is probably the perfect expression of the mingled respect and distaste with which the average literate Hoosier regarded the subject during his life.

To Theodore Dreiser

I PROPOSE WE DRINK to the honor or salvation, as you choose, of the man who made Kinsey possible; whose father, the child, grew up on the other side of the tracks and resented it bitterly; the black sheep among Indiana's authors, the prodigal son who never came home; the greatest American novelist of all, a voice crying in the wilderness—or, a mere reporter and a bad one, with no sense of shame, whose shocking frankness gave hypocrisy the tinge of virtue. Whatever the judgment, the fact remains he assisted powerfully in changing the course of this country's literature. He pioneered a new school of realism which has won many followers, and he fought persistently to defend its point of view. Faulkner, Hemingway, Caldwell, Farrell, and Steinbeck have him to thank for their relative freedom to present life as they see fit, despite would-be censors. He gave the censors battle, and he gave them cause. Never at peace with the world or himself, this man was full of conflicts and contradictions. He believed that most lives are failures and that human beings are powerless to change their destinies; yet he became a worker for social reform. He was a free-thinking individualist, yet he joined the Communist party and believed Stalin was a truly spiritual person. This most controversial of Indiana writers once wrote: "In short, I catch no meaning from all I have seen, and pass quite as I came, confused and dismayed." To his more discriminating followers, he was a brooding, clumsy, earthbound giant, of little talent but much genius.

The following passage from Dawn is an example of Dreiseriana which gives sidelights on his family life, the Sullivan and Evansville of his day, his brothers and sisters—most notably on his brother Paul. Also, and inevitably, there is some clinical survey of the innermost feelings of the young Dreiser and a critical glance at some of those who happened to come in his way at this period in his youth.

THEODORE DREISER

Dawn

Boarders or no boarders, this effort of my mother's to keep this humble home and this fragment of a family together must have spelled complete defeat had it not been for an arrival and a source of aid which I shall now recount.

But before I do this, I wish to say that it was at this very impressionable period, and because of the various events I have narrated, that I became mentally colored or tinged with a sense of poverty and defeat and social ill-being in connection with our family that took me years and years, and then only in part, to overcome, and traces of which I still find darkly ensconced in certain corners of that subconscious which is a part of the deeper and more mysterious self of me. For years, even so late as my thirty-fifth or fortieth year, the approach of winter invariably filled me with an indefinable and highly oppressive dread, and that at periods when I needed not to be in dread of anything that winter and poverty, or the two of them together, could do to me. Similarly, any form of social distress—a wretched, down-at-heels neighborhood, a poor farm, an asylum, a jail, or an individual or group of individuals anywhere that seemed to be lacking in the means of subsistence or to be devoid of the normal comforts of life—was sufficient to set up in me thoughts and emotions which had a close kinship to actual and severe physical pain. At such times I felt not only an actual physical heart pain but a heavy, sinking sensation at the pit of my stomach, which all but unfitted me for any serious work I might have in hand. In sum, so immeasurably depressed was I by encounters with poverty or misery in any form anywhere that I was always feeling called upon to relieve it, to do something about it, the while my better judgment often told me there was little beyond the bare necessities—food, shelter, clothing—that one could offer to anyone without, in part at least, altering their very mental and physical texture.

I also early realized, in this connection, that where health and mentality go together, there is a positive joy in working, the while I also realized that nature handicaps people most damnably and then tosses them into the vortex of life to sink or swim. And this caused me to pity all such and to be inclined toward the belief that poverty and rags, while not always the symbols of social injustice, were nevertheless connected, in part, with economic maladjustment somewhere as well as social ignorance, though how anybody less than God himself was to arrange for the proper social equipment of every individual was beyond me. The creative forces that bring life to the surface spectacle which we behold are certainly to blame. Be that as it may, I still feel that I can clearly retrace to Sullivan and the last winter we spent there, the genesis of my awesome fear of winter and cold and want of good clothes and good food, which, spectre-wise, marched at my heels for years.

For it was during that last winter that my mother appeared to lose faith in this earnest and very decent adventure of hers and to sink back and down into a kind of dumb despair. The necessity of once more taking in washing—the local coal mine having shut down—and of running credit accounts at the stores, also of seeing her children carry coal and wood, and hearing them and herself denounced as "trash" by such ne'er-do-wells as the Thompsons and others, was sufficient, I take it, to depress anyone. Add to it the final problem of boarders who did not always stay and did not always pay, and you have a composite burden which must have been more than difficult for her to bear.

And yet I know now how valueless and, worse yet, ironic, at this time are mere compliments and filial pity, to say nothing of social and family respect, when extended to her, and especially in connection with the social and spiritual debt due her, by myself and the other members of her family at least. The courage, the charity, the affection, the complete subjection to the so-called "social contract" which must have been involved in her incentive! Add to all this the fact that for the first twenty years of their lives, all of her children appeared to be lacking in any trace of what might be called a social or constructive sense, that they mooned and dreamed and fiddled away their time, and you have a spectacle that must have frightened and made sad a woman of greater constructive force than was hers.

For, as I have indicated, she was never one who might have been called mentally incisive, nor had she ever had any of the advantages open at this day, educationally speaking, to the children of the very poorest. And already she had suffered enough blows and defeats and disasters to dissipate the fighting strength of even a stronger and more capable woman. And yet here she was, hidden away in this rag of a town, seeking to make a living for herself and her three younger children, to say nothing of some of the older ones as they appeared from time to time.

That final winter in Sullivan, though! The boarding and rooming venture finally failed—too large food portions, very likely, for the amount charged—and very soon she was refused credit (and that quite justly, I assume) at every grocery store. There was a period also at this time during which my father was out of work, though he stayed on in Terre Haute looking for something to do. And all of the older children were literally compelled to depart and seek work elsewhere, because there was nothing for them here. I recall a Christmas that passed with scarcely a toy worth mentioning (some little things sent by a sister from Chicago) and no candy or candles or any of the things which make the feast of the Christ-child worth while. I recall being sent to the distant mill to buy fifteen cents' worth of cornmeal, because it was cheaper there and one got more of it. I recall cornmeal mush eaten without milk because we had none. I recall clothes so old and so made over and patched that they were a joke. Even the rent was long overdue, though we were allowed to stay on because she did the washing of the landlord's family and hoped to pay eventually in that way, I presume.

And then, behold, a miracle! That eldest brother Paul, who after having been forbidden the shelter of the family roof in Terre Haute had disappeared and attempted to carve out a career for himself, returned, and that in the nick of time in so far as the affairs of his mother were concerned. His story is much too long to relate here;

it belongs in a novel, which I shall never find the time to write. After leaving a local Catholic school for boys, in which, by the aid of a priest, he had been placed at the time of the blowup in my father's affairs—so that he might study for the priesthood and so place himself in life—he had led a most checkered career. He had decamped from said school six or seven months after entering, and made his way on foot to that same Switz City in Indiana which was the terminal of the narrow-gauge railroad on which Jim Westfall worked, in search of a farmer friend (possibly a distant relative of mother's) in the hope that he would give him work. He found the farmer, but the work proved to be toil of the most back-breaking sort, and without reward save in food and shelter. He had to sleep in a haymow, and there was never a cent for clothes or entertainment in any form. (I am quoting from notes which he gave me a few weeks before his death.) The food was poor and he had to get up before daylight in order to do many chores before the real work of the day began. By night, he said, he was so weary that he could think of nothing save his hayloft, so that he might get sufficient rest to permit him to rise early and go through another such day.

So one night, when he was possessed of little more than rags and absolutely no money, he left, this time to walk to Indianapolis, sixty or seventy miles away, in the hope of enlisting aid from a Catholic priest who once had ministered in Terre Haute, and whom he knew. And this man proved to be a real Samaritan. He not only bought him a suit of clothes but gave him a room and meals in his parish house and some money wherewith to make a new attempt. But before that, what a sad journey for one so temperamental and inexperienced and emotional as was he at the time! Applying to one farmer for a meal on his way, a dog was set upon him. Applying to another at dusk for a night's lodging, he was ordered off at the point of a pitchfork, his wretched clothes giving him the appearance of a tramp, no doubt. For the most part he went hungry and slept in the open or under the shelter of some hay or straw stack. In Indianapolis he was picked up by the police as a vagrant, and only saved from a term on the rockpile by the appearance of the priest whose name he gave. (And this the future author of "On the Banks of the Wabash.")

In Indianapolis, fortunately enough, once his appearance and mental attitude were thus repaired, he was able to connect himself with an itinerant cure-all company, a troupe or wagon caravan which traveled gypsy fashion from city to city or rather from small town to small town, and sold "Hamlin's Wizard Oil" to the yokels. By this time he had discovered that he could sing and play in a rather amusing fashion; that is, he could accompany himself on an organ or piano; and it was this skill that brought him the opportunity to join this troupe.

And so he journeyed with this aggregation over Ohio, Indiana and Illinois, gradually winning for himself a better position. For he soon found that he could also write the type of comic song that the yokels loved to hear. Also that with the aid of a burnt cork make-up, he could positively convulse his auditors. This earned him some fame as a minstrel, so much, indeed, that the manager raised his salary and bound him by contract for three years. At the end of that time, though, he accepted a flattering offer from one of the best minstrel companies of that day, starting in Cincinnati as a blackface monologist, interlocutor and "end man." And now, after several years of this—and with a definite measure of popularity attending him—he appeared in Sullivan, and at the very time when his mother's affairs were at the lowest ebb.

But why, I once asked him? His reply was that for four years before this he had been dogged by a desire to see her; he had been haunted by the feeling that all was not well with her. So at last finding himself within reasonable distance of Terre Haute, he had gone there, only to find that she had removed to Sullivan, for which place he boarded the first train he could get. . . .

CHAPTER XXI

WHEN I THINK of my brother Paul, I often think of Gray's thought in regard to unknown Miltons and Caesars walking obscure ways in obscure places. For here was one of those great Falstaffian souls who, for lack of a little iron or sodium or carbon dioxide in his chemical compost, was not able to bestride the world like a Colossus. (And how narrowly many others miss infinitely better fates than are actually theirs!) I can think of him now, with his large range of sympathies and interests, as easily condensed or elaborated into a Henry VIII, say, or an Omar (of the Caliphate) or a shrewd Saladin or a Leo X. A little more selfishness, a little more iron or licithin, maybe; as it was, with these missing, he could only sing, jest and grow fat.

Even at this time, this strolling minstrel—who already at twenty-four had acquired a rotundity of girth that was good to look upon— had achieved the distinction of having had issued "The Paul Dresser Songster," a slim, gaudy pamphlet containing comic songs supposed to have been original with him and which he sold on royalty to such members of his audience as cared to buy. (Note the change of the name "Dreiser" to "Dresser." He thought this more pronounceable and suitable to his stage life.)

And now, cap-a-pie as to clothes—fur coat and silk hat—he arrived in our depleted home. I shall never forget the excitement his visit created. As I have said, our fortunes were at their lowest ebb, my mother at her wit's end. Al, Janet and Eleanor had gone to Chicago to seek work; Ruth and Amy had returned to Terre Haute to seek employment. This left my mother and us three youngest alone and waiting aimlessly for something to turn up. It was a cold, snowy day in February. Late in the afternoon there was a knock at the door, and there, to mother's amazement, stood her lost and presumably erring son. As she said afterwards, she scarcely recognized him; he had grown so much stouter and no doubt the fur coat and silk hat confused her. But the uncertainty was not for long, and then came embraces and tears, the while we children stood about and listened to tales of his success in the great world without, and then within the hour witnessed a most palatable change for all of us. For at once, of course, he relieved mother of her most pressing wants with ready cash, and thereafter so long as he was able, sent her money every week. In fact, for a period of ten years thereafter, or until her death in 1890, he never failed in this.

Only to me, the arrival of this brother was the same as the arrival of a total stranger—or nearly so—and yet, fascinatingly enough, a stranger who was more like a fairy godfather or the well known occidental Santa Claus. As I have said before, he was like the sun, or a warm, cheering fire. He beamed upon us all, and when he left (as he did, after only a few hours, but promising faithfully to return soon), he gave Ed and me copies of "The Paul Dresser Songster," with his picture on the cover just above the price (ten cents)! It contained all sorts of comic and sentimental jingles and underneath each was printed: "Copyright Willis, Woodward & Company, New York, N. Y." (And so he was connected with that big city, too!) And he spoke of a lot of his old but still good clothes which mother might make into suits for Ed and myself. And a week after he left, a box arrived, containing these clothes as well as a dress and slippers for mother and many groceries—a development or phase of prosperity which left me fairly agape. Later came new shoes and hats for each of us and a complete outfit for Trina, who was to "make her first communion" at the small Catholic Church. The labor of washing and ironing and taking care of boarders and roomers which had so harassed my mother for these several years was given over, never again to be resumed by her in this world, thanks be, and I trust in no other. Her heavy gloom was replaced by a normal optimism and sunny geniality, for given the least aid, she emanated rays of humor and hope.

Perhaps the conception of a fate or fortune in the affairs of men— an interfering hand that beyond our understanding or willing makes or mars our inconceivably petty lives—was at this time born in me. At any rate, this change from a gnawing, driving misery to the ease and relief that comes with a little money, was sufficient to burn itself forever in my memory, and there it remains to-day. My mother's tears of relief! Her son's loving, helpful arms! Truly, I think it is better to give than to receive!

And truly, I think there is nothing in life more wonderful than the tang of new experiences in childhood. The world is all so strange, so mysterious and full of promise. Our soul, or essence, whatever its previous state or lack of one, appears to come fresh from an entirely different realm, intensely avid and curious as to this one. And the impressionable slate or wax it brings is so clean, so unmarred. On it may be written anything, and so forcefully and enduringly. And youth does not crave the truth, only its dreams and illusions— which is well enough. For what a dreary world it would be if it did! Youth prefers and seeks mostly the vague, expansive, uncertain imaginings which crowd its mind, always so much more wonderful than reality itself.

And now, following Paul's departure, a new element or person- ality was injected into our lives, a woman whose relationship to Paul was probably one of the motivating causes for our removal to Evansville the following spring or summer. This Annie Brace (alias Sallie Walker) was, if I must confess it, the keeper or owner of a very successful, even imposing, "house of ill repute" in Evans- ville—a "madam," no less—but still young and very beautiful, as I came to see for myself. Somewhere she had encountered Paul and becoming enamored of him, was seeking at this time to join her life with his, and did, as it later appeared, for a time. Having heard from Paul, no doubt, as to his mother and her whereabouts and condition, she now hastened to make social and affectional capital with both him and his mother by coming to see her. As I recall her now (for I was always about and watching), she was a handsome woman of perhaps twenty-seven or eight—which seemed very old to me at the time—very dark as to hair and eyes and rounded and graceful as to figure, and with, as it seemed to me at the time, an exotic taste for black. The assumption, on my part at least, was that she was in mourning. But those clear, incisive, black eyes, and the exaggerated whiteness of her face and hands! I recall her sitting in our front room and beaming warmly on my mother, the mother of her lover. It was a brief visit between trains. Say that at best she spent an hour with us, but thereafter came boxes of groceries and baskets of fruit and packages of cloth, together with a number of cast-off and rather remarkable garments, the source and exact use of which were not discovered by my mother for some time, if ever.

And then, the following spring or summer, the actual removal of our family, or very fragmentary portion of a family, to Evans- ville, traceable, no doubt, to the kindly, if self-interested, desire of this Annie Brace to win or maintain an affectional control over Paul while he was so keen to do something for his mother. Whether he saw through this, or seeing felt it to be satisfactory, I do not know. Certain it is that he fell in with the proposal, first made by her to mother and later to him, and which in the course of a few months she engineered to a successful conclusion. First there was an extended visit—four or five days—on the part of Paul to our home in Sullivan, and then, in late May or early June, we left for Evansville.

In connection with this particular removal, though, are some facts which relate to the hodgepodge which life makes of what we are pleased to term morality and immorality, and of this I now prefer to speak. For although this particular change was effected as much as abetted by perhaps the reigning courtesan of her region, working through the always vulnerable emotions of my very good brother, still at the time the change was brought about, my mother knew no more of Annie Brace than she knew of anything else in connection with her eldest son's immediate past. And whether or not she knew, it is my conviction that it would have made no least difference in her opinion of his right to his particular interests or affairs. For and although concerned always with the necessity and duty of keeping step with the social and economic standards of whatsoever community she was a part—herself working most and hardest to maintain them—still where her grown children were concerned, she was never one to pry into their affairs. In their youth it was that she had had her say, but never to the extent of demanding interest in or respect for the hard and fast conventions of narrow-minded or socially biased persons. Human beings, as she often indicated in many ways, had trouble enough in maintaining themselves without being harried further by finicky and non-understanding social opinion or social notions. Knowing much, and this by direct experience, of the driving passions and weaknesses that affect us all, she was far too generous and innately understanding to criticize much. Rather, if her own or the children of others erred, it was because, as she usually insisted, of many things, most of which they could not help or forfend against, and it was her emotional fate as well as spiritual duty to continue to love them. She might quarrel and sigh, and even cry, but in the end they were her children and she bowed to the instinct that drew her to them.

But how intense was my own elation at the thought of change and seeing more of the world! Sullivan had been satisfactory enough at one time and another, though we had seen some grim hours there, but oh, to be up and away! I remember the packing, the seeing about boxes and a drayman to transport our few belongings to the freight office. And then at last the great day! I recall looking at the tall, scarred, eagle tree in the field and thinking that I should miss it. Also there was the problem of the future of our two dogs, Hound and Rover, which troubled me not a little, for it was finally decided that they were to be abandoned to a roving fate, because, forsooth, we lacked leather straps and collars wherewith to control them en route or the money to have them expressed. (These were trifling matters, I presume, which could not be brought to the attention of our successful brother.) At best, they were used to poverty and want and probably fared just as well without us. I hope so.

I recall the long, slow junketing of a five o'clock local train from Sullivan to Evansville, and of passing ten or twelve small villages, most of them less important even than Sullivan. One, Princeton, a resort of sorts, impressed me as being exceedingly alive and flourishing, with carriages to meet people at the trains and bright store windows seen through the trees. And with Vincennes came memories of Sue Bellette and the fire-house and Tinby. And at one other station, Paxton, came the vision of a certain family there whom we chanced to know. A wonderful ride!

But transcending all this by far was the novelty of entering a city of so considerable a size as Evansville. So slow was this train that it was nearly ten o'clock before we finally reached our destination, and by then I had grown too sleepy to realize much of what was going on about me. But at sight and sound of numerous engines and engine bells and the clattering of cars—all part of a big yard we were entering—as well as the sight of gas lamps flaring in the night, I sat up and took a renewed interest in life. Came a Union Station, capacious and lively, the terminal point of several roads, and here, with a crowd of others, we were ordered to get off. And then the wonder of a city night scene! Those poor scum back in Sullivan, I thought! What could they know of a place like this? A city! And such a city! And they had dared to look down on us! If only they could see us now, gloriously entering this city, a city such as they might never have the privilege of entering!

We were not allowed to wander about, though, or meditate too much in this fashion, for there at the train was this amazing brother and son, who now led us through a glowing waiting-room to the street (East Main Street), where were, as it seemed to me at the time, great crowds and countless lights and vehicles and street cars and brightly-lighted shops. True, the street cars were small, drawn by one lone mule and in charge of one man as conductor and driver, but what would you? They had bright-colored bits of glass at the top near the roof and bright brass handles. Even now I can see myself hanging onto the hand or skirt of my distrait and pestered mother (who was, no doubt, as wide-eyed and wondering as ourselves), as led by Paul we boarded one of the cars labeled "Salt Wells" and rode off to unravel the mysteries of our new home.

Neither my mother nor any of us had been given the slightest inkling as to what our new home was to be like. Imagine, then, our surprise and delight when after some piloting along a dark street we came upon a small one-and-a-half story brick cottage, set in a neatly-fenced big yard, with a barn and chicken run at the back! And flowers in the foreground! About the house and yard also a wide, grass-covered common which stretched unobstructed to a distant wood on one side and a far-off railroad yard on another, for we were at the edge of the city. South and westward was the city, the sky glowing with its lights. And entering, we beheld a completely-furnished home. No shabby makeshifts and leavings here, as at Sullivan. Instead, in the dining-room a shining new table with a complete set of chairs, and in the parlor, not only parlor furniture but a piano! Carpets on the floors, new carpets, and in the kitchen a shining cookstove, with dishes and an ample array of cooking utensils!

Quite like one who has seen a fairy wave her wand and work a miracle, stood my mother, looking at it all from first one doorway and then another. And behind her, patting her shoulder, because she was crying, my brother Paul. Blessed are the merciful, for, verily, they have their reward! Paul, the good son, the loving brother: write his name high among those who have wrought for affection's sake. Jailbird, writer of pointless ballads, singer of trivial songs—even so, write his name large as one who loved his fellowmen!

In the midst of these wonders—almost a surfeit of them—we went to bed, and next morning arose to new glories. I shall never forget the intense delight I felt in stepping out onto the lawn of our back-yard and over the low fence to view the city, the great common, the new life. And bright and early came Paul again, to suggest and direct. To Ed and myself he brought a ball and bat; to Trina some gewgaw of some kind. To the piano also he went and played some of his latest compositions, folderol comic songs, but how wonderful to us! So the new hours began to slip by and Sullivan to sink into the dim and misty past, never to rise or obtrude itself again.

CHAPTER XXII

THOSE FIRST DAYS in Evansville! Looking back on it now, it seems a kind of dream city—made so, of course, by my very fervid and youthful imagination. A marvelous river, a sylvan creek, trees, birds, flowers, open common, spires, towers, sunlight and moonlight; indeed, a perfect swirl of youth and life in which everything moves as in a dream, sentient and delightful.

It was a splendid thing, in a city of this size, to live in the last house, or almost the last house, of a region not inconvenient to the city heart and yet blessed with all of the idyllic charm of the country. It was so remote and quiet and rural and yet so convenient to everything. Inside its brown picket fence in the centre of the great common of grass, it possessed congruity and charm. (Returning years later, I found the common all built in and this little house crowded tenementwise without yard or tree into a close row of commonplace cottages.) A good brick walk with which East Franklin Street was paved led out to it. Gaslamps and water-plugs were near at hand. The mail-carrier, the milkman, the newspaper boy, and now and then a peripatetic policeman, were to be seen, the latter only accidentally and peradventure. Why should a policeman waste his time wandering about pleasant, grass-grown suburbs when he could idle much more comfortably in a saloon?

About half or three-quarters of a mile to the south of us were the tracks and switching yards of a railroad that ran from Evansville to Louisville, and on which later my brother Al worked for a little while as "butcher" or train-boy, selling candies and magazines. Between our house and that road was level grass, starred with white clover and a few fine, broad-branched trees. And to the east also was grass, with a house or two farther out. And beyond it all at one point an immense red brick pottery, with a number of kraal-like kilns of great size showing over a low wall of brick. And to the north was open common, with a pond here and there. And beyond, nothing but grass and well-favored trees, until one came to the muddy Pigeon Creek, a tributary of the Ohio, where were the Devil's Elbow and the Yellow Banks—swimming holes—and pockets on either side of dam and falls where bass and perch and other fish were to be had in great quantities. To the west was the city proper, a straggling, sprawling affair, with the east end of Main Street trailing to within two or three blocks of our door, and Blount's Plough Works, with giant hammers beating steel bars into ploughshares and belching flame and smoke, often by night as well as day.

And then, to the extreme west of the city, and bounding it, was the wide-surfaced, yellow-bodied Ohio River, rolling its enormous flood from the Alleghenies and the States of Ohio and Kentucky and Indiana into the Mississippi at Cairo. Never shall I forget the first day I beheld it, from the end of Main Street, which debouched upon an enormous sloping levee, paved with great grey cobblestones and stocked with enormous piles of cotton in bales, groceries and hardware in boxes, and watermelons and other fruits and vegetables in piles or crated, boxed, bagged or barreled. Among these were little artificial streets or lanes, along which traveled constantly scores of small mule-drawn drays driven by Negroes in sleeveless cotton undershirts and belted trousers gripped tightly about the hips. At the foot of the levee, where it met the water, were long, brown wharves or floating docks, anchored lengthwise of the shore, and lashed to those again, a number of the old-time, stern wheel river steamers, with their black double stacks, double and treble decks, gilt and red or blue or green decorations, and piles of freight being taken on or unloaded. It was the first active river scene I had ever beheld, except for pictures in our school geography.

And so, the glory of that first summer! The sense of newness, strangeness, mysteries to be explored, together with freedom and content with life! White clouds in the sky, trees, grass, a river and creek, journeys to far, mysterious parts of the city! Life went around in a circle of delicious and yet vain imaginings. And what a splendid company of playfellows we found here! At last Ed was in his glory, relieved, I am sure, and for the first time in his life, of my dreamy and all too meditative temperament and now able to pick and choose his own companions. . . .

But these new boys were, in the main, so good-natured and agreeable, a fun-loving and essentially democratic crew. They were always about with a proposal for a game of some kind. The matter of girls was as yet—in quite all of us, I think—a dormant instinct, or at least a sealed mystery. Certainly girls, to me at least, were no more at that time than boys, if as much, just another type of creature but not suitable for athletic games. At about this time, too, I was beginning to read, in an idle, indiscriminate way, an odd mixture of books which I found in the loft of our new house. These comprised such works as Gray's "Elegy," "The Deserted Village," "The Traveler," "Wanda," by Ouida, and Lytton's "Ernest Maltravers." And how I did enjoy them! It may seem strange, but it was as if I had met up with things I had long known and loved and understood. I did not know all of the words and did not trouble to look them up, yet I am sure that I gathered the import of most of that which I read. I can neither understand nor explain it, seeing that I was but between ten and eleven years of age. Yet so it was.

And at the very same time, if you will believe it, I began to read with interest *The Family Story Paper*, *The Fireside Companion* and *The New York Weekly*, all romantic periodicals which flourished at that time and sample copies of which were thrown over our fence almost weekly. Finding one lying on our front lawn one day, I picked it up and began reading one of those dramatic introduc-tions by which the reader is lured to "continue in our next." Forth-with I was lost. I just had to see what became of the poor but beautiful working-girl who was seized by thugs on her way to work and driven, gagged and blindfolded, to a wretched shanty far out on the Hackensack meadows, where she was confronted by her lust-ful and immoral pursuer. Having from either my mother or Paul extracted the required nickels, I proceeded every Friday or Saturday to the nearest news-stand to purchase, as might a drug addict, this latest delight.

But along with these also I was introduced, by some of the youths who gathered in the shade of our barn, to "Diamond Dick," "Brave and Bold," "Pluck and Luck," "Work and Win" and those other predecessors of the later "Nick Carters," "Frank Merriwells," etc. . . . It was a colorful world which they presented, impossible from a practical point of view and yet suggesting that freedom of action which we so often experience in dreams. How often at that time I trotted over the plains of Africa or Australia or Asia with these famous boy heroes whose names I have long since forgotten, but who possessed some practical device or other—iron horse or buggy or man, and bullet or arrow-proof jacket and suits even—in which one could travel in safety, if not peace, and, at the same time, defy and destroy all manner of savages and wild animals, and so with impunity invade the wildest, the most dangerous and therefore the most fascinating regions! At times, in short, I became so excited over the wonder of the life pictured that I would become intensely dissatisfied with the life I was living and was all for running away and finding a device of my own—a horse, a covered wagon, a bicycle, anything—and so seeing the world. But always practical considera-tions arose and interfered—money for one thing; parting from mother, Ed and others of the family. So instead I went along tamely enough, to school and church, and contented myself with baseball or fishing or reading of the deeds and adventures of newer and even grander heroes. . . .

CHAPTER XXVI

D URING ALL OF THIS TIME the most interesting figure in our family, to me and the others, was Paul. He was our bright and progressively growing and glowing luminary.

I have told of one of the reasons why he came to Evansville and then chose to remain there. Yet all of the time we were there I saw this Annie Brace (or Sallie Walker, as she was locally known) but twice, and then only for moments; once sitting in front of our door in a carriage and another time when I was sent to deliver a basket of preserves, the gift of my mother. And from this one fact alone, I have long since deduced that my mother could not have known of the nature of the business conducted by Annie Brace, for in every thought and direction connected with her younger children, she was always concerned lest our contacts be other than such as would tend to improve our social standing, to strengthen rather than weaken our interest and faith in the value of such social customs and rules as she understood and held to be valuable.

Still, on this one occasion I was thrust into the very centre of this so-called "den of iniquity," although I think my mother's intention was that I was to deliver my basket at the door and come away without parley of any kind. (There was a note in the basket which was supposed to explain everything.) I found the place with some difficulty, wandering up a long street which paralleled the Ohio River and provided some striking views. I rang the bell and before I could explain was ushered into an entryway by a Negro servant and told to wait. Nothing loath, and curious as to the character of the place (I only knew of such things by hearsay), I stared about until the Negro returned and told me to follow her, that my brother wanted to see me. I was then led upstairs and along a passage to a suite of charmingly furnished rooms which commanded a splendid view of the river. It was hot and bright in this semi-southern world, and there was Paul, in the trousers of a light, summery suit and a silk shirt, making his morning toilet. With him was his Annie, in a pink and white, heavily beflounced dressing gown, and surveying me with an amused if not very much interested eye. The rooms—living-room, bedroom and bath—were not yet made up for the day, but to my uninformed eyes they were beautiful, everything in them rich and wonderful, a marvelous place. Striped awnings were at the window to shut out the hot morning sun, and the living-room was furnished with comfortable-looking wicker furniture, covered with tan linen. There were potted plants and a piano, strewn with music. Silver-backed toilet articles graced a dresser in the nearby bedroom, and beyond this was a bathroom such as I had never seen before, large and bright and equipped with toilet accessories in great profusion. It seemed a kind of fairyland. . . .

The thing that I wish to make plain, however, in connection with Annie Brace is that once the secret of her profession was known to me, I guarded it as a great mystery, saying nothing of all I had seen to my mother or anyone else. During my visit to her house I was treated very genially by my brother, who gave me some money to spend on my way home. Pagan that he was, never economically or socially adjusted anywhere, he seemed to think nothing of my being there or of what I had seen.

In the course of time, however, it appeared to have become known, at least in our immediate neighborhood, that this handsome, well-positioned brother of ours was in some way connected with this institution; and along toward the end of our second summer, I received a shock in connection with Paul and his affairs which brought the matter of public opinion very much to the fore. I was passing the home of that Harry Truckee previously mentioned as he was whitewashing his front fence. "Hey, Thee!" he called, "What's the name of that woman your brother lives with downtown?" He was a sly and shifty-eyed youth, and on this occasion there was something about the way he spoke which warned me that he was about some ferrety business. Surprised and taken aback by this direct assault, I hardly knew what to say. Since no one, even in the family, had ever ventured to refer to the matter, if they knew, I had come to believe that it might still be a dark secret to others. I know I flushed and made some jumbled reply that I knew nothing about it, whereupon he followed up his first inquiry with a bold, irritating: "Aw, get out!" and then added: "Sure about that?"

"Certainly, I am sure about it," I retorted, for I was never in the least overawed by Truckee.

"Well, other people seem to know about it," he went on. "Ever heard of Sallie Walker?" There was a malicious look in his eye which simply defied contradiction. Still I denied knowing her, though I had seen that name over Annie Brace's door and guessed then that it must be she.

"You're a funny fella," he continued. "Never heard of Sallie Walker! Why, everybody knows her. She keeps a fast house down on the waterfront. You ask your brother sometime, he'll tell yuh. They say she's stuck on him and he lives there."

He smiled pleasantly and yet defiantly as if to say: "Put that in your pipe and smoke it!" and went on whitewashing. I turned away, a little sick, and went on about my errand with a keen sense of having been placed in a very embarrassing position. My thoughts were about as follows: Yes, Paul lives with Sallie Walker, and I know it. And Harry Truckee knows it. And he knows that I know it. But who is Harry Truckee? Trash! And his family? Trash! Paul has a big name. His pictures are all over town on the theatre billboards. He writes songs and lives at the St. George when he wants to and supports us and gives us things. And Sallie Walker is a beautiful woman. I wish I were as fine and prosperous as Paul and that some beautiful woman would fall in love with me. But it's too bad to be found out. But what difference does it make? He's not hurting anybody, and neither is she, and they're both good to us.

But there was never a word from any other source in Evansville. Every day or two Paul would appear at our home and stay for lunch or dinner, sometimes even all night. He loved to sit near mother or follow her about as she worked, telling her funny stories or asking her advice in some problem or plan. Often during the summer he would play ball with Ed and myself. Always he brought something: a watermelon, ice cream, candy, books, papers. At Christmas and Fourth of July it was he who made the day for us, bringing great bundles of toys or huge packages of firecrackers—rockets, pinwheels and the like. And often he would give us all tickets to see this or that show at the Apollo, which, of course, included himself. (It was seeing him on the stage and going behind the scenes that later prompted Ed, Al, Trina and myself to give a minstrel show in our barn, incidentally infecting all of the children in the audience with chicken lice!)

For by the end of the first summer, Paul was already a part of a stock vaudeville or minstrel organization which held the boards winter and summer at the Apollo—later the Evansville Opera House. In this connection he served not only as "end man" but betimes interlocutor, monologist, song and dance man, and I know not what else. The fences and billboards everywhere attested to his popularity. Large red and yellow and black single-sheets bore his picture and the legend: "Paul Dresser, Comedian—Evansville Opera House—Week of . . ." And nightly, before the show, or of an afternoon, he was to be found, along with friends of the stage, the sporting and news-paper worlds, about the lobby or bar of the old St. George Hotel, at that time Evansville's principal hostelry. I often sought him out there, with a note from my mother or to get tickets he was holding for us, or to perform some small errand for him, and I always carried away an impression of a man perfectly dressed, his suits and linen fresh and well-fitting, his ties and socks and shoes of the latest mode. Also, before the end of the first winter, he connected himself with a local semi-comic weekly—*The Evansville Argus*—as a para-grapher. His weekly column was copied into other papers east and west; he used to bring them out to the house for us to see.

You may well guess what all this meant to me. For was this not my own brother, strong and rich, a veritable bulwark, as it seemed to me, against further misfortune? He loved us and would see that we did not have to suffer. What other thing could make any brother anywhere half so important? . . .

Ah well, nothing can be gained by concealing the facts of the case: Theodore Dreiser's brother

PAUL DRESSER

composer of "On the Banks of the Wabash," was not a model either of thrift, sobriety, or morality—but he was generous of both heart and purse through the many years in which his family needed help and he could give it. Broke and well-nigh unlamented, Paul died at fifty, his career as a singer, actor, and composer almost forgotten.

Paul Dresser's music is not great, as musicians count greatness; it is only loved as great music seldom comes to be. The lyrics he provided are sentimental—sometimes painfully so—and printing them alone, without their music, would be unfair to the memory of their composer. But listen to his songs as they can be presented by a barber shop quartet or by a ballad singer mellowed to the proper degree and you know why Paul Dresser, the good-hearted, free-spending minstrel man, may very well live as long as the elephantine genius who was his brother. Some of those songs besides that which hymns the Wabash are familiar to most folks—especially those who have lived a half century or so: thousands upon thousands have thrilled, one way or another, to "The Letter That He Longed For Never Came" and "Just Tell Them That You Saw Me"—hundreds of thousands more to the classic which celebrated "Sal," the kindhearted Evansville Madam.

Let us give a little prayer for Paul Dresser, safe in the Hereafter— may the notes of his celestial harp blend well with the mellow tenor that charmed minstrel audiences in minstrelsy's greatest days!

"Some folks are born great, others achieve greatness, and still others wear a wide braid on ther nose glasses."

—Abe Martin's TOWN PUMP

"Th' safest way t' double your money is t' fold it over once an' put it in your pocket."

—Abe Martin's ALMANACK FOR 1909

"While goin' after fishin' worms in a field where his wife wuz plowin' Tipton Bud found a Indian dart."

—Abe Martin's ALMANACK

"Another distinguishin' feature about the school of experience is this—when you're through you're through."

—Abe Martin's BROADCAST

"Ther seems to be somthin' about bein' a good dutiful husband that causes him to toe in."

—Abe Martin's TOWN PUMP

CHAPTER TWELVE

Hoosier Genre

Homemade short stories were scarce in the state up to the time, in 1875, when Maurice Thompson published his first collection under the title Hoosier Mosaics. Admirers have professed to see, in some of these, the forerunners of a style which became most popular in the day of O. Henry. Whether Thompson's little book actually influenced the development of the American short story is questionable; there was only one edition and it was evidently a small printing and not widely circulated. Thompson himself seldom used the form after he was established as a writer, and upon those few occasions without great success.

Whether or not it is of significance as to structure, there is entertainment and good writing in

MAURICE THOMPSON

Was She a Boy?

No matter what business or what pleasure took me, I once, not long ago, went to Colfax. Whisper it not to each other that I was seeking a foreign appointment through the influence of my fellow Hoosier, the late Vice-President of the United States. O no, I didn't go to the Hon. Schuyler Colfax at all; but I went to Colfax, simply, which is a little dingy town, in Clinton County, that was formerly

called Midway because it is half way between Lafayette and Indianapolis. It was and is a place of some three hundred inhabitants, eking
out an aguish subsistence, maintaining a swampy, malarious aspect,
keeping up a bilious, nay, an atra-bilious color, the year round, by
sucking like an attenuated leech at the junction, or, rather, the
crossing of the I.C. & L., and the L.C. & S.W. railroads. It lay
mouldering, like something lost and forgotten, slowly rotting in the
swamp.

I do not mean to attack the inhabitants of Colfax, for they were
good people, and deserved a better fate than the eternal rattling
the ague took them through from year's end to year's end. Why,
they had had the ague so long that they had no respect for it at all.
I've seen a woman in Colfax shaking with a chill, spanking a baby
that had a chill, and scolding a husband who had a chill, all at
once—and I had a dreadful ague on me at the same time! But, as I
have said, they were good people, and I suppose they are still. They
go quietly about the usual business of dead towns. They have
"stores" in which they offer for sale calico, of the big-figured, orange
and red sort, surprisingly cheap. They smoke those little Cuba sixes
at a half cent apiece, and call them cigars; they hang around the
depot, and trade jack-knives and lottery watches on the afternoons
of lazy Sundays; they make harmless sport of the incoming and
outgoing country folk; and, in a word, keep pretty busy at one thing
or another, and above all—they shake.

In Colfax the chief sources of exciting amusement are dog fights
and an occasional row at Sheehan's saloon, a doggery of the regular
old-fashioned, drink, gamble, rob and fight sort—a low place, known
to all the hard bats in the State.

As you pass through the town you will not fail to notice a big
sign, out-hanging from the front of the largest building on the principal street, which reads: "Union Hotel, 1865." From the muddy
suburbs of the place, in every direction, stretch black muck swamps;
for the most part heavily timbered with a variety of oaks, interspersed with sycamores, ash, and elms. In the damp, shady laby-
rinths of these boggy woods millions of lively, wide awake, tuneful
mosquitoes are daily manufactured; and out from decaying logs and
piles of fermenting leaves, from the green pools and sluggish ditch

streams, creeps a noxious gas, known in that region as the "double refined, high pressure, forty hoss power quintessential of the ager!" So, at least, I was told by the landlord of the Union Hotel, and his skin had the color of one who knew.

Notwithstanding what I have said, Colfax, in summer, is not wholly without attractions of a certain kind. It has some yellow dogs and some brindle ones; it has some cattle and some swine; it has some swallows and some spotted pigeons; it has cool, fresh smelling winds, and, after the water has sufficiently dried out, the woods are really glorious with wild roses, violets, turkey-pea blossoms, and wild pinks. But to my story.

I was sitting on the long veranda of the Union Hotel, when a rough but kindly voice said to me:

"Mornin', stranger; gi' me a light, will ye?"

I looked up from the miserable dime novel at which I had been tugging for the last hour, and saw before me a corpulent man of, perhaps, forty-five years of age, who stood quite ready to thrust the charred end of a cigar stump into the bowl of my meerschaum. I gave him a match, and would fain have returned to Angelina St. Fortescue, the heroine of the novel, whom I had left standing on the extreme giddy verge of a sheer Alpine precipice, known, by actual triangulation, to be just seven thousand feet high, swearing she would leap off if Donald Gougerizeout, the robber, persisted further in his rough addresses; but my new friend, the corpulent smoker, seemed bent on a little bit of conversation.

"Thankee, sir. Fine mornin', sir, a'n't it?"

"Beautiful," I replied, raising my head, elevating my arms, and, by a kind of yawn, taking in a deep draught of the fresh spring weather, absorbing it, assimilating it, till, like a wave of retarded electricity, it set my nerves in tune for enjoying the bird songs, and filled my blood with the ecstasy of vigorous health and youth. I, no doubt, just then felt the burden of life much less than did the big yellow dog at my feet, who snapped lazily at the flies.

"Yes, yes, this 'ere's a fine mornin'—julicious, sir, julicious, indeed; but le' me tell ye, sir, this 'ere wind's mighty deceitful—for a fact it is, sir, jist as full of ager as a acorn is of meat. It's blowin' right off'n ponds, and is loaded chock down with the miasm—for a fact it is, sir."

While delivering this speech, the fat man sat down on the bench beside me there in the verandah. By this time I had my thumbs in the arm holes of my vest, and my chest expanded to its utmost—my lungs going like a steam bellows, which is a way I have in fine weather.

"Monstrous set o' respiratory organs, them o' your'n," he said, eyeing my manoeuvres. Just then I discovered that he was a physician of the steam doctor sort, for, glancing down at my feet, I espied his well worn leather medicine bags. I immediately grew polite. Possibly I might ere long need some quinine, or mandrake, or a hot steam bath—anything for the ague!

"Yes, I've got lungs like a porpoise," I replied, "but still the ague may get me. Much sickness about here, Doctor—a—a—what do they call your name?"

"Benjamin Hurd—Doctor Hurd, they call me. I'm the only thorer bred botanic that's in these parts. I do poorty much all the practice about here. Yes, there's considerable of ager and phthisic and bilious fever. Keeps me busy most of my time. These nasty swamps, you know."

After a time our conversation flagged, and the doctor having lit a fresh cigar, we smoked in silence. The wind was driving the dust along the street in heavy waves, and I sat watching a couple of lean, spotted calves making their way against the tide. They held their heads low and shut their eyes, now and then bawling vigorously. Some one up stairs was playing "Days of Absence" on a wretched wheezing accordion.

"There's a case of asthma, doctor," I said, intending to be witty. But my remark was not noticed. The doctor was in a brown study, from which my words had not startled him. Presently he said, as if talking to himself, and without taking the cigar from his mouth:

" 'Twas just a year ago to-night, the 28th day of May, 'at they took 'er away. And he'll die afore day to a dead certainty. Beats all the derned queer things I ever seed or heerd of."

He was poking with the toe of his boot in the dust on the veranda floor, as he spoke, and stealing a glance at his face, I saw that it wore an abstracted, dreamy, perplexed look.

"What was your remark, doctor?" I asked, more to arouse him than from any hope of being interested.

"Hum!—ah, yes," he said, starting, and beginning a vigorous puffing. "Ah, yes, I was cogitatin' over this matter o' Berry Young's. Never have been able to 'count for that, no how. Think about it more an' more every day. What's your theory of it?"

"Can't say, never having heard any thing of it," I replied.

"Well, I do say! Thought everybody had hearn of that, any how! It's a rale romance, a reg'lar mystery, sir. It's been talked about, and writ about in the papers so much 'at I s'pose 'at it was knowed of far and wide."

"I've been in California for several years past," I replied, by way of excuse for my ignorance of even the vaguest outline of the affair, whatever it might be.

"Well, you see, a leetle more'n a year ago a gal an' her father come here and stopped at this 'ere very hotel. The man must 'a' been som'res near sixty years old; but the gal was young, and jist the poortiest thing I ever seed in all my life. I couldn't describe how she looked at all; but everybody 'at saw her said she was the beautifulest creatur they ever laid eyes onto. Where these two folks come from nobody ever knowed, but they seemed like mighty nice sort of persons, and everybody liked 'em, 'specially the gal. Somehow, from the very start, a kind of mystery hung 'round 'em. They seemed always to have gobs o' money, and onct in awhile some little thing'd turn up to make folks kinder juberous somehow 'at they wasn't jist what they ginerally seemed to be. But that gal was fascinatin' as a snake, and as poorty as any picter. Her flesh looked like tinted wax mixed with moonshine, and her eyes was as clear as a limestone spring—though they was dark as night. She was that full of restless animal life 'at she couldn't set still—she roamed around like a leopard in a cage, and she'd romp equal to a ten-year-old boy. Well, as mought be expected, sich a gal as that 'ere 'd 'tract attention in these parts, and I must say 'at the young fellows here did git 'bominable sweet on her. 'Casionally two of 'em 'd git out in the swamps and have a awful fight on her 'count; but she 'peared to pay precious little 'tention to any of 'em till finally Berry Young stepped in and jist went for 'er like mad, and she took to 'm. Berry was r'ally the nicest and intelligentest young man in all this country. He writ poetry for the papers, sir—snatchin' good poetry, too—and had got to be talked of a right smart for his larnin', an' 'complishments. He was good lookin', too; powerful handsome, for a fact, sir. So they was to be married, Berry and the gal, an' the time it was sot, an' the day it come, an' all was ready, an' the young folks was on the floor, and the 'squire was jist a commencin' to say the ceremony, when lo! and beholden, four big, awful, rough lookin' men rushed in with big pistols and mighty terrible bowie knives, and big papers and big seals, and said they was a sheriff and possum from Kaintucky. They jist jumped right onto the gal an' her father an' handcuffed 'em, an' took 'em!"

"Handcuffed them and took them!" I repeated, suddenly growing intensely interested. This was beating my dime novel, for sensation, all hollow.

"Yes, sir, han'cuffed 'em an' took 'em, an' away they went, an' they've not been hearn of since to this day. But the mysteriousest thing about the whole business was that when the sheriff grabbed the gal he called her George, and said she wasn't no gal at all, but jist a terrible onery boy 'at had been stealin' an' counterfeitin' an' robbin' all round everywhere. What d'ye think of that?"

"A remarkably strange affair, certainly," I replied; "and do you say that the father and the girl have not since been heard from?"

"Never a breath. The thing got into all the newspapers and raised a awful rumpus, and it turned out that it wasn't no sheriff 'at come there; but some dark, mysterious kidnappin' transaction 'at nobody could account for. Detectives was put on their track an' follered 'em to Injun territory an' there lost 'em. Some big robberies was connected with the affair, but folks could never git head nor tail of the partic'lers."

"And it wasn't a real sheriff's arrest, then?" said I.

"No, sir, 'twas jist a mystery. Some kind of a dodge of a band of desperadoes to avoid the law some way. The papers tried to explain it, but I never could see any sense to it. 'Twas a clean, dead mystery. But I was goin' on to tell ye 'at Berry Young took it awful hard 'bout the gal, an' he's been sort o' sinkin' away ever sence, an' now he's jist ready to wink out. Yonder's where Berry lives, in that 'ere white cottage house with the vines round the winder. He's disp'rit sick—a sort o' consumption. I'm goin' to see 'im now; good mornin' to ye."

Thus abruptly ending our interview, the doctor took up his medicine bag and went his way. He left me in a really excited state of mind; the story of itself was so strange, and the narrator had told it so solemnly and graphically. I suppose, too, that I must have been in just the proper state of mind for that rough outline, that cartoon of a most startling and mysterious affair, to become deeply impressed in my mind, perhaps, in the most fascinating and fantastic light possible. A thirst to know more of the story took strong hold on my mind, as if I had been reading a tantalizing romance and had found the leaves torn out just where the mystery was to be explained. I half closed my eyes to better keep in the lines and shades of the strange picture. Its influence lay upon me like a spell. I enjoyed it. It was a luxury.

The wings of the morning wind fanned the heat into broken waves, rising and sinking, and flowing on, with murmur and flash and glimmer, to the cool green ways of the woods, and, like the wind, my fancy went out among golden fleece clouds and into shady places, following the thread of this new romance. I cannot give a sufficient reason why the story took so fast a hold on me. But it did grip my mind and master it. It appeared to me the most intensely strange affair I had ever heard of.

While I sat there, lost in reflection, with my eyes bent on a very unpromising pig, that wallowed in the damp earth by the town pump, the landlord of the hotel came out and took a seat beside me. I gave him a pipe of my tobacco and forthwith began plying him with questions touching the affair of which the doctor had spoken. He confirmed the story, and added to its mystery by going minutely into its details. He gave the names of the father and daughter as Charles Afton and Ollie Afton.

Ollie Afton! Certainly no name sounds sweeter! How is it that these gifted, mysteriously beautiful persons always have musical names!

"Ah," said the landlord, "you'd ort to have seen that boy!"

"Boy!" I echoed.

"Well, gal or boy, one or t'other, the wonderfulest human bein' I ever see in all the days o' my life! Lips as red as ripe cur'n's, and for ever smilin'. Such smiles—oonkoo! they hurt a feller all over, they was so sweet. She was tall an' dark, an' had black hair that curled short all 'round her head. Her skin was wonderful clear and so was her eyes. But it was the way she looked at you that got you. Ah, sir, she had a power in them eyes, to be sure!"

The pig got up from his muddy place by the pump, grunted, as if satisfied, and slowly strolled off; a country lad drove past, riding astride the hounds of a wagon; a pigeon lit on the comb of the roof of Sheehan's saloon, which was just across the street, and began pluming itself. Just then the landlord's little sharp-nosed, weasel-eyed boy came out and said, in a very subdued tone of voice:

"Pap, mam says 'at if you don't kill 'er that 'ere chicken for dinner you kin go widout any fing to eat all she cares."

The landlord's spouse was a red-headed woman, so he got up very suddenly and took himself into the house. But before he got out of hearing the little boy remarked:

"Pap, I speaks for the gizzard of that 'ere chicken, d'ye hear, now?"

I sat there till the dinner hour, watching the soft pink and white vapors that rolled round the verge of the horizon. I was thoroughly saturated with romance. Strange, that here, in this dingy little out-of-the-way village, should have transpired one of the most wonderful mysteries history may ever hold!

At dinner the landlord talked volubly of the Afton affair, giving it as his opinion that the Aftons were persons tinged with negro blood, and had been kidnapped into slavery.

"They was jist as white, an' whiter, too, than I am," he went on, "but them Southerners 'd jist as soon sell one person as 'nother, anyhow."

I noticed particularly that the little boy got his choice bit of the fowl. He turned his head one side and ate like a cat.

When the meal was over I was again joined by Doctor Hurd on the veranda. He reported Berry Young still alive, but not able to live till midnight. I noticed that the doctor was nervous and kept his eyes fixed on Sheehan's saloon.

"Stranger," said he, leaning over close to me, and speaking in a low, guarded way, "things is workin' dasted curious 'bout now—sure's gun's iron they jist is!"

"Where—how—in what way, doctor?" I stammered, taken aback by his behavior.

"Sumpum's up, as sure as Ned!" he replied, wagging his head.

"Doctor," I said, petulantly, "if you would be a trifle more explicit I could probably guess, with some show of certainty, at what you mean!"

"Can't ye hear? Are ye deaf? Did ye ever, in all yer born days, hear a voice like that ere 'un? Listen!"

Sure enough, a voice of thrilling power, a rich, heavy, quavering alto, accompanied by some one thrumming on a guitar, trickled and gurgled, and poured through the open window of Sheehan's saloon. The song was a wild, drinking carol, full of rough, reckless wit, but I listened, entranced, till it was done.

"There now, say, what d'ye think o' that? Ain't things a workin' round awful curious, as I said?"

Delivering himself thus, the doctor got up and walked off.

When I again had an opportunity to speak to the landlord, I asked him if Doctor Hurd was not thought to be slightly demented.

"What! crazy, do you mean? No, sir; bright as a pin!"

"Well," said I, "he's a very queer fellow any how. By the way, who was that singing just now over in the saloon there?"

"Don't know, didn't hear 'em. Some of the boys, I s'pose. They have some lively swells over there sometimes. Awful hole."

I resumed my dime novel, and nothing further transpired to aggravate or satisfy my curiosity concerning the strange story I had heard, till night came down and the bats began to wheel through the moonless blackness above the dingy town. At the coming on of dusk I flung away the book and took to my pipe. Some one touched me on the shoulder, rousing me from a deep reverie, if not a doze.

"Ha, stranger, this you, eh? Berry Young's a dyin'; go over there wi' me, will ye?"

It was the voice of Doctor Hurd.

"What need for me have you?" I replied, rather stiffly, not much relishing this too obtrusive familiarity.

"Well—I—I jist kinder wanted ye to go over. The poor boy's 'bout passin' away, an' things is a workin' so tarnation curious! Come 'long wi' me, friend, will ye?"

Something in the fellow's voice touched me, and without another word I arose and followed him to the cottage. The night was intensely black. I think it was clear, but a heavy fog from the swamps had settled over everything, and through this dismal veil the voices of owls from far and near struck with hollow, sepulchral effect.

"A heart is the trump!" sang out that alto voice from within the saloon as we passed.

Doctor Hurd clutched my arm and muttered:

"That's that voice ag'in! Strange—strange! Poor Berry Young!"

We entered the cottage and found ourselves in a cosy little room, where, on a low bed, a pale, intelligent looking young man lay, evidently dying. He was very much emaciated, his eyes, wonderfully large and luminous, were sunken, and his breathing quick and difficult. A haggard, watching-worn woman sat by his bed. From her resemblance to him I took her to be his sister. She was evidently very unwell herself. We sat in silence by his bedside, watching his life flow into eternity, till the little clock on the mantel struck, sharp and clear, the hour of ten.

The sound of the bell startled the sick man, and after some incoherent mumbling he said, quite distinctly:

"Sister, if you ever again see Ollie Afton, tell him—tell her—tell, say I forgive him—say to her—him—I loved her all my life—tell him—ah! what was I saying? Don't cry, sis, please. What a sweet faithful sister! Ah! it's almost over, dear—Ah, me!"

For some minutes the sister's sobbing echoed strangely through the house. The dying man drew his head far down in the soft pillow. A breath of damp air stole through the room.

All at once, right under the window by which the bed sat, arose a touching guitar prelude—a tangled mesh of melody—gusty, throbbing, wandering through the room and straying off into the night, tossing back its trembling echoes fainter and fainter, till, as it began to die, that same splendid alto voice caught the key and flooded the darkness with song. The sick man raised himself on his elbow, and his face flashed out the terrible smile of death. He listened eagerly. It was the song "Come Where My Love Lies Dreaming," but who has heard it rendered as it was that night? Every chord of the voice was as sweet and witching as a wind harp's, and the low, humming undertone of the accompaniment was perfection. Tenderly but awfully sweet, the music at length faded into utter silence, and Berry Young sank limp and pallid upon his pillows.

"It is Ollie," he hoarsely whispered. "Tell her—tell him—O say to her for me—ah! water, sis, it's all over!"

The woman hastened, but before she could get the water to his lips he was dead. His last word was Ollie.

The sister cast herself upon the dead man's bosom and sobbed wildly, piteously. Soon after this some neighbors came in, which gave me an opportunity to quietly take my leave.

The night was so foggy and dark that, but for a bright stream of light from a window of Sheehan's saloon, it would have been hard for me to find my way back to the hotel. I did find it, however, and sat down upon the verandah. I had nearly fallen asleep, thinking over the strange occurrences of the past few hours, when the rumble of an approaching train of cars on the I.C. & L. from the east aroused me, and, at the same moment, a great noise began over in the saloon. High words, a few bitter oaths, a struggle as of persons fighting, a loud, sonorous crash like the crushing of a musical instrument, and then I saw the burly bartender hurl some one out through the doorway just as the express train stopped close by.

"All aboard!" cried the conductor, waving his lantern. At the same time, as the bartender stood in the light of his doorway, a brickbat, whizzing from the darkness, struck him full in the face, knocking him precipitately back at full length on to the floor of the saloon.

"All aboard!" repeated the conductor.

"All aboard!" jeeringly echoed a delicious alto voice; and I saw a slender man step up on the rear platform of the smoking car. A flash from the conductor's lantern lit up for a moment this fellow's face, and it was the most beautiful visage I have ever seen. Extremely youthful, dark, resplendent, glorious, set round with waves and ringlets of black hair—it was such a countenance as I have imagined a young Chaldean might have had who was destined to the high calling of astrology. It was a face to charm, to electrify the beholder with its indescribable, almost unearthly loveliness of features and expression.

The engine whistled, the bell rang, and as the train moved on, that slender, almost fragile form and wonderful face disappeared in the darkness.

As the roar and clash of the receding cars began to grow faint in the distance, a gurgling, grunting sound over in the saloon reminded me that the bartender might need some attention, so I stepped across the street and went in. He was just taking himself up from the floor, with his nose badly smashed, spurting blood over him pretty freely. He was in an ecstasy of fury and swore fearfully. I rendered him all the aid I could, getting the blood stopped, at length, and a plaster over the wound.

"Who struck you?" I asked.

"Who struck me? Who hit me with that 'ere brick, d'ye say? Who but that little baby-faced, hawk-eyed cuss 'at got off here yesterday! He's a thief and a dog!—he's chowzed me out'n my last cent! Where is he?—I'll kill 'im yet! where is he?"

"Gone off on the train," I replied, "but who is he? what's his name?"

"Blamed if I know. Gone, you say? Got every derned red o' my money! Every derned red!"

"Don't you know anything at all about him?" I asked.

"Yes."

"What?"

"I know 'at he's the derndest, alfiredest, snatchin'est, best poker-player 'at ever dealt a card!"

"Is that all?"

"That's enough, I'd say. If you'd been beat out'n two hundred an' odd dollars you'd think you know'd a right smart, wouldn't ye?"

"Perhaps," said I. The question had a world of philosophy and logic in it.

The shattered wreck of a magnificent guitar lay in the middle of the floor. I picked it up, and, engraved on a heavy silver plate set in the ebony neck, I read the name, Georgina Olive Afton.

George Ade and Kin Hubbard were professional humorists good enough for Indiana—and thus any place—but there were others whose literary output has tickled the risibilities of us natives fully as much, and they—the others—didn't aim it that way at all: they fancied themselves as serious. Sometimes, indeed, they were downright pugnacious when they spoke of the superiority of their private muses over those, let's say, of Riley. Some of them were supremely vain of their non-existent genius—and that was fine: no conscience need trouble itself if its owner laughs at pride taking a prat fall, and the falls of some of the proudest who succumbed to the Hoosier literary urge were spectacular indeed!

There was, chiefest of them all,

JAMES BUCHANAN ELMORE

Bard of Alamo, in the Balhinch district of Montgomery County, poet and novelist but chiefly poet, and what a poet.

I feel so strongly on the subject of Elmore and his works, my admiration is so deep-rooted, that I again find it necessary to speak in the first person for a bit—the cold impersonal third cannot express my sentiments. I honestly believe that, except for an incurable complacency; an absolute, mulish refusal to learn anything from others, a monumental self-satisfaction, Jim Buck Elmore could have become a really great poet before the eighty-five year span of his life ran out in 1942 and they laid him to rest near his beloved Alamo.

After all it takes some measure of genius to generate such lines as—

> "He absconded to Cincinnati, and dentistry took,
> And left a true love he willfully forsook,
> To pine in true nature—a false, fickle friend,
> He never intended his ways for to mend."

None but Elmore (since the extinction of the breed of New England Puritans who composed grave-stone verse in the seventeenth century) could have produced—

> "But there they laid on the crimson snow—
> Their hearts have ceased to ebb and flow;
> Quite as cold as a frozen chunk,
> With a lady's heart upon a stump."

—a poet who can do a thing like that does not just happen; in my opinion, he is foreordained and created, for some good purpose! If he chooses to neglect the opportunities by which he might harness that genius, direct that dash and verve more wisely, the fault for his failure lies squarely upon his own shoulders.

But did Jim Buck Elmore really fail? I have often wondered.

Isn't it better to be the real, genuine, eighteen carat Bard of Alamo rather than an imitation Tennyson, as were so many of his contemporaries? Isn't it better to create something that is superlatively awful, rather than only mill-run awful and thus undistinguished? Jim Buck's poems are still widely read and frequently recited—can that be said of any appreciable amount of the verse which appeared in the Century in the 'nineties? Or in the snooty little literary quarterlies last year? I don't know the answers to these idle questions—and I'm afraid I don't care; I still worship at the Elmore shrine.

James B. Elmore published his own works—and sold them, too, until prosperous old age rendered such operations both undignified and unnecessary. When he died an admirer recalled him in his prime:

"It is Saturday or circus day or a fiesta or gala day of some kind. He has one of those little satchels with patent-leather finish, made especially for carrying diapers . . . it was fastened around his neck with a strap. It lay open like he was selling peanuts and in it nestled at least 50 anemic looking red books about the size of a McGuffey Primer.

"This book contained the current sampling of his poetic works, unexpurgated and including, maybe, the pathetic little story about the poor little gel who had so much trouble working in the overalls factory and the far greater troubles she had with the unprincipled roues who worked in the overalls.

"The book sold for 75¢ and I don't think that James B. had to work those stony acres of his very hard, for many's the time I've seen him start on the long trip back to Alamo with his moth eaten horse and buggy and his diaper compact innocent of a single immortal tome. And I often wondered who was the smarter, the wise guy who laughed at his poesy, or the Bard, with his pocket full of bucks, jogging homeward his dusty way laughing at the suckers who bought his books?"

The question is proper and the answer favors the poet. Elmore's estate, very modestly appraised at a value of $50,000 at the time of his death, was worth fifty per cent more then; is now worth three times that figure. Not bad, for a poet, even for a poet who indulges in a little plowing on the side.

But it is not the life of James Buchanan Elmore which we should consider here, it is his work. First in the heart of every admirer comes

The Monon Wreck

OUR LAST RIDE

The train is coming yonder, near,
The conductor calls the station clear,
Then outward move the busy throng
Ready for their stepping on.

A signal waved says all is well,
And now we hear the parting bell:
The engineer opes the steam chest throes,
Then swifter than a dart she goes.

She glides along quite at her ease,
The swiftness causes a gentle breeze;
The wheels are creaking on the frosty rails,
Just like a bird she nimbly sails.

One mile is passed and all is fun;
Two miles are made—the thing is done:
We are crossing over Sugar Creek bridge,
And starting on the graded ridge.

She strikes against a broken rail,
When all the cars it does derail,
And down they plunge into the deep,
A depth of more than sixty feet.

She rolled over just afore and aft,
The occupants turning like a shaft,
Before she reaches this mournful place,
Where each the other's soul embraced.

A silence fell upon the crew,
As if they knew not what to do;
Then came sad and lamenting cries
From a wreckage of cars as flames arise.

Tears are flowing thick and fast
From every one of the mangled mass;
And, laying there, we hear their prayers,
Asking the Lord to relieve their cares:

"Our Heavenly Father! wilt Thou draw near,
And hear our woe in supplication here;
Save us from this wreck of flame,
Where dearest comrades have been slain."

To the nearest town a messenger made,
While on the ground the dead are laid.
Oh, how terrible are the moaning sighs,
With pitiful appeals and last good-byes!

But there they laid on the crimson snow—
Their hearts have ceased to ebb and flow;
Quite as cold as a frozen chunk,
With a lady's heart upon a stump.

Which was so far from her native home,
The ancient city of old Rome;
Never again to reach that clime,
And hear the bell of St. Peter's chime.

And now the flames begin to light
The demolished cars, which adds to fright,
For fear that all will burn to death.
Oh, God! Intervene and save the rest!

And yonder in the wreck I see
A man that's pinioned down by the knee,

And hear him moaning and to say:
"Cut, oh, cut my leg away!"

But a jackscrew from the mail caboose
Is now applied and lets him loose,
With many thanks to these brave men—
For greater heroes ne'er have been.

There was a mother, frantic and wild,
Looking for her little child,
Which in her fright had run away
To the nearest house of that sad fray.

And as that mother paced to and fro,
She found some footprints in the snow,
And, leaping onward with breathless bound,
Her loving daughter soon was found.

And such a meeting ne'er has been—
It moistened the eyes of the bravest men,
While in her arms she clasped so dear
The object of her joy and fear.

But four are dead—they speak no more:
The Savior has their souls in store,
Awaiting of the Judgment Day,
Where all is good, or sad dismay.

"A newspaper picture makes anybuddy look guilty."

—Abe Martin's ALMANACK

"Ther's many a slip twixt th' blue prints an' a new house."

—Abe Martin's ALMANACK

"What's become o' the ole-time workman that spit on his hands?"

—Abe Martin's BROADCAST

She was born in Arkansas and educated in Michigan but, once located in Spencer, Indiana,

MARGARET WEYMOUTH JACKSON

became Hoosier to the core. She had served on the editorial staffs of several farm papers—including that of Farm Life in Spencer—before she began writing the short stories and novels which have added up to an impressive total and which have appeared in the country's most widely circulated periodicals. She is at her best when she writes of a midland world of which Spencer (or a town very like it) is the center and the outer borders are marked by municipalities which could be Indianapolis, Greencastle, Crawfordsville, and Bloomington; of scenery similar to that of Brown county, the North Fork of White River, and the Vigo county coal fields.

Telling plain tales of average citizens in such a locale, she could not possibly avoid treatment of the strange manifestations which mark that annually recurring period of Hoosier madness, the high school basketball season. One of basketball's most tragic problems, that of the boy who is too short to make the team, is discussed in

Hour of Victory

GENE ALCOTT WALKED north on Main Street in the near-zero cold of New Year's afternoon, clad in white duck trousers, a maroon pull-over sweater and a windbreaker shorter than the sweater. He wore white socks and old brown loafers, a round cap made of alternate sections of maroon and white stuck on the back of his curly black head. He walked proudly, as he had the right to do, for his trousers were clean as new-fallen snow, his shoes were polished, he himself was scrubbed within an inch of his life, and his whole ensemble proclaimed him to the crowd which streamed toward the gymnasium as a high-school cheerleader, and therefore a personage of no small significance.

Actually, however, Gene's feelings were complex and by no means as cheerful as his exterior would indicate. He was glad to be a cheerleader. He appreciated it, but it was, he knew, a sop. He wasn't big enough to make the team. In junior high he had been the first man on the team, the high-point man. He had been as big as the others then, bigger than some. But he was almost through growing, and the others hadn't even started. Now they had all outgrown him, one or two by as much as a foot. Though he had the heart of a lion, though he hewed and hacked his way in and out and never relaxed for a moment, he couldn't make it any more. He was, at sixteen, only five feet four, and he weighed a hundred and thirty pounds, and he was simply too small and too light for a team already endowed with skill. The coach had a long talk with Gene, and Gene accepted the coach's judgment.

It was tradition in Hilltown to have girl cheerleaders. Always there were two or three of the prettiest girls in school to lead the cheering. The school took pride in these girls. When the team went into tournament play it was customary for the newsmen to come around and get a couple of shots of Hilltown's cheerleaders. They had good costumes, well-made, not too short or fancy, or too theatrical, and the girls, under Mr. Mumford's firm hand, disdained any of the floor-show type of cheerleading and just got out there and led the high school into a pandemonium of sound.

But this year the guys on the team had an idea of their own. Every boy in school got back of Gene, and they made him a cheerleader. So that for the first time in its history Hilltown had a boy and two girls.

The girls didn't like it very well, and they let Gene know it. They held out on him. They told him to lead one yell and they would lead the next. They sat close together, chins in hands, knees pressed together, their pretty hair, their bright maroon jumpers and white silk blouses making them as attractive as flowers. Gene sat beside them—on sufferance. Gene had ideas. He wanted to work things out with the girls. He had an idea for a locomotive and a way to lead it that would really skyrocket the whole school. The boys always yelled for him, but the girls in the bleachers—some of them anyhow—followed the girls, and they didn't respond as well to him as to Mary and Betty, so that the sound lacked that fine shrill frenzy that makes a cheering section all it should be.

But there was more than that to Gene's discomfort. No one had ever said a word to him at home, but he knew as definitely as though he had been hit in the face that his father was disappointed that he was a cheerleader and not on the team. Perhaps because of Hilltown's tradition, perhaps because his father had once played on the maroon-and-white five, he was a little ashamed of Gene. He felt that the boy was in a situation not masculine, not rugged. Gene knew this, and it robbed him of satisfaction. But he couldn't give it up. There was something stubborn in himself, something that held him where he was. He wanted to work it out with Mary and Betty, and he wanted to get the cheering section really razzle-dazzled.

But he wasn't getting anything done at all except just to be mulish and miserable. Mary, he felt, would have strung along with him. She was always good-natured and pleasant to him. It was Betty who influenced her, kept her from cooperating. Gene liked Mary. He liked her better than any other girl in school, and it made him mad that she didn't have enough spunk to tell Betty where to get off, to side with him and make Betty come to terms. All this warfare was between the three cheerleaders and no one else seemed aware of it.

This afternoon Gene's father was coming to the game, his first of the winter. Gene's Uncle Ned was home, and he had been on the team that went to the semi-finals twenty years ago, the team they still talked about in Hilltown, and he never missed the New Year's Day game with Stone City. So Gene's father, who had stopped going to the games, since Gene wasn't even on the second team, would be there today. It added the last difficult complication to Gene's feelings. For Gene knew his father would be mortified when Gene got up and turned his back somersault and led the yells. Gene's face felt red, and not only with cold. Actually, for a minute his eyes misted. He loved his father blindly. He wanted his respect. But he wasn't big enough or heavy enough for the team and he was better off where he was. He liked the cheering section. He felt that his mother understood—a little, anyway. She went to all the games with a woman friend. But how could he tell his father what it meant when he flung his hand up and they were still and he flung it down and they roared?

There had never been a bigger crowd in the gym. It was a bright cold sunny day, and everyone felt the urge for holiday. It was the New Year's Day of all New Years. Practically all Stone City had turned out for the game, and Hilltown was in there, packed to the rafters, from babies in arms to grandfathers. The Stone City team was big and strong, and averaged an inch or two taller, a few pounds heavier and about a year older than the Hilltown team. They were undefeated, and slated to win the Valley tournament. Big, rugged boys with a new young coach full of ideas. The Hilltown team had heart, but they were spotty. They had lost games they should have won, and won games they should have lost. There wasn't a senior on the team. "Next year," the town said, "the boys will be seasoned, and we'll have a team." It was the best they could hope for. But they were loyal. These were their boys and they had faith in them.

Gene took his place on the front row in the middle of the cheering section. The girls, Mary and Betty, weren't in sight yet. The third team, the junior-high five, were playing, and they had their own cheerleaders. Gene watched the game and watched the crowd and looked for the girls. His windbreaker laid aside, his cap on his knee, his maroon sweater glowing with color, he began to feel good in spite of himself, began to feel a slow, even pulse beating up in him. "The old one-two," he muttered to himself, "The old locomotive." He felt sharply a thing he had felt only vaguely, with unknown longing, before. It was coming along, just a little at a time, and almost consciously he held it back—for the big game. He saw his mother come in with their neighbor, and she waved at him. His father and uncle came in together and stood talking in the crowd at the end of the floor.

Gene was nervous. The gym was filling so rapidly that there wasn't going to be a seat left for his father. He wanted to go tell his father to sit down. The crowd was pouring up both stairways now, and the band had taken over the stage. The second team came out on the floor, and his father and uncle still stood there, talking to Mr. Mumford. But Gene didn't want to parade around in his cheerleader clothes, as though asking for attention. He didn't want his father looking at him, a little surprised, as he had looked when Gene came down for lunch, thinking—even if he didn't say so—that that was a hell of a getup for a grown boy. So Gene just sat where he was. Mary and Betty joined him, and they were beautiful, with bright fair hair shining and brushed smooth, their white gym shoes and white silk blouses gleaming in the sunlight.

Mary sat beside Gene, and Betty beyond her. Mary smiled at Gene and asked him if he wanted to take the first yell. Betty glanced at him briefly, impersonally. There were people, he supposed, who would think Betty was the prettier of the two girls. But Mary had such a pleasant face. Her eyes were darkly blue and set under a brow that bulged just a little, so that she had a way of looking at you that was like a little kid, both kind and bright.

Gene's heart beat faster, and he said to Mary, "We ought to get together, for the team's sake." He leaned beyond her, and said to Betty, "Look, why don't we all get out there and yell? You take the middle—"

"Oh, Gene, we can't yell that much. How would it look? You go ahead."

Gene got up without any more argument, put up a hand and gave the crowd the signal, danced a little sideways in his old loafers, and he got a good yell out of them. He felt it in his arms and hands. They gave him a good cry for the team, and Gene led the traditional "Hello, Stone City!"

He returned to his seat, and at once the two girls were out there with Betty's idea of a locomotive.

Then Stone City's cheerleaders—three girls—hurled themselves about. They had a routine which Mr. Mumford described as "painful." But Stone City had a team.

The second team won its game and the big boys came out. Now it was really time to take the gym apart, and the slow beat that had been coming up in Gene began to take possession of him. He cajoled the crowd, he wheedled and coaxed them with a flat upturned palm. He spread himself out, and the crowd came back for him. It was the best yell of the afternoon and it sent the big team off.

Gene sat down and looked for his father. He couldn't see him anywhere. Then he saw his uncle, and his father beside him. They were crowded in at the end of the press box, the scorekeeper's bench. They were old letter men, and Mr. Mumford had made room for them there. His father was directly opposite Gene, facing him, right across the playing floor. He was looking at Gene strangely, as though he had not seen him for a long time. Shyness overcame the boy. All at once it struck Gene that he might never be any bigger than he was now. Oh, he might grow another inch or two. But he might be as he was thé rest of his life. He was healthy, he was strong and well, he was good in school and had nothing to regret except this. He felt his whole being resist and repel the accompanying suggestion of failure. Even if he never grew another half inch, it need not destroy him, make him lack all that he wanted out of life. There was more to a man than inches, he told himself savagely. But he sat there, humped a little, and let the girls take over the cheering.

The team, like Gene, fought a losing battle. They were unable to hit the basket. After heartbreaking tries to get the ball, they would miss. Or the ball would go into the basket and out again; it would bounce from one side of the rim to the other and down to the floor.

The crowd began to chafe and yell at the referees. The fans' mouths were down. There were always a few who couldn't bear to lose, and who became angry and even a little ugly. The Stone City side was jubilant, noisy, yelling for its team. The Hilltown team came into the second half, licked. Gene saw it. He just sat there and let the girls run it. He saw the heartbreak in the faces of the boys he had played with, felt their courage going out of them. The boys who had made him a cheerleader! The thought stung him. The old one-two, that old locomotive, began beating in his head, in his wrists. His stomach felt taut. The girls sat down beside him. Mary turned to him. Her dark blue eyes were full of tears.

"Oh, Gene," she said, "can't you do something?"

Gene looked at her. He felt sparked. And he saw that Betty had quit and couldn't do more. Hilltown took time out, trying to pull themselves together.

Gene got up. He forgot his father. He forgot the girls. He went out there, and he looked back at the Hilltown bleachers, and all at once his pulse quickened, the fever burned him. He began to clap his hands; he called out to them, he went sideways, he got everyone to clapping; they were all clapping with him, calling with him.

Gene left the floor. He denied gravity. He bowed his legs, he bent his knees, he walked on the sides of his feet, walked on his ankles. He bobbed up and down like a cork. His head bobbed, his elbows fluttered, he rocked from side to side. He called and called to them, and all the time he was clapping, clapping, clapping and they were clapping with him, yelling with him. There was not one who wasn't with him. Stone City was suddenly silent—stunned. The clapping was a roaring clatter of sound. The walls of Jericho must surely tumble.

Then he had them in his hand. He knew to the split second when he had them. He flung up his arm; he spread his fingers and silenced them, a complete, a perfect silence, and then up he went into the air, and when he came down they roared with him, a lion's cough of sound—just one big "Aitch!"

He had them clapping again; he had them crazy. He gave them the signal and they came back for him; they couldn't help themselves. A high clear "Aye!" rang through the gym and on around the world.

There he was way down at one end, and way back at the other end, and they were all clapping again and going right along with him.

They spelled "Hilltown" out. They proclaimed it, and when the last big "En!" had rung through the vaulted gym, Gene gave them one word more, one big word, "Fight!" and it was all over.

There was a surge of joy, of buoyancy. The crowd laughed out loud, delighted with themselves and with him. It was the breaking of a dam, the spilling out of all their energy and courage and sound. It was dancing and it was singing. It was art, and they loved it.

It was impossible for any team to fail to feel that surging life of the spirit, that buoyant moment. Everyone felt happy, relaxed. Never mind the score! The whistle blew. The Hilltown boys began to hit. Nothing could stop them now.

Gene sat in the last booth in the drug store, with Mary and half a dozen others crowded in. Gene was against the wall, held fast there by his friends. Mary was beside him, drinking from his straw. Jack Fowler, the biggest boy in the school and the afternoon's high point man, came back and leaned over and pounded Gene on the back. The coach came back and thanked him. Mary begged him to promise to teach her and Betty the new locomotive he had talked about. Everyone was happy, the game was saved, and Gene was dizzy with ideas. Just as a girl sometimes makes the amazing discovery that she doesn't have to be pretty, so now, he had made the discovery that there were other things than inches.

And more than that. He was still dazzled with the look on his father's face, with his father's arm around his shoulder, with his father walking out of the gym with him, wanting everyone to know Gene was his boy.

But with all this complexity of joy, there was something he was holding back until he got alone in his own room. He was holding back the echo of that great controlled shout, that moment when he was out of the world and took the town with him. It was something that would recur for him in other times and ways, he knew. He would never lose it now.

———

One Indiana gentleman has enjoyed a distinguished career as a novelist, commentator, essayist, critic, and public official and continues to go strong. Born in Aurora and educated at Franklin College and Oxford University

ELMER DAVIS

is anxious lest, in the furious growth of population in the central and northern sections of the state, the Ohio river country be forgotten. He reminds us that

We Lived in Indiana Too

BY THIS TIME, I suppose, everybody in Indiana knows that the state also includes the river counties; and everybody in the river counties knows that they belong to Indiana. People up-state drive down to the banks of the Ohio, on Sunday afternoons, to look at the scenery—the beauty of the flat upstate landscape has been praised by Mr. Tarkington, but people who live there seem occasionally to want something different; and people from the river counties are apt to pile into the car for a week-end in the excellent state parks, farther north, which were unknown when I was a boy. Indeed, most of up-state Indiana was unknown to us residents of the river counties when I was a boy, forty years and more ago: as we were unknown to the people farther north who shared with us the designation of Hoosiers. Indiana was traditionally—a tradition spread far and wide by Hoosier novelists—a flat country, with no hills except in Brown County (and in those days even they had hardly been penetrated by explorers) and no rivers but the Wabash. Hardly anybody had ever heard of the Ohio and its hills. (Not till I went to college up-state did I realize that those hills were not hills at all, but only out-size gullies washed in the plateau by creeks going down to the river.)

Yet it was a river country, a hill country, that I grew up in—a country so different from the rest of the state, in those days, that I should have known practically nothing about Indiana if I hadn't got my education at Franklin College. For which there was good reason. The first settlers of Indiana came in two waves—those who crossed the river from Kentucky (with Virginia or North Carolina origins a generation farther back) and those who came down the river from Pittsburgh, in the days when rivers were the only dependable means of transportation. Some of the Kentuckians went on farther north, though they had pretty well thinned out by the time they got to the latitude of Indianapolis; but many of them stayed on the other side of the river where they first landed. As for the Pennsylvanians, they were river men who settled on the river banks.

My home town, Aurora, was largely the creation of two families— the Holmans who came across from Kentucky and the Gaffs who came down the river. When I was a boy few of us but the politicians knew anything about Indiana, yet all of us were conscious of belonging to the river culture, which, from Pittsburgh and St. Paul down to New Orleans, was pretty much of a piece—and different in every state from the culture of the land-locked regions behind it. Aurora was to be sure a special case; it lay on the fringes of the tri-state metropolitan complex of Cincinnati, and in those days at least its citizens felt themselves far more Cincinnatians than Hoosiers. (Cincinnati, "the city" par excellence of my boyhood, still seems to me more of a home town than any place in Indiana—even Aurora, now that most of the people I used to know are dead.) But above all we were conscious of belonging to a river country, a river culture, that had peculiar characteristics of its own.

All that is gone now, and for good reason—it grew when the rivers were the only means of transportation, it survived, not too greatly weakened, in the days of the railroads; but it died in the age of the automobile. In my boyhood the river counties (our county, at least) were painfully trying to recover from the panic of 1893 (and then, about the time they began to see their way out of the woods, from the panic of 1907). There had been a time when they were the most prosperous, and the most civilized part of Indiana, while the upstate pioneers were still clearing away the woods and draining the swamps. Then the railroads began to take away the steamboat traffic, cornfields began to sprout up-state where forests had been, and the river counties went into a decline. The river bottoms were as good corn land as you could find anywhere (they were also the only possible locations for ball parks, so that as late as June you usually had to have ground rules—two bases on a hit into the backwater in left field). Later people found they were good for tobacco, too; they were not very extensive, and the hills were not good for much except apple orchards and hay. There was some small-scale manufacturing; but my own town, at least, didn't begin to make a good living again until (after I had left) it developed as a market center for the hay and tobacco trade, and more recently has gotten some of the overflow of prosperity from the great distilleries at Lawrenceburg, four miles away. It looks far more prosperous now than it did in my boyhood. Yet it is the same kind of prosperity that you can see in any flourishing town from Pittsburgh to Denver; there is no longer anything distinctive about it.

Well, what used to be distinctive about it? Largely a matter of age—not much age, of course, but age enough to count in those

days. The river counties belonged to the early decades of the nineteenth century, up-state Indiana to the middle. I once attempted to
summarize it, for a visiting savant from Boston, by saying that down
on the river we were wearing pants and reading the classics while
people up-state were still hunting the mastodon with stone axes.
He refused to accept this; he insisted that if southern Indiana wore
pants, then or now, they were Tom Lincoln's pants; and that the
shiftlessness and footlessness of Tom Lincoln is to this day the
dominant characteristic of the inhabitants of those parts. He was
wrong; he did not know the river counties. All he had seen of
southern Indiana was a town far from the Ohio, or even the Wabash
—a town which owes its fame largely to Dr. Kinsey—with occasional
side trips into Brown County, now quaintified up for the tourist
trade. The river counties, I maintain, used to be different.

It is hard to put that difference into words; which may be why
nobody has ever put it into words, though there have been men
from the river counties who might have done so. Yet there was a
difference we could feel, even if we couldn't express it—a sense of
background and belonging. Occasionally the architects managed to
express it better; the Lanier house at Madison is now a state memo-
rial; and the Gaff house at Aurora, lately voted by the Institute of
Architects the best specimen of its type in the country, has at least
been put on ice for the time being as the clubhouse of the Veterans
of Foreign Wars. Other old houses thereabouts have been rehabili-
tated; but people die and their children move away. There are good
new houses in the river towns, but they look like good new houses
in Muncie or Kokomo, or any other town in the vast area of the
Mississippi Valley which the automobile has made all one piece;
there is nothing distinctive about them.

The up-stater may sniff scornfully that there never was anything
distinctive about us at all; that it was only a myth we created to
compensate for our poverty when up-state farmers were getting rich.
But it wasn't all a myth. We produced few of the state's great men;
our best in politics was William Steele Holman, our best in science
Harvey Wiley, our best in literature David Graham Phillips (far
better than he is now rated, as a social critic if not as a novelist).
But there was a sense of settledness, of background, of tradition,

even if it was only a few decades older than the tradition of our fellow citizens in the flat country to the north; a shabby-genteel tradition, perhaps, old families (old by the Middle-Western time scale) living in old houses that had seen better days, but still keeping up their standards. And all around us all the time the beauty of the river and the hills—not such a unique and breath-taking beauty as the less traveled among us were taught to believe it was, but a very satisfying landscape none-the-less. We all knew that we had something even if we couldn't quite say what it was—except, of course, that it was not money.

So I stick to my story. We were wearing pants when the up-staters still went around in bearskins, even if we all wear the same kind of clothes now.

"Constable Newt Plum's son-in-law up at Indynoplus has opened a cut-rate meat shop fer salaried people."
—Abe Martin's ALMANACK FOR 1909

"Atlas had a great reputation but I'd like to have seen him carry a mattress upstairs."
—Abe Martin's TOWN PUMP

"Why don't women reformers begin on ther sisters?"
—Abe Martin's TOWN PUMP

"I don't believe I ever heard anybuddy say they wanted a Christmus card for Christmus."
—Abe Martin's TOWN PUMP

"Chef Dan Moss, o' the New Palace hotel, tried carrots without peas but they didn't git over."
—Abe Martin's BROADCAST

"I kin always tell a feller who has married a good housekeeper by the way he brightens up when I speak kindly to him."
—Abe Martin's TOWN PUMP

—and then there was

ERNIE PYLE

the GI's columnist of World War II, who had been known before he achieved his greatest fame in that capacity as a newspaper man who signed his daily feature "The Vagabond from Indiana."

Pyle's home folks lived over around Dana, in the Wabash Valley along the Indiana-Illinois border and about half-way between Evansville and Hammond. Except that it's not quite far enough from the black land of the Illinois prairies, Dana would be about as near average Indiana as any place you could think of. Since it, too, produced a famous writer, maybe it is average Indiana in spite of its proximity to the Sucker State.

Here Ernie Pyle talks of his home folks and their neighbors.

Home Country

I DON'T KNOW whether you know that long, sad wind that blows so steadily across the thousands of miles of Midwest flatlands in the summertime. If you don't, it will be hard for you to understand the feeling I have about it. Even if you do know it, you may not understand.

To me the summer wind in the Midwest is one of the most melancholy things in all life. It comes from so far and blows so gently and yet so relentlessly; it rustles the leaves and the branches of the maple trees in a sort of symphony of sadness, and it doesn't pass on and leave them still. It just keeps coming, like the infinite flow of Old Man River. You could—and you do—wear out your lifetime on the dusty plains with that wind of futility blowing in your face. And when you are worn out and gone, the wind—still saying nothing, still so gentle and sad and timeless—is still blowing across the prairies, and will blow in the faces of the little men who follow you, forever.

One time in 1935, when I was driving across Iowa, I became conscious of the wind and instantly I was back in character as an

Indiana farm boy again. Like dreams came the memories the wind brought. I lay again on the ground under the shade trees at noon-time, with my half hour for rest before going back to the fields, and the wind and the sun and the hot country silence made me sleepy, and yet I couldn't sleep for the wind in the trees. The wind was like the afternoon ahead that would never end, and the days and the summers and even the lifetimes that would flow on forever, tiredly, patiently.

Maybe it's a bad job, my trying to make you see something that only I can ever feel. It is just one of those small impressions that form in a child's mind, and grow and stay with him through a life-time, even shaping a part of his character and manner of thinking, and he can never explain it.

There's another impression that has come up with me out of childhood: I have a horror of snakes that verges on the irrational. I'm not afraid of being killed by a snake. It isn't that kind of fear. It's a horrible, unnatural mania for getting away, and it is induced equally by a six-inch garden snake and a six-foot rattler.

Ask my mother. She'll tell you the snake story, probably. In all the years, she never failed to tell it over again when I came home on a visit.

I was a little fellow, maybe four or five. My father was plowing at the far end of our farm, a half mile from the house. I was walking along behind the plow, barefooted, in the fresh soft furrow. He had just started the field, and was plowing near a weedy fence row. Red wild roses were growing there. I asked my father for his pocket-knife so I could cut some of the roses to take back to the house. He gave it to me and went on plowing. I sat down in the grass and started cutting off the roses.

Then it happened in a flash. A blue racer came looping through the grass at me. I already had my horror of snakes at that tender age—it must have been born in me. I screamed, threw away the knife, and ran as fast as I could. Then I remembered it was my father's knife. I crept back over the plowed ground till I found it. He had heard me scream and had stopped. I gave him the knife and started back to the house.

I approached the house from the west side, where there was an old garden all grown up in high weeds. I stopped on the far side and shouted for my mother. When she came out to see what I wanted, I asked her to come and get me. She said I should come on through by myself. I couldn't have done that if it had killed me not to. She ordered me to come through, and I began to cry. She told me that if I didn't stop crying and didn't come through, she would whip me. I couldn't stop, and I couldn't come through. So she came and got me. And she whipped me—one of the two times, I believe, that she ever whipped me.

That evening when my father came in from the fields, she told him about the crazy boy who wouldn't walk through the weeds and had to be whipped. And then my father told her about the roses and the knife and the snake. It was the roses, I think, that hurt her so. My mother cried for a long time that night after she went to bed.

It has been more than thirty years since that happened, but to this day when I go home my mother sooner or later will say, "Do you remember the time I whipped you because you wouldn't walk through the weeds?" And then she will tell me the story, just as I have told it here, and along toward the end she always manages to get the hem of her apron up around her eyes, just in case she should need it, which she always does.

My mother would rather drive a team of horses in the field than cook a dinner. But in her lifetime she had done very little of the first and too much of the latter. She has had only three real interests—my father, myself, and her farm work. Nothing else makes much difference to her. And yet, when I left home in my late teens, to be gone forever except for brief visits, she was content for me to go, because she knew I was not happy on the farm.

My mother is living proof that happiness is within yourself; for a whole lifetime she has done nothing but work too hard, and yet I'm sure she has been happy. She loves the farm there outside Dana, Indiana. She wouldn't think of moving to town, as the other "retired" farmers do. She would rather stay home now and milk the cows than to go to the state fair. She is the best chicken raiser and cake baker in the neighborhood. She loves to raise chickens and hates to bake cakes.

After she and my father had been married thirty years, they took a trip east and saw Niagara Falls. She didn't want to go and was glad to get back home, but did admit she enjoyed the trip. The highlight of the journey, which included Washington and New York, was a night in a tourist cabin near Wheeling, West Virginia. Is was fixed so nice inside, she said, just like home. She talks about it yet.

My mother probably knows as little about world affairs as any woman in our neighborhood. Yet she is the broadest-minded and most liberal of the lot. I don't remember her ever telling me I couldn't do something. She always told me what she thought was right, and what was wrong, and then it was up to me. When I was about sixteen I forgot and left my corncob pipe lying on the window sill one day when I went to school. When I got home that night, she handed me the pipe and said, "I see you're smoking now." I said, "Yes." And that was all there was to that. She thinks it's awful for women to smoke, but I imagine if she had a daughter who smoked she'd think it was all right.

She is a devout Methodist and a prohibitionist. Yet she and my father voted for Al Smith in 1928, because they thought he was a better man than Hoover. Some of their neighbors wouldn't speak to them for months because they voted for a Catholic and a wet, but they didn't care. They are always doing things they think are right.

My mother has quite a temper. I remember once when the liniment man came, and said we hadn't paid him for a bottle of liniment. My mother said we had. The man said we hadn't. So my mother went and got the money, opened the screen door, and threw it in his face. He never came back.

She always tells people just what she thinks. A good many of our neighbors have deservedly felt the whip of her tongue, and they pout over it a while, but whenever they're in trouble they always thaw out and come asking for help. And of course get it. My mother is the one the neighbors always call on when somebody gets sick, or dies, or needs help of any kind. She has practically raised a couple of kids besides myself. She has always been the confidante of the young people around there.

I started driving a team of horses in the fields when I was nine. I remember that first day perfectly. My mother had gone to a club meeting, but she came home in the middle of the afternoon and brought me a lunch of bread and butter and sugar out to the field. And also, I suppose, she wanted to make sure I hadn't been dragged to death under the harrow.

She played the violin when she was younger, but she gave it up after I took one term of lessons. I gave it up too. You should have heard me.

My mother doesn't realize it, but her life has been the life of a real prairie pioneer. You could use her in a book, or paint her picture, as one of the sturdy stock of the ages who have always done the carrying-on when the going was tough.

She isn't so well any more, but she seems to work harder than ever. We try to get her to rest, but she says, "Oh, the work has to be done." We say, "Yes, but you don't have to do it. Supposing you were gone; the work would still be here, but you wouldn't have to do it." But she doesn't understand what we mean.

Perhaps you have heard of my father. He is the man who put oil on his brakes when they got to squeaking, then drove to Dana and ran over the curb and through a plate-glass window and right into a dry-goods store.

My father is also the man who ran with Roosevelt in 1932. He ran for township trustee, was the only Democrat in the county who lost, and was probably the happiest man who listened to election returns that night. He couldn't think of anything worse than being township trustee. The reason he lost was that all the people figured that if he was trustee he wouldn't have time to put roofs on their houses and paint their barns and paper their dining rooms and fix their chimneys, and do a thousand and one other things for them. I guess when my father is gone that whole neighborhood will just sort of fall down.

He used to work as a hired hand way over on the other side of the Wabash River. When he was courting my mother, every Sunday he would drive a horse six miles to the river, row a boat across, and then ride a bicycle ten miles to my mother's house. At midnight he started to reverse the process. Mother figured he either loved her or else was foolish and needed somebody to look after him, so she married him.

My father has never lived anywhere except on a farm, and yet I don't think he ever did like the farm very well. He has been happiest, I think, since he started renting out the farm. Ever since then he has been carpentering and handy-manning all about the neighborhood. He is a wizard with tools, where other people are clumsy. He is a carpenter at heart.

Once when he was a young man, my father did start out to see the world. He went to Iowa to cut broom corn, but broke a leg and had to come home. He never went anywhere again till he was fifty-five, when he went to California to see his brother. He sat up all the way in a day coach. Later he went to New York, so he has seen both oceans.

When he was in Washington he kept butting his head against those big glass cases that hold exhibits in the Smithsonian Institute. The glass was polished so clean he couldn't see it. We all thought it was awfully funny. He got a splitting headache from it.

We got our first automobile in 1914. We kept it up in the north end of the wagon shed, right behind the wagon. At the south end of the wagon shed there was a big gravel pit. One day we came home from town, my mother and I got out at the house, and father went to put the car away. We saw him make the circle in the barn lot, and then drive into the north end of the shed. The next instant, the south end of the shed simply burst open, a wagon came leaping out, and with one great bound was over the cliff and down in the gravel pit. My father said he never did know exactly what happened.

He is a very quiet man. He has never said a great deal to me all his life, and yet I feel that we have been very good friends. He never gave me much advice, or told me to do this or that, or not to. He bought me a Ford roadster when I was about sixteen, and when I wrecked it a couple of weeks later he never said a word. But he didn't spare me either; I worked like a horse from the time I was nine.

He never shows much emotion, and he has never seen a big-league ball game. Yet my mother came home one afternoon during a World Series, and caught him sitting in front of the radio, all by himself, clapping and yelling for all he was worth.

My father is now getting a little deaf. Mother says he can always hear what he isn't supposed to hear. If my father doesn't like people, he never says anything about it. If he does like people, he never says much about that either. He is very even-tempered. If he has an enemy in this whole country, I have yet to hear about it.

He doesn't swear or drink or smoke. He is honest, in letter and in spirit. He is a good man without being at all annoying about it. He used to smoke cigars, but he quit the Fourth of July that Johnson fought Jeffries in Reno—I think it was 1908. The event didn't have anything to do with it. His holiday cigar simply made him sicker than usual that day, so he quit.

"It seems like you can't buy anything any more that lasts as long as th' ole one."

—Abe Martin's ALMANACK

"Who remembers th' good ole fashioned days when th' only time you smelled bacon wuz when you passed a workin' man's home?"

—Abe Martin's ALMANACK

" 'He'll be jest six months ole the next time slot-machines are suppressed,' said Mrs. Lafe Bud, when somebody admired her new baby."

—Abe Martin's TOWN PUMP

"Jest when I git to thinkin' this is the greatest nation on earth some rotten book comes out an' takes it by storm."

—Abe Martin's TOWN PUMP

CHAPTER THIRTEEN

Hoosierland in the Sinful 'Twenties

JULIET V. STRAUSS

Juliet Virginia Humphries Strauss came very, very near to being what a Hoosier dyed-in-the-wool, pure-bred, cantankerous—and possibly hide-bound—likes to believe is the typical female of the species. She had no folderol, no foolishness, about her. She said what she thought and she did not hesitate to think in fields esoteric. Underneath she had outcroppings of that romantic streak which underlies most of our kind, but unlike the majority she let these show on the surface upon occasion—and therein lay her special charm.

She was born at Rockville, Indiana, in 1863; at eighteen she married Isaac Strause, editor and owner of the Rockville Tribune (whose name she insisted on spelling in the original German form, though he, the weaker vessel, had tried to anglicize it); she helped on the paper, kept house, taught school, and lectured—in her later years—to bolster the family budget.

According to Edward Bok (whose Ladies Home Journal profited from her talent for setting down common-sense opinions on paper) she began to write for The Indianapolis News over the signature of "A Country Contributor" in 1903, and in 1908 was discovered by him, the discerning Bok, and invited to submit material to his omnipotent guide to those who aspired to female refinement and to improvements in homemaking.

Mr. Bok knew what he was about, no one ever questioned that, and although his Ladies Home Journal may have slipped a bit from the place of unchallenged pre-eminence in 1908, the writings of the "Plain Country Woman" who was Mrs. Strauss make as good sense now as they did when he and his Journal were at their highest power.

Juliet Strauss was a gallant gal, a fit contemporary for Tarkington, Ade, and Kin Hubbard, as is demonstrated in this essay from

The Ideas of a Plain Country Woman

CHAPTER XVI THE SIN OF TRYING TO BE TOO
GOOD

A VERY DEAR FRIEND of mine said to me the other day with a cadence of gentle melancholy in her tone, "I have very few pleasures in this world." I glanced quickly up at her to see if she was consciously "putting on" or if she really thought that what she said was true. The tie between us is of the sort that is thicker than water and I wouldn't hesitate a moment to invite her to come off her perch, or even to assist her to descend by forcible means, if I thought it would do any good. My sisters and I were brought up in a holy horror of "putting on," and were always on the lookout for the slightest hint of affectation in voice or manner. Our wits were sharpened to the detection of the faintest tinge of sentimentalism— the merest swaying of the form in walking—the most infinitesimal wag of head—the slightest suggestion of taking ourselves seriously or making the most of a situation.

We dreaded the laughter and sarcasm that were the sure retribution of posing—so we held to plain facts until it really amounted to a fault. Plain dealing can be overdone, and truth itself employed unnecessarily. However, I saw that the woman believed what she said—but I laughed anyway—openly and derisively. We were on the way home from a session of bridge whist and were going for a drive .the next afternoon; the next day after that was the euchre club; some friends had telephoned that they were coming in to spend the evening: the poor soul who had no pleasures was hastening home to strike a light to the wood fire in her big, pleasant hall, to draw a pitcher of cider and put it in the refrigerator for her guests. Her girl was getting supper; nobody was sick; the winter coal laid in; her cellar full to overflowing with good things for the coming winter. And so I laughed at her because she had so few pleasures in this world.

I never did admire the attitude of the cross-bearing child, or the idea of being a pilgrim and a stranger in this vale of tears. As for me I am so native to my element that everything appeals to me with a sort of pleasure. As we walked along the street that afternoon a thousand little consciousnesses thrilled me with a sense of pleasure. The clear sunset, the fresh September breeze, with just the hint of wood smoke on its breath, the rustle of the leaves on the maple trees that make our town a sylvan home, with all the suggestions the word implies—the long vista of the street under the arching branches, the flight of blackbirds coming home to roost, the familiar houses wherein dwell the neighbours (and every one around as dear as a relation!), the motion of walking, the function of breathing— the myriads of memories and realisations, reminiscent and antici- patory, folded in the convolutions of the brain and faintly expressing themselves in the sensations of the hour.

I wondered how the woman had come to let these things lose their effect upon her—and then it suddenly came to me that she had done so by trying to be good! How many people have done the same thing, let the long list of martyrs, religious fanatics, inmates of monasteries, convents and lunatic asylums reply! I am of the earth, earthy, and I am glad of it. This world is my home while I stay in it, and, to tell the truth, I do not care if that is forever and ever. Let me change to a beech tree or a quaking aspen, or a red bird or a fish, so I may keep this joy when the wind blows and the rain falls and the sun shines on the riffles of the creek, or sinks in a sea of gold behind the scant fringe of our fast-thinning Indiana woods.

As a race we are given to hypochondria. It was a part of the religion of our ancestors. We were to taboo pleasure—to take up our cross— in short, to make ourselves a terror to the young and a burden to ourselves in the mistaken idea that we were gaining something by it. Women are particularly given to this form of martyrdom. They accept the cares of life as trials, when they might just as well make joys of them, and they show a servile respect to grief that must be trying to Him who sends sorrows as blessings to such as will have them so. There is a vast difference in the way grief comes to us— but it is a belief of mine that the more strongly we allow our element to claim us, the closer we live to the life of the body, the easier it is to bear the natural griefs that flesh is heir to. For this reason it is all important to keep to the simple joys of living and loving—let the little daily cares—the seemingly inconsequent things, be dear to you, and let life itself be dear to you—as dear as it will—never spurn its pleasures, and above all, know when you have them. Realise your blessings before it is too late—and never say you have few pleasures so long as a year of youth is left and you love anybody in the world or anybody in the world loves you. Youth means much besides mere youngness—it is a thing we may keep or lose.

I am an unorthodox soul who doesn't go to church, an unconventional person who is always transgressing social rules and customs, a lax housekeeper, working by fits and starts, a somewhat indiscreet talker, given to plain speech and open confession. The truth is, however, I am not needed at church. If I were, I should go. I never went to a revival meeting in my life, but what a paralysis fell upon the spirit of the occasion. Not a conversion, not a testimony, not a hand-shaking, or a walk-around takes place while I am inside the doors. There is always a painful and perspiring effort on the part of the evangelist. Embarrassing silences come in which one can hear a pin drop. Nobody rises for prayer, not a sinner goes to the mourner's bench, the meeting stands at a deadlock—though the night before there was a great awakening. I am always seized with the idea that it is up to me to do something, but I don't quite know what it is. It would be insincere for me to rise for prayer; my voice is too much cracked by long disuse to raise a hymn on a sudden and risk carrying it till the others recover from their surprise and join in one by one.

I feel a sympathy for the hero of the old story about the stranger who happened in when the preacher was discoursing on the sheep and the goats. "And who will be the goats?" he demanded in old-style pulpit oratory—"and who will be the goats?" The silence after the reiteration of this question was so prolonged and impressive that the stranger, being of an obliging disposition, rose and remarked: "Well, mister, rather than have the performance stop, I'll be a goat." I always feel an intense willingness to be a goat or anything else that will help matters along, but I haven't the talent for it some way, and once out in the open air with my limbs freed from the terrifying limitations of the pew in which there is no opportunity for action except to rise while singing the last verse or when the preacher asks all who want to go to heaven to stand up, I decide for the hundredth time, that browsing out along the highways and hedges is my best chance.

Not that I do not respect church-going people or the sentiment that takes them there. I was never for carrying coals to Newcastle— there are so many good women who go to church—one less is scarcely noticed. If I were a man, now, and could make a spot of tweed or cheviot among the silks and voiles, I think I should go, but then there are so many fine things I would do if I were a man, it really seems a pity I wasn't one.

In regard to being good, what a joke it will be on me if at the end I find my philosophy wrong, and that I made a mistake in merely being thankful and appreciative, and in accepting the little gratuities of life as blessings and being glad over them! What if I have to go back and learn it all over again and know that my delight in every wayside weed and flower was a pagan joy—my rapture in the sunshine only a passion which we leave behind—my being happy, like the apples, when the south wind blows, merely a sensuous response to the call—what call? How faint and far—how reminiscent and prophetic—ah, we cannot know for certain which part of us is nearest God or when we are spurning the divine!

At any rate, I am convinced that there is no virtue in having few pleasures. Everything is a pleasure that belongs properly to our element. We should be normal souls, not struggling against our destiny, and as such the functions of life are naturally pleasurable and we should not despise them. I was getting dinner the other day, when it suddenly struck me what a jolly thing it was to be doing. I was hungry, for one thing, and that made it better. And it

was cool enough to make the kitchen fire not ungrateful. I had
rushed down at a quarter past eleven to scare up something for
dinner. I made a little peach cobbler, fried a skilletful of tomatoes,
cooked mashed potatoes, fried ham with cream gravy, made soda
biscuits, and put a dish of crisp white celery and a shaky mould of
my new crabapple jelly on the table.

I have a mania for waiting till the last minute and then racing
like mad to get the meal on the table. This is contrary to all authorities on housekeeping—and maybe that is why I like to do it.
I never could plan ahead for days in advance. I am sure I shouldn't
enjoy things to eat if they were not prepared on the impulse of the
moment, but as I say, it suddenly occurred to me what a fine state
of affairs it was to be hungry and have something to cook and some
loved ones to share the meal with one! There was pleasure in every
motion of flying around the kitchen, satisfaction in being able in a
few minutes to evolve a good meal from the raw material, delight
in the warmth and fragrance of the room, with the clear sunlight
and crisp autumnal air outside. Would any woman who can do this
dare to say she has few pleasures?

But aside from these homely delights—that we should all allow
to be as dear to us as they wish to be—there are so many others.
I am just woman enough to like to go to a tea, or reception, or
large evening company or card party, or picnic, or anything else
that comes along. Here in a very "poky" little village, far from great
cities and social centres, my friends and I have been free to have
fun in our own way, and we have had it. The gypsy picnics we used
to have remain bright spots in our memories. I was detailed, with
two dignified gentlemen, to fry the potatoes. Later, my sister-in-law
and I quarrelled over frying the eggs, and finally we all sat down
to a feast for the gods—seasoned by hunger and the novelty of the
occasion. Often, four good cronies took long afternoon drives and
spread our little supper table on the shorn grass of the meadows,
where the long shadows of little thickets on the west of us stretched
canopies of shade for us. I took my samovar and made coffee, and
between you and me, the poor lady who has not many pleasures
was always one of our number.

We have an old horse who paces in harness, and is so lazy we can scarcely beat him out of a walk, but when one puts the saddle on him quite early on an autumn morning and strikes out the big road, he really has some pretty fair gaits. He can "rack" a little and has a nice little lope—if one were not a bit afraid he might stumble—but why cross the bridge, or go over the horse's head before the time comes? All the blisses of a lifetime are crowded into an autumn morning ride.

I believe in many pleasures as a safeguard to morality. I doubt the virtue of allowing seeming duty to intervene between one and a personal pleasure. Much preaching has instilled into our minds the idea that it is our duty to make other people happy. I doubt that it is as much our duty as to make ourselves happy. Happiness is infectious, and happy people spread the contagion. Some of the most disagreeable people I know are devoted to the idea of making others happy. To this end they are always hauling out some impossible person and making him wretched by trying to mix him up with people who are not congenial. They are always frowning upon other people's pleasures, always reminding them of neglected duty. They are opposed to gossip, and look askance at gaiety, and their patronage is fatal to the young, for it places any person whom they seek out in the light of a beneficiary. I firmly believe if they put in the time having high jinks just for their own amusement, they would do more good in the world. For the gay and bright need not be unkind, nor can the happy be selfish or the selfish happy. It is useless to undertake to make people happy by being persistently kind to them. If they are bright they will be happy in their own way; if they are dull you cannot improve them. They will only demand more than you have to give and turn sulky if you do not instantly produce it.

No woman who lives in a sweet home in a shady country town with pleasant friends around her, with books to read and horses to drive and good things to eat, and work to do, has a right to say she has few pleasures. We all have our griefs, our heartaches, our woes, but we should not live in them. One day at a time is the way to live. (Oh, irrevocable days if we could have you back again!) As for me the fast fleeting days hold so many pleasures I scarcely know which to seize as it hurries along! Eheu fugaces!—and the day is done! I am glad, however, I went with my friend to drive yesterday and that we stole the peaches that hung so temptingly over the roadway. To be sure, they were clings and a trifle sour, and I got peach fuzz down my neck, but how we laughed when I rolled down the grassy bank with the bough that had broken in my hands, and how warm the sunlight was, and how blue the hills in the distance looked! Tomorrow may hold another laugh like that—who knows?

The Lost Generation (and what a lot of unsalable tripe that "Lost Generation" phrase was!) grew up and achieved respectability in Indiana, as elsewhere—in spite of the purse-mouthed prophecies of its elders, bellyaching like Billy Sunday himself in an effort to fasten blame for the blunders of their own feigned rectitude upon their sons and daughters.

After World War I the elders set up almost every conceivable hurdle on the path to virtue: unenforceable Prohibition, a new-rich economy, the worship of wealth and an example of wild speculation; but in the early 'twenties, especially in Indiana, they introduced a new hazard to public morality. Then it was, under the leadership of a few opportunists, some gangsters, and a goodly number of politicians, that the more wool-headed and less independent among them began to join the newly-recreated Ku Klux Klan by thousands and tens of thousands. That the young people of the "Lost Generation" survived this piece of dangerous idiocy perpetrated by their elders and most severe critics; that, indeed, they had more hand than any other group in laughing it out of existence, was the final trial by fire. Let us hear no more of the sins of the "Lost Generation"!

It was in the nineteen-twenties that people in Indiana began to make a serious effort to fasten responsibility for their personal shortcomings upon those twin scapegoats of the psychologist, Heredity and Environment. Hitherto disorderly behavior had been attributed to a lack of piety, to innate cussedness, to a temporary lapse or—in the case of the very young—sometimes to worms.

The new doctrine, which had been introduced simultaneously by Chautauqua lecturers and some of the Hearst publications, was (and is) not universally accepted by Hoosiers. One of the dissenting voices is that of our old friend, that apostle of reason, Kin Hubbard, speaking through Police Matron Lide Hanger.

KIN HUBBARD

Abe Martin's Town Pump

THE RELATION OF ENVIRONMENT
TO CRIME

BY

POLICE MATRON LIDE HANGER

SPEAKIN' OF ENVIRONMENT an' its relation to crime, I have recently completed an investigation o' the homes o' seventeen boy bandits an' I found ever'thing modern an' up-to-date. Pianners an' radios adorned ever' home. I found no evidence o' brewin', an' what literature I found layin' about wuz the sort now found in all homes. What fathers I met all seemed to be industrious an' sober, an' in two o' the homes I found mothers who appeared to be o' fair quality. In the home o' Wesley Purviance, eighteen, who recently shot four fillin' station keepers in one night, I found three Bibles an' an uncompleted water-color picture entitled "The Breath o' Spring." Wesley is quite an artist as his cell walls testify. Wesley's mother still bakes bread, an' the home shows many evidences o' gentle blood. While Wesley's father has never been active in Boy Scout work, he's regularly employed, an' stands well with his grocer. I've never been fooled by environment. Mrs. Tilford Moots's uncle, well-to-do an' highly respected at seventy-four, raised himself. His father wuz hanged fer horse stealin' when he wuz two years ole, an' his mother abandoned him an' run off with a hatchet slayer. He wuz put in a home where ther wuz already seven children. Later, at the age of eight, he wuz apprenticed to a lively couple who loved to entertain. He spent five of his most impressionable years in this atmosphere. At the age o' thirteen he took employment in a barber shop where he remained two years. Next we find him workin' in a livery stable. At the age o' seventeen, havin' never touched liquor or terbacker, he took up the art of solicitin' life insurance. Today he's the president of a big life insurance company an' is livin' happily with his original wife, whom he picked out of a laundry, an' they're surrounded by good children an' ever' luxury. What a contrast ther is in the lives of Mrs. Tilford Moots's uncle an' Mort Pine, who is on the way home from Ecuador to face the charge o' wreckin' a whole community. Mort Pine wore curls till he wuz fourteen years ole. His father wuz an upstandin' man who never went to circuses, while his mother devoted her whole gentle life to uplift work. Mort played with a pony instead o' the boys. He had a private tutor, an' spent his summers at Lakeside, O. He wuz carefully an' systematically shielded from ever' bad influence durin' the oat-sowin' period. He wuz placed in a bank an' soon become a cashier. He interested himself in ever' commendable public activity. He would often brave the most inclement weather, day or night, to help the unfortunate, an' his Bible class had grown till it wuz almost unwieldly. Widows would seek him out before their husban's wuz cold an' intrust their meager inheritances with him. He wuz the trusted guardian of ever' worthy fund. One May day he fell in with the promoter of a perpetual motion contrivance. With all the cunnin' an' deftness of a born criminal he managed to cover up his peculations, forgeries, an' jugglin' till ther wuz only $91 left in the bank. This he stole, an' with a valuable red-headed stenographer he disappeared. It wuz three months before the community would believe that ther wuz anything irregular, but by that time Mort wuz safely in Ecuador.

The 'twenties were a time of unrest, even in life's normal aspects: all that promotion, speculation, and a something in the air which urged people to go somewhere else and do something different were the marks of the era.

One man, recently married and settled down in Muncie to write, saw this as most natives could not. For

C. E. SCOGGINS

had already been a great many places and done a great many things. There has been some question, in view of this wandering before and since his period of residence in Muncie, as to whether Mr. Scoggins should be considered an Indiana author at all. As the final authority upon that matter the judgment of that gentleman himself could hardly be questioned. This is what he says:

"Yes, I did live some years in Indiana, and at one time almost considered myself a Hoosier. I was born in Mexico and raised in Texas, though, and call myself a Texan for convenience—to avoid explaining that I'm not technically a Mexican. I have also lived some years in Florida and Spain, to say nothing of several spent batting around Latin-American countries, and now twenty more in Colorado. So in trying to pin me down on the map, just let your conscience be your guide. . . .

"*The Red Gods Call* you may fairly ascribe to Indiana; it was written in Muncie, where I began my career as a professional writer— after thirty years of making a living any way I could, and acquiring the disease called 'the itch to tell.' My wife's a real Hoosier, but our daughter's a Florida Cracker, and now I've almost learned to call myself a Coloradan—and don't ask how the three of us happened to get together. You may safely assume that it's a long story."

To take advantage of Mr. Scoggins' liberality in the matter, he becomes hereafter, insofar as I am concerned, an Indiana author. He is a good one. He can spin a tale of adventure as lively as the very best, and he can—as a result of his own adventurous life, his observant eye, and what must be very painstaking research—make the wildest romantic venturing appear entirely plausible. These, if you please, are qualities that make great novels.

Mr. Scoggins in his first highly successful novel launched his action from a small Indiana city which he called "Milo." Now Milo could only be Muncie since, as the introductory action opens in 1912, there stands an electric sign at the railroad station which reads "Milo Offers More." Muncie had such a sign, save for the difference in the

name, and took a kidding before it was removed which the inhabitants of middle age must still recall quite clearly. Mr. Scoggins' book
touches Muncie only at the beginning and at the end—in between,
the action is far from the Hoosier scene. But since his hero shows
signs of the unrest which began a few years before but came to a head
in the 'twenties, and since it is such a good yarn in whole or in part,
let us look at a selection from

The Red Gods Call

PROLOGUE

A SONG IN THE NIGHT

CHAPTER I

I WAS A CALIPH ONCE. Yes, once in the very manner of the good
Harun himself I befriended a homeless vagabond, fed him and
clothed him and dazzled him with my wealth and kindness; but there
must be some difference between ancient Bagdad and Milo, Indiana.
It didn't work out just right.

It was June, I remember, because I was at the station to meet
Martha, who was coming home from Vassar. It was June; out along
Madison Avenue the elms were green, and people were beginning
to sit on their porches in the evenings, and honeysuckle was in
bloom. June, 1912, it must have been, because that year I was president of the Live Wire Club and we put up that big electric sign
at the station—Milo Offers More.

No doubt you've seen it, passing through? It was new then, and
that evening the station agent forgot to turn it on.

I remember Martha kissed me before the whole crowd, as calmly
as if we were already married. It made me feel a little blank; I don't
know why. Maybe I'd thought she'd be excited about it, or shy, or
something; but she kissed her mother, and then me, and then Andy
her demon brother, and three or four of the girls, and got into her
mother's car and drove off talking a mile a minute; and I stood there
wishing something were different, I don't know what. Business was

good and Martha was lovely, and I was one of Milo's rising young men; but it didn't seem so very much to cheer about, after all. I suppose caliphs often feel that way.

So I noticed that the sign wasn't lighted, and you may believe I spoke about it.

In those days people moved when Howard Pressley spoke. Far down the train the conductor was already wailing "Bo-o-o-oard!" when it blazed out, every bulb doing full duty. Having seen to this, I was turning away, when I became aware of an entirely illegal passenger who sat on the blind platform of the baggage-car, blinking and shrinking in the sudden glare of that splendid slogan.

"Well, greetings, Weary!" I said with my unfailing wit.

The train moved. He relaxed and grinned.

"Does it?" he murmured.

"Does what what?" I inquired intelligently.

"Offer more," he said, waving a bland farewell.

Yet not, alas, farewell. Jerry the station cop knew the unlawful uses of the blind-baggage platform; Jerry the lynx-eyed knew I was not given to conversing with empty space. Violently the hand of the law fell on the ankle of the transgressor. Violently they rolled across the concrete into the parking space, and for a minute you couldn't see the taxicabs for the dust.

The vagabond came out of it. Unfortunately I was in his way. "Oof!" said I, and "Whoa!" said Jerry; and the train departed.

"Ho, hum," sighed the vagabond. "Welcome to Milo, Gus!"

I felt a little to blame. No, I will tell the truth: I had never seen a hobo in high-laced boots and wide gray hat; he looked like a character out of a Wild West movie; he was grimy, but he was lean and broad-shouldered, and he had a jaw.

Have I said that life seemed orderly and dull? I was diverted.

"Gus," I said, "you take the words out of my mouth! If we'd known you were coming, we'd have furnished a softer cop for you to fall on."

Jerry was not amused; a hobo by the railroad's brim a simple vagrant was to him. Said he vengefully, "Come along. Git goin', Gus!"

Selling real estate teaches you to think fast. I walked with them round the corner into the shadow; I spoke confidentially to Jerry and offered a certain soothing argument, and Jerry kept on walking.

Yes, ten dollars was all I thought I was going to pay for one Arabian Night's entertainment, Indiana edition!

"Here's my car," I said. "Hop in."

Now that I had my vagabond I didn't know just what to do with him. Feed him, I supposed, and learn the sad story of his life. "Hungry?" I asked him.

His voice, a leisurely barytone with a sort of western nasal quality, fitted his picturesque appearance, but his words were somewhat hackneyed.

"Old-timer," he said, "I take this mighty kind of you, but don't get me wrong. I ain't exactly a hobo."

"Of course not," I sighed. "I take it, though, you wouldn't refuse a meal?"

"I could eat a wolf," he admitted, "raw. But if it's all the same to you, let's go somewhere and shell out a few cinders first. Mamma! That engine burns lots of coal."

He seemed to find a certain humor in his grimy discomfort; maybe he was some special kind of hobo, after all. I drove round to the side entrance of the Park Hotel, prudently avoiding the lobby, and smuggled him up to my rooms.

"Gosh!" he murmured, gazing.

Right there, I can see it now, was where I got the caliph feeling—princely, you know, all generous and noble. Through his eyes I saw the true magnificence of my own bachelor quarters; by pleasing contrast I felt my own importance in the world. "There's the bathroom," I told him. "Go as far as you like."

What is there about bathrooms that makes people sing? He hummed, this vagabond, disjointedly at first, sputtering and splashing; then you could follow an odd, foreign-sounding melody. It took hold of you; it made you somehow wistful; but I got to thinking about Martha, I don't know why, and forgot to listen. Martha, and long summer evenings at the country club, where she and I would slip away alone. Down the fifth fairway where it drifts into the woods, our feet falling silent and our voices hushed, through a vale drowned in shadow to a velvet knoll under the moon. Martha, and the lights and laughter sweetly remote across the stillness. A new hot longing thrilled me. I had not meant to go to her this evening; she would prefer to rest after her trip. And yet—

I looked at my watch. The bathroom door opened.

"Say," cried my vagabond, refreshed, "can I use a slug of this alcohol rub here on the shelf? This is the first time I been clean for a week, and I feel reckless!"

He was naked, and, by Jove, he was a powerful specimen! No wonder the burly Jerry had found him hard to hold. His shoulders were thick and round, with little bulging veins that showed not an ounce of fat; his flanks were spare and hard, and his skin as white as a baby's. I had thought he was dark, but that was only soot and sunburn. He was indeed a special kind of hobo. From a sooty bundle he fished clean, if rumpled underclothes, and he had a razor too.

"Old-timer," he cried zestfully, "now this is some way for a white man to live! What do these diggings set you back—or do you own this dump?"

That was his manner of speaking—crude; forceful, but crude. I was moved to maintain my status as a caliph. I mentioned, not too conservatively, the sum I surrendered monthly to the management, and he whistled so respectfully that I was almost consoled for not owning the Park Hotel.

I had a sudden pleasing fancy. I almost laughed. "Wait a minute!" I said, getting up. "You're about my size. Wonder if you could wear my shoes?"

"Huh?" said he.

"Hobnailed boots," I explained tactfully, "while admirable for—er—general touring purposes, aren't exactly appropriate for dining."

He grinned. Even in his rumpled underclothes, I tell you, the fellow was picturesque, his white teeth showing boyishly in his lean brown face.

"For a fact," he observed, "I been missin' meals right regular lately. Maybe it's my boots."

Even as I opened my wardrobe door the idea grew on me. But I didn't laugh. Casually, in the true manner of a caliph, I tossed him my dinner jacket and its accessories; reserving for myself, as was fitting, the superior formality of tailed coat and white tie. Now that was all in order, wasn't it? Purple and fine linen, as I understand it, are part of a caliph's stock in trade. Very properly, too, the studs baffled him and the cut of the vest dazzled him.

"Oh, mamma!" he murmured. "Jerry, Jerry, pinch me quick!"

But I didn't laugh. I was kindly, tactful. I skilfully adjusted his tie and turned to put the finishing touches on my own.

Then quite suddenly it came to me that there was nothing much to laugh about. My face seemed more than usual—well, not fat, but roundish; and my brisk dignified carriage did make my—you know— my front stick out a little. I looked like what I was in those days, a prosperous young business man. But he! In my very own clothes, which fitted him badly enough, this fellow Hardy was distinguished. Yes, Hardy he said his name was; Gus Hardy. He had gone moody, pacing restlessly about the room; he carried his hands in his pockets and his wide shoulders loose; and his brown face, lighter across the forehead, gave him the look of one of those big-game hunters you see at banquets. I made mental note to wear a hat that summer, playing golf, so my forehead would stay white that way.

Yes, I perceived a difference between Bagdad and Milo, Indiana. In Bagdad everybody knows which is the caliph.

"Where did you get that sunburn?" I asked him.

He answered absently, gazing out the window, "Guatemala, I reckon."

I give you my word I didn't know where Guatemala was, only had a vague notion that it was one of those hot countries. And he laid no emphasis on it; rather he seemed lost in some somber train of thought; yet when he spoke that word he wrapped it in glamor. He didn't, if you know what I mean, speak it in English at all. The syllables came clipped and liquid off his tongue, like the murmur of deep quiet water, and for a moment you saw a land far off and strange.

That, of course, was my cue to command him, "Now tell me the sad story of your life. Begin!"

I led him to the dining-room and planted him at a secluded table, and even though I couldn't think of a graceful way to get at it— looking across rose-lighted linen at that brown face and gentlemanly shirt-front. The New York-like elegance of the Park Hotel did not lend an atmosphere; all the modern caliphs I could recall seemed to have operated in quaint greasy chop-houses and saloons.

"Sorry I can't offer you a drink," I said. "Local option, you know."

He nodded absently, gazing about the room. It was a little late for diners; there were only the Andersons, and the Naylors with an out-of-town guest, and a few traveling men.

I tried again. "Pretty hot in Guatemala, eh?"

"Hot enough on the coast. In the mountains, no."

"You were in the mountains?"

"Quezaltenango. Railroading."

There it was again, the crisp liquid murmur of syllables that conjured up visions. "It doesn't sound like a place where there'd be a railroad," I said.

"There ain't, yet. Never will be, maybe. We're trying to find a way through."

And he seemed to think he had said it all.

"Jungle?" I prompted.

"Mountains. One of those places God forgot to finish—ten thousand feet up and no way to get down. The Indians say He had a lot of land left over and just dumped it there."

"Oh!" I said. "Indians. Hostile?"

He grinned absently, making a negative gesture with one forefinger—he was always doing something with his hands. "Mayas," he said, curling the word so quaintly that I had to ask him how it was spelled.

"Oh," I said, "Mayas!"

"Yeah. Ever see any of the Maya ruins? Quirigua, for instance?"

He asked it simply, as if you might walk down the street any day and see Maya ruins.

I repeated after him, "Keereegwah?" as if searching my memory; but the flatness of my own syllables humbled me.

"Old," said Gus Hardy. "Old when the Spaniards came; old when Christ was born; nobody knows how old. Ball courts, two hundred feet between walls, where they played a game like basketball. Platforms for sacrifice, where they cut men's hearts out so their crops would grow. Palaces and temples—empty these two thousand years and more."

His eyes came back to mine, and I remember that they were intensely blue.

"Makes you feel queer," he said. "Makes you feel like a man lived about a minute—like a fly. Here's Quirigua, a station on the white man's railroad. A United Fruit Farm, with switch-engines shunting around, loading bananas for the States; and over here this place that was a city when Pilate washed his hands. Big sandstone pillars sticking up, carved all over—some kind of writing, they claim—and a Maya king at the top. With whiskers," he said, looking at me.

"Flat faces and slant eyes. And whiskers; but no Maya, no Indian has a hair on his face to-day. Where did they come from, those fellows? Where did they go?"

I could see the Naylors and the Andersons watching us, wondering, no doubt, why we wore evening clothes—while Gus Hardy wondered what had happened when the world was young.

"Stone temples around a court—standing there, still solid after twenty centuries of jungle rot. They didn't know how to build an arch; they had to make the rooms little and the walls thicker at the top so a slab of stone would reach; but they had mortar that's better than any we know.

"And some of those slabs are granite—granite, half a ton to a slab, and no granite formation in a hundred miles! No trucks, no wheel roads; nothing but manpower. How did they do it—and why?"

I doubt if I knew, even then, what we ate. With short crude strokes he wiped out for me the Central America of O. Henry and Richard Harding Davis, its funny little republics and palms and revolutions; building instead a grim old empire, fixing me with the flame of imagination on his brown face.

"Makes you feel queer," he said. "You go out through these banana groves, the light seeping sort of wet through those big flimsy leaves. Quiet, only a switch-engine clanking somewhere, and the lazy whack of some nigger's machete. Quieter and quieter, the jungle choking you, and no sound but your horse's hoofs squashing along the trail. And you come out on this place—this place where kings walked alive. Hot, you know, and still; so still you can hear the jungle growing to swallow it again, creeping up under your feet, crowding in, smothering you. Like something alive and wicked, waiting, eternally waiting to swallow the things men do. And you run into a big idol squatting in the brush; half frog, half tiger—grinning; and you hear a switch-engine whistle and you jump. I promise you, you jump."

His talk drifted. Chucho, Huehuetenango, Retalhuleu, I can remember yet the flavor of those names! Black beaches and the endless thunder of giant combers on the sand; steaming lowland, and plateaus in the sky where cloud seas flowed below you and the sun burned you through icy air. Distance and space and color, through which rode white men, laughing, conquering. The Mayas, survivors of an ancient race—you saw them trotting in from the hills on market day; the women with slant-eyed, flat-faced babies on their backs and burdens on their heads, the men loping along under loads that would try the strength of a mule. Dumb! Stupid! The life crushed out of them! Building nothing, knowing nothing of their fathers who set monuments to bearded kings.

Gus Hardy fell silent, and I looked with strangeness on the deserted dining-room of the Park Hotel. With strangeness I saw that it was not yet ten o'clock. It seemed that hours might have passed.

"You're going back?"

I remember yet the vicious little hiss of his cigarette drowning in his coffee-cup, the abrupt gesture of his lean brown hand.

"As fast as I can travel," he said. "Let's get out of here. I—oh, I don't know. I get restless, sitting still."

It's odd, now, to think that I might have given him a dollar or so and directed him to some lodging-house. It's odd. I give you my word I had forgotten that he was a hobo, that the very shirt that lent him dignity was mine. I saw a man like Kipling's Findlayson, C. E., a heroic figure from the outposts of civilization—his blue eyes moody, oppressed by the small-town elegance of the Park Hotel. And—

Can you see this? Once on a Saturday afternoon, playing up to the eighteenth green at the club, there was a sunset that made me forget the game. A flat purple cloud towering up and up, its ragged edges all afire, the sky vast and pale and stained with savage color; the dark woods and the house in that eerie light were lonely somber things; it took you like a wild and magnificent foreboding. And

Martha came down from the veranda to wave to us, one sweet note of white in that sinister gorgeous picture. I remember how I hurried my long shot to the green, hurrying to be with her, to share it with her; and we lost the hole, and my partner was very sarcastic about it, and Martha didn't care for the sunset after all; said it made her shiver.

You know? A little bird swinging on a twig in the sunshine, a moment in a book where a man has written better than he knows, a great actress weeping—there is little you can say about it, but you must know that there is some one who sees. Here I had this Gus Hardy full of strange talk—this blue-eyed, brown-faced painter of visions.

I looked at my watch. With an engaging air of aimlessness I said, "What say we take a little spin?"

CHAPTER II

AND AS I DROVE I forgot to point out the prosperity of our business section, our handsome residences, our well-kept lawns. The feeling of strangeness persisted; oddly I felt as if I were returning from far journeys to a quaint familiar place; returning after loneliness and labor, to the soft welcome of a woman's eyes and hands. Have I said that it was June? Out along Madison Avenue the elms were green. The lighted windows looked very homelike through the trees; now and then some one sang out to me, neighbor fashion, from a veranda; the odor of honeysuckle trailed across our faces, and the sound of Rita Nelson's piano drifted out to us as we passed.

I forgot to tell Gus Hardy that the Nelsons were Milo's richest family. Oddly, in my official capacity as president of the Live Wire Club, I was thinking that we should make more of streets like this, and less of the smoke of our many factories. What is it, after all, that every man wants? A home.

I spoke of this to Gus Hardy, and he sighed.

"Yeah," he said, "that's so. But what you going to do when you get restless, and the sun goes down slow like it does up here, and you get homesick sitting on your own front porch?"

"Pretty tame, I guess," I admitted, "for fellows like you."

"It—oh, I don't know!" he said. "You feel like there ain't enough room outdoors, or enough stars in the sky. It's all so tight and settled, and the people all the same, and you don't fit. That's it; you don't fit. And you get to thinking; and something happens, some little thing. You wouldn't believe— This time it was a woman singing."

A woman singing! On this romantic note we came to Martha McAllister's house; and I saw what I had hoped for, a light in the living-room. I checked the car.

With a masterly imitation of sudden impulse I said, "Want to drop in here a minute?"

"Huh?" said Gus Hardy, staring, and after a moment, "Here?"

The McAllister house did me credit. It was not so large as to be formidable, but it was wide and comfortable looking, with a veranda that seemed to invite and welcome you. Gus Hardy made no objection; he said nothing at all.

Wherefore I shouted cheerily, "Hello! Anybody home?"

Martha's bright head bobbed up at the open window and her bright voice answered me. I think I forgot to notice whether Gus Hardy followed me. She met me at the door, laughing, scolding me.

"This is a nice time of day! I thought you weren't coming. I didn't care if you never came," she said, and wrinkled her small nose in the most entrancing impudence. "Sitting here in my very newest, nicest dress. Like it?"

That was Martha—quick, dancing you lightly out of your own mood into hers. I wondered why I had thought it was a rather solemn moment—following her into laughter, feeling a little slow and heavy and masculine. I did indeed like her dress; it looked like the stuff of misty moonbeams, caressing her. What should I say about it?

I became aware of Gus Hardy's brown impassive face. I said, "Martha, let me present—"

Her clear eyes widened and her dainty brows went up. She had thought, of course, that I came alone; instantly I knew that I ought to have come alone. All at once I knew how a married man feels who cheerily produces an unexpected guest at dinner. It came to me that the business of being a lover was not so simple as selling real estate; I should have to put my mind to it.

Have I said that Martha was lovely? Dainty, the fine and fragrant product of tender care. And Gus Hardy, hobo! Instantly I knew that she could never understand the caliph feeling; that for her he must be not less than he seemed, with his grave brown face and the dignity of his borrowed clothes. Presto! Vanished the vagabond; appeared the distinguished naturalist and explorer.

"—my old friend Hardy—Hardy Logan, you know, the great Hardy Logan you've heard me talk so much about. Just back from his expedition up the Amazon, bug hunting, you know. I didn't tell you, did I, old man, that Miss McAllister came in on the same train with you? Or maybe you saw each other," I said hysterically, thinking of Martha in her Pullman and Gus Hardy crouching in a swirl of cinders on the blind-baggage platform. "That's how I happened to be at the station. Lucky, eh?"

Then I had to stop for breath—ready to break out again if Gus Hardy should fail me. Without a flicker his grave eyes accepted the nomination; he bowed, a stiff, foreign sort of bow; he looked at me and grinned, a slow easy grin.

"Lucky," he said, "is the very word I was trying to think of."

"The Hardy Logan? How nice! I'm dreadfully thrilled!" Not even Vassar could ever give Martha a vocabulary.

I remember I laughed a good deal. I made mental note to try grinning slow that way myself, after the golf season was advanced and I was properly sunburned.

Following Martha into the room I whispered in his ear, "Great! Keep it up. I'll explain later."

He murmured, "You don't hunt bugs up the Amazon, old-timer. They hunt you."

And I laughed again. "You've been there? Fine!"

I mean, I felt as if I had deftly mastered a delicate situation. Before Mrs. McAllister my vagabond clicked his heels and bowed again; even Andy, the demon brother, was so impressed that he forgot to be funny about the unusual splendor of our attire. In Milo, you understand, evening clothes are distinctly the mark of an occasion.

Well, I can see it now; distinctly that was one!

Mrs. McAllister was placidly sewing or embroidering or something; I said, "Andy, Mr. Logan knows all about Indians. Indians that cut men's hearts out!" and let nature take its course, which left me free to enjoy a little attention from Martha.

"It seems years and years since Easter," I murmured tenderly.

"Does it?" said Martha.

"—and anyway, I thought you'd be tired after your trip—"

"—so you brought him along to make sure you wouldn't be bored?"

"Ah, don't be angry! I couldn't help it. Hadn't seen old Hardy for years and years—"

"The same years?" said Martha.

And you'd have thought, to look at her, that we were having a sprightly and amusing bit of persiflage. She even smiled. Once, long ago, I had stupidly cut a dance with her, and she had smiled like that. Sweetly. Oh, much too sweetly. Why can't women be frank and straightforward—like a man?

But she was very gracious to Gus Hardy. "Do you know," she said, "I never met an entomologist before?"

"A who?" said Gus Hardy. "Oh," he said, and looked at me and grinned. "No, ma'am, Buck's got that wrong. I'm an engineer."

"Who's Buck?" piped up Andy.

"Why, Buck," said Gus Hardy, and jerked his head at me.

I draped one arm over the back of my chair and tried to look like Buck. "Yeah," I said carelesslly, "I doubt if Gus every knew my given name. Always called me Buck."

"Gus who?" inquired the insatiable Andy.

"Hardy. I mean, Mr. Logan. Gus, we used to call him, Gloomy Gus, you know. By Jove," I said brightly, "it's like seeing a man returned from the dead! Here I thought old Gus was way up the Amazon somewhere, chasing bugs—"

"No," said Gus firmly, "you got that wrong, Buck. I was going up there to work for a German company building a railroad. But in

Rio I met a poor devil that had just come from there, all shot to pieces he was—"

"Arrows or guns?" demanded the bloodthirsty Andy.

"Fever. And he gave me damned good advice."

"Here!" I protested. "Old man, remember you're in a civilized country now!" But nobody seemed to hear me.

"He told me about those Dutchmen. Offered good money, they did, and caught their suckers; but getting the money, or getting away after they got you, was something else again. Country no white man could live through and they owned all the boats. They worked you till the fever picked your bones and shipped you out feet first. No, thanks! Not any for Gus Hardy," he said; adding serenely, "Logan."

"Can I call you Gus?" begged Andy.

"You bet!" said Gus Hardy, and took that freckled imp by the neck and shook him as if he were a puppy.

And Andy liked it! He wriggled and kicked and rolled off the davenport and sat grinning up at Gus Hardy like a puppy adoring his master.

"Andrew," said Mrs. McAllister, "you mustn't annoy Mr. Hogan."

"Logan," I corrected.

"So that's why I didn't go far up the Amazon. I drifted over into Colombia and got a job with a mining company, and after that I hooked up with this outfit in Guatemala. That's how you lost track of me. Buck," he said critically, "you're living too soft. You're getting fat."

Now that wasn't tactful, was it? Or necessary. I was just thinking that he showed great presence of mind in shifting the scene of his adventures to familiar ground, but this was carrying realism too far.

Said Mrs. McAllister, "Oh, Mr. Hogan—"

"Logan," I said, and then I had to breathe and let my front stick out again.

"—do tell us about Central America! Every winter we look at folders, and last winter we almost went: Havana, and Puerto Barrios, and Puerto Limon, and the Canal," she said, making such heavy weather of the names that I, having heard Gus Hardy pronounce them, shuddered. "Tell me, are they as heavenly as they sound?

Palms," she chanted, "and eternal summer, and maybe we'd run into a revolution."

Maybe that's where Andy got his bloodthirsty disposition. I, Howard Pressley, would have choked rather than laugh in Mrs. J. F. McAllister's face, but Gus Hardy openly grinned. She stopped talking and waited meekly for him to speak.

"No, ma'am. Not exactly heavenly. Havana's all right if you can stand high prices, but Barrios and Limon, they're hot and they're dirty and you'll see more beggars than revolutionists. Anyway, I hope so. A revolution ain't always as funny as it sounds."

"Oh, Mr. Hogan—"

"Logan," I said.

"—have you been in one?"

"No longer than it took me to get out," said Gus Hardy.

It was all wrong. I had brought him that he might show them visions; and there he sat, holding the center of the stage, his laconic phrases stripping every shred of glamour from the things he had seen.

"No, ma'am," he said; "fever and dirt and homesickness ain't exactly my idea of heaven."

I tried to put him on the track. "Tell them about the ruins at Quirigua," I prompted, "and the old empire of the Mayas."

I thought I spoke those exotic words with almost his own fluid curling crispness, conjuring up—before my own eyes, at least—the dank green shadows of banana groves with bronzed white men riding through them, a switch-engine clanking somewhere, and somewhere the lazy thwack of a machete. The jungle, blind and malignant and invincible; and here, steeped in the hot stillness of centuries, the ruins of a lost and forgotten civilization. Those great stone pillars, carved with grotesque symbols, meaning—what? And the images of kings. Huge idols crouching in the stealthily springing undergrowth, half frog, half tiger, grinning. The jungle, waiting to swallow the things men do.

But Gus Hardy, gazing moodily about the room, did not seem to hear.

I PROTESTED AGAIN, "Surely there's more to the tropics than fever and dirt and homesickness!" And his eyes came with somber irony back to mine.

"Yes," he said, "there's work. And when work's done you can get drunk, or play poker with a gang of homesick hardshells. Romantic, ain't it?"

"The way you tell it," I said with biting sarcasm. "But the atmosphere, the background, man! The sense of immense antiquity, of space and color, of—of—"

Mrs. McAllister said gently, addressing Gus Hardy, "Howard has the romantic mind."

Imagine that. The romantic mind—me! You'd have thought it was I who had spoken rhapsodically of palms and revolutions and eternal summer!

I said with dignity, "Well, I guess Hardy doesn't find it quite so bald as he makes it sound. He's been away a couple of months and he can't wait to get back. On his way back now—as fast as he can travel."

"Truly?" said Martha, looking at Gus Hardy.

He shrugged his shoulders. " 'They all come back,' " he said. "That's what we say down there: 'They all come back.' "

"You like it?"

"I hate it," said Gus Hardy. "That is, I know I hate it. Homesick, every man jack of 'em, having pipe dreams about getting enough money to come home and live in the States. 'God's country,' " he murmured with a faint, one-sided, deprecatory grin.

There was something disarming and appealing about the fellow. I had to remind myself that not three hours ago I had seen him thrown off a train.

"Quite a few of us manage to live here and make our money as we go along," I said coldly.

"Oh, sure! That's only the way we string ourselves. We know well enough we don't fit. We don't even try to keep money when we get it. Look at me—making good money, off and on, ever since I was eighteen; and—"

He was inviting them to consider the case of Gus Hardy, hobo; not content with wrecking the character I had given him—what with unblushing profanity and references to the dissolute pastimes of his kind—now he had forgotten who he was supposed to be. I leaped in.

"By the way, old man—"

"—and what do I do with it? Play poker with it. Buy liquor with it. Spend it like a kid the minute I hit civilization. Why, I only meant to stop a few days in New York—"

It was Andy who derailed the train of revelation, demanding: "Gus, will you teach me to play poker? Will you, Gus? I know the names of all the cards. I could learn easy. I—"

"Andrew!" exclaimed his mother.

"Git out!" laughed Gus Hardy, and rumpled Andy's hair. "A young squirt like you talkin' about poker! When you're twenty-one I'll teach you."

"You goin' to live here?" cried Andy eagerly.

"Well," said Gus Hardy, "how old are you now? Eleven? I'll be back in about ten years. You remind me, will you?"

"Andrew, bedtime!"

She was properly firm. Andy went out, dragging his feet, kicking a rug before him. In the hall he turned.

"Gus," he appealed, "now that's a promise!"

"It's a promise," affirmed Gus Hardy, and laughed, and quickly crossed himself and kissed his thumb and blew the kiss heavenward; and suddenly was grave again, that moody, far-away look dropping like a shadow on his brown face.

"Buck," he said, "reckon we'd better drift?"

I give you my word that it seemed natural for him to call me Buck, natural for him to be here, like a wanderer returned, in Martha McAllister's house. Yes, my imaginary long-lost chum was too life-like by half.

"Perhaps we'd better," I agreed, rising with alacrity.

Mrs. McAllister and Martha spoke in the same breath and were still talking when I got through. "But, my dear man, you've only just come!" and "Don't be silly! We've heard Hardy Logan, and Hardy Logan, and Hardy Logan for ages, and now we've got him you're not going to take him away so soon!"

I tried to hoist Gus Hardy with my eyes, but the scoundrel had taken up Martha's guitar and sat absently fingering the strings.

"It's late," I protested. "We only dropped in for a minute."

"You made a great impression on Andrew," said Mrs. McAllister, "Mr. Hogan."

"Logan," I corrected feebly.

"He's a fine kid," said Gus Hardy.

What could I do? I sat down again. "I see you still play the guitar, Gus," I said.

"I always thought," he said, "some day I'd have a kid like that. A regular young Gringo, freckled and pug-nosed and popping out all over with questions."

"Play something, Gus," I urged.

"And a house like this, on a street like this."

"Why not?" said Martha, too courteous.

He would have told her why not; I saw it in his eye and in the thoughtful tightening of one corner of his mouth.

With hectic heartiness I broke in, "Sell you one any time, old man. Got several on my list. But how long could you stand being tied to a house?"

He was lifting his hand from the strings and setting it down again, so that they whispered dolorously from chord to chord under his palm.

"Yeah," he said, nodding, "that's so."

"It gets in your blood—the tropics," I explained. "Gus was just saying a while ago that he could never stay put any more. Gets restless. Gets homesick sitting on his own front porch. Too dull, too tight and settled for him—after a country where you do as you please and nobody cares. Eh, old man?"

"Nobody," said Gus Hardy, that faint ironic grin tightening one corner of his mouth.

"Not enough room outdoors, nor enough stars in the sky. And the sun goes down too slow; and something happens, some little thing. Tell them about the woman singing," I said, remembering. "Beautiful, of course?"

"No," said Gus Hardy. "She was fat and greasy, but she could sing. They all can, those folks."

Absently he touched a light bass note, and then a deeper one; snapped a finger down on a fret, slurring it, and plucked the treble strings in an odd provocative rhythm.

Looking at Mrs. McAllister he said gravely, "This is a circus for me. I'll remember it, many's the time."

"We hope you will," said our hostess, "Mr. Hogan."

"Logan," I said mechanically. "Play something, Gus!"

"The woman sang," prompted Martha.

"I don't know if I can explain it," said Gus Hardy. "She was the cook in a Mexican restaurant, way out Broadway, you know. I got to hanging around there after my money gave out, because it was cheap. No, that ain't the truth. I was hungry for Spanish—everybody talking English all the time, and always in a hurry. Hungry for something that reminded me of the hot country."

"You said you hated it," said Martha.

"No, ma'am. I said I knew I hated it. But you can't always remember what you know," he said, and was silent, his eyes appealing to her for understanding. You'd have thought I was hardly among those present.

"You were telling us about the song of the cook," I said.

"Well, I had a big time for a while. Lots of friends while I was spending, but after that I—got lonesome. Walked around trying to find a place that felt like outdoors, and I saw this Mexican joint. Got to hanging around there, spinning yarns with the owner—from Durango he was, and homesick too. A fat guy named Murgia. And this woman used to sing.

"One song she liked—I've heard it many a time out in the hills. At night, the stars burning four times as close as they do here, and the mountains big and dark, and off yonder the native women singing. Like this."

He hummed, his brown fingers touching that staccato measure

with the blurred bass. He hummed; and you felt the loneliness and heard, far off, the native women singing.

"Made me remember," he said, looking at Martha. "The old gang's out there now, plugging away, taming the country God forgot to finish. Mountains as far as you can see, the sun hot and the air thin and cold." He stopped, groping for words; with irony he grinned and gave over the effort and set down the guitar. "So I hit out," he said. "Reasonable, ain't it?"

"Sing it!" said Martha.

Still I didn't see what the fellow was doing. I only had an uncertain, childish wish to be disagreeable.

"Yes," I said, "sing it! It must be wonderful."

Simply, without reluctance or apology, he took up the guitar again. He sang almost under his breath—looking at Martha.

Odd, how that melody took hold of you. It was pitched in a plaintive unfinished key—a minor I believe they call it—and it sounded wistful and hopeless. Somehow it told us things Gus Hardy had no words to say. Age-old, ineffable sadness; mountains heaped under a great star-sprinkled sky, and a strange, wild, simple people that lived on, bewildered, after their ancient world was dead. I wanted to be near to Martha to take her hand; but she was looking at Gus Hardy. Her lips were parted and her eyes absorbed, listening.

Then, then I knew what he had done. I had brought him here that he might show them visions; and he had shown them instead, shamelessly and without reserve, himself—brown and hard and wistful and appealing, a vagabond with the glamour of far countries on him. I knew how sleek and dull I looked beside him. I, Howard Pressley, dealt in my little city lots; his were the jungles and the mountains and wide plateaus in the sky. His voice deepened and softened and died away on that strange unfinished note.

"Very nice!" I said, and myself was shocked at the harshness of the sound.

"Sh!" said Martha, for his fingers were still plucking at the strings, running up a little golden interlude.

CHAPTER IV

Yes, now i knew that sharp hot thing that twisted in me. It was rage. What right had she to look at him like that? And he sang to her. As if I were a stuffed figure, sitting there—as if he were alone with her in some star-shining stillness, he looked into her eyes and sang. It wasn't decent. Americans don't make love that way.

You saw a high-walled garden and a lover at his lady's window. A garden very far from Milo, Indiana; a lover who sang though he knew the night might well have eyes of death; sang as a bird sings, softly, but with a throb that was like tears in your throat. The red coal of rage melted within me. I wanted something, something great and sweet and wild and forever unattainable; and I had a crazy impulse to laugh—feeling the absurdity of great longings in that comfortable, well-furnished room.

I tell you, a fellow that can sing like that ought to be restrained by law. I was glad when he stopped. "Bravo!" I said.

You know the startled feeling you have when you speak aloud in an empty room? It was like that. Martha looked at me, a queer, vague, misty look; Gus Hardy sat with his brown hands listless on the guitar; Mrs. McAllister sighed and took up her sewing or knitting or embroidery or whatever it was, and nobody said a word.

Briskly, trying to break that inertia, I looked at my watch, and rose, saying, "By Jove! I'd no idea it was so late," though I knew perfectly well.

Gus Hardy got up and stood looking about him, for his hat, I supposed, forgetting that we had come bare-headed. I reminded him; he only shook his head, smiling that faint one-sided smile.

"You'll come often while you're here," Martha commanded him.

Gus Hardy looked at me.

"He insists he has to hit the trail tomorrow," I said.

Gus Hardy bowed, murmured "Good night, ma'am. Good night, Miss Martha. Much pleasure," and marched out.

"Ha, Ha," I said lightly, to cover the crude abruptness of his exit, "quaint fellow, old Gus. This sort of thing's a little out of his line."

But the atmosphere absorbed that effort like a sponge, leaving me futile and fat and dull, my actual presence less vivid than the knowledge that Gus Hardy had been there. Under the hall lamp I saw Martha's eyes still full of the mist of dreams.

"Martha—"

"Yes?" she whispered, gazing into the darkness that had swallowed him.

"I think I'd better tell you."

Her eyes cleared and cooled and came to me.

"He's just a hobo. A vagabond. I picked him up when they kicked him off the train. Out of the gutter," I said, savagely glad to have it out and smash the glamour that incased him. "He seemed an amusing sort of fellow so I dressed him up and fed him. I don't know why I brought him here. That's all."

I stood, you might say, with my head bared to the lightning, but nothing struck.

"I don't know the man from Adam," I said, sinking my teeth into the words. I had little practice being savage in those days and there was intoxication in it. "He's told us what he is. A waster. A gambler. A ne'er-do-well. But he's seen things and done things and the world's a big place to him. Big," I said, and borrowed a gesture from Gus Hardy, "do you understand? Big!"

"I don't care," said Martha; "I think he's nice. You can tell it by his eyes. He looks at you just like a sweet little boy, lost and homesick and so grateful."

"Eyes!" I raged. "My goodness, woman, didn't you hear a word I said?"

"Oh, yes. Ed Willis told me you—picked him up."

Imagine that! Knowing all the time, and pretending to remember all about a non-existent Hardy Logan. I don't know which enraged me more, the officiousness of Ed Willis or the duplicity of the woman.

"Oh!" I said; which hardly covered the case.

"It seemed a funny thing for you to do," she said with gentle, unflattering emphasis. "I thought at first he really was an old friend of yours. I couldn't imagine your doing it for a perfect stranger—and it didn't help to boom Milo a bit, did it?"

And while I struggled with that she spoke again, gazing into the darkness.

"Howard, imagine," she murmured, "living like that! Always alone, and lonely, nothing to look forward to, nobody that cares. Homesick for a home that isn't anywhere, just drifting on and on— I never thought how it would be. It meant so much to him, being here in a nice American home. Did you see him, just looking and looking, storing up every little thing to remember?"

"He was looking for his hat," I muttered.

"Howard," she said, "must he really go away tomorrow? Can't you find something for him to do?"

Well, I mean, imagine that if you can.

The soft air of June came through the open door, a breath from wide starry spaces and the good smell of growing things, and showed me the feeble uselessness of rage. It had always been like this. It would always be like this. She was a woman; she was like a lovely child, content to live between four walls. I had brought her visions and she had seen only a lean brown face and wistful eyes. Lonely! I laughed, not mirthfully. Even now the odor of honeysuckle can make me somehow sad.

"Lonely," I said, "lonely! The worst loneliness of all is to bring you my thoughts and feelings and see them flatten out and wither into nothing. Time after time. I never seem to learn."

"But you get excited about such funny things," said Martha. "Howard, I've been thinking—"

Gus Hardy spoke only once on the way back to the hotel, to ask if we had no speed laws in Milo; and I saw then that I was ripping along Madison Avenue at fifty miles an hour— I, president of the Live Wire Club, that stood for law and order if it stood for anything.

Again, while he was divesting himself of his borrowed splendor, he rose briefly from the depths of his moody silence:

"Sorry I had to run out on your bug-hunter yarn. Thought I'd better play safe. Oh, I could have talked like a bug hunter for a little while, but sooner or later I'd be sure to slip."

"It doesn't matter," I told him listlessly. "It didn't get over anyway. I had to tell them who you were."

After a time I became aware that he was sitting with his shirt half off, staring at one spot on the rug.

"Well," I inquired, "got any plans, old man?"

"Buck," he demanded, "is that your girl?"

Emptying my pockets, I dropped into a drawer a neat but expensive ring. "No," I said.

Silence, and yet more silence. I lighted a cigarette and yawned. Gus Hardy looked up, and then I saw how his blue eyes were shining with the light of dreams.

"Buck," he said softly, "old-timer, I like this town."

Yes, it's a good little town, Milo. It is not Bagdad. No man is born a caliph, to thrust his hand untouched into the wheels of another's destiny. But it's a good town. It grows, already its dignity is beyond the use of slogans. You remember the electric sign at the station that used to proclaim to the public that "Milo Offers More"? It just says "Milo" now.

I saw it afterward and had to laugh, remembering. I laughed again when I saw Gus Hardy. He's not so lean as he was, and his sunburn is lighter and runs clear up to his hair; he plays golf bareheaded, he tells me. It seemed odd to think that I myself used to take such chances with the sun.

I asked him if he remembered that song, and he said "What song?"

I hummed a few notes of it, and he remembered. While he was thumping the piano and trying to sing it Martha came into the room. She is still pretty, if you like that placid, fair, young-matronly type; and she introduced me to a pug-nosed, freckled young Hardy who swarmed all over me and buried me under an avalanche of questions, calling me Uncle Buck, while Gus beamed complacently over his shoulder and said "h'm, h'm" for the words he had forgotten.

I got restless listening. Milo's a good little town, but too—you know—too tight and settled. The people are too much the same and there isn't enough room outdoors. There's an old Spaniard on the western slope of the Andes, now, who knows the use of quiet days.

His house is in a saddle of the seaward ridge. Westward the dim blue arch of the Pacific climbs; eastward the dark green chasm of the Zorro Valley fades into the blue of the great inland ranges, reaching away into the silver ageless peace of ice and snow. A man's country, that. They think in leagues instead of city blocks, and neighbors are not so many but that every stranger is a friend. Come weary to any man's door and his house is yours.

A rare old fellow is this Fernandez del Valle; and he has a daughter, and she sings.

The stars come very close about that hacienda in the hills; in the courtyard are flowers and a fountain that lulls you with soft monotony, and the girl sings. Her eyes are age-old mystery and the melting flame of youth; and her voice touches you with longing, great and sweet and wild and forever unattainable. Fancy Gus Hardy trying to sing that song!

" 'Let's eat where ther hain't no durn women. Cigarette smoke makes me sick,' said Tell Binkley, as he took a tornado insurance prospect to lunch."

—Abe Martin's BROADCAST

Probably it was inevitable that the college student of the 'twenties came in for the greatest body of criticism—and he found that prominence quite to his taste (unless my memory fails me). Here he is, as seen in retrospect by himself. It is an alumnus of Indiana University who speaks; the recipient of a degree in law, he was, but he strayed far from the haunts of the Oyer and Terminer, of the Writ and the Tort. Probably he has not used the full appellation since, but the diploma awarded to him by a tolerant—even an admiring—alma mater was engrossed

HOAGLAND HOWARD CARMICHAEL

Here I must again abandon discreet anonymity and resort to the first person. For I, the commentator, underwent Education in the same era as Mr. Carmichael (though on a different campus), and I feel that the historical record must be kept straight, even if I must violate my characteristic modesty to straighten it.

Either the years have inflamed the tone of Carmichael's rose-tinted glasses or life on the Wabash College campus in the 'twenties was a bit less exotic than that at Indiana University, down the Monon. Maybe the Jordan River ran stronger waters than did Sugar Crick in those days, maybe it was only the greater proximity of Brown County and its moonshine industry; in either case, college days at Bloomington, as recorded in Carmichael's reminiscences, seem to have been several shades gaudier than they were elsewhere in the Hoosier state. Almost every campus then harbored its quota of the deliberately, if mildly, odd who strove to live up to the standards which they believed were expected of The Lost Generation. But around the Book Nook, just off the Indiana University campus, I remember noting as an occasional visitor that there did seem to be more than a standard quota of strollers among the painted clouds. If life was livelier there, if sanity was at a greater premium, the responsible factor was probably the genius of Hoagy Carmichael's music and the fey philosophy of the Bent Eagles—and in Carmichael's brilliant maturity one cannot help but wonder if it was not he, rather than his revered friend Moenkhaus, who was actually the moving force behind the Eagles?

In spite of the possible inflations of memory, much of Carmichael's little book reads like gospel to one who trifled in halls of learning circa 1920–1925. All collegians in Indiana admired the music of great, high-brown, Reg Duval and his Indianapolis orchestra and of Jordan's deeper brunette band from Louisville. (Jordan was "Louisville Style" jazz and that, for a brief period, was as significant as "Chicago" or "tailgate" or the other categories about which the pseudo-cognoscenti of jazz still speak with hushed reverence.) We all flocked to hear the Wolverines, when the opportunity offered, and the Original Dixieland, and the Syncopating Five, and the Mound City Blue Blowers. Carmichael not only heard their music, he absorbed it— along with a law course.

But he didn't function as a lawyer; instead he has been, in a pleasantly varied career, a radio and recording artist, a writer of movie scripts, an actor and always a composer—of Star Dust, Rockin' Chair, Lazybones, Two Sleepy People, Georgia On My Mind, Hong Kong Blues and dozens of others—most of them tremendously successful.

His is a screwy account of a screwy era, as witness this following scene on the Indiana campus, complete with Book Nook inmates, from Hoagy Carmichael's

The Stardust Road

Have you ever seen the big maples? The trunks are sometimes three feet in diameter and they shoot straight up, barren of branches, for some forty or fifty feet and then they spread out into a huge umbrella of limbs and foliage. Hundreds of these and an equal number of large beech trees shade the Indiana campus. For many years there were no walks—just natural paths winding among the trees. Several of these led to a street that borders the campus on the east, called Sorority Row, and here is where the quartets and jazz bands serenaded at night.

A low stone wall borders the campus on the south. This is the "spooning wall" and is usually dotted by quiet indiscernible couples late at night who have stopped there on the way home from the Book Nook or a picture show. To the north of the campus, bounding Dunn Meadows and the old athletic fields, runs the famous Jordan River. Famous because of its high-sounding name and yet its waters—a foot deep in floodtime—barely trickle during the dog days of August. But never let it be said that this jaded stream produced nothing. It did. Crustaceans. Crawdads I mean, by the thousands. We kids were not barefoot boys with rod and reel, we were barefoot boys with tin can for scooping them up. Fishing for crawdads is an art. It's like catching a fly with your hand and almost as difficult. Indiana Avenue is the other boundary and thereon stands the Book Nook.

The Book Nook was a little house originally. It was situated hard by the campus on Indiana Avenue and it really was a book store. Gradually it had grown and been added to until it seated a hundred or so coke-guzzling, book-laden, high-spirited students. There new tunes were heard and praised; lengthy discussions were started and never quite finished. There the first steps of the toddle were taken and fitted to our new rhythm. Dates were made and hopes were born. Jordan's band continued playing for the local dances and sometimes they could be prevailed upon to stay over and play for a Sunday afternoon session in the Book Nook. *"Shake it and break it, and hang it on the wall"*—that was the Sunday ritual.

Let me take you gently by the hand and lead you into the Book Nook on a normal afternoon. That little guy, over there, flogging the piano—that could be me. The one with the long nose and the exerted purple face. And the large freckled youth with the saxophone, the one making those long blue notes, that's Batty De Marcus. The high-cheekboned unshaved youth perched yonder in a booth, that's Moenkhaus, composing a poem, perhaps, for we hear his weird coyote-howl laugh even above our efforts.

A few couples are seated in booths at the far side and Pete Costas, the proprietor, is punctuating his English with Greek epithets because Klondike Tucker, the Negro chef, has balled up an order.

Wad Allen is curved into a seat across from Monk, and the thing he toys with, stroking sensuously, is a piece of lemon meringue pie. All Bent Eagles love to pat a lemon meringue pie—though blueberry will serve in a pinch.

Those round yellow objects arising as the twilight creeps softly upon the scene? Why, those are grapefruit rinds hurled at me because my music has grown too sedate.

I dodge the grapefruit rinds and stop. Monk is going to read his creation. There is a moment of quiet. Quiet fraught with expectancy. Nerves too tight. Minds keyed to vistas beyond the horizons of so-called rational thought.

Monk reads:

> Blooters, thou knowest no Heaven
> Blooters, thou knowest only us
> Bugs, men, whores and fowls—
> They are the Children of Heaven.

There are wild yells. Wad Allen shrieks his appreciation. I hear in my ear a voice. The voice of a non-Bent Eagle. It is a plaintive voice, timid with query.

"What does it mean?"

I turn and smile pityingly. This poor guy doesn't know what those immortal lines convey.

"It means just what it says," I hear Wad Allen say. "Just *exactly* what it says."

That's normal.

It is also normal for the Book Nook to be nearly deserted and for Moenkhaus and Wad Allen and myself, and Harry Hostetter, too, to be there. We talk of things we are puzzled about. We confess bewilderment and doubts and fears and we never laugh at each other. We wonder where we are going.

"I'm going to be a lawyer," I say firmly. "Jazz is okay, but—"

Harry interrupts. "Thanksgiving comes but once a dozen," he says, looking at Monk. "But what we call jazz comes but once."

"It originated in the South," Wad says. "Buddy Bolden blew hot jazz for the Creole dances. They get most of the credit for it."

"Jazz" meant "play it faster." Buddy put a hat over the bell of his horn to get fuzzy effects and Freddie Kepet, another Creole, brought his band to the Columbia Theatre in New York about 1911 and showed 'em how to use a mute. They liked their music more in keeping with their climate though—slow and raspy.

"I hear they put Buddy in an asylum," I say and I hope with all my heart that they didn't take his horn away from him. "Law is the best."

"Buddy Bolden, the Original Creole Band, and the Original Dixie-land Band were preceded by at least two people I've heard of," Harry says. "One was blind Tom Harney. He was a sort of prodigy on the piano, around Lexington and Louisville. . . . That was back in the eighties and early nineties . . . he was feeble-minded too. He played his real hot licks as an introduction to his concert. He was great, but he wasn't original except when he played it wrong—but, oh, so right—as an attention rouser."

"So what?" Monk says lazily. "Hogwash isn't any too bright, and he plays them all wrong. As a matter of fact," he admits modestly, "I am perhaps the greatest piano player who ever fell off the Matter-horn."

I like jazz . . . kinda like law too . . . like people. . . .

"I'm wondering what Buddy Bolden had in his brain when he blew the introduction to what is now *Tiger Rag*?" I say.

Monk yawns. "Who cares? I'm going to die any day now."

And he did die. Just a year before Bix, also, strangely, the same year Buddy Bolden, now an old man, finally went to the place where nobody's crazy.

They got Buddy, but they never got us. A lot of people listened to us and were dubious and we knew it. But they never *proved* we were nuts.

We like to walk along the streets and see people watering their lawns and we like to hear the rumble of the ice wagon and the querulous barking of a familiar dog. These sounds are right. We *know* they are right and perhaps they make us afraid.

Certainly, we were a little afraid one night several years later in New Castle, Indiana. Our college band was at its peak and we were very full of our music and of ourselves. It got around to Christmas— the third Christmas for my last college band. The real band "Carmichael's Syringe Orchestra," we called it.

"Alas," Wad Allen says, "a herd of elephants are singing Christmas carols below our window."

None of us laughed, but we listened.

We have just played a dance. It is two o'clock in the morning and Wad has just come in. Somebody pulls the sliding doors in the dingy hotel room exposing an even dingier room, drab and cold.

There on a little table is a Christmas tree, dilapidated and maimed. One forlorn candle burning at the top of its scraggly branches. We stand looking at this little scrub and I finally muster all my courage to speak in an exaggeratedly deep voice.

"Well, well, look what we have here! Something for little Waddie Allen—'cause he's been a good little boy. And here's a surprise for Artie Baker. . . ."

A potato grater for Wad. A piece of rope for Art Baker. Someone gets a funnel. It is too much for us. No one yells an inanity. No one speaks. We look at the tree and the single candle shimmers and flickers and is reflected in the tears that stand, suddenly, in our eyes. We stand there, six little children of jazz, brave in long pants, and then the candle sputters out and we are afraid.

After a moment someone says something and we laugh. A little laugh.

Hoagland, these guys are your friends . . . they are the guys you want to play for. They are the ones who make you play. There's Wad, and Bridge Abrams, and the others, who played the dance along with you, and even though you aren't going to follow the beat of hot sweet sound, even though you're going to be a lawyer with solid fees and solid arguments, they're with you, in this room, on Christmas night and somehow you aren't lonely. But they come back to you Christmases; always they come back, and other times too, they are with you.

The band, the college band—one for all and all for one—and it wasn't corny.

Moonlight nights you hear the ghostly laughter, the silver-gleaming sound, the good talk. Rainy nights you remember. Fall nights you recall.

After education at the college level began in Indiana there followed, in order, debating societies, fraternities, mandolin clubs, co-eds, football teams, alumni associations and—inevitably—alumni banquets.

Comes an author, fervent and valuable alumnus of Purdue, who obviously knew all there was to know about these occasions upon which alumni gathered, and gather, and tells about it with cold and almost brutal frankness.

GEORGE ADE

describes in lucid detail

The Night Given Over to Revelry

ALL THOSE who had Done Time at a certain endowed Institution for shaping and polishing Highbrows had to close in once a Year for a Banquet. They called it a Banquet because it would have been a Joke to call it a Dinner.

The Invitations looked like real Type-Writing and called upon all Loyal Sons of Old Bohunkus to dig up 3 Sesterces and get ready for a Big Night.

To insure a Riot of spontaneous Gaiety the following Organization was effected:

Committee on Invitation.
Committee on Reception.
Committee on Lights and Music.
Committee on Speakers.
Committee on Decorations.
Committee on Police Protection.
Committee on First Aid to Injured.
Committee on Maynew.
Committee on Liquid Nourishment.

Each Committee held numerous Meetings, at the Call of the Chairman, and discussed the impending Festivities with that solemn regard for piffling Detail which marked the Peace Conference at The Hague.

The Frolic was to be perpetrated at a Hotel famous for the number of Electric Lights.

The Hour was to be 6:30, Sharp, so that by 6:45, four old Grads, with variegated Belshazzars, were massed together in the Egyptian Room trying to fix the Date on which Doctor Milo Lobsquosset became Emeritus Professor of Saracenic Phlobotomy.

Along about 7:30, a Sub-Committee wearing Satin Badges was sent downstairs to round up some recent Alumni who were trying to get a Running Start, and at 7:45 a second Detachment was sent out to find the Rescue Party.

Finally at 8 o'clock the glad Throng moved into the Main Banquet Hall, which was a snug Apartment about the size of the Mammoth Cave of Kentucky, done in Gold and various shades of Pink, to approximate the Chambermaid's Dream of Paradise. The style of Ornamentation was that which precipitated the French Revolution.

Beside each Plate was a blond Decoction named in honor of the Martini Rifle, which is guaranteed to kill at a Distance of 2,000 Yards. The compounding had been done in a Churn early that morning and the Temperature was that of the Room, in compliance with the Dictates of Fashion.

Those who partook of the Hemlock were given Courage to battle with the Oysters. These came in Sextettes, wearing a slight Ptomaine Pallor. On the 20th Proximo they had said good-bye to their Friends in Baltimore and for Hours they had been lying naked and choked with thirst in their little Canoes and now they were to enter the great Unknown, without pity from the Votaries of Pleasure.

Luckily the Consomme was not hot enough to scald the Thumbs of the jovial Stevedores who had been brought in as Extras, so the Feast proceeded merrily, many of the Participants devoting their spare Moments to bobbing for Olives or pulling the Twine out of the Celery.

The Fish had a French Name, having been in the Cold Storage Bastile for so long. Each Portion wore a heavy Suit of Armor, was surrounded by Library Paste and served as a Tee for two Golf Balls billed as Pommes de Terre.

It was a regular Ban-quet, so, there was no getting away from Filet de Biff aux Champignons. It was brought on merely to show what an American Cook with a Lumber-Camp Training could do to a plain slice of Steer after reading a Book written by a Chef.

Next, in accordance with honored Tradition, a half-melted Snow-ball impregnated with Eau de Quinine.

Just about the time that the White Vinegar gave way to the Ani-line Dye, a nut headed Swozzie, who could get into Matteawan without Credentials, moved down the Line of Distinguished Guests asking for Autographs. His Example was followed by 150 other Shropshires, so that for the next 30 Minutes the Festal Chamber re-sembled the Auditing Department of a large Mercantile Establish-ment.

During this Period, the Department of Geology in the University was honored by the appearance of a genuine petrified Quail. And the Head Lettuce carried the Personal Guarantee of the Goodyear Rub-ber Co.

Between the Rainbow Ice Cream and the Calcareous Fromage, a member of the class of '08, who could not Sing, arose and did so.

Then each Guest had to take a Tablespoonful of Café Noir and two Cigars selected by a former Student who had promised his Mother never to use Tobacco.

It was now after 10 o'clock and time to go Home. Those who had started to tune up along in the Afternoon were dying on the Vine. Others, who had tried to catch even on the $3 Ticket, felt as if they had been loaded with Pig Iron. Up at the Long Table enough Speakers to supply a Chautauqua Circuit were feeling of themselves to make sure that the Manuscript had not been lost. Each thought that he was the Orator of the Evening.

The Committee had put on the Toast Program every one who might possibly take Offense at not being Asked.

Also they had selected as Toastmaster a beaming Broncho whose Vocal Chords were made of seasoned Moose-Hide and who remembered all the black-face Gravy that Billy Rice used to lam across to Lew Benedict when Niblo's Garden was first opened.

After every 30-minute Address he would spend ten minutes in polite kidding of the Last Speaker and then another 10 Minutes in climbing a Mountain Height from which to present the Next Speaker.

Along about Midnight the Cowards and Quitters began crawling out of Side Doors, but most of the Loyal Sons of Old Bohunkus propped themselves up and tried to be Game.

Before 1 o'clock a Member of the Faculty put them on the Ropes with 40 Minutes on projected Changes in the Curriculum.

At 1:30 the Toastmaster was making Speech No. 8 and getting ready to spring the Oldest Living Graduate.

Protected by all the Gray Hair that was left to him, he began to Reminisce, going back to the Days when it was considered a Great Lark to put a Cow in the Chapel.

The Toastmaster arrived home at 3 A.M. and aroused his Wife to tell her it had been a Great Success.

MORAL: If they were paid $3 a Head to stand for it, no one would attend.

Muncie has given the world many distinguished products other than automobile parts and glass fruit jars: Emily Kimbrough for one, and Muncie should be proud of her! Of course she left Muncie for Chicago at an early age but she is still a Hoosier, and she calls attention to that distinction at every opportunity.

EMILY KIMBROUGH

How Dear to My Heart

ONE OF THE INCIDENTAL THINGS which had contributed to Daddy's financial overload was the box of dirt from Grandmother Wiles, but Mother did not know about that for years.

Grandmother Wiles was an imperious and an impulsive woman, and she and my Grandfather lived in Indianapolis. *He* was the gentlest of men, Daniel Hough Wiles; handsome, too, with thick, startlingly white hair when I knew him, and deep-set blue eyes which humor almost always lighted. He suffered from asthma, and the only time I ever saw him show a sign of ill humor was when anyone asked him how he felt, and even then it was the expression which exasperated him.

"I *feel* with my fingers, of course," he would snap. "How else *would* I feel?"

Or if he were too spent with coughing to be able to speak, he would wriggle his fingers impatiently at the offender, his mild, deep eyes cold.

"I *am* better, or I *am* worse," he taught me very clearly. "But that is *not* how I *feel*."

Mildness in Grandmother Wiles, however, was as infrequent as was his departure from it. Not that she was disagreeable; she had a lusty and infectious enjoyment of nearly everything, but she was volatile and violent. Ideas came to her more quickly than to most people, and the period of time between receiving and acting upon them was almost imperceptible.

When Mother was growing up and attending the Girls' Classical School, they lived on Delaware Street, and their neighbors were the Benjamin Harrisons. The gardens joined, I think, and one Christmas the two families made a little sentimental exchange of keys to the gate which separated them. Mother, even in reminiscence, always grew a little apprehensive over the telling of a meeting at this gate, so that I may easily be inaccurate about the details. However, Mr. and Mrs. Harrison moved to Washington to live in the White House, when he became President, and the house next door stood empty. One Summer evening, Grandmother, who was a passionate gardener—she could not conceivably have been an indifferent anything—was watering her flower beds after sundown. Suddenly a key turned in the lock of the garden gate, and when it opened, President Harrison stood on the threshold. Astounded, Grandmother cried out, "Why, Benjamin!" and turned the hose full force in his face.

He was astounded, too, and staggered from the impact into the shrubbery, revealing Mrs. Harrison just behind him.

"And *Mary*," Grandmother called, her voice high with pleasure at such a surprise—and diverted the nozzle with a jerk to Mrs. Harrison's countenance.

The little greeting evidently did not diminish for a moment the friendship between the two families, because it was in the Winter of that same year that the Daniel Wiles gave an "evening reception with dancing" for the Benjamin Harrisons, again home from the White House.

About an hour before the "evening" was scheduled to begin, Grandmother sat at her bureau under the ministrations of the French hairdresser—and how he had found his way out to Indianapolis I do not know. He went from house to house to "do" the ladies. Grandmother had on, over her corset cover and petticoats, a short, white dimity dressing sacque. Under the top petticoat she had on—I would have known, even if the hairdresser didn't—her bustle. She wore one until she died in 1926; said it took away the sagged and swayback look women were apt to get and she liked the warmth of it, too.

But on the night of the reception she was too warm in it, and even in the sheer dimity dressing sacque. Not that she gradually became aware of this. She jumped to her feet as the Frenchman was twirling his iron preparatory to a dart on another curl, shook both hands above her head—her most characteristic gesture—until the heavy gold bracelet on each wrist was shaken down toward the elbow, and announced that the house was too hot. That was all she said, and that very minute she was gone from the room, the Frenchman left twirling his iron.

What she did was to go straight to the cellar and look at the furnace. Grandfather Wiles said later, benignly, that he didn't suppose she had ever looked at it before. Her answer was that you needed only one look to see that it was too hot. Even the door was yellow red, so she opened it with an iron bar standing near by, filled a pail of water from the spigot in the corner, and threw it over the white-hot coals. The explosion must have knocked her ten feet or more, but when she sat up, she didn't seem to be hurt and the fire looked much lower, so she went back upstairs to finish dressing.

Her bureau was tall, walnut, with extended little round shelves and many little drawers, their handles made of glass drops. The mirror in the center was full length, and that was where she saw herself as she prepared to sit down again for the hairdresser to go on with his work. He was in no condition to go on with it—struck dumb and still waving his curling iron, but in a sort of warding off motion at her—and it was this curious gesture that made her lean toward the full-length mirror to see if her appearance was what ailed him. It was, indeed. From head to foot she was as black as the coal in the bin—all except the top of her head. That, well back to the crown, looked as bare and shiny as a darning egg.

When she had bathed—or, rather, scrubbed—she found, too, that her eyebrows and eyelashes were gone. Nothing could be done about them, but she demanded impatiently that the hairdresser devise a "coiffure" which would cover the bald area, and be sharp about it. She and Mr. Wiles must receive their guests in half an hour.

They did, too, with President and Mrs. Harrison beside them, both somewhat dazed at her transformation. Grandmother was only exasperated at the Frenchman in spite of the superhuman work he had done. She had had to find her smelling-salts for him. He had said he felt faint.

She was impulsive, too, on the day when the Bishop came to call, and he must have been the one to tell it. Hurrying downstairs in a pleasantly nervous flurry when she was told that he was in the parlor, she tripped on the top step and fell the entire length of the stairway. She fell sitting, and struck the highly polished floor at the base with such force that she careened across it, together with a small prayer rug which she had encountered there. She only came to a stop well inside the parlor. The Bishop, after a momentary pause of surprise, hurried over to help her to her feet.

"I have never, Bishop Cunningham," she protested, as she took his hand and rose, "come downstairs that way before!"

"Iona, the baby daughter o' Mrs. Leghorn Tharp, president o' the Colonial Bridge Club, wuz seriously crushed when a stack of unwashed dishes toppled over on her."

—Abe Martin's BROADCAST

"One good thing about the present-day cost o' livin'—the feller that fergits his change don't lose half as much as he used to."

—Abe Martin's BROADCAST

"Lester Moots and wife have merged with her parents."

—Abe Martin's BROADCAST

"Alcoholic psychosis is nothin' more or less'n ole D.T.'s in a dinner suit."

—Abe Martin's BROADCAST

CHAPTER FOURTEEN

Indiana Outdoors

Most Indiana people just naturally didn't love Nature much until pretty well after the Civil War. Up to that time Nature—the birds, beasts, bugs (all "varmints" to the pioneer), and even the trees and grass—had competed with the settler for the benefits of harvesting or destroying his livestock, field crops and garden sass.

You don't notice the beauty of the red-winged blackbird when he's working on your wheat; a fox appears efficient but not graceful as he runs away with your hen; potato bugs have brilliant enamel on their backs but they play hell with potatoes; a tree looks better cut up on the woodpile than killing your garden with shade; grass is all right in the pasture but it takes hard work to get it out of the corn rows.

However, as the country settled and folks had more time and even the wildest districts got tamed down somewhat, some Hoosiers began to talk about Nature with the capital N. Probably it was town folks, who didn't know anything about it, who took the most interest at first.

Thoreau had started the cult of nature-loving in New England and Maurice Thompson was a practitioner in Indiana. Some of his early writing on the subject concerned itself mostly with the South he had known as a young man, but in 1885 he published By-Ways and Bird Notes—which was just the sort of thing to inspire the amateur bird-watcher—and the next year his Boys' Book of Sports came out. Its sections on woodcraft, nature study, hunting, fishing, and camping sounded exactly the proper tone to inspire not only boys but their fathers, uncles and maiden aunts with a desire to get back in the wilds and to glory in the wilderness which their grandfathers had learned to hate and to conquer. Many such books have been published since, most of them stemming direct from Thompson's.

About 1900 the cult came into its own and, along with it, well informed on wildlife and ready to promote its even greater popularity as a study, came

GENE STRATTON PORTER

Gene Stratton-Porter (that hyphenated form was her own rendering, upon occasion, of the more prosaic Mrs. Charles Darwin Porter, nee Gene Stratton) was certainly one of the most widely read of Indiana novelists. Her works—The Song of the Cardinal, Freckles, A Girl of the Limberlost, Laddie, The Harvester and a couple of dozen others only a little less marvelously successful—were based upon an abiding love for the outdoors and a remarkably comprehensive knowledge of the wild life which survived within the swampy confines of the Limberlost country of northeast central Indiana.

Hers was the sort of lore understandable to anyone who ever searched an abandoned apple orchard for spring mushrooms, peered at a nest of robin's eggs, or walked home with a wilting handful of spring beauties and bloodroot. But it was adorned, besides, with a sprinkling of scientific terminology, which gave the reader a sense of intellectual well-being—as if he had known all the time that skunk-cabbage is really Ictodes foetidus.

Upon this framework and with her beloved Limberlost as background, Mrs. Porter began, in middle life, to construct her novels. From the first they had phenomenal sales. In the second and third decades of the twentieth century they were read by the majority of the fiction audience; even today they are enjoyed by many who are, if not the most discerning, at least among the nicest of readers. What matter if Mrs. Porter's plots are simple to the level of the nursery school? if her characters speak a language to their human associates, to their bird and animal acquaintances and—endlessly—to themselves which would be either incomprehensible or doubt-inspiring to any resident of the Limberlost of their day or ours? if they all managed to cultivate a radiant innocence which carried into their middle age and which amounted, in our eyes, sometimes almost to idiocy? Her books were soundly instructive, generally, in the ever-interesting ways of the woods and fields and their inhabitants; they gave, and still give, pleasure to millions—and anyway some books must be written which one can give to one's great-aunts at Christmas and on birthdays!

Here we have an example of Mrs. Porter at her best, reporting her observation of one of the woodland friends—without romantic trimmings.

The Song of the Cardinal

HE DARTED THROUGH the orange orchard searching for slugs for his breakfast, and between whiles he rocked on the branches and sang over his message of encouragement to men. The song of the Cardinal was overflowing with joy, for this was his holiday, his playtime. The southern world was filled with brilliant sunshine, gaudy flowers, an abundance of fruit, myriads of insects, and never a thing to do except to bathe, feast, and be happy. No wonder his song was a prophecy of good cheer for the future, for happiness made up the whole of his past.

The Cardinal was only a yearling, yet his crest flared high, his beard was crisp and black, and he was a very prodigy in size and colouring. Fathers of his family that had accomplished many migrations appeared small beside him, and coats that had been shed season after season seemed dull compared with his. It was as if a pulsing heart of flame passed by when he came winging through the orchard.

Last season the Cardinal had pipped his shell, away to the north, in that paradise of the birds, the Limberlost. There thousands of acres of black marsh-muck stretch under summers' sun and winters' snows. There are darksome pools of murky water, bits of swale, and high morass. Giants of the forest reach skyward, or, coated with velvet slime, lie decaying in sun-flecked pools, while the underbrush is almost impenetrable.

The swamp resembles a big dining-table for the birds. Wild grape-vines clamber to the tops of the highest trees, spreading umbrella-wise over the branches, and their festooned floating trailers wave as silken fringe in the play of the wind. The birds loll in the shade, peel bark, gather dried curlers for nest material, and feast on the pungent fruit. They chatter in swarms over the wild-cherry trees, and overload their crops with red haws, wild plums, papaws, blackberries and mandrake. The alders around the edge draw flocks in search of berries, and the marsh grasses and weeds are weighted with seed hunters. The muck is alive with worms; and the whole swamp ablaze with flowers, whose colours and perfumes attract myriads of insects and butterflies.

Wild creepers flaunt their red and gold from the treetops, and the bumblebees and humming-birds make common cause in rifling the honey-laden trumpets. The air around the wild-plum and red-haw trees is vibrant with the beating wings of millions of wild bees, and the bee-birds feast to gluttony. The fetid odours of the swamp draw insects in swarms, and fly-catchers tumble and twist in air in pursuit of them.

Every hollow tree homes its colony of bats. Snakes sun on the bushes. The water folk leave trails of shining ripples in their wake as they cross the lagoons. Turtles waddle clumsily from the logs. Frogs take graceful leaps from pool to pool. Everything native to that section of the country—underground, creeping, or a-wing—can be found in the Limberlost; but above all it is the chosen habitation of the birds.

Dainty green warblers nest in its tree-tops, and red-eyed vireos choose a location below. It is the home of bell-birds, finches, and thrushes. There are flocks of blackbirds, grackles, and crows. Jays and catbirds quarrel constantly, and marsh-wrens keep up never-ending chatter. Orioles swing their pendent purses from the branches, and with the tanagers picnic on mulberries and insects. In the evening, night-hawks dart on silent wing; whippoorwills set up a plaintive cry that they continue far into the night; and owls revel in moonlight and rich hunting. At dawn, robins wake the echoes of each new day with the admonition, "Cheer up! Cheer up!" and a little later big black vultures go wheeling through cloudland or hang there, like frozen splashes, searching the Limberlost and the surrounding country for food. The boom of the bittern resounds all day, and above it the rasping scream of the blue heron, as he strikes terror to the hearts of frogdom; while the occasional cries of a lost loon, strayed from its flock in northern migration, fill the swamp with sounds of wailing.

Flashing through the tree-tops of the Limberlost there are birds whose colour is more brilliant than that of the gaudiest flower lifting its face to light and air. The lilies of the mire are not so white as the white herons that fish among them. The ripest spray of goldenrod is not so highly coloured as the burnished gold on the breast of the oriole that rocks on it. The jays are bluer than the calamus bed they wrangle above with throaty chatter. The finches are a finer purple than the ironwort. For every clump of foxfire flaming in the Limberlost, there is a cardinal glowing redder on a bush above it. These may not be more numerous than other birds, but their brilliant colouring and the fearless disposition that keep them forever in evidence make them seem so.

The Cardinal was hatched in a thicket of sweetbrier and blackberry. His father was a tough old widower of many experiences and variable temper. He was the biggest, most aggressive redbird in the Limberlost, and easily reigned king of his kind. Catbirds, king-birds, and shrikes gave him a wide berth, and not even the ever-quarrelsome jays plucked up enough courage to antagonize him. A few days after his latest bereavement, he saw a fine, plump young female; and she so filled his eye that he gave her no rest until she permitted his caresses, and carried the first twig to the wild rose. She was very proud to mate with the king of the Limberlost; and if deep in her heart she felt transient fears of her lordly master, she gave no sign, for she was a bird of goodly proportion and fine feather herself.

She chose her location with the eye of an artist, and the judgment of a nest builder of more experience. It would be difficult for snakes and squirrels to penetrate that briery thicket. The white berry blossoms scarcely had ceased to attract a swarm of insects before the sweets of the roses recalled them; by the time they had faded, luscious big berries ripened within reach and drew food hunters. She built with far more than ordinary care. It was a beautiful nest, not nearly so carelessly made as those of her kindred all through the swamp. There was a distinct attempt at a cup shape, and it really was neatly lined with dried blades of sweet marsh grass. But it was in the laying of her first egg that the queen cardinal forever distinguished herself. She was a fine healthy bird, full of love and happiness over her first venture in nest-building, and she so far surpassed herself on that occasion she had difficulty in convincing any one that she was responsible for the result.

Indeed, she was compelled to lift beak and wing against her mate in defense of this egg, for it was so unusually large that he could not be persuaded short of force that some sneak of the feathered tribe had not slipped in and deposited it in her absence. The king felt sure there was something wrong with the egg, and wanted to roll it from the nest; but the queen knew her own, and stoutly battled for its protection. She further increased their prospects by laying three others. After that the king made up his mind that she was a most remarkable bird, and went away pleasure-seeking; but the queen settled to brooding, a picture of joyous faith and contentment.

Through all the long days, when the heat became intense, and the king was none too thoughtful of her appetite or comfort, she nestled those four eggs against her breast and patiently waited. The big egg was her treasure. She gave it constant care. Many times in a day she turned it; and always against her breast there was the individual pressure that distinguished it from the others. It was the first to hatch, of course, and the queen felt that she had enough if all the others failed her; for this egg pipped with a resounding pip, and before the silky down was really dry on the big terra-cotta body, the young Cardinal arose and lustily demanded food.

The king came to see him and at once acknowledged subjugation. He was the father of many promising cardinals, yet he never had seen one like this. He set the Limberlost echoes rolling with his jubilant rejoicing. He unceasingly hunted for the ripest berries and seed. He stuffed that baby from morning until night, and never came with food that he did not find him standing a-top the others calling for more. The queen was just as proud of him and quite as foolish in her idolatry, but she kept tally and gave the remainder every other worm in turn. They were unusually fine babies, but what chance has merely a fine baby in a family that possesses a prodigy? The Cardinal was as large as any two of the other nestlings, and so red the very down on him seemed tinged with crimson; his skin and even his feet were red.

He was the first to climb to the edge of the nest and the first to hop on a limb. He surprised his parents by finding a slug, and winged his first flight to such a distance that his adoring mother almost went into spasms lest his strength might fail, and he would fall into the swamp and become the victim of a hungry old turtle. He returned safely, however; and the king was so pleased he hunted him an unusually ripe berry, and perching before him, gave him his first language lesson. Of course, the Cardinal knew how to cry "Pee" and "Chee" when he burst his shell; but the king taught him to chip with accuracy and expression, and he learned that very day that male birds of the cardinal family always call "Chip," and the females "Chook." In fact, he learned so rapidly and was generally so observant, that before the king thought it wise to give the next lesson, he found him on a limb, his beak closed, his throat swelling, practising his own rendering of the tribal calls, "Wheat! Wheat! Wheat!" "Here! Here! Here!" and "Cheer! Cheer! Cheer!" This so delighted the king that he whistled them over and over and helped the youngster all he could.

He was so proud of him that this same night he gave him his first lesson in tucking his head properly and going to sleep alone. In a few more days, when he was sure of his wing strength, he gave him instructions in flying. He taught him how to spread his wings and slowly sail from tree to tree; how to fly in short broken curves, to avoid the aim of a hunter; how to turn abruptly in air and make a quick dash after a bug or an enemy. He taught him the proper angle at which to breast a stiff wind, and that he always should meet a storm head first, so that the water would run as the plumage lay.

His first bathing lesson was a pronounced success. The Cardinal enjoyed water like a duck. He bathed, splashed, and romped until his mother was almost crazy for fear he would attract a watersnake or turtle; but the element of fear was not a part of his disposition. He learned to dry, dress, and plume his feathers, and showed such remarkable pride in keeping himself immaculate, that although only a youngster, he was already a bird of such great promise, that many of the feathered inhabitants of the Limberlost came to pay him a call.

Next, the king took him on a long trip around the swamp, and taught him to select the proper places to hunt for worms; how to search under leaves for plant-lice and slugs for meat; which berries were good and safe, and the kind of weeds that bore the most and best seeds. He showed him how to find tiny pebbles to grind his food, and how to sharpen and polish his beak.

Then he took up the real music lesson, and taught him how to whistle and how to warble and trill. "Good Cheer! Good Cheer!" intoned the king. "Coo Cher! Coo Cher!" imitated the Cardinal. These songs were only studied repetitions, but there was a depth and volume to his voice that gave promise of future greatness, when age should have developed him, and experience awakened his emotions. He was an excellent musician for a youngster.

He soon did so well in caring for himself, in finding food and in flight, and grew so big and independent, that he made numerous excursions alone through the Limberlost; and so impressive were his proportions, and so aggressive his manners, that he suffered no molestation. In fact, the reign of the king promised to end speedily; but if he feared it he made no sign, and his pride in his wonderful offspring was always manifest. After the Cardinal had explored the swamp thoroughly, a longing for a wider range grew upon him; and day after day he lingered around the borders, looking across the wide cultivated fields, almost aching to test his wings in one long, high, wild stretch of flight.

A day came when the heat of late summer set the marsh steaming, and the Cardinal, flying close to the borders, caught the breeze from the upland; and the vision of broad fields stretching toward the north so enticed him that he spread his wings, and following the line of trees and fences as much as possible, he made his first journey from home. That day was so delightful it decided his fortunes. It would seem that the swamp, so appreciated by his kindred, should have been sufficient for the Cardinal, but it was not. With every mile he winged his flight, came a greater sense of power and strength, and a keener love for the broad sweep of field and forest. His heart bounded with the zest of rocking on the wind, racing through the sunshine, and sailing over the endless panorama of waving corn fields, meadows, orchards, and woodlands.

The heat and closeness of the Limberlost seemed a prison well escaped, as on and on he flew in straight untiring flight. Crossing a field of half-ripened corn that sloped to the river, the Cardinal saw many birds feeding there, so he alighted on a tall tree to watch them. Soon he decided that he would like to try this new food. He found a place where a crow had left an ear nicely laid open, and clinging to the husk, as he saw the others do, he stretched to his full height and drove his strong sharp beak into the creamy grain. After the stifling swamp hunting, after the long exciting flight, to rock on this swaying corn and drink the rich milk of the grain, was to the Cardinal his first taste of nectar and ambrosia. He lifted his head when he came to the golden kernel, and chipping it in tiny specks, he tasted and approved with all the delight of an epicure in a delicious new dish.

Perhaps there were other treats in the next field. He decided to fly even farther. But he had gone only a short distance when he changed his course and turned to the South, for below him was a long, shining, creeping thing, fringed with willows, while towering above them were giant sycamore, maple, tulip, and elm trees that caught and rocked with the wind; and the Cardinal did not know what it was. Filled with wonder he dropped lower and lower. Birds were everywhere, many flying over and dipping into it; but its clear creeping silver was a mystery to the Cardinal.

The beautiful river of poetry and song that the Indians first discovered, and later with the French, named Ouabache; the winding shining river that Logan and Me-shin-go-me-sia loved; the only river that could tempt Wa-ca-co-nah from the Salamonie and Mississinewa; the river beneath whose silver sycamores and giant maples Chief Godfrey travelled many miles to pitch his camp-fires, was never more beautiful than on that perfect autumn day.

With his feathers pressed closely, the Cardinal alighted on a willow, and leaned to look, quivering with excitement and uttering explosive "chips"; for there he was, face to face with a big redbird that appeared neither peaceful nor timid. He uttered an impudent "Chip" of challenge, which, as it left his beak, was flung back to him. The Cardinal flared his crest and half lifted his wings, stiffening them at the butt; the bird he was facing did the same. In his surprise he arose to his full height with a dexterous little side step, and the other bird straightened and side-stepped exactly with him. This was too insulting for the Cardinal. Straining every muscle, he made a dash at the impudent stranger.

He struck the water with such force that it splashed above the willows, and a kingfisher, stationed on a stump opposite him, watching the shoals for minnows, saw it. He spread his beak and rolled forth rattling laughter, until his voice re-echoed from point to point down the river. The Cardinal scarcely knew how he got out, but he had learned a new lesson. That beautiful, shining, creeping thing was water; not thick, tepid, black marsh water, but pure, cool, silver water. He shook his plumage, feeling a degree redder from shame, but he would not be laughed into leaving. He found it too delightful. In a short time he ventured down and took a sip, and it was the first real drink of his life. Oh, but it was good!

When thirst from the heat and his long flight was quenched, he ventured in for a bath, and that was a new and delightful experience. How he splashed and splashed, and sent the silver drops flying! How he ducked and soaked and cooled in that rippling water, in which he might remain as long as he pleased and splash his fill; for he could see the bottom for a long distance all around, and easily could avoid anything attempting to harm him. He was so wet when his bath was finished he scarcely could reach a bush to dry and dress his plumage.

Once again in perfect feather, he remembered the bird of the water, and returned to the willow. There in the depths of the shining river the Cardinal discovered himself, and his heart swelled big with just pride. Was that broad full breast his? Where had he seen any other cardinal with a crest so high it waved in the wind? How big and black his eyes were, and his beard was almost as long and crisp as his father's. He spread his wings and gloated on their sweep, and twisted and flirted his tail. He went over his toilet again and dressed every feather on him. He scoured the back of his neck with the butt of his wings, and tucking his head under them, slowly drew it out time after time to polish his crest. He turned and twisted. He rocked and paraded, and every glimpse he caught of his size and beauty filled him with pride. He strutted like a peacock and chattered like a jay.

When he could find no further points to admire, something else caught his attention. When he "chipped" there was an answering "Chip" across the river; certainly there was no cardinal there, so it must be that he was hearing his own voice as well as seeing himself. Selecting a conspicuous perch he sent an incisive "Chip!" across the water, and in kind it came back to him. Then he "chipped" softly and tenderly, as he did in the Limberlost to a favourite little sister who often came and perched beside him in the maple where he slept, and softly and tenderly came the answer. Then the Cardinal understood. "Wheat! Wheat! Wheat!" He whistled it high, and he whistled it low. "Cheer! Cheer! Cheer!" He whistled it tenderly and sharply and imperiously. "Here! Here! Here!" At this ringing command, every bird, as far as the river carried his voice, came to investigate and remained to admire. Over and over he rang every change he could invent. He made a gallant effort at warbling and trilling, and then, with the gladdest heart he ever had known, he burst into ringing song: "Good Cheer! Good Cheer! Good Cheer!"

As evening came on he grew restless and uneasy, so he slowly winged his way back to the Limberlost; but that day forever spoiled him for a swamp bird. In the night he restlessly ruffled his feathers, and sniffed for the breeze of the meadows. He tasted the corn and the clear water again. He admired his image in the river, and longed for the sound of his voice, until he began murmuring, "Wheat! Wheat! Wheat!" in his sleep. In the earliest dawn a robin awoke him singing, "Cheer up! Cheer up!" and he answered with a sleepy "Cheer! Cheer! Cheer!" Later the robin sang again with exquisite softness and tenderness: "Cheer up, Dearie! Cheer up, Dearie! Cheer up! Cheer up! Cheer!" The Cardinal, now fully awakened, shouted lustily, "Good Cheer! Good Cheer!" and after that it was only a short time until he was on his way toward the shining river. It was better than before, and every following day found him feasting in the corn field and bathing in the shining water; but he always returned to his family at nightfall.

When black frosts began to strip the Limberlost, and food was almost reduced to dry seed, there came a day on which the king marshalled his followers and gave the magic signal. With dusk he led them southward, mile after mile, until their breath fell short, and their wings ached with unaccustomed flight; but because of the trips to the river, the Cardinal was stronger than the others, and he easily kept abreast of the king. In the early morning, even before the robins were awake, the king settled in the Everglades. But the Cardinal had lost all liking for swamp life, so he stubbornly set out alone, and in a short time he had found another river. It was not quite so delightful as the shining river; but still it was beautiful, and on its gently sloping bank was an orange orchard. There the Cardinal rested, and found a winter home after his heart's desire. . . .

Sometimes a member of his family from the Everglades found his way into the orchard, and the Cardinal, having grown to feel a sense of proprietorship, resented the intrusion and pursued him like a streak of flame. Whenever any straggler had this experience, he returned to the swamp realizing that the Cardinal of the orange orchard was almost twice his size and strength, and so startlingly red as to be a wonder.

One day a gentle breeze from the north sprang up and stirred the orange branches, wafting the heavy perfume across the land and out to sea, and spread in its stead a cool, delicate, pungent odour. The Cardinal lifted his head and whistled an inquiring note. He was not certain, and went on searching for slugs, and predicting happiness in full round notes: "Good Cheer! Good Cheer!" Again the odour swept the orchard, so strong that this time there was no mistaking it. The Cardinal darted to the top-most branch, his crest flaring, his tail twitching nervously. "Chip! Chip!" he cried with excited insistence, "Chip! Chip!"

The breeze was coming stiffly and steadily now, unlike anything the Cardinal ever had known, for its cool breath told of ice-bound fields breaking up under the sun. Its damp touch was from the spring showers washing the face of the northland. Its subtle odour was the commingling of myriads of unfolding leaves and crisp plants, upspringing; its pungent perfume was the pollen of catkins.

Up in the land of the Limberlost, old Mother Nature, with strident muttering, had set about her annual house-cleaning. With her efficient broom, the March wind, she was sweeping every nook and cranny clean. With her scrub-bucket overflowing with April showers, she was washing the face of all creation, and if these measures failed to produce cleanliness to her satisfaction, she gave a final polish with storms of hail. The shining river was filled to overflowing; breaking up the ice and carrying a load of refuse, it went rolling to the sea. The ice and snow had not altogether gone; but the long-pregnant earth was mothering her children. She cringed at every step, for the ground was teeming with life. Bug and worm were working to light and warmth. Thrusting aside the mold and leaves above them, spring beauties, hepaticas, and violets lifted tender golden-green heads. The sap was flowing, and leafless trees were covered with swelling buds. Delicate mosses were creeping over every stick of decaying timber. The lichens on stone and fence were freshly painted in unending shades of gray and green. Myriads of flowers and vines were springing up to cover last year's decaying leaves. "The beautiful uncut hair of graves" was creeping over meadow, spreading beside roadways, and blanketing every naked spot.

The Limberlost was waking to life even ahead of the fields and the river. Through the winter it had been the barest and dreariest of places; but now the earliest signs of returning spring were in its martial music, for when the green hyla pipes, and the bullfrog drums, the bird voices soon join them. The catkins bloomed first; and then, in an incredibly short time, flags, rushes, and vines were like a sea of waving green, and swelling buds were ready to burst. In the upland the smoke was curling over sugar-camp and clearing; in the forests animals were rousing from their long sleep; the shad were starting anew their never-ending journey up the shining river; peeps of green were mantling hilltop and valley; and the northland was ready for its dearest springtime treasures to come home again.

From overhead were ringing those first glad notes, caught nearer the Throne than those of any other bird, "Spring o' year! Spring o' year!"; while stilt-legged little killdeers were scudding from cloudland their "Kill deer! Kill deer!" call. The robins in the orchards were pulling the long dried blades of last year's grass from beneath the snow to line their mud-walled cups; and the bluebirds were at the hollow apple tree. Flat on the top rail, the doves were gathering their few coarse sticks and twigs together. It was such a splendid place to set their cradle. The weather-beaten, rotting old rails were the very colour of the busy dove mother. Her red-rimmed eye fitted into the background like a tiny scarlet lichen cup. Surely no one would ever see her! The Limberlost and shining river, the fields and forests, the wayside bushes and fences, the stumps, logs, hollow trees, even the bare brown breast of Mother Earth, were all waiting to cradle their own again; and by one of the untold miracles each would return to its place.

There was intoxication in the air. The subtle, pungent, ravishing odours on the wind, of unfolding leaves, ice-water washed plants, and catkin pollen, were an elixir to humanity. The cattle of the field were fairly drunk with it, and herds, dry-fed during the winter, were coming to their first grazing with heads thrown high, romping, bellowing, and racing like wild things.

The north wind, sweeping from icy fastnesses, caught this odour of spring, and carried it to the orange orchards and Everglades; and at a breath of it, crazed with excitement, the Cardinal went flaming through the orchard, for with no one to teach him, he knew what it meant. The call had come. Holidays were over.

It was time to go home, time to riot in crisp freshness, time to go courting, time to make love, time to possess his own, time for mating and nest-building. All that day he flashed around, nervous with dread of the unknown, and palpitant with delightful expectation; but with the coming of dusk he began his journey northward.

When he passed the Everglades, he winged his way slowly, and repeatedly sent down a challenging "Chip," but there was no answer. The Cardinal knew that the north wind had carried a true message, for the king and his followers were ahead of him on their way to the Limberlost. Mile after mile, a thing of pulsing fire, he breasted the blue-black night, and it was not so very long until he could discern a flickering patch of darkness sweeping the sky before him. The Cardinal flew steadily in a straight sweep, until with a throb of triumph in his heart, he arose in his course, and from far overhead, flung down a boastful challenge to the king and his followers, as he sailed above them and was lost from sight.

It was still dusky with the darkness of night when he crossed the Limberlost, dropping low enough to see its branches laid bare, to catch a gleam of green in its swelling buds, and to hear the wavering chorus of its frogs. But there was no hesitation in his flight. Straight and sure he winged his way toward the shining river; and it was only a few more miles until the rolling waters of its springtime flood caught his eye. Dropping precipitately, he plunged his burning beak into the loved water; then he flew into a fine old stag sumac and tucked his head under his wing for a short rest. He had made the long flight in one unbroken sweep, and he was sleepy. In utter content he ruffled his feathers and closed his eyes, for he was beside the shining river; and it would be another season before the orange orchard would ring again with his "Good Cheer! Good Cheer!"

Indiana's great system of state parks attests to the fact that the Hoosier taxpayer loves the unspoiled landscape and is willing to pay tribute to his love with his dollars. But a surprising amount of natural landscape is preserved throughout the state by individuals, by clubs, and in many cases by nothing more than good fortune.

Wildlife is common, too, and in some rather surprising localities. Most small tree-shaded Indiana cities harbor a larger squirrel population than ever did an equal area of virgin timber. Fishing is good in every Indiana branch and puddle, though the size of the individual specimen varies in proportion to the habitat. Deer are a nuisance in some southern parts of the state, as are beavers in places in the north. Even metropolitan Indianapolis has its occasional excess of game, as witness

JEANNETTE COVERT NOLAN

Lines With a Hoosier Accent

INDIANAPOLIS FAUNA

I AM INTERESTED in reports of the astonishing number of gray squirrels now dwelling in the Hoosier capital's north side residential district. They say the squirrels have moved in, firmly established themselves on all the best sites, and seem determined to dispossess original property owners. The first several hundred to appear were cordially welcomed by their human neighbors—and were in general reasonably well-behaved. But as their ranks increased they grew arrogant and slightly drunk with power; they organized and unionized into a pressure bloc.

In short, the squirrels have changed from darling little creatures frisking on the greensward into something dangerously like a cohort of gangsters.

Now an attempt must be made to regulate their excesses, and in extreme cases offenders are being trapped and deported. There are even instances of the enactment of more severe penalties.

Recently a friend of mine emerged from her house in Woodstock and walked rapidly toward her car which was parked on the drive. As she crossed the lawn she saw a large gray squirrel with a thoughtful expression sitting in the grass near the car. My friend recognized him; for years he and his extensive family had occupied a nest in an oak tree on the grounds. In comradely fashion, the lady waved her hand to the squirrel.

He immediately scampered over and bit her on the ankle.

It was a wholly unwarranted attack and all the more amazing in that the lady had been always an indulgent hostess, never infringing upon the squirrel's privacy and refraining from complaint when occasionally the squirrel showed himself as somewhat less polite. After the wound had been dressed, the lady consulted with her doctor, her husband and certain civil authorities, and it was agreed that the squirrel was a public menace and must therefore be killed.

Very reluctantly the lady concurred in this majority opinion. The squirrel was a patriarch; she had been fond of him. If only he had told her that her use of the car interfered with some plan of his own, she would have gracefully yielded priority. She realized that he was old and crochetty, and she tried to excuse him by pleading that a multitude of domestic cares had worn his temper thin. On the day of execution the lady was most distressed—and she hasn't yet recovered her usual aplomb. To be bitten by your next-door neighbor is an experience difficult to weather happily; still worse is the witnessing of your neighbor's punishment.

A good many people are wondering how to account for the prevalence of the squirrels in Indianapolis. Well, I think our city has always exerted some attraction for the genus *sciurus;* this present situation is simply the repetition of event.

In August, 1822, when Indianapolis was an infant community, pioneer settlers here had their first furious bout with gray squirrels—and it was terrible while it lasted. Nobody knew where the squirrels had come from or where they were going, nobody knew anything except that suddenly the village swarmed with squirrels, closing in from all sides, swimming the White River in such hordes that the water seemed dyed the deep gray of their coats, racing through the streets, entering the houses, plundering and pillaging.

For days the ruthless invaders streaked through Marion County, laying waste the gardens and fields of grain, eating every edible thing in sight, trailing ruin in their wake. Horrified citizens combined to fight them, patrolling with guns, flailing with rake and hoe, digging entrenchments, baiting enormous traps. The boys and girls of Indianapolis were pressed into service to frighten the enemy with noise. Beating on tin pans, clanging cowbells, shouting at the top of their voices, the children marched up and down, back and forth; pandemonium reigned, the din was hideous—and the tide of squirrels swept on, unfrightened and unabating.

The onslaught was truly desperate, resistance seemed quite ineffectual, citizens seemed to wage a losing battle. And then, as suddenly as they had come, the squirrels vanished, the last regiments skittering off into the surrounding forest.

It's said that one old veteran sergeant paused in the middle of the Circle, laughed impudently, stuck out his tongue in a taunting gesture and cried *"Veni, vidi, vici!"* before rushing on to fresh conquest over the county line. Perhaps he was the progenitor of this ingrate who has just bitten my friend's ankle. I wouldn't be surprised.

———

Sticklers for fact may hold that Indiana has no legitimate claim at all to the citizenship of

EDWIN WAY TEALE

but sticklers are likely to be rather unpleasant people. Ignoring their quibbling is a pleasant duty, may even be considered a public service.

Certainly Teale spent his summers on his grandparents' farm at the edge of the Indiana dunes—a mile and a half from Lake Michigan and six miles from Michigan City—during most of his first sixteen years; certainly, also, he preferred the summer days at Lone Oak Farm to winter at his parents' home at Joliet, Illinois.

When we multiply, say, a dozen summers by three months each and add in the many Christmas holiday visits and the four years he spent as a student at Earlham College, Mr. Teale achieves a total residence which will, or should, justify at least honorary status as a Hoosier. It was the dune country that inspired and abetted the interest in natural history, aviation, and photography which have been the chief subjects of his pleasant and informative writing. In further evidence of his own acknowledgment of his roots in Hoosierdom he describes himself in the title of one of his best books as

Dune Boy

THE DEATH OF A TREE

For a great tree death comes as a gradual transformation. Its vitality ebbs slowly. Even when life has abandoned it entirely it remains a majestic thing. On some hilltop a dead tree may dominate the landscape for miles around. Alone among living things it retains its character and dignity after death. Plants wither; animals disintegrate. But a dead tree may be as arresting, as filled with personality, in death as it is in life. Even in its final moments, when the massive trunk lies prone and it has moldered into a ridge covered with mosses and fungi, it arrives at a fitting and a noble end. It enriches and refreshes the earth. And later, as part of other green and growing things, it rises again.

The death of the great oak which gave our Indiana homestead its name and which played such an important part in our daily lives was so gentle a transition that we never knew just when it ceased to be a living organism.

It had stood there, toward the sunset from the farmhouse, rooted in that same spot for 200 years or more. How many generations of robins had sung from its upper branches! How many humans, from how many lands, had paused beneath its shade!

The passing of this venerable giant made a profound impression upon my young mind. Just what caused its death was then a mystery. Looking back, I believe the deep drainage ditches, which had been cut through the dune-country marshes a few years before, had lowered the water-table just sufficiently to affect the roots of the old oak. Millions of delicate root-tips were injured. As they began to wither, the whole vast underground system of nourishment broke down and the tree was no longer able to send sap to the upper branches.

Like a river flowing into a desert, the life stream of the tree dwindled and disappeared before it reached the topmost twigs. They died first. The leaf at the tip of each twig, the last to unfold, was the first to wither and fall. Then, little by little, the twig itself became dead and dry. This process of dissolution, in the manner of a movie run backward, reversed the development of growth. Just as, cell by cell, the twig had grown outward toward the tip, so now death spread, cell by cell, backward from the tip.

Sadly we watched the blight work from twig to branch, from smaller branch to larger branch, until the whole top of the tree was dead and bare. For years those dry, barkless upper branches remained intact. Their wood became gray and polished by the winds. When thunderstorms rolled over the farm from the northwest the dead branches shone like silver against the black and swollen sky. Robins and veeries sang from these lofty perches, gilded by the sunset long after the purple of advancing dusk filled the spaces below.

Then, one by one, their resiliency gone, the topmost limbs crashed to earth, carried away by the fury of stormwinds. In fragments and patches, bark from the upper trunk littered the ground below. The protecting skin of the tree was broken. In through the gaps poured a host of microscopic enemies, the organisms of decay.

Ghostly white fungus penetrated into the sap-wood. It worked its way downward along the unused tubes, those vertical channels through which had flowed the lifeblood of the oak. The continued flow of this sap might have kept out the fungus. But sap rises only to branches clothed with leaves. As each limb became blighted and leafless, the sap-level dropped to the next living branch below. And close on the heels of this descending fluid followed the fungus. From branch to branch its silent, deadly descent continued.

Soft and flabby, so unsubstantial it can be crushed without apparent pressure between thumb and forefinger, this pale fungus is yet able to penetrate through the hardest woods. This amazing and paradoxical feat is accomplished by means of digestive enzymes which the fungus secretes and which dissolve the wood as strong acids might do. These fungus-enzymes, science has learned, are virtually the same as those produced by the single-celled protozoa which live in the bodies of the termites and enable those insects to digest the cellulose in wood.

Advancing in the form of thin white threads, which branch again and again, the fungus works its way from side to side as well as downward through the trunk of a dying tree. Beyond the reach of our eyes the fungus kept spreading within the body of the old oak, branching into a kind of vast, interlacing root-system of its own, pale and ghostly.

Behind the fungus, along the dead upper trunk, yellow hammers drummed on the dry wood. I saw them, with their chisel-bills, hewing out nesting holes which, in turn, admitted new organisms of decay. In effect, the dissolution of a great tree is like the slow turning of an immense wheel of life. Each stage of its decline and decay brings a whole new, interdependent population of dwellers and their parasites.

Even while the lower branches of the oak were still green, insect wreckers were already at work above them. First to arrive were the bark beetles. In the earliest stages their fare was the tender inner layer of the bark, the living bond between the trunk and its covering. As death spread downward in the oak, as freezing and storms loosened the bark, the beetles descended foot by foot. Some of them left behind elaborate patterns, branching mazes of tunnels that took on the appearance of fantastic "thousand-leggers" engraved in wood.

During the winter when I was twelve years old a gale of abnormal force swept the Great Lakes region. Gusts reached almost hurricane proportions. Weakened by the work of the fungus, bacteria, wood-peckers, and beetles, the whole top of the tree snapped off some seventy feet from the ground. After that the progress of its dissolution was rapid.

Finally the last of the lower leaves disappeared. The green badge of life returned no more. On summer days the sound of the wind sweeping through the old oak had a winter shrillness. No more was there the rustling of a multitude of leaves about our hammock; no more was there the "plump!" of falling acorns. Leaves and acorns, life and progress, were at an end.

In the days that followed, as the bark loosened to the base, the wheel of life, which had its hub in the now-dead oak, grew larger.

I saw carpenter ants hurrying this way and that over the lower tree-trunk. Ichneumon flies, trailing deadly, drill-like ovipositors, hovered above the bark in search of buried larvae on which to lay their eggs. Carpenter bees, their black abdomens glistening like patent leather, bit their way into the dry wood of the dead branches. Click beetles and sow-bugs and small spiders found security beneath fragments of the loosened bark. And around the base of the tree swift-legged carabid beetles hunted their insect prey under cover of darkness.

Yellowish brown, the wood-flour of the powder-post beetles began to sift about the foot of the oak. It, in turn, attracted the larvae of the Darkling beetles. Thus, link by link, the chain of life expanded. To the expert eye the condition of the wood, the bark, the ground about the base of the oak—all told of the action of the inter-related forms of life attracted by the death and decay of a tree.

But below all this activity, beyond the power of human sight to detect, other changes were taking place. The underground root system, comprising almost as much wood as was visible in the tree rising above-ground, was also altering.

Fungus, entering the damaged root-tips or working downward from the infected trunk, followed the sap channels and hastened decay. The great main roots, spreading out as far as the widest branches of the tree itself, altered rapidly. Their fibers grew brittle; their old pliancy disappeared; their bark split and loosened. The breakdown of the upper tree found its counterpart, within the darkness of the earth, in the dissolution of the lower roots.

I remember well the day the great oak came down. I was fourteen at the time. Gramp had measured distances and planned his cutting operations in advance. He chopped away for fully half an hour before he had a V-shaped bite cut exactly in position to bring the trunk crashing in the place desired. Hours filled with the whine of the cross-cut saw followed.

Then came the great moment. A few last, quick strokes. A slow, deliberate swaying. The crack of parting fibers. Then a long "swo-o-sh!" that rose in pitch as the towering trunk arced downward at increasing speed. There followed a vast tumult of crashing, crackling sound; the dance of splintered branches; a haze of dead, swirling grass. Then a slow settling of small objects and silence. All was over. Lone oak was gone.

Gram, I remember, brushed away what she remarked was dust in her eyes with a corner of her apron and went inside. She had known and loved that one great tree since she had come to the farm as a bride of sixteen. She had seen it under all conditions and through eyes colored by many moods. Her children had grown up under its shadow and I, a grandchild, had known its shade. Its passing was like the passing of an old, old friend. For all of us there seemed an empty space in our sky in the days that followed.

Gramp and I set to work, attacking the fallen giant. Great piles of cord wood, mounds of broken branches for kindling, grew around the prostrate trunk as the weeks went by. Eventually only the huge, circular table of the low stump remained—reddish brown and slowly dissolving into dust.

For two winters wood from the old oak fed the kitchen range and the dining-room stove. It had a clean, well-seasoned smell. And it burned with a clear and leaping flame, continuing—unlike the quickly consumed poplar and elm—for an admirable length of time. Like the old tree itself, the fibers of these sticks had character and endurance to the very end.

A knowledge of the natural products of the great outdoors can have its practical aspect, and James Buchanan Elmore was the man to ap-

preciate that fact. In lilting verse he sings of the humble spring greens and their specific virtues—and also of a maiden who knew her poke shoots when she saw them and feared not to bust her girdle in their gathering. Nature lore at its most inspiring is depicted by

JAMES B. ELMORE

When Katie Gathers Greens

The warm and pleasant days are come,
  And sweet May voices ring;
All hearts are full of fervent love—
  They tell me this is spring.
The young plants show their tender shoots,
  The day so pleasant seems;
It is a balm that cheers the heart
  When Katie gathers greens.

Much indoor life stagnates the blood,
  And makes a torpid liver;
But soon the sun sends piercing rays,
  And makes the leaflets quiver.
I long for viands tart and good
  To start arterial streams;
My heart leaps up with joy and hope
  When Katie gathers greens.

A mild cathartic, narrow dock,
  Out in the orchard grows;
And dandelion, whose wondrous leaves
  With nervine overflows.
Growing mustard in the garden
  Comes sweetly in my dreams.
And fills my heart anew with joy,
  When Katie gathers greens.

The purple poke top soundly sleeps;
  It is the last of all
To enter in such dainty food
  As changes bile and gall.
But yet it comes, though very late,
  And dots the waste like scenes;
Then comes the happiest day of spring,
  When Katie gathers greens.

Katie, I would that you might live
  And smile along your course,
And glean elixir's precious wealth
  From Nature's mystic source.
Though Doctor So-and-So might fail
  From slight replenished means,
The matron, lord, and lass rejoice
  When May brings back the greens.

CHAPTER FIFTEEN

Domestic Economy – In the Beginning

As Americans' interest in outdoor living continues to expand, there comes also an interest in how the pioneer—first American white to live really close to nature—went about it: how he found his way around in the big, dark woods, how he built his fireplace and his fire, what he cooked on it, and how he went about his cooking processes.

To a lesser degree, there is an interest in other domestic arts: how to make soap and dyes, how to weave cloth in the old way, and how to grow and process the materials for weaving.

A most thoughtful formula for the first problem—how to find one's way—is, strangely enough, written by a man still quite young who was reared in northern Indiana. By the evidence of his knowledge of the outdoors, he must have spent a good deal of time on the Kankakee River or its tributaries or on the Indiana dunes.

DAVID WAGONER

tells the secrets of STAYING ALIVE in a book of verse of the same title.

Staying Alive

Staying alive in the woods is a matter of calming down
At first and deciding whether to wait for rescue,

Trusting to others,
Or simply to start walking and walking in one direction
Till you come out—or something happens to stop you.
By far the safer choice
Is to settle down where you are, and try to make a living
Off the land, camping near water, away from shadows.
Eat no white berries;
Spit out all bitterness. Shooting at anything
Means hiking further and further every day
To hunt survivors;
It may be best to learn what you have to learn without a gun,
Not killing but watching birds and animals go
In and out of shelter
At will. Following their example, build for a whole season:
Facing across the wind in your lean-to,
You may feel wilder,
But nothing, not even you, will have to stay in hiding.
If you have no matches, a stick and a fire-bow
Will keep you warmer,
Or the crystal of your watch, filled with water, held up to
    the sun
Will do the same in time. In case of snow
Drifting toward winter,
Don't try to stay awake through the night, afraid of freezing—
The bottom of your mind knows all about zero;
It will turn you over
And shake you till you waken. If you have trouble sleeping
Even in the best of weather, jumping to follow
With eyes strained to their corners
The unidentifiable noises of the night and feeling
Bears and packs of wolves nuzzling your elbow,
Remember the trappers
Who treated them indifferently and were left alone.
If you hurt yourself, no one will comfort you
Or take your temperature,
So stumbling, wading, and climbing are as dangerous as flying.
But if you decide, at last, you must break through

In spite of all danger,
Think of yourself by time and not by distance, counting
Where ever you're going by how long it takes you;
No other measure
Will bring you safe to nightfall. Follow no streams; they run
Under the ground or fall into wilder country.
Remember the stars
And moss when your mind runs into circles. If it should rain
Or the fog should roll the horizon in around you,
Hold still for hours
Or days if you must, or weeks, for seeing is believing
In the wilderness. And if you find a pathway,
Wheel-rut, or fence-wire,
Retrace it left or right: someone knew where he was going
Once upon a time, and you can follow
Hopefully, somewhere,
Just in case. There may even come, on some uncanny evening,
A time when you're warm and dry, well fed, not thirsty,
Uninjured, without fear,
When nothing, either good or bad, is happening.
This is called staying alive. It's temporary.
What occurs after
Is doubtful. You must always be ready for something to come
    bursting
Through the far edge of a clearing, running toward you,
Grinning from ear to ear
And hoarse with welcome. Or something crossing and hovering
Overhead, as light as air, like a break in the sky,
Wondering what you are.
Here you are face to face with the problem of recognition.
Having no time to make smoke, too much to say,
You should have a mirror
With a tiny hole in the back for better aiming, for reflecting
Whatever disaster you can think of, to show
The way you suffer.
These body signals have universal meaning: If you are lying
Flat on your back with arms outstretched behind you,

You say you require
Emergency treatment; if you are standing erect and holding
Arms horizontal, you mean you are not ready;
If you hold them over
Your head, you want to be picked up. Three of anything
Is a sign of distress. Afterward, if you see
No ropes, no ladders,
No maps or messages falling, no searchlights or trails blazing,
Then, chances are, you should be prepared to burrow
Deep for a deep winter.

*Having followed Mr. Wagoner's instructions and reached our destina-
tion, we fell some trees and lay up our cabin. Those chores done, we are
ready to cook and eat—not to mention change our clothing.*

*One of the best works on these and related subjects did not see print
until 1951, when the Indian Historical Society brought it out as one of
its publications.*

*It is a minor masterpiece, this little book, A Home in the Woods, the
reminiscences of*

OLIVER JOHNSON

*who, aged a few months, was among the first crop to settle in the vicinity
of the new town which had been grandiosely designated "Indianapolis"
and designed to be the state's new capital. Oliver Johnson did not put
his reminiscences on paper; he only told his stories and left the writing
chore to his grandson.*

HOWARD JOHNSON

*did a workmanlike job, having an abiding interest in both the subject
and his grandfather, and he set the narrative down in what must have
been the old gentleman's exact words. Here, then, are facts of life circa
1822–30 set down in the pure, basic Hoosier. This is unlike what Eggleston and Riley heard or thought they recalled hearing, but it may still be
encountered in the neighborhoods surrounding Amo or Alamo or
Paragon, and it has a sound by no means unpleasant to the unprejudiced
ear.*

A Home in the Woods

THE FIREPLACE

Buildin a fire in a fireplace so it would throw out heat wasn't a matter of jist throwin in a armful of wood haphazardlike. There was only one way, and that was the right way.

First, you rolled in the back logs: as big a one for the bottom log as the fireplace would take, then a smaller one on top. For these logs we used green or partly seasoned timber so it would burn slow and last longer. Buckeye made good back logs. These backlogs not only protected the clay back wall of the fireplace but they would throw out lots of heat when the front fire became a mass of live coals. Green backlogs would last for several days.

The andirons, or dog irons as we called them, was then shoved up against the back logs. Then a good-sized piece called the forestick was laid across the front of them. Between the logs the fire was made. The forestick kept burnin pieces of wood from rollin out on the hearth and also let a draft under the fire.

Most fireplaces was right good sized so they would take big sticks of wood. One of our neighbors had one so big it almost took up all the end of the room. When he put on a new backlog, he drug it through the house with a horse that went in a door on one side and out a door on the opposite side. Then the log was rolled into the fireplace by hand.

At night you could keep a fire by bankin it down with ashes. In the mornin pull off the ashes and there was a good bed of coals to start a new fire. We had no matches them days, and it was a lot of trouble to start a fire with flint and steel, so we aimed to keep some logs burnin in the clearin most of the time for a place to get coals if the fire went out in the fireplace. If all fire was out at home, a boy was sent to a neighbor to borrow a shovelful of coals.

The fireplace was right handy when the women wanted to sweep the room. They would begin at the back of the room and sweep toward the hearth. All the dirt would be in the fire in short order. Though we had candles, a good blazin fire of an evenin would make enough light to work and read by. Fireplaces had the reputation of burnin your face and freezin your back, but there was nothin to hinder a person from turnin around if he was a mind to.

We lived mighty happy and contented in the early days. With a good snug cabin, a big fireplace, and a supply of corn meal on hand, there wasn't much to worry about. Our big family spent many a pleasant evenin settin around a blazin fire while the wind and the snow cut capers outside.

Pap would be settin in his usual place to one side of the fire, chewin terbacker, and spittin in the fire. He wasn't much to talk then. Sometimes he would set there by the hour and never say a word to anybody; just chew and look into the fire. I often wondered afterward what he was thinkin about, if he wasn't sometimes tryin to imagine what this part of the country would look like in the future. Pap was luckier than some of the older ones. He could read. If he could get hold of a newspaper, no matter if it was back date, he would read evenins. He had an old history of the world that he had read so much the pages was wore through where his thumb rested.

Us boys would pass the evenin cipherin on our slates, parchin corn, whittlin out something with our knives, or if you was big enough to handle a rifle, mouldin bullets. We could do most anything, jist so we didn't make any noise. That Pap wouldn't have. If any started, he just tapped his foot on the floor about three times. That was enough; we understood mighty well what it meant.

Mother and the girls would spin and knit. They was kept purty busy makin clothes for the family. Most everybody went to bed early and got up early them days. There wasn't much chance of wearin out your sociability of evenins.

Occasionally a neighbor and some of his family would drop in to set by the fire and chat a while. If there was any grown girls in the family and the visitors was men folks, it wasn't uncommon about bed time to hear the father say:

"Boys, step outside while the gals go to bed."

When you went back in the cabin, every girl was under the covers, head and all. And you didn't look too close at them, either.

Fireplaces not only furnished heat for the cabin, but there was where all the cookin was done.

Swingin from one of the jams was a crane fitted with three hooks of different length so a pot could be hung high or low over the coals for different heat. The crane could be swung out or in from the fire when puttin on or takin off a pot.

A iron pot or two, a skillet, or spider as we called it if it had legs, a griddle, and a squatty-lookin pot known as a Dutch oven about summed up the cookin tools needed for fireplace cookin. Hangin on the jam was a long-handled fire shovel and a pot hook for reachin in and takin off lids, so you wouldn't burn your hands.

When mother started a meal, everybody had to scatter back from the fireplace out of her way. She was a little woman, and it was a wonder how she could pick up them big heavy spiders with one hand and carry them around with such ease. And how she could handle the fire shovel—puttin just the right amount of coals around a pot to give the proper heat. And she never dropped the lids she lifted with the pot hook. Sometimes a few coals or a little ashes would get in the cookin, but that didn't matter; we thought it just helped season it some. While it wasn't a very handy place for the women to work, it was surprisin what a good meal could be scared up on a fireplace and with so few things to do it with. Their faces and hands got purty brown cookin before an open fire, but nobody thought anything of it for they all done the same work and all looked alike. If they had been any other color, we'd a thought they was either sick or aristocrats.

We wouldn't a lasted long without corn meal. Corn bread was our staff of life. For several years we had it in some form for breakfast, dinner and supper, never tirin of it. Corn Bread was made in several different ways. As I remember, there was corn dodger, which was corn meal mixed with water, salt, and butter and baked in a spider. Johnny cake was mixed the same way, but baked on a clapboard tilted up before the fire. Turnin a Johnny cake wasn't so easy to do. Mother would take hold of one end of the clapboard, give it a little shake to loosen the cake, then flip it up in the air to turn it over and catch it on the board. Then it was set before the fire again to finish bakin.

Hoe cake was mixed about the same as Johnny cake, flattened out with the hands, and put on a griddle to bake.

Corn pone was scalded meal mixed and put in a warm place to raise. Then it was mixed with punkin and let raise again. It was baked in the Dutch oven. Corn meal mush was a big favorite in the early days. Mush and milk was a common meal at supper time, and fried mush for breakfast. Many a time us children went to bed on a supper of mush and milk and not a thing else. Some people wouldn't think they could get along on corn bread every meal, but we did for years and grew up a right strong and husky bunch.

Lye hominy was another corn dish. It was corn grains soaked in lye made from wood ashes, biled until the hulls come loose and was rubbed off by hand, soaked in cold water until the lye was all out, then cooked.

We didn't have to worry much about meat. Some settlers brought hogs in when they took up land. They was turned loose in the woods to feed on mast and herbs they rooted out of the ground. Mast is acorns, beechnuts, chestnuts, and other nuts. The lard was so strong that mother used butter instead for cookin. The meat was strong, too, and there was plenty of wild game we liked better. At first, deer was plentiful and it was on the table so often we got tired of it. After I got big enough to handle a rifle, mother would often say to me:

"Son, I wish you would run down in the bottoms and get me a turkey for a change."

I wouldn't be gone more than a hour before I'd be back with a gobbler for her.

The woods was full of squirrels. You could go out most any time and get a mess. We used only the hind parts and the backs of em. There was also lots of grouse—pheasants, we called em—which we thought about the most tasty meat of all. Once in a while someone would kill a bear and divide it around among the neighbors; but that meat was sort of strong and oily. Fall Crick and White River was full of fish, like suckers, redhorse, cat fish, bass, perch, salmon, buffalo, and red eye. We didn't bother much with a hook and line. Pap always kept a good canoe. If we wanted a mess of fish, all we had to do was grab the gig, jump in the canoe, pole up and down the crick a few times; if the water was clear, you was purty sure to spear a mess.

Every family had some chickens. They took care of themselves, feedin in the woods and roostin in the trees. They was kept jist for the eggs. We considered wild turkey and pheasant much better to eat. The family cow furnished the main beverage as well as butter and cottage cheese for the family. Once in a while she was the start of a mighty good ox.

For emergencies mother would jerk venison and turkey breasts. The meat was sliced thin and hung over a bed of coals to half dry and half cook. Then it was hung in a cool place for future use.

It was a universal custom for the women to tend the garden, just as they always milked the cow. We had garden stuff of most all kinds. Potatoes and punkins was the most important. Tomatoes, called to-mat-us-es, was raised only for ornaments to set on the mantle; they was supposed to be poison then, so we never eat em. Punkins was used in several ways. They was stewed, put on plates, buttered and eat. Sometimes mother fried punkin. It was stewed, spread on clapboards and dried before the fire for winter use. We also made punkin molasses. The punkin was allowed to freeze, then the juice was squeezed out and boiled down. While mother was dryin the punkin I would beg a little of her, run it through the cullender, dry it before the fire, cut it into small strips and roll it into tight rolls. This was called punkin leather. It was mighty handy to slip in your pocket and nibble on at school.

One other important part of every garden was the two or three rows of terbacker to furnish the smokin for the old women and the chewin for the men folks. About all the men and bigger boys chewed terbacker.

Pap always made a good supply of maple sugar. The trees was tapped the same as the Indians did it, the sap ran out in handmade troughs dug out of the short cuts of logs, and it was boiled down in a big kettle until it grained into sugar. Pap would never waste any sugar water to make molasses. What he was lookin after was the sugar supply, as the maple sugar was the only kind of sweet'nin we had.

There was plenty of wild grapes, wild plums, and wild gooseberries in the woods. They was made into sass. But no pies, for there was no flour to make the crust. Wheat wasn't raised for several years. The ground was so new and rich it would grow up all straw and fall over by cuttin time without makin any grain. Besides that, the first grist mills had no way to bolt the flour. Then agin, I think the older people liked their three-times-a-day corn bread so well that they didn't want anything that would take its place. I remember when mother started makin wheat bread; Pap fussed around about it and said he would jist as soon skin a hackberry tree and eat the bark. Our first white bread was salt risin, for there was no yeast then to make any other kind. For biscuits, we made a substitute for baking powder by burnin corn cobs and usin the ashes.

Mother soon found that if she was goin to do much bakin for our big family she would have to get a bigger oven and one with more heat. So Pap went out back of the cabin and made her one. He first built up a platform out of puncheons, about eighteen inches high and four feet square. On this platform he made a holler cone out of clay. On one side was a door. Opposite the door and a little higher up was a hole for draught and smoke. The oven was heated by buildin a fire inside of good dry wood. When mother thought it was hot enough, she would rake out the fire and brush out the ashes as best she could. Then she would test the heat by throwin in a finger or two of flour. If the flour browned to suit her, she put in the bread and closed the door. The heat in the clay walls done the rest.

We didn't use store tea and coffee. It was hard to get, but the main reason was that everlastin shortage of money to buy with. Sometimes mother made tea from spicewood and sassafras. A right good substitute for coffee was made from parched corn.

Our table was mighty simple and plain, consistin of pewter plates, tin cups, iron spoons, knives and forks. The forks had but two prongs. From long usage some of the forks had a prong missin. Yet we got along purty well them days. We had our ups and downs, but nobody went hungry and nobody done much complainin. We just about lived off the land and was satisfied.

THE SPINNING WHEEL

WHEN I was a youngster, all our clothin was linen. We didn't have any sheep for several years on account of the wolves. Besides, the woods was so full of burrs, briers, and brush that the wool would a been ruined. A few of the older folks wore buckskin britches and huntin shirts, but Pap and mother saw that our family had linen clothes.

Most families put out a half acre or so of flax every spring so they could make their own linen. Flax grew somethin like wheat or grass. In the late summer when it was ripe it was pulled up by the roots and spread on the ground to dry. Then it was bound in bundles and stored away until fall, when it was again spread out on the ground to let the fall rains rot the inside or heart of the stalk. The outside fiber would remain firm. After the rottin process, it was again bound up and laid away until brittle cold weather, when it was run through a hand breaker. Then it was scutched or swingled by graspin a bundle in one hand and layin it across a solid board. With a wooden knife in the other hand it was whipped and beaten until all the dry heart of the stalk fell out leavin only the outside fiber.

The fiber was then drawn through a hackle, which was a board with a lot of sharp spikes stickin up, until all the seed and root ends was jerked off. Drawn through a finer hackle, the fiber split up into fine silky strands. The bunch of them was wound around a distaff and the flax was ready for spinnin.

To spin, one end of the distaff was stuck in a hole in the frame of the spinnin wheel. The spinner then started the wheel with her foot and with one hand started the flax by pullin a little from the distaff. With the other hand she fed it on to the reel. The thread was gauged as it passed through the fingers. If it felt too big it was jerked back to draw out the fiber thinner. If too small it was given a quick jerk from the distaff to feed on more. As the thread passed over the spinnin wheel it was twisted and wound on to a large spool. If a thread broke, the wheel was stopped, the two ends frayed out with the thumb and finger then pressed together, the wheel was started, and you couldn't tell where the break was.

The thread was reeled off in skeins and biled in lye to bleach and soften. It was now ready for the weaver. We didn't have a loom. Pap thought mother had enough to do takin care of a big family. So our weavin was done by a neighbor woman who made a business of takin in weavin. The linen cloth was made into dresses for the women and girls, and shirts and britches for the men and boys. Underwear was somethin the men and boys didn't have for several years, or until we started raisin sheep. We wore linen summer and winter. If you got too cold, you put on two shirts and two pair of britches—that is, if you had em.

All bed clothes, towels, table cloths, and women's stockins was linen. Mother spun her own thread for sewin. If we wanted a fish line, mother spun that, too.

Soon as we got to raisin sheep we had lots warmer clothin for winter. After shearin the sheep, which was done by the women, about an inch of wool was cut off to get rid of the burrs, and the rest was washed in soapsuds. When dry it was picked by hand into small loose and fluffy bunches. Then it was carded, or drawn through small sharp spikes much like the flax hackle, until the fine hairs was all pulled out straight. Then it was made into rolls and spun into thread same as flax was, only the spinnin wheel was bigger than the flax wheel. Mother had three small wheels and two large ones so the girls could help spin. When enough thread was spun, it was taken to the weaver and made into cloth. Sometimes mother colored the thread; then we had plaid goods.

Mother made us boys an everyday coat or jacket called a wamus. It buttoned in front like any other coat, but had a long, divided skirt, or tail, in the back. When we got cold we would bring the tail around and tie it in front. That also kept the tail out of the way when workin.

Instead of neckties, men wore a stock if they wanted to look dressy. It was a big silk or satin affair, sometimes pleated, that covered the chest and run over the shoulders and buttoned in the back. It extended up until it almost touched the ears. Pap had one but laid it aside; said it was too dressy for him. When I was about grown I picked it up and wore it out.

Men's hats was made in the hat shops in the towns. The prevailin hat for dress was the tall, bell-crown style. Some of them was a sight to see; they was so big and tall and hairy. For a dozen or more coon hides, a hatter would make you a hat out of half of them, keepin the other half for his pay. He sheared the hair off the hides and mixed it with a sticky preparation of some kind, beat it into a stiff mess and spread it over a form or hat block. More hair was spread on to make the nap. When they was smoothed up they looked purty slick, but when they got rained on they fuzzed up like an old mad coon for sure.

Pap never would wear one; said it made him feel stuck up. He always wore a plain, broad-rim wool hat. Boys wore that kind, too. Some coonskin caps was worn, but not many with the tail left on. They was worn only by men like Uncle Milt and others who hunted a lot and wanted to hang on to the Indun fightin days. In the summer time, boys went bareheaded mostly. If we wanted a straw hat, we braided long strips of wheat straws and got mother to sew them together, workin in the shape as she sewed. The first headwear for women was ordinary sunbonnets. Soon as dress goods was wagoned up from river towns they made bonnets about all shapes and colors imagined. Big red bandana handkerchiefs was also worn on the head by women.

Pap made all the shoes for our big family. He would work on shoes only of evenins. They was for winter wear. In the summer most everybody went barefoot, especially the women and children. Some wore moccasins made from ground hog hides. In the fall Pap would go to town and buy or trade for a half side of sole leather and a half side of upper leather. Mother's and his shoes was always made first, then shoes for the girls. Us boys come last. Sometimes he didn't get to us bigger boys until purty late in the fall. I guess he thought it made us tough and healthy to go barefoot in the frost. As I was the oldest boy, it would be up toward Christmas before I got any shoes.

Sometimes us older boys would go to school half a term barefooted. On frosty mornins in the fall we would heat a clapboard before the fireplace until it was almost charred, stick it under our arm and run through the frost until our feet began to sting. Then we threw the clapboard on the ground, stood on it until our feet warmed, grab it up and make another run. This way we would reach the schoolhouse in purty good shape, not sufferin much from the cold or thinkin much about it.

I remember goin over to Uncle Ben's one time to play with my cousins. (He was mother's brother.) We'd had a cold spell and the crick was froze over. I walked across the ice in my bare feet. Another time I remember when Pap finished my shoes on Christmas eve. I was so tickled with em I put em on, run out of the door and tore around the house to try em out. I forgot about the ice that had formed around the well and the water trough. When I hit that slick spot with them new shoes, I got a fall I never did forget.

Grown girls would want to fix up a little when they went to meetin on Sunday. They would carry their shoes and stockins in their hands until they come in sight of the meetin house, then slip em on. After meetin was over they wouldn't be more than out of sight when they'd take em off. They was mighty proud of their shoes, but they was so used to goin barefoot their shoes felt a mighty sight more comfortable carried in the hand.

CHAPTER SIXTEEN

Our Young Folks

A large percentage of "young folks" are juveniles, and to the term juvenile many, though not quite all, elders insist on adding the descriptive term delinquent. Of course, juveniles are not delinquent to any greater extent now than they were in times past—if as great.

Much of this unfavorable opinion is due to the fact that as we adults age, we tend to remember things that never happened and to forget unpleasant things that did. Happily, not quite all of us do so. A few years ago, a charming Hoosier gentleman who had reached his mid-eighties (without becoming in the least unpleasantly octogenarian) was seated at afternoon coffee with a group of his middle-aged friends when the conversation turned, as it often did, to juvenile delinquency.

The eighty-odd gentleman listened for a while, then slammed down his coffee cup and spoke his piece:

"I get so tired of listening to you kids talk like that. Hell's fire! You don't know what juvenile delinquency is! You should have lived in Waynetown in the 'Nineties, as I did; we knew about delinquency!"

We shall look at two maidens in this chapter, both of them more or less delinquent, but, strangely enough, the one historical personage of the two, representing a lass who flourished (and faded) in nineteenth century Greencastle, Indiana (and who must have tended to be a bit round of heel), was by her own evidence genuinely delinquent. The fictional character in the other selection was only mildly delinquent. What is more, she saw the error of her ways, while the nineteenth century true juvenile delinquent apparently never did so.

Let us begin with the earlier lady's case, not only because it is a sad one, beautifully set forth in verse by none less than

JAMES BUCHANAN ELMORE

(The Bard of Alamo)

but also because Elmore, besides the drama of his epic, has included in it a verse couplet unequalled in English letters since the days of Cowper. It is:

> He absconded to Cincinnati and dentistry took,
> And left a true love he willfully forsook,

So, without further delay, let us consider

Pearl Bryan's Fate

Pretty Pearl Bryan had an elegant home,
With flowers and green pastures whither she roamed;
Her face like a rosebud, and teeth snowy white,
A gem of pure beauty—a star of the night.

There came to this cottage, in care of Will Wood,
A wooer, Scott Jackson, an imp of the lewd,
And betrayed this kind maiden, her heart he did break,
Who laid down her life for a villain's sake.

He absconded to Cincinnati, and dentistry took,
And left a true love he willfully forsook,
To pine in true nature—a false, fickle friend,
He never intended his ways for to mend.

There came a quick message: "Oh! come to me, dear,
I never once thought how I treated you here.
Oh, come to me, darling. I'll make it all right;
Make your departure in shadow of night."

Shrill shrieked the whistle, she then bade adieus,
And soon there was flying this wonderful news.
She's safe in Queen City, a medium is found,
And her future destiny this witch does expound.

She goes to the station, her steps to retake,
Where Walling consoles her, which is a mistake.
A carriage is procured for making a drive,
When this poor girl is last seen alive.

A darkey was secured as coachman in disguise,
To the shores of Kentucky they quickly arrive;
These steeds of assassins are making good stride
To a place in the bushes, their mischief to hide.

The carriage is stopped by the side of the road,
Where two cruel wretches have landed their load;
With cocaine and dagger these fiends, 'tis said,
Relieved this poor damsel of a beautiful head.

When the moon's rays reflected the bright shining steel,
She fainted within and began for to kneel.
"Oh, God, save the distressed, and care for me quick!
Take me to heaven." Then came the death lick.

She sank on the leaflets, her blood stained the thyme;
Thus ended the most brutish of modern crime—
All for the lusts or passions of men,
Whose doom is the scaffold or work in the pen.

The darkey is frightened nigh unto death,
And flees with the horses that's throbbing for breath,
And leaves the two murderers afoot for to flee,
With the head in a satchel, as bloody as can be.

A search of their clothing reveals spots crimson red,
But where, Oh! where is the poor victim's head?
'Tis sunk in the river, or hid in the ground,
Never, 'tis supposed, by man to be found.

Now these Herods are landed inside of a jail,
And leave the old parents to weep and to wail
The loss of their darling, so dear unto them,
Slain by assassins—imps of good men.

A mob is now raising; they quake, it is said,
And feel the cold chills at the loss of their heads.
An appeal is now taken to Kentucky for fear
'Tis only a-hastening to meet the cold bier.

These men they must hang, the jury did say,
Until they are dead, a debt for to pay,
For killing a maiden just in her beauty and bloom,
And now lies headless in a mouldering tomb.

They ascended the scaffold—a ransom of blood;
The trap door is sprung, and Oh! what a thud!
Two bodies are swinging at the end of a cord,
Their spirits ascended to the court of our Lord.

No telling which way the spirits will go—
Whether 'tis up, or far, far below;
One thing is certain; 'tis better by odds
To be a good person, a child of God's.

Poor Pearl Bryan! But, as Mr. Elmore could have told her, "The wages of sin is death."

We had heard from Mr. Elmore on previous occasions, always speaking fluently and with wisdom and we have also heard once from the following writer,

JESSAMYN WEST

Miss West was born in Jennings County, Indiana, and it was probably no fault of hers that her family removed her and condemned her to grow up in California. She is no less a native born Hoosier, and we are proud of her. This is an extract from one of her several excellent novels,

Cress Delahanty

WINTER

Wʜɪʟᴇ ʜᴇʀ ᴍᴏᴛʜᴇʀ and father awaited the arrival of Mr. and Mrs. Kibbler who had called asking to speak to them "about Cress and Edwin Jr.," Mr. Delahanty reminded his wife how wrong she had been about Cress.

"Not two months ago," he said, "in this very room you told me you were worried because Cress wasn't as interested in the boys as a girl her age should be. In this very room. And now look what's happened."

Mrs. Delahanty, worried now by Mrs. Kibbler's message, spoke more sharply than she had intended. "Don't keep repeating, 'in this very room,'" she said, "as if it would have been different if I'd said it in the back porch or out of doors. Besides, what has happened?"

Mr. Delahanty took off his hat, which he'd had on when Mrs. Kibbler phoned, and sailed it out of the living room toward the hall table, which he missed. "Don't ask me what's happened," he said, "I'm not the girl's mother."

Mrs. Delahanty took off her own hat and jabbed the hat pins back into it. "What do you mean, you're not the girl's mother? Of course you're not. No one ever said you were."

Mr. Delahanty picked up his fallen hat, put it on the chair beside the hall table and came back into the living room. "A girl confides in her mother," he told his wife.

"A girl confides in her mother!" Mrs. Delahanty was very scornful. "Who tells you these things, John Delahanty? Not *your* mother. She didn't have any daughter. Not me. Cress doesn't confide in anyone. How do you know these things, anyway, about mothers and daughters?"

John Delahanty seated himself upon the sofa, legs extended, head back, as straight and unrelaxed as a plank.

"Don't catch me up that way, Gertrude," he said. "You know I don't know them." Without giving his wife any opportunity to crow over this victory he went on quickly: "What I'd like to know is why did the Kibblers have to pick a Saturday night for this call? Didn't they know we'd be going into town?"

Like most . . . John Delahanty stopped work early on Saturdays so that, after a quick clean-up and supper, he and his wife could drive into town. There they did nothing very important: bought groceries, saw a show, browsed around in hardware stores, visited friends. But after a week of seeing only themselves . . . it was pleasant simply to saunter along the sidewalks looking at the cars, the merchandise, the people in their town clothes. This Saturday trip to town was a jaunt they both looked forward to during the week, and tonight's trip, because of February's warmer air and suddenly, it seemed, longer twilight, would have been particularly pleasant.

"Five minutes more," said Mr. Delahanty, "and we'd have been on our way."

"Why didn't you tell Mrs. Kibbler we were just leaving?"

"I did. And she said for anything less important she wouldn't think of keeping us."

Mrs. Delahanty came over to the sofa and stood looking anxiously down at her husband. "John, exactly what did Mrs. Kibbler say?"

"The gist of it," said Mr. Delahanty, "was that . . ."

"I don't care about the gist of it. That's just what you think she said. I want to know what she really said."

Mr. Delahanty let his head fall forward, though he still kept his legs stiffly extended. "What she really said was, 'Is this Mr. John Delahanty?' And I said 'Yes.' Then she said, 'This is Mrs. Edwin Kibbler, I guess you remember me.' "

"Remember her?" Mrs. Delahanty exclaimed. "I didn't know you even knew her."

"I don't," said Mr. Delahanty, "but I remember her all right. She came before the school board about a month ago to tell us we ought to take those two ollas off the school grounds. She said it was old-fashioned to cool water that way, that the ollas looked messy and were unhygienic."

"Did you take them off?" Mrs. Delahanty asked, without thinking.

As a private person John Delahanty was reasonable and untalkative. As clerk of the school board he inclined toward dogmatism and long-windedness. Now he began a defense of the ollas and the school board's action in retaining them.

"Look, John," said Mrs. Delahanty, "I'm not interested in the school board or its water coolers. What I want to know is, what did Mrs. Kibbler say about Cress?"

"Well, she said she wanted to have a little talk with us about Cress—and Edwin Jr."

"I know that." Impatience made Mrs. Delahanty's voice sharp. "But what about them?"

Mr. Delahanty drew his feet up toward the sofa, then bent down and retied a shoelace. "About what Cress did to him—Edwin Jr."

"*Did* to him—" said Mrs. Delahanty aghast.

"That's what his mother said."

Mrs. Delahanty sat down on the hassock at her husband's feet. "Did to him," she repeated again. "Why, what could Cress do to him? He's two or three years older than Cress, fifteen or sixteen anyway. What could she do to him?"

Mr. Delahanty straightened up. "She could hit him, I guess," he ventured.

"Hit him? What would she want to hit him for?"

"I don't know," said Mr. Delahanty. "I don't know that she did hit him. Maybe she kicked him. Anyway, his mother seems to think the boy's been damaged in some way."

"Damaged," repeated Mrs. Delahanty angrily. "Damaged! Why, Cress is too tender-hearted to hurt a fly. She shoos them outside instead of killing them. And you sit there talking of hitting and kicking."

"Well," said Mr. Delahanty mildly, "Edwin's got teeth out. I don't know how else she could get them out, do you?"

"I'm going to call Cress," said Mrs. Delahanty, "and ask her about this. I don't believe it for a minute."

"I don't think calling her will do any good. She left while I was talking to Mrs. Kibbler."

"What do you mean, left?"

"Went for a walk, she said."

"Well, teeth out," repeated Mrs. Delahanty unbelievingly. "Teeth out! I didn't know you could get teeth out except with pliers or a chisel."

"Maybe Edwin's teeth are weak."

"Don't joke about this, John Delahanty. It isn't any joking matter. And I don't believe it. I don't believe Cress did it or that the boy's teeth are out. Anyway I'd have to see them to believe it."

"You're going to," Mr. Delahanty said. "Mrs. Kibbler's bringing Edwin especially so you can."

Mrs. Delahanty sat for some time without saying anything at all. Then she got up and walked back and forth in front of her husband, turning her hat, which she still held, round and round on one finger. "Well, what does Mrs. Kibbler expect us to do now?" she asked. "If they really are out, that is?"

"For one thing," replied Mr. Delahanty, "she expects us to pay for some new ones. And for another . . ." Mr. Delahanty paused to listen. Faintly, in the distance a car could be heard. "Here she is now," he said.

Mrs. Delahanty stopped her pacing. "Do you think I should make some cocoa for them, John? And maybe some marguerites?"

"No, I don't," said Mr. Delahanty. "I don't think Mrs. Kibbler considers this a social visit."

As the car turned into the long driveway which led . . . to the Delahanty house, Mrs. Delahanty said, "I still don't see why you think this proves I'm wrong."

Mr. Delahanty had forgotten about his wife's wrongness. "How do you mean wrong?" he asked.

"About Cress's not being interested in the boys."

"Oh," he said. "Well, you've got to be pretty interested in a person— one way or another—before you hit him."

"That's a perfectly silly notion," began Mrs. Delahanty, but before she could finish, the Kibblers had arrived.

Mr. Delahanty went to the door while Mrs. Delahanty stood in the back of the room by the fireplace unwilling to take one step toward meeting her visitors.

Mrs. Kibbler was a small woman with a large, determined nose, prominent blue eyes and almost no chin. Her naturally curly hair—she didn't wear a hat—sprang away from her head in a great cage-shaped pompadour which dwarfed her face.

Behind Mrs. Kibbler was Mr. Kibbler, short, dusty, soft-looking, bald, except for a fringe of hair about his ears so thick that the top of his head, by contrast, seemed more naked than mere lack of hair could make it.

Behind Mr. Kibbler was Edwin Jr. He was as thin as his mother, as mild and soft-looking as his father; and to these qualities he added an unhappiness all of his own. He gave one quick look at the room and the Delahantys through his thick-lensed spectacles, after which he kept his eyes on the floor.

Mr. Delahanty closed the door behind the callers, then introduced his wife to Mrs. Kibbler. Mrs. Kibbler in turn introduced her family to the Delahantys. While the Kibblers were seating themselves—Mrs. Kibbler and Edwin Jr. on the sofa, Mr. Kibbler on a straight-backed chair in the room's darkest corner—Mrs. Delahanty, out of nervousness, bent and lit the fire, which was laid in the fireplace. . . . Then she and Mr. Delahanty seated themselves in the chairs on each side of the fireplace.

Mrs. Kibbler looked at the fire with some surprise. "Do you find it cold this evening, Mrs. Delahanty?" she asked.

"No," said Mrs. Delahanty, "I don't. I don't know why I lit the fire."

To this Mrs. Kibbler made no reply. Instead, without preliminaries, she turned to her son. "Edwin," she said, "show the Delahantys what their daughter did to your teeth."

Mrs. Delahanty wanted to close her eyes, look into the fire, or find, as Edwin Jr. had done, a spot of her own on the floor to examine. There was an almost imperceptible ripple along the length of the boy's face as if he had tried to open his mouth but found he lacked the strength. He momentarily lifted his eyes from the floor to dart a glance into the dark corner where his father sat. But Mr. Kibbler continued to sit in expressionless silence.

"Edwin," said Mrs. Kibbler, "speak to your son."

"Do what your mother says, son," said Mr. Kibbler.

Very slowly, as if it hurt him, Edwin opened his mouth.

His teeth were white, and in his thin face they seemed very large, as well. The two middle teeth, above, had been broken across in a slanting line. The lower incisor appeared to be missing entirely.

"Wider, Edwin," Mrs. Kibbler urged. "I want the Delahantys to see exactly what their daughter is responsible for."

But before Edwin could make any further effort Mrs. Delahanty cried, "No, that's enough."

"I didn't want you to take our word for anything," Mrs. Kibbler said reasonably. "I wanted you to see."

"Oh, we see, all right," said Mrs. Delahanty earnestly.

Mr. Delahanty leaned forward and spoke to Mrs. Kibbler. "While we see the teeth, Mrs. Kibbler, it just isn't a thing we think Crescent would do. Or in fact how she *could* do it. We think Edwin must be mistaken."

"You mean lying?" asked Mrs. Kibbler flatly.

"Mistaken," repeated Mr. Delahanty.

"Tell them, Edwin," said Mrs. Kibbler.

"She knocked me down," said Edwin, very low.

Mrs. Delahanty, although she was already uncomfortably warm, held her hands nearer the fire, even rubbed them together a time or two.

"I simply can't believe that," she said.

"You mean hit you with her fist and knocked you down?" asked Mr. Delahanty.

"No," said Edwin even lower than before. "Ran into me."

"But not on purpose," said Mrs. Delahanty.

Edwin nodded. "Yes," he said. "On purpose."

"But why?" asked Mr. Delahanty. "Why? Cress wouldn't do such a thing, I know—without some cause. Why?"

"Tell them why, Edwin," said his mother.

Edwin's head went even nearer the floor—as if the spot he was watching had diminished or retreated.

"For fun," he said.

It was impossible not to believe the boy as he sat there hunched, head bent, one eyelid visibly twitching. "But Cress would never do such a thing," said Mrs. Delahanty.

Mrs. Kibbler disregarded this. "It would not have been so bad, Mr.

Delahanty, except that Edwin was standing by one of those ollas. When your daughter shoved Edwin over she shoved the olla over, too. That's probably what broke his teeth. Heavy as cement and falling down on top of him and breaking up in a thousand pieces. To say nothing of his being doused with water on a cold day. And Providence alone can explain why his glasses weren't broken."

"What had you done, Edwin?" asked Mrs. Delahanty again.

"Nothing," whispered Edwin.

"All we want," said Mrs. Kibbler, "is what's perfectly fair. Pay the dentist's bill. And have that girl of yours apologize to Edwin."

Mrs. Delahanty got up suddenly and walked over to Edwin. She put one hand on his thin shoulder and felt him twitch under her touch like a frightened colt.

"Go on, Edwin," she said. "Tell me the truth. Tell me why."

Edwin slowly lifted his head. "Go on, Edwin," Mrs. Delahanty encouraged him.

"He told you once," said Mrs. Kibbler. "Fun. That girl of yours is a big, boisterous thing from all I hear. She owes my boy an apology."

Edwin's face continued to lift until he was looking directly at Mrs. Delahanty.

He started to speak—but had said only three words, "Nobody ever wants," when Cress walked in from the hall. She had evidently been there for some time, for she went directly to Edwin.

"I apologize for hurting you, Edwin," she said.

Then she turned to Mrs. Kibbler. "I've got twelve seventy-five saved for a bicycle. That can go to help pay for his teeth."

After the Kibblers left, the three Delahantys sat for some time without saying a word. The fire had about died down and outside an owl, hunting finished, flew back toward the hills, softly hooting.

"I guess if we hurried we could just about catch the second show," Mr. Delahanty said.

"I won't be going to shows for a while," said Cress.

The room was very quiet. Mrs. Delahanty traced the outline of one of the bricks in the fireplace.

"I can save twenty-five cents a week that way. Toward his teeth," she explained.

Mrs. Delahanty took the poker and stirred the coals so that for a second there was an upward drift of sparks; but the fire was too far gone to blaze. Because it had not yet been completely dark when the Kibblers came, only one lamp had been turned on. Now that night had arrived the room was only partially lighted; but no one seemed to care. Mr. Delahanty, in Mr. Kibbler's dark corner, was almost invisible. Mrs. Delahanty stood by the fireplace. Cress sat where Edwin had sat, looking downward, perhaps at the same spot at which he had looked.

"One day at school," she said, "Edwin went out in the fields at noon and gathered wild flower bouquets for everyone. A lupine, a poppy, two barley heads, four yellow violets. He tied them together with blades of grass. They were sweet little bouquets. He went without his lunch to get them fixed, and when we came back from eating there was a bouquet on every desk in the study hall. It looked like a flower field when we came in and Edwin did it to surprise us."

After a while Mr. Delahanty asked, "Did the kids like that?"

"Yes, they liked it. They tore their bouquets apart, said Cress, "and used the barley beards to tickle each other. Miss Ingols made Edwin gather up every single flower and throw it in the wastepaper basket."

After a while Cress said, "Edwin has a collection of bird feathers. The biggest is from a buzzard, the littlest from a hummingbird. They're all different colors. The brightest is from a woodpecker.

"Does he kill birds," Mr. Delahanty asked, "just to get a feather?"

"Oh, no!" said Cress. "He just keeps his eyes open to where a bird might drop a feather. It would spoil his collection to get a feather he didn't find that way."

Mr. Delahanty sighed and stirred in his wooden chair so that it creaked a little.

"Edwin would like to be a missionary to China," said Cress. Some particle in the fireplace as yet unburned, blazed up in a sudden spurt of blue flame. "Not a preaching missionary," she explained.

"A medical missionary?" asked Mr. Delahanty.

"Oh, no! Edwin says he's had to take too much medicine to ever be willing to make other people take it."

There was another long silence in the room. Mrs. Delahanty sat down in the chair her husband had vacated and once more held a hand toward the fire. There was just enough life left in the coals to make the tips of her fingers rosy. She didn't turn toward Cress at all or ask a single question. Back in the dusk Cress's voice went on.

"He would like to teach them how to play baseball."

Mr. Delahanty's voice was matter-of-fact. "Edwin doesn't look to me like he would be much of a baseball player."

"Oh he isn't," Cress agreed. "He isn't even any of a baseball player. But he could be a baseball authority. Know everything and teach by diagram. That's what he'd have to do. And learn from them how they paint. He says some of their pictures look like they had been painted with one kind of bird feather and some with another. He knows they don't really paint with bird feathers," she explained. "That's a fancy of his. . . ."

"I'm sorry Edwin happened to be standing by that olla," said Mr. Delahanty. "That's what did the damage, I suppose."

"Oh, he had to stand there," said Cress. "He didn't have any choice. That's the mush pot."

"Mush pot," repeated Mr. Delahanty.

"It's a circle round the box the olla stands on," said Crescent. "Edwin spends about his whole time there. While we're waiting for the bus anyway."

"Crescent," asked Mr. Delahanty, "what is this mush pot?"

"It's prison," said Cress, surprise in her voice. "It's where the prisoners are kept. Only at school we always call it the mush pot."

"Is this a game?" asked Mr. Delahanty.

"It's dare base," said Crescent. "Didn't you ever play it? You choose up sides. You draw two lines and one side stands in the middle and tries to catch the other side as they run by. Nobody ever chooses Edwin. The last captain to choose just gets him. Because he can't help himself. They call him the handicap. He gets caught first thing and spends the whole game in the mush pot because nobody will waste any time trying to rescue him. He'd just get caught again, they say, and the whole game would be nothing but rescue Edwin."

"How do you rescue anyone, Cress?" asked her father.

"Run from home base to the mush pot without being caught. Then take the prisoner's hand. Then he goes free."

"Were you trying to rescue Edwin, Cress?"

Cress didn't answer her father at once. Finally she said, "It was my duty. I chose him for our side. I chose him first of all and didn't wait just to get him. So it was my duty to rescue him. Only I ran too hard and couldn't stop. And the olla fell down on top of him and knocked his teeth out. And humiliated him. But he was free," she said. "I got there without being caught."

Mrs. Delahanty spoke with a great surge of warmth and anger. "Humiliated him! When you were only trying to help him. Trying to rescue him. And you were black and blue for days yourself! What gratitude."

Cress said, "But he didn't want to be rescued, Mother. Not by me anyway. He said he liked being in the mush pot. He said . . . he got there on purpose . . . to observe. He gave me back the feathers I'd found for him. One was a road-runner feather. The only one he had."

"Well, you can start a feather collection of your own," said Mrs. Delahanty with energy. "I often see feathers when I'm walking through the orchard. After this I'll save them for you."

"I'm not interested in feathers," said Cress. Then she added, "I can get two bits an hour any time suckering trees for Mr. Hudson or cleaning blackboards at school. That would be two fifty a week at least. Plus the twelve seventy-five. How much do you suppose his teeth will be?"

"Cress," said her father, "you surely aren't going to let the Kibblers go on thinking you knocked their son down on purpose, are you? Do you want Edwin to think that?"

"Edwin doesn't really think that," Cress said. "He knows I was rescuing him. But now I've apologized— and if we pay for the new teeth and everything, maybe after a while he'll believe it."

She stood up and walked to the hall doorway. "I'm awfully tired," she said. "I guess I'll go to bed."

"But Cress," asked Mrs. Delahanty, "why do you want him to believe it? When it isn't true?"

Cress was already through the door, but she turned back to explain. "You don't knock people down you are sorry for," she said.

After Cress had gone upstairs Mrs. Delahanty said, "Well, John, you were right, of course."

"Right?" asked Mr. Delahanty, again forgetful.

"About Cress's being interested in the boys."

"Yes," said Mr. Delahanty. "Yes, I'm afraid I was."

There you are. Cress, with the kindest motives in the world, still, by the evidence of Edwin Jr.'s missing front teeth, became somewhat delinquent. And she with a father on the school board, even! You just never can tell, can you?

Young Hoosiers of whatever era are usually worth paying attention to, if only for the sake of plain morbid curiosity. Of late the nation's foremost Pied Piper seems to be a native Hoosier whose novels have steadily made the best-seller lists and have earned him a special place in the sympathies of America's young people.

KURT VONNEGUT, JR.

was born in Indianapolis in 1922, scion of a prominent German-American family of architects and ironmongers. He attended Public School No. 43 (the James Whitcomb Riley School) and Shortridge High School in Indianapolis, and went on to Cornell, where he studied biochemistry, Carnegie Tech for mechanical engineering, and Chicago, where he was an anthropology major. His experiences in World War II included being held as a prisoner of war during the fire-bombing of Dresden. After stints as a police reporter and a public relations writer, Vonnegut began to devote himself in earnest to the writing of fiction. He has taught "creative writing" at Iowa, Harvard, and the City University of New York. Beginning with Player Piano in 1952, he has dealt with the themes of technology, science, religion, and the manifold ingenious ways that man can be inhumane to man.

Vonnegut, as noted before, is a graduate of Shortridge, a public academy whose literary products include Booth Tarkington, Dan Wakefield, and Jeremy Larner. His recurrent preoccupation with his Hoosier origins and their influence on him is characteristically expressed in the following reflections on his own school days. Or, as Vonnegut himself might say much more pointedly, "And so it goes. . . ."

Times Change

REFLECTIONS OF A HIGH-SCHOOL
STUDENT FROM THE CLASS OF '40

I WENT TO Shortridge High School in Indianapolis, Indiana. It was
and still is one of the few American high schools with a daily paper. It
was fashionable to write. Everybody was crazy about writing, and I'm
writing still. So is Dan Wakefield, and so are a lot of other people who
went there. It is such an old paper that my mother used to be on its
staff, God rest her soul. Its name is the *Echo*, which is an honest name
for an officially sanctioned student newspaper. Everything I said in it
echoed off the grown-ups around me, which was all right with me back
then. Thinking back, I am not persuaded that I was a complete fool to
be content with echoing. I admired a lot of my teachers—still do. Many
of them are still teaching, and I pay them calls from time to time.

One thing that was lucky for me: my high-school years were from
1936 to 1940, and the Great Depression was still pretty mean, and the
smartest people in town had turned to teaching. I don't think the
smartest people do that anymore. Times change.

The poet of my graduating class had this to say in the front of our
yearbook, which incidentally celebrated the seventy-fifth anniversary
of the school:

"Where go the years?
But moments fleet, uncertain
That swiftly speed and disappear
From mortal view?
Where go the years?
To seek the darkness and to hide
Within the dust of old hall clocks?
Or ride forgotten moonbeams
To the sky?"

I don't laugh or even smile at that high-school poem now. Where *do* go the years? That's an excellent guess—that they ride forgotten moon-beams to the sky. The author was Phyllis Heidenreich.

Phyllis—where are you now?

I will tell you where a lot of our classmates are: they're in soldiers' graves. When I go back to Indianapolis, I sometimes stand beneath the great bronze casualty lists which are bolted to the walls in the entrance hall of Shortridge, and I read all the names, and I marvel silently, "My God—so that's what became of him . . . and him . . . and him . . . and him." It's easy for me to imagine that all those dead young men are lawyers and realtors and insurance salesmen and teachers and engi-neers and so on. And they're not.

I reread those casualty lists again very recently, made old friends and enemies stop mowing lawns and barbecuing steaks in my imagi-nation, made them climb back into their graves. And then I went downtown to a television station to promote a new book of mine. It was a pacifistic book. One of my television costars was the man in charge of the Indianapolis 500-mile Speedway Parade. Another was Little Richard, a black rock musician who had given The Beatles their start in international show business. He took them to Germany with him.

Little Richard was wearing an electric-blue dashiki, and he would periodically shout, even while the parade marshal or I was speaking, "Let it all hang out!" So I did let it all hang out, I expressed my disgust at the Vietnam war, said I had four sons of military age, that none of them was going, because it was an unjust war, and so on.

The next day, I heard that a beloved relative of mine was going around town saying he was shocked by my lack of patriotism. Well, he shouldn't have been. I was exhibiting the sort of patriotism that used to be taught, during the Great Depression, by the best teachers in the Indianapolis public schools. We were proud back then of our tiny standing Army, proud of our civilian wisdom in keeping the military in its place. We were horrified by war.

Times change.

I've wanted to record somewhere, for a long time, something easily forgotten: my generation was raised to be pacifistic, but it fought well in a war it felt was just. This is surely true of the pacifists in the present high-school generation: they aren't cowards, either.

And much of what they object to in contemporary society came into being during World War Two. That was when warlike thinking and Prussian attitudes toward unquestioning obedience became so popular. Too bad.

I wrote a piece for the *New York Times* not long ago, which contained some reflections on high school as it used to be. In it, I was amazed that a girl I had gone to school with was now Mrs. Melvin Laird, the wife of our Secretary of Defense. I quoted an Indianapolis friend on that subject:

"When you get to be our age, you all of a sudden realize that you are being ruled by people you went to high school with. You all of a sudden catch on that life is nothing *but* high school. You make a fool of yourself in high school, then you go to college to learn how you should have acted in high school, then you get out into real life, and that turns out to be high school all over again—class officers, cheerleaders, and all."

He was right.

High school is closer to the core of the American experience than anything else I can think of. . . . We have all been there. While there, we saw nearly every form of justice and injustice, kindness and meanness, intelligence and stupidity, which we were likely to encounter in later life.

Richard Nixon is a familiar type from high school. So is Melvin Laird. So is J. Edgar Hoover. So is General Lewis Hershey. So is everybody. . . .

CHAPTER SEVENTEEN

Law and Disorder

It will come as a profound surprise to many, but genuinely distressing times of trouble may even appear on rare occasion within the hallowed confines of Indiana. Even here there may occur kidnappings and gunplay and floods: very rarely, of course, but they have been known. All such unpleasantries—except floods—are believed to be perpetrated by persons born elsewhere, or at least likely to be found upon investigation to be the offspring of outlanders emigrated to our state by some vagary of careless fortune.

One of the best of such unpleasant episodes was written by

JOSEPH ARNOLD HAYES

of Indianapolis birth and Indiana University education, a highly successful full-time novelist and playwright for the past thirty-five years, sometimes writing in partnership with his wife, Marijane Johnston Hayes. He wrote the piece from which a selection follows as a novel, believed to be based on an actual episode. It was also produced on the stage and as a moving picture. In all three, it was received with enthusiasm and in all three forms it won major awards. Its opening scene especially merits attention—so let's look at

The Desperate Hours

THEY EMERGED from the woods a few minutes after dawn, a cold, moist dawn with a mist billowing up from the fields. There were three of them, their uniforms blending with the yellowing autumn green.

They paused only briefly, scanning the deserted highway that lay flat across the flat Midwestern country. At a signal from one—the tall, lean, young-looking man who walked slightly ahead of the other two, with his head tilted and his shoulders lifted at a defiant and slightly trium-phant angle—they proceeded swiftly, but not running, behind a screen of trees and underbrush, in a line parallel to the highway. In a very short time, and before anyone or anything else appeared on the road, they reached a farm. In the barn lot, one detached himself from the others, moving quickly, a small young man, even younger than the tall one but without the other's jaunty manner, and began to work on the wires under the hood of the late-model gray-colored sedan parked there. The other two moved swiftly but with stealth toward the barn. Inside, they came upon a middle-aged farmer, wearing blue overalls, shifting with pail and stool from one cow to another. The shorter of the two men—who was middle-aged and slower, but powerful-looking, with the ponderous forward-leaning gait of a bear—picked up an ax handle and stepped across the straw-littered, concrete floor. Before the startled farmer could utter a cry, the tremendous arms went up once, there was an ugly sound, and the farmer sprawled. Then the heavy man lifted the handle again, but the other stopped him with a short commanding gesture similar to the one he had used on the highway. He then knelt down by the unconscious but still breathing farmer and stripped him of his overalls.

They then went out of the barn, rejoined the boy who was now seated behind the wheel of the car with the motor purring. With no eyes upon it, the sedan slipped out of the barn lot, turned south, and became lost in the thinning mist.

All this had been accomplished with a minimum of effort, no waste motion and in the most precise and machinelike manner imaginable.

Word of this incident, and all that had preceded it but nothing that followed it, reached Indianapolis, seventy-two miles to the east, less than half an hour later. Almost immediately then a telephone rang in the bedroom of a small, neat cottage in one of the newer but un-pretentious subdivisions northwest of the city.

A rangy young man in green-striped flannel pajamas rolled over in bed, yawning, and then, not groping, reached across his unawakened wife and picked up the telephone. He spoke into it curtly, then listened briefly. "I'll be down," he said quietly. Wide awake at last, he replaced the telephone in its cradle and turned to the woman in the bed.

Her eyes were open now, and she crinkled her nose at him, stretching with an exaggerated display of well-being and satisfaction to cover up the sharp cut of apprehension that such phone calls always caused in her. She sat up, watching her husband climb into his dark suit. He was an extremely tall man, in his early thirties, with extremely thin arms and legs that in no way betrayed the wirelike twist of muscles that lay below the surface. He was talking as he dressed, and he spoke in a laconic sort of drawl, grumbling in such a way that she caught the thrust of emotion he was trying to subdue.

"Glenn Griffin, his kid brother and another con, a lifer by the name of Robish," Jesse Webb was staying. "Not more than an hour ago. From the Federal prison in Terre Haute." He strapped on his gun, gave the shoulder holster a quick pat, then pulled on his suit jacket, flipping it back once, with an automatic gesture so that the deputy sheriff's badge showed once, briefly, a dull glimmer in the dimness. "I'll catch a shave downtown, Kathie."

"You'll eat, too," she reminded him, and he turned to the bed, grinning slowly, his face suddenly very young.

"I reckon I'll eat, Kathleen Webb," he drawled, "if you say so."

But even as he spoke, the smile flickered, failed, and he bent quickly, kissed her, and turned.

Her voice caught him. "Is Glenn Griffin the one you—" She broke off when he paused in the bedroom doorway.

"He's the one," he said. "He had twelve years to go. I hope he heads straight for his old home town." He was rubbing the back of his narrow, lean, efficient hand, in that way he had, and Kathleen rose from the bed.

She walked with him to the front door. "But isn't this the last place he *would* come?" she asked reasonably, trying not to betray the slow knife-turn inside.

Jesse Webb, of the Marion County Sheriff's office, himself in charge this entire week because his superior, Sheriff Masters, had gone to South Carolina on a combined extradition case and hunting trip, turned to his wife in the doorway and explained why he thought, or hoped, that Glenn Griffin would come to Indianapolis. In the first place, he said, you had to bank on the homing-pigeon instinct in the criminal mind: a familiar town, even if their faces are known in it, gives them the illusion of security. They always think they know where to hide, although today all such rat holes would be turned inside out by nightfall. Then, too, there was the woman, name of Helen Lamar; she was thirty-five at least, ten years older than Glen Griffin himself, but important to him. And Jesse had a hunch she had the money.

"There's always a woman," Kathleen said, reluctant to release the slender arm with the taut muscles rippling in it.

"Not always, but if there is, it helps. If she's still in Indianapolis, I'll lay two to one she's the beacon will lead us straight to those three——" He clamped down on his tongue because Kathleen despised what she called "courthouse language." He stopped and caught her chin in his hand and again he kissed her lips, still warm with sleep, then strode toward the car parked in the driveway, his mind almost consciously waiting for the inevitable words from the door.

They came, floating in the chill, sharp air: "Good luck, darling."

He waved with one hand, unsmiling, and backed the Sheriff's car into the street, guiding with his other hand.

At that moment the gray sedan was cruising along in farm country that had begun to have a slight lift and roll to it. Glenn Griffin, wearing the faded blue overalls, was at the wheel. The middle-aged man sat beside him, his enormous hulk of head sunk between two permanently upthrust shoulders so that it seemed almost a part of his thick, heavy body. The boy, Glenn's younger brother, lay stretched out on the back seat, his head well down, his eyes closed.

But Hank Griffin was not sleeping. He was remembering the slow flat crawl in darkness over the hundred yards of bare ground with the walls and gun towers behind them; he was remembering the headlong, reckless crash of the three bodies through the comparative safety of the dark woods. His chest was lashed and scratched and his shirt front torn and slightly crusted with blood. There was a gash across his forehead and it had begun to throb. But worst of all, he was shuddering. Now that they were beyond earshot of any shrieking sirens, insistent, shrill and blood-curdling on the high walls, he could imagine the sound as if he had actually heard it. His rather short, tight-knit and very youthful body had begun to shake with crawling vibrations in every bone and muscle, and there was nothing he could do to stop it except grit his teeth together and lie there listening to Glenn and Robish in the front seat.

"You're going south," Robish was complaining in a heavy but querulous voice. "Indianapolis is northeast."

"I'm going southeast now," Glenn Griffin said easily, and the words leaped and flickered in that laughter that now colored every word he spoke and filled the car with an exultancy that moved like warmth over Hank in the back seat.

"Didn't you say Lamar was in Indianapolis? With the dough."

"She moved away last week. To Pittsburgh. If they can't locate her in Indianapolis, it'll take the heat off. They won't locate her."

"Where the hell we heading then?"

"Indianapolis," Glenn said quietly, mocking the man beside him, with the laughter still in his tone. "I got some business there, remember? But we're not walking into a roadblock from the west, pal. We'll circle all the way around and come in from the northeast some time this afternoon."

"Then what?"

"Then we'll find us a cozy spot. And I'll contact Helen."

"A cozy spot—like where?"

"You name it, Robish. Only no hangouts, see. They'll be watching all of them. No hotels, either. Pick a nice quiet house on a nice quiet street on the edge of town, say, with no other houses close by. Make it a big place, though, with soft furniture. Comfortable, scared people— a sucker who goes to work every day, maybe a kid in the family. Some place to take the stir-taste out of our mouths."

"Then what?"

"We wait."

"How long?"

"Till Helen gets there from Pittsburgh, P.A. Now shut up, Robish, let a guy enjoy his freedom."

In the back seat Hank heard Robish swear under his breath. Hank had to hand it to Glenn: he could certainly handle Robish. First, Robish had growled that they had to ditch the prison clothes; Glenn wouldn't listen. He'd get him clothes when he needed them—good clothes. Meanwhile, stay down. And then Robish had complained about not carrying a gun: it made him feel helpless. What if they ran into a roadblock? They wouldn't, Glenn had said, because nobody ever heard of these roads. As for the gun, they couldn't afford to pull a job and tip off their whereabouts; besides, Glenn had one, didn't he? A .38 revolver, taken from the guard who was now in the prison infirmary with a bump on his head, if nothing worse. Relax, Robish, and enjoy yourself.

But Hank was not relaxed. He was looking ahead. And he was picturing a house such as Glenn had described. After the clank of lock, the smooth mechanical sound of cell doors closing, the hard stiffness of concrete floors and metal bunks, he was imagining sinking down again into a deep soft chair, his feet planted on deep-tufted carpet, the warm and intimate reality of ordinary walls with framed pictures on them. As yet even the crisp, cold air that penetrated the closed windows of the sedan had not reached the valleys of memory where the harsh iron-tasting odor of the last two years still lingered like stench from a swamp. But in a house like that, he said to himself . . .

The Hilliards had bought their house on Kessler Boulevard because it was quite large compared to the new homes selling for slightly less money in the subdivisions. It had been worth the difference in price because, while fairly convenient to shopping centers and bus lines, it was remote enough from other homes to give the family a sense of privacy. Also, it was outside the city limits by only ten blocks, and the taxes were lower. In the eight years that they had occupied the house, they had come, without any of them ever being quite aware of it, to love every corner, stairstep and shingle. It would require another paint job in the spring, true, and the furniture, purchased new when Dan was released from the Navy after the war, showed some, but not much, evidence of wear and tear by two growing youngsters. Cindy, who was now nineteen, thought they should replace the living-room suite as soon as possible, but her mother, Eleanor, wasn't just sure. Even though they received a 20 per cent discount on furniture purchases because Dan was now personnel manager of the largest department store in town, they were living, Eleanor argued, in inflationary times and the furniture *was* comfortable. Besides, as she pointed out to Dan less than a week ago, Cindy might be getting married soon. Dan had said nothing—which was his way.

As Dan came down the stairs at 7:40 on this particular Wednesday morning, he was trying to look ahead to the complicated problems of the day at the office rather than give in to the nagging uncertainty, almost anxiety, he had begun to feel about his daughter, Cindy. Not that he had anything personal or in particular against Charles Wright. Perhaps, he chided himself, only a banked-down sort of envy. Dan had had to work for everything he had ever made, every cent. This house itself was evidence of how long and how hard. Without an education past the second year in high school, he had come to this. And he was proud—a hard pride that was compounded of a personal sense of accomplishment and of gratitude. Charles Wright, on the other hand, was not the sort of young man with whom Dan could ever feel comfortable. Chuck—as Cindy had come to call him after going to work as secretary in the law office where young Wright was already a junior partner—had had it all handed to him, everything easy. Fine. He was lucky. But he was also, Dan knew from hearsay and from certain knowledge, an irresponsible young man, more interested in fast sports cars, beautiful girls, and long, wine-drenched parties than in finding a solid place for himself in the life of the community. Very well, then, Dan was acting like a typical father, or as Cindy had chided, "a conservative old fogy."

In the kitchen the day's routine had begun almost an hour before. Ralphie, who dawdled over breakfast as though it were some sort of punishment for past crimes, was glaring at a half-full glass of milk. He looked up when Dan doubled up a huge freckled fist and placed the knuckles lightly against the soft ten-year-old cheek. Eleanor, whose face was rounded like her son's and who had passed along to him also her light-colored hair, smiled and placed Dan's steaming ham and eggs before him, then sat down across from him, at the kitchen table. Without make-up, she looked like a child herself, small and still slender.

"Lucille is sick," she announced, explaining the absence of the maid who usually came on Wednesday and Saturdays.

"Again?" Dan said. "Any gin missing?"

Eleanor frowned and shook her head in swift wifely warning, nodding to Ralphie, who lifted his eyes from the milk and grinned knowingly. "She's probably blotto," he said sagely.

"Where does he learn his language?" Dan inquired.

"Comic books," Eleanor said, buttering toast. "Television. Do you know what blotto means, Ralphie?"

"My name," Ralphie announced, punctuating each word with a click of his glass on the table, "is Ralph. R-a-l-p-h. There's no *y* on the end of it."

"Sorry, old fellow," Dan said.

"And blotto means tight. Tight means drunk. Have I drunk enough milk?"

Eleanor was laughing, behind her napkin, and nodding. Ralphie was up, jarring the table, kissing his mother's hair swiftly; then he turned grave eyes on Dan and gave him a swift salute, half defiance and half apology, and turned on his heel.

"I'll ride my bike. I've got a whole half-hour, almost." He disappeared onto the rear porch, clumped down the three steps and was gone. Dan heard the garage door sliding up and was reminded again that he had to oil the runner mechanism soon.

Eleanor said, "Our son Ralph, spelled R-a-l-p-h, is too old to kiss a man—that's you—good-bye or good night."

"Well," Dan said wryly, but feeling a pinch somewhere inside, "that seems to be that."

"A milepost," Eleanor said, her eyes on him steadily now, studying him.

"We seem to be flying past mileposts darned fast, old girl," he said.

What Eleanor saw was a man of average height with heavy shoulders, the bulk of his body fitting finely under the double-breasted suit; she looked into the familiar deep blue eyes and was conscious of the mahogany-red hair above and the freckles climbing over and across the rather broad nose and the deep fine lines that added, she thought, so much character to an otherwise very ordinary but very appealing face.

Reading his mind, she said, "Cindy'd like to ask him for Thanksgiving dinner, Dan."

Dan downed the last swallow of coffee, stood up, yanked at his suit coat like a boy dressed for a party and determined to impress.

"Should she?" Eleanor asked.

Dan shrugged, but not successfully. "Ellie, I don't want to jump in and start opposing this thing and get Cindy's back up. But—well, Thanksgiving's a sort of family day."

Eleanor lifted her face for his kiss, then walked to the kitchen window while Dan went out the rear door, his topcoat thrown over his arm instead of over his shoulders.

When she opened the window, the gusty warning of winter swept through the kitchen. She watched from an angle as Dan backed the blue car out of the garage, maneuvering it around Cindy's black coupe in the driveway. Then, for absolutely no reason at all except that it was a ritual between them, meaning at the same time more and less than the word itself, she called, "Careful. And I mean it."

His hat pulled at its usual not quite proper angle, Dan shouted back, "Close the window," and swept out of her line of vision.

Eleanor complied, as she did every morning, five days a week. She never caught colds, and Dan knew this, just as she knew that there was no particular reason for him to be careful. Careful of what?

As she set a fresh place for Cindy, Eleanor decided against mentioning Chuck Wright this morning, especially in view of Dan's unspoken rejection of the Thanksgiving-dinner idea. All the words that occurred to her seemed stereotyped and flat, anyway—that Chuck Wright had a reputation for being wild, that he was the type that would never settle down. Cindy would only reply again, from the summit of nineteen years, that you could blame the war for that, hinting at some great tragedy and dramatic feat that, if known, would explain Charles Wright completely and utterly and make him totally acceptable in every far corner of the land.

Eleanor flipped on the radio, punching the buttons one after the other, finally settling for a news report as she prepared to drink her second cup of coffee.

After listening for perhaps five minutes—her attention not caught by the report of three escaped convicts in Terre Haute or attracted by the warning that these men were armed and dangerous—she heard Cindy descending the uncarpeted back stairs that only the family used, her heels a quick tattoo. Eleanor turned off the radio and set down her cup. As soon as Cindy was out of the house, Eleanor's own day would really begin. . . .

By selecting only the most unlikely and untraveled back roads, the locations of which Glenn Griffin seemed to have traced on the flintlike surface of his mind, he had by now maneuvered the gray sedan all the way around the city, staying for the most part forty or fifty miles south, and later, twenty miles east. By noon, however, he was approaching the city on a small road northeast of town, a road so small that the actual boundary of the city was not designated by one of the black-on-white signs reading "INDIANAPOLIS, CITY LIMITS."

It was now ten minutes after twelve. Robish slept, snoring. Hank, in the back seat, had fallen into the habit of rubbing the palms of his hands down the sides of his shirt over his ribs as though to wipe off some invisible stain or slime that clung to the rough cloth. Driving, Glenn Griffin was whistling, softly, steadily.

It had taken more than six hour by this roundabout route to reach a destination only seventy-two miles from their starting point. But they had progressed without incident, as smoothly and easily as if they had been flying a plane over the hundreds of alert and watchful eyes.

All three had begun to feel the emptiness of hunger, but Glenn refused to stop. . . .

Eleanor Hilliard was about to go up the front stairs to change into her gardening clothes—too many leaves had fallen on the flower beds under the maples—when she heard the step on the porch. The front doorbell rang. She pushed a strand of light hair off her forehead and sighed. It was that blissful moment after lunch when Ralphie had returned to school and she felt a certain treasured sense of freedom until 3:30. The front door was a solid panel, without window, and although there was a safety chain attached to the door frame, she never bothered to use it. It annoyed her that anyone had come to the front door. The family and tradesmen normally used the side entrance, because it connected the driveway directly with the sun porch and was more convenient.

The man who faced her on the porch, a very young man with short-cropped but soft looking and glistening black hair, wore faded blue farmers' overalls and he was smiling almost apologetically. He looked boyish, and so miserable about his errand that Eleanor smiled, too.

"Sorry to bother you, ma'am," he said in a voice that was almost a whisper, "but I guess I've lost my way. I'm trying to get to the Bulliard Dairy. I know it's in the neighborhood, but——"

Then he stopped, and now he was looking over her shoulder into the sun-streaked front hall. The smile remained on his face, but a subtle alteration took place around the edges of his mouth, a tightening that froze the smile. Involuntarily, she turned.

After that, everything happened so fast and with such cool mechanical precision that she was paralyzed, mind and body, and that numb helplessness must have been what carried her safely through the next few minutes.

She heard the door behind her open, felt the knob hard against her ribs, then heard it close. The older man, who must have entered through the back door, turned from her and stomped up the stairs. A third man, much younger, who wore the same strange gray-green garb as the big fellow, appeared in the dining-room door, then walked swiftly, lightly through the entire downstairs section of the house, opening doors, closing them. Eleanor saw, without really comprehending, the black gun in the hand of the young man in overalls who remained with her in the hall. She thought of the small automatic upstairs, concealed in the coil of spring under Dan's bed. She felt then a scream accumulating, powerful and uncontrollable, in her parched, locked throat.

"Take it easy, lady," the young man beside her advised softly. "Take it easy. You open your mouth, your kid'll come home from school and find your body."

She could feel her mind take hold, with a sharp click in her brain, as of a switch thrown. Instead of screaming, she lifted her hand to her mouth and bit down hard on the back of it, so hard that she tasted blood. But the scream was choked off in the back of her aching throat.

The boyish man returned, not looking at her, and said, "All clear down here, Glenn." Without another word, or even a nod from the one called Glenn, the youngster turned and went through the dining room toward the kitchen.

Eleanor heard the back door open and close and then a motor grind over in the driveway. Only then, after he had left the room, the boy's voice reached her—young, casual, subdued. He might have been one of Cindy's young admirers speaking. The naturalness of that voice in the hurricane-center of nightmare filled her with an incongruous terror that not even the gun had aroused. Outside, she heard a familiar sound: the garage door descending on the metal runners that needed oiling.

Then, in the silence, the middle-aged man came down the stairs; he carried one of Dan's suits flung over one arm. His animal-like face wore an expression that might have denoted pleasure, but his yellowish-green eyes, lost between the slits in the bulbous pouches, seemed as depthless and opaque as marbles.

"Nobody home but the missus," the man reported.

Staring at Dan's tweed suit, Eleanor thought of her husband. Big, calm, reserved, never roused to anger. Even in the swift flood of panic and disgust—as she saw the older man's eyes crawl hungrily over her— the thought of Dan calmed her.

"Get in there, Robish," Glenn Griffin said, "and keep an eye open out front."

Robish, pulling his eyes from her, followed the order and went into the living room and dropped himself into the large chair half-facing the wide front windows. He uttered a huge sigh. The back door opened and closed again. All three of them were in the house, the car concealed in the Hilliard garage.

"Now," said the one named Glenn. "Now, Mrs. Hilliard. We got a phone call to make, you and me. I guess you got the idea now. I guess you know what'll happen, you let go with anything fishy while you're talking. Case not, though, listen. We're playing for keeps. We don't want to hurt nobody, specially kids. But when the little guy who owns that bike out there gets home . . ."

"What do you want me to do?" Eleanor asked.

Glenn Griffin grinned again. "Smart little lady. Hope the whole family's smart as you, Mrs. Hilliard. Now."

Leaning against the telephone table, Eleanor listened to the very explicit, low-toned directions. Then she picked up the phone, dialed Long Distance and for the first time noticed the strange bloody tooth marks on the back of her hand. She gave the operator a number that she knew she should remember but could not. A number in Pittsburgh, Pennsylvania....

All through the endless afternoon Eleanor Hilliard's mind returned again and again to the dust-covered gray sedan parked in the garage.

Ralphie arrived home at 3:30, but he didn't notice the closed garage door. She detained him in the living room, speaking swiftly and firmly. She had a terrible headache, she said; she had to have absolute quiet all afternoon; she was sorry, but he would have to go out and play until suppertime and he was not to come back until then. No, he didn't have to change his clothes, not today. But Ralphie was hungry—as usual. Then he was to go to the drug store, get a sandwich; she gave him the money. Puzzled at his mother, who never before had complained of a headache, but pleased at the chance to buy a drug-store sandwich on his own, Ralphie climbed on the bicycle and went spinning down the boulevard.

"Nice work, lady," Glenn said, replacing his gun in his pocket.

She looked at him without expression, feeling nothing now but the hard stone in the pit of her stomach. "If you keep eating up everything, I'll have to shop before supper."

"I got a few more questions now, Mrs. Hilliard."

Then the process started all over again. The questions . . . This daughter, this Cynthia, what time did she get home from work? Did she drive her own car? Was she ever late? Okay then, just let her walk in.

"You won't have to do a thing but keep quiet, see."

If Cindy saw the garage door at all, she did not stop to question why it was closed. At 5:18 she brought the coupe to a halt in the driveway, leaped out, and came into the living room through the sun porch. Eleanor was sitting stiff and still on the sofa. Glenn was standing, his ankles crossed casually, by the television set; the gun was in his hand. Robish was in the small combined library-den in the rear of the house, with the door between it and the long living room standing open. Eleanor could see him watching the driveway through the side windows. She knew that the young one, named Hank, was still in the kitchen, his eye on the back yard, listening to the news reports on the small radio.

Cindy burst in, in that way she had, always a little breathless lately, her checked coat flying, her hair flowing behind her. When she caught sight of her mother, she stopped, her hazel-flecked blue eyes snapping around the room, remaining a split second on Glenn Griffin.

Glenn grinned. "Come right in, redhead."

Before Eleanor realized that Cindy had moved, the girl whirled and started to retrace her steps, running this time.

"Okay," Glenn Griffin said easily, but his voice lifted, "we still got your old lady, sis."

Robish burst in from the den as Cindy's step faltered at the sun-porch door. She turned, slowly catching sight of Robish then, the big man planted in the center of the room, and, dismissing him instinctively, she faced Glenn Griffin, who had not moved a muscle.

"That's better, redhead," the tall young man said, grinning. "Now you're being real sensible." As his eyes flicked over her, the grin faded.

Cindy did not wilt, or go slack, or in any way indicate that she was terrified. She moved her feet one small inch further apart and glared. "What do you want?"

"Spitfire, too." Surprise colored his tone. "Not sensible like your old lady." Without taking his gaze from the girl, Glenn said, "Robish, get back to the window. The old guy's going to be pulling in any minute."

"I need a gun," Robish said.

"Get back there," Glenn Griffin told him, still not glancing at him, dismissing him.

"You think you can——"

"Now."

Robbish stayed only a second longer; then he turned about and disappeared into the gathering shadows of the den.

"Sit down, redhead," Glenn said, his voice hushed a little. "Sit down and let me explain the facts of life. With that hair, you might feel like getting real brave. You can do that, just about any time you feel like it. You might even get away with it, not get hurt at all. But that's not saying what'll happen to the old lady . . . or the kid brother . . . or the father. We're waiting for him now, see, so take off your coat and sit right down in that chair."

Without in any sense suggesting that she was following an order—without, in fact, removing her coat as commanded but glancing at

Eleanor with a hint of a reassuring smile that failed to come off—Cindy crossed to a chair and sat down. She even lighted a cigarette, steadily, returning the young man's arrogance by simply ignoring his presence.

"How long have these animals been here, Mother?" she asked.

Glenn laughed, a short explosive snort of sound, derisive and ugly.

"I've lost track of time," Eleanor said. "Some time after noon. Cindy . . ." She had meant to voice a warning, but she stopped herself. "There's another one in the kitchen."

"In other words," said Cindy, blowing smoke, "the house is crawling with them."

Eleanor was watching Glenn Griffin's face at that moment and she felt a tightening of her own terror; a hand clenched her heart. The young man's face, a faint unhealthy jaundiced pallor at all times, went icy white, colorless, and the flesh around his even white teeth drew back into a stiff grin. He seemed to stand there undecided for a long time, perhaps half a minute; then, soundlessly, he turned and, in that graceful feline glide of his, he walked into the hall and through the dining room toward the muffled chatter of the radio in the kitchen.

There he remained until the sound for which Eleanor's nerves had been tensed reached her.

"Griffin!" Robish barked from the den.

Glenn Griffin materialized again. "No lights now, not a word out of either of you. Got that?"

Eleanor nodded dumbly.

"Got that, redhead?"

Cindy had her eyes fixed on the wall beyond Glenn Griffin's poised body as he stood in the hall doorway. She seemed to look through him as though he were glass, or simply not present at all. Eleanor longed to put out a hand. This couldn't be. This was no time for Cindy's stubborn temper.

"He's trying to open the garage," Robish said. "You want me to grab him now?"

"Not with all those cars going by," Glenn said. "He'll come in." He lifted his voice. "You watching, Hank?"

"He's not coming in this way," the other's voice called from the kitchen.

Again Eleanor felt the scream gathering like some terrible inhuman force in her chest. She listened to the familiar footsteps, brisk and energetic even after a hard day: up the two steps, across the tiled sun porch. This time Glenn did not waste time: he pointed the gun directly at the door, directly at Dan Hilliard.

First, Dan saw his wife—a statue, pale, haggard. He stopped short. The room was filled with the fading blue-gray twilight. Then he saw Cindy, sitting straight, smoking, her small face angry and defiant. At once, he thought of Charles Wright: had Cindy announced something to Ellie? Only then, because there was the faintest sort of shadow movement from the direction of the hall, did Dan see Glenn Griffin. And the pointed gun.

He felt his breath hold, and before anyone could move or speak, although he felt Eleanor straining half out of her chair, he had the whole picture straight and clear. He recalled the news reports on the radio in the car less than fifteen minutes before; he realized he had been a fool for not comprehending as soon as he saw the gray sedan through the windows of the garage. But such a far-fetched thought would not have occurred to him. However, he wasted no time now in bewilderment or amazement or rebellion at the situation as it stood.

Eleanor saw the unnatural redness mounting her husband's craggy face, spreading violent under the tilted hat. Dan's mind, she knew, worked slowly but thoroughly, wasting no time on suppositions, moving straight ahead, but with caution, into whatever faced him. And she wondered, relaxing only a little, why she had dreaded this moment more than any other of the day. Before Dan spoke, she knew that his would be the first meaningful words that met Glenn Griffin all day.

"I suggest you put the gun away, Griffin," Dan said. "If you fire it, you'll have the whole neighborhood down on you in less than three minutes. The Wallings next door are home, and they'd hear the shot, even with the woods in between. If they didn't, someone driving by would."

The only sound in the dusky room was something between a whimper of hysteria and gasp of relief and gratitude from Eleanor. Dan felt a movement from the direction of the den, but he did not shift his eyes from Glenn Griffin's.

"You try something, mister, you all get it," a heavy, dull voice said from the den. "You dumb, mister?"

"No," Glenn Griffin said, very slowly. "He's not dumb at all, Robish." The odd grin was flickering into place. "He's a smart boy, smarter than we figured, maybe." There was an edge of warning in his quiet tone.

Then, repeating his daughter's words—as Eleanor, knowing them both so well, might have expected—Dan demanded: "What do you want?"

This time Glenn Griffin was not taken by surprise. "I don't want anybody to get hurt. What do *you* want, Pop?"

Dan crossed then, despite the gun, toward his wife; he placed a hand —large and freckled and tender—on her shoulder and simply let it rest there, relaxed. "That's what I want, too."

Glenn let go with a laugh at that; he dropped the arm holding the gun. "Now you talk sense. So I'm going to talk sense, too."

The room was deep in shadow now, and Dan listened in silence, feeling the shudders subsiding in Eleanor's shoulder. He didn't increase the pressure of his hand.

Glenn, striding in that slender catlike manner of his up and down the room, spoke in the unemotional manner of one who has known for months, perhaps years, exactly what he wants to say. Dan listened while the helplessness of his position seeped into him like some mysterious benumbing drug.

All they wanted—the three of them—was a safe place to stay till about midnight, at the latest two or three in the morning. They had some money coming, a lot of money, and when it arrived, they would go. It was as simple as that. In the meantime, life in the Hilliard house was to go on normally. In every way.

"Just like normal, see. You got it straight, folks?"

He spoke like an actor who had rehearsed his words many times. He moved around the room and his brows lifted and his face worked as though some invisible camera were on him, as though he were carefully but arrogantly trying in his behavior to live up to some picture of himself that he carried in his mind. Dan recorded all this, for whatever good it might do, his own mind noting everything in that indirect but almost infallible way he had of judging people. Dan reached one inevitable, stone-hard conclusion: these were not idle threats. This boy would kill one or all of them if anything went wrong. Once Dan had accepted this, fully, he acted upon it, but he could feel his legs shaking now, his body frozen and numb with helpelssness.

"We'll do whatever you say, Griffin," Dan said in a flat voice. "Only——"

"Yeah?"

"Griffin, what if I could get you the money you want? Right away, I mean. Tonight. *Before* midnight? Would you leave then?"

"You couldn't do it, Pop. I had a look at your bankbooks. You just don't have it."

"That sounds like a deal to me," Robish said from the darkness of the den. "We could get the hell out of here."

Dan noted also the urgency behind the invisible man's tone. "Maybe I could raise it. Somehow. What then, Griffin?"

"We're sticking," Glenn said.

"Yeah," the voice from the other room muttered sourly. "Sticking to wait for that babe. You'd risk our necks just to see that dame again."

Having unexpectedly created the breach, Dan stepped into it. "If this woman, whoever she is, knows where to come, how do you know the police won't be following her? It's as much to my advantage as yours now to avoid the police."

"What about that?" This time Robish emerged, planting himself at the far end of the room, his hulk of body bleak and hard in threatened mutiny. "The guy talks sense, Griffin. Hell, you can pick up a woman anywheres."

A flicker of bewilderment passed over the hard, young features of Glenn Griffin's face. He glanced from Dan to Robish. Then he whirled to Robish, the movement a dancer-shadow in the room. "I'm running the show, Robish. I thought we had that straight. We're staying, see, till Helen gets here. She's too smart to let the cops get on her tail. And she's got the kind of dough I got to have. And I got to have it here, see. Right in this town."

"You got no right to take these chances just so you can get a copper knocked off. What do I care somebody broke your goddamned jaw? That was a long time ago, anyway, and if this guy here can raise the dough——"

"No!" The word crackled. "You heard me, both of you." Slowly Glenn stepped toward Dan. "You, Hilliard, you lay off. I don't need no ideas from you. I got my own, and I got them all worked out and they been working fine."

"Ain't worth it," Robish snorted.

"I say it is, Robish. Where'd you be if it wasn't for me?" He spoke with his back to Robish, his eyes on Dan. "You'd be sitting down to that stew again, that's what, with a gun on you, and a guard breathing down your neck again. This way, *we* got the guns, and that's the way it's going to be." He was rubbing his cheek, feeling the hard ridge of tissue that now protected the mended bone. "And you, Hilliard, you're going to talk when I ask you something or when I tell you to talk. Otherwise, you're going to keep your trap closed. You love this woman of yours, you're going to play ball. Like you say, pal, it's as much your advantage as mine to keep any coppers away from here. Any red lights show in front of this joint, it's not going to be pretty" . . . .

Cutting you off after only a few "desperate hours" with many more still ahead is a dirty trick, isn't it? Better get yourself a copy to complete your knowledge—and to read over again in the future: it continues on the same high pitch to the last page.

Floods do not necessarily produce lawlessness—although a certain amount of activity inimical to the public weal may accompany them. To the second- or third-generation dwellers in the river bottoms, they are an annual occasion, like Christmas, and are often greeted philosophically if not with enthusiasm.

One family of record dwelling in a notably sound, two-story log house on the bank of the Ohio regularly ties its commodious johnboat to the front porch, retires to the second floor, eventually to the attic, and in years of very high water to the roof. It welcomes kinfolks less happy in the height of their quarters and prepares to sit out the "spell of risin'." They have high old times; especially if grandpa strings up his fiddle and pa has a full jug on hand. The hours flit by. The fun may even continue after the water falls, for through the rest of the spring they have a traditional game of chance, which consists of betting on what ma has cooked up when she opens one of the food cans which spent the high water in the cellar and had its label soaked off and floated to New Orleans, or at least Memphis. Ma claims innocence as to whether she is opening kidney beans or clingstone peaches, and sporting members of the family wager two bits on the question at appropriate odds.

Though there is tremendous loss of property (and some of life up and down the river), to many river-bank dwellers a good flood offers some entertainment.

WILLIAM EDWARD WILSON

native of Evansville, former newspaperman and long-time professor of English at Indiana University, has written several books about southern Indiana. The most graphic account of a high water we are likely to encounter appears in one of the best of these,

Crescent City

DAM 600 REPORTS

AT DAM 600, ten miles above Crescent City, the river stood at fifty-two feet.

"If it goes, Chief, I reckon we'll go with it," Mac said.

He stood in the doorway of the hut, a dark, bulging, burly figure in dungarees, heavy, black turtle-neck sweater, and blue pea jacket. He spoke without anxiety. He was merely stating a fact.

At the desk, the Chief nodded, laid down his pipe, and, picking up the telephone, called in his hourly report. A few minutes later, it came back on the radio.

Seven A. M. Dam Six Hundred, fifty-two feet. . . . Seven A. M. Dam Six Hundred, fifty-two feet. . . .

The two Coastguardmen went out together on the concrete bridge of their hut, which rose like a lighthouse in a sea of muddy, swirling water. From where the men stood, however, looking out over the desolate expanse that stretched in all directions as far as they could see, they had an illusion of racing swiftly against the current on the isolated structure, as if their bridge were not a lighthouse but the prow of a speeding ship. The water broke against it and hissed past in an ugly, foaming plume. Only by fixing their eyes on the stationary, protruding tops of trees in the distance could they halt the illusory motion. Both the dam and the locks were inundated, their location marked by eddying swells on the surface of the coffee-colored river.

"Take a look at those lines, will you, Mac," the Chief said.

Mac set off down the bridge beside the iron railing, but before he reached the power launch that was moored beside the hut, the Chief called after him.

"Belay it, Mac. Look!"

From behind a clump of treetops upstream, a house had swum out into the middle of what once had been the river's channel. A man clutching a dog was astraddle the roof peak. A chicken perched beside him. The Coastguardmen saw the man wave and they waved back at him, but there was no other way of communicating with him above the roar of the flood.

"Another one," Mac said.

"That makes four already this morning."

The Chief went into the hut and took up the telephone again. The line was still alive. Several minutes later, his message came back on the crackling radio.

Seven-O-Five. Man on housetop, floating past Dam Six Hundred. . . . Station Three, take over. . . . Seven-O-Five. Man on housetop, floating past Dam Six Hundred. . . . Station Three . . .

When the Chief came out on the bridge again, the house had disappeared downstream.

"He was still wavin' when I lost sight of him," Mac said.

The Chief rubbed the stubble on his chin.

"If she doesn't crest by three o'clock," he said, "we'll stick it out about two more hours after that. Then we'll shove off. Let's go look at those lines."

"If we're still here to shove," Mac said, following him.

WILFORD LINDESCHMIDT ANSWERS THE TELEPHONE

THROWING the dead electric bulb into the tangle of sumac across the road, Wilford Lindeschmidt walked around behind the signboard, turned the switch, and came back to inspect the results of his work. All the bulbs were burning. In the gray morning light, the sign glowed a pale yellow.

LINDY'S
HEATED CABINS
Barbecue Sandwiches Cold Drinks
Cigarettes
Candy

In spite of the thermometer, which registered forty-two, the January morning was raw and cold. Fog blew in patches down the deserted highway and clung to the bare branches of the trees on either side. Lindy glanced up at the sky speculatively. It sagged close to the earth, like a saturated gray blanket. One more drop of moisture, he thought, and it must rip from end to end and dump its load.

"What the hell," he said with a shrug, and, going around behind the signboard again, turned off the light and started across the graveled parking area toward the combined lunchroom and dwelling.

At twenty-eight, Wilford Lindeschmidt looked forty. In his shirt-sleeves and hatless, he walked with his hands in his pockets, his big, athletic shoulders hunched, his paunch sagging. Although his face was round and naturally good-humored, it was developing premature lines of anxiety and despair. He had the air of a man who is not so much settled in his way of life as resigned to it.

Halfway across the parking area, Lindy saw Slim Fergus come out of the tool shed and, standing at the edge of the bluff behind the row of cabins, motion to him.

"Wait a minute," Lindy said.

He went inside, where the soda fountain and the marble-topped tables gleamed in the dim light, took down a leather jacket from the hook behind the door, and came out again, running his arms into the stiff sleeves.

Without speaking, Slim pointed over the bluff. Lindy looked down, sucking on a toothpick as he contemplated the misty view of the city and the river below them.

"Must be damn near out to Forsythia Street," he said.

Slim Fergus nodded, drew a single cigarette out of a pocket inside his hunting jacket, and lighted it with one hand, ducking his head into the wind.

"Radio said it would crest today," Lindy remarked.

Slim sniffed.

"Maybe."

Lindy Lindeschmidt squatted at the edge of the bluff and began to identify the buildings and streets below—the New Century Hotel, the Marvin Library, the *Banner*, the courthouse. Near the inundated levee, the New Century seemed to be flooded up to the second story. The site of the old Pepper House, where a twenty-story building was to have risen back in the boom days, was a muddy lake. Through the branches of the trees that surrounded the tall, old houses, Audubon Street gleamed dully with shallow water, and beyond it, south of Whip-Poor-Will, the Negro shacks looked like a fleet of drifting houseboats. Most of the Clafford's Grove area, east of Forsythia, appeared to be dry, and the West Side of the city, bristling with factory smokestacks and church spires, and Hooverville, which clambered up the bluff, a rabble of tents and packing boxes and sheet-iron shanties, were safe. Beyond the city, as far as Lindy could see, the river spread southward, like a boundless gray ocean. A faint, feathery fringe of tree tops marked the Kentucky shoreline, but Lindy estimated that there was water over the Kentucky bottoms as far as Kratztown, ten miles away.

"Jesus!" he said, standing up and flicking the toothpick at the trunk of a larch nearby. "All this on top of everything else!"

"Prosperity's just around the corner," Slim mocked.

Lindy snorted.

"So's Christmas!"

He tapped a cigarette out of a fresh pack, took a light from Slim, and inhaled deeply.

"I fixed that light. Thought at first I'd take out every other damn bulb and cut the electric bill down, but, hell-fire, if I have to start saving on light bulbs, I might as well close up."

"Or sign up," Slim suggested.

Lindy glanced sidewise at Slim's solemn horse face, and his lips curled, sending his second inhale of smoke upward in a long plume.

"Oh, yeah?" he said.

Slim's sides shook silently.

"I'll be damned if I will," Lindy said. "Luke Floyd's got everything syndicated down in Crescent City, but I'll be damned if he's going to syndicate me. I'll burn the damn place down before I start paying him tribute." He took another drag on the cigarette. "First place," he added thoughtfully, "there's nothing to pay it with."

Slim's blue eyes danced.

"Business might pick up," he said. "Nice, quiet place for his gang to meet. I bet he doesn't dare let 'em come to his house. Juliana wouldn't have 'em."

"And me living at the point of a gun!" Lindy muttered.

Slim was silent, his face expressionless, but Lindy knew how he felt. Although he never said so, Slim agreed with him. Slim's own refusal to pay tribute had cost him his smoke shop in the city. Slim could cut corners like anyone else, when it came to the law, but when it came to people, he had principles.

"Floyd gave me fifty bucks last night," Slim said finally. "I guess forty-eight of it must have been a tip, unless you've raised your prices, but I put it all in the till."

"So I'll have to take it," Lindy said.

"In the till, it's revenue," Slim said dryly, "and now you can pay me last week's wages."

Lindy dropped his cigarette and ground it out with his heel.

"I hate to take that kind of money," he said. "I never did until last summer. I always did a clean business, strictly tourist. I used to turn away those damned high-school kids by the dozen. And older people, too. You'd be surprised at some of the combinations that used to turn up out here round midnight full of bathtub gin. You wouldn't believe me."

"Human nature don't change," Slim said.

"Well, I never took any of that kind of money till last summer. I even turned Luke Floyd away a half-dozen times. Then it was a question of have to or starve."

With narrowed eyes, Slim Fergus peered through the fog at Crescent City for a long time. Finally he said, "It's a funny thing. Twenty years ago, when I was barkeep at the old Pepper House, I got so disgusted with human nature one day that I got to figurin 'how me and old Jay

Holt with the *Gazette* and John Davis—he was prosecutor then, runnin' for his first term of Congress—how we could bust this town wide open and clean it up. But look at John Davis since. Lot of good it would have done. Look at John Davis. And look at what they did to old Jay Holt."

"I understand he's just about cleaned out—old man Holt. I heard he's going to lose that place of his on Cardinal Street."

"Jay Holt is a straight shooter."

"Yes. But I always did think the Marvin bank wouldn't have failed if he had stayed in it."

Slim shook his head.

"Nothin' could have stopped that bank from failing. That's why Jay Holt got out. He couldn't stand the monkey business that was going on—the kind of security they were accepting, for one thing. I heard later that he gave 'em hell one day at a director's meeting, and when they wouldn't toe the mark, he just pulled his resignation out of his pocket, threw it on the table, and walked out. That was a whole year before the bank failed. Anyhow, Jay Holt ain't no businessman."

"I had fifteen hundred bucks in that bank," Lindy said ruefully.

Slim laughed.

"I had three thousand. But I didn't lose it—not there, at least. When I heard Jay Holt had pulled out after bein' in there only such a short time, I smelled a rat and went down and drew my money out."

"I wonder why he never went into politics. He'd of made a damn sight better senator than John Davis, for instance."

"Jay Holt would last about five minutes in politics. First place, if he was senator, he'd go ahead and do what he thought was right, regardless of what people wanted, and you can't do that in politics—not here, anyhow. Jay Holt don't cram what he thinks down other people's throats, but he lives the way he thinks and be damned to you. He's all of a piece. I like a man that's all of a piece, good or bad. The only real sons of bitches in this world are those you can't depend on, guys that is one thing one minute and another another."

"I always liked him," Lindy said. "We used to live next door to him on Cardinal Street, till my old man got that fool notion of building farther out. If my old man hadn't done that, I wouldn't be taking Luke

Floyd's dirty money now." He tapped another cigarette out of the package, studied it for a second, and then put it back. "Who'd Luke have with him last night?"

Slim shrugged.

"I never see anything," he said. "I got bad eyes."

"Was it Carl Schmitt's widow?"

With cupped hands, Slim outlined a voluptuous figure in the air and nodded.

"Seems to me it's about time they busted up," Lindy said. "Luke don't usually stick to one woman as long as that."

"He's still married, ain't he?"

"Oh, that's different. It's the Clafford money that keeps him tied to Juliana—that and Juliana herself. He couldn't get along without that money, and, for some reason or other, she couldn't get along without him. I never could figure out why, except of course she's kind of off her trolley, everybody says. But a lot of good Luke Floyd does her. He's been two-timin' her ever since she got him out of the pen and married him. They say at one time it was Senator Davis's wife. And then it was that writer's wife. What's his name?"

"Pendleton?"

"That's it. They say he used to meet her in Chicago. Then, after that one—"

Slim put his hand on Lindy's shoulder.

"Look," he said, "we ain't goin' to stand out here in the wet and try to think of every round-heeled dame east of the Mississippi, are we?"

Lindy laughed.

"Well, if you're so anxious to get to work, Slim, maybe you'd better go and clean up that cabin they were in last night."

Slim started up the lane toward a cabin named Tulip.

"I think I'll get me a job down a Eulalie Plume's," he said, over his shoulder. "A nice, clean, professional job."

Lindy laughed again, humorlessly.

"O. K.," he said.

For several minutes, he remained by the larch at the edge of the bluff, staring blankly across the river. The fog was lifting, but the threat of rain was still in the sky. He had a roof over his head, at least, he was thinking. He and Slim could shoot groundhogs in another week, if they had to, and maybe next summer they could lay out a miniature golf course. They seemed to be the only thing that was making money these days. He was glad he was not married. Although he knew he never would be able to forget Cynthia Henderson, he was honestly grateful to her now for turning him down. He'd be happier if she had married Alan Charters instead of that snob Billy Davis, but there was one thing about it—as Mrs. Billy Davis, with all that dough, she was a whole lot better off than she would have been as either Mrs. Alan Charters or Mrs. Wilford Lindeschmidt. And for him, without a wife to worry about, these hard times were easier to take. So long as Slim Fergus stood by him, he'd get along all right. There was something about Slim that was comforting and strengthening, too. He liked Slim.

As he entered the back door of the main building, which housed the lunchroom and their living quarters, Lindy heard the telephone ringing above the blare of the radio. He took his time going through the kitchen and even paused to listen to an announcement.

Eight A. M. Dam Six Hundred, fifty-two and a half feet. . . . Eight . . .

In the lunchroom, he took down the receiver from the telephone on the wall. It was Jay Holt calling from the New Century.

"You know I'm in charge of relief headquarters down here, Lindy."

"Yeah, Mr. Holt. Anything I can do for you?"

"Well, yes, there is. Only I don't like to ask you. I've tried everything else I can think of."

"Go ahead. Shoot."

"It's about some refugees from the river bottoms. We've got a new batch of them here, and there isn't any room for them. We've filled up every inch of free space in the hotel."

"So you want me to take 'em up here in my cabins, that it?"

"If you could do it. There are about fifty."

"Be almost like having Coolidge back. I haven't had that many in my cabins since way to hell and gone. Send 'em up, Mr. Holt."

"There isn't any money in it for you, Lindy. We haven't got an extra cent. I know you're having a hard time, like everybody else, and—"

"Send 'em up, I said!"

There was a moment's silence at the other end of the line.

"There's another thing, Lindy," Jay Holt said finally. "They're all colored people."

Wilford Lindeschmidt did not answer at once. With a pencil stub, he sketched three elaborately tailed "K"s on a pad on the wall. Under them, he wrote the name of Luke Floyd and wreathed it with dollar signs.

Station Nine, the radio droned. *Permission obtained to break into Coombs Warehouse. . . . Station Nine . . .*

Lindy laughed, scrawled a four-letter word across the scribbled sheet, tore it from the pad, and wadded it in his palm.

"Hell," he said into the telephone, "they're human, ain't th-y? Send 'em up. . . ."

One P. M., the radio announced. *Dam Six Hundred, fifty-five feet, still rising. . . .. One P. M. . . . .*

EARLY EARD ENDS HIS VOYAGE

AT TWO O'CLOCK, the man who had floated past Dam Six Hundred at 7:05 A.M. was forty miles below Crescent City. The dog and the chicken were still his only companions. The man's house had taken a short cut across the Kentucky bottoms, eluding the rescuers from Station Three, floated over what once had been Kratztown, and rejoined the main current of the river there.

The man was fifty-three years old. His name was Early Eard. He was born in a house built on stilts in the first bottoms twenty-seven miles up the river from Crescent City and had lived there all his life. It was the same house on which he was now afloat. His father was a veteran of the Confederate Army who had never owned a slave and had always suffered from the institution of slavery, which made him an economic overplus. His mother had carrot-colored hair and smoked a pipe and, as a measure of frugality, nursed her eight children until they were three years old, if her milk and the children survived as long as that. Only four of the children did survive—Early and three girls. Contrary to the widely accepted belief about such people as the Eards, Early had never had incestuous relations with any of his sisters or unnatural relations with beasts or fowls, possibly because he knew nothing of the theory that life follows literature. He was no reader of literature and had almost no life to speak of. In fact, at fifty-three, Early Eard was still a virgin. Of his appetites, hunger was always so predominant that his sexual urge had no opportunity to flourish.

In the flood of 1913, Early Eard's house was completely inundated and his mother and two of his sisters were drowned, but Early and the third sister were rescued and taken to shelter in a village ten miles away. When the waters receded, the house was still sound, standing on its stilts in the scored bottomland like a crane. A year later, Early's third sister was kicked by a mule and died. In 1917, a draft board sought out Early, examined him, and informed him that he was unfit for military service. That was the only time in his life that he ever came in contact with his government. Until that time, he had not known there was a war in progress, and since that time, he had never inquired who fought it or who won. His voyage on the roof peak of the house in which he was born had, at two o'clock on this January afternoon in 1932, carried him farther away from his birthplace than he had ever traveled before.

There is little more that could be said about Early Eard at the age of fifty-three, except that he had red hair, like his mother's now turned a rusty gray, pale-blue eyes, a severe pain in his coccyx from sitting astride the roof peak for twenty hours, and the middle finger missing from his left hand. He could not explain how he lost the middle finger, for the accident happened when he was a baby and his mother had given him so many versions of the maiming that he never was sure which was the true account. He believed, however, that his oldest sister had chopped the finger off with a hatchet. He could neither read nor write and he had never possessed more than seven dollars in his life. He had never heard of Herbert Hoover, who was President of the United States on the day that he floated down the river on his housetop; in fact, he did not know there was such an office as the Presidency. If asked who God was, he would probably have made a long face and pointed solemnly at the sky.

At ten minutes past two, Early Eard did what, for twenty hours, he had been numbly afraid he would do. He fell asleep and slid down the roof into the water with his dog still in his arms. The dog swam in a straight line for fifty feet before it drowned. Early Eard could not swim.

His head never reappeared above the surface of the churning, brown water. The chicken remained on the roof peak, intermittently pecking at the lice under its wings and ruffling its feathers to shake off the wetness. Three miles farther downstream, it was rescued by a Negro named Ben Todd, who that same night wrung its neck and gave it to his wife to fry for supper.

Unprejudiced as we aim to be, we must admit that Indiana at least holds place with lesser states (we recognize the fact that there is no other kind) in the matter of mayhem committed by motor car.

One of our promising young writers records such an event and its effect on on-lookers in four poems.

JOHN WOODS

was born and spent his boyhood in Morgan County, Indiana, a pretty fortunate circumstance as is evidenced by similar occurrences in the lives of such disparate fellow citizens as Paul V. McNutt, John Dillinger, and even your humble petitioner, all of whom enjoyed similar good fortune. Woods received his baccalaureate and a master's degree from Indiana University and is a Professor of English at Western Michigan University.

THE DEATHS AT PARAGON, INDIANA

1. *Sandra, the waitress*

Sun streaked the coffee urn
And wrote AL'S LUNCH across the cups.
I saw no harm in summer then,
And held against the scorching sun
A spring, touching the deepest earth,
That trickled in the bearded tub
Behind the store. But nothing holds
When fire levels on the frying concrete.

Thermometer said, "Go easy, girl.
Dodge trouble." And so I fed
The truckers, watching the tube of coffee
Twitch along the urn, the street
Repeat itself across the mirror.
I washed an egg beneath the tap.

Then, too sudden for the mind,
The car came rolling, spraying parts
And boys across the road outside.
He came, and comes forever, sliding
Headfirst into the curb, bursting.
The egg broke below my hand.
O this to say: his arms was bent
Behind his back; dust and leaves
Crawled downstream in the gutter.
O this to hope: someday his staring
Eyes will close upon my dream.

2. *Goss, the ambulance driver*

My head goes spinning in the siren,
But I hold the road. Muscles
Keep the old shapes. When oaks
Are ripped by lightning, tip to root,
Will sap spring out until the tree
Hangs wrinkled as an inner tube
From junkyard fences? Dr. Sweet,
This Siren calls: "I am the cross
Your training binds you to." But hear,
One behind is crucified
Upon a steering wheel, and bleeds
His heart away. Sew on him
A year, and he will lie unbuckled.
But now to drive this ambulance
With all my riders emptying
Behind me.

O this to say:
Lives are balloons; and when the moorings
Drop, the wind takes you sailing.
Like inner tubes, they round around
Their hold on air. O this to cry:
Someday the wind goes slack, and they
Go spinning like my passengers.

3. *Chauncey, the junk man*

Scatter me, wind. I am the king
Of bang and rattle, of fall apart
And rust in weeds. Here is where
Things wobble off to. My offerings
Come sailing from back doors: wires
Distracted into sparks, handles
That give you pains, and broken holders.
If I were mayor, every matron
Would come unglued and hit the spot
With all her joints aglow. But I
Can coax a shape in anything,
And make it stick, and tend and solder.

O this to say: today I dragged
A mash of wheels and sparking sides
Into my shed. First I cluttered
Ledges with all unwired cubes;
Then I festooned rafters with
The unlinked flexible. But when
I gathered shape into my brain,
I cowered under fenders, reeling.
The shape was fall and spin and blast.
The shape was death. I let it go.

4. *Doctor Sweet*

Yesterday I fished for bass,
But now I fish for breath in bones
Clasped as bottom roots. The pulse

Nibbled like a chub but got
Away. All five of you are dead.
Light beaks my eyes, and edges
My knives with fire. Though I link
You by my chart, you'll dangle empty.
Even Chauncey, with his shed of parts,
Can never make you run. I know
He'll tow your flattened car away
And hang its pieces from his roof
Like sausages and collarbones.
I fear he'd bandage you with earth.

I know those visitors below.
They come to lynch you with their pity.
You left them with their loves and debts,
Responsibility and guilt.
This mob of tears will not forgive.
O now I give you to their hands
For burial in summer's earth.
O this to hope: that you will never
Wake upon an empty world
And cry for love, and hear no answer.

Only a few paragraphs back we mentioned the name of John Dillinger, Morgan County's bad boy. He may not have been its worst one, in a final analysis; but he certainly tried.

DAVID WAGONER

poet and novelist whose boyhood was spent in Indiana, did an excellent piece on Dillinger's final come-uppance and its scene. The present writer can testify to the accuracy of the setting as described by Mr. Wagoner, as he himself witnessed the event (not knowing that Dillinger was playing the lead) from the seventh floor of a neighboring hotel. In the book New and Selected Poems, we find

The Shooting of John Dillinger Outside the Biograph Theater, July 22, 1934

Chicago ran a fever of a hundred and one that groggy Sunday.
A reporter fried an egg on a sidewalk; the air looked shaky.
And a hundred thousand people were in the lake like shirts in
    a laundry.
Why was Johnny lonely?
Not because two dozen solid citizens, heat-struck, had keeled
    over backward.
Not because those lawful souls had fallen out of their sockets
    and melted.
But because the sun went down like a lump in a furnace or a
    bull in the Stockyards.
Where was Johnny headed?
Under the Biograph Theater sign that said, "Our Air is
    Refrigerated."
Past seventeen FBI men and four policemen who stood in
    doorways and sweated.
Johnny sat down in a cold seat to watch Clark Gable get
    electrocuted.
Had Johnny been mistreated?
Yes, but Gable told the D.A. he'd rather fry than be shut up
    forever.
Two women sat by Johnny. One looked sweet, one looked like
    J. Edgar Hoover.
Polly Hamilton made him feel hot, but Anna Sage made him
    shiver.

Was Johnny a good lover?

Yes, but he passed out his share of squeezes and pokes like a
    jittery masher

While Agent Purvis sneaked up and down the aisle like an
    extra usher,

Trying to make sure they wouldn't slip out till the show was
    over.

Was Johnny a fourflusher?

No, not if he knew the game. He got it up or got it back.

But he liked to take snapshots of policemen with his own
    Kodak,

And once in a while he liked to take them with an automatic.

Why was Johnny frantic?

Because he couldn't take a walk or sit down in a movie

Without being afraid he'd run smack into somebody

Who'd point at his rearranged face and holler, "Johnny!"

Was Johnny ugly?

Yes, because Dr. Wilhelm Loeser had given him a new profile

With a baggy jawline and squint eyes and an erased dimple,

With kangaroo-tendon cheekbones and a gigolo's mustache
    that should've been illegal.

Did Johnny love a girl?

Yes, a good-looking, hard-headed Indian named Billie
    Frechette.

He wanted to marry her and lie down and try to get over it,

But she was locked in jail for giving him first-aid and comfort.

Did Johnny feel hurt?

He felt like breaking a bank or jumping over a railing

Into some panicky teller's cage to shout, "Reach for the
    ceiling!"

Or like kicking some vice president in the bum checks and
    smiling.

What was he really doing?

Going up the aisle with the crowd and into the lobby

With Polly saying, "Would *you* do what Clark done?" And
    Johnny saying, "Maybe."

And Anna saying, "If he'd been smart, he'd of acted like Bing
 Crosby."
Did Johnny look flashy?
Yes, his white-on-white shirt and tie were luminous.
His trousers were creased like knives to the tops of his shoes,
And his yellow straw hat came down to his dark glasses.
Was Johnny suspicious?
Yes, and when Agent Purvis signalled with a trembling cigar,
Johnny ducked left and ran out of the theater,
And innocent Polly and squealing Anna were left nowhere.
Was Johnny a fast runner?
No, but he crouched and scurried past a friendly liquor store
Under the coupled arms of double-daters, under awnings,
 under stars,
To the curb at the mouth of an alley. He hunched there.
Was Johnny a thinker?
No, but he was thinking more or less of Billie Frechette
Who was lost in prison for longer than he could possibly wait,
And then it was suddenly too hard to think around a bullet.
Did anyone shoot straight?
Yes, but Mrs. Etta Natalsky fell out from under her picture hat.
Theresa Paulus sprawled on the sidewalk, clutching her left
 foot.
And both of them groaned loud and long under the streetlight.
Did Johnny like that?
No, but he lay down with those strange women, his face in the
 alley,
One shoe off, cinders in his mouth, his eyelids heavy.
When they shouted questions at him, he talked back to
 nobody.
Did Johnny lie easy?
Yes, holding his gun and holding his breath as a last trick,
He waited, but when the Agents came close, his breath
 wouldn't work.
Clark Gable walked his last mile; Johnny ran half a block.
Did he run out of luck?

Yes, before he was cool, they had him spread out on dished-in
    marble
In the Cook County Morgue, surrounded by babbling people
With a crime reporter presiding over the head of the table.
Did Johnny have a soul?
Yes, and it was climbing his slippery wind-pipe like a trapped
    burglar.
It was beating the inside of his ribcage, hollering, "Let me out
    of here!"
Maybe it got out, and maybe it just stayed there.
Was Johnny a money-maker?
Yes, and thousands paid 25¢ to see him, mostly women,
And one said, "I wouldn't have come, except he's a moral
    lesson,"
And another, "I'm disappointed. He feels like a dead man."
Did Johnny have a brain?
Yes, and it always worked best through the worst of dangers,
Through flat-footed hammerlocks, through guarded doors,
    around corners,
But it got taken out in the morgue and sold to some doctors.
Could Johnny take orders?
No, but he stayed in the wicker basket carried by six men
Through the bulging crowd to the hearse and let himself be
    locked in,
And he stayed put as it went driving south in a driving rain.
And he didn't get stolen?
No, not even after his old hard-nosed dad refused to sell
The quick-drawing corpse for $10,000 to somebody in a
    carnival.
He figured he'd let *Johnny* decide how to get to Hell.
Did anyone wish him well?
Yes, half of Indiana camped in the family pasture,
And the minister said, "With luck, he could have been a
    minister."
And up the sleeve of his oversized gray suit, Johnny twitched
    a finger.

Does anyone remember?
Everyone still alive. And some dead ones. It was a new kind of
   holiday
With hot and cold drinks and hot and cold tears. They planted
   him in a cemetery
With three unknown vice presidents, Benjamin Harrison, and
   James Whitcomb Riley,
Who never held up anybody.

CHAPTER EIGHTEEN

Further Thoughts on Schoolin'

Although we have taken an earlier look at the process of education, we should consider the thoughts of the Johnsons, grandfather Oliver and grandson Howard, on the grammar schools of the early day. After all, Oliver Johnson had been through the mill and the thoroughness with which he describes its processes and the care which Howard Johnson apparently took to record his recollections accurately give them interest. In any case, Oliver probably knew a great deal about early school, while Eggleston, writing of The Hoosier Schoolmaster, was experienced only as a door-to-door Bible salesman at the time he wrote. He had attended a small town school only two or three years—and it, at Vevay, Indiana, was probably one of the better ones. He had not had much chance to witness the travail with which schoolmastering was beset.

So let us look at

A Home in the Woods

THE THREE R's

Early schools wasn't much. If a neighborhood wanted a school they got together and started one. I reckon I was about seven years old (1828), and my sister Louisa, who was the oldest of us children, was about nine when Pap and some of the neighbors got together and decided to build a schoolhouse and start some learnin for their youngsters.

There was no danger from Induns any more. They had left except for now and then some friendly ones travelin or comin to trade. The neighbors held a meetin and elected three men to be trustees. Pap was one of them. The trustees was to build a schoolhouse, hire a teacher and provide for his board. All questions comin up between the master and the patrons was to be settled by the trustees.

Pap offered a location for a school on the north part of our place which was about centrally located for most families, although some of the children would have a long walk through the woods. The men and the big boys of the neighborhood got together and in a few days built a log house without a cent of outlay from anybody. The room was about twenty feet square, plenty big enough to take care of the twenty or thirty boys and girls who would be comin. On one side of the buildin was a door. Opposite it was the master's chair and table, both handmade. In one end was a big fireplace. In the other end was a rough board shelf put on wood pins that stuck out from the logs. This was the writin table. For light a log was taken out just above the writin table and wood strips pinned up and down across this openin. Greased paper was fastened between these strips. When you went to the writin table you had to climb over the top of the benches so as to set facin the table.

The benches was made from slabs split from logs. Legs was put in the flat side, leaving the round side up for us to sit on with our short legs. One leg was put in the middle of the bench to keep the boys from teeterin. Them benches got purty tiresome after settin a long time. They also got purty slick on top from our slidin around on them. If you wanted to rest your back you could sort of hunker down with your elbows on your knees and slide back a little to get your feet off the floor. Once in a while a scholar would slide back too far, lose his balance, and flop he would go on his back on the hard puncheon floor. We had no desks. Your two books and your slate was kept on the floor under your bench. No one had any certain place to set. On cold days the big boys and girls would give the benches nearest the fire to the little ones.

Teachers, or schoolmasters as we called them, was somewhat of a problem to get. Nearly all of them was single men. They wasn't lookin for land or a permanent location, like men with families. They was more of a rovin class. Some was right well educated and turned out to be mighty good fellers. Some times we got a master who wasn't as bright as some of the big scholars. It appeared like they had failed at everything else and then took up teachin. There was no such thing then as a woman teacher. It wasn't a woman's job, any more than milkin a cow was a man's job. Then again it took purty much of a man to handle the big boys and girls.

The only way we got any schoolmaster was to wait until one come along lookin for a place. If the trustees took a notion to him, which they generally did, they told him to draw up his article and go around in the neighborhood and see what signers he could get. If he got enough signers to satisfy him he was hired. The article usually offered a term of three months, December, January, and February, and he got his board and pay. The charge for a full term was fifty to seventy cents a scholar. Some families would sign up for only half a term for big boys, because they had to help at home cuttin wood, goin to mill, and such. Some little folks lived so far away that they was signed up for half a term, as they could go through the woods only during good weather.

Durin the term the master boarded around different places. A big family, with several children in school, boarded and roomed the master longer than a small family.

After our first log school was built and we was lookin forward to our first school, no master came along. There was a young man in our neighborhood who said he could teach the school. He wasn't the best feller in the world and he didn't get many signers, but the trustees was so anxious to get the school goin that they hired him anyway. He taught about two weeks when the new buildin caught fire at night and burned to the ground. It caused quite a flurry in the neighborhood. Some said the master was careless. Anyway, that ended my first school term.

The next fall rolled around and no new schoolhouse was built. Some wanted a school while others was unconcerned whether their young-sters got any learnin or not. Finally a man named Hawkins, who lived about a mile and a half northwest of us, said he would have a school at his cabin if people wanted it. He was gettin up in years, but had taught some in his younger days. He lived in a double cabin with jist his wife at home; that give him room to hold school in his kitchin or livin room. The trustees told him to go ahead and sign up what scholars he could. Even though it was a long trip through the dense woods for Louisa and me, Pap signed for us.

Master Hawkins was a big fat man, jolly and good natured. He wasn't very strict, and we done about as we pleased. I reckon we learned a little at that. If the weather was bad at noon we set around where we pleased to eat our dinner, while Mrs. Hawkins went ahead and got their dinner as if we wasn't there. Anything like a nice day and us scholars got outside to eat. I don't think there was more than twelve or fifteen of us going to that school.

Somethin funny happened at that school along toward the end of the term when the sun was warmin things up. Master Hawkins had a habit of settin in the doorway during the noon hour when the sun shined down nice and warm and takin a nap. Us scholars was playin around out in front of the cabin, when someone noticed a frog hoppin along purty close to the master. We soon saw the cause of its hurry when a garter snake come crawlin from under a puncheon that laid out in front. The master always wore buckskin britches that stood out at the bottom like a sailor's trousers. Well, the frog spied the master's legs a stickin out there on the ground and them big open britches which I reckon he took for a holler log. In he went for a good place to hide. That cold frog on the master's bare leg was mighty awakenin, for he grabbed his britches leg with both hands and danced around like a wild man. We tried to tell him what it was, but he couldn't hear anything. Mrs. Hawkins come runnin out when she heard the racket and got him in the house. He was kinda got when he shed his britches and found a frog squeezed to death. We all had a good laugh at the master, and he took it in good humor, but we noticed he didn't take any more naps in a open door.

The winter that sister Louisa and me went to the Hawkins school we traveled all the way through the thick woods. There wasn't any road, so Pap blazed a trail for us. We didn't have any trouble goin or comin until long about the last of the winter. One mornin it was snowin; one of them heavy wet snows that sticks to the trees and everything else it falls on. Mother was uneasy about sendin us, but Pap thought we would get along all right. Things was purty white when we started out, but we trudged along for quite a piece before we noticed that the trail and the blazed places was gettin harder to see all the time. That was when we wandered off the trail. We wasn't much excited about it, as we knew a young man who lived about straight east from the school-house and by that time would have reached school. So we decided to head straight north and pick up his trail in the snow, which we did, or thought so.

The snow was fallin harder all the time and his tracks didn't show very plain, but we figured we could get to school before they was covered up. After follerin them a while we come to a big tree top and a lot of bushes all covered with snow. The tracks sheared off and went around them and didn't straighten out but kept on windin and twistin around. At first we thought the young man must be lost. Then we thought the tracks might be that of a bear. We both started to cry, knowin we was lost. But both bein purty hardy youngsters and knowin quite a little about the way of the woods, we soon braced up and decided to foller them tracks, since they would take us some place. We kept on windin around through the woods for quite a while. Finally we came out into a clearin and there right before our eyes was a cabin.

We was so tickled we couldn't hold ourselves. We was so turned around and upset we was sure we never saw that cabin before in our lives. We ran up to the door and knocked and who should open it but Aunt Polly, Uncle Milt's wife, our nearest neighbor. She took us in and petted us up some and sent us home. We found that the tracks we had been follerin was made by Aunt Polly's cow as she browsed around the woods on her way home.

Pap and mother was some excited about our story, and tickled too. Pap wanted to know why we didn't take time to eat our dinner, as it was after noon when we reached home. We hadn't thought about eatin anything; we had just clung to our dinner buckets all the way. We learned afterward that when the young man whose tracks we was follerin had come to that big tree top, he walked straight through under the snow on almost dry ground. Aunt Polly's cow went around the bushes, and we got switched off.

There was a new turn in school matters the year after we went to the Hawkins school. The next spring some families from Pennsylvania and

Maryland settled on land over to the east of us. They was right thrifty people. They couldn't think of a country without schools for their children, so they started in right way on buildin a schoolhouse for school that fall. They got together with Pap and Uncle Ben and others on our side of the crick, and this time the school was located on Uncle Ben's land across Fall Crick.

School started off that winter with a new master, who was a stranger to our parts, and a goodly number of scholars. It was the first organized school, if it could be called such, that was held in our neighborhood. Readin, writin, 'rithmetic, and spellin covered the full course of studies. A Webster's spellin book served for both readin and spellin; half the page was spellin words and the other half was readin lesson. A Pike's 'rithmetic, a slate and a slate pencil finished the equipment of a scholar. On the writin table was foolscap paper, quill pens and ink. We made our own pens and ink. Black ink was made by bilin down the bark from a soft maple tree. Red ink was made from pokeberries.

School took up about six o'clock in the mornin. People believed in gettin a full day out of a master when they hired him. School would open by the master callin:

"Come to books!"

Then we all started a rush and a scramble for our seats. It didn't make any difference how much noise you made, just so you set down some place. The first lesson in the mornin was 'rithmetic. We just worked our problems to get the right answer. Scholars would be strung out through the book accordin to how bright they was, no two of them on the same lesson. Some would get purty well through the book, while others never got very far. Sometimes one of the older scholars could solve a problem the master couldn't.

About the middle of the forenoon and agin in the afternoon the master would say:

"Get your writin lesson."

Then there was a scramble for the writin table. The little ones, of course, didn't write. The master had a copy ready for each scholar. He would give instructions how to hold the pen and how to shape and shade the letters. More attention and more interest was given to writin than any other study unless it might be spellin.

To recite spellin, the scholars was called out, one at a time, and asked how far they got. That might be as far as you pleased. Then the master had you spell and pronounce from the book. Then he would take the book and pronounce to you, and you spelled.

Readin was gettin up and rattlin off the lesson. Some would read a whole lesson without a pause and in about two breaths. Little attention was given to punctuation. The only corrections was on pronouncin or leavin out or substitutin words. If the master got short of time you might read twice a week, and then again it might be twice a day, just as he felt about it.

Little ones had primers. Their only work was to learn their A, B, C's. About the only time they got to recite was when the master got through with the big scholars in time. Then he would call one up and stand him between his knees. With a pointer he would point out a letter for the scholar to name. Little ones recited all the way from once a day to once a week. In most of the early schools, scholars studied out loud. That sure made a terrible uproar in the room. Some tried to see how much noise they could make. I remember one girl who could drown out any voice in the room when she was gettin her spellin. When she opened up, you'd just as well lay your book down.

Early schoolmasters was mighty strict in some things and used the gad purty often, especially if they was in a bad humor. They wasn't very particular about your lessons or how much you stayed away from school, for they didn't have to bother with you then. We caught it for a lot of things that struck the master's fancy to give someone a lickin for.

TURNING OUT THE MASTER

While every family recognized Christmas in a religious way, there was no doins at home in the way of givin presents or celebratin the day. We went to school Christmas and New Year's if they fell on a week day, just the same as any other day. But it was a custom, common in all country schools, for the master to give his scholars a treat and a vacation when Christmas come around. No presents was handed out, and there was no such things as candy and oranges. A master's treat was generally the same every Christmas: apples and ginger cakes.

Sometimes a master made no preparation or straight out refused to give a treat. Then it was the custom for the scholars to lock him out or turn him out on Christmas mornin, and keep him out of the school-house until he did agree to treat. This was so much a custom that the trustees and the parents upheld the scholars in such actions. Usually the masters we had was ready on Christmas morning with their treat, and we spent the day eatin apples and ginger cakes, playin games and havin a jolly good time.

Everything had been goin on right well with our school for several years. Then come the fall the trustees had trouble findin a school-master. None showed up in our neighborhood, so they got Mr. Brown to teach. He and his family was among the Marylanders I mentioned before who had moved in over to the east of us. He was also one of the leaders in buildin the new schoolhouse and had taught school back in Maryland. Mr. Brown made a good master, we all liked him, and every-thing went along all right until Christmas. Us scholars hadn't said any-thing to him about a treat. He was such a good man we never doubted but what he would be on time with his apples and ginger cake. The day before Christmas we talked of presentin him with an article to sign to make sure what he was goin to do, but changed our minds and decided to come to the schoolhouse by daybreak and prepare to turn him out if things didn't go our way.

We didn't know that Mr. Brown knew nothin of the Hoosier cus-tom. We was all in the schoolhouse bright and early next mornin, door barred, waitin for him. One of his boys must have got wind of what we was goin to do, for he showed up instead of Mr. Brown and said his pap sent him down to see if what he'd heard was true. We told him it was and to go back and tell his pap he was locked out until he brought a treat. When the boy reported back, Mr. Brown flew into a rage. Mrs. Brown come runnin down to Uncle Ben's and said her husband was carryin on somethin awful, swearin like a sailor, somethin he didn't do, and shakin his fists and sayin no mob could keep him out of his school-house. She said he was loadin his horse pistols also, and would Uncle Ben go up and talk to him. Well, Uncle Ben went back with her and ex-plained to Mr. Brown the way things was done out here and that all he had to do was take a little treat down and give the youngsters a vacation and all would be well. He also hinted that horse pistols was the wrong tools to use in our parts.

Mr. Brown didn't show up on Christmas day, but the next day he was on hand, pleasant as you please, with apples and ginger cake and a jug or two of spruce beer, which was a drink made by these German settlers from the east. We had a fine day of it after all. Mr. Brown held no grudge and seemed to enjoy himself as much as any of us.

The closest we ever come to a real fight was when we turned Mr. Linch out. He was a big, raw-boned, sandy-haired Irishman, middle-aged and a bachelor. He had a terrible bad temper. When he got mad he would lay on the gad unmercifully. A few days before Christmas we noticed Mr. Linch goin round and fixin the winders so they could be fastened on the inside. We knew then that he was gettin ready to shut us out if we demanded a treat. We never said a word until the day before Christmas, then knowin we had a tough customer to deal with, we drew up an article coverin everything we expected the next day and asked him to sign it. He flatly refused and give us to understand that he intended doin nothin. We didn't argue the matter, but us big boys and girls made plans to get to the schoolhouse before daybreak and take possession ahead of Mr. Linch.

Christmas mornin we was all there on time. We built a fire in the fireplace, then we barricaded the door by pilin all the benches up against it. We didn't have to wait long before we saw him comin down the road with his ax on his shoulder and a bunch of kindlin under his arm. He soon saw someone had saved him the trouble of buildin a fire. Mr. Linch stuttered some when he got mad. When he found he couldn't get in and heard us inside, he said:

"Wha- wha- what does this me- mean?"

We told him to come around to the winder and we would tell him. This he did, and we handed him a revised article which called for two bushels of apples and two dozen ginger cakes. We also added to the article that he would not punish any scholar for his part in turnin him out. He give us a dirty look and tore the article to pieces.

"Y- Y- You can go to hell!"

Then he walked around to the door and started on it with his ax and never stopped until he had beat it into kindlin. He never knew that some of us big boys was standin each side of the door armed with a club apiece if he come in usin that ax. When he saw our barricade and that it was useless to break through it, he threw down his ax and started down the road, never sayin a word.

Pap knew all about our plans and about the middle of the forenoon he came down to the schoolhouse to see how the land lay. When he saw the splintered door and heard our story, he got plenty mad.

"Any man who acts like that needs a good lickin."

Pap sent all the small scholars home, but told us bigger ones to stay until the next day. He said he would bring our supper and breakfast to us, and for us to stay and whip the old rascal out. We spent Christmas night at the schoolhouse and until noon the next day, but no Mr. Linch showed up, so we all went home.

In a day or two we got word that Mr. Linch went from the schoolhouse to a cabin about two miles north where they sold whisky. There he stayed a day or so, drinkin and carousin and wound up with a fight. To make matters worse for me, Mr. Linch was boardin at our house at this time. About a week after Christmas he showed up. Pap went to the door and asked him what he wanted. He looked a sight, haggard and holler eyed, and his clothes showed burns where he had been knocked into a fireplace, we supposed. He said he wanted his carpetbag and to cross the crick.

The crick was froze over so we couldn't use the canoe and the ice wasn't thick enough to bear a man's weight. Pap give him his carpetbag and told me to get the gray mare and take him across at the ford, where it wasn't froze over. I was purty shaky when I rode up and told Mr. Linch to mount behind me. When we crossed the crick I knew he would like to drown me for the part I took in turnin him out, but he never opened his head, nor did I. When we got across, he slid off the mare, started down the road and didn't even look back. That was the last any of us ever saw Mr. Linch. That was also the end of school for that term.

Boys and girls could go to school just as long as they wanted to, or as long as they paid for their term. Some would be grown and of age. I think a lot of us kept goin to school more for a pastime and to get away from the monotony of home life than we did for book learnin. I was one of them grownups in the last school I attended. Our schoolmaster was a young man named Gill. He was the most likeable master we ever had, pleasant, agreeable and right smart. He didn't do much lickin either. Us big scholars thought of him more as a chum than a master. He got so chummy that one of the big girls become "his gal."

Along toward Christmas we begun to wonder what kind of a treat
Mr. Gill had in store for us, never once thinkin he would fail us. But to
our surprise, the day before Christmas come around and not a word
about a treat from Mr. Gill. I always thought he intended to treat us,
for he didn't act like other masters had when they took a solid stand
against it. I think he wanted to hold out on us just for the sport of it;
might be he just wanted to match wits with us and show us how game
he was.

Christmas mornin we was all on hand bright and early. Doors and
winders was barred. Then we waited for Mr. Gill to come. About the
usual time here he come walkin out of the woods into the clearin in
front of the schoolhouse. There he stood a while, takin in the situation.
I don't think he was fooled much, for he smiled and turned around and
started to leave. We was ready for that move by havin one of our best
runners standin by the door ready to catch him if he tried to get away.
When we caught him, he fought and kicked so bad and give us such a
tussle that we had to tie him up and carry him back to the schoolhouse. We presented our article, but he flatly refused to sign it. Some
mischievous youngster spoke up.

"Why not take him down to the crick and stuff him under the ice?"

Well, before anybody could say no we was on our way with him tied
up as he was. We cut a hole in the ice and threw a couple of rails across
it. Then we took his coat off and tied a rope to his feet so we could pull
him back before he would drown and laid him on the rails. Before we
jerked the rails out from under him we agin asked him if he was ready to
sign the article. He said he would drown before he would sign. All of a
sudden a voice came from the crick bank.

"Boys, don't do that. That is too exposin."

It was the trustees, who had been watchin us all mornin to see that
we didn't go too far in our part of the game. I know I was mighty glad
to hear that voice and I think the others was, too. The master almost
had us whipped out that time. As for Mr. Gill, I could never figure out
how far he would have gone with his part of the game. Sometimes I
wonder if he didn't see them trustees before we did and was puttin his
trust in them.

We took Mr. Gill off the rails, put his coat back on him and carried
him back to the schoolhouse and set him up against a tree while we

went inside to consult on our next move. We decided to let the big girls snow ball him a while. That didn't work either, for his gal got to cryin and carryin on so the other girls just quit for feelin sorry for her.

Mr. Gill now demanded that we turn him loose, although he refused to sign our article. I reckon we was just about as determined a bunch of youngsters as you could get together. We was raised by people who was that kind ahead of us. So we refused to let him go.

While we was discussin what to do next, we looked up the road and there come a big drove of hogs on their way to a Ohio River town market. A good many of these hogs was half wild. They had been brought in from the woods, half fattened and full of fight, especially the boars with their long tusks. All at once the thought struck us: why not lay the master out in the road and let the hogs pass over him!

When we laid him in the road we give him another chance to come to our terms. Still he refused, although we noticed he got mighty pale. We backed off and watched as the hogs went by. The first bunch would smell and root him some and go on. Then they wasn't so particular about walkin around him. Finally one of them rough lookin, long-tusked, half-wild boars come up purty close and started pawin the ground, sniffin and chompin his jaws like he was goin to jump right on him. That was more than Mr. Gill could stand. He called to us to come and get him, that he would give us our treat.

It was now noon. School went right on after noon as if nothing unusual had happened. The next day Mr. Gill give us one of the finest treats we ever had. We sure earned it.

———

To those of us who appeared so late on the scene that traveling photographers were wont to photograph every class each year and to offer prints of the result for sale to the victims, the school class picture is a familiar, often horrifying, memory.

As classes advanced in years and iniquity, the photos became even more horrifying than the physiognomies of the class members warranted. There was, always, the class cut-up who either crossed his eyes or stuck out his tongue just as the pictorial artist uncovered his lens. In case the class was numerous enough to warrant lining up for a panorama view, the camera, standing still, rotated from one side to the other, causing those figures in the center to increase in bulk while those at the ends were reduced according to the law of perspective. In a panorama view of the class, or entire student body, some merry-andrew, usually owning jug-ears and freckles, preempted a place at the end where the setting of the camera indicated the action was to start. After the camera had begun the photograph and had moved on, the jester withdrew behind his fellow-students and, causing some little disturbance, doubled over and dashed to the opposite end of the line in time to assume his original pose and to appear in the finished picture twice.

The pictures were sold by the school principal, when completed, usually for twenty-five cents to a dollar each. Our school, harboring an excessive number of suspicious minds, was convinced that the principal had grown rich through hoarding the commission we knew he must receive.

Members of the first grade must have been innocent of either such capers or such suspicions, and it was a picture of that grade, taken some six decades ago, which was, long after, treasured by

SAMUEL YELLEN

Professor Yellen was born in Lithuania but educated in the United States. He has been a member of the Indiana University faculty since 1929 and now holds the position of University Professor Emeritus of English.

First Grade, Room 1, South Case School

There I stand, second row, fourth from the right,
Arms rigid at my sides, obedient,
A scholar, though perhaps not erudite,
My eyes upon the camera eye intent.

Rebuke or guile has forced each banal pose.
One wears the hackneyed toothless grin, and one

Out of brand-new shoes, like a flower, grows.
One girl sits scowling, a wee Amazon.

All the trappings of innocence are here:
Curls and ribbons, stockings hanging in rolls,
Starched dress, sailor suit, protruding ear.
But who would say that these are simple souls?

One is perplexed, contempt curls on one lip,
One has known terror, one has learned aplomb,
One smirks in fraudulent good-fellowship,
One is withdrawn in philosophic calm.

But I, or rather he who bore my name—
He surveys me with enigmatic face.
Likeness there is, yet we are not the same;
For he stands there, and I am in this place.

That stranger in the prim wide-collared blouse
Is, so Wordsworth said, Father of the Man.
I tell you from my shaded prison-house,
Out of that ugly duckling came no swan.

Why have I no keepsake of one small heart
Beating out the minutes of that lost day?
Whence came these trackless seas to hold apart
The Man here and that forlorn castaway?

Little Father, there is no turning back;
I go my journey at a grim command.
But you I carry in my haversack;
Together we go on, though not hand in hand.

*But learning does not end with grade school in Indiana. Higher educa-
tion is rampant. It must rank among the state's top ten industries, or
perhaps we would be more proper to term it a profession, and the ways
in which it operates are mysterious and wondrous to the uninformed.
Times and truths change, even in the groves of Academe, so in some*

respects the picture which follows, painted circa 1957, will appear out-
dated. In others, sadly, it will seem strictly au courant. Professor Yellen
has "seen the elephant" from all angles. In his The Passionate Shepherd:
A Book of Stories *appears the instructive*

The Mystic Presences

As for Eliot Wentworth, whose dismissal (or rather, to employ precise legalistic jargon, failure of reappointment) agitated our faculty last spring, I happen to be in a position to say that, once the sequence of events was set going, the poor bastard never had a chance. Indeed, unwittingly I was the trigger mechanism that started the chain reaction. Of course, when the inevitable moment came, we went through all the prescribed motions of considering his case objectively, weighing the evidence carefully, and forming an impartial judgment. There is, after all, no place like a university for going through all the motions simply to arrive at a foregone conclusion. And, I suppose, it is only fair to add that a few naïfs among us actually have faith in the motions. Nevertheless, the outcome was as predetermined as if young Eliot Wentworth were the pawn of Fate, Destiny, the Norns, the Will of Heaven, Kismet, Character, Heredity, Instinct, Circumstance, the Unconscious, or any other of the mystic presences man has invented to justify his own blunders and mishaps. But then, my view should be taken at a discount. Not without a modicum of truth, Eliot used sardonically to call me Prof Harry Sanders That Lovable Old Cynic.

No doubt I might have tossed a monkey wrench into the Wheel of Fortune. As chairman of the Department of Sociology and Anthropology, I could have insisted that Eliot be kept on. I had nothing to lose. I am sixty-three, only scant years from retirement. An old bachelor, having given no hostages and having put money in my purse, I could have forced the issue. And for a while, I must admit, I was foolishly tempted. When you get along in years and have no family, you are a lonely man. It was as if I had suddenly been presented with a brilliant

son and a charming daughter-in-law to fuss over me. Eliot and his wife
Sharon had youth and freshness. They pumped vitamins into me. They
were an elixir, a fire where I could warm myself. However, good sense
won out. Sure, I could have rammed Eliot down the Dean's throat. But
the Dean would never have promoted him, and the poor bastard
would have remained the perennial assistant professor growing the
long sharp nose of disappointment. Besides, in the final analysis, the
Dean was right.

It is the law in Yarmouth, Carlyle once wrote, that every herring
hang by its own head. I am perfectly ready to hang by mine. Yes, the
responsibility lies with me. In fact, not only was I the unwitting trigger
mechanism, but, as you will see, when it came right down to it, I cast
the deciding vote. I could have made the fight and got Eliot his tenure.
On the other hand, if I *were* misjudging the Dean's temper, the whole
affair might have blown up in our faces.

How can you convince the unknowing public that the linen you are
washing may be just slightly soiled? Or that a kind of experiential wisdom resides in the cultural pattern which rejects someone like Eliot?
Yes, I could have raised a mighty fuss. And all for what? To get Eliot
a tenure contract. These days all you hear about is tenure, as if it were
the passport to Zion. Well, I may not be lovable, but I guess I am an
old cynic. In *theory*, once you are on tenure, you cannot be dismissed
except after open trial, and only on charges of treason, immorality, or
incompetence. However, there are more ways than one of skinning a
professor. As for the sense of security that tenure is alleged to give you,
I can refer you to the pleasantry current on our campus: you spend
your thirties worrying about the treason clause, your forties worrying
about the immorality clause, your fifties worrying about the incompetence clause, and your sixties worrying about retirement.

No, the essential point was that Eliot was still at an age—thirty-two
—when I could get him another berth. Provided, obviously, that he
departed without too much of a stink. Besides, I realized that I myself had been guilty of a stupid mistake. Indeed, two stupid mistakes.
In the *affaire Wentworth*, the original sin was probably mine. With
those three syllables *probably*, I pay my respects to the factor of Eliot's
personality, to the ever-present variables, *and* to the mystic presences.
Thank God for *probably*. Even with that sedative, I lost many a night's

sleep. After all, even a lovable old cynic knows when he has behaved shabbily.

I recall the cold bright morning last January when Eliot dropped into my office to exchange amiable insults. On an impulse, which I was soon to regret, I tossed a folder across the desk. It was instantly recognizable as one of those folders descending upon a chairman like a flock of birds each spring, containing the photograph, the official transcripts and credentials, and the weary letters of recommendation, sent out by the graduate schools peddling their latest crop of Ph.D.'s. This one, from Chicago, was a very early robin indeed. And for good reason. The candidate happened to be a Negro, and they were going to need plenty of time to place him. If ever.

"How about hiring *this* baby," I asked prankishly, "and changing the complexion of the department?"

As soon as Eliot looked at the photograph and saw the Negroid face, he said in an acid voice: " 'And Laughter holding both his sides.' "

That was his favorite comment on a bad joke or an ornate piece of pedantry. It was one of the things I rather liked about him. He was refreshing. (*Fresh!* my colleagues would snort.) Agreed that Eliot sometimes rubbed us the wrong way. He *did* rub through the incrustation of the stale, the pretentious, the solemnly timid. And another thing. How many of our sociologists could have thrown out a verse from Milton? As Eliot stood there with the cold flat morning light on his narrow face, I found myself contrasting him with our standard product. He was no slave to the professional cliché, and he *had* done some reading. Nowadays we no longer read Hobbes, Locke, Machiavelli, Rousseau, Aristotle, even Sumner and Boas. All we read is one another's textbooks, monographs, and reprints. Reproduction by cross-sterilization! Well, well, my dotage must be upon me. Forgive this digression into an old-fashioned viewpoint.

When I saw how seriously engrossed Eliot was in the folder, I realized that I had blundered. With an offhand manner, I tried to take it from him. But he merely frowned, stepped back, and went on with his study. Somewhat annoyed with him (and myself too), I beheld him at his least attractive. Certainly his posture would have taken no prize. Not quite six feet in height, spindly, his shoulders stooped, his chest collapsed, he looked consumptive. And his *clothes!* He was apt, as on that morning, to be wearing *black* shoes (unshined) with a *brown* suit (unpressed). His head, however, compelled attention. Nose and chin were firmly cut. Thick brownish-black hair parted on one side and a heavy tangle of eyebrow deepened and swarthiness of the face. And dark-brown eyes looked out from under the drooping eyelids with a quizzical irreverence, an irreverence arising, as I had come to understand, not out of personal bitterness, but rather out of a need to shield his own honesty in a world of sham and cant. Without the mockery of his eyes, his face would have seemed saturnine, almost sullen. What never failed to astonish me was that this unpolished specimen had done both his undergraduate work and his doctorate at *Princeton!*

By every token, he should have enjoyed an immediate academic success. His training was excellent, his mind keen. His very name and family should have been a warrant of soundness. And yet, even though the market was tight, Michigan had given him the heave-ho after the customary three-year probation. Three years are, of course, time enough for the man's slip to show. Perhaps my colleagues had been right in questioning his appointment. Perhaps their doubts had been more than a rationalization of their fears for their little bailiwicks. Perhaps that sixth sense of the academic world had detected the unreliable, the nonconformist, the odor of the stake. I could readily understand why Michigan had unloaded him, however reluctantly. Was it, indeed, wise to take a chance when you could procure the safe article? And Eliot was difficult. He was not quite the do-gooder so abhorred by present-day sociologists, but he *was* the gadfly type, even if he did lack the unpleasant self-congratulatory air which so many of that type have. To add to the difficulty, a small trust fund gave him an income which, while not sufficient for a man with a wife and child to flourish on, was just enough to deprive him of the useful virtue of docility ordinarily bestowed upon one by the providence of financial exigency. For instance, he spoke up his convictions brusquely, without paying the small toll of hesitation, circumlocution, and qualification demanded by academic propriety. As on that January morning.

"Say, this fellow really *is* first-rate," he said, looking up from the folder. "You've got to hire him, Harry."

"Now hold your horses," I said with an uneasy laugh. "You know we can't hire a Negro."

"Why not?"

"Don't be infantile, Eliot! Do I have to point out to you that this is not Liberia, but the good old U.S.A.?"

"Do I have to point out to the eminent Prof Sanders that this is a university, not a country club? We've even got a couple on the basketball team."

I sighed. I knew I was in for it. "Listen to reason, Eliot. The great day hasn't dawned yet. You don't go out and hire a Negro the way you buy a standing rib roast. You've got to look at the broader picture."

That last *was* a fatuous remark, and I suppose I deserved Eliot's grimace of disgust. "For Christ's sake, Harry, you're not going to turn into a god-damned administrator right before my eyes!"

Nevertheless, the grimace and the words stung, and I committed my second blunder. "Where have you been the last two and a half years?" I demanded sharply. "I thought I hired a trained *anthropologist*, not a starry-eyed English professor. Haven't you been observing the mores around you? May I inquire whether you have ever seen a Negro in one of our local barber shops? Or in one of our local restaurants?"

I stopped short. For looking at Eliot's face, I instantly realized that the poor innocent had *not* noticed. And for once, he was speechless. He was in a state of moral shock. It was clearly a case of "Came the light." His eyes had been opened.

Of course, once Eliot created that scene in Corbin's and then got himself interviewed by the local newspaper, his doom was sealed. In the life scholastic, the only public scene you create is to read a paper at the American Sociological Society, and the only interview you give is to *The New York Times*, whose liturgical style swaddles all improprieties. While I was myself not a witness to the scene in Corbin's, I had a detailed account from a colleague who happened to be there; and having also twice by chance been present at similar scenes, I can easily picture what took place.

Let us set the stage. Occupying a fine old red-brick house, Corbin's is the most elegant restaurant in town, listed by both Duncan Hines and the A.A.A., with a refined air and subdued sound, food a little too spiritualized for my taste, and Corbin himself always on the premises playing the character part of Mine Host. Enter, at about six thirty, the height of the dinner hour, Eliot, pale with resolution, accompanied by an extremely nervous Negro graduate student in Music who (poor bastard) has been persuaded to undergo this public humiliation on behalf of his people. Follows the stage business of craning of necks by the diners, among whom are some of the town's leading citizens. Corbin bustles forward to Eliot: "I'm very sorry, sir, but we're just about to close for the evening, and we're not seating any more patrons." Meanwhile, the waitresses, on cue, turn off the outside lights and pull down the front window shades. That was Corbin's effective way of dealing with this kind of situation. He would remain imperturbably polite and bland in the face of all protests, and he would lock the front door and surrender whatever business might yet have come to him that evening.

As Walter Scott remarked, a pedagogue is a man among boys and a boy among men. By bad luck, the boy Eliot had stumbled among men. The local sheet, as we all know, is the tool of the Democratic machine. Its editor was happy to be given this opportunity to embarrass not only the university, but also the Governor of the state, a Republican whose re-election depended on the large Negro vote in the industrial centers. Such are the sordid details. No one but Eliot was surprised to discover his interview about the incident in Corbin's boxed on page one in 14-point boldface. Eliot trotted out the usual platitudes and put them through their paces to remind us that our great Constitution guarantees equal rights to all citizens of the state, regardless of race, creed, or color. Even as I squirmed, I could not help being entertained at observing how the individual had been submerged in the role. The interview did not sound like Eliot at all. It sounded like any Indignant Liberal.

You may wonder whether I am not doing young Eliot an injustice. Having resided for only two short years in a community with an extravagantly ramified structure (plus the superimposed stresses of town and gown), how was he to be cognizant of all the boxes within boxes and wheels within wheels? But, after all, he *was* an anthropologist, with a brain and 20–20 vision. I must confess to a certain disappointment in him. Sent out to do a study of an Indian tribe, he would have come back smelling like a wigwam and loaded down with penetrating notes. Nonetheless, in his own everyday surroundings he proved to be as unobservant as a medieval mystic contemplating his own navel. There must be some anticatalyst in the university medium which retards the process of maturation. Take a salesman, a lawyer, or a candlestickmaker at age thirty-two. He would not have fallen into that error. Even after a casual reading of the newspapers, he would have been aware of the local folkways and of the political set-up. And he would have known that while our Board of Regents might overlook a moderate amount of immorality and a rather sizable amount of incompetence, it would not overlook violations of the first of the academic commandments: Don't be a troublemaker.

The day the interview appeared, I called Eliot into my office and we came as close to a stormy scene as I have ever come. "What precisely did you hope to accomplish by that silly business at Corbin's?" I demanded.

Eliot, looking sallow and strained, smiled at me for a moment before replying. "Put it down to heedless misguided youth, Harry. Someone has to get the old mule Society moving."

"I must say, Eliot, that the gadfly type has always been a puzzle to me. Indeed, I might well have voted to give Socrates the hemlock, if only to get rid of a public nuisance. How can an otherwise sensible person, mindful of the multiplicity of our social forces and the complexity of their interplay, presume to attempt to put the world in joint and make a fictive Justice prevail?"

"That, gentlemen, is the question before us," said Eliot dryly.

I snorted my annoyance. "Eliot Wentworth, one of God's angry men!"

"No, Harry," he said quietly. "I don't enjoy being a public spectacle, and I think I know what I may be in for. But I can't help myself. I can't just stand by. I guess I'm one of those for whom the bell tolls. Some He made beasts of the field, and some He made fowls of the air."

"Okay. I admit we're not alike. I suppose that ultimately, unless you go in for the Freudian claptrap, it must come down to a problem in physiology. Given the right sort of test tube, flask, and Bunsen burner, one could work out the reaction that generates such a head of steam. But that question still plagues me: What did you hope to accomplish?"

"It all depends on whether you believe in social progress. *Someone* has to stir things up to prevent paralysis from setting in." Then he smiled mockingly. "At the very least, I added a little drama to the drab existence of the Administration."

That last crack made me cross. "Now who do you think battles with the Legislature for your salary check, and stands between you and all the bigots and jackasses in the state? You might recollect that elementary law of Society, the Law of the Fleas. Big fleas have little fleas. Conversely, little fleas dwell on big fleas. I carry you, the Dean carries me, the President carries the Dean. Equal rights is just a parcel of words to you. The poor bastard out there on the firing line is the President."

"Sure, sure," Eliot replied impatiently. "That's what he gets paid a princely stipend for."

The scene in Corbin's, I remember, occurred on a Wednesday evening, and the interview appeared on Thursday. The following Monday morning I received a phone call from Dean Hendricks inviting me to have lunch with him. I had been expecting that call. I could imagine the conferences over the week-end between him and the President, between the President and the Publicity Director, and very likely between the Governor and one or two of the Regents. That noon I met the Dean at the Faculty Club and we took a table to ourselves in the Ship, over against the sloping timbers between the farthest porthole and the elaborately spoked wheel. Spawned by the daydream of a landlocked architect, the Ship would have foundered in Farmer Brown's Pond, the only body of water in our vicinity. However, there, amid the ship's lanterns, the captain's chairs, the carved bas-relief of winches and capstans, and the other nautical accouterments, the faculty entertained visiting firemen and the Dean broached delicate matters with departmental chairmen.

Although the Dean is exactly my age, you wouldn't guess it. If I say so myself, he looks like an old man. As he sat across the table from me, the bald head with the red-rimmed eyes and the raw wrinkled neck sticking up above the white collar put me in mind of an ancient buzzard. Our conversation proceeded in accordance with immemorial practice, each topic keeping pace with a course in the luncheon. Thus Saturday night's basketball game came in with the vegetable soup; and the prospects for an early golf season, with the veal birds. Eliot came in rather abruptly with the dessert.

"Sanders, did you know Wentworth was going to put on that restaurant act?"

"Of course not, Dean. Wouldn't I have stopped him?"

The Dean studied me severely for a moment. "I don't need to tell you that it has caused the President considerable embarrassment. It couldn't have come at a worse time." He paused to swallow a spoonful of cherry-colored gelatin, then went on in a lowered tone. "What I'm about to tell you is in the strictest confidence. I hope that business of Wentworth's doesn't upset the apple cart. It has caught us in the middle of rather delicate negotiations." His voice trailed off, as though he had suddenly thought better of letting me in on the top secret.

In vain did I search those watery faded-blue eyes. Were there really negotiations? And if so, what were they? Or was the old buzzard simply bamboozling me? I have to acknowledge that I was no match for the Dean. Not only did he have all the advantage of status, but his veined relic of a face rebuffed every attempt of mine to read it. However, I did surmise how the Dean's remarks were going to conclude. By now I could do a definitive treatise on the ritualistic expressions accompanying the academic sacrifice.

"What kind of a fellow is Wentworth anyway?" he asked, as he took out a cigarette. I was already busy filling my pipe.

"Well, Dean, he's not a genius. How many geniuses have we got? But he *is* the most promising young anthropologist I've come across in several years."

The Dean lit his cigarette and then turned his bleached eyes on me. "I wonder if he isn't going to turn out to be a troublemaker." With that, poor Eliot was as effectively sacrificed as if an Aztec priest had torn out his bleeding heart and held it up still beating for the multitudes to behold.

If I go on with this story, it is because, notwithstanding its already ascertainable denouement, it holds a roadside interest. There is a resemblance here to watching a Greek tragedy. While we fully know the destiny in store for the protagonist, yet the actual working out of that destiny is attended by fascinating variations and surprises. And there were even a few surprises for *me*, although I was, in a sense, the agent of the Fate calling the turns.

Toward the end of February, I held the customary meeting of our six full professors in the department to pass on promotions, new appointments, and dismissals. Ordinarily, had I been seeking someone's promotion, I would have had them over to the house during the evening, with a good blaze in the fireplace and a decanter of Scotch to soften the resentments and grudges which had accumulated in their very human breasts over the months. But this time I called the meeting for a Saturday morning, and in our seminar room. Aside from the irritation of giving up a Saturday morning to departmental business, I wanted those cheerless bare walls painted an institutional tan and the scratched dusty table and floor to work upon them. Alas, such are the petty dodges a chairman must employ to bring about the decision he knows to be in the best interest of his department. Of course, I had prudently made some preliminary calculations of how the vote might go, and I was fairly positive that Eliot would be dismissed (or rather, not rehired) by a count of four to two. That would have been most agreeable to me, since it would have spared me the unpleasantness of casting a deciding vote and would have made it possible for me (with a decent display of reluctance) to bow to the judgment of my staff. But I was not to be spared.

As I sat at one end of the table that morning and looked around at my colleagues, I felt like a clumsy craftsman surrounded by his botch-work. How had I in my sixteen years as chairman managed to get together so sorry a collection? I remember Eliot saying to me after the first occasion when he met the full professors all together: "Man, you sure can pick 'em! Where'd you get the *menagerie?*"

Rather huffily I retored: "We may not be Princeton or Columbia, but that's as good a group of men as you'd find at any of our sister institutions."

"Oh, sister!" Eliot cried.

And I couldn't help laughing. It was, in part, their appearance. I sometimes wonder by what malicious handiwork we academics turn into such freaks. What intaglio process makes the smooth young flesh sink in with the years to bring into sharp relief the hidden quirks, cranks, and crazes, and transforms us into caricatures of ourselves? Well, I suppose I'm no beauty either. However, what dejected me as I looked around the table was the thought of how much talent had leaked out somewhere along the way. Here were men expertly trained and able enough, yet what a disappointment when measured against their early promise. What had happened? Why had they dribbled away (yes, and sold out) their gifts for such trifling gains? Browning's Andrea del Sarto would have shaken his head sadly at them. Their grasp had far exceeded their reach.

The good Lord deliver me from being judged by a jury of my colleagues. I have sat on too many such juries and seen the mystic presences of Academe operate (fortunately, as chairman, above the fray). I have watched spite, rancor, jealousy, guile, jobbery, self-approval, and self-righteousness assert themselves through the thin disguises. Oh, we do no worse unto one another than we are done by! And yet, unbelievable as it may seem, one factor somehow cancels out another, a proper balance is achieved, and generally a sound verdict is reached. As in the case of the University vs. Assistant Professor Eliot Wentworth. Two votes came through for Eliot according to expectation, those of Jolliffe and MacPherson. Jolliffe is our Crime and Social Disorganization man. Even Eliot, who had originally dubbed him the Hairless Jesus, had come to respect him. How that mild spirit succeeds in getting along with murderers, dope fiends, second-story artists, counterfeiters, grifters, prison wardens, and hard-boiled cops is the everlasting marvel of our university administration. Of all the professional Christians I have known, he is the sole exemplar of the meek and lowly of heart. Had Eliot been a safe-cracker or an imbecile, he would still have had Jolliffe's vote. As for MacPherson, our Anthropologist, he is a blunt pragmatic Scotchman, who was then just back, gaunt and brown, from another of his expeditions to Yucatan. With his acquired tolerance for the extremes of human culture and convention, he would not have cared whether Eliot was a polygamist or a cannibal. By yard-stick and abacus, he had computed Eliot's published articles as he might have measured a pyramid or a cranium. And the resulting figures had proved fully adequate.

I had, of course, written off those two votes. They were easy enough to predict. The great surprise, and indeed embarrassment, for me was furnished by Atkinson (Social Theory). In this instance a bookie could have made a killing. I would have offered odds of 20 to 1 that Atkinson would howl out a bitter *No*. I am sure that Eliot's epithet "the Bearded Lady" had come to his ears. How he must have paced the floor, straggly beard aquiver, before he could swallow his mortification and render a just verdict. (Or, as the lovable old cynic in me suggests, did he cast that vote for Eliot out of hostility to *me* and what he thought I might wish?) Well, admirable as this triumph of the human spirit might be, there was no doubt that the Bearded Lady had presented me with an awkward problem. I had come a long way from being permitted to bow reluctantly to the judgment of my staff. I now *had* to have all the three other votes even to be given the chance as chairman to cast the deciding vote. Otherwise, I would be put in the extremely painful position of having to *override* my colleagues in order to get rid of Eliot.

Luckily, there *is* a certain predictability in human behavior and, aside from one anxious moment, the others came through as I had made book. Take Rausch, our Population and Statistics man. Observing him that Saturday morning, the way a woman might observe her husband after a decade and a half of marriage, I asked myself: "How in the world did Rausch ever look good to me?" He has an overstrained waxen face and a stammer. And he is vain, incredibly so, vain as only a pedant can be. He was my first important appointment; all I can say in my defense is that in his middle thirties he had seemed a brilliant catch and I had had to outbid both Nebraska and Duke for him. However, I had failed to detect the secret core of timidity or insecurity which was later to drive him into a series of safe little articles, an endless succession of inconsequential population studies dug out of the census figures for the counties, towns, and villages of our state. The kind of problem this eminent scholar set for himself was, How do villages under 500 compare with towns between 500 and 2,000 in the percentage of children joining the Boy Scouts and Girl Scouts? Or, What percentage of the population of Stark County ranged according to income levels are high-school graduates? Since our state has a hundred counties and hundreds of towns and villages, these invaluable little studies could go on forever. And did.

It is a sad spectacle. Yet which department cannot boast its Rausch? Most of us on the faculty, when we glance at the long list of titles in his annual bibliography, recognize it as a case of compulsive scholarship, smile tolerantly, and think: "There but for the grace of the great god Neurosis go I." But not Eliot. That *enfant terrible* found it behooved him to ask one afternoon: "Dr. Rausch, what is the percentage of left-handed crapshooters in Elkinsville?" Rausch never forgot that. And when the time came to sit in judgment, he stammered with an earnest mien radiating impartiality: "It's true that Wentworth does have a kind of superficial flair, but do you think his approach to things is really at bottom a scholarly one?" Ah, but those fifty-year-old wattles fluttered with repressed fury.

Another interesting case was Dobbs (Family and Marriage). Dobbs is tall, erect, and clean-cut, an earlier handsomeness casting an air of distinction over his sixties, though his ashen hair has gone very thin. He enjoys a reputation with the ladies, and he dresses elegantly, going in for pearl-gray vests and Homburgs. (Eliot christened him the Clothes Horse.) He is a smooth number and nobody's fool. I remember his once saying to me, after he had been needled by Eliot: "Sure, Harry, you as chairman can afford to have a jester around. But we others at court can't regard him with precisely the same favor." Tracing his initials with his finger tip in the dust of the seminar table, Dobbs also put on the mask of impartiality. What he said was: "I suppose Wentworth is clever enough, but it seems to me that he's dispersing his energies." Now that was good, coming from Dobbs. The only energy *he* disperses is in knocking over the bottle in bottle pool at the Faculty Club. But here again, part of the picture was hidden. I knew what was eating *him*. Sharon! Yes, at a faculty dance she had once turned down a little proposition of his. I knew this because she had confided in me.

That leaves me with Frobisher, who handles our work in Methods. Everyone knows him for my yes-man. A tall black-haired fellow in his late forties, with a neat black mustache, Frobisher looks like a foreign diplomat. It is, incidentally, not *me* he yesses, but my status. He would do shameless flipflops to vote the way his Chairman wishes. And apparently he has worked out a rationale for himself which makes him impervious to amazed stares and sly smiles. Eliot addressed him once as Mrs. Bloom, to his great mystification, since he had never heard of Joyce nor of that notorious last chapter in *Ulysses*. While I can't say I respect Frobisher any more than his other colleagues do, I must confess that a chairman often finds a yes-man extremely useful.

Strangeful enough, it was Frobisher who furnished the anxious moment. Indeed, he gave me quite a turn. The trouble was that I neglected to take into account the power of the conditioned reflex. For two years now I had conditioned Frobisher so that Eliot Wentworth's name was the signal for a chant of approval. That is why I was almost caught off base. Taking it for granted that I was all for keeping Eliot, Frobisher launched into his paean: "It seems to me that Wentworth is an extraordinarily bright young man, in many ways just the sort we want to build into a strong department like ours. Of course, the training he got at Princeton is really excellent. And he puts it to good use. I read that last monograph of his, and I must say it's of a quality you'd expect from a much older man." I suppressed a morbid prompting to let Frobisher run on, to see exactly how far he *could* go and still manage to scramble back over to the other side of the fence. But I knew I could not indulge myself, and I arranged my face in a frown. Sensitive as litmus paper, Frobisher reacted instantaneously. I didn't like doing that to him, but it was necessary. Never have I admired his adroitness as much as then. With hardly a pause, he changed pace almost in mid-sentence: "And, nevertheless, good as Wentworth is, the unfortunate fact is that he happens to be in a field where we already are exceptionally strong (this with a half-bow to MacPherson). Perhaps it would, after all, be wisest to let him go elsewhere and to look around for a young man we can try out in one of the other fields."

As you can see, I had my opportunity to cast the deciding vote. Of course, I was prepared to ride out the inevitable buzzing among the faculty. After all, they recognized a cause-and-effect sequence when they saw one. They had heard about the scene in Corbin's and had read Eliot's interview; now they took note of the failure to reappoint. However, it is not hard to ride out a tempest in the faculty teapot. That is part of a chairman's job. Fortunately, the buzzing is all noise and no sting. Eliot served as a conversation piece at the Faculty Club and at the spring cocktail parties. There was even a salutary cathartic effect: each speaker was furnished a cloak underneath which he could get his own grievances, real or imagined, off his chest. But despite all the talk and the sympathetic head-shakings, not one went to bat for the poor bastard. And to my surprise, breaking the news to Eliot was not rough at all. In fact, he was *gentle* with me, as though I were the one getting the bad news. "If you can take it, Harry," he said, "I can." Whether he was letting me off easy because he liked me or because he felt sorry for me, I couldn't tell. In any case, we got him comfortably settled elsewhere.

But Fate had reserved one last twist. It still remained for Prof Harry Sanders That Lovable Old Cynic to receive a kick in his lovable old rump. I remember that whenever Eliot was about to impart an especially ironic morsel, he used to say: "This one is going to *kill* you!" Well, this one certainly killed *me*. Early last month the faculty assembled in Zoology Hall, appropriately surrounded by the pickled and bottled specimens in the glass cases lining the walls, for its first meeting of the fall semester. That is the occasion on which the various departmental chairmen introduce their new staff members. As I looked around to see what toll the past summer had taken of my colleagues, I was given a shock that sent the blood flaming to my cheeks. There not more than five rows behind me was a *black face!* And not even a brown or tan that might pass for a Hindu, but an uncompromising coal black.

To make matters worse, the black face was right next to Dirks, chairman of Chemistry, and, as everyone knows, a hard-bitten illiberal Republican. Even though I understood how desperate a situation Chemistry confronts these days in procuring staff, I couldn't shake away the fact that Dirks the Republican Chemist had done what Sanders the Sociologist had been too timid to do. I was mortified. What would Eliot think when he found out? Might I after all, have hired the Negro as he suggested, and spared myself all the heartache and tossing? Or, contrary to my skepticism, had Eliot's little act of provocation produced this result, and had some intimation come down from the Republican Governor to the Republican Chemist? In either case, I felt that I had sacrificed Eliot to a phantom, that the Dean had made a monkey of me. Nor was it merely that my *amour-propre* was wounded. I suddenly realized how acutely I missed Eliot, and Sharon too. I was an old and lonely man. I *needed* them, their youth, their vigor, their honesty. Even Eliot's mockery had been a tonic to me. I had cheated myself, and at the close of a fairly honorable career had lost my peace of mind to boot.

I explain my reaction at such length only to account for a foolish bit of behavior I might otherwise not have been guilty of. The knife *was* turning in me. Hence it was that a week or so ago when I met the Dean at the Faculty Club I invited him to have lunch with me. We boarded the Ship and sat at the same table between the farthest porthole and the wheel; and we ate veal birds again, from their toughness probably the same hatch we had had before. All the time I was well aware that I was about to do something silly. (If I could really pump Hendricks, would he have got to be Dean?) But I was gripped by an impulse beyond my control. And I suppose I did not improve matters by becoming coy and trying cajolery.

"Dean," I said, "I don't know whether you ever ran across a story called *The Lady, or the Tiger?* It used to be a favorite in high-school English classes."

The Dean looked up at me, nodded, and said: "Frank Stockton." Then he bent his head back to his food.

"Well, you may recall how it ends," I went on. "The reader never does find out whether the poor bastard out there in the arena finally gets the lady or the tiger. Somehow I was put in mind of that story the other day at the faculty meeting when Dirks introduced that new assistant professor of his. Just as a matter of curiosity, Dean, last winter when you and I were talking about Eliot Wentworth, were you already negotiating for the black chemist? Or did Wentworth's little piece of agitation put the heat on and make you look around for one as a political gesture? Come on, Dean, which was it? Just between us girls."

The Dean remained silent, occupied with carving his veal bird. He put a forkful into his mouth and chewed deliberately, looking down at his plate. I counted the number of times those jaws chomped (eleven), and watched the progress of that mouthful as it moved along the raw wrinkled neck and down into the gullet. At last he lifted his relic of a face to mine and regarded me with those watery red-rimmed eyes. And all I got out of the old buzzard was a slow elaborate wink.

CHAPTER NINETEEN

Foreign Affairs – As Viewed
Through the Sycamores

One of the favorite coarse—and untrue—criticisms of Hoosiers offered
by residents of Rhode Island, Arkansas, California, and other outland
states is that Hoosiers tend to be provincial, uninterested in the affairs
of Europe, Africa, and northwestern Asia.

Such a charge is, of course, totally groundless. The Hoosier mind
mainly tends to embrace the universe; in such cases where it does not
express its opinions, that is due to the belief that foreign affairs are
really of only secondary importance. If a Hoosier feels himself to be
short of knowledge of European affairs, he quickly masters the subject
by means of an eighteen or thirty-six day tour of the continent.

Two young ladies who learned almost all there was to be known
about France were

CORNELIA OTIS SKINNNER AND
EMILY KIMBROUGH

The two young ladies had just completed college when they elected to
travel on the continent. Miss Skinner was not Hoosier bred, but she was
so fortunate as to have more knowledge of Indiana virtues than most
outlanders; Miss Kimbrough had the advantage of having begun life as
a resident of Muncie. Their joint impact, on France especially, must
have left its mark: certainly France and the French impressed them, as
is evidenced by the most amusing book they produced. One may hope
that the girls did not permit exaggeration to mar their narrative. It

would sorrow one deeply to learn that the episode of the New England-produced and -edited Ladies Rest Tour Association guide book for American females touring abroad did not actually recommend lodgings in the Rouen bordello which the pair patronized—safeguarded by the Madame who sequestered them out of the line of heavy traffic on the third floor, where they were disturbed only by the merry shouts from below them.

We give you a passage from

Our Hearts Were Young and Gay

THE RAILWAY which bore us from St. Valery was the "Chemin de Fer de la Manche" which we never called by any other name than "The Road of Iron of the Sleeve." . . . The one daily train winds its way in leisurely fashion through the Normandy countryside, stopping at every village and crossroads and occasionally in the middle of a wheat field for no apparent reason, unless perhaps the engineer takes a sudden fancy to pick a few poppies. At Rouen it gives up, the gallant little engine is detached (doubtless after being duly congratulated) and the cars are coupled onto a less colorful, through line to Paris. We decided to break the trip and enlarge our cultural vista by stopping off in Rouen for the night, and why our experience in that historic town didn't leave its mark on the rest of our lives is proof positive that there must be a special Providence set apart to watch the faltering steps of such ninnies as we. However, we got through the day before that action of Providence was needed.

We checked our lugagge at the station and with Baedekers in hand, open like hymn books, went on foot about that lovely ancient city. . . . We took the first narrow winding street, and almost at once found ourselves in the Place de l'Hôtel de Ville. It and that other Gothic gem, the church of St. Ouen, rose before us. On either side little shops nestled under the overhanging eaves of ancient buildings, as they must have in the days of the Guilds. A peasant in a black smock and sabots pushed along a cart loaded with exquisitely arranged cabbages, and a scissors grinder made known his presence in a weird unintelligible cry which might have been in the language of the Norman Dukes. The sky was flecked with small, attenuated clouds, and in the soft air, to brand the scene as being French, was that distant scent of open sewage which, curiously enough, one comes in time to like. Suddenly, miraculously we were in the Middle Ages, or rather, *le Moyen Age*. Past the Palais de Justice and down the rue Jeanne d'Arc, under the Tower which also bears her name, where her pitiful trial took place, and then at last we were in the old Market Place, standing on the spot where that guileless girl from Domremy was burned to death. It was Emily's first experience of the sort. She stood in the center of that beautiful and heartbreaking square murmuring, "This is the place. This is the very place." And quietly, unpremeditatively, we both stooped down and touched the cobblestones. We were moved to the point of wanting to burst into loud sobbing. For all our conscientious sight-seeing there had, up to now, been a certain deliberately planned quality to our appreciation. Our response to things, while enthusiastic, had been anything but hyper-sensitive. But we responded now to Joan of Arc, a girl of our own age. We responded with all the warmth and ache of our young hearts. This was what we'd come abroad for, this breathless moment, when we put down our hands to touch the spot where a momentous and agonizing hour of history had passed.

We wandered on down the rue de la Grosse Horloge and on to where the little thirteenth century houses nestle, as if for sanctuary, about the great Cathedral. We lifted our eyes to the flamboyant façade, and then up and up and ever up, following the soaring line of that "tallest finger toward heaven," the *Tour de Beurre*, and something inside us was stirring too profoundly for us to express except in simple phrases. Emily with a catch in her breath said gently, "You know, back in Indiana there's a lovely phrase of yearning. People say, 'I hope I get to go.' Well, I've gotten to go, and here I am standing in front of the Cathedral in Rouen, France . . . Europe!"

We went up the steps and through the door, and the vast nave unrolled almost audibly before us, and all along in the dark side-chapels were the wavering lights of tapers as tremulous as ourselves. Near the holy water font sat a black-hooded nun. Her face was pallid and as long drawn out as those of the carved saints in their narrow niches, and she kept repeating in a low, harsh whisper, "Pour les pauvres, Mesdames, pour les pauvres!" I bought a candle from her and although I didn't know much about such ceremonies, I placed it on a little spike beside the others which flickered before the shrine of Joan. She hadn't been canonized for very long and it was sweet to think of her coming into the eminent name of St. Joan. For all my Universalist forbears I went down on my knees to thank her and France and God for letting me be there. It was only after a little while that I felt suddenly self-conscious and got to my feet, looking about to see if anyone had noticed me. But the only person I saw was Emily, who on the opposite side of the shrine was also getting to her feet. She, too, had put a candle there and had said her prayer. Without a word we went on together toward the Lady Chapel.

Halfway up the nave we were accosted by an old harpy who was sitting behind a table of lighted tapers. She called out something to us and when we paid no attention, left her place, ran after us and started clutching at our sleeves. She was pointing at the small postern door opening onto the spiral stairway to the belfry. We must climb up to the top, she said. Why we felt it incumbent upon us to obey her, is as incomprehensible as why we felt obliged to tip her 50 centimes for issuing this unpleasant order. Emily and I both detest heights to such a degree that even climbing a step-ladder makes us sick at our stomachs, but we let ourselves get pushed and shrilled into that Stygian tunnel. The door slammed to behind us and there was no alternative but to climb. Up the worn stone steps we trudged in pitch darkness except at infrequent moments when a slit of light from a mullioned window revealed the nasty fact that we were leaving *terra firma* further and further below us. Up and up we wound our panting way and yet we seemed to be getting nowhere. Round and round like slow-motion squirrels in an elongated cage. It began to take on a quality of nightmare and we each suffered an attack of that paralyzing childhood phobia, the feeling that we were being chased from behind by "something awful." Even as a grown woman when I find myself in the dark, I have an unfortunate tendency to think up all sorts of Poe-like horrors. I don't believe in ghosts but I become suddenly afraid of them, and a myriad of old wives' superstitions cross my mind. How I'd derived the notion I can't imagine, but at that point I heard myself telling Emily that if cathedral bells started ringing while you were in the belfry, the vibrations would drive you mad. Emily, who in addition to her other terrors was undergoing an acute spell of claustrophobia, collapsed onto the step she was treading and managed to croak, "Is it time for the bells to ring?"

"How should I know when the bells ring?" I snapped.

"What about the Angelus?" Emily said. "You know, that painting."

Fear, I concluded, had caused her to take momentary leave of her senses and I asked her what the heck a painting had to do with it.

"They heard bells, didn't they, those peasants? And Millet was French; he must have known when French bells ring. It was the end of the day in that picture and it's the end of the day now. Unless . . ." she added with a note of hysteria, "we've been climbing all night and are starting out on tomorrow."

I could offer nothing more helpful than the information that back home in Bryn Mawr the angelus used to ring at six. Emily asked was it six now and I said I didn't know, because by the dim light from one of those window slits it was apparent my watch had stopped. Emily said, well, hers was going but it was in her safety-pocket, and pulling up her skirt, she started frantically plunging into her overstuffed sporran. In the midst of this activity there suddenly caught up with us a group of five or six other tourists, poor yokels like us, trapped by the crone two or three miles below. They didn't look any too happy, either.

Their presence eased our panic and Emily came hastily back out of her money belt. "Keep close to them," she hissed. "There'll be less danger of going mad if the bells ring."

"What makes you think so?" I said.

"There'll be more of us together," she said. "That will make it harder for the vibrations to concentrate." This was an example of Emily's reasoning at its best, but it seemed rather reassuring at the time. We followed along with the others and in a minute or two were laughing and skipping our way to the top.

We came out into fresh air and a dazzling sunset. I guess there must have been a magnificent view too but we didn't dare look. However, we gazed with delight at the sky and some charming carvings in the balustrade and felt so relieved to be again in the open, we never noticed when the other pilgrims left. Suddenly we were aware that they'd gone and we were alone on the summit of that great cathedral. Then, as if twenty minutes previously we hadn't worked ourselves up into a sufficient wax, we began, in a spirit of fun and fantasy, a little series of supposings. What if, one of us suggested, we were up here at the top and no one else had come. The bells had not made us mad because we were outdoors when they rang. But we were alone . . . nobody knew we were up there. Even the old crone had gone home. The situation offered endless possibilities and, inspired by the fascination of horror, we went on elaborating. Suppose, for instance, in the confusion of turrets, buttresses and pinnacles we couldn't find the door to the stairway or, having found it, suppose it proved to be locked? In such an event we'd call loudly but who could hear us at that height? We waved and wig-wagged but nobody saw us. It was growing dark and eventually we were forced to spend the night huddled against a cornice. Next day, we went on to say, was a holiday and the door remained locked. Again we waved our handkerchiefs, and again to no avail, so we started taking off our clothes and signaling with them but still the passers-by in the street far, far below never looked up. Then, we conjectured (and by now the tale had taken on a ghoulish reality), we dropped our garments piece by piece down over the edge, hoping someone would investigate whence they were falling. But there was a strong breeze blowing and most of them caught in transit on gargoyles and projecting bits of masonry, and still nobody noticed. We became crazed with fright and hunger. There remained nothing for us to do but step forth onto that dizzy parapet, closing our eyes and clinging frantically to one another and a fragile stone pinnacle. And there we stood, stark naked in the wind and weather. For a time nothing happened, and then from far down below we heard a murmur of voices which swelled into a mighty roar. We didn't dare open our eyes, much less let go of the pinnacle in order to wave. We just stood there motionless, trusting that curiosity would force some of the populace to come up. We would be shamed, even possibly arrested, but we'd be saved. But not a soul ever came up! Word went round that a miracle had come to pass and that we were holy manifestations. The bishop declared the view of us from the square below a point of pilgrimage, and as further expression of reverence, ordered the passage-way to the belfry locked and barred, for no human must ever profane the spot where we stood. We died there, of course.

What we actually did was to scare ourselves so with this little flight of fancy, we shot back into the tunnel like rabbits to their warren, clattered down the spiral stairway and catapulted through the door and on past the old troll so fast we blew out her tapers.

We were exhausted after this, so we returned to the station, extracted our over-night bags from the check room, and, footsore and weary, plodded to the place where we planned to spend the night. I wonder now what gave us such endurance. But we felt it would not have been in keeping with the surrounding atmosphere of antiquity to have taken a taxi. If we had, it is doubtful if the driver, provided he were a God-fearing family man, would have abandoned us at that address.

We had acquired the address through my mother. Mother was a joiner. She would join any organization of which her friends were presidents or committee members, provided, of course, the dues weren't excessive. Once having joined, she seldom did much about her affiliations, and dear knows never dreamt of going to any meetings, but she kept on joining others because, she'd explain, she thought they might prove useful sometime and besides such nice women belonged to them. One of her enthusiasms was an instructive little endeavor known as "The Ladies' Rest Tour Association." Its purpose was to provide lists of comfortable but inexpensive and, of course, highly respectable lodgings for ladies traveling alone and unprotected through Europe. It publishes a monthly pamphlet which contained sprightly articles penned by certain of the itinerant members, telling about the cosy inn one of them had found in Avignon, recommending a highly intellectual pension in Perugia, or putting fellow travelers on the trail of a Swiss tea room where the coffee was "just like home." There was also issued a general European lodging list for the use of members only, they being supposedly on their honor not to pass the information along to any outsider (one of the aims of the society was to "keep Europe unspoiled"). Mother had culled the adress of a Rouen boarding house out of this invaluable pamphlet and had sent it to us. She may have written it down wrong, or the Ladies' Rest Tour publication may have been guilty of a misprint, but it was clear someone had blundered, for the hostelry provided to be one which had very little to do with "rest" and Lord knows nothing remotely to do with "ladies." As surely as we were what our mothers would have called "nincompoops," that house was one which our mothers also would have called "of ill repute."

We rang the bell and after a time the door was opened a crack by a frowsy maid who didn't seem to want to let us in. But we smiled and said, *Bon soir* and blandly asked to see *La Madame* (meaning "landlady"). The maid looked slightly astonished and walked off, returning in a second with the landlady, who looked even more astonished. She was awfully dressy and luridly made up, hardly the type one would associate with the Ladies' Rest Tour and the elderly New England gentlewomen who supported it. We told her we'd like a room for the night, a seemingly simple demand but one which obviously increased her astonishment, for she stepped back in a blank manner and gave no reply. I was afraid she thought that two girls arriving alone and on foot might detract from the gentility of her pension, so, to establish our respectability, I told her that her house had been recommended to us as just the place for *deux jeunes filles*. She murmured a faint *Ah?* and beckoning us to follow, led us down a hall. It was lined on either side with smallish rooms, rather elaborately decorated. Some of the doors were open, and we caught glimpses of the other guests who seemed quite surprised to see us and we were indeed surprised to see them. They all appeared to be young women in very striking evening dresses. This was certainly unusual, but we concluded they must all be waiting to go out to a dinner-party. It never once occurred to us that we weren't exactly in keeping with the *ton* of the place, I, in my Buster Brown panama and Emily in her pepper and salt tweeds.

Madame led us up several flights of stairs and allotted us a modest room quite removed from the more elaborate ones below. She explained we'd be more *tranquille* there. Then, in a faint, far-away voice, she asked how we'd happened to come to her place. We told her we'd read all about it in a book published by an American society. She hadn't said much up to now, but this item of information caused her to lose all power of articulation, for she opened and closed her mouth several times but nothing came forth. Finally, with a wan, Camille-like wave of the hand, she backed out of the rooom and closed the door. Her behavior had been very odd, but with our faith in the Ladies' Rest Tour ever bright, we dismissed her as being a "character."

We washed, went out and found a quiet near-by restaurant where we dined. We were less shy about going into restaurants than we'd been in London, possibly because there were no other places in which to eat. Then we returned to our snug abode. The frowsy maid, still looking astonished, admitted us, and we went down the long hall, tiptoeing because the doors were all closed now, and we didn't want to disturb anybody. We could hear the sound of laughter and music coming from a back room but we felt too tired to join in the fun, so we climbed the flights of stairs and went to bed. We were very comfortable but I couldn't help thinking that this was an eccentric sort of pension, and Emily remarked that it lacked that "homey" quality of the one in St. Valery.

Once in the night we woke with a start. People were walking in the corridor outside, we could hear a man's voice and someone tried the handle of our door. Then we heard Madame speaking sharply to whoever it was and evidently she pulled him away. We thought it very nice and motherly of her to be up watching out for her boarders, but just in case we might be disturbed again we did take the precaution of pushing the bureau against the door. After which we slept the sleep of babes.

The following morning, bright and eager as daisies, we rose, packed and asked for the bill. Madame told us it was not her custom to make out a formal account but she named a sum which was most reasonable, and as we paid it we told her what a pleasant sojourn we had had there and how we'd most assuredly recommended her establishment to all our friends. Her eyes glazed over a bit at that, and faintly she asked us if we'd have the *bonté* to give her the name of the American *Société* which had informed us about her. She would like, she said to write to them. We gave her the name and address of the Ladies' Rest Tour Association, and left her to start what, we trust, proved to be an interesting and illuminating correspondence.

At the station we waited a considerable time for the Paris train. We always waited an interminable time for trains. I guess that was my fault. I can't control my mania for getting to stations way ahead of schedule. I confess to this failing only because Emily, who is co-author, insists that I do. (She, incidentally, likes to arrive just in time to swing aboard the observation car as it whizzes by.) In those days I was even worse. Emily used to say that the moment I discovered the hour for a train departure, I reacted the way a hunter in India must when he comes across fresh tiger tracks. He rushes home with the thrilling news of his discovery and starts laying plans. He packs his provisions, gets his equipment in order, makes calculations regarding the weather and sets forth to a snug look-out. There he lies in wait for a night or two until his tiger happens along. This, she vowed, was my normal behavior when lying in wait for a train. Therefore, at Rouen, we went to the station after breakfast and had a very nice early lunch there later on. After that I decided it was about time for us to go out on the platform in order, to continue Emily's unfortunate metaphor, to be within closer range when our train should come prowling up to its water-hole. It was a judgment on her that at this point she all but lost the means of continuing any further her European trip.

The Cathedral was just visible above the distant rooftops. Emily, standing on tiptoe at the edge of the platform, pointed at the *Tour de Beurre* in an exalted and lofty gesture. This was a moment to remember, she said, we must try to fix it in our memories. We didn't have to try very hard. Her pocket book was a grey suède "envelope" fastened, not too securely, with a blue enamel clasp. It had a strap across the back through which to slip one's hand, a detail which was considered particularly smart. Shallow and not very large, the thing was intended to hold only a few bare necessities. But that day Emily had rammed it to bursting point. It was replete with coin purse, comb, cigarette case, wads of postcards, a Roger and Gallet pomade lipstick and one of those compacts which came in a small cardboard box with a tiny puff and powder in cake form known as a "Dorine." In addition to all this, she had transferred to it the entire contents of her money-belt—passport, traveler's checks, jewelry, even those much thumbed letters from Aunt Huda and Uncle Lloyd; because, she said, going to Paris and all, you couldn't tell what you might be asked for. At the moment of her skyward gesture her hand was through the strap and the purse was upside-down. Gazing at the distant spire she was saying, "You know, it's so lovely, I feel as if something were about to burst," and those were the truest words she ever uttered, because something did. It was the chic enamel clasp, and her purse opened out wide in the manner of a steam shovel. The contents clattered down with the rush of a rock-slide and disappeared from view. For a moment we stood there, stunned by the cataclysm, then we both squatted at the edge of the platform and peered down at the tracks a good distance below. There they were. All of Emily's possessions scattered along ten feet of the roadbed. Her letter of credit in transit had opened out, money and coins were strewn over the stones like oats in a plowed field, her Roger and Gallet pomade was wedged between two spikes, even her "Dorine" had fallen to pieces and the puff was resting jauntily on a gleaming rail. I straightened up just in time to jerk her back as a train roared in past her nose and on top of all her possessions. At that precise instant, the Paris train, the one we'd been stalking for five or six hours, sneaked in behind us on the other side of the platform. Our porters, to whom Emily had been referring as our "beaters," galloped up to arm themselves with our baggage and to tell us we must despatch ourselves as the train waited only a few minutes.

We told them what had happened and they in turn bellowed the information to one another and the fast collecting crowd. Other travelers hurried up, waiters dashed forth from the station restaurant, even the ticket agent ran out anxious to get in on the news first hand. We pointed, and the porters gesticulated energetically at the collection of Emily's worldly goods strewn below the railway carriage. Then everyone began to offer advice. One could, they said, back up the train, but someone else objected that the mail was being unloaded and such *mouvement* would derange the postal agents, to say nothing of the objects of this lady. Someone else made the helpful remark that she might salvage what was left of her little numbers after the train had gone which, *évidemment*, would be some fifteen minutes after the hour of departure of the Paris train. A waiter put in the gallant suggestion that if the gravity of the situation were made sufficiently clear, the Paris train might wait. But the ticket agent shouted in righteous indignation that the Paris train had never waited for anyone except M. Poincaré and the waiter was an imbecile. No, there was nothing for us to do but wait there until the train had gone, the train which was not the Paris train, for example; then the lost objects could be salvaged unless already ruined, *bien entendu,* by the passage of the train, that one, in effect, which was not the Paris train, of course, is it not? In that case even the young lady's passport would no longer be of any use and she would have forfeited her right to remain in the country; or, came the note of cold native logic, to leave it. This was a fine point for debate, one after their own hearts, and they were just settling down with fervor for an all-day discussion when a voice like a fog horn resounded above the bedlam. "Me voici!" it roared and it came from below the platform. Peering down the narrow gap between it and the train we located its owner, a burly workman, his baby blue smock billowing out around him, stretched out flat on his stomach between the wheels. He was gathering in Emily's possessions, passport, money, letter of credit, even the Roger and Gallet pomade and the scattered parts of her "Dorine." Everyone watched and spurred him on with heartening suggestions, and he himself held forth in an oration upon his own audacity, ingenuity and general good sense. By some miracle the Paris train waited. Perhaps there was an extra amount of baggage that day. Certainly no one made any attempt to hold it. I myself think it waited because the engineer was hanging out the cab window watching and didn't want to miss anything.

The workman backed out from between the wheels, which mercifully remained stationary, trotted around the engine, up some steps at the far end of the platform and ran to us triumphant, his hands and pockets full of Emily's little treasures. The crowd, with murmurs of admiration and relief, hustled us over to the Paris train. Emily, grateful to the verge of tears, kept spluttering hybrid phrases of the "Merci *ever* so much" variety, pressing more and more money into the kindly, outstretched hand. He assured us such exertion was nothing for such a man as he and that he loved America. He had never been there but he knew well "Charlot" Chaplin and Gloria "Svanson." However, in all honesty he must confess that he had not been able to retrieve quite all. Down there, lying in a particularly dangerous spot, was a fifty franc note. It was reposing itself between the wheels and any minute now the train would be leaving. He could not, even for America, risk his life further. He had to think of his family and to invite any more danger would be unreasonable. Emily, frankly weeping by now, agreed that indeed he had already dared too much, and pressed more money into his liberal hand, this time for his family. He thanked her and bowed and said he must now return to work. A humble artisan, we told each other, who had done such a magnificent thing with no thought of himself. It made us feel noble and warm. Our train started to move, we yanked loose the window strap and leaned out for one last look. There under the other train which was placidly taking on water and would not leave for another half hour, was our hero workman. He was just backing out from between the wheels and as we passed, he stood up and waved good-bye with the fifty franc note in his hand.

Not that Hoosiers confine themselves solely to frivolous notes on travel in foreign lands; they can handle the most profound geopolitical themes as well. They do not necessarily confine such subjects to boxes on the editorial page, nor do they insist that they be composed by persons whose names are adorned with Ph.D.s. A sports writer will do, or a humorous columnist; all being Hoosier, the results are uniformly telling. See thoughts on Middle East troubles as published in the Indianapolis Star for October 23 and November 12, 1973. What world figure among political scientists could paint a more graphic picture?

BOB COLLINS

writes

Referee Again Saves Israel From Victory

Y EARS AGO there was a fighter out of London named Phil Scott. He was big, could hit like a mule and had amazing speed for a heavyweight.

And the British thought they had a world champion until a few chinks in his armor were discovered. Like sometimes the wind from a missed punch hyperventilated him, and after a solid connection, you could hear the glass breaking in Liverpool.

His ability to get his chin in front of fists won him a spot in boxing memorabilia as "Fainting Phil Scott."

And I thought about old Phil often the past week or so as the Arabs kept announcing crushing triumphs until they began claiming a moral victory for escaping annihilation.

They're fast—and tricky—but they can't take a punch. They finish on their feet only because—for some strange reason—they are allowed to bring their own referees.

And the referees always declare it no decision on the grounds that their guys made a mistake showing up in the first place, and request that everybody retire to a neutral corner.

Then the judges reprimand the Israelis for defending themselves, and we all settle back and wait for the Arabs to get brave again.

This time, however, I think they blew it. They quit with their goal—getting the Israelis out of the Holy Land—in sight.

In just a few more days they all would have been in Cairo.

And a few days later, he has further thoughts on matters transpiring in the same area.

Oh, Henry Really Has Tales to Tell

For several years the world has been awed by the spectacular success of Henry Kissinger's personal diplomacy.

Obviously he has discovered a new way. He turns tigers into tabby cats and some of the world's most stubborn demagogues into models of reason.

But how? I figured that, whatever his methods, they had to be unique. And the other day I think I found the answer.

There was a picture of Henry holding hands with the ugliest Arab I ever saw.

How shrewd. How simple. Why didn't somebody think of it 2,000 years ago?

Think about it. There are few men who will stay argumentative if another man is holding their hand. Believe me, they are too busy worrying about more immediate and personal problems.

Now that the secret is out, I hope the government releases more pictures—like Henry hugging Mao or Henry having a candlelight dinner with Brezhnev or Henry taking a moonlight stroll with Tito.

I can see dictators and oil barons, prime ministers and generals, crumbling before Kissinger's onslaught.

And I can envision conversations like, "Yes, Yes, I'll talk to Golda Meir," or, "So, OK, OK, we'll pay cash for the wheat and settle our World War II debts," or, "I will write a personal letter recommending Chiang Kai-shek for the Nobel Peace Prize."

"If you will promise never again to hold my hand in public."

CHAPTER TWENTY

Epilogue

Casting about for a peroration of some sort, one finds that Indiana's own George Ade produced about as good a description of Hoosiers and Hoosierland as may be found.

In his Single Blessedness and Other Observations, published in 1922, the following sketch appears. It seems to a native and long-time resident to apply about as well today as it did when Ade wrote it. Every now and again Hoosiers have a state's right to an outburst of unabashed chauvinism. Ade's the man to rare back and holler, for as the Sage of Hazelden might have said, "He who Tooteth Not his own Horn, the Same shall not be Tooted." Here's how it goes.

Indiana

INDIANA HAS A SAVOUR not to be detected in Ohio. It is decidedly un-Michigan-like. Although it tinges off toward Illinois on the west and Kentucky on the south, the community is neither nebulous nor indefinite. It is individual.

Indiana is not Out West or Way Down East or Up North or south in Dixie.

It is true that, west of the Platte River, Indiana is supposed to be under the wither and blight of Eastern decay. Conversely, as one leaves Columbus, Ohio, and moves toward the region of perpetual sea-food,

617

he encounters people to whom Terre Haute and Cripple Creek are synonymous.

The Hoosier refuses to be classified by those who lack information. He knows that his state is an oasis, surrounded by sections. Our people are clotted around the exact centre of population. Boston is not the hub. It is a repaired section of the pneumatic rim.

When a state is one hundred years old (Indiana is beyond the century mark) it escapes the personal recollections of the pioneer, and is still so young that newspapers do not burn incense before the grandchildren of eminent grandparents.

We have grown some ivy, but we have not yet taken on moss.

Indiana has made history, but it figures that the present and the future are more worthy of attention than a dim and receding past.

Indiana has cemeteries and family trees, but does not subsist on them.

If the Hoosier is proud of his state, it is because the state has lived down and fought down certain misconceptions. Even in Cambridge, Massachusetts, the fact that Indiana produces more gray matter than hoop-poles is slowly beginning to percolate.

For a long time the Hoosier was on the defensive. Now he is on a pedestal.

Forty or fifty years ago the native son who went travelling owned up to an indefinite residence somewhere between Chicago and Louisville. To-day the Hoosier abroad claims Indiana fervently, hoping to be mistaken for an author.

The Indiana man respects his state because it has grown to importance and wealth without acquiring a double chin or wearing a wrist watch.

The sniffy millionaire and the aloof patrician do not cause any trembles in the state of Indiana.

Even our larger cities have no thoroughfares shaded by the gloomy strongholds of caste. Some of the more enterprising comrades are unduly prosperous, but they continue to reside in homes.

The state is short on slums and aristocratic reservations. In other words, we are still building according to specifications.

The number of liveried servants residing within the boundaries is incredibly small and does not include one person born on the banks of the Wabash.

We have a full quota of smart alecks, but not one serf.

Because Indiana is not overbalanced by city population and is not cowed by arrogant wealth and has a lingering regard for the cadences of the spellbinder, an old-fashioned admiration for the dignified professions, and local pride in all styles of literary output, the Hoosier has achieved his peculiar distinction as a mixed type—a puzzling combination of shy provincial, unfettered democrat and Fourth of July orator. He is a student by choice, a poet by sneaking inclination, and a storyteller by reason of his nativity. . . .

Your passer-by looks out of the car window and sees the Hoosier on the depot platform, necktieless and slightly bunched at the knees. According to all the late cabaret standards, the Hoosier is a simpleton, the same as you observe in the moving pictures.

Alight from the train and get close to our brother before you turn in your verdict.

Forget that he shaves his neck and remember that many a true heart beats under galluses.

Pick out a low, roomy box on the sunny side of the general store and listen with open mind, while he discourses on the crops, and bass fishing, and preparedness for war, and General Lew Wallace, and Christian Science, and how to find a bee-tree. Do you want a line on Booth Tarkington or Albert Beveridge or Tom Taggart? He will give you the most inside information and garnish it with anecdotes.

The Hoosier may wear the wrong kind of hat, but he is alert on men and affairs and living doctrines. For sixty years the state has been a crucible of politics. It was a buffer between crowding factions all during the Civil War.

Just as the Hoosier emerges from the cradle he is handed a set of convictions and learns that he must defend them, verbally and otherwise. So he goes into training. He may turn out to be a congressman or a contributor to the magazines, but even if he escapes notoriety he will always be a belligerent, with a slant toward the intellectual.

What happened away back yonder to make Indiana different? Listen! There were two migrations early in the nineteenth century.

From the seaboard there was a movement to the west. From the Carolinas and the mountain regions there was a drift northward across the Ohio River. Indiana was settled by pioneers who had the enterprise to seek new fields and the gumption to unpack and settle down when they found themselves in the promised land.

Indiana is a composite of steel mills and country clubs, factories and colleges, promoters and professors, stock-breeders and Chautauqua attractions, cornfields and campuses. It grows all the crops and propaganda known to the temperate zone.

If a high wall could be erected to inclose Indiana, the state would continue to operate in all departments, but the outsiders would have to scale the wall in order to get their dialect poetry.

Here's to Indiana, a state as yet unspoiled! Here's to the Hoosier home folks, a good deal more sophisticated than they let on to be!